THE HISTORY OF WORLD THEATER
From the English Restoration
to the Present

THE HISTORY OF

WORLD THEATER

FROM THE
ENGLISH RESTORATION
TO THE PRESENT

Felicia Hardison Londré

A Frederick Ungar Book

CONTINUUM / **NEW YORK**

1991

The Continuum Publishing Company
370 Lexington Avenue
New York, NY 10017

Printed in the United States of America

Library of Congress Cataloging-in-Publication Data

Berthold, Margot, 1922–
 [Weltgeschichte des Theaters. English]
 The history of world theater / Margot Berthold : [translated by
Edith Simmons from the original German].
  p. cm.
 Translation of: Weltgeschichte des Theaters
 "A Frederick Ungar book."
 Originally published: New York : Ungar, c1972
 Includes bibliographical references.
 Contents: From the English Restoration to the present /
Felicia Hardison Londré.
  ISBN 0-8264-0485-5
  1. Theater—History. I. Londré, Felicia Hardison, 1941–   From
the English Restoration to the present. 1991. II. Title.
PN2104.B413 1991
792'09—dc20   90-1742
                                                    CIP

The quotation from *Faust,* copyright © Translation/Stage adaptation 1988 by Robert David MacDonald,
is used by kind permission of Tessa Sayle, Literary and Dramatic Agency.

Frontispiece photograph of Douglass Stewart as Witch Doctor in *The Emperor Jones* courtesy of Missouri
Repertory Theatre, 1988. All other photo credits are given with the captions.

Contents

Preface

In Nature everything is connected, everything is interwoven, every-thing varies with respect to everything else, everything fluctuates when confronted with something else. But given this infinite multiplicity, Nature can be fully grasped only by a limitless intellect. In order for more limited minds to take full advantage of their share of this enjoyment, they must have the ability to set for themselves arbitrary limits that do not exist in Nature—the ability to dismiss some things from consideration and to refocus their attention as the spirit moves them.
—Gotthold Ephraim Lessing, *The Hamburg Dramaturgy*,
   No. 70

The guiding premise behind this book could not be stated more succinctly than in these words borrowed from Lessing. In history, as in Nature, I believe, "everything is connected." It is not necessary to see a direct causal relationship between one event and another, but rather to recognize the multiplicity of connecting strands in a vast web of human endeavors linked across time and space. We can see in our own time how the catastrophic events and gradual changes occurring in Beijing or Moscow have repercussions around the world. Less apparent though no less real are the effects that such waves on the tide of history have on the lives of ordinary people in Kansas City or Timbuktu. Because of events in China, for example, Missouri Repertory Theatre doesn't get to bring in an internationally renowned Chinese director to do Shakespeare, and the season's bill is changed; instead of *King Lear,* the company presents *Born Yesterday.* What difference does it make in the lives of thousands of Kansas City theatergoers if they see *Born Yesterday* instead of *King Lear*? What is the difference in the careers of actors who are or are not hired for one or the other show? Of course, the historian's assessment of events can be based only upon what did happen. "What might have been" is the subtext of history, an imaginative exercise for the reader, analogous to the actor's imaginative exploration of the possibilities of characterization beneath his spoken dialogue. The point is that history evinces a mysterious interlocking of forces that may seem unrelated at first sight. As Eugène Scribe shows in his play *Le Verre d'eau,* a mere glass of water spilled at an inopportune moment can precipitate a war between two great nations.

The history of theater in particular must be concerned with interconnecting elements. In no art more than theater is there such a blending of all the arts. Theater is a nexus of rhetorical, poetic, mimetic, pictorial, musical, and architectural arts and crafts. Never in history has the theater developed in isolation from other human activities: politics, religion, economics, science, and sociocultural norms. What appeared on the stage at any given time and place was the product of a complex of factors that included audience demographics, the theater's system of patronage or management, the physical facility, the intellectual context articulated by critics and theorists, and so on. To situate historical developments in the theater within these various constructs across space and time has been an ambitious, if not always attainable, goal of this book.

As an aspect of this interconnectedness, the historian often hears individual voices speaking to him or her across time. Lessing's comment from the past, for example, directly addresses my present purpose. History is made by people. No matter how remote in time, they had fundamentally the same "senses, affections, passions" as we do. Their contributions to the development of the theater, however much in service to an ideal of art, were to some extent determined by their personalities, their individual drives, and their relationships with other people. The greatest and most innovative artists were certainly influenced by and/or rebelling against the efforts of a host of lesser-known artists who went before, or who took parallel but less visible paths, or even those who turned off on side roads and found themselves at dead ends. Without espousing a "great lives" approach to theater history, I have tried to keep the individual artist or craftsman at the center of my study. The individuals who come to the fore in my narrative are not always the ones who were considered most important in their own time. Some earned posterity's belated recognition for seminal contributions that were not immediately recognized as such. Some find their places here as representatives of a certain direction of energies in a given period. Some are here to redress a balance; for example, I have tried to bring into the overall picture some awareness of women in other areas of theater besides acting, and of the achievements of certain unjustly neglected African American artists, and of important artists whose renown was spread only within the linguistic boundaries of their infrequently translated languages. These people and a host of others along with all of us involved in theater today form a network of interconnected efforts so vast that it "could only be grasped by a limitless intellect."

This brings us to the second part of Lessing's statement: "Limited minds . . . must have the ability to set for themselves arbitrary limits that do not exist in Nature—the ability to dismiss some things from consideration and to refocus their attention as the spirit moves them." Written history, like art, cannot exactly replicate the reality it sets out to elucidate. Limits must be defined. Like art, history is a matter of selection and arrangement. The artist and historian both select their material from reality's infinitude and then present it according to appropriate organizing principles. It is a question of where to put the frame around the subject and then how the elements should be composed within the frame. My framing of the various topics covered in this book has not been uniform; that is, the size of the frame has differed according to the inherent demands of the material as well as the point of view I bring to the material. In cinematic terms, I have conceived this book as a combination of wide-angle shots framing broad vistas and close-ups focusing upon certain subjects in greater detail.

With reference to my "point of view," I have exercised deliberate restraint in the use of contemporary critical filters; that is, material on women in the theater or popular entertainments or aristocratic patronage can be handled apart from a narrowly feminist or Marxist or élitist perspective. The ideal of Montaigne in his *Essais*—to be *ondoyant et divers*—seems closest to my intention; I have also attempted to present names, dates, and ideas with "fluidity and variety." However, I have tried to remain particularly alert to evidence of cross-cultural interactions. In the amassing of evidence, the fact that I read French, Spanish, and Russian, but not German, Italian, Polish, or the Scandinavian languages sets up certain involuntary biases in my coverage, and in some respects I may have overcompensated in my concern to give the theaters of the latter languages a fair share of attention. At the same time, I am deeply disturbed at the impossibility of giving a "fair share" to the rich theatrical traditions of so many other countries, even within Europe, which has been the major focus of this book, not to mention those of Africa, Asia, the Middle East, South America, and the South Pacific. As all modern theaters become increasingly interconnected—especially through the good offices of organizations like the International Theatre Institute and gatherings like the International Women Playwrights Conference in 1988—I am confident that fair coverage will be forthcoming.

One other factor has had a major impact upon the shaping of this book. That is its originally intended function as a companion volume to Margot Berthold's *A History of World Theater,* which was first published in German, and published in English translation by Frederick Ungar in 1972. The original plan was to subtitle my volume *From the Eighteenth Century to the Present.* However, that would have left out seventeenth-century England and its vital Restoration theater. Therefore, I took it upon myself to cover the Restoration in this volume's chapter 1, the only chapter I devote exclusively to a single country. Although each historian has an individual style and historiographical method, my volume was written with the format of the original volume in mind.

A work of this scope necessarily relies heavily upon secondary sources, although one can periodically touch bases with primary sources. In addition to the work of other scholars represented in my bibliography, I owe a great intellectual debt to the many exciting and dedicated scholars who are actively expanding the boundaries of theatrical studies, uncovering new evidence, articulating new methodologies for the use of evidence, and generally making theatrical scholarship such a lively and fascinating arena in which to work. It is, of course, impossible to name all those whose stimulating conference papers, published articles, and informal discussions have influenced my thinking during the last decade, but I cannot refrain from mentioning a few: Ed Amor, Steve Archer, Peter Arnott, Rose Bank, Judith Barlow, Alexei Bartoshevich, Jerry Birdman, Kasimierz Braun, Eugene K. Bristow, Jarka Burian, Kalman Burnim, Harry G. Carlson, Marvin Carlson, Sharon Carnicke, Gay Gibson Cima, Peter Davis, Jill Dolan, Weldon Durham, Bob Erenstein, Bill Esper, Dan Gerould, Costas Gianakaris, Glenda Gill, John Golder, Spencer Golub, Roger Gross, John Harty, Roger Herzel, Frank Higgins, Errol Hill, Burnet Hobgood, Wiebe Hogendoorn, Norris Houghton, Cynthia Jenner, Al Kalson, Larry Kaushansky, Margaret Knapp, Michal Kobialka, Philip Kolin, Bill Kuhlke, Colby Kullman, Alma Law, Liu Haiping, Marc Maufort, Cary Mazer, John McCormick, Rex McGraw, Michael Meyer, Tice Miller, Emmanuel Molho, Cesare Molinari, Jim Moy, Patricia O'Connor, Nicholas Paley, Richard Pettengill, Tom Postlewait, Joseph Roach, Arnold Rood, Roberto Sánchez, Roby Sarlós, Guillermo Schmidhuber, Claude Schumacher, David Schuster, Virginia Scott, Laurence Senelick, Vidas Siliunas, Sam Smiley, Tatiana Shakh-Azizova, Inna Solovieva, Ludmila Starikova, Boleslaw Taborski, Juli Thompson, Georgi Todorov, Richard Trousdell, Anna Tsipeniuk, Andrew Tsubaki, Gary Vena, Ron Vince, Carla Waal, Wang Yiqun, Ken Washington, Daniel J. Watermeier, Al Wertheim, David Whitton, Simon Williams, Don Wilmeth, Barry Witham, Alan Woods, Yoshiteru Kurokawa, and Phyllis Zatlin. In particular, I should like to acknowledge the special debt that my generation owes to Oscar Brockett, whose *History of the Theatre*, now in its fifth edition, paved the way for so much else that has been accomplished in the last three decades; his tolerance for all points of view and his generosity in sharing the fruits of his research experience have been a special inspiration to me in this undertaking.

My work was also aided by two University of Missouri–Kansas City

Faculty Research Grants. For their encouragement and assistance, I should like to thank Henry A. Mitchell, vice-chancellor for International Affairs; Gordon Seyffert, assistant director of the Center for International Affairs; Eleanor Schwartz, vice-chancellor for Academic Affairs; Marvin Querry, acting dean, Office of Research Administration; Max Skidmore, dean of the College of Arts and Sciences; Burton Dunbar, associate dean of Arts and Sciences; David Weinglass, professor of English; Tom Peters, reference librarian. My colleagues in theater at UMKC have been a constant source of support and kindness: Joseph Appelt, Bruce Bacon, Max Beatty, Jacques Burdick, Jerome Butler, Francis Cullinan, Susan Dinges, Mila Jean Ehrlich, John Ezell, Robin Humphrey, George Keathley, Jennifer Martin, Robert Meagher, Dale Rose, Dennis Rosa, Vincent Scassellati, Ron Schaeffer, Doug Taylor, Chester White, Ewa Wielgat. Also at UMKC and Missouri Repertory Theatre I should like to thank Danny Baker, Tess Brubeck, Martin Coles, Trudi Fendi, Jenny Ferris, Ross Freese, Gene Friedman, Mary Guaraldi, John Dunn, Philip blue owl Hooser, Laurie Jarrett, Gerald Kemner, Kay Kuhlmann, Audrey Newton, Larry Pape, Kent Politsch, Rits Ritson, Stewart Skelton, Bob Thatch, Jan Waller, and Jean Wilson. In some way or another, everything I have done since joining the UMKC faculty in 1978 was nurtured by my great privilege of working in close association with Patricia A. McIlrath, chairman of the UMKC Department of Theatre and artistic director of Missouri Repertory Theatre until her retirement in 1985. The continuing friendship of this great lady of American theater is one of my greatest joys.

A number of other people have been very helpful to me as I worked on this book. Among these are Sonia Moore of the American Center for Stanislavski Theatre Art; Gerald Freedman, artistic director, and Bill Rudman and Margaret Lynch of Great Lakes Theatre Festival; Jon Jory, artistic director, and Michael Dixon, dramaturg, of Actors Theatre of Louisville; Peter Sellars and Jim Ingalls of the Los Angeles Festival of the Arts; Mel Tolkin, screenwriter; Jeanne Newlin, curator of the Harvard Theatre Collection; Lisbet Grandjean, director of the Copenhagen Theatre Museum; Gabrielle Heller of the International Theatre Institute-France; Martha Coigny, director, Lynn Gross, Louis Rachow, and Elizabeth Burdick of the International Theatre Institute–U.S.A. Center; Rose Marie Moudouès of the Société d'Histoire du Théâtre; Kado Kostzer and Alfredo Arias; Nuria Espert; Anatoly Mitnikov, dramaturg at the Mossoviet Theatre; Mark Rozovsky, director of the Nikitski Vorot Theatre; Alexei Bartoshevich, secretary of the Soviet Theatre Workers Union; Vyacheslav Nechaev, director of the Scientific Theatre Library, Moscow; Ying Ruocheng and Ying Da of the Beijing People's Art Theatre; Cecilia Olveczky, dramaturg at Det Norske Teatret; as well as my friends Fernando Arrabal, Andrée Chedid, Terry Dwyer, Steve Fish, Steve Hemming, and Gary Lenox. I should also like to thank my editor, Evander Lomke, for his unflagging encouragement and patience, and to pay a special tribute to the late Frederick Ungar whose high standards and humanist values are evident in the product of his publishing company.

Certain people had a seminal influence on my sense of theater and of history. My father, the late Colonel Felix M. Hardison, United States Air Force, took me to the theater, taught me the pride and responsibility that goes with being an American, and sent me off to see the world. Of the many superb teachers I've had, two were instrumental in forming my approach to theater and generating lasting intellectual excitement: Firmin H. Brown and John Ezell. Needless to say, my thinking has also been informed by countless students. Nor have my children Tristan and Georgianna ever lacked opinions on anything.

Finally, I want to express my appreciation to those who read the manuscript, pointed out my errors, and suggested improvements. Judith Milhous's expertise was invaluable to me in the sections on Restoration and eighteenth-century English theater; her generosity in taking so much time from her own work to comment upon these sections is deeply appreciated. Similarly, Ron Engle helped me through the sections on German theater. Venne-Richard Londré was my first reader, rounded up many of the illustrations for me, and helped out in countless other ways. My friend Dan Watermeier also read the entire manuscript, offered numerous perceptive suggestions, and kept me going when history seemed endless.

The Stuart Court and Restoration England

INIGO JONES AND STUART COURT ENTERTAINMENTS

Before the Restoration, England's strongest link with the continental stage was the Stuart court masques that were produced for the king and queen at Whitehall. Inigo Jones, who designed virtually all of those lavish entertainments between 1605 and 1640, traveled twice to Italy and France where he studied the architectural and stage design achievements of Andrea Palladio, Vincenzo Scamozzi, Bernardo Buontalenti, and others. Jones adapted Italian techniques of perspective painting, changeable scenes, and machinery for flying effects to the limited facilities of the Banqueting House at Whitehall, and he made the first use of a proscenium arch in England. Although his spectacular court masques had little apparent effect upon London's public and private theaters at the time, Jones's innovations were later to be an impetus for the new kind of theater that was to emerge during the 1660s.

Like its continental counterparts (the French *ballet de cour* and the Italian *intermezzo*), the Stuart court masque combined music, dance, poetry, and painting. Jones went even further by incorporating architecture into some of his presentations, as in *Time Vindicated* (1623), which represented on stage the exterior of the Whitehall Banqueting House, the very building (designed by Jones) in which the masque was being performed. The magnificence of the masques was a celebration of monarchy, as were the works of numerous other artists—especially painters and musicians—upon whom the pre-Commonwealth Stuart kings, James I and Charles I, both bestowed their patronage.

Queen Anne, the Danish-born wife of James I, commissioned Inigo Jones's first masque and later initiated the idea of the antimasque as a "spectacle of strangeness" to heighten by contrast the beauties of the main feature. Following a precedent set at the French court, the queen herself appeared as the principal dancer in some of the masques. The king was the essential audience member, the "divine" source of harmonious opulence that the masque reflected back upon himself. Ben Jonson's poetry injected a moralizing tone into the entertainment, since his allegorical texts upheld the ideal virtues that their majesties were supposed to embody.

Such elaborate exercises in self-congratulation were confined to the court, however, and could neither dazzle ordinary citizens nor distract them from the increasing religious factionalism and economic hardship that affected their way of life. Indeed, the notorious extravagance of the costly masques drew the public's attention to corruption and decadence in high circles. The resulting disillusionment found oblique expression in the many Jacobean tragedies that used a foreign setting, often Italian, to depict vice and depravity at court. Those dark, horrific dramas, along with the satirical "city comedies" that reflected a growing cynicism among merchants and professional men, were performed in the surviving Elizabethan-style public theaters (The Red Bull, Globe, Fortune, and Hope) or in the higher-priced private theaters (Blackfriars, Whitefriars, Phoenix/Cockpit in Drury Lane, and later the Salisbury Court). It speaks well of the reign of James I that such energetically skeptical works were regularly produced in spite of the fact that he had placed the playhouses under direct control of the royal household. In 1625 Charles I succeeded to the throne and married Henrietta Maria, sister of Louis XIII of France. No masques were performed during the first six years of his reign, even though Charles had led masquing dances at his father's court since 1618. Only after England had concluded peace treaties with France and Spain were the court masques resumed, and peace is a predominant theme in the ones performed between 1631 and 1640. It is interesting, too, that all of the Caroline masques—like Van Dyck's many portraits of the king—were confined to the period of personal rule by Charles I, the eleven years following his 1629 dissolution of Parliament. By stressing England's peace while the Continent was embroiled in the Thirty Years War, the masques symbolically justified the policies of the monarchy by divine right.

Although his English subjects were displeased by the king's marriage to a Catholic and by his employment of many foreign artists and craftsmen, Charles I and Henrietta Maria together established a foothold for Baroque art in England and set a standard of taste that would be reasserted after the Restoration. Not only was the painter Van Dyck induced to settle in England, but Rubens was commissioned to paint ceiling panels for the Whitehall Banqueting House. Those panels, showing the apotheosis of a Stuart king into a sublime Baroque heaven, would have been the ideal complement to the sumptuous masques per-

Inigo Jones (1573–1652) designed the third Whitehall Banqueting House, which was completed in 1622. This second-floor room, with its elegant classical proportions, was used for court masques until it was discovered that smoke from the torches was ruining the ceiling panels that were painted on commission by Peter Paul Rubens. Courtesy of the Department of the Environment, London.

Britannia Triumphans (1638) by Sir William Davenant was the first masque to be staged in a temporary masquing house built in the courtyard near Whitehall Banqueting House, which was no longer used for masques after 1635. The first scene, shown here, included a vista of the river Thames and the city of London. Devonshire Collection, Chatsworth. Reproduced by permission of the Chatsworth Settlement Trustees.

formed in the hall below except for one factor that had been overlooked: smoke from the torches used in the masques threatened to damage the painting. Performances were suspended for three years while Inigo Jones designed and supervised construction of an adjacent Masquing House at Whitehall, which was inaugurated in 1638.

Both Charles and Henrietta Maria were accomplished dancers, but the nature of the masque meant that there had to be a royal spectator; thus the king and queen took turns dancing in masques that each offered to the other. The allegorical union of Mars and Venus that they represented was also a reflection of the queen's considerable influence in political matters as well as in polite behavior. Under Charles I, the masques were lengthened with more dancing and became more directly tied to current issues, perhaps as a kind of rationalization of the king's policies. This was especially true after Inigo Jones and Ben Jonson quarreled in 1631 over whether spectacle or poetry took precedence in the masque. Jonson then ended the twenty-six-year collaboration, and Jones triumphantly elaborated his spectacular effects over texts contributed by more tractable poets: Aurelian Townshend, Thomas Carew, James Shirley, and, most importantly, William Davenant. Although Jones was constantly perfecting his machinery, his pictorial content correspondingly declined in originality; often he even borrowed directly from engravings of scenery designed by Buontalenti's pupils, Giulio and Alfonso Parigi, for ducal festivals in Florence.

The inspiration was French, however, when Jones designed three pastoral plays commissioned by Queen Henrietta Maria. Conceived by her as a means of importing the refined etiquette of platonic love that was fashionable at the French court, Racan's *Arténice* was presented in French for the court of Charles I in 1626. Seven times the scene alternated between two idealized rural settings, a woods and a village. These scenes included several transformations of the moon, and thunder and lightning effects. The production culminated in a view of the River Thames with Somerset House, the queen's residence, where the play was staged—a clever metaphorical tying together of the romance of the pastoral and the real world of the court. *Arténice* is a landmark production in English theater history on two counts. It was the first spoken drama presented on a perspective stage with changeable scenery, and it was the first time that a lady (the queen herself) played a speaking role on an English stage. The scandal of her appearance in a non-dancing role may account for the seven-year delay before a second pastoral play was performed.

By the time he designed sets and costumes for *The Shepherd's Paradise* (1633), an English pastoral by the Francophile author Walter Montague, with a running time of nearly eight hours, Jones was drawing upon engravings by the French artist Jacques Callot. That influence is clear in a French-style formal garden scene for this production. Ostensibly intended to afford the queen an opportunity to practice her English, *The Shepherd's Paradise* gained notoriety when it was linked to the phrase "Women-Actors, notorious whores" in William Prynne's *Histriomastix*, a 1,000-page pamphlet with a correspondingly long subtitle: *The Players' Scourge. . . . Wherein it is Largely Evidenced . . . by the Concurring Authorities and Resolutions of Sundry Texts of Scripture; of the Whole Primitive Church, both under the Law and Gospell; of 55 Synodes and Councels; of 71 Fathers and Christian Writers; . . . of above 150 Foraigne and Domestique Protestant and Popish Authors. . . ; of 40 Heathen Philosophers, Historians, Poets; . . . and of Our Own English Statutes, Magistrates, Universities, Writers, Preachers, That Popular Stage-Plays (the Very Pompes of the Divell Which We Renounce in Baptisme if We Believe the Fathers) are Sinful, Heathenish, Lewde, Ungodly Spectacles, and Most Pernicious Corruptions; Condemned in All Ages, as Intolerable Mischiefes to Churches, to Republickes, to the Manners, Mindes, and Soules of Men. And that the Profession of Play-poets, of Stage-playes, are Unlawfull, Infamous, and Misbeseeming Christians* (1632). The zealous Puritan protested in vain that the queen was not his intenc.ed target; he was disbarred, stripped of his academic degree, fined, imprisoned, and had his ears cut off.

Since Prynne had been a barrister, the king engineered a display of loyalty by the legal profession in the form of a magnificent masque, *The Triumph of Peace* (1634), composed by James Shirley in consultation with a committee from the four Inns of Court. The masque itself was preceded by a public procession composed of hundreds of lavishly costumed footmen, gentlemen on horseback, musicians, and other performers riding on chariots. The extravagance of this spectacle—probably the most splendid show of Charles I's reign—pointed up a financial reality: the wealth of the country was already passing into the hands of professional men and merchants, whereas the Crown without a Parliament was limited in its ability to raise money.

The following year brought the third and last of the queen's pastorals, *Florimène*, an anonymous French play once again on the subject of platonic love. It was performed in French by Henrietta Maria's ladies, in honor of the king's birthday; the queen remained a spectator this time, since she was in her last month of pregnancy. Several drawings by Jones and his assistant John Webb have survived to give an idea of this production, which was much praised for its graceful charm.

On a stage built at one end of the great hall at Whitehall, Jones placed a frontispiece (a proscenium emblematically conceived for the particular production) decorated with cupids rendered in the free and easy French manner. Behind that was a "standing scene" of trees and

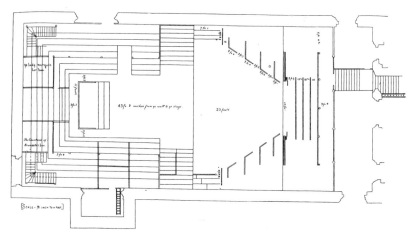

This copy of Inigo Jones's plan for the arrangement of the hall and the stage for the pastoral Florimène (1635) shows the disposition of book-wings and backshutters for the standing scene. From Les Masques anglaises (1909).

The "border" that framed the scene for Florimène, as shown in Jones's ink drawing, was a "Pastorall invention, proper to the subject, with a figure sitting on each side, representing a noble shepheard and sheapeardess, playing on Rurall instruments, over them Garlands held up by naked Boyes, as the prize of their Uictory. Above all, ranne a large Freese, and in it children in severall postures, imitating the Pastorall Rights and sacrifices, in the midst was placed a rich compartment, in which was written FLORIMENE." The scene depicted here consists of "Groves, Hils, Plaines, and here and there scattering, some shepheards cottages, and a far off, to terminate the sight, was the mayne Sea, expressing this place to be the Isle of Delos." Devonshire Collection, Chatsworth. Reproduced by permission of the Chatsworth Settlement Trustees.

cottages formed by four angled wings (book wings) on each side of the stage; that is, the downstage face of each of the eight angled wings was parallel with the front of the stage while the angled faces of the wings projected toward a central vanishing point. Behind the farthest upstage pair of wings, the ones set closest together, were the backshutters. Backshutters were painted panels that slid in grooves or tracks on the stage floor from both sides of the stage to meet at center. *Florimène* had two pairs of backshutters, one directly behind the other, which allowed two different "shutter scenes," one with a vista of the Isle of Delos that was specifically designed to complement the standing scene, and the other with a view of the Temple of Diana. Even greater scenic variety could be achieved by retracting both pairs of backshutters to reveal the "backscene," which may have constituted as much as one-third of the upstage area. When the backscene was revealed, it was set with a "scene of relieve," which meant that profiled or cut-out flats were set before a painted backdrop to give an illusion of depth. When shutter scenes and scenes of relieve were alternated in production, the relieves could be changed while a shutter scene was being performed. *Florimène* had scenes of relieve depicting each of the four seasons.

Jones's experiments with stage machinery culminated in the last masque before the civil war, *Salmacida Spolia*. Performed in January and February of 1640, shortly before lack of money necessitated Charles's convening of Parliament, this masque was a dazzling and optimistic exercise in self-delusion. The myth that peace and prosperity were axiomatic in a land blessed with a divinely empowered king was reified in scenic splendor surrounding the persons of both Charles I and Henrietta Maria. It was possible for their majesties to dance roles in the same masque, because the queen's mother, Marie de Medici, was there to sit in the throne of state. After twenty separate musical numbers, the king was finally discovered seated on a golden Throne of Honor, surrounded by his lords and by statues of ancient heroes. Then the queen made her entrance: she and her ladies were revealed by the parting of the clouds on high in the backscene. Seated upon another cloud, they were flown in and landed on the stage floor. The king and his lords led them out into a dance while the vacated cloud was "drawne awaye over ye sceane."

William Davenant wrote the last four court masques by Inigo Jones, and it was he, along with John Webb, who would carry Jones's scenic innovations forward—across the Puritan-controlled eighteen-year hiatus in English theatrical development—to set a standard of production in the Restoration theater. The son of an innkeeper at Oxford (midway between Stratford-upon-Avon and London), Davenant had fueled his literary ambitions by not denying the rumor that he was the illegitimate

John Webb (1611–72) worked closely with Jones on Salmacida Spolia *(1640) by Sir William Davenant, the last court masque performed before the civil war that led to the establishment of the Commonwealth. The king danced the role of Philogenes, wearing a costume "of watchet, richly embroidered with silver, long stockings set up of white; their caps with scrolls of gold, and plumes of white feathers." Devonshire Collection, Chatsworth. Reproduced by permission of the Chatsworth Settlement Trustees.*

Scene 5 of Salmacida Spolia *represented a great city and clouds with deities in the sky. The cloud that descended to the right side of the stage carried two persons, while that on the left carried three. The "greate Cloud with 6 persons in it" was pulled from the right side into the center. When the song ended, the two clouds on the sides were raised up again. Devonshire Collection, Chatsworth. Reproduced by permission of the Chatsworth Settlement Trustees.*

son of William Shakespeare. Writing complimentary verse and several successfully produced plays, he worked his way up to the court. He wrote his first masque, *The Temple of Love* (1635) in the same year as his comedy, *The Platonick Lovers,* which reflected Henrietta Maria's cult of platonic love. Although Davenant (who had lost part of his nose to syphilis) may have intended the play as a gentle mockery of love on a purely spiritual plane, it must have pleased the queen, for she not only watched the King's Men perform it at court, but set a precedent by going to see it performed at Blackfriars in 1636.

The benefits of giving invitational performances at court led theater companies to pander to court tastes, thus contributing to a decline in dramatic literature from the vigor of Jacobean fare to the artifice and refinement of Caroline drama. However, some scholars see in plays like *The Platonick Lovers* or Richard Brome's *The Love-Sick Court* or Philip Massinger's *The Bashful Lover* (1636) a deliberate use of the court's own language in order to penetrate that closed world with some corrective criticism. In any case, there is ample evidence that Charles I loved the theater as he loved all the arts: he saw an average of twenty-five productions a year, suggested the plot of James Shirley's *The Gamester* (1633), and accorded top priority to Inigo Jones's conversion of the royal Cockpit at Whitehall into the Cockpit-in-Court Theatre in 1629. The Cockpit-in-Court was intended for use by professional companies rather than for court masques, and thus it had no provision for scenic machinery.

Davenant's collaborations with Inigo Jones on the court masques gave him a taste for scenic spectacle, and he believed there was a market for it among the general public. In 1639 he obtained a royal patent to construct a theater and form a company "to exercise action, musical presentments, scenes, dancing, and the like." It is clear from the warrant that he was planning to produce music drama featuring Italian-style painted-perspective changeable scenery. That theater, however, never came into being, as Davenant encountered unexpected difficulties in getting financial backing. Instead, he took over the management of the King's and Queen's Boys at the Drury Lane Cockpit, or Phoenix, Theatre. He ran it for only a year, April 1640 to May 1641, while carrying out other duties in the Royal Army, so he had no opportunity to install the scenic machinery he wanted. When civil war broke out in 1642, Davenant served the Royalist cause, for which he received a knighthood in 1643. He was imprisoned twice, found a wealthy widow to marry for money, and lived for a time in France before resuming his theatrical activities.

THE COMMONWEALTH PERIOD

The civil war between the Roundheads (Parliamentarians and Puritans) and the Cavaliers (Royalists) continued until 1646, ending in defeat for the king, who was executed for treason in 1649. That public event, witnessed by a huge throng at Whitehall, was described by one Puritan as "a Tragedie at the Banqueting-house, where he had seene and caused many a Comedy to be acted upon the Lord's Day." The queen, her sons Charles and James, and many Royalists lived in exile in France during the Interregnum. There they had the opportunity to see elaborate productions like the machine plays mounted by the Italian "great magician" Giacomo Torelli, who came to Paris in 1645.

Meanwhile, theatrical development came to a standstill in England, although sporadic performances continued to be given. In 1642, the Puritans in Parliament had succeeded in passing a resolution "that while these sad Causes and set times of Humiliation doe continue, publike Stage-playes shall cease, and bee forborne." The Globe Playhouse was torn down in 1644. In 1647, actors began performing openly again at the Salisbury Court, Fortune, and Cockpit/Phoenix Theatres, but Parliament responded with an ordinance "for the better Suppression of Stage-plays, Interludes, and Common Players" under which any actors caught performing were to be imprisoned and arraigned as rogues. That ordinance was strengthened in 1648 with provisions for demolishing the playhouses and fining spectators caught attending performances.

The dismantling of the interiors of the remaining theaters and the soldiers' raids on performances were discouragement enough to impel some actors to go abroad to practice their profession. The best known of these was the irascible actor-manager George Jolly, whose hot temper made it difficult for him to keep a company together. The earliest record of his activity on the Continent shows that he was in Germany with a company of fourteen actors in 1648. He is known to have toured to Poland and Sweden in 1649–50, then to Vienna; he may also have performed for Charles II in Frankfurt in 1655. Especially active in Eastern Europe was a company led by John Wayde and William Roe, which included Dutch and German actors as well as English.

Another way of circumventing the anti-theater laws was to perform "drolls." These were short comic scenes extracted from longer popular plays, such as "Merry Conceits of Bottom the Weaver" from *A Midsummer Night's Dream* or "The Grave-Makers" from *Hamlet*. Drolls could be presented inexpensively at private gatherings, at country fairs, in taverns, or even on "Mountebancks Stages at Charing Cross, Lincolns Inn

Fields, and other places . . . with Loud Laughter and Great Applause." In such situations the spectators could disperse quickly if the authorities arrived. One especially popular performer of drolls was "the incomparable *Robert Cox,* who was not only the principal Actor, but also the Contriver and Author of most of these Farces." He apparently created a series of pieces centered upon characters like Simpleton the Smith, John Swabber, and Hobbinat. Among his choice bits was a turn as Young Simpleton "with a great piece of Bread and Butter" making much of the fact that a man cannot be left undisturbed to "eat a little bit for his Afternoon's Lunchin'." His popularity was enough to pack the Red Bull Theatre, where his last recorded performance was cut short in 1653 by soldiers who had been alerted by some jealous rope-dancers. Cox died in 1655, but a collection of his drolls was published about that time. The most important collection of drolls, *The Wits, or Sport upon Sport,* was published by bookseller Francis Kirkman in 1672.

The arts in general fared badly during the Commonwealth in England because of the loss of aristocratic patronage as well as the Puritans' prohibition of activities that could be construed as frivolous. Weddings became solemn occasions unmarked by dancing or feasting, and Christmas was merely another working day unless it fell on Sunday. Church hymns were allowed, although the sumptuousness of organ music was considered "popish." Ornamentation—whether in music or in the decorative arts or in dress—was associated unfavorably with the Baroque impulse that emanated from Catholic countries. Much support for the Puritans came from the merchant class, whose trade with the Calvinist Low Countries oriented them to a more homely style in home furnishings and architecture. Despite his nearly thirty years of important contributions to English architecture, Inigo Jones lost his position as Surveyor of Works in 1643. Scorned as the "contriver of scenes for the Queen's Dancing Barn," Jones died in poverty in 1652. Luckily, his vast collection of drawings and books with his marginal annotations passed into the possession of his nephew-in-law and disciple John Webb.

The church sermon, often quite lengthy, became the dominant mode of expression along with its literary counterpart, the essay. Numerous important essayists promoted the Parliamentarian view, while Thomas Hobbes was one outstanding thinker who shared the royal family's exile. Poets also fell into two camps: Cavalier love lyricists like John Suckling, Robert Herrick, and Richard Lovelace versus Parliamentarian authors of philosophical poems. John Milton, the greatest writer of the age, supported the Commonwealth cause and was perceived in Europe as its spokesman, although he had written a masque in his youth. Milton's *Comus* (1634), which had been performed by the earl of Bridgewater's three children at Ludlow Castle, extols Christian tem-

The frontispiece to Kirkman's The Wits, or Sport upon Sport *(1672) shows characters from several different drolls that were performed during the Commonwealth. Among them, at the front of the stage are Falstaff and the Hostess from Shakespeare's* Henry IV, Parts 1 and 2. *This drawing may not accurately represent an actual stage of the period, but it does offer some indications of stage lighting.*

perance even as it acknowledges the hedonistic attractions of evil.

The Commonwealth's suppression of plays seemed justified to some because of the theater's royal patronage as well as its historic connection with the Catholic Church. Lacking such associations and appealing largely to the masses, bearbaiting was allowed to continue throughout the Interregnum. Leslie Hotson contends that London supported two bear gardens—arenas where spectators watched half-starved bears brutally attacked by savage dogs. Other amusements available to Londoners were games of tennis and bowls. Tennis was played, in England as on the Continent, in indoor courts: rectangular buildings with windows set high in the side walls and lined with spectators' galleries. During the Interregnum, two tennis courts—Gibbons's and Lisle's—stood in Lincoln's Inn Fields, which became a popular recreation area. Both of those buildings were to be important in the re-establishment of theatrical practice in England.

DAVENANT'S PRE-RESTORATION PRODUCTIONS

Even before the 1660 restoration of the English monarchy, Sir William Davenant diplomatically effected a gradual restoration of theatrical entertainment. Calling upon certain well-placed friends in Oliver Cromwell's administration, Davenant appealed to their interest in music and described the educational possibilities of "moral representations," thus securing their protection in his endeavor. On May 23, 1656, he offered a public performance entitled *The First Day's Entertainment at Rutland House,* an "Entertainment by Musick and Declarations after the manner of the Ancients." About 150 people paid five shillings apiece to attend a one-and-a-half-hour performance in Davenant's own home, a mansion that had been confiscated by the Cromwell regime when its Catholic owner died. A stage with a purple and gold curtain was set up at one end of a narrow room, and—following an English tradition that went as far back as the Tudor interludes performed in fifteenth-century banqueting halls—the musicians were placed above the scene. The substance of the dialogue between two Athenians was an argument for and against "opera." The favorable verdict for opera was cleverly supplemented by songs honoring Cromwell as Lord Protector and making fun of the French.

By September of that same year, Davenant was ready to go a step further. *The Siege of Rhodes,* "a Representation by the Art of Perspective in Scenes and the Story Sung in Recitative Musick," was performed at Rutland House on a stage with an ornamental proscenium and eleven-foot-high scenery, including movable backshutters, designed by John Webb. This was the first public performance in England using scenery in the Italian mode. The five acts were called "entries," a term carried over from the masques to define the work as a musical performance rather than a play. Since the injunction against stage-players was still in effect, the cast was composed of seven singers and musicians, including one woman. The shock of that first public appearance of an Englishwoman in a dramatic role was mitigated by the casting of her own husband, Edward Coleman, in the role of the character's husband. The crowds and armies that figure in the story were simply painted on the shutters or backdrops. The space was too small to permit dancing even if Davenant had dared to go that far, and yet the influence of the Stuart court masque is clear. Although Davenant later alluded to *The Siege of Rhodes* as an opera, his purpose was not to launch English opera as a genre, but to bring back legitimate drama. It is probable, according to Edward J. Dent, that Davenant had originally written it as a play; in fact, the great poet-playwright John Dryden would later signal it as the prototype for the Restoration genre known as heroic drama.

Davenant's next goal was to get his work into a public building. He won permission to do so by proposing a work that would support the cause of Cromwell's war with Spain. The resulting musical presentation, short on narrative and long on propaganda, was based upon *The Tears of the Indians,* an inflammatory book dedicated to Cromwell and published in London in 1656 as a sensationalistic exposé "of the Cruel Massacres and Slaughters of above Twenty Millions of innocent People; Committed by the Spaniards." Davenant's production, *The Cruelty of the Spaniards in Peru,* "Exprest by Instrumentall and Vocall Musick, and by the Art of Perspective in Scenes, &c.," opened in July 1658 at the Phoenix/Cockpit in Drury Lane. The interior of the theater, which had been destroyed by soldiers in 1649, was now repaired. Apparently, Davenant even installed some rudimentary machinery, for the text of the work includes the following indication: "a Rope descends out of the Clouds, and is stretched to a stiffness by an Engine, whilst a Rustic Air is played, to which two Apes from opposite sides of the Wood come out, listen, return; and coming out again begin to dance; then, after a while, one of them leaps up to the Rope, and there dances to the same Air, whilst the other moves to his measures below. Then both retire into the Wood. The Rope ascends." *The Cruelty of the Spaniards in Peru* was evidently little more than a musical variety show.

In the winter of 1658–59, again at the Drury Lane Cockpit, Davenant staged *The History of Sir Francis Drake,* an action-packed play with musical accompaniment. It had six entries with flat painted scenes depicting various activities of West Indian natives. Although the story

Sir William Davenant (1606–68) is one of few major figures who carried on theatrical activities both before and after the Commonwealth. His nose was partially disfigured by syphilis.

involved the rescue of a captive bride, the play was performed by an all-male cast. The briefly glimpsed "Beautiful Lady ty'd to a Tree, adorned with the Ornaments of a Bride, with her hair dishevelled, and complaining, with her hands towards Heaven" was either a painting on a backdrop or a mute figure in a *tableau vivant.*

   That same season, Davenant boldly revived *The Siege of Rhodes,* this time for the broader public of the Cockpit, to which he brought John Webb's scenery. However, there was some sentiment that he might have gone too far. After the death of Oliver Cromwell and the accession of his son Richard, a Parliamentary committee was appointed to investigate whether the operas had overstepped the bounds into the realm of "stage-plays." Performances at the Cockpit seem to have continued, although Davenant was arrested and imprisoned for a few weeks in 1659 along with many other conspirators who had plotted an uprising on behalf of the exiled king. With the arrival of General Monck in London in February 1660, there was little doubt that the reopening of the theaters was imminent. Davenant obtained a lease on Lisle's Tennis Court and departed for France to win the king's support for his long-repressed theatrical ambitions.

THEATER COMPANIES

Charles II entered London in a triumphal procession, joyfully welcomed by cheering crowds, on May 29, 1660. Three companies had already begun offering regular performances of plays: one led by Michael Mohun at the Red Bull, another company under John Rhodes at the Cockpit, and another under William Beeston at Salisbury Court. Sir Henry Herbert, who had been Master of the Revels under Charles I, was reasserting the authority of his old office. In addition, George Jolly soon returned from the Continent, eager to resume work in London. Sir William Davenant sized up the situation and decided that he had the best chance of coming out on top in the theatrical power struggle if he joined forces with Thomas Killigrew, a playwright who had spent several years in the service of the king in exile and had acquired the title of King's Jester. Davenant also had the advantage of possessing the patent for a theater, which he had obtained from Charles I in 1639.

By the end of the year Davenant and Killigrew had won the right to form the two theater companies that would monopolize the London stage into the eighteenth century. They immediately set about choosing their actors from the companies that were no longer authorized, fitting out theater facilities, and producing plays, although the documents that formally granted their royal patents were not obtained until 1662–63. Thomas Killigrew was patented to run the King's Company, whom he recruited largely from Mohun's company along with some others of the generation of pre-Commonwealth actors. In addition, two young actors joined Killigrew: Thomas Betterton, who soon transferred to Davenant's company and became the leading actor of his generation, and Edward Kynaston, one of several men who specialized in female roles in those early days before a sufficient number of actresses could be brought into the profession. For three seasons the King's Company performed on a simple platform stage in Gibbons's Tennis Court, which was renamed the Theatre Royal in Vere Street.

Davenant's patent established the Duke of York's Company. Most of his actors were young and came from John Rhodes's company. He opened the Duke's Theatre in Lincoln's Inn Fields (formerly Lisle's Tennis Court) with a revival of *The Siege of Rhodes,* now expanded and presented as part 1, followed by a second day's performance of a sequel, part 2, to which a second woman's role was added. No drawings exist for the second part, but the published text suggests a variety of scenes painted on shutters and possibly a scene of relieve. The prologue further hints that Davenant, like artists in all periods, chafed at the discrepancy between funding for the military and funding for the arts:

Oh Money! Money! if the WITTS would dress,
With Ornaments, the present face of Peace;
And to our Poet half that Treasure spare,
Which Faction gets from Fools to nourish Warr;
Then his contracted Scenes should wider be,
And move by greater Engines, till you see
(Whilst you Securely sit) fierce Armies meet,
And raging Seas disperse a fighting Fleet.

The king, the duke, and other nobility attended the opening performance. One performer, John Downes, was so overcome by stage fright that he gave up acting and became the company's bookkeeper/prompter; his recollections, published as *Roscius Anglicanus* in 1708, provide an invaluable record of theatrical activity on the Restoration stage.

Hoping to rival the production values of the operas staged at Davenant's theater, Killigrew built a new Theatre Royal in Bridges Street in 1663. Although the King's Company concentrated on legitimate drama rather than operas, its inauguration of changeable scenery enlivened the competition between the two theaters. Both theaters suffered severe financial setbacks when they were ordered closed in 1665 because of the Great Plague, which devastated London for a year and a half, claiming 100,000 victims among a population of 500,000. Scarcely was the plague under control when, in September 1666, the Great Fire broke out that destroyed four-fifths of London. Amazingly, both theaters were spared.

Another problem was the encroachment of George Jolly upon the two patentees' territory. The obstinate Jolly had obtained special permission in 1660 to perform at the Cockpit, but after two seasons took his company—mostly composed of actors from Beeston's troupe—on tour. Davenant and Killigrew took advantage of his absence to cheat him out of his London rights, so that Jolly's license was revoked in 1667 when he attempted to resume performances there after the plague. Finally he was mollified by being given the management of the Nursery, a training ground for young actors for both of the patented companies. The Nursery company used various facilities, including the former Theatre Royal in Vere Street.

Davenant's management of the Duke's Company was based upon personal involvement in all areas; through sound financial policies and clear contractual assignments of responsibilities, he maintained a generally high level of morale among members of his company. Certainly, he was the leader in innovative approaches to production, which Killigrew then imitated. Killigrew tended to leave the running of the King's Company to shareholders, and discipline was lax. Although there were organizational differences between the two patent companies, both were composed of senior actors, who held shares in the company stock, and some hired junior actors. Actresses belonged only to the latter category, and indeed they were always paid far less than men of comparable popularity and experience.

Judith Milhous has calculated that there were about two hundred performance days in a normal theater season, and that an exceptional run of a new play might be about eight or ten performances; this meant that fifty or more different plays would be presented each year; some of these were new plays but most were holdovers from previous seasons. These figures varied, of course, with changes in the economic climate and in production trends from the 1660s to 1700.

When Sir William Davenant died in 1668, his son Charles inherited the patent, which his mother held for him until he was seventeen; however, the actual management and artistic decisions were capably handled by senior company members Thomas Betterton and Henry Harris. After a decision was made to construct a larger theater with more complex stage machinery, Betterton traveled to France to study the scenic mechanisms in use there. In 1671 the Duke's Company moved into the Dorset Garden, a magnificently equipped new theater near the Strand. Twice as big as Lincoln's Inn Fields Theatre, it was the largest (approximately 140 feet long by 57 feet wide) theater of the Restoration period and included an apartment for Thomas Betterton on the top story at the front of the building.

Only eleven weeks after the Duke's Company vacated Lincoln's Inn Fields, the King's Company moved into it, for the Theatre Royal in Bridges Street had been destroyed by a fire that also burned up the company's ten-year stock of scenery and costumes. Despite difficulties in financing, they eventually built the Theatre Royal in Drury Lane, which opened in 1674. That building remained in use for over a century, until it was demolished in 1791 and replaced by a larger Drury Lane Theatre on the same site.

Restoration theater architecture and scenic conventions were a product of the long evolution from Tudor banqueting halls and Eliza-bethan/Jacobean playhouses merged with the devices of the Stuart court masque; they were also obliquely influenced by French theatrical practice as observed by the English nobility in exile during the Interregnum as well as by subsequent emissaries like Betterton. The French influence may have been a factor in the reduced capacity of the Restoration theaters (about 500–700 in the tennis court theaters and up to 1200 at the Dorset Garden, as opposed to around 2,000 in the earlier Eliza-bethan public theaters), and in a seating pattern that reflected a social hierarchy. The pit, or main floor of the auditorium, was occupied by young gallants, government officials like Samuel Pepys, some ladies, and some women of ill repute, all of whom were jostled together on backless benches covered with green cloth. Surrounding the pit at stage level

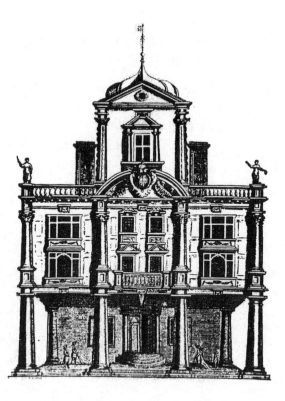

The Duke's Theatre in Dorset Garden was built for Davenant's company in 1671. This façade underwent a number of modifications over the years, and little is known about the interior. George Wilkenson, Londina Illustrata *(1808–1825).*

were the boxes; in the center box sat the king and his companions, while the side boxes were mostly filled with "ladies of quality." Ordinary citizens took places in the middle gallery and in the even less expensive upper gallery. Those citizens who did sit in the pit would be likely to put their wives and daughters in the middle gallery. Servants attending "persons of quality" would take the low-priced upper-gallery seats.

The Tudor and Elizabethan practice of placing the musicians above the stage was continued at least at the Dorset Garden Theatre. The frontispiece of the court masques now took the form of an ornate permanent proscenium. The old convention of using two doors at the back of a bare performance space for all entrances and exits evolved into the Restoration theaters' use of "proscenium doors"—at least one, and possibly two, on each side of the proscenium—opening onto a deep apron. That bare forestage, which served as the basic playing area, was twenty-one feet deep at the Drury Lane Theatre and probably about the same at the Dorset Garden. Architecturally, the Restoration theater was a hybrid form that most resembled the Elizabethan/Jacobean private theaters like Blackfriars in the auditorium and forestage areas, and the Stuart Court stage in everything behind the proscenium.

PRODUCTION VALUES

It was in the scenic settings behind the proscenium that Restoration theater made its greatest advance over anything previously seen on a public stage in England. The basic technology was that pioneered by Inigo Jones in the court masques in an effort to reproduce effects achieved by the French and Italians. Instead of adopting the Italian "chariot and pole" method of scene shifting, which involved centrally operated machinery beneath the stage floor to move entire sets of wings into or out of view, Jones and his successors relied upon stagehands to push the backshutters in or out, to place and replace scenic units behind the backshutters for scenes of relieve, and, eventually—after "standing side-scenes" gave way to changeable wings—to set new pairs of wings in their supporting wooden tracks or "grooves" on the stage floor. A production could feature any number of "flat scenes" simply by drawing apart the two halves of a backshutter to reveal another painted shutter behind it, but "set scenes" with cut-out relief units and ground rows could only be alternated with flat scenes that would mask the placement or removal of set pieces. Also in the scenic area behind the proscenium were all the flying effects, the machinery for which was apparently patterned after that used on the Continent. Recent research by Colin Visser and John Orrell has shown that as early as 1661 a touring French troupe must have rigged some flying mechanisms at the Cockpit in Drury Lane.

Despite descriptive stage directions in published play texts, frequent entries on theater in the diaries of Samuel Pepys, and some pictorial materials, present knowledge about elements of production in Restoration theater is sketchy. For example, the five engravings by Dolle of scenes from Elkanah Settle's *The Empress of Morocco,* as produced at the Dorset Garden in 1673, constitute the only extant pictorial evidence concerning the interior of that theater with scenery on the stage. Thus it seems unusual that so many specialists have avoided detailed analysis of them. Two scholars (Richard Southern, in the *Revels History of Drama in English,* and Jocelyn Powell in *Restoration Theatre Production*), who have attempted to explain—applying the published stage directions to the illustrations—how these scenes were realized on stage, do not seriously question old assumptions that these scenes were all composed of wings, borders, and backshutters. It is certainly possible, as Powell suggests, that the act 2, scene 1, vista of a river could have been a scene of relieve: "The architecture at either side and the great ships immediately behind could be painted on the same wing, or the architecture could be cut out in relieve and the ships painted upon a wing behind. The sea, with the rest of the fleet and the boat coming ashore, might be painted on shutters, as in *The Siege of Rhodes,* or might be practical, with the ships passing on grooves between the turning waves."

Act 4, scene 2 of *The Empress of Morocco,* is a Masque of Hell, a play-within-the-play, and thus it is logical that this is the only one of the five engravings that depicts a curtain drawn up near the top of both sides of the frame. That it could not have been, as Southern suggests, "the regular front curtain of the theatre which had been unintentionally omitted from the other illustrations" is borne out by the fact that one of the flying demons is moving in front of that curtain while the other's hand is behind the curtain. Southern goes on to point out that "no wings or borders are indicated but presumably these would show rocks and clouds respectively." Considering the careful attention to detail with which these five settings are rendered, as well as the fact that there is no other pictorial evidence of such elaborate scenes on the English Restoration stage, it seems logical to place more trust in Dolle's accuracy of depiction, especially since an interpretation based primarily upon the illustrations is not necessarily contradicted by the printed stage directions.

Proceeding from the pictorial evidence, I suggest that at least one and possibly as many as four out of five of the settings represented may have been simply painted illustrations that served as backgrounds to the action on the forestage. Several factors support this conjecture. First, there was a tradition of using scenery as a purely emblematic production value. Southern himself has shown (in *Changeable Scenery*), for example, that "Davenant did not introduce scenery as an illusionistic setting but, instead, thought out quite a profound conception of it as an accompaniment to the exposition of the plot used in a sort of counterpoint." Second, it was not unusual in Restoration theater to paint people on the scenery; indeed, even if the river scene for *The Empress of Morocco* had been a scene of relieve as described by Powell, it would have included the painted figure standing on the prow of the ship as well as the rowers of the tiny boat on the water at center. The discrepancy in the size of the figures in the various settings also argues against their being representations of live actors in the settings; this is especially apparent in the size differences between the prison scene and the Hell scene. Third, the amount of activity shown in the Hell scene and in the palm-tree scene would not have been performed within the setting behind the proscenium arch while a twenty-foot deep forestage separated that action

Dolle's engravings of settings for the five acts of Elkanah Settle's The Empress of Morocco *(here and facing page) as produced at the Dorset Garden Theatre in 1673, show the musicians' gallery above the proscenium opening. A small portion of the forestage with the first of two pairs of proscenium doors is also visible. The setting for act 1, above, was a prison scene. The Harvard Theatre Collection.*

Left, act 2 of The Empress of Morocco *is described as "the Prospect of a large River, with a glorious Fleet of Ships, supposed to be the Navy of Muly Hamet, after the Sound of Trumpets and the Discharging of Guns." The Harvard Theatre Collection.*

Right, the palm tree setting for act 3 of The Empress of Morocco *might have been a flat painting of dancers around a tree, used as an emblematic reinforcement of the live-action dancers on the forestage. The Harvard Theatre Collection.*

Left, act 4 of The Empress of Morocco *contains a masque of Hell, "in which Pluto, Proserpine, and other Women-Spirits appeared seated, attended by Furies; the Stage being fill'd on each side with Crimalhaz, Hametalhaz, Q. Mother, and all the Court in Masquerade." The Harvard Theatre Collection.*

Right, the final tableau at the end of act 5 of The Empress of Morocco *shows Crimalhaz "cast down on the Gaunches, being hung on a wall set with spikes of Iron" while Abdelcador tells the just, triumphant Prince Muly Hamet: "See the reward of Treason; Death's the thing / Distinguishes th' Usurper from the King." The Harvard Theatre Collection.*

from the audience. Fourth, the palm-tree setting can scarcely be explained otherwise than as a flat illustration, and this is presumably why most scholars have simply avoided discussing it. Southern does courageously tackle it (in the *Revels History*): "What is remarkable is that it shows us no wings and no borders and no backscene at all! Indeed the illustration is one of the most curious in scenic history." He concludes that Dolle took artistic license in concentrating on representing the dance spectacle while ignoring the surrounding scenery. The stage directions for this scene are:

> The scene opened. A State is presented, the King, Queen, and Mariamne seated, Muly-Hamet, Abdelcador, and Attendants, a Moorish Dance is presented by Moors in several Habits, who bring in an artificial Palm-tree, about which they dance to several antick Instruments of Musick; in the intervals of the Dance, this Song is sung by a Moorish Priest and two Moorish Women: the Chorus of it being performed by all the Moors.

A logical interpretation of this sequence is that the shutters for the previous scene opened, allowing the extras to carry the "State" or throne onto the forestage; it will be noted that no throne is shown in the engraving. The dancers would also carry onto the forestage a small portable palm tree. Then the painted scene would slide in behind them, with its painted dancers and large painted palm tree emblematically reinforcing the live dancers and prop tree. Another reason for suspecting that the scene is merely a flat illustration is that nothing we know about Restoration costuming suggests that live performers would have appeared in such uniformly designed exotic costumes, which also would have been uncharacteristic in featuring bare legs and feet.

The question of whether the width of the Dorset Garden Theatre could have accommodated closable shutters within a few feet behind the proscenium arch—that is, would there have been room to draw them off to the sides?—has been debated in a series of articles by Robert D. Hume and John R. Spring. Even if this were not possible, the proscenium opening could have been filled by sliding in two shutters from each side of the stage. Furthermore, it is known that painted drop curtains were in use by 1690 and there is nothing to contradict the possibility that they could have been used as early as 1673 for *The Empress of Morocco*. In any event, there is at present no way of knowing with any certainty exactly how those scenes were represented. My own guess is that the prison, palm-tree, and Hell scenes were flat painted illustrations and that the river and the torture settings were scenes of relieve.

Samuel Pepys, unfortunately, ended his diary several years before that production, for the scarceness of his comments on scenic spectacle other than to note that this or that play was "done with scenes" might suggest that any visual interest in a production was noteworthy. Indications are that there was great latitude in the way different productions were staged, some apparently very minimally, others dazzling in their spectacular effects achieved with machinery. After a visit backstage in March 1666, for example, Pepys noted that "the Machines are fine, and the paintings very pretty." An illustration that can be linked with one of Pepys's comments is for *The Island Princess*, which he saw on January 7, 1668/9: "It is a pretty good play, many good things being in it—and a good scene of a town on fire." The scene painted with a town on fire also depicts a crowd of people on the canvas.

Comedies were costumed in contemporary dress, so efforts were made to reflect the high fashion of the audience. The Restoration renewed English consumerism, partly as a reaction against the drabness of Puritan garb and partly because England's expanding foreign trade made little luxuries more readily available than ever before. Ribbons, laces, plumes, brocades, fur muffs, periwigs, fans, snuffboxes, swords, perfumes, dressing-table and tea-table accessories all became everyday necessities for ladies and gentlemen. Actors and actresses showed off as much of such finery as they and their companies could afford, and often created a bit of stage business to feature some item. The companies built up large stocks of costumes, but individual performers were expected to flaunt gorgeous accoutrements lavished on them by their wealthy admirers. King Charles II lent his coronation robes for at least two different productions. Tragedies were costumed even more extravagantly than comedies to reinforce the exoticism of their settings. The one essential for a tragic hero was feathers on his head, for these could quiver very effectively in scenes of "rant." Women, too, liked to adorn themselves and the posts of their beds with feathers. A green baize cloth spread on the floor protected the investment in extravagant costumes when actors had to do death scenes.

Daylight coming through windows in the theater was a source of illumination, as curtain time was around three-thirty in the afternoon during most of the Restoration period. Additional light came from chandeliers of candles suspended over the forestage, behind the proscenium, and in the auditorium. There may have been as many as six hoops with twelve candles on each one hanging quite low over the forestage and thus obstructing the view from the galleries. At first the candles were tallow, which dripped on the audience, and they were unpleasantly smoky, but later both theaters were spending more to have wax candles. The auditorium remained well lighted during the performance, although some dimming of stage lights was possible for special effects. This could be done by stagehands snuffing out candles mounted behind the scenes or by a device that allowed the footlights to be dropped below the level of the stage floor.

RESTORATION AUDIENCES

Charles II loved the theater, and his tastes had a great deal to do with the way it developed in the early years of the Restoration, both on stage and in the auditorium. Having spent most of his years of exile at various courts of Europe (except for an adventure in Scotland and the north of England in 1650–51, from which—traveling in disguise—he had barely escaped with his life), he enjoyed the company of witty, literate, cosmopolitan courtiers. He gathered about him a coterie of nobility and gentry, who lived in or near the palace. Well educated and strongly oriented to French fashions, the "Court" set the trends in social matters as in the arts. John Dryden, in his "Essay on the Dramatic Poetry of the Last Age," credited the king with setting an example that led to "an improvement of our Wit, Language, and Conversation" over that of the previous generation in England. The cultivated tone of Charles II's court was similarly reported at second hand by essayist John Dennis:

> That Reign was a Reign of Pleasure, even the entertainments of their Closet were all delightful. Poetry and Eloquence were then their Studies, and that human, gay, and sprightly Philosophy, which qualified them to relish the only reasonable pleasures which man can have in the world, and those are Conversation and Dramatick Poetry. In their Closets they cultivated at once their Imaginations and Judgements, to make themselves the fitter for conversation, which requires them both.

Dennis went on to point out that the main topic of conversation was "the Manners and Humours of Men," which made the nobility particularly adept at judging and appreciating comedy. Certainly, much the same could be said about the court of Charles II's contemporary, Louis XIV.

A retinue of courtiers (often including one of the mistresses he flaunted publicly, as did Louis XIV) accompanied Charles II during his frequent attendance at both theaters. He applauded the French practice of allowing women to perform publicly—even in male roles or "breeches parts" that showed off their legs; passed along some lavish court costumes to the players; lent his royal musicians for special productions; and even suggested ideas for plays, often based upon the plots of French or Spanish works with which he was familiar. A few plays were written by members of an inner circle known as the Court Wits: George Villiers, duke of Buckingham; John Wilmot, earl of Rochester; Charles Sackville, Lord Brockhurst; Sir Charles Sedley; Sir George Etherege; and others. Although Charles II always valued polite manners and a behavioral code of honor for gentlemen, their often shocking escapades and vulgar language were reflected in the amorous adventures and bawdy jokes that constituted many of the comedies.

Closely patterning itself upon the court was the "Town." This group was composed of wealthy and fashionable people who lived around Covent Garden, St. James's Square, or the Strand, and frequented the court. These people spent their ample leisure time riding in Hyde Park, walking in the Mall or St. James's Park, conversing in coffeehouses (coffee, tea, and chocolate all became available in the 1650s), going to concerts, dancing, gambling, and attending the theater to see characters from their own social milieu on stage. Much has been written debating whether or not the flagrant sexual intrigues of the comedies that were the main staple of Restoration theater accurately reflected the mores of the Town. Since most marriages were made as a matter of social or financial convenience rather than romantic inclination, infidelities were probably not unusual, especially in the loose moral climate created by the pleasure-loving king in reaction against the years of hardship. We know that, further down on the social scale, Samuel Pepys was often unfaithful to his wife. In an age when life expectancy was relatively short, and twenty-five was considered over the hill, a feverish attitude of living for the moment prevailed, reinforced by the materialism of Thomas Hobbes's influential *Leviathan* (1651). From Hobbes's work, too, came one of the basic premises of Restoration comedy: laughter is caused "by the apprehension of some deformed thing in another, by comparison whereof they suddenly applaud themselves." The Town probably encompassed some who enjoyed feeling morally superior to the libertines and cuckolds of the comedies as well as those who laughed indulgently at the ridicule of old-fashioned behavioral decorum.

One of the most visible components of the Town audience was the young gallant or rake who came to the theater to show off—and, perhaps, to make an assignation. From the pit, a rakish youth could ogle the ladies in the side boxes and send Mrs. Mary Meggs (the licensed theater concessionaire, also known as Orange Moll) or one of her orange wenches to deliver the gift of an orange to one of them. Although they were nominally gentlemen, these sixteen- to twenty-five-year-olds occasionally pushed their way into the theater without paying and let their rowdiness get out of hand. Nor did they feel any compunction about loudly criticizing a play during the performance. Perhaps they were allowed to get away with it since it lent an element of spontaneity and variety for the many spectators who returned to see the same play several times. Moreover, wit was a social asset that was prized second only to money, and the extemporaneous critique was a means of displaying wit. A gallant whose wit did not sparkle quite as much as he fancied it did, or one who overdressed to make an impression, was known as a fop.

A third major segment of London life was the "City," a prosperous concentration of trade and capital. This sober, hardworking business community created a sound financial basis for trading firms like the Hudson's Bay Company and the East India Company, and for the eventual establishment of a modern banking system. During the early years of the Restoration, the rising merchant class avoided the theater. Not only were their Puritan sensibilities at odds with the behavior they perceived as immoral on stage and in the audience, but they were often mocked in the plays as a form of Cavalier revenge on the class that had supported Oliver Cromwell. A certain tension between the Town and the City is understandable, since so many Royalists' estates had been confiscated during the Interregnum and were never recovered. As the years went on, however, it appears that more and more citizens were drawn to the theater. Certainly it was in the theaters' interest not to alienate the monied segment of society. For example, the last lines of the prologue to John Dryden's 1673 comedy *Marriage à la Mode* express a desire to appeal to all three social components:

> For that's one way, howe'er the play fall short,
> To oblige the town, the city, and the court.

Citizens included small tradesmen and shopkeepers as well as wealthy merchants. Samuel Pepys's diaries take increasing note of their presence, as in his entry for 1 January 1667/8:

> I after dinner to the Duke of York's playhouse, and there saw *Sir Martin Marr all*, which I have seen so often, and yet am mightily pleased with it and think it mighty witty, and the fullest of proper matter for mirth that ever was writ. And I do clearly see that they do improve in their acting of it. Here a mighty company of citizens, 'prentices, and others; and it makes me observe that when I begun first to be able to bestow a play on myself, I do not remember that I saw so many by half of the ordinary 'prentices and mean people in the pit at 2s-6d a piece as now; I going for several years no higher than the 12d and then the 18d places, and though I strained hard to go in then when I did—so much the vanity and prodigality of the age is to be observed in this perticular.

Pepys himself was of a fringe group loosely associated with the Town: government officials, Parliamentarians, literary men, country gentry and their families, military officers, lawyers, and other professionals.

In 1663 Pepys noted that it had become a fashion among the ladies to wear vizard masks during the play and that after the performance he went with his wife to the Exchange to buy her a vizard. By the end of the century, however, the vizard seems to have had an unsavory connotation, as implied in James Wright's *Historia Histrionica* (1699): "Of late, the playhouses are so extremely pestered with vizard-masks and their trade, (occasioning continual quarrels and abuses) that many of the more civiliz'd part of the town are uneasy in the company, and shun the Theatre as they would a house of scandal." Finally, in 1704, Queen Anne prohibited the wearing of vizard masks in the theaters. Nevertheless, women of ill repute seem to have been a presence in the theater from the beginning. Pepys noted, for example, on February 4, 1666/7: "I had sitting next to me a woman the likest my Lady Castlemayne that ever I saw anybody like another; but she is a whore I believe, for she is acquainted with every fine fellow and called them by their name, Jacke, and Tom—and before the end of the play fished to another place."

Although this print dates to a century later than the Restoration, the Orange Girls' manner of selling fruits and flirting with male theatergoers changed little. From Modern London *(1804), published by Richard Phillips.*

Right, Samuel Pepys (1633–1703) appreciated the scene of the town on fire when he saw a revival of John Fletcher's The Island Princess *(1621), with some additional scenes, in 1669. This illustration showing people painted on the background is the frontispiece to Tonson's* Beaumont and Fletcher.

PLAYS DURING THE REIGN OF CHARLES II

The general broadening of audience composition over the four decades of the Restoration period was reflected in an evolving repertoire of plays. There is considerable variety among the 400 plays written by 180 different authors between 1660 and 1700. The types of drama that are considered most characteristic of the Restoration—heroic tragedy and risqué comedy—were mainly written in the 1670s; it had taken nearly a decade of experimentation with genres, and testing of audience response, to develop a generation of playwrights in tune with the time.

When the theaters reopened in 1660, there were no active playwrights from the pre-Commonwealth period still alive, other than Davenant and Killigrew themselves. Needing material quickly, Davenant and Killigrew relied for the first two seasons almost exclusively on old works by Beaumont and Fletcher, Shakespeare, Ben Jonson, James Shirley, Richard Brome, Thomas Heywood, Philip Massinger, John Webster, William Rowley, Thomas Middleton, and others. When Killigrew and Davenant negotiated for the rights to produce old plays, Davenant was put at an extreme disadvantage, for the Lord Chamberlain granted him the rights to only eleven old plays, mostly by Shakespeare, as well as his own plays that had previously been performed at Blackfriars. Killigrew apparently got all the other old plays. Davenant was therefore under greater pressure than Killigrew both to popularize those old plays with scenes and music, and to acquire new plays as soon as they could be written. This explains why, between 1660 and 1664, as Robert D. Hume has pointed out, the Duke of York's Company staged twenty-two new plays, while only twelve of the plays in the much larger repertory of the King's Company were new ones.

Another way of obtaining plays quickly was to translate and adapt foreign works, especially Spanish and French ones. One of the earliest of these was Sir Samuel Tuke's *The Adventures of Five Hours* (1662), based upon Calderón's comedy of intrigue, *Los Empeños de Seis Horas*. The English version was enlivened with some topical allusions concerning the Dutch, against whom the English were waging a trade war that would soon escalate into full-fledged warfare. Presented by the Duke's Company, with an amazing run of thirteen consecutive performances, this was the first very successful drama of the Restoration.

The greatest number of such adaptations were from French originals. French romances by La Calprenède, Mademoiselle de Scudéry, Madame de Lafayette, and the Abbé de St. Réal were the basis for love-and-honor plays by John Dryden, Nathaniel Lee, Aphra Behn, Lord Orrery, Thomas Otway, and others. French neoclassical tragedies by Pierre Corneille and Jean Racine, written in twelve-syllable rhymed couplets called alexandrines, prompted a spate of rhymed-verse heroic tragedies in English—until John Dryden announced in 1677 that he was abandoning the unnatural form, and others followed suit. Above all, Molière inspired a wealth of plot ideas for Restoration comedies by Thomas Shadwell (most notably *The Libertine* from *Dom Juan*), Edward Ravenscroft (*The Citizen Turned Gentleman* from *Le Bourgeois gentilhomme*, among others), William Wycherley (*The Plain Dealer* from *Le Misanthrope*), Aphra Behn, Susannah Centlivre, and Thomas Otway, to name a few.

John Dryden, as well as being a poet, critic, and satirist, was the first professional dramatist to write for the new theaters. His life, 1631–1700, encompassed the Restoration period, and he represented its full range of dramatic styles, often as the trailblazer. Born into a Puritan family, he wrote an elegy on the death of Cromwell, but became a firm Royalist under Charles II, and converted to Catholicism under James II. Despite appearances, he was not an opportunist, but sincere and moderate in his beliefs; the subject about which he wrote most passionately throughout his life was the English language, most notably in his *Essay of Dramatick Poesy.* When Davenant died in 1668, Dryden succeeded him as poet laureate.

Dryden's early plays were produced by the King's Company, beginning with an adaptation, *The Wild Gallant* (1663), which failed. He launched heroic tragedy as a genre with his popular *The Indian Queen* (1664), a grandiose love-and-honor play written entirely in rhymed couplets. Each of his five heroic tragedies, the best of which are *The Conquest of Granada* (1670) and *Aureng-Zebe* (1675), featured an almost superhuman hero and his equally imposing antagonist alternately expressing high-flown sentiments and battling mightily in an exotic locale. After five acts of terrible travails, these plays usually ended happily. The baroque artifice of the form (essentially a play of ideas decked out with extravagant gestures and visual opulence) appealed to the Cavalier audience's obsession with codes of behavior, especially in terms of an individual's role within a rigid social structure. Heroic tragedy offered physical action, drums and trumpets, for sword-wearing, pistol-carrying gentlemen of a generation whose country had been engaged in one war or another fairly constantly; and at the same time it provided something to tantalize the intellect. This speech by Almanzor, hero of *The Conquest of Granada,* exemplifies the genre's baroque juxtaposition of a raging passion and the rational analysis of it:

> Forgive that fury which my soul does move;
> 'Tis the essay of an untaught first love:
> Yet rude, unfashioned truth it does express;
> 'Tis love just peeping in a hasty dress.
> Retire, fair creature, to your needful rest;
> There's something noble labouring in my breast:
> This raging fire, which through the mass does move;
> Shall purge my dross, and shall refine my love.

Refinement was a major concern of Dryden as well as of his audience. However overblown heroic tragedy may seem to the modern reader, for the Restoration spectator it offered a subtle interplay of topical allusion and fanciful idealism, of what Jocelyn Powell has called "a self-conscious dialogue between life and the stage."

Apart from Dryden's heroic tragedies, the best examples of the genre are Roger Boyle, earl of Orrery's *Mustapha, Son of Solyman the Magnificent* (1665), Elkanah Settle's *The Empress of Morocco* (1673),

Thomas Otway's *Alcibiades* (1675), John Crowne's *The Destruction of Jerusalem by Titus Vespasian* (1677), Nathaniel Lee's *The Rival Queens* (1677) and *Mithridates* (1678), and Thomas Southerne's *The Loyal Brothers* (1682). Heroic tragedy was satirized brilliantly—though not fatally—in 1671 with the King's Company's production of *The Rehearsal* by George Villiers, duke of Buckingham, and three other wits. The main target in *The Rehearsal* was Dryden himself, transparently represented by a character named Mr. Bayes, a poet who conducts the rehearsal of the play within the play. Comedian John Lacy, who played Mr. Bayes, was coached in Dryden's mannerisms. The inner play featured characters like Drawcansir, a travesty of Almanzor, who spouted such lines as "I drink, I huff, I strut, look big and stare; / And all this I can do, because I dare," and Volscius, whose love-versus-honor dilemma is summed up in the choice between whether to put on both boots (Honor) or none (Love)—a soliloquy that culminates in his hobbling away with one boot on.

With *All for Love* (1677), Dryden turned from heroic to neoclassical tragedy. Dryden professed "to imitate the divine Shakespeare," but—having read Nicolas Boileau's influential *L'Art poétique* (1674)—he strictly observed the unities, of time, place, and action, as well as the decorum of the neoclassical drama that already dominated the French stage. Dryden's blank-verse version of the Anthony and Cleopatra story concentrated the action into the last day of their lives and employed only ten characters. That economy of means and rigidity of form pointed the way for other dramatists like Nathaniel Lee with *The Rival Queens* (1677), Thomas Otway with *The Orphan* (1680) and *Venice Preserv'd* (1682), John Banks with *The Unhappy Favorite; or, The Earl of Essex* (1681) and *The Island Queens* (1684), and Thomas Southerne's *Oroonoko* (1695). These later tragedies also contained an element of pathos or sentimentality that would gradually gather strength and come to dominate the tragedy of the eighteenth century.

Another genre to which Dryden contributed was "English opera," also called "dramatic opera," which differed from Italian opera primarily in its use of spoken dialogue rather than recitative. The genre was launched in 1673 at the Dorset Garden Theatre with an operatic version of *Macbeth*, about which little is known. The King's Company countered early in 1674 with a French opera (described in John Evelyn's diary, January 5, 1674, as "an *Italian Opera* in musique, the first that had been in England of this kind"), *Ariane, ou le mariage de Bacchus,* performed in French, but it was not successful with the public. A month later, the Duke's Company scored one of its greatest successes with an "English opera" based on *The Tempest*. Shakespeare's play had been adapted by Davenant and Dryden in 1667, and it was further revised by Thomas

Shadwell for the 1674 version, *The Tempest; or, The Enchanted Island,* with instrumental music by Matthew Locke and new vocal music by James Hart and Pietro Reggio, as well as songs by John Bannister from the earlier production. Just as important as the music were the spectacular visual effects utilizing all the technological resources of the Dorset Garden. In *Restoration Theatre Production,* Jocelyn Powell discusses probable maneuvers of the flying machines and the alternating images of order and disorder produced by the changes of scenery to create what he calls "a dialogue of sensuality and reason that is at the soul of the age." Among the Dorset Garden's other operatic spectaculars, for which the price of admission was doubled, were Shadwell's *Psyche,* Charles Davenant's *Circe,* and Dryden's two dramatic operas: *Albion and Albanus* (1685) and *King Arthur* (1691). Dryden was also successful at comedy. His *Sir Martin Mar-all* (1667) was an adaptation of an earlier adaptation by the duke of Newcastle of Molière's *L'Etourdi* and Quinault's *L'Amant indiscret,* which Dryden made into a vehicle for James Nokes. In low comedy, Nokes "shook you to a Fatigue of Laughter," according to Colley Cibber, for "when he debated any matter by himself, he would shut up his Mouth with a dumb studious Pout, and roll his full Eye into such a vacant Amazement, such a palpable Ignorance of what to think of it, that his silent Perplexity (which would sometimes hold him several Minutes) gave your Imagination as full Content as the most absurd thing he could say upon it." The blundering Sir Martin Mar-all, who kept accidentally giving away the schemes in which he was involved, became Nokes's best-loved role, and the play was a favorite of Samuel Pepys. After one of the first performances, in August 1667, Pepys noted in his diary: "It is the most entire piece of Mirth, a complete Farce from one end to the other, that certainly ever was writ. I never laughed so in all my life; I laughed till my head [ached] all the evening and night with my laughing, and at very good wit therein, not fooling. The house full." Another entry, nine months later, reveals his unflagging enthusiasm for the play: "Thence to the Duke of York's House to a play, and saw Sir Martin Marr all, where the house is full; and though I have seen it I think, ten times, yet the pleasure I have is yet as great as ever, and is undoubtedly the best comedy ever was wrote." *Sir Martin Mar-all* was revived frequently for over twenty years.

Restoration comedy reached its peak of brilliance, 1668–78, not in comedy of humors like *Sir Martin Mar-all,* but in comedy of wit or, bluntly, "sex comedy." Although he declared himself unsuited to the genre, Dryden contributed to it one outstanding example (as well as lesser-known, smuttier works like *The Kind Keeper, or Mr Limberham,* 1678); his *Marriage à la Mode* (1672) is a witty and spirited commentary on the game of sexual intrigue. It employed one of the major conventions of the genre, the "gay couple." The plots of these plays usually involved bringing together a handsome young gallant, who was devoid of moral scruples but skilled at operating within accepted boundaries of the social code, and an attractive young woman who was completely in control of her emotions. Often the comedies featured two gay couples; since the liberated young ladies of the period flounced about town in pairs, the libertines found it most convenient to do the same. The union of the would-be lovers might be thwarted by a parent who wished to arrange a different match, or a heavy guardian who managed the inheritance of one of them, or an older woman (over twenty-five) who refused to recognize that her affair with the young rake was over, or—if the young woman was already married—a husband whose suspicions were aroused. The gay couple's coming to an understanding was also complicated by the fashion for concealing any genuine affection; the clearest indication that a lady and gentleman were meant for each other was an equal matching of wits in lively repartee. The victims of the cynical wit of these comedies were the outsiders, anyone who did not fit into the tight inner circle of the fashionable people: country folk, merchants, clergymen, cuckolded husbands, older women who were still trying to compete with young ones, and foolish fops.

First among the Restoration dramatists who excelled at comedy of wit was Sir George Etherege. As a gentleman and intimate of the court, "Easy Etherege" dabbled at playwriting only as a hobby to show his wit. He was the creator of the rakish hero of Restoration comedy with the character of Sir Frederick Frollick in his first play, *The Comical Revenge; or, Love in a Tub* (1664). *She Would if She Could* (1668) follows Courtall and Freeman about the vividly depicted fashionable locales in London. Eight years later, Etherege wrote his third and final play *The Man of Mode; or, Sir Fopling Flutter* (1676), which is probably the best and most characteristic of all the comedies of wit, as well as the most graceful. Its fashionable hero, Dorimant, was said to be a thinly disguised portrait of the roguish cavalier John Wilmot, earl of Rochester. Equally memorable are the lovely and coolheaded Harriet, the older and uncool Mrs. Loveit, and the title character, an exquisitely delineated comic fop. All three of Etherege's plays were successful in production.

William Wycherley tried to be a gentleman-amateur playwright like Etherege. The first of his four plays, *Love in a Wood; or, St. James's Park* (1671), adopted the style Etherege had set, but he subsequently developed his own, more cynical tone. *The Gentleman Dancing Master* (1672) borrowed its plot from the contemporary Spanish dramatist Calderón. Wycherley's ribald masterpiece, *The Country Wife* (1675), remains today the most frequently performed of all Restoration comedies. In it, the rakish Horner concocts a scheme for gaining easy access to married women without fear of reprisals from the husbands he cuckolds. An intertwining plot line traces the futile efforts of Mr. Pinchwife to keep the simple country girl he married from learning of, much less adopting, the lascivious habits of the town. "Manly Wycherley" wrote his darkest satire in *The Plain Dealer* (1676), which is partly inspired by Molière's *Le Misanthrope*. Although its hero, Manly, is a plain-dealing individualist who wants no part of the town's hypocrisy, he ultimately engages in some sexual deception. Critics have long debated whether Wycherley intended his comedies to pander to the jaded sensibilities of the coterie audience or to serve as moralizing exposés of a flagrant immorality. Whatever his purpose—and it could embrace both possibilities—he set about it with such explicitness in his risqué situations and dialogue full of double entendres that his comedies are considered to be among the most lewd of the genre.

Also judged "indecent" by subsequent generations was Aphra Behn, the first Englishwoman to earn her living by writing, and, along with Dryden, one of the most frequently produced authors of the period. The bawdiness of her comedies went so far as to show scenes in brothels,

Aphra Behn (1640–89) was the first Englishwoman to make her living as a playwright. This portrait of "the divine Astrea" is engraved from a portrait attributed to Mary Beale.

as in *The Town Fop* and *The Rover,* both written in 1677, at the peak period for licentiousness in comedy. Many of her plays were quite successful, but the fact that she was a woman was held against her. Two women of the preceding generation, Katherine Phillips ("the Matchless Orinda") and Margaret Cavendish ("Mad Madge"), the duchess of Newcastle, had shocked their contemporaries by allowing some poems to be published under their own names. In addition, Phillips translated two plays of Corneille, and the duchess published a collection of unproducible plays in 1662; but both women were wealthy amateurs. Mrs. Behn, an impoverished widow, wrote out of necessity. In defense of her *Sir Patient Fancy* (1678) she noted "that it was bawdy, the least and most excusable fault in the men writers, to whose plays they all crowd, as if they came to no other end than to hear what they condemn in this, but from a woman it was unnatural." Some years later, John Dryden referred to Mrs. Behn as "writeing loosely, and giveing, if I may have leave to say so, some scandall to the modesty of her sex. I confess, I am the last man who ought, in justice, to arraign her, who have been myself too much a libertine in most of my poems." Among the other popular comedies of "the divine Astraea," as she was nicknamed, were *The Amorous Prince* (1671), *The Feigned Courtesans* (1679), *The False Count* (1681), *The City Heiress* (1682), and *The Lucky Chance* (1686). She also tried her hand at tragicomedies, tragedy of intrigue like *Abdelazer; or, the Moor's Revenge* (1677), historical comedy like *The Roundheads* (1682), and her very successful farce *The Emperor of the Moon* (1687).

Several other writers contributed to the apogee of comedy of wit in the 1670s. Although Thomas Shadwell is most often remembered for his comedies of humors in imitation of Ben Jonson, he joined the mainstream of that decade with *Epsom Wells* (1627), *The Virtuoso* (1676), and *A True Widow* (1678). A recently discovered comedy, *The Frolicks; or, The Lawyer Cheated* (1671), brings to light an amateur woman dramatist, Elizabeth Polwhele, about whom virtually nothing is known. Songwriter Thomas D'Urfey's *A Fond Husband* (1677) was wittily salacious enough to bring Charles II to the theater for three of the first five performances. The king was also fond of John Crowne's coarse comedy *The Country Wit* (1675), but Crowne's only play to win lasting appreciation was *Sir Courtly Nice; or, It Cannot Be* (1685). Thomas Otway contributed to the craze for sex-comedy with his racy *Friendship in Fashion* (1678). Edward Ravenscroft, whose most popular work was the farcical *London Cuckolds* (1681), had begun his playwriting career by adapting Molière comedies to the brittle conventions of Restoration society, most notably with *The Cit Turned Gentleman* (1671), which at the same time adumbrated the incipient trend toward social mobility between the classes (i.e., citizens, or "cits," moving into the ranks of gentlemen, and gentlemen beginning to go into business).

A CHANGING REPERTOIRE

The rapid decline in explicit sex scenes after 1678 may be attributed not only to social mobility and a changing audience composition, but also to the sobering effects of the "Popish Plot" of that year. Although the Popish Plot was a soon-discredited fabrication put forward by Titus Oates, a man of questionable character in league with several other anti-Jesuit zealots, their wild stories of a Catholic conspiracy to assassinate the king and murder all the Protestants in London gained public currency. It generated widespread unrest, which led to the execution of about thirty-five innocent Catholics over the next three years. It also precipitated the Exclusion Crisis, a series of Parliamentary attempts to exclude the king's Catholic brother James, the duke of York, from succeeding to the throne. To insure James's rightful place, Charles II dissolved Parliament, and public opinion supported the triumph of the court party (or Royalists, henceforth known as Tories) over the country party (Whigs). Charles II died in 1685. James II arrogantly attempted to reassert an absolutist monarchy, as though the civil wars and Commonwealth had never happened. Three years later, a group of Protestant nobility invited James's son-in-law, the Dutch Prince William of Orange, to lead an army of rebellion in England. William landed with a force of fifteen thousand men, but there was no battle. James II fled to France. The "Glorious Revolution" of 1688 that brought William and Mary to the English throne was a bloodless one.

That eventful decade generated few plays of lasting stageworthiness. Some dramatists turned to writing political propaganda plays like Shadwell's *The Lancashire Witches and Teague O'Divelly the Irish Priest* (1681) or Thomas D'Urfey's *Sir Barnaby Whigg* (1681). Those who continued to write comedy showed considerably less proclivity to glamorize libertinism. The single most important new play of the 1680s was a new kind of tragedy, Thomas Otway's *Venice Preserv'd* (1682). Otway had tried heroic tragedy and neoclassical tragedy, and then discovered the possibilities of blank-verse "domestic tragedy." His unrequited love for the actress Elizabeth Barry prompted him to write a vehicle for her special talents; the first result was *The Orphan* (1680), followed by his masterpiece. Although *Venice Preserv'd; or, A Plot Discover'd* is set in a foreign country and in an earlier period, its veiled allusions to the English political situation are evident, especially in the satirical portrait of the earl of Shaftesbury, a contentious leader of the Whigs who fell from grace in 1681, as the unscrupulous old senator Antonio. The famous, so-called Nicky-Nacky scene between Antonio and Aquilina is almost Elizabethan in its use of bawdy farce as relief from the intense pathos of the tragedy. Above all, it is the expansive rendering of emotion on a personal level that adumbrated the sentimental tragedy of the eighteenth century and insured this play's long stage life.

The theater companies had already entered a period of turmoil. The King's Company was demoralized by Killigrew's bad management even after moving into their fine new Theatre Royal in Drury Lane in 1674, and their habitual disorderliness threatened the company's stability. Matters became serious enough that in 1676 the Lord Chamberlain ordered a silencing of Drury Lane so that its management could be reorganized. The disarray continued, however, as the company slid further and further into debt. Finally, in 1682, after swords were drawn and some were wounded in a fight between senior and junior actors, the Drury Lane was closed. In May of that year, Thomas Killigrew's son Charles entered into an agreement with Charles Davenant, Thomas Betterton, and William Smith of the Duke of York's Company, by which the two patents were to be combined in a joint organization.

The United Company, which lasted for twelve years, 1682–94, enjoyed the freedom from competition gained from performing in only one theater at a time, but operated under the disadvantage of having to make rental payments on both theater buildings: seven pounds for the Dorset Garden and three pounds for the Drury Lane out of every performance day's receipts from either house. Most productions were staged at the Drury Lane, while the larger and better-equipped Dorset Garden was used only occasionally for large-scale efforts requiring elaborate machinery. One Dorset Garden production was Dryden's expensively mounted opera *Albion and Albanus,* which lost the company a great deal of money when political events of 1685 drew the public's attention away from theater. Furthermore, without the stimulus of competition, there was a drastic decline in the number of new plays presented. According to Judith Milhous, the United Company mounted no more than three or four new plays each season in the five years after 1682, whereas the two competing theaters had previously given London a total of eighteen to twenty-four new plays every year.

Theater management problems did not end with the formation of the United Company. In 1687 Alexander Davenant bought a controlling share of the company from his brother Charles and appointed his inexperienced brother Thomas as manager—at twice the salary that Betterton and Smith had been paid for the job. Thomas Betterton, the company's leading actor, was apparently altruistic enough to serve as an unofficial and uncompensated advisor to young Thomas Davenant, but his good will could not stem the tide of difficulties. Charles Killigrew soon initiated a long suit against the theater over the method by which his shares had been calculated, as well as other matters covered in detail in Leslie Hotson's book. Late in 1693 it was discovered that Alexander Davenant had bought his share with borrowed money and had even sold the same property twice! When he fell behind on his loan payments, he fled to the Canary Islands. His creditors, Christopher Rich and Sir Thomas Skipwith, revealed that they actually owned the patent as well as shares in the company. Rich then took over the financial management of the debt-ridden United Company and set about initiating certain economies that offended the actors. In November or December 1694, Thomas Betterton and fourteen other actors filed with the Lord Chamberlain a fifteen-point list of grievances. The patentees quickly responded with a point-by-point reply. (Both documents are reprinted in Judith Milhous's *Thomas Betterton and the Management of Lincoln's Inn Fields, 1695–1708.*) Actors and management could work out no basis for reconciliation, even though the death of Queen Mary imposed a three-month suspension of performances. The power struggle between Betterton and Rich culminated in the Actors' Rebellion of 1695. Within a year and a half after Christopher Rich's installation as manager of the United Company, Thomas Betterton and eleven other rebellious actors obtained a special license to perform apart from the patented company. Betterton's well-established reputation as an actor and his connections with "People of Quality" enabled him to raise money to re-equip Lincoln's Inn Fields, which had not been used as a theater since the King's Company vacated it in 1674.

After the official mourning for Queen Mary ended, Drury Lane reopened with a revival of Aphra Behn's *Abdelazar; or the Moor's Revenge.* It was received unenthusiastically, perhaps because the young actors who remained with Rich had not yet won a following. Betterton and the other experienced actors at Lincoln's Inn Fields had the exceptional good luck to open with William Congreve's *Love for Love* (1695), which ran for thirteen straight performances and contributed strongly to a resurgence of comedy of wit in the 1690s. That second wind for the genre had begun in 1691 with Thomas Southerne's *The Wives Excuse,* which had not been popular but had helped pave the way for Congreve's extraordinarily successful first play, *The Old Batchelor* (1693), and his second, *The Double Dealer* (1693).

Congreve was an Englishman who had grown up in Ireland and shared a tutor with Jonathan Swift at Trinity College in Dublin. He wrote only five plays—four comedies and a tragedy—all produced before he was thirty. His comedies were as risqué as many a play of the 1670s, but he was best loved for his fullness of characterization and for the finest wit and most felicitous turns of phrase since Etherege. Although *Love for Love* has remained his most often revived work, Congreve's comic masterpiece is undoubtedly *The Way of the World* (1700). This, his last play, features the most memorable "gay couple" in all of Restoration comedy: the lovely, artful Millamant and the rakish, smitten Mirabel. The sparkling dialogue sequence in which they impose upon each other their conditions for marriage epitomizes Restoration society's image of itself: the self-possession of their exquisite repartee masks any softness of feeling. That very brittleness—along with an excessively convoluted plot—may account for the play's tepid reception, for by 1700 the tide was already turning toward sentimentality.

Among the writers encouraged by Congreve were two of the "female wits" of the 1690s, Mary Pix and Catherine Trotter. In one fifteen-month period in 1695–96, six new plays by women writers were produced in London. The first, *She Ventures and He Wins,* opened Betterton's 1695 season at Lincoln's Inn Fields, but nothing is known about the "young lady" who wrote the comedy under the pseudonym "Ariadne." The first of the so-called "female wits" was Catherine Trotter, who was only sixteen when her tragedy *Agnes de Castro* (1695) was presented and won a favorable reception at Drury Lane, thus helping to establish a revival of the earlier heroic tragedy genre. Trotter had already published a novel at fourteen and would go on to see four other plays—three more tragedies and a comedy—produced and published. Mary de la Rivière Manley had her first two plays, a comedy and a tragedy, produced in March and April of 1696. The comedy, *The Lost Lover,* was produced at Drury Lane and failed. The tragedy, *The Royal Mischief,* was in rehearsal at Drury Lane when Mrs. Manley withdrew it and gave it to Lincoln's Inn Fields instead; it ran for six performances, although some ladies who saw it found the villainess Homais—played by Elizabeth Barry—excessively passionate. Manley also wrote two more plays and some "scandals." Mary Griffith Pix began with a tragedy, *Ibrahim, the Thirteenth Emperor of the Turks,* produced at Drury Lane in May 1696, followed within the year by a comedy of intrigue, *The Spanish Wives.* She may have written as many as a dozen plays, several of which were revived in the eighteenth century.

Trotter, Manley, and Pix all professed a debt to Aphra Behn, who had paved the way for women playwrights. Nevertheless, they found themselves the butt of a satire, *The Female Wits, or, The Triumvirate of Poets at Rehearsal,* by an unknown author, produced at Drury Lane early in the 1696–97 season. Mrs. Manley's high-handed transfer of *The Royal Mischief* to the rival theater in the previous season provided the focus for some rather savage ridicule, but the young, well-read Trotter and the fat, outgoing Pix were also recognizable in the characters of Calista and Mrs. Wellfed. The attack fortunately did not deter Susannah Centlivre from writing for the stage a decade later. Her nineteen plays were chiefly comedies with moral lessons, including her long-popular *The Busy Body* (1709).

Colley Cibber's *Love's Last Shift* (1696) has been signaled as the pivotal play that retains the outward form of Restoration comedy of wit while focusing on a moral dilemma that elevates character over plot. That very popular play, in which Cibber himself played the foppish Sir Novelty Fashion, centered upon a young husband, Loveless, and the loyal loving wife he abandoned to pursue a life of pleasure; she wins him back by secretly taking the place of a prostitute to spend the night with him. That fifth-act reformation of the libertine after "four acts for your coarse palates" suggests that Cibber was trying to have it both ways— pleasing the coterie and moralists alike. Ten months later, again at Drury Lane, a sequel was presented; *The Relapse* (1696) by John Vanbrugh showed Loveless slipping again into libertinage while his wife is courted by the fop, who has bought himself the title of Lord Foppington. Such freshly conceived characters as Miss Hoyden and Sir Tunbelly Clumsey helped to gain the play its success. The morally ambiguous tone of *Love's Last Shift* and *The Relapse* is indicative of that decade's uncertainty about the requirements of a fickle audience.

Vanbrugh had a second great success with *The Provok'd Wife* (1697), which makes it clear that illicit love was no longer seen as a matter of course, but had to be rationalized. The abuse suffered by the title character at the hands of her boorish husband, Sir John Brute, is offered as justification for her giving in to a young blade's importunities. Other than *The Relapse* and *The Provok'd Wife*, Vanbrugh's plays were adaptations, mostly from French originals. He also served many years as a soldier, and he distinguished himself as an architect with such Baroque designs as Blenheim Palace in Oxfordshire, Castle Howard in Yorkshire, Grimsthorpe Castle in Lincolnshire, and the Queen's Theatre, Haymarket, which became London's first opera theater.

The shift in prevailing attitudes is further exemplified in the comedies of George Farquhar, a Dublin actor who left the stage after accidentally wounding a fellow actor. He then went to London and got his first play, *Love and a Bottle* (1698), produced at Drury Lane. His second play, *The Constant Couple; or, A Trip to the Jubilee* (1699), combined the verve and flair of comedy of wit with the morally gratifying reform of the rakish Sir Harry Wildair. It was given a remarkable fifty-three performances in the seven months of its first season, and Farquhar got four "third nights" (the third performance of a new play was traditionally a benefit for the author). The role of Sir Harry remained a popular one throughout the eighteenth century, especially when performed as a "breeches role" by Peg Woffington in the 1740s and 1750s.

Farquhar's last and best two comedies usher in the eighteenth century like a breath of fresh air in a hothouse: *The Recruiting Officer* (1706) and *The Beaux Stratagem* (1707) are actually set outside London, in Shrewsbury and Lichfield respectively. The latter play includes a sympa-

George Farquhar (1677–1707) wrote his last comedy, The Beaux' Stratagem, *in 1707. The scene is set in the gallery of Lady Bountiful's country house near Lichfield, but the illustration suggests a generic baroque interior. From* The Works of the Late Ingenious Mr George Farquhar *(1711).*

thetic older woman, Lady Bountiful, who is pleased to live in the country. The young gallants Aimwell and Archer are far less coldly self-seeking than their counterparts in comedies of the 1670s. The heroine is a lovely young woman unfortunately married to a drunken boor (hence her name, Mrs. Sullen). The play ends with the granting of a "divorce," which under English law at the time meant "separate maintenance." Thus, although Mrs. Sullen could not become legally free to marry Archer, their leading a final dance together allows an ambiguous interpretation of their future relationship. Mrs. Sullen was played by a young actress, Anne Oldfield, whom tradition said that Farquhar had discovered in a tavern when he heard her reading aloud some passages from Beaumont and Fletcher. He recommended her to Christopher Rich, and after a few seasons she was playing leading ingenue roles at Drury Lane.

RESTORATION ACTORS AND ACTRESSES

One of the glories of Restoration theater was its actors and actresses. Their on- and offstage personalities come to life for us through the many references to be found in diaries, memoirs like the *Apology for the Life of Mr Colley Cibber, written by Himself,* and other scattered records. We cannot reconstruct, of course, exactly what the acting style of the period was like except in generalities based upon the play texts and what is known about the physical conditions of the playhouse. Documents of the period abound with references to vocal qualities and line readings as much as to visual effects. Spoken delivery seems to have been rather cadenced, especially in tragedy, perhaps influenced by the French vocal style used in delivering alexandrines. The importance of gesture and formal poses by the actor might also be traced to a French influence epitomized by René Descartes's *Les Passions de l'âme* (1649), which discussed external signs of the passions in its treatment of the relationship between the mind and the body. Similar ideas were propounded in Englishman John Bulwer's pair of treatises on hand gestures, *Chirologia* and *Chironomia* (1644): "The lineaments of the body do disclose the disposition and inclination of the mind." In any event, there was a self-consciousness about performance, a kind of complicity between actor and audience as if they were winking at each other over the character and situation on stage. Most actors had no thought of living the part, but preferred to take the spectators into their confidence to share an idea about a character. The artifice or gamelike quality of the performance was precisely what Restoration audiences seem to have best appreciated, and it is particularly exemplified by the rhymed prologues and epilogues that framed every play. These were genuine "plums" for the actors who got to speak them, because they placed the actor alone on stage, directly addressing the audience in clever turns of phrase, usually concerning the theater itself. There was no better way of getting on intimate terms with one's constituency.

Among the many distinctive stage personalities were "the four B's": Thomas Betterton, his wife Mary Saunderson Betterton, Elizabeth Barry, and Anne Bracegirdle. Thomas Betterton was by far the leading actor of his time as well as a theater manager and adapter of plays. His acting career began with the reopening of the theaters in 1660 and lasted until his death in 1710 at the age of seventy-four. In addition to roles like Hamlet and King Lear in old plays, Betterton created major roles in 130 new plays. Colley Cibber was lavish in his praise of Betterton's vocal work and his ability to portray a variety of characters, and that judgment is corroborated by the accounts of others who saw him act. According to Cibber, "Betterton never wanted Fire and Force when his Character demanded it; yet, where it was not demanded, he never prostituted his Power to the low Ambition of a false Applause. . . . In all his Soliloquies of moment, the strong Intelligence of his Attitude and Aspect drew you into such an impatient Gaze and eager Expectation, that you almost imbib'd the Sentiment with your Eye before the Ear could reach it."

Mary Saunderson married Betterton in 1663 and was always known as "a Woman of an unblemish'd and sober life." She made her debut as Ianthe in the 1661 revival of *The Siege of Rhodes,* and it is by that name that Samuel Pepys always referred to her in his diary. She was probably the first woman ever to play the roles of Juliet and Ophelia. According to John Dryden's description of a character she played, she was "of a middle

Below, left, the popular comedian Joe Haines (d. 1701) was particularly noted for his delivery of the epilogue he wrote for Thomas Scot's The Unhappy Kindness; or, a Fruitless Revenge *(1697). Wearing the costume of a horse officer, he addressed the Drury Lane audience mounted on an ass. Thomas Brown,* Works II *(1719).*

Thomas Betterton (1635–1710), right, the outstanding actor of the Restoration period, is shown here in the role of Hamlet as he sees the Ghost in Gertrude's chamber. Nicholas Rowe's edition of The Works of Mr William Shakespeare, *5 (1709).*

The vivacious Nell Gwynn had to leave the stage when she became the mistress of Charles II. This engraving after Gascar shows Nell with her two sons by the king and typical baroque architecture of the period. Courtesy of the British Museum.

stature, dark-coloured hair, the most bewitching leer with her eyes, the most roguish cast! her cheeks are dimpled when she smiles, and her smiles would tempt a hermit." When she lost her attractiveness in middle age she gracefully gave up playing romantic roles, although it was the custom for performers to "possess their parts" throughout their careers. She and Betterton also taught acting. She died in 1712 and was buried beside her husband in Westminster Abbey, an unprecedented honor for members of the theatrical profession.

The beginnings of Elizabeth Barry's career are obscure and unreliably reported, but she eventually emerged as the greatest tragic actress of the Restoration. The turning point in her career apparently came after some alleged personal instruction by her lover, the earl of Rochester. Her earliest recorded role was Draxilla in *Alcibiades* (1675) by Thomas Otway, her would-be lover whose amorous advances she repeatedly spurned, although she was said to have rejected very few others. Superb as she was in the heroic tragedies of Dryden and Lee, it was Otway who gave Barry her greatest roles, ones that emphasized "the softer Passions": Monimia in *The Orphan* and Belvidera in *Venice Preserv'd*. "In the Art of exciting Pity she had a Power beyond all the Actresses I have yet seen," wrote Cibber, "or what your Imagination can conceive." Not long after retiring from the stage, she died of a bite from her lapdog.

Anne Bracegirdle was also lucky in the roles written for her by an admiring playwright. She played leading roles in all five of William Congreve's plays. Of her Millamant in *The Way of the World* Colley Cibber wrote that "all the Faults, Follies, and Affectations of that agreeable Tyrant were venially melted down into so many Charms and Attractions of a conscious Beauty." The musical quality of her "laughing voice" was also very appealing.

The pert, pretty Nell Gwyn was probably not an exceptional actress, but her vivacity made her very popular with audiences; she was especially liked in "breeches roles" (male roles played by women as a means of showing off shapely legs). Pepys overheard her say that she was "brought up in a bawdy house to fill strong waters to the guests." As an orange girl at Drury Lane, she became the mistress of actor Charles Hart of the King's Company. Given a small role by Killigrew, she quickly won favor in madcap comic roles, though Pepys remarked on "how ill she doth any serious part." Eventually the king himself took her as one of his mistresses and she retired from the stage.

Henry Harris, Betterton's comanager at Dorset Garden until his retirement in 1681, acted leading male roles with a lighter touch than Betterton; he apparently displayed a quick wit off the stage as well as on, as noted by Pepys who often conversed with him at Will's Coffee House or over a private dinner. The good-looking, melodious-voiced William Mountfort played both tragic and comic lovers to perfection, and was mourned by theatergoers and colleagues alike when he died at thirty-three, the innocent victim of a swordfight over Mrs. Bracegirdle. Samuel Sandford, an excellent actor, was consistently cast as the villain, says Cibber, "for, having a low and crooked Person, such bodily Defects were too strong to be admitted into great or amiable Characters." Cave Underhill, "a jolly and droll companion" and much-loved comic actor, continued performing into his eighties; his favorite role was the Gravedigger in *Hamlet*. Another popular comedian, Joe Haines, especially delighted audiences with his delivery of prologues and epilogues, many of them written by himself. Moll (Mary) Davis enlivened her roles for the Duke's Company with singing and dancing specialty numbers; one of her songs so charmed the king that he took her as a mistress. These and many another actor and actress captured the affections of London theatergoers, but stories about the loose living of many of them fueled the moral outrage of reformers until matters came to a head in the 1690s.

THE COLLIER CONTROVERSY

The average, nontheatergoing citizen had long regarded the playhouses as hotbeds of lewdness, but—rather than risk sounding like a

Puritan—refrained from speaking out against them. Although the court of William and Mary set a very different moral tone from the courts of Charles II and James II, the king and queen held rather passive attitudes toward the theater. Thus, the 1690s revival of sex comedy continued unchecked, although the tide was clearly turning at all levels of society. A Society for the Reformation of Manners was founded in 1692. In his "Preface to *Prince Arthur*" (1695), Sir Richard Blackmore, the royal doctor and an author of dull epic poems, condemned the gentleman character in comedy as "a Derider of Religion, . . . a Person wholly *Idle*, dissolv'd in Luxury, abandon'd to his Pleasures, a great Debaucher of Women, profuse and extravagant in his Expences." The Young Lady character, he wrote, "entertains the Audience with confident Discourses, immodest Repartees, and prophane Raillery. She is thoroughly instructed in *Intreagues* and *Assignations,* a great *Scoffer* at the prudent Reservedness and Modesty of the best of her Sex."

It was widely reported that "some squeamish females of renown" muttered objections to the "blasphemy and bawdy" in Vanbrugh's 1696 comedy *The Relapse.* The following year, Vanbrugh's *The Provok'd Wife* was performed with a tongue-in-cheek prologue, spoken by Mrs. Bracegirdle, that anticipated petty attacks by those who did not grasp the author's satiric intention:

> Since 'tis the intent and business of the stage
> To copy out the follies of the age,
> To hold to every man a faithful glass
> And show him of what species he's an ass,
> I hope the next that teaches in the school
> Will show our author he's a scribbling fool.
> And that the satire may be sure to bite
> Kind heaven inspire some venomed priest to write
> And grant some ugly lady may indite.

Vanbrugh's prologue was prescient, for the attack that finally took effect was that of a "venomed priest," a nonjuring clergyman; (nonjurors objected as a matter of conscience to taking oaths of allegiance to William and Mary; they were deprived of office, but left in peace).

Jeremy Collier's *A Short View of the Immorality and Profaneness of the English Stage* (1698) was a diatribe in six long chapters against the theater as he saw it. It advanced a moral purpose for the drama: "The business of Plays is to recommend Virtue, and discountenance Vice." However, Collier often veered off into aesthetic considerations and failed to see that exaggeration and satire on the stage might also serve a reforming purpose. Despite its flaws, the work commanded attention by its very conviction and vehemence—and because many agreed that his complaints against the stage had some validity. Collier objected to "Smuttiness of Expression" particularly among female characters and in the prologues and epilogues "design'd to justify the Conduct of the Play." He dealt with "the Profaneness of the Stage" in two particulars: cursing and swearing, and the abuse of religion and Holy Scripture. In his chapter on "The Clergy abused by the Stage," he attacked Vanbrugh for the scene in *The Provok'd Wife* in which "Sir John Brute puts on the Habit of a Clergyman, counterfeits himself drunk, quarrels with the Constable, and is knock'd down and seiz'd. He rails, swears, curses, is lewd and profane to all Heights of Madness and Debauchery." (That Collier's words hit their mark is borne out by the fact that Vanbrugh himself later revised the scene to have Brute disguise himself in his wife's clothes instead of a clergyman's.) Collier further offered examples from the plays to show how "the Stage-Poets make their principal Persons vicious, and reward them at the End of the Play."

Among the immediate replies to the *Short View* were William Congreve's *Amendments upon Mr Collier's False and Imperfect Citations* and George Farquhar's *The Adventures of Covent Garden*. The latter opined "that Mr Collier showed too much Malice and rancour for a Church man, and his Adversaries too little wit for the Character of Poets; that their faults traversed would show much better; Dullness being more familiar with those of Mr Collier's Function as Malice and ill nature is more adapted to the Professors of wit." It is generally agreed that the best riposte came from critic John Dennis in *The Usefulness of the Stage to the Happiness of Mankind, to Government, and to Religion* (1698). Collier reattacked with *A Defense of the Short View,* and Vanbrugh joined the polemic with his *Short Vindication of the Relapse and the Provok'd Wife, from Immorality and Profaneness, by the Author* (1699). Vanbrugh agreed that the drama ought to serve a moral purpose, but disagreed on the means: "The Stage is a Glass for the World to view itself in; People ought therefore to see themselves as they are: if it makes their Faces too Fair, they won't know they are Dirty, and by consequence will neglect to wash 'em."

The "Collier controversy" raged on for a quarter of a century, engendering pamphlets and commentaries by about eighty different authors. The final blows were struck in the "war of pamphlets" by William Law's *The Absolute Unlawfulness of the Stage Entertainment fully Demonstrated* (1726) and another of John Dennis's several treatises on the subject, *The Stage Defended, from Scripture, Reason, Experience, and the Common Sense of Mankind for Two Thousand Years* (1726). By then, however, audience composition, economic exigencies, and other social factors had made their own marks on the dramatic repertoire. Depending upon one's viewpoint in the matter, the eighteenth century was to be an age of gentility and sentiment or an age of stultifying banality.

The Eighteenth Century

FRANCE AND ENGLAND
ON THE PATH TO ENLIGHTENMENT

France is the touchstone of European theater in the eighteenth century. Everything that happened elsewhere was either in imitation of—or, in some instances, self-conscious reaction against—the styles and standards set by French aesthetic theory, dramatic literature, and theatrical practice. However, those standards had largely been set during the preceding century, France's *Grand Siècle*. The long reign (1643–1715) of Louis XIV had not only established France's political hegemony and provided a model of monarchy that would be imitated by a host of rulers, great and small, for several generations, but had attained such a pinnacle of artistic achievement in the writings of Corneille, Racine, Molière and others, and in the staging of operas and court ballets, that it would prove difficult even for France herself to evolve beyond those prestigious set forms. While the French had adopted the Italian baroque style in the staging of elaborate musical productions, neoclassicism remained the ideal in architectural decor as in the "regular" forms of dramatic literature. The Comédie Française, founded in 1680, continued well into the eighteenth century to base its repertoire on seventeenth-century neoclassical tragedies and comedies. Neoclassicism thus was identified with French cultural superiority, even when that mode of expression lost its brilliant edge in the waning years of Louis XIV's reign.

A questioning of those traditional artistic values in France began as early as the 1680s, with the Quarrel of the Ancients and the Moderns. The Ancients advocated continuing imitation of classical antiquity, which also reflected the stable social order under the great "Sun King." The most notable statement of their case was Nicolas Boileau's *Art of Poetry* (1674), in which, after taking to task what is known as the "Golden Age" drama of Spain, Boileau bragged:

But we, committed to the rule of reason,
Unfold the plot with art's concision.
Through unity of time and place and action,
Audiences stay rapt in total satisfaction.

The Moderns, on the other hand, rejected absolutes and upheld the possibility of advancing the arts through questioning and change. Although the polemic spread to England (as exemplified in essays by Sir William Temple and William Wotton), it died around 1700 without a clear victory for either side. However, certain works published during that period were gradually to permeate European consciousness with the Moderns' kind of skepticism toward established order. Bernard de Fontenelle's *Conversations on the Plurality of Worlds* (1686) championed the notion of intellectual progress and helped to popularize the study of science, which others subsequently placed in opposition to religion. Isaac Newton's *Principia* (1687), in demonstrating that the universe functions like "clockwork" according to observable mathematical principles, also fueled a general loss of metaphysical faith. Pierre Bayle, one of the thousands of French Huguenots driven into exile by Louis XIV's revocation of the Edict of Nantes in 1685, argued persuasively in his widely read *Historical and Critical Dictionary* (1697) that no human belief can be taken as absolute dogma, a view that further undermined the authority of the church. Perhaps most influential of all in the realms of both aesthetics and politics was *An Essay Concerning Human Understanding* (1690), in which John Locke asserted that human knowledge does not derive from God-given absolutes but from the senses and from experience. Thus was sown the seed of a revolutionary idea: that all men are created equal.

The intellectual ferment precipitated by such thinkers came to fruition only after the death of Louis XIV, for he had become increasingly religious in his old age under the influence of Madame de Maintenon, whom he had secretly married in 1683. Indeed, her clout was such that the company of Italian *commedia dell'arte* players that had resided and performed in France for two generations was sent back to Italy in 1697 for its implied insult to her when they announced a play entitled *The False Prude*. Louis XIV was succeeded in 1715 by his five-year-old great-grandson Louis XV. Acting as regent for the boy, Philippe d'Orléans reversed France's long-standing foreign policy by forming alliances with England and Holland, thus easing the flow of ideas between France and England. Although given to debauchery (and thereby setting a fashion for *libertinage* among the nobility whom he restored to a more privileged status than they had enjoyed under Louis XIV), the regent was a man of taste with a strong interest in theater. In 1716 he

Italian Comedians (*ca. 1720*) *by Antoine Watteau. In that period of rampant* thé-âtromanie, *the players were one of Watteau's favorite subjects, especially Gilles—an avatar of the* commedia dell'arte's *Pedrolino—shown here taking his curtain call. National Gallery of Art, Washington, DC, Samuel H. Kress Collection.*

recalled the Italian players to Paris and reinstalled them in the Hôtel de Bourgogne.

Philippe d'Orléans also collected Italian art, but it was the rococo paintings of Antoine Watteau that epitomized the Régence period (1715–23). Watteau had trained under a scene painter, Claude Gillot, and often depicted characters from the Italian comedy. His *fêtes galantes* like "The Embarkation from Cythera" featured elegantly attired aristocrats in outdoor settings. Such graceful combinations of artifice and nature retained subtle references to classical antiquity while giving rein to an indulgent sensuality. They also captured the spirit of playacting in life that permeated aristocratic behavior of the time. Ultimately it was not enough for ladies and gentlemen to make a show of manners and dress; they discovered the pleasure of performing for their friends in the great halls of their houses. Fueled by the intense "theatromania" of the day, such *théâtres de société* became widespread. Voltaire, for example, performed in private theatricals in his houses in Paris and at Ferney, his casts

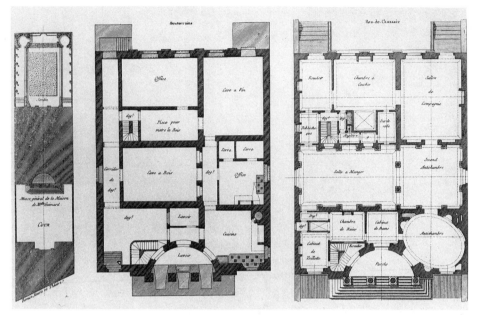

Plans of the house and theater built for the infamous Mademoiselle Guimard in Paris. (a) The site plan shows the irregularly shaped theater fronting on the rue de la Chaussée d'Antin, an inner courtyard, the mansion with its semicircular porch, and a garden in back. (b) The basement level of her house includes the kitchen, laundry room, wine cellar, and storeroom for firewood. (c) On the ground floor are the reception rooms and a dining room.

Plans of La Guimard's house and theater (continued):
(d) The colonnaded dining room is shown in cross section. (e) The first floor above ground level is mostly bedrooms.

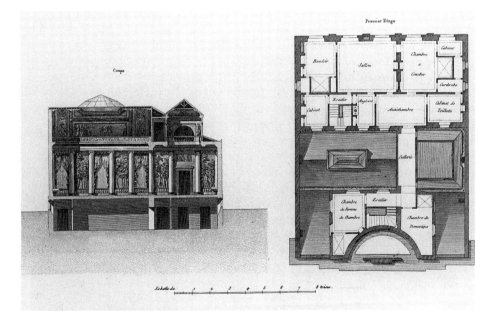

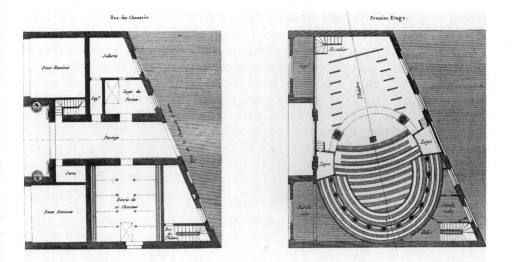

Plans of LaGuimard's house and theater (continued):
(f) At street level the theater building functions as a carriage house with a porte cochère leading into the courtyard. (g) The first floor of the five-hundred-seat theater shows access by two staircases, one for spectators and one backstage.

Plans of La Guimard's house and theater (continued):
(h) Additional seating on the upper level of the theater. (i) Cross section of the stage and auditorium, also showing the drive-through passage from the street to the inner courtyard.
C. N. Ledoux, L'Architecture.

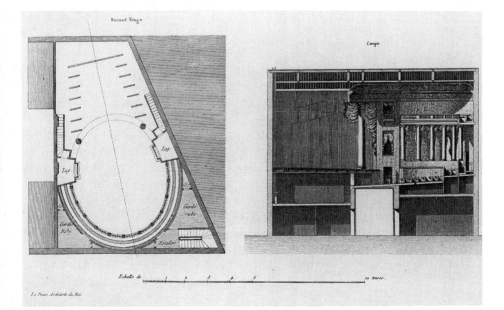

composed of other amateurs alongside guest professional artists like Henri-Louis Lekain. Some gentry wrote their own plays, usually comedies, to showcase themselves and their own interests. For some, private theatricals served as a pretext to indulge in risqué language and behavior that would be out of bounds in polite society; such were the short ribald pieces that Beaumarchais wrote for Madame de Pompadour's husband, for performance at the château d'Etioles. On the other hand, decorum prevailed at the château de Sceaux in 1714–15 when the Duchesse du Maine presented a series of Grandes Nuits de Sceaux consisting of performances of plays by Racine, Molière, and others, in which she herself appeared. A few screens sufficed to approximate the simple settings that were used for such neoclassical plays at the Comédie Française: a *palais à volonté* for tragedy or a *chambre à quatre portes* for comedy. By midcentury, however, the vogue for theatricals among the leisured classes was bringing about the construction of "private theatres" in many homes—just in time to feature the more specific settings appropriate to the new dramatic genres that gradually eroded neoclassicism's hold on the French theater.

Perhaps the most renowned of all Parisian private theaters was the one built for Mademoiselle Guimard, a leading dancer at the Opera. Designed by Claude-Nicolas Ledoux and financed by several of her lovers, the theater fronted on the rue de la Chaussée d'Antin; the ground level served as a carriage house, with a passage from the street into the courtyard that linked the theater with Mademoiselle Guimard's exquisitely appointed mansion, which became known as the "Temple of Terpsichore." A well-equipped stage and a 500-seat oval auditorium charmingly decorated by Jean-Honoré Fragonard occupied the second and third floors of the theater annex. So fashionable were Guimard's programs of opera, mime, and drama (including plays written for her by Charles Collé and dramatic proverbs by Louis Carmontelle), despite the fulminations of the church and the objections of the established theaters, that even ladies of the court ventured there, their reputations preserved by discreet access to certain boxes with identity-concealing grillworks across the front. It was said also that men of the church with a weakness for theater often used such boxes.

Although middle-class Parisians were scandalized by reports of the smutty plays shown at theaters like that of la Guimard, they too occasionally formed dramatic circles for staging private theatricals. As early as 1705 a group of young people, hoping to earn some pocket money, put together a production of Corneille's *Polyeucte* in the back room of a grocer's shop in the Faubourg Saint Germain. When Madame du Gué, a wealthy woman of the quarter, heard ecstatic reports of the performance of the leading role by a fifteen-year-old beauty named Adrienne Lecouvreur, she invited the little company to present the play in the courtyard of her mansion for her society friends. Zealous to protect its monopoly on classical tragedy and comedy, the Comédie Française quickly got the lieutenant general of police (whose office was charged with jurisdiction over Paris theaters) to put a stop to the endeavor, but not before Adrienne Lecouvreur had earned enough notice to launch her remarkable career.

Theatrical activities for all classes of society paralleled the rise of the *salon* as a carefully staged milieu for serious exchange of ideas. In the Paris *salons* of bright, enterprising women like the Duchesse du Maine, Madame de Lambert, Madame de Tencin, Madame du Deffand, Madame Geoffrin, and Julie de Lespinasse, philosophers and playwrights enjoyed a freedom of expression that censorship—officially instituted in 1701—did not permit in their writing for publication and public performance. French nobility mingled with intellectuals of bourgeois origin not only in the *salons* but also in the newly popular cafés where lively discussions of artistic and moral concern took place over

Left, Charles Coypel painted the great French actress Adrienne Lecouvreur (1692–1730) as Cornelia in Corneille's The Death of Pompey. *Her instinctive approach to playing the classics for genuine emotion as opposed to declamation affected audiences deeply. From a private collection.*

Right, le Légataire universel *(1708), a lively comedy of immoral financial intrigue, is the masterpiece of Jean-François Regnard (1655–1709), who is considered the best of Molière's successors. Here a rascally valet impersonates a wealthy invalid and dictates a false will to a notary. Courtesy of Collections de la Comédie Française.*

imported coffee, tea, and chocolate. Economic questions were debated at the Club de l'Entresol (a French imitation of English clubs) until it was ordered closed in 1731. The injustices of the French taxation system, whereby nobles were exempt from paying taxes and a class of financiers or tax-collectors known as *fermiers-généraux* enriched themselves at the expense of the increasingly miserable Third Estate, inspired a number of dark satirical comedies with money as the major motive. Among the most notable of these were Jean-François Regnard's *Le Légataire universel* (The Universal Heir, 1708) and Alain-René Lesage's *Turcaret* (1709). The title character of the latter play is a ruthless, unscrupulous financier who is finally duped by his valet. Tax-collectors tried to get the play banned, but the Dauphin insisted upon its performance at the Comédie Française, where the audience—nobleman and bourgeois alike—laughed uproariously at the scathing but well-recognized portrait.

Both the French and English economies suffered serious upheavals in 1720 with the failure of John Law's investment scheme in France and the bursting of the South Sea Bubble in England. In France, the rapid gains and losses of huge fortunes encouraged a frivolous cynicism and extreme licentiousness among the aristocracy. For the most part, they escaped being satirized in the theater because it was their tastes that prevailed in the legitimate theater. In England, by contrast, an increasingly wealthy merchant class promoted the bourgeois values of hard work, honesty, and frugality. Those attitudes are best illustrated by Sir Richard Steele's *The Conscious Lovers* (1722) and George Lillo's *The London Merchant* (1731). The latter also reinforced pride in a system that allowed the middle-class businessman to achieve a key position in the social structure by earning money. Satire thrived on the English stage, especially in Henry Fielding's spirited political lampoons of the 1730s. In those decades the French neoclassical influence also remained strong in England, as exemplified by Susannah Centlivre's borrowings from Molière for her *Love's Contrivance* (1703) and from Regnard's *Le Joueur* for *The Gamester* (1705), or Edmund Smith's Racinian *Phaedra and Hippolytus* (1707), or Joseph Addison's extremely popular blank-verse tragedy *Cato* (1713). Gradually, however, the tide of influence turned the other way, that is, from England to France.

Besides the French Huguenots who had fled to England and regularly wrote home about the exhilarating freedom of English thought and institutions, several influential French writers visited England. Voltaire's years of exile there, 1726–28, gave rise to his *Philosophical Letters* (1734). The work upheld so many aspects of English civilization as examples for the French that its publication provoked a violent storm of protest from the authorities. Voltaire fled from Paris to escape arrest, and his book was publicly burned. One of the wittiest of French social critics was Montesquieu, whose *Persian Letters* (1721) satirized manners and mores by viewing them from the perspective of two Persian tourists in France. Montesquieu's 1729–31 stay in England allowed him to observe the workings of a constitutional government based upon the principle of separation of executive, legislative, and judicial powers, which he described in *On the Spirit of Law* (1748). While such currents of thought gradually coalesced to shape a generation of French philosophers, there were also subtle indications of English influence impacting upon France's sacred neoclassical ideals in the theater. Although Voltaire later repented of his early enthusiasm for Shakespeare, the English penchant for exotic locales in legitimate drama was picked up in many of Voltaire's own plays. Philippe Destouches replaced the cynicism of his early comedies with sentimental moralizing in the plays he wrote after his 1717–23 diplomatic service in England. While the French remained justifiably proud of the Comédie Française as their one legitimate theater (founded in 1680, but already a bastion of tradition, taste, and top-quality performances of old plays), they felt a mingled fascination and repulsion toward the excesses of English theater. That "anglomania" led to a plethora of English plays performed in French translation, especially in the second half of the century. On balance, however, the century probably saw more French plays translated or adapted into English versions than vice versa.

ITALIAN OPERA, FAIR THEATERS, AND THEIR MUSICAL OFFSHOOTS

Italian opera, created in the 1590s by the Camerata of Florence, spread throughout Italy and to other capitals of Europe within half a century. The first public opera house, San Cassiano, was built in Venice in 1637. The early music-dramas of Claudio Monteverdi were soon surpassed by the melodic Baroque extravagances of such composers as Alessandro Scarlatti in Italy and Jean-Baptiste Lully in France. The opera's fantastic tales set to Baroque music found their complement in the opulent visual effects created by Italian stage technicians and designers like Giacomo Torelli and Gaspare Vigarani, both of whom took their expertise to Paris in the mid-seventeenth century. There, in 1672, the Italian born Lully jockeyed himself into the position of director of the Royal Academy of Music. When Molière died in 1673, Lully was able to get an injunction against the use of music on the legitimate stage and to take over the Palais Royal theater for his spectacular musical productions with scenes and machines designed by Carlo Vigarani (son of Gaspare

Vigarani). Molière's former company had to move into a tennis court, while the Palais Royal served as the home of Paris opera, rent free, for ninety years.

By the eighteenth century, *opera seria* was the staple of court theaters as far afield as Scandinavia and Russia. The Italian influence had become especially entrenched, both musically and scenically, in Germany as well as France. In Italy, opera so dominated the performing arts that there was little legitimate theater of consequence; since the ever-popular *commedia dell'arte* still relied heavily upon improvisation, most dramatists found it more rewarding to devote themselves entirely to writing librettos. English opera, the hybrid form launched by William Davenant's *The Siege of Rhodes,* gradually disappeared from the repertoire after the death of Henry Purcell, while Italian singers appeared with increasing frequency in London. In England, the fad for full-scale opera sung in Italian began in earnest with the arrival of George Frederick Handel in 1710. The German-born composer had studied in Italy but made his career in England. Beginning with his phenomenally popular *Rinaldo* (produced at the Queen's Theatre in 1711), he wrote thirty-six operas in thirty years. Handel produced his operas with Italian singers, which included the rival sopranos Francesca Cuzzoni and Faustina Bordoni as well as the century's greatest *castrato*, Farinelli; but the vogue for *opera seria* in England was eroded by other musical entertainments (ballad operas, burlettas, comic operas, pasticcios, and other specialties) that arose from the rival London theaters' efforts to attract larger audiences. In 1737 Farinelli was hired by the Spanish court to sing four songs a day for the melancholy Felipe V, which he did for ten years. Then Fernando VI appointed Farinelli director (1747–59) of the magnificent court theater, El Buen Retiro. Even popular audiences in Spain, faced with a choice between Italian opera and French neoclassical plays, gravitated to the opera.

In France the evolution of musical theater intertwined with entertainment forms at the popular *théâtres de la foire*. Since the Middle Ages, the annual Paris fairs of Saint-Germain (February to March) and Saint-Laurent (July to September) had offered simple entertainments: rope-dancers, gymnastic demonstrations, performing animals, and the like. When the Italian players at the Hôtel de Bourgogne were expelled from France in 1697, entrepreneurs at the fairs began to test the waters, first helping themselves to the exiled troupe's *commedia dell'arte*-based scripts and then inventing parodies of tragedy and opera. To entice audiences inside their show-booths or theaters, they offered *parades*—short buffooneries using vulgar language—on an outdoor platform or balcony, while admission was collected for the main show. Both the Comédie Française and the Opera invoked their privileges to prevent the fair

Italian commedia dell'arte *was an important source of material for the fair theaters in early eighteenth-century Paris. Harlequin, with his black mask and diamond-patterned costume, figures prominently in this scene from* The Princess of Carizme. *From LeSage and D'Orneval,* Le Théâtre de la foire *(1722–1723).*

performers from speaking dialogue or from singing and dancing except on a tightrope. Charles Alard and other fair-theater producers were constantly inventing elaborate subterfuges to get around the restrictions. One contrivance was the *pièce à écriteaux:* extras would unscroll banners on which the dialogue was written in large letters. There might be between twenty and fifty such scrolls for each act of a three-act play. Another ploy was to get the audience to sing popular songs appropriate to the pantomimic action on stage. In 1709 Alard won permission from the Opera to use music, dance, and spectacle in return for a hefty fee. In *comédies à vaudevilles* the actors' lines were sung to popular tunes; (the word "vaudeville" is sometimes said to come from the French *voix de ville,* a way to have a stage "voice" within the "city" limits; more likely, it derives from the drinking songs known as *vaux-de-Vire* that had originated in the valley of the Vire in the fifteenth century). *Comédies en ariettes* were plays with specially composed tunes. Alard's privilege was renewed in 1715, and that year marks the first use of the term *opéra comique.* The term refers to a uniquely French type of opera using spoken dialogue instead of recitative to connect the songs; it was not necessarily comic, but could be sentimental, pastoral, historical, even political.

Although the Comédie Française initiated a new order for the suppression of the fair theaters in 1719, they proved irrepressible. When they had the right to speak monologues but not dialogues, one actor would speak while another responded in gestures. The restriction could also be circumvented by having actors alternately step into view from the wings to say a line and retreat from view while another actor entered to speak the response. The one-speaker rule was cleverly lampooned in Alexis Piron's *Arlequin Deucalion* (1722); an actor alone on stage evoked the mythological Deucalion after the flood, recreating mankind out of mute stones thrown over his shoulder.

Meanwhile, the Italian players had returned to Paris, now led by Luigi Riccoboni, and settled again into the old Hôtel de Bourgogne. After the twenty-year hiatus, however, there was no longer much market in France for *commedia dell'arte,* so Riccoboni's troupe began imitating the popular offerings of the fair theaters. They soon added some French actors to the company, but their fortunes really took a turn for the better with the 1720 production of *Arlequin poli par l'amour* (Harlequin Refined by Love) by Pierre Carlet de Chamblain de Marivaux. For the next twenty years Marivaux gave the Italians a new play almost every season, providing excellent roles for the lovely leading actress Sylvia and for the beloved Thomassin, who so nimbly played the clown. So fresh and original was Marivaux's graceful banter in these delicate studies of awakening love that the style became known as *marivaudage.* The subsequent rivalry between the Italian players and the Comédie Française was ridiculed in a satirical *opéra comique* by Alain-René Lesage, who had broken with the Comédie Française after their production of *Turcaret;* his *La Querelle des théâtres* (War of the Theaters, 1723) was one of about a hundred pieces he wrote for the fair theaters beginning in 1712. In 1723 Louis XV attended a fair theater performance, thus implicitly sanctioning their existence. That same year he granted the Italians an annual subsidy and the title *Comédiens ordinaires du roi.* However, they were always familiarly known as the Comédie Italienne, even though the troupe was mostly French by the 1740s.

The opposition faced by the Parisian fair theaters was similar to that

Left, this show booth at Bartholomew Fair of London advertises a biblical tale complete with an illusionistic beheading, but it apparently includes a Harlequin. McKechnie, Popular Entertainment Through the Ages.

Right, in this illustration of a Parisian-fair theater production entitled Harlequin, Defender of Homer, *the scholars in academic robes face the bookcase labeled* Ancients *while the young women turn toward the bookcase labeled* Moderns. *From LeSage and D'Orneval,* Le Théâtre de la foire *(1722–23).*

of their counterparts in London. There too the licensed theaters repeatedly attempted to squelch any infringements upon their monopoly. As relics of medieval commercial practices, the fairs relied upon sideshow entertainment to attract customers to buy the wares on sale there. Bartholomew Fair, the oldest seasonal fair of London, with its origins in the twelfth century, almost from the beginning had used jugglers, tumblers, ballad-singers, and other entertainers to enliven its commercial transactions. Such diversions even survived during the Commonwealth. By the eighteenth century, booths for the performance of plays and drolls were appearing alongside the conjurors, freak shows, puppets, and an amaz-

Left, Les Sincères *(The Sincere Ones, 1739) by Marivaux was staged at the Comédie Française in the 1950s by Vera Korène. Robert Hirsch and Jeanne Moreau played leading roles. Courtesy of French Cultural Services.*

Right, Pierre Carlet de Chamblain de Marivaux (1688–1763) wrote over thirty-five charming romantic comedies between 1706 and 1757. Among the perennial favorites are The Double Inconstancy *(1722),* The Second Surprise of Love *(1727),* The Game of Love and Chance *(1730), and* The Dispute *(1744). Courtesy of French Cultural Services.*

Bottom, Marivaux's Le Triomphe de l'amour *(Triumph of Love, 1732) was produced at the Théâtre National Populaire in 1956. Pictured are Maria Casarès as Léonide, Daniel Sorano as Harlequin, Monique Chaumette as Hermidas, and Georges Wilson as Dimas. Courtesy of French Cultural Services.*

ing variety of performing animals. In 1700 the Court of Common Council forbade acting in fair-booths, but the regulation was largely ignored. Thereafter, Bartholomew Fair usually included between two and six theatrical booths, and a number of actors from the patent theaters performed there "unofficially" every summer. Among these was Drury Lane's popular comedian William Penkethman, familiarly known as "Pinky," the hilarious master of many faces. At Mrs. Mynn's booth in 1707, the aging Restoration dramatist Elkanah Settle presented a version of his *Siege of Troy*, which had been in the repertoire at Drury Lane. This extravagant production used "scenes, movements, and machines" with spectacular effect, but the serious dialogue was abridged and replaced by vulgar language and slapstick action similar to that of the French *parades* and Italian *commedia dell'arte*. Among the play's marvels was a seventeen-foot-high gilt Trojan horse out of which forty soldiers made their entrance with drawn swords. As in Paris, such fair entertainments appealed to all social classes. Other London fairs that at various times defied the legitimate theaters in presenting drolls and plays were May Fair, Tottenham Court Fair, and Southwark Fair.

For the Paris fair theaters, the outstanding writers besides Lesage and Piron were Louis Fuzelier and Charles-Simon Favart. Fuzelier's 237 plays written alone or in collaboration showed considerable variety; in the twelve-month period between April 1725 and April 1726, for example, he supplied fifteen different plays for all six of the public theaters that were operating in Paris: the Opera, the Comédie Française, the Comédie Italienne, the Opéra Comique at the Saint-Laurent fair, the Opéra Comique at the Saint-Germain fair, and a theater run by Englishman John Risner during the Saint-Germain fair. Most typical of his style were his "irregular," episodic plays for the *théâtre de la foire*, in which performance values took precedence over literary values.

Charles-Simon Favart had a more refined literary sensibility; he began writing for the unofficial theater in 1734 and gained a steady following as he evolved away from satire toward greater sentimentality. The popularity of his *Acajou* (1744) caused the Opera to revoke the fair theaters' right to use music for a fee. The ensuing brouhaha over control of *opéra comique* brought an injunction against the genre from 1745 to 1752. The fair theater was again reduced to rope-dancing, although it used the grand title *Théâtre d'Opéra-Comique Pantomime*. With his theater closed, Favart formed a touring company. He married Marie-Justine Chantilly, a charming actress-singer whose brilliant career was marred only by the unwelcome attentions of Adrienne Lecouvreur's erratic and violent-tempered lover, the Maréchal Maurice de Saxe, who had summoned the troupe to entertain him during his military campaign in the Low Countries. By the time the injunction against *opéra comique* was lifted, the Favarts had joined the Comédie Italienne. There, Madame Favart made theatrical history in 1753 when she shocked audiences by wearing an authentic peasant costume with wooden shoes for her role as a country girl in her husband's *Bastien and Bastienne*. Previously, the peasants and shepherdesses of the stage had been costumed as if they were dukes and duchesses. Madame Favart's initiative was taken up at the Comédie Française by Lekain and Mademoiselle Clairon, who were already working toward a more natural style of acting; they were the first on the legitimate stage to wear costumes suited to the character, the historical period, and the geographical locale. For Voltaire's *Orphelin de Chine* (The Orphan of China, 1755), Clairon had a "Chinese" gown designed by Boucher. Mme. Favart then one-upped Clairon by importing authentic harem clothes from Constantinople for Favart's *Les Trois sultanes* (Three Sultanas, 1761), a musical gem in which a sultan is instructed in polite behavior toward women.

Favart also wrote librettos for the new Opéra Comique that Jean-Louis Monnet opened in 1753. Monnet hired Arnoult, the king's own engineer-machinist, to construct a theater, and had the ceilings painted by François Boucher. At about the same time, an event that would strongly influence the development of the *opéra comique* took place, not at Monnet's Opéra Comique or at the Comédie Italienne, but at the Opera. In 1752, an Italian troupe known as the Bouffons performed Giovanni Pergolesi's *La serva padrona* (The Servant as Mistress, 1731) at the Paris Opera. The production was immensely popular, but it touched off a pamphlet-war: *la guerre des bouffons*. With *La serva padrona*, the French were introduced to *opera buffa*, a comic opera form using sung recitative, which had developed as a humorous offshoot of *opera seria*. At issue was whether French opera should continue in the heroic Baroque tradition then epitomized by French composer Jean-Philippe Rameau or whether it should follow the international trend led by the Italians toward greater spontaneity of melody and an affecting simplicity of plot and characters. The queen favored the Italian style while the king's pro-French stance was supported by several prominent figures who held forth from the "king's corner" of the Palais Royal theater at each performance. Jean-Jacques Rousseau joined the battle on the Italian side as librettist and composer of *Le Devin du village (The Village Soothsayer)*, a one-act comic opera in the Italian style (using the fashionable rustic setting and peasant characters) produced at the Paris Opera in 1753. This was the work that inspired Favart's parody, *Bastien and Bastienne*. After a season or two of Italian operas, however, French national pride reasserted itself and the Italian influence was largely diverted from the Opera to the *opéra comique*. Thus we see the impulse for Madame Favart's simple peasant costume in 1753. Her husband lampooned the Italian style in a popular musical parody entitled *Un Caprice amoureux; ou Ninette à la cour* (1755), and yet the Italian influence was evident in his subsequent work. Like Favart, Michel-Jean Sedaine wrote many popular *opéra comique* libretti idealizing the humblest levels of society. On the international front, Pergolesi's lively, humorous piece had the effect of loosening up the more ponderous aspects of serious opera, and it paved the way to the operas of Christoph Gluck and Wolfgang Amadeus Mozart.

Because the Opéra Comique and the Comédie Italienne were offering similar fare, rivaling each other for the same audiences, the two companies were joined in 1762. Thus the Comédie Italienne got the monopoly on *opéra comique*, which also brought certain restrictions. To minimize competition with the Opera, they were not allowed to sing in Italian, nor could they use choruses, which were a feature of traditional French opera; "continuous music" between songs was also forbidden. As a genre, *opéra comique* still seemed "unnatural" to many theorists of the 1760s, since it was neither tragic nor comic and since it juxtaposed dialogue and music. There was, however, considerable variety in the repertoire of plays and *opéras comiques* presented by the combined company; the offerings could be in verse or prose, serious or comic, anywhere from one to four acts in length, and of French or Italian origin.

The greatest boost to the repertoire of the Comédie Italienne came in 1761 with the arrival in Paris of the great Italian playwright Carlo Goldoni. For twenty years Goldoni had been delighting Venetian audiences with his sharply observed comedies depicting the various social classes with which he had come in contact in his practice of law. Through his plays like *Arlecchino, servitore di due padroni* (The Servant of Two Masters, 1743), and *La locandiera* (The Mistress of the Inn, 1753), he had sought to overcome two hundred years of outworn *commedia dell'arte* conventions: he abolished the use of masks in his plays and demanded that actors adhere to the text instead of improvising. Rejecting the *commedia*'s stock characters, he moved steadily toward greater realism in characterization. He was glad to leave Venice, however, when the invitation came from Paris, because he felt that his managers were cheating him and that his reforms were being undermined by Carlo Gozzi's *fiabe* (fairy-tale plays). In such fantasy plays as *L'amore delle tre melarance* (The Love of Three Oranges, 1761) and *Turandot* (1762), Gozzi championed the use of masks and other *commedia* devices. The sunny-dispositioned Goldoni was also disillusioned by his rival's libelous attacks and their acceptance by the public. In Paris, Goldoni provided a steady stream of plays in both Italian and French, bringing his total output to over 150 comedies and earning him the sobriquet "the Italian Molière." But his royal pension disappeared with the French Revolution and he spent his last years in poverty.

I Rusteghi (The Boors), a comedy by Carlo Goldoni, as performed in Venice in 1760, shortly before he settled in Paris. The setting, representing the Rialto, is mostly painted on the backdrop.

A seventeenth-century Russian puppeteer supports the puppet stage on his head while his upper body is concealed in a sack. The seated man behind him plucks a musical instrument held on his lap.

Supplied with librettos by Goldoni, Favart, and Michel-Jean Sedaine along with original music composed by André-Ernest-Modeste Grétry, Egidio Duni, François Philidor, and Pierre Monsigny, the Opéra Comique—still called "the Italians" by many Parisians—thrived. In 1783 the company built a new theater—which they named after Favart—on the Boulevard des Italiens, and the long history of the Hôtel de Bourgogne came to an end. The company's stability was threatened in 1789 when several performers seceded to join a company formed by the queen's hairdresser Leonard Autié and the violinist Giovanni Viotti. Sponsored by the queen's brother, the Théâtre de Monsieur was also known by the street name of its location: Théâtre Feydeau. A bitter : ivalry between the Favart and the Feydeau ensued—until the French Revolution brought the demise of both troupes. The Opéra Comique was reconstituted in 1801 from surviving members of both troupes. The present-day Opéra Comique, located just off the Boulevard des Italiens, was built in 1835 and bears the name Salle Favart.

As in Paris and London, fair theaters flourished in the larger cities of Germany and Poland, and throughout Russia. They were an important influence on the development of Wolfgang Amadeus Mozart's early career as an operatic composer. During the European tours of his childhood, he was exposed to the frothy music of Paris fair-theater composers like Monsigny and Philidor. The one-act opera *Bastien and Bastienne* (1778) that Mozart composed when he was twelve was based upon Favart's *opéra comique* of that title. His earliest commissioned operas were for the carnival theaters of Milan (*Mitridate, rè di Ponto*, 1770) and Munich (*La finta giardiniera*, 1775; *Idomeneo*, 1781). His final masterpiece for the lyric stage, *Die Zauberflöte* (*The Magic Flute*, 1791), was written for the kind of theater that grew out of the fairground tradition. Emanuel Schikaneder, the actor-singer-impresario who commissioned it and wrote the libretto, ran a popular theater in Wieden, a suburb of Vienna, where he presented a repertory of musical fairy tales. The role of Papageno drew upon aspects of Hanswurst, the traditional clown character of German fairbooth performances.

Although most city fairs died out by the end of the eighteenth century, Russian fairs continued to be important all during the nineteenth century, still featuring the traditional wandering entertainers called *skomorokhi*—clown-minstrels who sometimes also exhibited trained bears or gave handpuppet shows using a little stage perched on the puppeteer's head (the puppeteer himself concealed in a body-bag). The most popular figure in Russian puppet theater was Petrushka, a clown figure who appears in Russian texts from the early eighteenth century to Igor Stravinsky's *Petrushka* (1911), a ballet with a fairground setting.

With the decline of the Paris fairs, many fair-performers found a new home on the Boulevard du Temple, a pleasant tree-lined promenade that gradually became a year-round entertainment area. As Parisians of all social classes began taking their late-afternoon strolls on the Boulevard du Temple, it became a mecca for street vendors of every variety. By the nineteenth century it was lined with theaters, cafés, and restaurants, and would eventually give rise to the epithet "boulevard theater" to denote commercial theater of broad, popular appeal. The first entrepreneur on the boulevard was Jean-Baptiste Nicolet, an acrobat who had performed regularly at the fairs of Saint-Germain, Saint-Laurent, and Saint-Ovide. When a new lieutenant general of police, M. Sartines, took office in 1759, Nicolet seized the opportunity to win permission to offer variety entertainments in a rented room on the boulevard. Little by little his presentations escalated from acrobatics and monkey shows to rope-dancers and marionettes in the permanent theater he built and named *Salle des grands danseurs*. He had a famous monkey who would lead processions along the boulevard to the theater and there act out current events. Once Nicolet costumed the monkey in a dressing gown, nightcap, and slippers like those worn by François-René Molé, a popular-favorite comic actor at the Comédie Française, and taught the monkey to mimic the actor's gestures. Finally Nicolet dared to offer plays performed by live actors, capping a trajectory that had given rise to the popular saying, *"De plus en plus fort, comme chez Nicolet"* (From one excess to the next, like Nicolet). He hired Toussaint Gaspard Taconnet, a heavy-drinking actor-stagehand-cum-playwright (whose favorite expression was *"Je te méprise comme un verre d'eau"* (I scorn you as I would a glass of water), to create some earthy farces, which proved enduringly successful with audiences.

While the vulgarity of Taconnet's work attracted crowds, Nicolet's occasional foray onto classical terrain was met with relative indifference, according to Goldoni. Goldoni relates in his *Mémoires* how he found himself to be the only audience member when he was enticed into that theater by the announcement of a play on the subject of Coriolanus. Just before the opening curtain, the actor who was to play the title role asked to borrow Goldoni's sword for his performance. (As a gentleman, Goldoni was entitled to wear a sword, whereas the actor was not.) Then Goldoni had to sit through a rope-dancing act and two comic skits before he got to see his sword brandished on stage in the one-act *Coriolanus* by an unknown author. Of course, the Comédie Française attacked such ventures; thus, in 1772, Nicolet was summoned to show his wares in a performance before Louis XV and Madame du Barry. The performance earned his theater the title *Grands danseurs du roi*, which Nicolet retained until the Revolution. Nicolet died in 1796, and his theater became the Théâtre de la Gaîté.

Nicolet's initiative was soon taken up by others. In 1769 Nicolas Audinot opened the second permanent theater on the Boulevard du

Above, Jean-Baptiste Nicolet ran this theater at the Saint-Germain Fair before he moved to the Boulevard du Temple. Among the performers in the parade *on the balcony is the* commedia dell'arte-*inspired white-faced clown Gilles. Courtesy of French Cultural Services.*

Scenes from drames, *parodies, or* pantomimes *performed at the Théâtre des Grandes Danseurs in 1781. At lower left is a scene from* L'Elève de la Nature, *a one-act comedy with music that drew upon ideas in Rousseau's* Emile. *From Felix Gaiffe,* Le Drame en France au XVIIIe siècle.

Temple. He called it the Théâtre Ambigu because of the ambiguous nature of the entertainments devised to skirt the Comédie Française's restrictions. Audinot is credited, for example, as the inventor of the *pantomime dialoguée*, certainly ambiguous in its implication that a "pantomime with dialogue" is something other than spoken drama. His rivalry with Nicolet led him to expand from marionettes to parodies performed by children. Some spectators were scandalized, but most were amused to hear the foul language of the unofficial theater spoken by children. Another enterprise in the very center of Paris brought puppets and children together on the same stage at the Théâtre des Beaujolais. The theater opened to the public in 1784 with performances by marionettes about four feet tall known as *bamboches,* skillfully manipulated from above by brass wires, while actors spoke and sang their lines from the wings to the accompaniment of a twenty-piece orchestra. Sculpted and costumed to resemble specific performers at the Comédie Française, Comédie Italienne, and Opéra, and backed by elaborate scenery and machine effects, the *comédiens de bois* (wooden actors) regularly attracted adult audiences to fill the theater to its capacity of eight hundred. Eventually the entrepreneurs, Célestin Delomel and Jean-Nicolas Gardeur, hit upon the idea of using six- to ten-year-old children to dance among the marionettes and mimic their movements. Success proved the undoing of the Beaujolais, as it provoked the official theaters to agitate for new restrictions. Since two or more actors were needed for each marionette character (at least one to pull the wires and one to speak the lines), Lieutenant General of Police Lenoir in 1788 prohibited the use of more than one actor per role and further outlawed singing or speaking from the wings.

Among other early theaters on the Boulevard du Temple were the Théâtre des Associés, opened in 1774; the Variétés Amusantes, 1778; and the Délassements-Comiques, 1787. The latter theater offered essentially the same fare as the others, but it had unfortunately opened under the newly appointed and particularly zealous lieutenant general of police, M. Lenoir, who imposed a gauze curtain between performers and audience. The tearing of that gauze was one of the most celebrated symbolic acts that occurred on January 13, 1791 when the Revolutionary Assembly passed a law granting all theaters full liberties.

ENGLISH THEATER UNTIL THE LICENSING ACT OF 1737

The early decades of the eighteenth century were a period of flux in English theater. While the Collier controversy raged on, various forms of dramatic entertainment were tried as alternatives to Restoration comedy. Several changes in management at the licensed theaters as well as the appearance of a number of short-lived unlicensed theaters tested the limits of the patent system. When the century began, the two officially sanctioned theaters in London were the Drury Lane, still run by the ruthlessly profit-minded Christopher Rich, and Lincoln's Inn Fields, which Thomas Betterton and an actors' cooperative had operated since the Actors' Rebellion of 1695. The 1699–1700 season saw them rivaling each other in a final fling at sparkling comedy of wit: George Farquhar's *The Constant Couple; or, A Trip to the Jubilee* packing the house at the Drury Lane, and William Congreve's masterpiece *The Way of the World,* under-appreciated in its initial run, at Lincoln's Inn Fields. Thereafter, the two theaters' strategy for luring audiences tended toward supplementing the full-length play with a variety of other entertainments like pantomimic interludes, vocal and instrumental music, acrobatics, contortionists, rope-dancing, and animal imitations. By the 1720s, the short comic afterpiece emerged as the most popular complement to the main play. Whether it took the form of farce or satire, the afterpiece brought a welcome release through laughter after the sentimentality of comedy and the pathos of tragedy from which middle-class tastes were leaching the comic bite or tragic grandeur.

In 1705 Betterton's company moved into a new theater, the Queen's Theatre in Haymarket, designed by architect-playwright Sir John Vanbrugh, who had obtained a license for it. Although the company was favored by the discriminating members of the Kit-Kat Club, the theater was soon deemed better suited to opera than to legitimate drama. Under Vanbrugh's influence, the two patent companies were reunited at Drury Lane in 1708, leaving the Queen's Theatre free to become the first English opera house. At Drury Lane, however, Christopher Rich's repressive policies continued and, once again, the actors complained. The result was the 1709 "silencing" of Drury Lane. The theater remained closed until November 1710, when it reopened under a triumvirate of actor-managers: Colley Cibber, Robert Wilks, and Thomas Doggett (the latter being soon replaced by Barton Booth). In 1714 the patent for Drury Lane was issued to Sir Richard Steele, who allowed the triumvirate free rein. Their management maintained a relative stability and prosperity until 1732. Meanwhile Christopher Rich died, leaving his son John Rich to carry out his project of rebuilding Lincoln's Inn Fields.

The sumptuously decorated New Theatre in Lincoln's Inn Fields opened in 1714 as a second patent house. Unable to compete with Drury Lane in legitimate drama, the uneducated but nimble-bodied John Rich (using the stage name "Lun") won a popular following with his annual pantomimes in which he played the mutely expressive Harlequin. The English pantomime probably originated with John Weaver's action-ballet

The Loves of Mars and Venus, offered as a supplement to the main bill at Drury Lane in 1717. To this concept Rich added elements borrowed from the Italian *commedia dell'arte* troupes that had long visited London, and from a couple of Parisian fair-theater performers, Sorin and Baxter, who brought a piece entitled *The Whimsical Death of Harlequin* to London. Rich's innovation was to incorporate magical stage effects "such as the sudden transformation of palaces and temples to huts and cottages; of men and women into wheelbarrows and joint-stools; of trees turned into houses; colonnades to beds of tulips; and mechanics' shops into serpents and ostriches." The stories recounted through clowning, acrobatics, song, and dance ranged from classical mythology to contemporary news reports of colorful criminals. In one of Rich's most famous sequences, Harlequin was hatched from an egg. An eyewitness recalled that "from the first chipping of the egg, his receiving motion, his feeling the ground, his standing upright, to his quick Harlequin trip round the empty shell, through the whole progression, every limb had its tongue, and every motion a voice, which spoke with most miraculous organ, to the understandings and sensations of the observers." While men of letters like Alexander Pope (in *The Dunciad*) deplored such vulgarization of dramatic art, even Drury Lane—despite the higher inclinations of the snobbish Colley Cibber and, later, David Garrick—succumbed to the pressure of the box office and offered the "monstrous medleys" as "crutches to our weakest plays."

John Rich's second great contribution to the English stage was the ballad opera. It was he who presented *The Beggar's Opera* by John Gay at the Lincoln's Inn Fields theater in 1728 and thereby launched a tremendous vogue for dramatic satire with snatches of song set to popular airs. Dr. John Christopher Pepusch, musical director of Lincoln's Inn Fields, arranged the sixty-eight songs, some only two or three lines in length, and composed an overture. Subtitled "a Newgate pastoral," the play used a lowlife setting to spoof the artifice of Italian opera and its trite love intrigues. The rivalry of Polly Peacham and Lucy Lockit for the love of the highwayman Macheath echoed the real-life competition between two temperamental Italian sopranos, Francesca Cuzzoni and Faustina Bordoni, who had actually come to blows on the stage of the Queen's Theatre (renamed King's Theatre with the accession of George I in 1714) at the final performance of Giovanni Bononcini's *Astianatte* in 1727. Less blatantly, *The Beggar's Opera* also attacked the political corruption in Sir Robert Walpole's administration. The public's response was unprecedented, sustaining thirty-two consecutive performances and a total of sixty-two performances in the first season. The play was revived the following season by the regular company as well as by a cast of children called the Lilliputians. The public was avid for souvenirs like fans and mugs painted with scenes from *The Beggar's Opera;* indeed, anything with the word "beggar" in it attracted interest. Samuel Johnson noted the current saying: *The Beggar's Opera* made "Gay rich and Rich gay," Gay's sequel, *Polly* (1729), was banned from production by Walpole, but the popularity of the genre continued unabated for about eight years and fifty more ballad operas. *The Beggar's Opera* earned Rich enough to build a new theater, the Covent Garden, which opened in 1732.

At Covent Garden, John Rich continued to offer a variety of entertainments besides his pantomimes and ballad operas. A single evening's bill might include a Shakespearean tragedy and a burlesque of some literary or topical subject. Several of Handel's operas premiered there as well as his oratorio, *Messiah* (1743). Drury Lane, in order to compete, was forced to recognize that there were "many more Spectators than Men of Taste and Judgment" and that a pantomime on the bill would at least have the virtue of exposing a greater number of spectators to partake of "a good Play than could be drawn without it." Besides the business acumen of the versatile manager-playwright-comic actor Colley Cibber, the Drury Lane had a major asset in Anne Oldfield. That comely actress with a "sweet, strong, piercing, and melodious" voice was extremely popular in both comedy and tragedy. Cibber particularly praised her distinct pronunciation but further asserted that the spectator was always "as much informed by her eyes as her elocution." Offstage she was as genteel and elegant as a woman of quality, but her characterizations were vivid in their individuality of "air and manner." Although actors were considered socially inferior, their activities both on and offstage were a subject of public interest, for they were regularly reported in newspapers like Sir Richard Steele's *Tatler* (1709–11), *Spectator* (1711–12), and *The Theatre* (1719–20), Aaron Hill's *The Prompter* (1734–36), as well as numerous other weekly and monthly journals.

The fortunes of the two patent theaters were complicated by the sporadic appearance of unlicensed theaters. Temporary playhouses in suburban areas like Greenwich and Richmond Hill drew audiences in the summer months. Concert rooms and fair booths occasionally offered plays. After moving to Covent Garden, John Rich sometimes rented Lincoln's Inn Fields to various troupes. A series of playhouses opened in Goodman's Fields, tapping an audience at some distance from the patent theaters; the most prosperous of these was the New Theatre in Ayliffe Street under Henry Giffard's management from 1732 to 1742. But the most serious threat to the patent theaters' hegemony came from a second theater in Haymarket, built by entrepreneur John Potter in 1720. Much smaller than the nearby King's Theatre, which was now restricted to an operatic repertoire, the new playhouse was dubbed Little Theatre in the

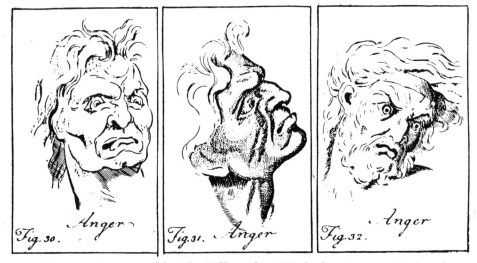

This expression engraved by John Williams for A Method to Learn to Design the Passions *(1734), based upon an earlier French work by Charles Lebrun, is typical of many eighteenth-century attempts to codify human emotions and their external expression. Such works had enormous influence upon the acting style of the period. Courtesy of the Department of Rare Books and Special Collections, The University of Michigan Library.*

Hay. Its status was not seriously questioned as long as it operated without a permanent company, serving mainly as a home for visiting foreign troupes, English amateur theatricals, and variety performances. But

Robert Hume pinpoints the 1728–29 season as a harbinger of change in the status quo. In that season the Little Haymarket ran twenty-three different plays for 115 nights in comparison to Drury Lane's sixty-eight plays in 195 nights and Lincoln's Inn Fields's forty-nine plays in 156 nights. The significant factor was that sixty percent of the Little Haymarket's offerings were new plays, as opposed to only two new main-pieces at Drury Lane and three at Lincoln's Inn Fields.

The Little Haymarket presented a wide variety of plays, but is best remembered for its hospitality to the satirical plays of Henry Fielding. Unable to peddle his plays at the legitimate theaters, Fielding vented his frustration in *The Author's Farce* (1730), a satire on the Drury Lane and its management, to which he soon appended an afterpiece: a burlesque of heroic tragedy entitled *Tom Thumb*. Fielding's subsequent plays at the Little Haymarket included *Rape upon Rape* (1730), a comedy with elements of social satire; *The Tragedy of Tragedies* (1731), a revision and expansion of *Tom Thumb;* and *The Welsh Opera* (1731), an audaciously satirical ballad-opera afterpiece. Although Fielding's next satirical ballad opera, *Grub-Street Opera,* was suppressed, the popularity of his burlesques—and of others like Samuel Johnson of Cheshire's *Hurlothrumbo*—got Fielding's burlesque *Covent-Garden Tragedy* (1732) staged at Drury Lane. Because Colley Cibber's Whig sympathies were well-known and Drury Lane would not risk offending Walpole's government, Fielding eschewed satire in favor of comedy in his seven new plays that were produced at Drury Lane in 1732–33. (One of these was *The Miser,* based upon Molière's play, with English characters and setting.)

During the stormy period of the Drury Lane patent's transition in 1732–33, Fielding remained there while most of the actors rebelled against the new management and went to the Little Haymarket. In 1734 the patent was bought by Charles Fleetwood and the actors returned to Drury Lane, having won several concessions. But Fielding had to go back to the Little Haymarket to get his *Don Quixote in England* staged. In 1736 Fielding rounded up some undistinguished actors and formed his own company to present his *Pasquin,* "A Dramatick Satire on the Times: being the Rehearsal of Two Plays, viz. A Comedy call'd *The Election;* and a Tragedy call'd *The Life and Death of Common Sense.*" *Pasquin* contained Fielding's most pointed political humor to date as well as some spirited digs at the patent theaters' managements; it became his greatest box-office hit, successful enough to allow the raising of prices during the initial run. Fielding's last major work for the theater, also presented at the Little Haymarket, was *The Historical Register, for the Year 1736* (1737), a metatheatrical construction of skits intended, as the character Medley says, "to ridicule the vicious and foolish customs of the age, and that in a fair manner, without fear, favour, or ill nature, . . . [and] to expose the reigning follies, in such a manner, that men shall laugh themselves out of

Left, Hogarth's engraving of The Laughing Pit *shows lighted candles in the auditorium and the spikes that prevented spectators from climbing onstage. Elderly rakes in the side boxes display undue interest in the orange wenches who sold refreshments. From Karl Mantzius,* A History of Theatrical Art, *vol. 5 (1909).*

Right, the great satiric dramatist Henry Fielding (1707–54) is caricatured in this portrait by William Hogarth. Courtesy of The British Museum.

them before they feel that they are touched." The overt attack on Prime Minister Walpole certainly helped to sell tickets, and thus this play has long been singled out as the prime impetus for passage of the Licensing Act of 1737.

Many factors, however, economic and social as well as political, influenced Parliament's passage of the Licensing Act of 1737, which severely damaged the British theater for two centuries. Vincent J. Liesenfield's book on the subject elucidates the bill's historical context and provides its complete text. In summary, the Licensing Act prohibited the presentation or performance of any "interlude, tragedy, comedy, opera, play, farce or other entertainment of the stage" for hire, gain, or reward except by authority of a Royal Patent or a License from the Lord Chamberlain. It further provided that any new play and any addition to old plays be submitted to the Lord Chamberlain for prior approval at least fourteen days before performance. The immediate effect of the re-establishment of government-regulated theater monopolies was to put the Little Haymarket, Goodman's Fields, and other such theaters out of business, and to end Henry Fielding's career as a playwright. The long-term effect was disastrous: it suppressed healthy competition among theaters and stifled the incentive to risk money on new plays. Although the monopolies would be ended by the Theatre Act of 1843, the censorship provision remained in effect, with some modifications along the way, until 1968.

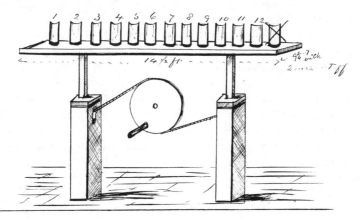

H. R. Eyre, manager of the Theatre Royal at Ipswich in the 1880s, compiled a scrapbook, Interesting Matter Relating to Scenery, Decoration, etc., of the Theatre Royal, Tacket Street, *which includes this diagram illustrating how footlights—either candles or oil lamps with reflectors—could be lowered below stage level to darken the scene. Suffolk Record Office.*

Eyre's scrapbook also contains this nineteenth-century illustration of eighteenth-century footlights in a provincial theater. The man on stage is trimming the wicks so that the candles would not sputter and drip during the performance. Suffolk Record Office.

TWO GIANTS AND A NEW GENRE

By midcentury, the general evolution of social attitudes away from cynicism and self-interest, toward humanitarianism, sentimentality, and virtue, had become evident in the theaters of France and England. Despite the championing of classical tragedy by Gian Vincenzo Gravina and Scipione Maffei in Italy, Nathaniel Lee and Joseph Addison in England, Johann Christoph Gottsched in Germany, and Voltaire in France, the venerable genre was losing its purity. Imitations of Corneille and Racine had become stale exercises in verse without poetry. Prosper Jolyot de Crébillon attempted to reinvigorate tragedy by injecting horror, as in his *Rhadamiste et Zénobie* (Rhadamisthes and Zenobia, 1711). The theoretical treatises of Antoine Houdar de la Motte advocated abandonment of the neoclassical unities, but he was unable to do so in his own tragedies, including his successful *Inès de Castro* (1723). Ironically, the evolution of the genre from classical grandeur to domestic pathos was largely the doing of one of classical tragedy's staunchest defenders, Voltaire. Comedy also evolved away from its classical definition to become *comédie larmoyante* or "tearful comedy," a sentimentalized treatment for which the French *honnête homme* and the English merchant were both the subject and the audience. In France, Pierre Marivaux led the way toward the focus on feelings, but the stage was subsequently taken by moralizing comedies that lacked his delicate touch; among the more popular were Philippe Destouches's *Le Philosophe marié* (The Married Philosopher, 1727) and *Le Glorieux* (Vainglorious, 1732), and Nivelle de la Chaussée's *Le Préjugé à la mode* (The Fashionable Prejudice, 1735). Morality onstage was also good business for an English public whose tastes in reading were turning away from the hard-edged satire of Swift and Pope to Richardson's *Pamela; or, Virtue Rewarded* (1740). Finally, the trends toward tragedy of pathos and tearful comedy converged in a new dramatic genre: *le drame,* also known as *drame bourgeois* or "middle-class drama."

Those changes are reflected in the work of two giants of the century: the philosopher-playwright Voltaire and the actor-manager-playwright David Garrick. Although neither was a leader in the movement to make art subject to the emotions, their prodigious talents and visibility distinguished them as rallying figures for the spirit of the times. Garrick, for example, in 1757 received a letter from a clergyman who wrote: "I honor you for your repeated endeavors in stemming the torrent of vice and folly. You do it in a station where most men, I suppose, would think you might fairly be dispensed with from bearing your part in the duty of a good citizen on such a necessary occasion, but it is for this that I chiefly honor you." Similarly, Voltaire's plays became more and more oriented to serving a moral purpose, especially after *Mahomet* (1742). "True tragedy is the school of virtue," he stated.

Voltaire's literary career began and ended with the tragic genre: *Oedipus* in 1718, *Irène* in 1778, and he wrote twenty-five others in the intervening sixty years. Although he constantly upheld the ideals of Racinian tragedy, Voltaire contributed to the development of the *drame bourgeois* through his almost begrudging assimilation of certain aspects of English theater. His ambivalent attitude is evident in his "Discourse on Tragedy" (1731), a letter to Lord Bolingbroke that was published as a preface to his tragedy *Brutus:* "I have endeavored at least to transplant into our scene some of the beauties of yours; at the same time I am satisfied that the English theatre is extremely defective." He granted that the English had some "admirable scenes" in those "wild pieces" that were wanting in purity and decorum of action and style, but at the same time he described French tragedies as "conversations rather than the representation of an event," and deplored the "excessive delicacy" that obliged the French to narrate events instead of showing them on stage. "The English are more fond of action than we are, and speak more to the eye," he continued; "the French give more attention to elegance, harmony, and the charms of verse. It is certainly more difficult to write well than to bring upon the stage assassinations, wheels of torture, mechanical powers, ghosts, and sorcerers."

Voltaire expanded the scope of French tragedy beyond the Greek, Roman, and biblical settings of his seventeenth-century models to Jerusalem *(Zaïre)*, Peru *(Alzire)*, Mecca *(Mahomet)*, Assyria *(Semiramis)*, China *(The Orphan of China)*, and, perhaps most tellingly, France itself *(Adelaïde of Guesclin* and *Tancrède)*. Also unprecedented on the French stage was the philosophical substance of his tragedies, especially concerning religious questions. Political philosophy was expounded in his *Les Guèbres; ou la Tolérance* (Fire-worshippers; or, Tolerance, 1769), through lines like these:

> I think like a citizen, act like an emperor,
> I hate the fanatic and the persecutor.

Despite his reputation as a satirist, Voltaire was capable of creating passionate outbursts and touching moments of pathos that adumbrate the final stage in the evolution of a tragedy for the masses: melodrama.

Voltaire's plays figured prominently in the theater's twin tendencies toward greater specificity in the stage setting (as opposed to the generic columns suggesting antiquity in the traditional *palais à volonté*) and more

Le Glorieux (Vainglorious, *1732*) was the comic masterpiece of Philippe Destouches. The actors are Grandval, Quinault-Dufresne, Mademoiselle Labette, and Mademoiselle Quinault. Engraving by N. Dupuis after N. Lancret. Reynaud, Musée rétrospectif.

Voltaire believed that his tragedy Semiramis *(1748) was ruined by the presence of the spectators on stage as sketched here, seated behind balustrades on both sides. From a private collection.*

elaborate scenic effects. His introduction of onstage deaths by poisoning and of ghostly apparitions was undoubtedly a product of his exposure to Shakespeare. The exoticism of his settings—which cried out for the geographically or historically evocative costumes that Lekain and Mademoiselle Clairon introduced—might be seen as a transferral of French operatic production values to the legitimate stage. Indeed, because of its elaborate scenery and machinery, the stage of the Opera had long been free of the encumbering presence of spectators, while Voltaire frequently attacked in print the continuation of that practice at the Comédie Française. "The benches meant for spectators on the stage constrict the stage and render any action almost unfeasible. They are why the stage decoration . . . is rarely suited to the play," he wrote as early as 1731. In 1748 he blamed the crowd of seated and standing spectators on stage for the failure of his elaborately mounted *Semiramis.* In that production, for example, so thick was the crowd of *petit marquis* standing at the back of the stage that the ghost of Ninus could not leave his tomb until someone called out, "Make way for the ghost." Voltaire's long campaign finally paid off, and he is generally credited with the removal of spectators from the French stage in 1759. In this he had the help of his friend, the leading actor at the Comédie Française, Henri-Louis Lekain. Other members of the company resisted, because they were unwilling to take a loss of revenue from the approximately 140 high-priced seats, but Lekain worked with a benefactor, the Comte de Lauraguais, to achieve a remodeling of the theater that added places elsewhere to compensate for the removal of stage seating.

Voltaire's sensitivity to production values must have stemmed in part from his experience in amateur theatricals. Wherever he lived over the years, Voltaire had his own theater—on rue Traversière in Paris, at Cirey, les Délices, and Ferney—where he himself could perform, often in his own plays. It was to Voltaire's active involvement in theater that Lekain owed his career.

Short and not considered handsome, Lekain was physically unsuited to tragedy, but Voltaire perceived the inner fire and intelligent expressiveness of the twenty-year-old goldsmith's son in a performance at one of the three *sociétés bourgeoises,* or amateur public theaters, in Paris in 1749. Voltaire brought Lekain to live in his house, provided him with lessons, played opposite him in a performance organized by the duchesse du Maine at Sceaux, and continued to encourage him after a disappointing debut at the Comédie Française in 1750. Lekain was not received into the company until 1752, but he soon eclipsed Jean-Baptiste de Grandval, who had been the leading tragedian there for twenty years. Other outstanding actors who enjoyed Voltaire's encouragement included Hippolyte Clairon, Marie Dumesnil, Jeanne Gaussin, and Adrienne Lecouvreur. Voltaire was at the latter's bedside when she died in 1730 without repenting her theatrical profession, which meant that the church would refuse to allow her burial in consecrated ground. A police officer and two porters disposed of her body by night in an unmarked spot on the banks of the Seine. Voltaire's elegy "On the Death of Mademoiselle Lecouvreur" was both a loving tribute to the actress and an indignant denunciation of the French clergy. It called attention to the contrasting treatment of England's leading actress, Anne Oldfield, who died that same year and was accorded a state funeral and burial in Westminster Abbey.

During his quarter-century of exile in Switzerland, Voltaire often received visits from his Paris friends, including Lekain and Clairon, who performed in his private theater. When he finally returned to Paris at the age of eighty-three to attend the premiere of *Irène*, Voltaire was especially looking forward to a reunion with Lekain, but the great actor had died suddenly only two days earlier. In counterpoint to his grief, Voltaire enjoyed the tumultuous adulation of crowds wherever he went in Paris. At the performance he attended of *Irène*, Jean-Baptiste Brizard and Françoise Vestris came to his box to crown him with laurel. After the final curtain, the entire company gathered on stage around a bust of Voltaire, also crowned with laurel. He died in Paris two months later.

The invention of *le drame* as a distinct genre can be pinpointed in the publication of two plays and their accompanying manifestos by Denis Diderot: *Le Fils naturel* with "Dialogues on *The Illegitimate Son*" (1757) and *Le Père de famille* (The Father of the Family) with "On Dramatic Poetry" (1758). Like other Enlightenment philosophers, Diderot saw theater as a means of moral instruction in a time when morality was emotionally based and virtue was equated with sensitivity. Appealing to man's reason, natural goodness, and sentiment, *le drame* would be at once moving and edifying through its depiction of contemporary middle-class life, as in the sentimental bourgeois family scenes by Diderot's favorite painter, Jean-Baptiste Greuze. In striking a balance between comedy's focus on domestic life and tragedy's seriousness of tone, *le drame* would emphasize conditions and relationships over characters. It would portray not only such professions as the philosopher, the businessman, the politician, the citizen, the financier, the nobleman, and others, but also relations among the father of the family, the husband, the sister, the brothers. "Each of us has a station in society," Diderot wrote, "but we deal with people of all stations." For example, his statement of theme for *The Father of the Family* was "wealth, birth, upbringing, duties of parents toward their children, and of children toward their parents, marriage, the bachelor, everything that has to do with the status of the father of a family." In effect, *le drame* exceeded its moralizing function and served to vindicate the solid contributions to the nation by a middle class that suffered so many hardships of social inequality.

Several artists depicted the so-called apotheosis of Voltaire at the sixth performance of his play Irène *by the Comédie Française in its theater in the old Salle des Machines. This engraving of Mademoiselle Vestris crowning Voltaire with laurel on stage is a bit fanciful. The crown was actually placed on his head by the actor Brizard as Voltaire sat in his box before the performance, and Mademoiselle Vestris crowned a bust of Voltaire on stage after the tragedy. She also spoke the verse inscribed here, which declares that Voltaire should not have to wait for the dark shore in order to enjoy the honor of immortality, and that the honor is all the more meaningful in that it is France that confers it. Courtesy of Collections de la Comédie Française.*

Brunetti designed this set for Irène *with a painted vista of the sea and towers beyond the architectural arcades. Voltaire was reportedly very pleased with the design. The engraving depicts the crowning of a bust of Voltaire after the sixth performance. Courtesy of Collections de la Comédie Française.*

Diderot proposed innovations in form as well as content. Although he did not attack the classical unities, he called for freedom from servile observance of "rules" for dramatic art. The drama should not be composed of alternating comic and tragic scenes, but maintain a uniform tone to convey the tears and laughter of everyday life. It was more important to sustain a mood than to excite an audience with *coups de théâtre,* and a realistic atmosphere should be supported by careful attention to settings, costumes, and stage composition. Instead of standing in a semicircle facing the audience, the actors should move about and group themselves into natural-looking tableaux. Prose dialogue should replace verse, and the actor—liberated from the artifice of verse—should develop a correspondingly natural style that would incorporate sighs, groans, exclamations, and pantomimic business.

Those plays and manifestos were written at a difficult juncture in Diderot's career. In 1746 he had undertaken the ambitious project of putting together a vast compendium of contemporary knowledge to which experts in all fields contributed. The philosophers supported this *Encyclopaedia* as a means of demonstrating human progress through knowledge, but the church's attacks on it began with the publication of the first volume (containing entries on atheism, *âme,* and other "a" words) in 1751. For volume 7 (1757), Jean d'Alembert contributed an article on Geneva, in which he deplored that city's having banned theater for fear of corrupting its youth. Spearheading the controversy over that article was Jean-Jacques Rousseau's "Letter to d'Alembert on the Theatre," which refuted the claim for theater as an agent of civic virtue. This led to the resignation of d'Alembert from the editorial staff, along with Jean-François Marmontel, who had written many of the *Encyclopaedia's* articles on theater and drama. Despite an injunction against further publication of the *Encyclopaedia,* Diderot continued to work on it. He was finally able to publish volumes 8 through 17 and distribute them clandestinely to subscribers in 1766.

Although it was the publication of Diderot's plays that had launched the serious genre, *The Father of the Family* was not performed until 1761, and *The Illegitimate Son* failed at its premiere in 1771. Diderot fell into such poverty that he sought a buyer for his private library; it was generously purchased by Catherine the Great of Russia, who allowed him to keep it during his lifetime. His five-month visit to her court swayed him to acceptance of the concept of "enlightened despotism." The library sent to Russia after his death contained thirty-three volumes of unpublished manuscripts, including *The Paradox of Acting* (ca. 1773), an important treatise not published until 1830, on the roles of intuition and intellect in performance.

Diderot's ideas of *le drame* were taken up in the ponderous plays of Louis-Sébastien Mercier and in the early full-length plays of Beaumarchais as well as in their critical essays. The most successful example of *le drame* following Diderot's precepts was *Le Philosophe sans le savoir* (Philosopher without Knowing It, 1765) by Michel-Jean Sedaine. It centered upon a successful businessman who had obscured the fact of his nobility in order that, as a good father of a family, he might transmit to his children virtues that do not depend upon title. In a touching scene with his son, he extols his chosen position in life: "No matter what pressing concerns cause our kings to take up arms and go to war, catching everything up in it and dividing Europe, still the businessman— English, Dutch, Russian, or Chinese—remains my closest friend. We are like a silken tissue over the surface of the earth, each of us a thread tying our nations together and leading them back toward peace by commercial necessity. That, my son, is what it means to be an honest businessman." Although *le drame*—the genre as Diderot conceived it—disappeared by the end of the century, many of its elements can be detected in the Romantic drama of the early nineteenth century.

In the realm of theoretical debate, one of the liveliest but least-known arenas on the Continent was Spain. The Spanish *comedia* (any full-length play, usually in three acts, as opposed to the five-act neo-classical tragedy or comedy) had flourished throughout the century known as the Golden Age, which ended with the death of Pedro Calderón de la Barca in 1681. The "irregular" *comedia* retained its popularity with audiences well into the eighteenth century despite increasing attacks by proponents of French neoclassicism, led by Ignacio de Luzán. Although Luzán admired the plays of Lope de Vega and Calderón, he realized that the once-glorious *comedia* had sunk to a deplorable level of taste and, in his *Poetics* (1737), he prescribed neoclassicism as the means of revitalizing Spanish theater. In this he was supported by a French-influenced periodical, *Diario de los literatos* (1737–46). But critics like Marcelino Menéndez y Pelayo and others upheld Spanish popular tradition with all its vulgar excesses. In 1765 the *autos sacramentales* were suppressed by royal decree; these lavishly produced religious allegories had survived since the sixteenth century, but could not withstand on the one hand the church's objection to increasing elements of profanity and, on the other hand, the neoclassicists' attacks on a form that both violated the unities and contradicted the spirit of the Enlightenment.

The polemic between neoclassicists and nationalists continued in Spain throughout the 1700s. Although no outstanding play was written to illustrate the doctrine, neoclassicism achieved significant influence, gradually gaining ground—at least in theory—in a battle that had already been won in France a century earlier. By the time Luzán lived in Paris, 1747–50, the trend toward sentimentalization of comedy and tragedy was well under way there. Despite his former championship of the concept of purity of genre, Luzán was swayed by the popularity of

Nivelle de la Chaussée's *The Fashionable Prejudice* (1735), and he even translated that *comédie larmoyante* into Spanish. Thus did a strong current of sentimentalism flow into Spain's fledgling neoclassicism. The best of the Spanish authors of neoclassical moralizing tragedy was Nicolás Fernández de Moratín, who surpassed even Vicente García de la Huerta y Muñoz, author of the popular *Raquel* (1772), largely by the quality of his verse. One popular author working against the grain of French influence, Ramón de la Cruz, revived the *sainete*, a short, often racy, comic piece with music that formerly served as an afterpiece to the *comedia*. Cruz also popularized the *zarzuela*, whose origins went back to the musical allegories presented by Calderón at Felipe IV's hunting lodge, the Palacio de la Zarzuela; in Cruz's hands the *zarzuela* moved closer to operetta, mocking neoclassicism and taking its subjects from contemporary working-class Madrid life. Culminating the century's artistic progress were five neoclassical comedies by Leandro Fernández de Moratín, son of the tragic poet. In a style reminiscent of Molière or Goldoni, and displaying an enlightened sensibility, the younger Moratín gave Spain its best plays since the Golden Age, most importantly *La comedia nueva, o el café* (The New Comedy; or, The Café, 1792) and *El sí de las niñas* (When a Girl Says Yes, 1801). He also made the first Spanish translation of *Hamlet* directly from the original (1798), and he wrote a history of Spanish theater that was published posthumously.

In England the rallying figure for the new sensibility was not primarily a playwright or theorist like Voltaire, Diderot, and Luzán, but an actor: David Garrick. Through his compelling style of acting, his managerial astuteness, and his moral authority, Garrick dominated the English stage for thirty years, until his retirement in 1776. His meteoric rise to prominence began with his appearance as Richard III at Goodman's Fields, an unlicensed suburban London playhouse, in 1741. Henry Giffard, the theater's proprietor, was circumventing the Licensing Act of 1737 by selling tickets to a "Concert of Vocal and Instrumental Musick, divided into Two Parts." Between the two parts of the concert was "perform'd gratis" Shakespeare's *Richard III* and a one-act ballad opera. Although the announcement stated that the role of King Richard was played by "a Gentleman (Who never appear'd on any Stage)," Garrick had served a brief anonymous apprenticeship in a few small roles. In contrast to the heroic, declamatory acting of the established performers of the day, Garrick individualized his villain, revealing through his facial expressions and bodily action the moment-to-moment workings of the inner man. Garrick's approach may well have been influenced by Charles Macklin's unprecedented portrayal, only eight months earlier, of Shylock as a believable, fully characterized tragic figure instead of as a clown; certainly Macklin's and Garrick's relatively "natural" styles, allow-

Shakespeare's Richard III was the role that launched the career of David Garrick (1717–79) in 1741. His expressive face and gesture are captured in this oil painting by William Hogarth. National Museums and Galleries on Merseyside, Walker Art Gallery.

David Garrick played Hamlet for over thirty years, but audiences never ceased to thrill to the terror of his first encounter with the Ghost, as depicted in this painting by Benjamin Wilson. The Folger Shakespeare Library.

ing the audience a sense of psychological intimacy with the character, were in tune with the changing spirit of the times. In his important study *The Player's Passion,* Joseph R. Roach has shown how Garrick's expressive genius emerged from a sociological context in which the external signs of inner emotion were apprehended from a scientific perspective. The enthusiastic word-of-mouth reports of Garrick's Richard III drew audiences to Goodman's Fields in such numbers that the Drury Lane and Covent Garden theaters suffered sharp declines at the box office. Garrick was quickly invited by Charles Fleetwood to join the Drury Lane company. Although Goodman's Fields was forced to close, other would-be theatrical entrepreneurs followed Giffard's example in finding creative ways to get around the restrictions of the Licensing Act of 1737.

Garrick made his Drury Lane debut in 1742, but did not settle permanently there until 1747, when he became the joint manager and patent holder with James Lacy; it was Garrick's leadership during the next twenty-nine years that brought the Drury Lane to its peak of prestige and prosperity. The preceding five years saw him performing not only at Drury Lane but also at the Smock Alley Theatre in Dublin and, for the 1746–47 season, at Covent Garden. The Smock Alley Theatre hired him along with Peg Woffington and Henry Giffard for the summer of 1742 in a successful effort to triumph over its rival Dublin patent house, the theater in Aungier Street. Garrick and Woffington were well matched on stage, but their private liaison lasted only three years. They played opposite each other as Lear and Cordelia, Richard III and Lady Anne, Hamlet and Ophelia, as well as in the comedies that were the spirited Peg's forte. At Aungier Street, not even the popular James Quin and Susannah Cibber could draw audiences away from Smock Alley. The Irish-born Quin, known as "the bellower," was already well established as London's leading actor in the old-fashioned grand style. (It is worth noting how many luminaries of the London stage had come from Ireland; besides Woffington and Quin, there were such leading actors as Charles Macklin, Spranger Barry, Thomas Dogget, and Robert Wilks; actor-playwrights Thomas Sheridan, Arthur Murphy, and Susannah Centlivre; and playwrights Richard Steele, George Farquhar, Isaac Bickerstaffe, Richard Brinsley Sheridan, and Oliver Goldsmith.)

The differences between Garrick's and Quin's styles became especially apparent in 1746 when they performed together in Nicholas Rowe's *The Fair Penitent.* According to playwright Richard Cumberland, who saw the production in his youth, James Quin used "a full deep tone, accompanied by a sawing kind of action, which had more of the senate than of the stage in it," and "he rolled out his heroics with an air of dignified indifference." On the other hand, "little Garrick, young and light, and alive in every muscle and feature," came "bounding on the

The Irish-born Peg Woffington (1714–60) acted from childhood and eventually became David Garrick's leading lady for a time. One of her greatest successes was the breeches role of Sir Harry Wildair in Farquhar's The Constant Couple *(1699). Crawford,* The Romance of the American Stage.

James Quin (1693–1766), "the bellower," represented the best of the heroic style of acting that went out of fashion as Garrick introduced greater subtlety. The costume worn by Quin as Coriolanus in this 1749 engraving is a typical habit à la romain *with the "forest of feathers" used by tragic heroes. Courtesy of The British Museum.*

stage. . . . Heavens, what a transition!—it seemed as if a whole century had been stept over in the transition of a single scene." Garrick stood only five feet four inches tall and did not have a powerful voice, but he more than compensated for those handicaps by the agility of his vocal inflections, bodily actions, and emotions. The *Gentleman's Magazine* of October 1742 reported that his voice was "capable of all the passions, which the heart of man is agitated with, . . . easy in its transitions, natural in its cadence"; it noted also his attentiveness to whatever other character might be speaking, as well as his remaining in character after he finished his own speeches. Besides giving a powerful impression of naturalness, Garrick's acting was distinctive in its physicality: pantomimic business, use of hand props, movement, and above all his expressive eyes in a face that Samuel Johnson said was "never at rest." In his *Essay on Acting* (1744), Garrick defined acting as "an Entertainment of the Stage, which by calling in the aid and Assistance of Articulation, Corporeal Motion, and Occular Expression, imitates, assumes, or puts on the various mental and bodily Emotions arising from the various Humours, Virtues, and Vices incident to human Nature."

Garrick's contributions to the English stage went beyond his innovations as an actor. He has been dubbed "the grandfather of modern directing," because he conducted disciplined rehearsals and guided his cast in their interpretation of roles. As manager of the Drury Lane, he supervised an average of sixteen tragedies, thirty comedies, and twenty-five afterpieces each season. He was also a prolific author of comedies, farces, and afterpieces, some of which long remained among the most popular offerings in the Drury Lane repertoire; among those were the farce *The Lying Valet* (1741), the pantomime *Harlequin's Invasion* (1759), the burletta *A Peep Behind the Curtain* (1767), and *The Clandestine Marriage* (1766) written in collaboration with George Colman the Elder. He further functioned as a play doctor of both old and new plays. Although he carried on the Restoration tradition of performing altered versions of Shakespeare's plays, his own adaptations of the texts generally brought them closer to the originals. Garrick's devotion to Shakespeare led him to plan a Shakespeare Jubilee in Stratford-upon-Avon to celebrate, only a few years late, in September 1769, the bicentennial of Shakespeare's birth. Unfortunately, heavy rains curtailed the three days of processions, ceremonies, fireworks, a horse race, and a ball. Garrick had financed much of the undertaking out of his own pocket, but recouped the loss by writing a spoof of the Stratford event, a comic afterpiece that achieved a record run of ninety-one performances that season. This piece, *The Jubilee* (1769), found fun in the confused mingling of local townsfolk, London actors, and a hapless Irishman who came to the jubilee but

The ticket to the Shakespeare Jubilee held in Stratford-upon-Avon in 1769 bears the signature of David Garrick's devoted brother George, who assisted him in production and administrative business. The Folger Shakespeare Library.

could get no lodging; it also incorporated a lavishly staged procession of highlights from nineteen of Shakespeare's plays.

In 1751 Garrick made his first trip to Paris, which awakened in him a lasting interest in French culture. One result was his invitation of the great French balletmaster Jean-Georges Noverre to bring his company of dancers to present their elaborate production of *Les Fêtes chinoises* at the Drury Lane. The fantastical exotic sets and costumes capitalized on a European mania for Rococo *chinoiserie*. Indeed, *The Chinese Festival* came to London in the same year that Voltaire wrote his play *The Orphan of China* (1755). But the timing was not right for intercultural exchange, as English popular sentiment was already turning against France three months before the outbreak of the Seven Years War. King George II enjoyed the dance spectacular, but rioting in the audience grew increasingly destructive with each performance. (Disturbances in the theater were not uncommon in eighteenth-century England; there were, for example, the Little Haymarket riot of 1749, the Half-Price Riots of 1763, and the Old Price riots of 1809. On the Continent too it was usual to have guards posted in the auditorium to keep order.) When the war ended in 1763, Garrick returned to the Continent for a grand tour lasting two years. On this trip he established lasting friendships with several of the leading French actors; his subsequent correspondence with Lekain is warmly affectionate. Jean Monnet, manager of the Opéra Comique, subsequently kept him up to date on French theater developments, giving Garrick the impetus for certain technical innovations at

Below, the "Fitzgiggo riot" at Covent Garden in 1763 occurred during a performance of Thomas Arne's opera Artaxerxes, when Thaddeus Fitzpatrick, "a gentleman of independent fortune," led some ruffians onto the stage to protest the management's decision to abolish the custom of half-price admissions for the latter half of the show. This print also provides a clear illustration of stage boxes and side doors, candle hoops over the stage, and actors using only the front of the stage. Courtesy of The British Museum.

Above, left, Thomas Gainsborough's painting of "Garrick Standing with the Bust of Shakespeare" (1769) evokes Garrick's admiration for the Shakespeare plays. Although David Garrick cut and adapted the plays to his own purpose, he brought the texts closer to the original than any other eighteenth-century performer. The Folger Shakespeare Library.

Below, left, the "wing lights" mounted on the back of a flat for this German production of Lessing's Minna von Barnhelm are similar to those used on the English stage at this time. However, methods of scene shifting differed in England and on the Continent. Using the continental chariot-and-pole system, this wing would be moved along in its groove by means of a wagon beneath the stage floor. Gothaer Theaterkalender.

Right, David Garrick and Mrs. Pritchard enacted Macbeth in contemporary dress; his calves are probably padded for shapeliness. The Gothick style of the stage setting was fashionable in the late eighteenth century. Engraving by V. Green from a painting by Zoffany (1776), the Folger Shakespeare Library.

Drury Lane. Thus, in 1765, Garrick amazed and delighted audiences with a more brightly lit stage and an absence of unpleasant tallow-candle smoke. He did this by eliminating the overhead hoops containing dozens of candles and mounting, instead, "wing lights" on the backs of the side flats. These oil lamps backed by reflectors could be swiveled on brackets to increase or dim the lights. These improvements were further refined by designer Philippe DeLoutherbourg, who in 1772 joined Garrick's company upon Monnet's recommendation.

Drury Lane was remodeled three times under Garrick's management. In 1747 he enlarged the auditorium, increasing its capacity by 25 percent to 1,268 spectators. He began at the same time his long-unsuccessful efforts to curtail the selling of places on stage and "behind the Scenes." Not until 1762 did he finally end the practice of allowing spectators on stage, when—following Voltaire's example—he offset the potential loss of income at actors' benefits by again enlarging the auditorium to raise its capacity to 2,206. The greatest improvements were effected in 1775 when architect Robert Adam widened the proscenium opening to thirty feet, improved the acoustics, and added a neoclassical facade to the building; what most pleased audiences, however, was Adam's beautification of the interior decor with new paneling on the front of the boxes, a painted ceiling, and pillars "inlaid with plate glass on a crimson and green ground." That refurbishment enabled Garrick to sell his patent profitably when he retired the following year. His farewell performance on June 10, 1776, packed the house. His address to the audience afterward so moved them to tears that they would not allow the afterpiece to be played.

Garrick's predominance over the epoch does not obscure a host of others who made it an age of great acting despite its dearth of plays of lasting literary value. As early as 1741, Luigi Riccoboni claimed in his *Historical and Critical Account of the Theatre in Europe* that "the best actors in Italy and France come far short of those in England." After Peg Woffington, Garrick's leading lady was Hannah Pritchard, who excelled at vocal effects in comedy as well as in her greatest role, Lady Macbeth. Garrick also played opposite Susannah Cibber, a popular interpreter of pathetic roles. Mary Ann Yates distinguished herself in tragedy by her elaborate gestures of the hand and arm. Frances Abington won a following for her elegance of dress as well as for her witty interpretations of coquettes like Beatrice in *Much Ado about Nothing* and Lady Teazle in *The School for Scandal*. The high-spirited comic actress-singer Kitty Clive delighted audiences and dismayed critics as Portia in the trial scene of *The Merchant of Venice,* by her mimicry of well-known London lawyers. Charles Macklin, who had led the way toward a more "natural" approach to acting and costuming on the eighteenth-century English stage, continued to act until he lost his line-retention ability at the age of ninety. Spranger Barry, a tall, attractive leading man with a fine voice, specialized in classical roles. In 1751, Barry and Garrick both played Romeo at the two rival theaters for twelve consecutive nights; some theatergoers reportedly liked to watch Spranger Barry as the tender lover in the first three acts at Covent Garden, and then rush to Drury Lane to catch the darker nuances in Garrick's impassioned interpretation of the last two acts.

One factor that encouraged such a blossoming of talent was the lively critical writing on theater in a plethora of daily, weekly, and monthly newspapers and magazines. The practice of publishing regular reviews of theater productions with commentary on the acting might be credited to Addison and Steele's pieces on theater in the *Tatler* and the *Spectator*. Polemics on dramatic theory were launched when authors like John Dennis and Alexander Pope wrote letters to the editors of various journals. In the twice-weekly *Prompter* (1734–36), the first publication devoted largely to theater, Aaron Hill employed a combination of editorializing, constructive reviewing, satire, and discussion of the art of acting to promote higher standards of taste. At midcentury, Samuel Johnson's intellectual leadership weighed in against neoclassical restrictions on the drama, but, unfortunately, he paid little attention to the contemporary stage in his periodicals, the *Rambler* and the *Idler*. Arthur Murphy, an actor-playwright-translator, published theater criticism as well as general essays on theater in his *Gray's Inn Journal*. In addition to theatrical coverage in the mass media, dozens of treatises on acting were published in England, including translations of a number of earlier continental studies of the passions and their expression in the muscles of the face and body.

Undoubtedly the greatest tragic actress of the English stage was Sarah Kemble Siddons (1755–1831). She grew up in a family of strolling players and, at eighteen, married actor William Siddons, who was to become her business manager. After an unsuccessful London debut opposite Garrick in 1755, she and her husband returned to touring in the provinces for six years. She was employed for a time by the greatest of the provincial theater managers, Tate Wilkinson, who ran the York circuit of theaters in northern England. A number of such theaters received royal patents between 1768 and 1788, and Wilkinson used his as a base for developing the talents of promising artists like Mrs. Siddons, her brother John Philip Kemble, and the gifted comic actress Dorothy Jordan, all of whom went on to stardom in London. Wilkinson worked tirelessly for thirty years to raise the status of the actor in the provinces and was repaid by the increasing willingness of established actors to perform on the road during the summer. With his help, Mrs.

David Garrick's short stature contrasts with the taller Spranger Barry, who often played young lovers at Drury Lane in the 1740s, before moving to Covent Garden in 1750. Appearing with them in The Roman Father *(1750) by W. Whitehead are Mrs. Ward and Mrs. Pritchard. The Folger Shakespeare Library.*

Sarah Siddons (1755–1831) as Mrs. Beverly and John Philip Kemble (1757–1823) as Mr. Beverly are shown at a moment of extreme pathos in act 5 of Edward Moore's The Gamester *(1783). Courtesy of The British Museum.*

Siddons advanced to an engagement at the Theatre Royal in Bath, the most fashionable city outside London and the setting for Richard Brinsley Sheridan's comedy *The Rivals* (1774). Sheridan, who had bought a share of Garrick's patent and succeeded him in the management of Drury Lane, persuaded Mrs. Siddons to return to London in 1782. She opened in one of her great pathetic roles, *Isabella; or, The Fatal Marriage,* Garrick's adaptation of a 1695 play by Thomas Southerne based upon a novel by Aphra Behn, which provided a role for Siddons's eight-year-old son Henry. Her powerful, compelling performance launched a wave of "Siddonian idolatry" and lifted Drury Lane from its box-office slump. The following season John Philip Kemble made his Drury Lane debut as Hamlet. Although the intellectual Kemble lacked his sister's apparent spontaneity and emotional range, he and Mrs. Siddons towered above all others as the leading exponents of classical grandeur in acting.

In 1788 Kemble became acting manager of the theater under Sheridan, who was by then devoting his time—and the theater's revenue—to a career in politics. Lord Byron was later to sum up Sheridan's career thus: "He has written the *best* comedy *(School for Scandal),* the *best* drama *[The Duenna]* . . . , the best farce (the *Critic*—it is only too good for a farce), and the best Address (Monologue on Garrick), and, to crown all, delivered the very best Oration (the famous Begum Speech) ever conceived or heard in this country." Sheridan's brilliant *School for Scandal* (1777) marks the apogee of wit and humor over sentiment in the century's running battle between the two approaches to comedy. "Laughing comedy" was favored also by Oliver Goldsmith in his "Essay on the Theatre" (1773) and in his play of the same year, *She Stoops to Conquer.* The Drury Lane repertoire was further enhanced by the Shakespeare productions Kemble introduced; but differences with Sheridan brought Kemble's defection to Covent Garden in 1796. After 1794 Sheridan was operating the largest theater in Europe, and in order to make a profit he tended to pander to less sophisticated tastes with offerings like *Pizarro* (1799)—adapted by Sheridan from August von Kotzebue's melodrama *The Spaniards in Peru*—which achieved a run of thirty-one consecutive performances, or Frederic Reynolds's *The Caravan; or, The Driver and His Dog* (1803), a musical afterpiece in which a performing dog named Carlo nightly jumped into a tank of water to rescue a child from drowning.

Because of structural deterioration, the 117-year-old Drury Lane was torn down in 1791. While the company made temporary use of the theaters in Haymarket, a vast new Drury Lane was constructed by Henry Holland, who was also commissioned to remodel Covent Garden. Completed in March 1794, Holland's magnificent Drury Lane, with a capacity

John Philip Kemble (1757–1823) is portrayed here as Rolla in Pizarro (1799), as adapted by Richard Brinsley Sheridan from a melodrama by Kotzebue. The excitement of such scenes as that of Rolla escaping over a bridge with the child on his arm ensured the play's popularity for over sixty years. The Victoria and Albert Museum.

"Old Prices," "No Catalani" (Catalani was an Italian singer), and "No Private Boxes" proclaimed signs in the auditorium during the Old Price Riots at Covent Garden in 1809. To quell disturbances, the magistrates read the Riot Act from the stage. Courtesy of the Royal Opera House Covent Garden.

of 3,611, boasted the latest technology for scenic spectacle but also incorporated in its stage floor a board from the old stage that Garrick had trod. The increased size of the theater made it more suitable for extravagant productions like *Pizarro*, to the loss of serious drama. This third Drury Lane theater was short-lived; despite such safety devices as an iron curtain and tanks of water in the roof, it burned down in February 1809, only five months after Covent Garden had been destroyed by fire. Kemble had invested heavily in Covent Garden, but Sheridan suffered total financial ruin from the loss of the underinsured Drury Lane. Stoically watching the conflagration from a nearby coffeehouse, Sheridan flashed his wit even in the face of disaster: "May a man not take a glass of wine by his own fireside?"

The great age of actors in England drew to a close with the retirement of Mrs. Siddons in 1812 after a farewell performance of her greatest role, Lady Macbeth. George Frederick Cooke, the powerful but unreliable actor of satanic roles like Richard III, and the first English "star" to tour to America, died in 1812. Sheridan died in 1816. Kemble retired in 1817, his spirit perhaps broken by the Old Price Riots at Covent Garden in 1809, which had lasted sixty-seven nights despite his attempts to arrive at solutions to the mob's demands for the abolition of private boxes, for dismissal of a recently hired Italian singer, and for ticket prices that would force the theater to operate at a loss. A new epoch was heralded in 1814, when Edmund Kean made his debut at Drury Lane, displaying in his acting the Romantic sensibility that was to sweep all the arts in the early nineteenth century.

THEATER ARCHITECTURE
AND PRODUCTION VALUES

It was said in the eighteenth century that one went to England for good acting and to southern Europe for fine theaters. Italy had long held the lead in theater architecture, scene design, and stage machinery. As Italian opera spread throughout continental Europe, so too did the Italian proscenium-arch theater with its settings composed of flat painted wings and backdrops, and its chariot-and-pole method of scene shifting, all of which had been developed by the first half of the seventeenth century. The first wave of construction, in the early seventeenth century, consisted largely of private court theaters in which the auditorium could double as a ballroom. The proscenium arch posed no artificial barrier in these palace theaters, as the singers and dancers—usually courtiers—descended steps from the stage to mingle with their

peers on the floor. While this kind of private but opulent musical entertainment had its English equivalent in the Stuart court masque, there
was no similarity in the way the public theaters developed in England
and on the Continent. Until Garrick remodeled Drury Lane, English
theaters were relatively unadorned and uncomfortable (and they retained the U-shaped auditorium while continental theaters evolved toward an egg shape). Italian public theaters, however, carried on the
court theaters' tradition of baroque splendor.

Beginning with San Cassiano in 1637, sixteen public opera theaters
opened in Venice by 1700. With 356 new works presented in the 1700–
1701 season alone, competition among the Venetian theaters was keen,
and ticket prices decreased during the eighteenth century. Although
none of those early theaters has survived, eyewitness descriptions attest
to their magnificence. Like the court theaters, they were constructed
without permanent seating in the *parterre*. The practice of dividing the
galleries into private boxes is believed to have begun in Venice, where
jaded opera patrons used their boxes for playing cards, supping, and
conversing during most of the four-hour-long operas, paying attention
only to the arias or to the most spectacular scenic effects. At the first
private theater in Rome, the Tor di Nona (1660), the boxes had privacy
screens across the front. When reports of scandalous activity behind the
screens reached Pope Innocent XI, he ordered the boxes converted into
open galleries; in 1697, under Innocent XII, the theater was razed. But
the opera craze continued unabated, while architects of theaters in
Bologna, Genoa, Naples, and elsewhere experimented with various auditorium configurations for optimum acoustics and sightlines.

By 1700 the characteristic look of the baroque theater was set, with
the horseshoe-shaped auditorium as the most distinguishing feature.
This meant that the majority of the spectators—those in the side boxes
and galleries as well as those at either side in the *parterre*—were not
looking at the proscenium-framed stage picture as it was designed to be
seen. Instead of getting the full effect of a carefully executed perspective
scene, most were able to glimpse the backstage machinery beyond the
painted wings. Surely this demonstrates a deliberate acknowledgment of
the artifice of the theater as well as a concession to the elegant theatergoer's overriding interest in being seen by others in the audience.
The "conversational" arrangement of the seating in a candlelit auditorium gave a sense of shared intimacy among spectators and performers. If one or more Venetian opera houses had chandeliers that could be
raised into a recessed ceiling to darken the house during the performance, that practice did not catch on; indeed, many spectators brought
their own tiny candles by which to follow the libretto in little booklets
that could be purchased at the entrance—and certainly to illuminate

Perspective view of the mechanics and construction of the interior of a theater. Gabriel Dumont, Parallèle de plans des plus belles salles de spectacles.

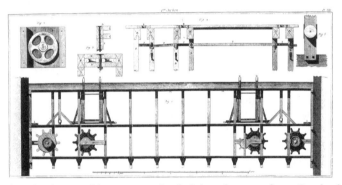

Cross section showing machinery at two levels below the stage floor. On the first level beneath the floor are the chariots that roll on tracks; their poles extend up through grooves in the floor, and the scenery is mounted on them. Beneath the chariot level are the rotating drums by which pulleys move the chariots forward or back. From the Encyclopédie *of Diderot and d'Alembert.*

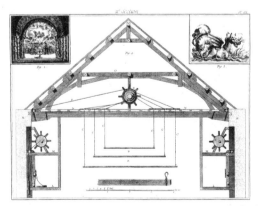

Cross section showing the rigging for flying apparatus on stage. B in the drawing is labeled "a graduated series of three bases for glory cars." Upper right is the setting for the Palace of Love with the largest glory descending from the heavens. Upper right is a dragon with flames used in the same setting. From the Encyclopédie *of Diderot and d'Alembert.*

Giuseppe Bibiena (1696–1757) designed this characteristic setting for theatrical festivities on the occasion of the wedding of Elector Frederick Augustus III of Saxony and Maria Josepha of Austria on August 20, 1719, in Dresden. The Metropolitan Museum of Art, the Elisha Whittelsey Collection, The Elisha Whittelsey Fund, 1951.

their own faces in the process. The standard illumination in a baroque theater before the 1750s consisted of five or six hoops or chandeliers (each holding about twelve candles) in front of the proscenium and, over the stage area, a row of two chandeliers for each wing opening. The candles were lit just at curtain time in order to insure their lasting throughout the performance. In the latter half of the century, the overhead chandeliers were eliminated in favor of candles with reflectors mounted behind the wings. Most theaters were also equipped with a row of oil lamp footlights, and candle brackets were affixed to the front of the boxes. The smelly, smoky, and drippy tallow candles eventually gave way to more expensive but cleaner white wax and, finally, spermaceti candles. Even the latter were prone to drip hot wax unless the snuffer remained alert to the task of keeping the wicks trimmed.

One family name is inextricably linked with the central European proliferation of Italian baroque theater architecture and stage decor: Galli-Bibiena. Three generations of Bibienas dominated the combined field of theater architecture and scene design. Ferdinando Bibiena began the dynasty's achievements in the 1680s with the scenery he created for the historic Teatro Farnese (built in 1619 by Aleotti, the inventor of sliding wings). In 1712 Ferdinando was summoned to Vienna to design court spectacles for the Hapsburg Emperor Charles VI. With his son

Giuseppe, Ferdinando created one of the most magnificent of all such displays, an opera-ballet, *Angelica vincitrice di Alcina* (1716), staged by torchlight in the Favorita gardens (now the Theresianum). Among its dazzling effects were a richly decorated palace rising from a seemingly empty fishpond, a battle on the water between "two fleets of little gilded vessels" while airborne infernal spirits swarmed around them, and "a hundred richly dressed dancers." In sum, reported a visiting English eyewitness, there was "a great variety of machines, and changes of the scenes, . . . performed with a surprising swiftness."

Among the finest architectural achievements of the Bibienas were the much-admired Verona Filarmonico (1720) by Ferdinando's brother Francesco, the Teatro Communale of Bologna (1763) by Ferdinando's son Antonio, and the court theater at Mannheim (1742) by Antonio's brother Alessandro. Giuseppe, aided by his son Carlo, also constructed the baroque-verging-on-rococo Margrave's Opera House at Bayreuth (1748) within an existing shell by a French neoclassical architect; an impression of intimacy prevailed in its highly ornamented auditorium-ballroom (capacity one thousand), while its stage was the largest and best equipped in Germany.

As scene designers, the Bibienas ranged even further afield; their works and influence were seen in Italy, Spain, Austria, Germany, France, Bohemia, Poland, Portugal, Sweden, Russia, and the Netherlands. Most of the settings they designed were architectural and gave the illusion of vast space. The illusion of depth had long been realized by Italian painters of scenes in perspective using a central vanishing point. Ferdinando Bibiena added a new dimension with his invention of *scena vedute in angolo* or *prospettivo per angolo*, using two or more vanishing points to the sides of the stage picture, somewhere beyond the proscenium arch. The innovation afforded an escape from symmetry that was characteristic of baroque style; as such it was picked up by some Italian designers, most notably Filippo Juvarra, but won fewer converts among the neoclassically oriented designers of France and northern Europe. Furthermore, although Ferdinando's first treatise on angle perspective, *Architettura civile* (1711), became one of the best known of many Italian works of design theory, it was maddeningly inexplicit concerning his methods. Thus it was the Bibiena family that remained most closely identified with those surprising—perhaps even unsettling—overscaled vistas of vaulted arches and galleries leading off in various directions.

Italy boasted other dynasties of architect-scene designers, notably the Galliaris, the Quaglios, and the Mauros. Bernardino Galliari trained a generation of Milanese scenographers in perspective scene painting and created court festivals and stage settings from Sardinia to Berlin, but won his greatest acclaim for the drop curtain with scenes of Bacchus and

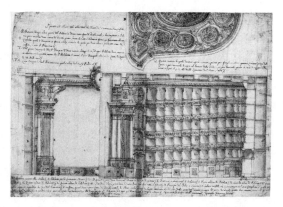

*Francesco Bibiena (1659–1739) designed the Teatro Filarmonico in Verona (1720),
which was long signaled as one of the best-conceived theaters in Italy. Its five tiers of
projecting boxes rise gracefully toward the rear of the auditorium. Audiences entered the*
parterre *through doorways (labeled* A *on this drawing) next to the proscenium instead of
at the back of the auditorium. The gap created between the boxes and the proscenium
ensured that actors waiting in the wings would not be visible from the side boxes. Cooper-
Hewitt Museum, New York.*

*Plan of the Teatro Reggio
(Royal Theatre) attached to
the king's palace in Turin.
Opened in 1740, it was
considered one of the finest
theaters in Europe. At the
back of the stage area is a
separate section for fireworks.
Gabriel Dumont,* Parallèle
de plans des plus belles
salles de spectacles.

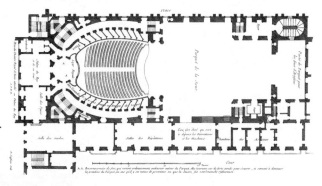

*Pietro Domenico Olivero's painting
of the interior of the Teatro Regio in
Turin shows the opening night
performance of Metastasio's opera*
Arasce *on December 26, 1740.
Some audience members follow their
librettos while others converse or buy
refreshments. In the center aisle
stands an armed guard to keep
order. Museo Civico di Torino.*

Ariadne that he designed for the Teatro Reggio in Turin. That important theater, designed by Benedetto Alfieri and opened in 1740, assimilated the best elements of earlier Italian theaters while incorporating an innovative concave ceiling. Members of the Bibiena and Galliari families both contributed scenic designs to this standard-setting theater whose relatively restrained decor prefigured the neoclassical style. Turin's reputation as a center of theatrical activity rested also upon Juvarra's service there as chief architect for Victor Amadeus II of Savoy, until he took his talents to Spain in 1735. Less grandiose than the Bibienas, Juvarra's best scene designs were probably those executed between 1708 and 1714 for the marionette theater he built in Cardinal Ottoboni's Palazzo della Cancelleria in Rome.

Although the Italian baroque influence was felt everywhere in continental Europe, the German court theater was by far the most receptive to its extravagance and relied heavily upon numerous visiting Italian designers. Vienna's first opera house was built in 1652 by Giovanni Burnacini. This was followed by opera houses in Munich (by Santurini, 1657), in Hamburg (by Girolamo Sartorio, 1678), and in Mannheim (by Lorenzo Quaglio, 1778). One of the gems of German eighteenth-century architecture was the rococo Residenztheater (1753) in Munich. This theater in the Elector's palace was designed by a French-trained architect, François de Cuvilliés. However, its stage machinery was the work of an Italian, Giovanni Paolo Gaspari, who additionally devised a mechanism that allowed the auditorium floor to slope for theater seating or be raised flush with the stage for court balls. Italian designers contributed also to some of the earliest Polish theaters: a 1748 opera house in Warsaw, the Teatr Narodowy (1765), and the Slonim opera house (1780). Giacomo Quarenghi built two theaters in Russia, the tiny Hermitage Theater in the Winter Palace for Catherine the Great (1786) and the ballroom-theater in Ostankino Palace for Count Sheremetyev (1795). Jacopo Fabris worked in Karlsruhe, Hamburg, London, and Berlin before settling in Copenhagen in 1746; his *Manual of Theatre Architecture and Machinery,* not published until 1930, is an important compendium of information on early eighteenth-century scenic practice. Baldessare Orsini also wrote a handbook based upon his own experience: *The Stage of the New Teatro del Verzaro* (1785). In it he described not only the perspective techniques for thirteen different stock settings (for example, royal chamber, temple, street, courtyard, dungeon, harbor, woods), but also his use of color to give an impression of three-dimensional relief to the setting. His descriptions suggest a limited palette—muted or grayed colors that would not detract from the performers—and this accords with other evidence of eighteenth-century scene painting such as the surviving backdrops of the theaters at Drottningholm and Gripsholm.

Gradually—especially in the latter half of the eighteenth century—French designers and architects began to rival and even surpass their Italian mentors. One of the first was Jean Bérain, who served as *dessinateur de la Chambre et du Cabinet du Roi* (director-designer of court festivals) from 1675 until his death in 1711. Although he carried on the scenic traditions established by Giacomo Torelli and Gaspare Vigarani, Bérain's personal flair—especially evident in his stylish costumes with elaborately plumed headdresses—soon epitomized French taste. He began by designing costumes for two operas, *Thésée* and *Atys,* for which Carlo Vigarani created the settings. When Vigarani retired, Bérain also took charge of machinery and decor for the operas produced by Lully at the Royal Academy of Music. He called upon the Italian machinist Rivani for help with the ballet *Le Triomphe de l'amour* in 1681, but by 1683 was designing his own machinery for the impressive Chariot of the Sun in the opera *Phaeton.* The famous rocking motion of Phaeton's chariot as mechanical horses pulled it across the sky in that court opera even spawned a parodic version for the mass audience, *Le Cocher maladroit* (The Clumsy Coachman), at the fair theater. In his set and costume designs for over fifty operas, Bérain effected the transition of French style from baroque to rococo. The work of his son, Jean Bérain *fils,* who succeeded him in the royal post, is scarcely distinguishable from that of the elder Bérain.

Bérain *fils* was followed by Servandoni. Born in Florence of French parentage, Jean-Nicolas Servan used the more prestigious Italianate form of his name when he designed for festivals in Paris, London, Vienna, Stuttgart, Bordeaux, and Bayonne. Servandoni was hailed as an innovator of the French stage when he adopted the *scena per angolo* in his designs for the Royal Academy of Music. Until then, French scenery had been rigidly symmetrical with up to eighteen pairs of wings placed, approximately one meter apart, parallel to the front of the stage and diminishing in height toward the rear of the stage. Using Bibiena's methods but eschewing the excessive ornamentation, Servandoni created an illusion of actual space by the angled placement of flats and by allowing the upper part of the setting to disappear from view as if too high for containment within the proscenium-framed picture. A major advantage noted by the *Mercure de France*'s critic at the first of Servandoni's operas, *Orion* (1728), was that the spectator no longer glimpsed the backstage space beyond the wings; on the other hand, mechanical scene shifts were not possible and Servandoni's sixty-some opera settings had to be carefully plotted for manual placement on stage. At the same time, however, Servandoni demonstrated a special talent for marvelous scenic transformations in his ten "mute spectacles" *(spectacles muets)* for the mammoth Salle des Machines in Paris. There, each year from 1738 to

Jean Bérain designed the setting and machinery for Lully's opera Phaéton, *which was performed for the court at Versailles in January and at the Paris Opéra in April of 1683. The scene depicted in this engraving is "The Fall of Phaéton." Archives nationales, Paris.*

This surviving sketch shows the mechanism by which Phaeton's chariot appeared to fly as if drawn by horses prancing in air. As in the modern theater, the actor wears a safety harness. Archives de France.

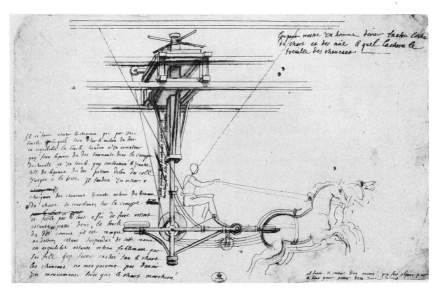

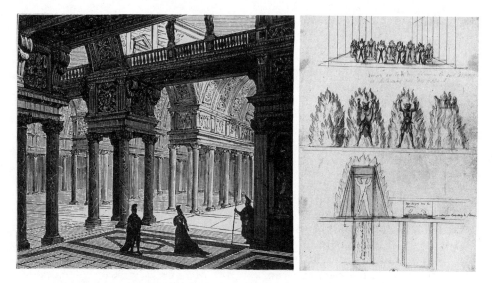

Left, this setting by Jean Servandoni illustrates his use of the scena per angolo, *which he introduced to the French stage. Germain Bapst,* Essai sur l'histoire du théâtre *(1893).*

Right, the records of the Menus plaisirs du Roy, *1752, include this study for a machine effect from the studio of Jean Bérain. This effect of flames and of infernal creatures rising from stage traps was one aspect of a production number featuring the four elements and Sky, Earth, and Hell. Courtesy of the Archives Nationales, Paris.*

Below, this rendering for a setting by Gabriel de Saint-Aubin (1724–80) is typical of those seen at Versailles with classical motifs reduced to human scale. Courtesy of French Cultural Services.

1742 and from 1754 to 1758, he created a fantastic display of scene changes and lighting effects on a mythological or religious subject, all to musical accompaniment, with nonspeaking actors to complete the visual impression.

François Boucher, who was to become better known for his easel paintings, was chief scenic artist for the Opera from 1744 to 1748. He excelled at two genres of painted backcloths: the charming sunlit, flower-carpeted bucolic settings before which silk-ribboned shepherdesses sang and danced in the fashionable "pastoral" operas like *Issé* (1742), and oriental fantasy settings for the equally fashionable *chinoiseries* like Rameau's *Les Indes galantes* (1735) or Noverre's *Les Fêtes chinoises* (1755). That graceful rococo style was continued by artists like Louis-René Boquet, J. B. Martin, Pierre-Adrien Paris, and Dominique-Francois Slodtz, all of whom contributed at various times to the state-subsidized entertainments under the rubric of the *Menus Plaisirs,* which included performances by the Royal Academy of Music, the Comédie Française, or the Comédie Italienne in Paris as well as festivals and temporary decorations officially arranged for the king at Versailles or Fontainebleau. Despite unlimited funding, the *Menus Plaisirs* at court usually consisted of such standard fare as balls, ballets, fireworks, and visits by the Paris companies.

More successful in galvanizing the attention of Louis XV and his court were the theatricals privately organized by the king's mistress, Madame de Pompadour, in the so-called Théâtre des Petits Cabinets that she fitted up in 1747 in a gallery of the *petits appartements* at Versailles. Since there was room for only fourteen spectators, invitations were highly prized to see the plays and operas performed by meticulously rehearsed courtiers (subject to fines for coming late to rehearsal), with the very talented Pompadour always singing or acting the leading role. The success of the endeavor led to the construction in 1748 of a larger theater that could be set up or dismantled in about fourteen hours in the well of the Ambassadors' Staircase. This theater won a wide reputation for its high standards of professionalism with productions like *Issé,* for example, which had originally been produced at the Opera and was revived at Versailles in 1749 with Madame de Pompadour in the title role of the nymph Issé. The six speaking roles performed by courtiers were supported by a corps of dancers, two thirteen-voice choruses, and a thirty-piece orchestra. Each of the five acts had a different setting: a peasant cottage, Issé's palace and gardens, a forest, a grotto, an isolated pavilion. The five-year existence of the Théâtre des Petits Cabinets saw sixty-one different works given a total of 122 performances. Unfortunately, the overtaxed public could perceive those court theatricals only as an extravagance, which clouded any appreciation of Madame de Pompadour's extraordinary role in the promotion of the arts in eighteenth-century France. This remarkable woman, born Jeanne-Antoinette Poisson and married at twenty to LeNormant d'Etioles, entered the nobility—being granted the title Marquise de Pompadour—by captivating the king with her charm and intellect. As his official mistress and trusted confidante, she was able to draw upon the treasury to patronize painters, sculptors, and poets. A voracious reader, she built up a personal library of over 3,500 volumes, and she was probably instrumental in making it possible, through her intercession with the king, for Diderot's *Encyclopédie* to resume publication after it had been banned. Although she was a constant target of criticism, la Pompadour continued to exercise her power in service to the arts for twenty years; the founding of the Sèvres porcelain factory remains one of her great contributions to the decorative arts of France.

Despite Madame de Pompadour's encouragement, the Opera at the Palais Royal was sinking ever deeper into debt due to the cost of mounting its elaborate productions with huge casts, multiple settings, and machine effects. Efforts to bolster the box office centered upon offering a wide variety of musical genres, with much emphasis on the increasingly popular ballet. In addition to the traditional lyric tragedies, there were opera-ballets, comedy-ballets, *ballets bouffons,* heroic ballets, heroic pastorals, regular pastorals, Italian intermezzi, and *spectacles coupés* made up of selections extracted from longer works. In 1750 the Palais Royal theater was thoroughly cleaned and redecorated, but still the Royal Academy of Music could not cope with its deficit; the Parisian municipal government finally discharged the debt in 1757 in order to keep the operation going. Even the total destruction of the Palais Royal by fire in 1763 could not close down the Opera. A temporary home was hastily constructed for it inside the Salle des Machines. Jacques-Germain Soufflot built an entire theater—stage, auditorium, and vestibule—within the stage area of the huge theater in the Tuileries Gardens next to the Louvre. Opened in 1764, the Théâtre des Tuileries housed the Opera for six years while a new building was constructed on the old Palais Royal site.

In 1770, when the Opera moved into its sumptuous new theater with the latest in stage machinery (all of which was to burn down in 1781), the vacated Théâtre des Tuileries in the Salle des Machines became an interim home for the Comédie Française. Expecting to stay only a few months until a new theater could be built for them, the company remained twelve years. Many found it even less accommodating than the cramped facility they had been using since 1689 in the former Rue des Fossés-Saint-Germain (today the Rue de l'Ancienne Comédie), which had been declared unsafe. In place of the nauseating stuffiness described by Louis-Sébastien Mercier in the old building, the Théâtre des Tuileries proved so cold that Lekain became ill from what he

Cross section of the small theater that was home to the Comédie Française from 1689 to 1770, on the rue des Fossés Saint-Germain (today the rue de l'ancienne Comédie) in the Latin Quarter. From the Encyclopédie *of Diderot and d'Alembert.*

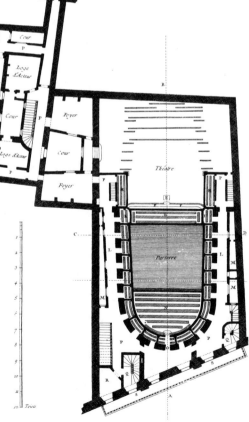

Plan of the theater vacated by the Comédie Française in 1770. It was small and awkwardly situated between adjoining buildings, and after nearly a century of use it had become unsafe. Spectators stood in the parterre; nearest the stage was the parquet section (labeled G on the plan) with three rows of benches; at the back of the parterre was an elevated amphitheater section (N) with benches. Other features are: (E) opening for the prompter, (F) orchestra, (H) balconies, (I) king's box, (K) queen's box, (L) corridor to the boxes, (M) light wells, (O) entrance to the amphitheater, (P) passages, (Q) stairs to the second and third levels of boxes, (R) actors' lodging, (S) balcony over the street. From the Encyclopédie *of Diderot and d'Alembert.*

described as "the dampness rising from the underground vaults of the theatre." Nevertheless, this was the site of two major theatrical events of the period: the premiere of *The Barber of Seville* in 1775 and the apotheosis of Voltaire in 1778. This theater is also associated with a change in basic terminology: previously stage left had been called *coté du roi,* because the king's box was on the right side of the proscenium arch, and the queen's box, *coté de la reine,* was on the spectators' left; now stage left began to be called *coté cour,* because it was on the side of the theater toward the Carousel Courtyard, and stage right, *coté jardin,* was nearest the Tuileries Gardens. After the French Revolution, the terms "court" and "garden" were applied to all theaters in preference to "king's side" and "queen's side." It is perhaps ironic that during the revolutionary period the royal family was incarcerated in this very theater before being transferred to the Conciergerie.

During the protracted negotiations for construction of a new Comédie Française by architects Peyre and Wailly, the theatromania that permeated all social classes in France led to the construction of a number of large provincial theaters of architectural importance. Most of them continued a trend begun with the Berlin Opera House built in 1741 by Georg Wenzeslaus von Knobelsdorff for Frederick the Great, featuring the theater as a prominent public building apart from a palace or other uniform-façaded complex. This practice was also advocated in the 1760s by the great balletmaster, Jean-Georges Noverre, who had worked in court and public theaters all over Europe and found none to his satisfaction. Although better known for his controversial proposals for reform of the ballet, Noverre also published essays on theater architecture, which were influenced by Count Francesco Algarotti's theoretical commentaries and by his own practical experience. Upholding function and public safety over aesthetics, Noverre called for free-standing theaters that would allow more convenient access and would reduce the dangers of fire. Another trend—seen in such French theaters as those of Metz (1751), Montpellier (1752), Lyon (by Soufflot, 1754), Brest (1767), Nancy (1771), Besançon (by Ledoux, 1778), Bordeaux (1780), Amiens (1780), Rheims (1785), Marseilles (by Ledoux, 1785), Nantes (1788)— was the enlargement of narrow corridors into vestibules and, in some cases, replacement of the earlier spiral stairs tucked into the corners, by a grand staircase. Ground plans for several of these theaters are reproduced in Gabriel Dumont's *Parallèle de plans des plus belles salles de spectacles d'Italie et de France, avec des détails de machines théâtrales* (1773), which illustrates the incorporation of Italian elements alongside French innovations. In the Lyon theater, for example, Soufflot introduced the elliptical auditorium to France, which had until then—long after Italian architects had settled on their horseshoe configuration—retained the U-shaped galleries derived from the old tennis courts. Indeed, the Lyon theater can be considered the watershed after which applied theater architecture became a topic for serious study in France.

The finest flowering of late eighteenth-century French theater architecture was achieved in two theaters, one private and one public: Jacques-Ange Gabriel's royal opera house at Versailles (1770) and Victor Louis's Grand Théâtre de Bordeaux (1780). Despite the splendor of the palace and the many entertainments that had been staged there under Louis XIV and XV, there had never been a permanent theater at Versailles. Besides Madame de Pompadour's makeshift arrangements in the *petits appartements,* a number of other temporary auditoriums had been fitted up, the most elaborate having been for Voltaire and Rameau's opera-ballet *La Princesse de Navarre* (The Princess of Navarre) in the palace's indoor equestrian arena on the occasion of the dauphin's wedding in 1745. Louis XV finally approved Gabriel's plans for a court theater in 1753, but the country's financial difficulties prevented its completion until the impending marriage of the future Louis XVI to Marie-Antoinette provided the necessary impetus. Philippe Quinault and Jean-Baptiste Lully's *Persée* (Perseus) opened the theater in 1770 and was described as "the triumph of the machinist." The blue-and-gold theater itself was an aesthetic triumph for all time with its subtle blending of rococo and neoclassical decorative elements in carved wood, painted to look like marble. Like other private theaters in eighteenth-century France, it bore a striking resemblance to interior church architecture, in this instance to the chapel at Versailles, except that—as if in tacit acknowledgment of priorities—the marble was real in the chapel. Gabriel's innovation was the progressive recession of each of the three tiers rising above one another in elliptical shape. Although it was stripped and remodeled several times during the next century, the Versailles opera house was lovingly restored to its original state in the 1950s. A second extant theater at Versailles was constructed in 1780 by Richard Mique in a separate building near the Petit Trianon for private performances by Marie-Antoinette and her intimates.

The third outstanding French neoclassical theater architect besides Gabriel and Ledoux was Victor Louis, designer of the Grand Theatre of Bordeaux (1780). Construction began in 1773, but work was halted periodically by shortages of funds and civic disputes; a 1777 document referred to the work-in-progress as "scandalous luxury and certainly disproportionate to the size of the town and to the means of its inhabitants." Even before it was completed, the fame of the monumental edifice attracted royal visitors like Emperor Joseph II of Austria. The town's commitment, despite considerable opposition, to siphoning so much money into a public theater while sacrificing a much-needed city

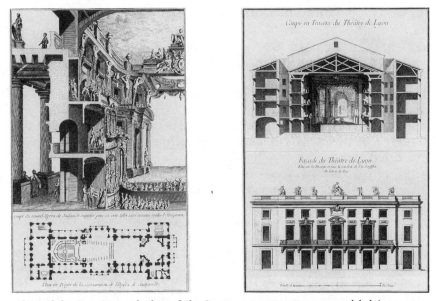

Above, left, a section and plan of the Stuttgart court opera as remodeled in 1759 to increase the seating capacity. Although the passages to the boxes remained quite narrow, a new foyer and staircases were added in keeping with the increasing role of theater as a p'ace to socialize. From the Encyclopédie *of Diderot and d'Alembert.*

Above, right, cross section and classical facade of the theater of Lyon (1754). Built by Soufflot in an open space facing the city hall, it was an early example of a freestanding theater. The building incorporated two cafés. From Gabriel Dumont, Parallèle de plans des plus belles salles de spectacles.

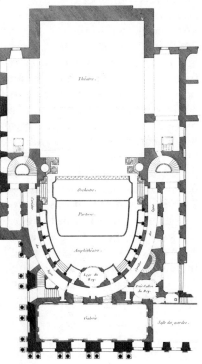

Plan of the opera house in the palace at Versailles (1770), designed by Jacques-Ange Gabriel. One of the distinctive features of this rococo gem is the squared-off parterre within the horseshoe-shaped auditorium. From Gabriel Dumont, Parallèle de plans des plus belles salles de spectacles.

hall and other buildings has been variously interpreted as a manifesta-
tion of the rapid growth of the bourgeois theatergoing public or as one
of the last ill-considered extravagances of the *ancien régime*'s profligate
despotism. In any case, what the influential Pierre Patte's *Essay on Theatrical Architecture* (1782) called "the most magnificent of modern theatres" still stands as one of the great architectural achievements of the
period. The twelve corinthian columns of the relatively sober facade
supported a covered portico for carriages, while small shops (to help the
structure pay for itself) were built into either side behind the flanking
colonnades. In addition to a café on the lower level, the theater had a
great many separate rooms, some 168 for activities directly related to
production, plus 144 income-producing rooms such as the shops and a
number of apartments rented to actors.

The Grand Theatre of Bordeaux was open to the public at all hours,
and crowds of people took advantage, often congregating noisily in the
vestibule during the day to the annoyance of those who would have
preferred to reserve the building to the uses of art. It also housed a small
concert hall and a ballroom, both of which disappeared in nineteenth-
century remodelings. In the entry hall Louis boldly placed a grand
staircase of a scale that had hitherto existed only in palaces; it was
described by a contemporary as "a monument within a monument." In
contrast to the austere grandeur of the facade and entry hall, the auditorium itself was sumptuously decorated in white, blue, and gold with
cantilevered boxes projecting forward of the supporting columns. The
domed ceiling was to become characteristic of French theater architecture as opposed to the flat ceilings of English theaters. Louis was among
the first to admit that his experiment with the shape of the auditorium
did not work; it was a perfect circle clipped off by the musicians' space in
front of the apron. That idea and the view-restricting columns at either
side of the proscenium were to disappear from the theaters Louis subsequently built in Paris: the Théâtre des Beaujolais (1783), which Louis
himself enlarged in 1791 to create the basic structure for what is today
the Théâtre du Palais Royal; a block away, on the site of the former
Opera at Palais Royal, another theater (1790), which is today the Comédie Française; and, facing the Bibliothèque Nationale, the magnificent
but no longer extant Théâtre National (1793), which was later renamed
Théâtre des Arts and was taken over by the Opera in 1794.

The history of Paris theater buildings becomes rather complex after
the second Opera at Palais Royal went up in flames during a performance of Gluck's *Orpheus* on June 8, 1781. That summer the Opera used
the small former theater of the Saint-Laurent fair while a new theater
was hastily erected at Porte Saint-Martin to meet the October 31 deadline
proposed by Marie-Antoinette. Architect Samson-Nicolas Lenoir em-

The Grand Théâtre de Bordeaux (1780) by Victor Louis was the most magnificent of all the freestanding theaters in France. Although the square has since been lowered and steps now lead up to the entrance, the façade originally allowed for carriages to drive behind the columns to deliver theatergoers to the door. This engraving also illustrates another mode of transportation: the sedan chair. Centre Régional de Documentation Pédagogique Bordeaux, Pierre Bardou.

This cutaway illustration of the interior of the Grand Théâtre de Bordeaux shows the domed ceiling and boxes projecting forward of their supporting columns. French theaters at this time still featured the "standing pit." Musée Condé, Chantilly (Photographie Giraudon).

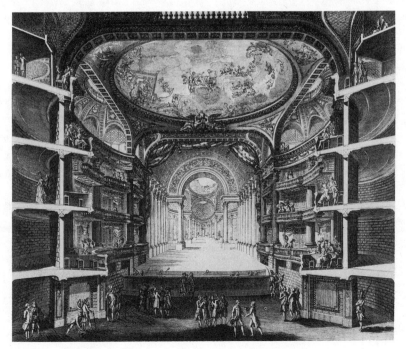

Left, of the three Paris theaters built by Victor Louis, the one intended for the Opera at Palais Royal (which instead became the Variétés Amusantes and, later, the Comédie Française), completed in 1790, is especially interesting as the first theater to use cast-iron supports for the balconies, as revealed here after the fire of 1900. From Jean-Hughes Piettre in Victor Louis et le théâtre.

Right, this view from the back of the stage shows the performers on the apron with the flat painted cutout scenic units behind them. The Palais Royal theater that Victor Louis designed for the Opera looked like this when it opened in 1790. Although the outer walls of today's Comédie Française remain as Louis designed them, the interior is now completely different. Courtesy of Collections de la Comédie-Francaise.

Below: Victor Louis's Palais Royal theater opened in 1790 as the home of the Variétés Amusantes. When the Comédie Française moved here in 1799, the interior had already undergone extensive damage during the Revolution. Courtesy of Collections de la Comédie-Francaise.

ployed two construction crews laboring around the clock, spent twice the amount budgeted, and perhaps compromised on safety, but the Opera season went on. The structurally weak Porte Saint-Martin was strengthened in 1782 and the Opera used it until 1794, at which time the company moved into Victor Louis's Théâtre National/Théâtre des Arts, where it remained until 1820. Meanwhile, Louis had been commissioned by the ambitious duc de Chartres, who hoped to get control of the *Menus Plaisirs,* to build a theater at the Palais Royal for the Opera. (Chartres inherited his title, duc d'Orléans, in 1785; during the French Revolution, he renounced his nobility and took the name Philippe Egalité.) Reminiscent of the Grand Theatre of Bordeaux but much refined, Louis's elegant theater, completed in 1790 (the first ever to use cast iron for its structural supports), suffered the indignity of being rented out for the low entertainments of the "Variétés Amusantes" when Chartres lost his bid for the Opera.

During the same period, the Comédie Française finally acquired its long-delayed new theater; the company's departure from the Théâtre des Tuileries marked the end of theatrical performances at the Salle des Machines. The two architects, Marie-Joseph Peyre and Charles de Wailly, had submitted plans for a new theater as early as 1768, but various disputes prevented the project from getting under way until Louis XVI's brother donated the site near the Luxembourg Gardens and took responsibility for construction costs. The left-bank location was considered inconvenient by some, but it actually placed the theater in the midst of the salutary intellectual and artistic ferment that was just beginning to animate the Latin Quarter. The building was appropriately grand, as befitted the *Comédiens du Roi.* At the inaugural ceremonies in 1782, the actor Dorival referred to it as "the new Temple that royal munificence has raised to the glory of dramatic art."

The auditorium was a slightly elongated circle in which the most noteworthy feature was the provision of benches in the *parterre,* where spectators had traditionally stood. This was the first legitimate theater in Paris so equipped, and many missed the greater spontaneity of the "standing pit." Since the time of Molière, the spectators standing in the *parterre* (men only) had constituted approximately half of the total attendance at any performance and had exercised considerable influence over the fate of new plays. However, the audience composition was changing in the last decades of the century. The middle-class theater enthusiasts and intellectuals who had filled the *parterre* before the 1770s either improved their financial status enough to move up to the second tier of boxes or were heavily infiltrated by a less educated class of theatergoers who moved down from the top gallery. In any case, many observers reported a lowering of standards of taste and behavior in the *parterre,* and guards were often hired to keep order there. It is possible that the introduction of benches in the *parterre* was intended, along with raised admission prices (from twenty sous for standing room to forty-eight sous for a seat), to inhibit the rowdy element there, thus widening the social gap between legitimate theatergoers and the populace that gravitated toward the entertainments on the Boulevard du Temple. Louis-Sébastien Mercier, a playwright and one of the liveliest commentators on the theater of his day (as well as a champion of the lower orders), noted in his *Tableau de Paris 1783–1788:* "The audience was forced to sit and has fallen into lethargy. The flow of ideas and feelings has been impeded; the electric contact between stage and pit has been broken, and all because the introduction of benches prevents the spectators from rubbing shoulders and putting their heads together. In former days, an almost incredible enthusiasm stirred the pit, and the general excitement lent to theatrical performances an interest they no longer have. Nowadays, that tumult has given way to calm silence and disapproval." Nevertheless, with the Revolution, the "standing pit" was to disappear from all French theaters, as it had much earlier in England.

The Comédie Française's theater of 1782 also incorporated the latest safety features, as the perennial danger of fire in the theaters had finally become a matter of public concern after the Palais Royal conflagrations of 1763 and 1781. At the instigation of an experienced machinist named Boullet from the Opera, Peyre and Wailly's theater became the first to install an iron curtain that would seal off the stage from the auditorium in the event of fire. Boullet, who was later to publish his practical recommendations in an *Essay on the Art of Constructing Theatres, their Machines and their Operations* (1801), also recommended a round-the-clock corps of guards and firemen assigned to every theater. Most theaters were already being provided with tanks of water on the roof, and this precaution too was taken at the new Comédie Française, along with a basement pump and 350 feet of leather hose. State-of-the-art lighting was another feature of the theater, following suggestions made by the famous chemist Antoine-Laurent Lavoisier for the use of reflectors in the auditorium as well as behind the wings. The auditorium was illuminated by a large central chandelier instead of many tiny ones. Two years after its opening, this theater became one of the first to replace the candles on the chandelier with Argand lamps, which were invented in 1784. These were oil-burning lamps with chimney devices that rendered them virtually smokeless.

Peyre and Wailly's fine theater was home to the Comédie Française for only eleven years. After a hiatus brought by the revolution, the company was installed in 1799 in the theater at the Palais Royal that had been used by the "Variétés Amusantes." That theater has been modified and restored many times since then, but today's Théâtre Français, home of the Comédie Française, is essentially the building that Victor Louis designed. Similarly, Peyre and Wailly's theater, which became known through most of its existence as the Odéon, looks today not very different from the original edifice, in spite of major fires in 1799, 1808, and 1818.

In Madrid there were only two permanent public theaters, both survivals of the Golden Age open-courtyard type of facility called *corrales*. Both were finally torn down after a century and a half of use. The Corral de la Cruz, constructed in 1579, was replaced with a modern theater in 1743, and the Corral del Príncipe (1582), in 1745. Although the new theaters were modeled after French theaters, Moratín noted in his historical overview that production values remained as slipshod as they had been in the *corrales*. More interesting architecturally was the theater built in Felipe IV's palace near Madrid, El Buen Retiro (1632). Cosimo Lotti designed the partitions between the boxes to slant toward the stage to allow better sightlines. In addition, the back wall of the theater could be opened to provide a vista of the palace gardens as a scenic effect, or fireworks could be set off there as part of the finale. Moratín described the use of the theater during the period that Farinello directed it: "For one opera, the stage was decorated entirely with crystal; on another occasion the hall was illuminated with two hundred chandeliers; in the opera *Armida placata* the stage represented a delightful place with eight fountains of natural water, one of which sent a jet seventy feet into the air. Among the trees could be heard the song of a multitude of birds, most skillfully imitated."

As the wave of theater construction swept northward on the Continent in the latter half of the century, it tended to combine Italian machinery with French neoclassical architecture and stage design. The second Schouwberg Theatre of Amsterdam, for example, was built in 1665 in the Italian baroque mode, but its stage decor showed more and more of the French classical influence during its 107-year existence; the third Schouwberg (1774) was a decidedly classical structure, yet it was fitted out with a full battery of Italian machinery.

The need for theater buildings in Scandinavia, both public and private, grew in the wake of increasingly frequent visits by touring companies, beginning in Denmark with residencies of English comedians in the sixteenth century, and German and Dutch players in the seventeenth century. By the eighteenth century, the courts of both Denmark and Sweden were eagerly receiving French troupes that would lend them prestige. For a company headed by Claude Rosidor, King Charles XII of Sweden converted the royal tennis court (Bollhuset) into a public theater and sent to Paris for settings from Jean Bérain's studio;

beginning in 1700, plays by Corneille, Racine, Molière, and their successors were performed in French in the 800-capacity theater (with a standing pit and spectators on stage). Similarly, the Danish court hosted the long residency (1700–1721) of a French troupe headed by René Magnon de Montaigu.

After his many years of supplying French theater at the Danish court, Montaigu moved to the public sector, joining forces with another Frenchman, Etienne Capion, who had already won a patent to present spoken performances by a German company and to construct a public playhouse on Lille Grønnegade street in Copenhagen. In 1722, the French/German company won permission to perform in Danish and immediately invited an eminent satirical poet and professor of philosophy and history to write for the company: Ludvig Holberg supplied twenty-seven enormously successful comedies for the first five-year phase of the theater's existence. After a twenty-year ban on theatrical activity in Denmark, the company—with Holberg as artistic advisor—was revived as the Danish Royal Theatre and given a new playhouse on Kongens Nytorv (1748). Holberg then wrote six darker comedies before his death in 1754. Although he was nicknamed "the Molière of the north," Holberg was not merely an imitator of French neoclassical comedy, but drew upon various sources of inspiration, including—as in his masterpiece, *Jeppe paa Bjerget* (Jeppe of the Hill, 1722)—baroque elements of the German Jesuit theater. The remainder of the century saw major progress in both Sweden and Denmark (Norway was part of Denmark until 1814) toward developing a native theatrical tradition alongside imported foreign works.

Architecturally, the most important theaters in Scandinavia, indeed the best-preserved eighteenth-century court theaters anywhere, are Drottningholm (1766) and Gripsholm (1782) in Sweden. Drottningholm Court Theatre was commissioned by Lovisa Ulrika, sister of Frederick the Great, whose marriage to the future King Adolf Fredrik took her away from the centers of Enlightenment where she had grown up enjoying abundant theater and social interaction with intellectual leaders like Voltaire. The first theater built on the grounds of the Drottningholm summer palace saw performances by touring companies of French players and Italian opera performers, but it burned down in 1762. A second theater on the site (1766) was built by Swedish architect Carl Fredrik Adelcrantz, decorated by the French court painter Adrien Masreliez, and equipped with machinery by the Italian technician Donato Stopani. Behind the unadorned, neoclassical facade of the free-standing theater is a beautifully proportioned auditorium of painted wood, and a stage house fully equipped with glory car, stage traps, wave-rollers, wind and thunder devices, swiveling reflectors for the candles behind the wings,

C. F. Christensen's painting shows part of the stage and auditorium of Copenhagen's Royal Theater (Det Kongelige Teater) in 1830. In performance is Jacob von Thyboe *by Ludwig Holberg (1684–1754). Teatermuseet, Copenhagen.*

The stage of Drottningholm Court Theatre (1766) is seen here with a late-eighteenth-century neoclassical palace setting designed by Lorens Sundström (1737–1776) for a musical divertissement. *Drottningholms teatermuseum.*

Left, a view from the back of the stage of Drottningholm Court Theatre showing two sets of wings at each position, with a cloud border above. At the far right is a pivoting pole with wing lights. The floor is heavily trapped. Drottningholms teatermuseum.

Beneath the stage at Drottningholm Court Theatre (right) are the undercarriages that roll on wooden tracks corresponding to grooves in the stage floor. The poles on these "chariots" go up through the grooves to support the flat painted wings. The turning of a central winch below stage can achieve a complete change of scenery in ten seconds. Drottningholms teatermuseum.

and machinery for achieving a complete shift of backdrop, borders, and wings in ten seconds. The sixty-five-foot deep, raked stage matches in depth the steeply raked auditorium with its thirty-two rows of benches, the last few rows of which were reserved for "valets and barbers of the Court, members of the kitchen and household staff." The auditorium is distinctive in its lack of galleries and in its extra width in the lower half, nearest the stage. Although it does have three boxes projecting from each side wall, the king and queen normally sat in front-row armchairs. The building also incorporates twenty-four dressing rooms where actors were lodged during the summer. In 1791, the gifted French architect-designer Louis-Jean Desprez added a banquet room with French windows overlooking the English gardens; its present-day use as a foyer for the theater is enhanced by the Swedish summer's long hours of daylight, so that intermission may bring the added spectacle of sky effects from the sun's position low on the horizon. Drottningholm Court Theatre's remarkable state of preservation is owed to the fact that it fell into disuse not long after the assassination of the actor-playwright King Gustav III (reigned 1771–92) and served only as a storage facility until theater historian Agne Beijer "rediscovered" it in 1921. Besides the wooden machinery in perfect working order, the theater held another treasure of historical importance: thirty stage settings consisting of 183 side-wings and twenty backdrops, including some painted by Desprez and at least one by Carlo Bibiena.

Lovisa Ulrika's son Gustav III gave Sweden a brief but dazzling golden age in all the arts, and he can be considered the father of Swedish theater. He enjoyed acting in court theatricals, but his overriding concern was to encourage the development of a native tradition—especially in playwriting—instead of relying so heavily upon French artists. To that end, he not only wrote numerous comedies and historical dramas himself but commissioned the first Swedish opera, *Thetis and Peleus* (1773), and the first verse drama in Swedish on a Swedish subject, *Birger Jarl* (1774) by G. F. Gyllenborg. He founded the Royal Opera, for which he first had Stockholm's Bollhuset renovated (reducing its capacity to five hundred), and then commissioned Adelcrantz to build it a permanent home (1782) with many architectural features inspired by Soufflot's Théàtre de Lyon. Adelcrantz also built for Gustav III a tiny theater designed to fit inside a round tower at Gripsholm castle; in 1782 Erik Palmstedt enlarged the facility by filling the tower space with a semicircular auditorium while the stage area extended into the adjoining queen's wing. The Gripsholm theater remains an architectural gem with its Ionic columns and its mirrors at various angles between the side columns to create a suggestion of baroque spatial complexity within the neoclassical order of the design. The half-domed ceiling is patterned with caissons, some of which—opposite the stage—can be propped open to provide an "invisible" upper gallery for servants. Although the Gripsholm stage is smaller than that at Drottningholm, it is equally well equipped for rapid scene shifts and other effects. Eight complete stage settings from the 1780s survived at Gripsholm. Apparently, the same scenery was often transferred among the court theaters and the Royal Swedish Opera, as a setting designed for Gripsholm could easily be enlarged for Drottningholm by adding a pair of wings near the backdrop. Desprez's famous settings for the opera *Queen Christina* (1785), for example, were designed for Gripsholm, but later used at Drottningholm.

As early as 1737, Swedish players had performed publicly under royal patronage at Stockholm's Bollhuset, but Lovisa Ulrika found them not up to her standards and replaced them with French actors and Italian singers. Gustav III also turned to French artists to set standards for the native work he hoped to encourage. Indeed, Sweden's first great

The Swedish Royal Opera's first star performers, Carl Stenborg (1752–1813) and Elizabeth Olin, were painted by Pehr Hilleström in a scene from Gluck and Calzabigi's Orpheus and Eurydice at the Bollhuset in 1773. Stenborg, as Orpheus, leads Eurydice out of a vividly depicted Hades. Courtesy of the Royal Swedish Opera Archives and Collections.

The French designer Louis Jean Desprez (1743–1804) spent the greater part of his career designing stage settings for the Swedish King Gustav III. This is one of several etchings and watercolor renderings of his famous setting, the garden of the Count de la Gardie, for act I of Queen Christina (1785), a historical drama by Gustav III. Courtesy of Statens Konstmuseer—Nationalmuseum.

Desprez's surviving backdrop is shown on the stage of the tiny theater at Gripsholm castle where King Gustav III's play Queen Christina *premiered in 1785. Courtesy of the Statens Konstmuseer—Nationalmuseum (Photograph: Alexis Daflos).*

comic actor, Lars Hjortsberg, was trained by Monvel and his French company during a five-year residence from 1781. Another Swede, Carl Stenborg, achieved prominence in the Royal Opera and later in the court dramatic performances presented by Gustav III's Society for the Improvement of Swedish Speech. Stenborg performed the title role, for example, in the patriotic lyric tragedy *Gustav Wasa* (1786), composed by Johann Gottlieb Naumann to the Swedish verse of Johan Kellgren and presented at the Royal Opera with settings by Desprez. That enormously successful work also marked the beginning of a Shakespearean influence that was to overtake French neoclassicism in Swedish dramaturgy. However, French style remained in evidence even when a patent for the foundation of the Royal Dramatic Theatre (Dramaten) at first restricted it to original Swedish plays. Using the Bollhuset, the Dramaten opened in May 1788 with Gyllenborg's *Sune Jarl.* Five plays by Gustav III were also produced in the first season. After some administrative renegotiations, the company was able to launch into the production of comic operas of French origin. The first of these, in September 1789, was *Soliman II,* an adaptation of Favart's *Les Trois sultanes* rendered into Swedish verse by the pre-Romantic poet Johan Gabriel Oxenstierna. This became the prototype for a peculiarly Swedish genre, *drama med*

The Orangerie Theatre in Warsaw's Łazienki Park is one of Europe's best-preserved eighteenth-century theaters. Photograph by Zbigniew Raplewski.

The stage is on an island, separated by water from the auditorium, in the eighteenth-century outdoor theater of Łazienki Park. The baroque "water palace" of King Stanislaw Poniatowski is seen in the background. Photograph by Felicia Londré.

sang, in which music and dance served mainly to advance a compelling spoken drama. The short, plump Hjortsborg won particular acclaim in the role of Osmin, guardian of Soliman's seraglio; he remained with the Dramaten until his death in 1843. The Dramaten was closed for a season after Gustav III's assassination and the Bollhuset was torn down, but the company reopened in 1793 in a new six-hundred-seat facility that was built for them in the Royal Arsenal. None of the eighteenth-century Swedish public theaters—Bollhuset, Arsenal, or the original Opera theater—has survived.

Among the surviving eighteenth-century court theaters of Europe not mentioned elsewhere are those of Rosersberg palace in Sweden, Christiansborg palace (today a theater museum) in Copenhagen (1767), Český Krumlov of Schwartzenberg in southern Czechoslovakia (1766) and Litomisl in northern Czechoslovakia, Ludwigsburg castle near Stuttgart in West Germany (1758), and two theaters in Łazienki Park: the Orangerie and an outdoor theater with an island stage, built for Poland's last king and great patron of the arts, Stanislaw Augustus Poniatowski, both on the palace grounds in Warsaw (1792).

In England, a few public playhouses survive to illustrate some aspects of late Georgian theater architecture, but most underwent major alterations, and the only one that gives a clear sense of its eighteenth-century state is the small Georgian Theatre of Richmond, Yorkshire (1788). It formed part of a provincial circuit that included playhouses in Harrogate, Beverley, and other towns. A significant feature of this theater is the absence of any forestage extending beyond the proscenium; thus the actor was by this time performing within the setting rather than declaiming before a scenic picture. The auditorium's stark simplicity, like that of most other theaters in the provinces and even to an extent in London, testifies to the English audience's relatively greater absorption in the action on stage as opposed to the total aesthetic impact of the theatergoing experience that was sought by their continental counterparts.

Nor was eighteenth-century English scenic art as highly developed as all that followed in the wake of the Italian baroque masters on the Continent. In fact, the only surviving original stage designs for a particular production on the English stage in the first half of the century are those of Sir James Thornhill, a leading decorative painter in the baroque style, who left four settings for an opera, *Arsinoë, Queen of Cyprus,* that was produced at Drury Lane in 1705. Apart from the spectacular effects contrived for pantomimes, the English theater relied largely upon stock scenes that were interchangeable from one play to another, with such typical locales as a city street, a garden, a room in a palace, a forest, a prison. Even those settings were often marred by lackadaisical scene

In 1705, Sir James Thornhill (1675–1734) designed four new scenes for Drury Lane's production of Arsinoë. *The first, shown here, is a moonlit garden composed of two pairs of assymetrical wings and a back scene. Victoria and Albert Museum.*

shifters who might carelessly mix scenic units—mismatching, in style of painting or locale, the backscene, wings, and borders—so that the audience saw "dull clouds hanging in a lady's dressing room" or "trees intermixed with disunited portions of the peristyle." Even as late as the 1790s, in a Drury Lane production of *Richard III* "Bosworth Field was a delightful little farmyard," and in *The Merchant of Venice* "plenty of trees gave evidence in the Hall of Justice." The English stage's continuing use of backshutters ("flats") that were manually slid along in upper and lower supporting grooves meant that the very center of the painted background became grimy with handprints where the two units came together. Even worse, occasionally, the two halves of the backscene did not match at all! Certain theaters may have installed the Italian-style chariot-and-pole mechanism for shifting the wings, but, in general, the English stage required a great many stagehands to effect scenic transformations, and their various operations were cued by a complicated system of bells, whistles, buzzers, and clappers, some of which must have been audible to the audience.

Under such conditions, only two scene designers, DeLoutherbourg and Capon, were able to distinguish themselves. Both had the good fortune to work for managers who paved the way toward making "new scenes" for new plays almost to be expected by the end of the century. William Capon designed for John Philip Kemble at Drury Lane and Covent Garden; beginning with the 1794 *Macbeth* that inaugurated the third Drury Lane theater, he pursued an interest in "antiquarian" scenery that presaged the next century's increasing attention to historical and geographical accuracy. Philippe Jacques de Loutherbourg, an Alsatian landscape painter, was hired by David Garrick for the 1772–73 season at Drury Lane and began immediately to have an impact on theatrical practice. His exclusive contract was renewed every year until 1781, when he turned to other projects after a salary dispute with Sheridan. For *A Christmas Tale* (1773), a pantomime based upon Favart's *La fée Urgèle*, DeLoutherbourg depicted a craggy mountain vista far more atmospheric than anything that had ever before been painted for the English stage, and he enhanced the illusion of depth by the irregular placement of set pieces and ground rows realistically painted like rocks. His "broken scenes" also incorporated "cut cloth" for the backscene, that is, a double backcloth with cut-outs in the downstage one. DeLoutherbourg's innovative skill in lighting the stage was evident in a garden scene for that same production. Cued by the line, "all my senses are in disorder. . . . Even now my eyes are deceiv'd, or this garden, the trees, the flowers, the heav'ns change their colours to my sight," the scenery suddenly changed from green to vivid red, "resembling fire." DeLoutherbourg achieved this "effect of enchantment" by rigging screens of colored silk on pivots that rotated them into position "before concentrated lights in the wings."

Transparent scenery was another of DeLoutherbourg's favorite devices: cut-out sections of backcloth were replaced with gauze and lit from behind. In *Selima and Azor* (1776), for example, the heroine was shown a vision of her father in a mirror, but when she tried to speak to him, the vision abruptly disappeared; the mirror was a transparency in the painted canvas wall, and the vision could be made to appear and disappear by lighting or darkening the area just behind the gauze. DeLoutherbourg's twelve scenes for the pantomime *The Wonders of Derbyshire* (1779) suggest what is meant when he is credited (or blamed) for the theater's evolution from rhetorical to pictorial art, as well as for the decline of architectural settings in favor of landscapes. He traveled to Derbyshire to sketch characteristic views, which he then reproduced on stage as fully and faithfully as possible, using changes of lighting to evoke different times of day. His attention to picturesque detail that made even English countryside seem exotic establishes him as a forerunner of Romanticism. Most exotic of all perhaps was the one production he designed for Covent Garden on his only return to theatrical work after leaving Drury Lane; this was *Omai; or, A Trip Round the World* (1785), an extravagant pantomime based upon the South Sea voyages of Captain Cook (who had brought a Tahitian native—a "noble savage," in the view of contemporaries—named Omai back to England with him). One ocean

Philip DeLoutherbourg (1740–1812) opened his Eidophusikon in London in 1781 and used it to continue the experiments with lighting and special effects that he had begun as a stage designer at Drury Lane. For five shillings apiece, up to 130 people could watch the amazing transformations to musical accompaniment and other sound effects. Courtesy of The British Museum.

setting in that brightly colorful production was apparently composed of forty-two separate pieces of scenery.

Besides spearheading the movement toward greater realism in stage settings, DeLoutherbourg's most significant legacies to the theater were in the realm of lighting. By brightening the illumination of the stage, he nudged the theater toward acceptance of the darkened auditorium during performance. After he left Drury Lane, he continued his experiments with lighting effects on a small (six feet wide by eight feet deep) moving-panorama stage that he called the Eidophusikon. There, unencumbered by actors or stagehands, he could create scenes like dawn over London with moving clouds, an erupting volcano, a storm at sea with sound effects, and "a view in the Mediterranean, the Rising of the Moon contrasted with the Effect of Fire." The Eidophusikon was enormously popular for about two years, after which, as admissions waned, DeLoutherbourg gradually returned to his first love, landscape painting.

THE BIRTH AND GROWTH OF RUSSIAN THEATER

Although the rich folklore of Slavic culture generated many quasi-dramatic customs and rituals, the formal beginning of Russian theater history dates back only to 1672. Russian drama had not developed as other European drama did, from liturgical drama intended to enliven the incomprehensible Latin of the mass, because Russian Orthodox church services were celebrated in Old Church Slavonic, which was close to the vernacular. There are some sparse records of ecclesiastical dramas like the biblical story of "The Children in the Fiery Furnace" having been performed inside the church, but these died out in the seventeenth century, as did the few examples of school dramas that were introduced from Poland. Native Russian school dramas would finally find popular audiences in the first half of the eighteenth century, long after their European prototypes had disappeared from the boards. The earliest literary plays in Russian did not appear until 1673 *(Of King Nebuchadnezzar, the Golden Calf, and the Three Youths Not Burned in the Furnace)* and 1685 *(The Comedy Parable of the Prodigal Son);* both were written by Simeon of Polotsk, a poet as well as an enlightened and scholarly monk who advocated separation of art and theology. By the latter half of the seventeenth century, however, Russians had begun to travel abroad and they brought back accounts of European theater they had seen. Intrigued by what he heard about those baroque scenic spectacles, Tsar Alexey Mikhailovich turned to a colony of German merchants who had settled on the outskirts of Moscow and ordered the Lutheran minister to put on a play for him.

Drawing upon his experience of school dramas in Germany, Johann Gottfried Gregory dramatized the biblical story of Esther and presented it at the Tsar's summer palace on October 17, 1672. A cast of sixty-four, sumptuously costumed, performed the seven-act play incorporating musical numbers and featuring improvised comedy skits between the acts. Although Father Gregory's cultivated German was clumsily rendered into Russian, and the Russian was further garbled by the German actors, the Tsar sat spellbound throughout the ten-hour performance of *The Comedy of Artaxerxes.* The tsarina, in whose honor her husband Alexey had commissioned the work, had to stand and peer through a curtain to watch the quasi-feminist tale. Father Gregory was well rewarded for his effort (some sable skins and the honor of kissing the Tsar's hand), and he was encouraged to start a theater school the following year. Father Gregory presented several more plays based upon the Bible, as well as secular and musical works. The deaths of Father Gregory in 1675 and Tsar Alexey in 1676 brought a twenty-six year hiatus in the development of Russian theater.

The next effort was similarly short-lived: in 1702 Peter the Great built a special theater and lodgings inside the Moscow kremlin for a company of German actors he imported from Danzig. Under Johann Kunst they produced German farces and began training some Russians to perform. Kunst died in 1703, but the theater struggled on for three years, offering plays in an incomprehensible mix of German and Russian to an indifferent Moscow public. Meanwhile Peter was building a new city on the northern marshes between the Gulf of Finland and Lake Ladoga; in 1712 the government offices were transferred to St. Petersburg, which also became the major theatrical center of Russia until the mid-nineteenth century. Peter's aim had been to use theater as an instrument for popularizing his reforms that were intended to bring Russia up to date with western Europe, but audiences remained small and confused. More fulfilling than theater for Peter's propagandistic purposes were some literary efforts like Feofan Prokopovich's allegorical tragicomedy *Vladimir* (1705).

Theater again fell into neglect until Anna came to the throne in 1730. Although her personal tastes ran to freak shows and grotesqueries, her reign did mark the first appearance of an Italian *commedia dell'arte* troupe before the Russian public. Italian opera was introduced by the Neapolitan composer Francesco Araia, who spent two decades in Russia; he composed the first opera on a Russian text, Aleksandr Sumarokov's *Cephalus and Prokris* (1755). A French balletmaster, Jean-Baptiste Landé, with support from Empress Anna, established a school of ballet. French neoclassicism was held up as an ideal by Caroline Neuber when her troupe played St. Petersburg in 1739–40, presenting Corneille and Racine in German. An important step toward the emergence of a neoclassical Russian drama—following the verse tradition of Racine's tragedy and Molière's comedy—was Mikhail Lomonosov's system of versification for the Russian language, which was introduced in 1739 and quickly won favor. One of the most brilliant scientific minds of all time, Lomonosov can also be credited with standardizing a Russian literary language apart from the traditional and restricting Old Church Slavonic. He wrote two tragedies, *Tamira and Selim* (1750) and *Demophont* (1752).

Empress Elizabeth (reigned 1741–62) brought the first French theater company to Russia and oversaw the switch from German to French culture as the predominant influence on the Russian nobility. Her reign also launched the careers of the first two Russian-born theater professionals: Aleksandr Sumarokov and Fyodor Volkov. Sumarokov was the first Russian nobleman to devote himself to literature and the first to write neoclassical tragedies in Russian. The success of his *Khorev* (1747) as staged by the cadets at the Military Academy for Nobility brought an invitation from Empress Elizabeth to perform the tragedy at court. Promoting himself as "the Russian Racine," Sumarokov slavishly imitated French neoclassical form and borrowed its themes. Inspired perhaps by Voltaire's ambiguous attitude toward Shakespeare, he wrote a neoclassical adaptation of *Hamlet* (1748), reducing the cast to eight characters, only five of them from Shakespeare. In 1756 Sumarokov was

Fyodor Grigorievich Volkov (1729–63), "the father of Russian theater," was a talented intuitive actor who also helped Sumarokov run the first permanent public theater in Russia.

appointed director of the first permanent, public, professional, state treasury-subsidized theater for the performance of secular plays. Elizabeth created this theater, located in a stone house of Vasily Island in St. Petersburg, to provide a home for the talented young actor-producer Fyodor Volkov. The son of a provincial merchant, Volkov had organized a company of amateur actors in his hometown to put on plays in a barn. News of that Yaroslavl theater's popularity reached the empress and in 1751 she invited the troupe to St. Petersburg. Elizabeth then decreed that Volkov and his most promising fellow actors be enrolled at the Military Academy for Nobility to raise their educational levels. Upon completion of his studies, Volkov took on the functions of artistic director/production manager at the Russian public theater for which Sumarokov served as an executive director. This was the beginning of Russia's Imperial Theatre system, which lasted until the 1917 revolution.

French tragedies and comedies continued to serve as models for a rapidly burgeoning Russian drama throughout the eighteenth century. Molière's influence is evident in both prose and verse comedies from Sumarokov to Fonvizin; among these are Vladimir Lukin's *The Wastrel Reformed by Love* (1765), Yakov Kniazhin's verse comedies *The Braggart* (1786) and *The Eccentrics* (1790) as well as his comic opera *Neschast'e ot karety* (Misfortune from a Coach, 1779), and perhaps even Vasily Kapnist's satirical *Yabeda* (Chicanery, 1798). Contemporary French authors were also imitated: Vasily Maikov's *Themistes and Hieronyma* (1773) borrowed heavily from Favart's *Les Trois sultanes,* and Nikolay Nikolev's *Sorena and Zamir* (1784) was based upon Voltaire's *Alzire.* In the 1760s, Ivan Elagin initiated the long-lived practice of appropriating the plots and dialogue of successful French plays but making the characters and customs familiarly Russian. Although her own plays strayed considerably from neoclassical strictures, Catherine the Great (reigned 1762–96) set an example of respect for French culture, carrying on a voluminous correspondence with Diderot, Voltaire, and other encyclopedists. The French Revolution later scared Catherine off the path of the Enlightenment. In the year of the storming of the Bastille, Kniazhin wrote *Vadim Novgorodski* (Vadim of Novgorod, 1789), a poetic tragedy expressing republican sentiments; published posthumously, in 1793, it was ordered burned by Catherine. However, Gallomania remained a fact of Russian life and art (and a frequent subject for satire in the theater) well into the nineteenth century.

Theater flourished under Catherine the Great, although her reign began with the untimely death of Volkov at age thirty-five. He had organized a lavish outdoor pageant, *The Triumph of Minerva,* to celebrate Catherine's coronation in 1763, but caught a fatal cold while rehearsing in exceptionally severe weather. Volkov was succeeded as director of the Russian Public Theatre by his friend Ivan Dmitryevsky, the finest actor of his day in both male and female roles. (Female roles were sometimes played by men, due to the scarcity of women inclined to theatrical work.) A highly cultivated man, Dmitryevsky was also the author of over forty plays, a translator, an art historian, and a teacher who traveled to western Europe to study acting techniques that he could transmit to his disciples. There was a story that at a social gathering with the greatest English actor David Garrick and the greatest French actor Henri-Louis Lekain, Garrick demonstrated his ability to blush, turn pale, or shed tears at will, but Dmitryevsky one-upped him by trembling and fainting so convincingly that the others became frantic to aid him—until the Russian laughingly disabused them. Dmitryevsky was succeeded in the Russian Theatre directorship by Peter Plavilshchikov, an outstanding actor, who also wrote plays with special emphasis on bourgeois and peasant settings and characters.

A Bolshoi Theatre for opera and ballet was constructed in St. Petersburg in 1773, and in 1779 an Imperial Theatre School there began training actors as well as singers and dancers. The Hermitage Theatre in the Winter Palace, designed by Italian architect Giacomo Quarenghi, opened in 1787 and continued to be used for private court theatricals, often performed by the imperial family, until the 1917 revolution.

Love scenes like the one depicted in this eighteenth-century Russian woodcut were largely borrowings from the French drama of the period.

A play in performance in St. Petersburg, Russia, around 1790. The setting is simple by Western European standards, and the prompter's head is visible.

Catherine also set up an Imperial Theatre Administration to oversee both court and public theaters; its censorship function was greatly strengthened after the French Revolution put an end to Catherine's liberal impulses. While foreign companies in St. Petersburg were generously subsidized, privately owned public theaters like those of Knipper and Medoks in Moscow were allowed to go bankrupt when they could not compete with the increasingly popular serf theaters. In the provinces, Imperial-administered theaters managed to proliferate without financial support.

Following Catherine's lead, many of the nobility—with time on their hands, since Catherine had released them from the responsibilities of service to the state that Peter the Great had imposed—opened private theaters in their palaces or on their country estates. Soon it became fashionable to own theater, ballet, or opera companies composed entirely of serfs. Serf theater flourished for about fifty years, roughly from the 1770s to the 1820s. There were some isolated instances of serf theater right up until the emancipation of the serfs in 1861, but the last large company of serfs was bought by the Imperial Theatres of Moscow in 1806. The quality of these theaters varied considerably, as did the treatment that the serf performers received at the hands of their masters. Perhaps the most ostentatious productions were those of Prince Nicholas Yusupov, owner of 21,400 serfs. Although he kept full dramatic, opera, and ballet companies on his sumptuous estate of Arkhangelskoe near Moscow and often scandalized Moscow audiences by their licentiousness, he also served as director of Imperial Theatres in the 1790s.

Another well-known, and more conscientious, serf-theater entrepreneur was Count Nikolay Petrovich Sheremetyev, who inherited, with his father's estate of Kuskovo, a theater, a vast inventory of stage settings, costumes, and props, and a company that he forged into an excellent artistic ensemble. Among the 230 serf actors, singers, and dancers in his main company was the lovely Parasha, or Praskovya Ivanovna, to whom he gave the stage name Zhemchugova, meaning "pearl." She made her debut in a *comédie en ariettes* in 1779, when she was twelve. Her greatest role was that of Eliane in Grétry's *Les Mariages samnites* (The Samnite Marriages, 1776), one of many *opéra comique* libretti that Sheremetyev had brought back from a formative visit to Paris with his serf librarian and later production manager, Vasily Voroblevsky. The heroine is a Samnite woman who courageously protests the women's lack of choice in marriage and then disappears as the enemy attacks the city; in the finale, the mysterious visored warrior who saved the Samnite general's life in battle is revealed to have been Eliane. This production also brought out the talents of Tatiana Shikova, who was given the stage name Granat,

Left, Praskovya Ivanovna (1767–1803), shown here in costume for The Samnite
Marriages, *was the leading actress in the huge company of serfs owned by Count
Sheremetyev. He gave her the stage name* Zhemchugova, *meaning* Pearl. *Courtesy of
The Bakhrushin Museum, Moscow.*

Right, another portrait of Zhemchugova as Eliane in The Samnite Marriages *was
painted several years later. Ostankino Palace Museum.*

meaning "garnet;" she long reigned as the leading dancer in Sheremetyev's serf company. Catherine the Great attended several productions at Kuskovo, and once remarked to her host that *The Samnite
Marriages* was "absolutely the most splendid production that has ever
been staged."

Sheremetyev fell in love with Zhemchugova and built for her a
theater on another estate near Moscow, at Ostankino. The entire Ostankino Palace remains a superb example of eighteenth-century craftsmanship, with parquet floors, tile stoves, ceiling paintings, and patterned
silk wall coverings all created by serf artisans. At the center of the palace
is the ballroom that can be converted into a two-hundred-seat theater by

removing raised sections of the floor, leaving another floor four feet lower for the audience's chairs. The intact floor comprising the greater part of the ballroom then became the seventy-eight-foot-deep stage. Machine rooms under the stage and in the ceiling above the auditorium were operated by twenty-six serfs under the direction of the serf mechanic F. I. Pryakhin. The theater was inaugurated in 1795, and *The Samnite Marriages* was revived there in 1797. Sheremetyev married Zhemchugova in 1801 after concocting a claim to nobility for her (using the surname Kovalyeva). As a countess, she could no longer appear on stage. Zhemchugova died in childbirth in 1803, her husband six years later. No longer used after Sheremetyev's death, the theater may be seen today in its ballroom configuration.

One eighteenth-century playwright stands apart from the others for the literary merit and theatrical advances of only two plays. Denis Fonvizin's early orientation was to the German enlightenment, but he learned French in order to read Voltaire. Employed in a bureaucratic post as a translator, he gained familiarity with a range of western European drama that influenced his two important comedies of character: *The Brigadier* (1769) and *The Minor* (1782). Both reveal his concern for various social ills that were condoned by Catherine: an ignorant and irresponsible gentry given to avarice, hypocrisy, baseless adulation of anything foreign, and brutal treatment of their serfs. Recognizing especially the authenticity of the characterization of the Brigadier's wife, Fonvizin's liberal-minded protector Count Nikita Panin described *The Brigadier* as "the first comedy written about our manners and customs." Even more successful was *The Minor,* the earliest Russian play that still reaches the stage. Compensating for some rather tedious moralizing passages is a gallery of comical character portraits including Mitrofan, the doltish adolescent of the title; his gross parents, the Prostakovs; the pig-obsessed Skotinin; the long-suffering serf nanny; and the charlatans hired to tutor "the minor." For three decades, these characters found their way into other authors' works. Fonvizin, however, spent his last years writing courageous political tracts and seeking to define his own life according to the Enlightenment's precepts of virtue.

THE GROWTH AND REBIRTH
OF GERMAN THEATER

Even though it was a German effort that gave the Russian theater its initial jolt, theater in Germanic lands was lagging behind that of the rest of Europe by more than a century. The spread of Humanism from

Renaissance Italy had certainly made its impact in the German universities, but the only direct link between scholarship and theatrical activity there—in contrast to the lively interaction of artists and scholars in France, Italy, and England in the sixteenth century—was in the didactically conceived school dramas attended by parents and perhaps some other middle-class townspeople. The Protestant schools that multiplied after the Reformation began by teaching Latin through simple productions of Latin texts by Plautus and Terence, then settled into dramatizations of Bible stories in the vernacular, similar to Father Gregory's *Comedy of Artaxerxes* at the Russian court. After 1540, Jesuit schools countered the Protestant effort with allegorical plays upholding Catholic doctrine. Whether audiences understood the Latin texts or not, the Jesuit plays impressed their message through lavish spectacle: huge casts in full costume, music, dance, movable scenery, and realistically painted depictions of infernal torments awaiting the sinner. In the long run, the Jesuit theater far surpassed the Protestant in importance and even had an impact on secular, vernacular theater as Jesuits were asked to assist with court productions at Munich, Vienna, and elsewhere. The Jesuit school drama's union of intellectual import and sensory impact would prove to be an exception in the German approach to the arts until their sudden blossoming (or, in theater, a sudden merging of literary and entertainment values) in the 1770s. From the mid-sixteenth to the mid-eighteenth century, the stagnant situation in German theater tended to be obscured by the continuing tradition of Jesuit school drama along with two other forms of theatrical activity.

The second form that carried forward strong elements of medieval theater was open-air performances by strolling players. Italian *commedia dell'arte* players made extended visits to Vienna and Linz as early as 1568, and were followed by many other companies in the southern German states, which remained Catholic after the Reformation. Still more influential were the so-called English Comedians, companies composed of ten to fifteen actors and six musicians who toured in the Protestant north from 1592. The appellation "English" carried a certain prestige, but these troupes may well have incorporated some Dutch performers and elements of a Dutch "grotesque" acting style in their presentations of overblown murder and revenge intrigues with comic relief, all improvised upon the plots of Elizabethan plays. Gradually, the form was taken over by German players, who called such pieces *Hauptaktion* or *Haupt-und-Staatsaktion* and presented them on a bill with a farcical afterpiece *(Nachspiel)*. The *Hauptaktion* ("mainpiece") was supposedly serious, but the serious action came to be punctuated repeatedly by the crude antics of a vulgar clown named Hans Wurst. This "Jack Sausage" character can be traced back to late medieval carnival festivities like the famous annual event in Nuremberg that featured *Fastnachtspiele* (Shrovetide plays) and various low entertainments. Whatever traits he may have assimilated from Harlequin or the Dutch Pickel-Herring over the years, Hans Wurst remained distinctly Germanic and a perennial favorite with audiences. His bawdy irreverence added special zest to the *Haupt-und-Staatsaktion,* which included "state scenes" showing life-styles of the rich and famous to titillate the humblest spectator's imagination. The most famous Hans Wurst was the Austrian Josef Anton Stranitzky, who gained a popular following as a fairbooth performer in Vienna's New Market. In order to oust him from the fairbooth, which was considered a fire hazard, the city council obtained the emperor's permission to build a theater for him. Stranitzky ran the Kärtnertor, Vienna's first municipal theater, from its opening in 1710 until his death sixteen years later, entertaining audiences from all social classes with his foul mouth and shticks like dropping his pants.

Italian opera was the third major type of theater that filled the vacuum until the time was right for a native German dramatic art. From opera's first appearance in Germanic territory, at the court of the archbishop in Salzberg in 1618, it was less accessible to the general public than school drama or strolling players, because it remained largely the work of foreign artists and was, for a long time, confined to court theaters. At first, temporary stages were set up in palace reception halls. These gave way by the mid-seventeenth century to permanent court theaters that permitted expansion of both the Italian machinists' efforts and their noble patrons' egos. The fact that "Germany" was composed of over three hundred different principalities, duchies, and electorates meant considerable jockeying for cultural pre-eminence among those local rulers, each of whom fancied his court a mini-Versailles. Some of them did open their theaters to the paying public, and this generated enough interest to support public opera houses in Hamburg from 1678 to 1738 and in Leipzig from 1693 to 1720; but in the long run, the populace (and many aristocrats too) preferred Hans Wurst.

Given the strong tradition of school drama, the ubiquitousness of strolling players, and the example of Italian opera, what impeded the development of a German literary drama beyond medievalism? The contempt with which theatrical practice was regarded by men of letters was certainly a factor. The two most frequently cited reasons are the lack of German political unity (along with the corollary lack of a single great cultural center like Paris or London) and the total devastation wreaked upon the population by the Thirty Years War (1618–48) in addition to several other wars of religion and succession fought on German territory. Indeed, it took the Germans over half a century to recover from the ravages of the terrible Thirty Years War. At the same time, the

Left, Josef Anton Stranitzsky (1676–1726) was the most famous interpreter of the earthy clown character Hanswurst. In this scene, according to the couplet, he is asking if he can sign up to stay in Vienna. In contrast to Hanswurst's comic outfit with yellow pants and green hat, the noble figure of the lord wears the habit à la romaine *that is typical of neoclassical tragedy.* Die Theater Wiens *(1899).*

Right, Caroline Neuber (1697–1760), a charming comic actress, waged a long, lonely battle to raise the standards of the German theater of her day. Elias Gottlob Hausmann's portrait of her was made in 1744, when she was forty-seven. Courtesy of the Deutsches Theatermuseum, Munich.

religious divisions of the sixteenth century evolved into the political struggles of the eighteenth century, between the Hapsburg dynasty in the south and the Hohenzollerns in the north.

Germany had also been linguistically divided until Martin Luther's translation of the Bible (1534) forged a standard German language from the various provincial dialects. That language was consolidated, Goethe was later to observe, by the theater; stage diction *(Bühnenaussprache)* set a standard and provided a base upon which a literature could be built, but the process took time. In fact, it may have been retarded by attitudes like that of one of the Enlightenment's leading figures, Frederick the Great, the Hohenzollern ruler of Prussia, who preferred to speak and correspond in French, using German only to address his dogs, horses, and servants. He hired Italian singers for his court operas, saying he would rather listen to the neigh of his horse than singing in German. Even the eminent philosopher-scientist Gottfried Wilhelm Leibniz, first president of the Berlin Academy (founded in 1700), wrote in Latin or French instead of his native German. As late as the last decades of the seventeenth century, fifty percent of all books printed in Germany were in Latin (and eighty percent were on religious subjects). Thus, the great fermenting of ideas that comprised the German Enlightenment long remained on a scholarly plane, in a philosophical realm apart from native artists and their audiences. A heroic effort was required finally to bring together literature and practical theater in the second half of the eighteenth century.

A trailblazer in that difficult task was Johannes Velten, a university-educated actor, whose troupe toured widely in the 1680s and introduced adaptations of French neoclassical plays, especially ones by Molière. Such a program depended heavily upon support from the aristocratic circles that embraced French culture for its social prestige. With the elector of Saxony as his patron, Velten worked to better the standard of acting in his troupe by moving toward more emphasis on scripted material and correspondingly less improvisation. The next ones to carry on such efforts were a scholar, Johann Christoph Gottsched, and an actress-manager, Caroline Neuber, *née* Weissenborn, who formed an uneasy alliance in 1727. Gottsched, a professor at the University of Leipzig, earned a reputation as "literary dictator" of the German Enlightenment through his editorship of two periodicals and his other writings on arts and letters, most importantly *Versuch einer kritischen Dichtkunst* (*Attempt at a Critical Ars poetica,* 1729). His main concerns were to uphold the moral function of art and to promote the general public's acceptance of French neoclassical precepts for German drama. He deplored the coarse material and false acting of the strolling players. In 1725, however, when the Haack-Hoffmann troupe (a continuation of Velten's former company) appeared in Leipzig, the *tour de force* performance of a young actress playing four different breeches roles in one play so impressed him that he began to envision theater as a possible instrument for the spread of his ideals. Reviewing Caroline Neuber's work in his "moral weekly," he suggested that the theater might espouse the same goals as that periodical: "the correction of uncouth behavior, foolish habits, and low literary taste." Nothing came of this until Johan Neuber and his young wife formed their own company and obtained a license for the Saxon circuit along with the privilege of calling themselves "the Royal Polish and Electoral Saxon Court Comedians." Accepting Gottsched's guidance, they added translations of Corneille and Racine to their repertoire. In 1731, they produced Gottsched's *Der sterbende Cato* (The Dying Cato), which was little more than a conflation of translated passages from English and French tragedies on the subject; its success can be attributed less to the text than to the troupe's acting, the fashionable costumes donated by the people of rank whose support Frau Neuber astutely cultivated (the enormous plumed hat she wore was a special attraction), and perhaps also to the novel association of mere players with such a prominent scholar.

Neuber maintained high standards for her company, offstage and on. In a 1735 letter to Gottsched, she wrote: "Whichever plays we perform, my concern will be for the betterment of the aims and reputation of German society as a whole in all my plays. I shall never pursue my own advantage without at the same time furthering society's ends, particularly since I see here, if only dimly, an opportunity to be recognized as prepared to accomplish something useful and worthwhile." Besides insisting on her players' exemplary behavior (in a day when the acting profession was virtually synonymous with drunkenness, brawling, and sexual misconduct), she disciplined them to memorize their lines instead of improvising as other troupes did. Under Gottsched's influence and in accord with their classically derived repertoire, they found an acting style based upon Gottsched's notion of French declamation with rhetorical gestures. It is difficult to see how Gottsched reconciled that style, which came to be known as "the Leipzig school" of acting, with his ideal of fidelity to "nature," but at least the sacrifice of spontaneity brought a gain in unity of style within a production, as well as a step toward thoughtful conceptualization of a role. Neuber's great talent as a comic actress nudged the expanding repertoire more and more toward comedy; the selections ranged from Molière to Marivaux to *comédie larmoyante*.

Still, audiences preferred the comic afterpieces; Frau Neuber herself wrote many of these scenarios for improvised clowning by a Harlequin. Eventually another company—one that specialized in Harlequinades—found greater favor with the public and even succeeded in 1737 in taking over Neuber's venue in Leipzig. She responded by writing a curtain raiser in which the clown was apparently forced to remove his traditional parti-colored costume and was banished from the stage. Weaning German audiences away from their attachment to the vulgar clown character had been one of Neuber's and Gottsched's common goals. In other areas, however, there was increasing friction between them, leading to a final quarrel and break in 1739, when Neuber refused to replace the company's memorized version of Voltaire's *Alzire* with a new translation by Gottsched's wife. Disillusioned by her apparent lack of progress in raising the public's level of taste, Neuber closed the 1740 season in Hamburg by rebuking her audience from the stage. Then, on the invitation of Empress Anna, the company traveled to St. Petersburg; but their Russian residency was cut short by the empress's death after only six months. Before she departed for Russia, one of Neuber's best actors, Johann Schönemann, defected to start his own company, which operated as a rival to hers upon her return to Saxony. Schönemann even won Gottsched's support, while the embittered Neuber wrote a curtain raiser, *Der allerkostbarste Schatz* (The Very Most Expensive Treasure, 1741), that effectively ridiculed Gottsched by caricaturing him as a censorial bat-winged night watchman. Neuber was even reduced to resuscitating her nemesis, the clown; but costuming him in white did not disguise the fact that she was capitulating to the demands of an uncultivated public. Her retirement years were spent in abject poverty. During her final illness, she was turned out of her lodgings because the homeowner did not want the stigma of an actor's dying beneath that roof. Thus, at her death in 1760, Caroline Neuber could not realize the significance of the contribution she had made toward the German theatrical renaissance that would come about in little more than a decade.

Gottsched may have been a less attractive personality than Neuber— and his wrongheadedness in advocating German imitation of the French interpretation of classical Greek drama later brought forth an invective from Lessing that has forever tarnished Gottsched's reputation—but his contribution was also considerable. Between 1740 and 1745 he published *Die Deutsche Schaubühne*, six volumes of plays by Ludvig Holberg, Joseph Addison, and various French neoclassical dramatists in German translations by himself, his wife, and his students; more importantly, it included plays by a generation of fledgling German playwrights, disciples of Gottsched in their early attempts to conform to French neoclassical strictures. Among them was Johann Elias Schlegel's *Hermann* (1741), set in classical Rome, but noteworthy as the first German "patriotic drama." Like others, Schlegel eventually rejected Gottsched's narrow program. Schlegel's change of heart came when he served as secretary to the Saxon ambassador in Copenhagen and observed preparations for the opening of the Danish Royal Theatre in 1748. His resulting essays argued in favor of the establishment of a national subsidized theater, and they pointed up the importance of allowing each nation to discover its own set of dramatic conventions to reflect the taste and manners of its people.

Three of Neuber's actors formed their own companies and carried on many of her ideals and practices: Johann Friedrich Schönemann, Heinrich Koch, and Konrad Ackermann. When Schönemann left the Neuberin in 1740, he had the advantage of working with three exceptionally talented actors, each of whom was to make a mark on German theater history: Sophie Schröder blossomed as his leading actress until she and Konrad Ackermann left to form their own company in 1741. Schönemann's third outstanding actor was Konrad Ekhof, who remained with the company until 1757, and returned after it was taken

The performance in progress at the Comedien-Haus in Nuremburg, ca. 1730, may be one by Carolina Neuber's troupe or some other touring company. The first verse given below is spoken by the prince and princess at stage center; the second verse is spoken by the four fools. Courtesy of the Deutsches Theatermuseum, Munich.

This modest building constructed by Konrad Ackermann was the home of the short-lived Hamburg National Theater, 1767–68, where Gotthold Ephraim Lessing (1729–81) served in a capacity that began to define the role of the dramaturg or literary manager in professional theater.

over by Koch the following year. Ackermann suffered many hardships before finally getting his own eight-hundred-capacity theater in Königsberg in 1755. During the Ackermann troupe's early years on the road, Sophie Schröder was rejoined by the hard-drinking husband she had left when she became an actress. Her son Friedrich Ludwig Schröder, born in 1744, made his stage debut at the age of three before Empress Elizabeth on a tour to Russia, and it was there that the widowed Sophie Schröder married Ackermann in 1749. Their Königsberg facility was the first private theater in Germany devoted exclusively to legitimate drama, but the Ackermanns' tenure was soon interrupted by the Seven Years War. Touring widely, their troupe distinguished itself by its early identification with the trend toward sentimental domestic drama. Among their successes was the premiere of Gotthold Lessing's *Miss Sara Sampson* (1755) with the ten-year-old F. L. Schröder in the role of the child Arabella.

In 1764 Konrad Ekhof left Koch's troupe to join the Ackermanns, whose repertoire of bourgeois drama suited the "natural" style of acting Ekhof had been developing in contrast to the "Leipzig style" of his former colleagues. Over the next decade, Ekhof earned the epithet "the father of German acting" for his compelling characterizations as well as for his efforts to improve the social standing of actors. He and F. L. Schröder (who would rise to preeminence in the 1770s) were certainly the greatest German actors of the century. With Ekhof adding luster to his company, Ackermann gambled on Hamburg as a likely city to support a permanent resident theater. On borrowed money he leased the site of the city's old Opera House, tore it down, and built a rather simple theater in its place. It opened in 1765 with a play by Friedrich Löwen, followed by a full season of French, English, Italian, and German plays supplemented by ballets. When the weary Ackermann gave up the enterprise a year later, it was Löwen who rallied a consortium of twelve Hamburg citizens to buy out Ackermann. The new venture, which incorporated most of Ackermann's troupe, called itself the Hamburg National Theatre. The lofty title was in keeping with the stated aims: to raise the status of actors and maintain an excellent company by paying them well, to encourage a German national drama, and—in keeping with the ideals of the Enlightenment—to raise the moral tone of society. Although Löwen appointed himself artistic director, he proved ineffectual, and company leadership devolved upon its leading actor, Konrad Ekhof. Besides the financial shakiness of the project, it was plagued by internal dissension, often involving actress Sophie Hensel, a favorite of the public, who was also the mistress of the theater's chief backer, Abel Seyler. Performances were given in two series, April to December 1767 and May to November 1768, before the enterprise collapsed. Ackermann reassumed the management of his former troupe, which his stepson F. L. Schröder took over after Ackermann's death in 1771. Ekhof joined a new company formed by Seyler and toured until 1774, when the duke of Gotha gave him and several others of his troupe a permanent home in his court theater. Ekhof functioned as artistic director there until his death in 1778, after which the company disbanded. However, the brief existence of this first fully subsidized German court theater for legitimate drama set an example for subsequent similar undertakings. As a prototype for the future, the Gotha Court Theatre far outshone the Hamburg venture.

The one great legacy of the short-lived Hamburg National Theatre was a major work of dramatic theory, the *Hamburgische Dramaturgie* (1769). Its author, Gotthold Ephraim Lessing, served that theater in the capacity of *dramaturg* (literary advisor). Indeed, he may be considered the first ever to hold such a position, forming the essential link between scholarship and artistry. He was already well established as a playwright (beginning in 1748, when Neuber produced one of his early comedies) and as Germany's leading literary critic (his collected works up to 1755 had been published in six volumes), when the founders of the Hamburg National Theatre invited him to join the staff as resident playwright. Lessing preferred not to be bound to write plays according to a schedule, but he was hired anyway with the idea that his name would lend prestige to the theater. Besides advising on the selection of the repertoire and offering background research on the plays and their authors (just as modern dramaturgs do), Lessing undertook to publish a twice-weekly commentary on the theater's activities. His one hundred essays that comprise the *Hamburg Dramaturgy* evolved beyond a critical register of productions into what W. H. Bruford called "a greater influence on the German drama than any other critical work." In the early essays, Lessing's assessments of specific production elements—for example, his analysis of Ekhof's acting (no. 3), or Madame Löwen's interpretation of a role (no. 25)—establish the interdependence of the text and the performance. As the work progresses, it becomes more theoretical, partly because Lessing's publication schedule could not keep pace with the productions as they opened and perhaps also because he was becoming distanced from the practical side of theater as the organizational problems escalated. Many essays are re-examinations of Aristotle's *Poetics,* from which Lessing proceeds to discussions of the nature of tragedy and his claim that the French neoclassical rules actually violated Aristotle's intentions. However, essays 84 through 89 demonstrate his profound respect for Diderot's theories of the *drame.* And larded throughout are his praises for Shakespeare. He occasionally touches upon the backwardness of German drama: "The Greeks felt themselves animated by their stage with such intense, such extraordinary emotions, that they could hardly await the moment to experience them again and again, whereas we are conscious of such weak impressions from our stage that we rarely deem it worth time and money to attain them" (no. 80). His last essay, published a year after "the sweet dream of founding a national theater here in Hamburg has already faded," communicates his disillusionment even as he expresses the hope that in the long run his efforts toward freeing German drama from French rules would not have been in vain.

Despite Lessing's critical stance, at least three of his four major plays adhere easily to the classical unities as defined by the French; the fourth and last, *Nathan the Wise* (1778), is a loosely structured dramatic poem on the theme of religious tolerance. All four plays exhibit the moral sensibilities of a critical thinker of the Enlightenment and may be considered the foundation for modern German drama. Where they differ from neoclassical models is in their focus on middle-class characters and settings; this was a crucial factor in building middle-class audiences for the great blossoming of German theater in the 1770s. *Miss Sara Sampson* (1755) was labeled a *bürgerliches Trauerspiel* (domestic tragedy) and bore the influence of Samuel Richardson, whose novels were quite popular in German translation, and of Denis Diderot. Its title character is a middle-class young woman who is poisoned by her seducer's former mistress, and yet her dying concern is for the care of the mistress's little daughter Arabella. Its long popularity with the public was heralded by the premiere: "the audience sat listening, as still as statues, for three and a half hours, and wept." The other tragedy, *Emilia Galotti* (1772), again features a virtuous middle-class heroine, her father, and a seducer; this time, however, the seducer is a prince and lacking in redeeming qualities. The title character's courage and her resourcefulness in rallying her passive father to thwart the aristocrat's wrongful designs led some to see a political subtext in the play.

Lessing's mature comedy, *Minna von Barnhelm* (1767), remains one of the most frequently revived of all German plays. Premiered by the Hamburg National Theatre only four years after the end of the Seven Years War, the play was remarkable for its realistic depiction of the aftermath of war. The main story is enriched with a wealth of telling details like the landlord's spying for the police, the Prussian state's failure to provide for the war widow, the unprincipled French mercenary who fought for the Prussians, and the unsettled atmosphere of the town which swarms with discharged soldiers. The central characters are Minna von Barnhelm, a plucky and resourceful Saxon heiress, and Major von Telheim, who served as an officer in the Prussian army but was unfairly given a dishonorable discharge because of a misunderstand-

Gotthold Ephraim Lessing's philosophical drama Nathan the Wise *continues to speak to modern audiences. Die Brücke company, sponsored by the Goethe Institute, gave over sixty performances of this production in North America, Asia, and Australia. Pictured are Peter Lühr in the title role and Gardy Brombacher as Daja. Courtesy of the German Information Service.*

Minna Von Barnhelm *is probably the most frequently performed of Lessing's plays in the modern theater. This production featured Wolfgang Arps as Major von Telheim, Gisela Peltzer in the title role, and Ingrid Andree as Franziska. Courtesy of the German Information Service.*

ing brought about by his generosity. The recent victory of the Prussians over the Saxons lends a topical aspect to the battle of the sexes. Minna and Telheim had earlier become engaged, but their union is now imperiled by Telheim's exaggerated ethical sensibilities, which come close to making him a tragic figure within the comedy. Their reconciliation at the end not only expresses Lessing's desire for a transcending harmony between the former enemy states, but it prefigures one of the major philosophical concerns of the generation to follow: the dichotomy between reason (Telheim) and the senses (Minna).

Lessing's advocacy of Shakespeare was not an isolated voice. In 1741 C. W. von Borck had made a creditable attempt to translate *Julius Caesar* into German. That same year saw publication of the first German appreciation of Shakespeare, by J. E. Schlegel (not to be confused with his nephew A. W. Schlegel who did Romantic translations of Shakespeare in the early 1800s). But the effectiveness of those early efforts was limited, because the plays themselves were scarcely available except as they had been plundered and deformed over nearly two centuries by strolling players. The first reasonably faithful renderings into German were Christoph Martin Wieland's prose translations of twenty-two of the plays, published in Zurich (1762–66). Another decade of effort by both a scholar and an artist was necessary to popularize Shakespeare, and those efforts formed a major current in the flow of ideas that became the *Sturm und Drang* (Storm and Stress). The scholar was Johann Gottfried von Herder, whose important essay *Shakespear* (1773) celebrated him as a great "natural" poet—that is, true to nature—because his works reflect his own time and culture and geography rather than attempting to conform to criteria set up by the ancient Greeks. The artist was Friedrich Ludwig Schröder, who in 1776 began introducing Shakespeare's plays into the repertoire of the Hamburg company he had inherited from his stepfather Ackermann. Although Schröder had been rather a scapegrace acrobat-comedian in his youth, he matured quickly upon taking over the troupe and welded a disciplined ensemble that took on an adventurous repertory. He did take liberties in adapting Shakespeare's texts, but he also succeeded in winning public acceptance of the "irrational" drama. His first Shakespearean offering, an abridged and altered *Hamlet,* was extremely popular, but in the same season the "over-tragic tragedy" of *Othello* caused many in the opening-night audience to faint at the "scenes of horror." According to an eighteenth-century historian: "The box doors were heard opening and shutting, as people left or were carried out of the theatre." Alterations announced for the third performance gave *Othello* a happy ending. However, Schröder did not always cave in to the public; he was capable of living up to Herder's dictum that it was the theater's job to form the public's taste, not the public's prerogative to impose its taste on the theater. When the 1777 production of *Henry IV* was poorly received at its premiere, Schröder came onstage after the final curtain and announced: "In the hope that this masterpiece of Shakespeare, which depicts different manners from our own, will be better understood on further acquaintance, we will perform it again tomorrow." And he kept it in the repertoire. In three seasons, 1776–79, Schröder staged nine Shakespeare plays.

Along with his stagings of Shakespeare, Schröder did more than any other theater practitioner to support the literary *Sturm und Drang* movement. He produced several plays by the young, volatile, middle-class writers who emerged so forcefully in the 1770s in rebellion against

Left, Friedrich Ludwig Schröder (1744–1816), a powerful actor of the "Hamburg school" of acting, promoted Shakespeare's plays there and elsewhere. He is shown here as Falstaff in Berlin in 1780. From Literatur und Theaterzeitung *(1780).*

Right, Friedrich von Klinger (1752–1831) helped to launch the Storm and Stress movement with plays like The Twins *(1776), which was awarded a prize for best play of the year. In this scene from act 4, the impetuous, violent Guelfo, having just killed his twin brother, is repelled by his own image in the mirror and cries:* Zerschlage dich, Guelfo! *("It's all up with you, Guelfo!"). Courtesy of the Deutsches Theatermuseum, Munich.*

Josef Platzer began designing for the Vienna Burgtheater in 1791. This set for a reception hall illustrates the technique he devised for creating an illusion of depth within an interior setting: an open archway in the upstage wall, beyond which was hung another painted backdrop. Courtesy of the Deutsches Theatermuseum, Munich.

the established values of rationalism. Inspired by Rousseau as well as Shakespeare, they proclaimed "nature" as an ideal over beauty. They seconded Herder's appreciation of the German *Volk*, the humble people whose folklore and songs were a truer expression of national culture than the studied amusements of polite society. They glorified individualism, impulsiveness, and feelings. *"Gefühl ist alles!"* (Emotion is everything!), proclaimed Friedrich von Klinger, the playwright who gave the movement its name. He had written a play entitled *Der Wirrwarr* (Confusion, 1776), but changed it to *Sturm und Drang* as more descriptive of the turbulent passions in that drama (it ends happily) of thwarted lovers during the American War for Independence. The *Sturm und Drang* writers had no prescribed agenda other than to break free of outmoded restrictions; thus the plays exhibit considerable variety. Perhaps their most common characteristic, besides intensity of feeling, is looseness of dramatic construction. An extreme case is the play that launched the movement and brought overnight fame to its author upon its publication in 1773: Johann Wolfgang von Goethe's *Götz von Berlichingen*. This historical drama based upon the autobiography of the sixteenth-century knight has nearly thirty speaking characters plus dozens of extras, requires fifty-six scene changes (about thirty different settings are specified), and covers a period of several years. Produced by Schröder in Hamburg in 1774, *Götz von Berlichingen* gave great impetus to the movement. Thus, when the word spread that Goethe had begun a play about Faust, Heinrich Leopold Wagner hastened to write his own play based upon the tragic Gretchen episode; *Die Kindermörderin* (The Childmurderess, 1776), is one of the more compelling plays of the time, but Goethe got the best of him, it was said, when he named Faust's factotum "Wagner." Other major "Storm and Stress" plays are: Friedrich Klinger's *Die Zwillinge* (The Twins, 1776), Jakob M. R. Lenz's *Der Hofmeister* (The Tutor, 1774), and *Die Soldaten* (The Soldiers, 1776), and Johann Anton Leisewitz's *Julius of Tarento* (1776), and Friedrich Schiller's *Die Räuber* (The Robbers, 1781) and *Kabale und Liebe* or *Luisa Miller* (Love and Intrigue, 1783).

The 1770s brought not only a spirited new German dramatic literature but also the turning point away from strolling players as the primary source of legitimate drama and toward a system of state-supported permanent theaters with resident companies in major towns. The Gotha Court Theatre had planted the idea of theater as a socially beneficent enterprise. The idea was taken up first by Emperor Joseph II in Vienna. In 1776, in order "to encourage the development of good taste and to improve manners and morals," he created a Deutsches Nationaltheater in the Burgtheater, which had served as court theater for the Hapsburgs since 1741. He envisioned it run as a "republic of actors," but when this did not work he invited F. L. Schröder to direct it. Schröder's four years there, 1781–85, added two hundred plays to the repertoire and raised the Vienna Burgtheater to a front-rank theater. Then Schröder returned to Hamburg—thus giving the name "Hamburg style" to his company's realistic acting—for the remainder of his illustrious career. The National and Court Theatre (Hof- und Nationaltheater) of Mannheim was founded in 1779 by Prince Elector Karl Theodore. Under the directorship of Baron Heribert von Dalberg, the Mannheim theater's greatest triumph was the premiere of Schiller's *The Robbers* in 1782, one of the most significant events in German theater history. After 1817, as the court's deficit mounted, the city government little by little took over, so that this became Germany's first municipal theater. Berlin's Nationaltheater was established in 1786 and successfully run by Karl Theophil Dobbelin. Many others followed, and by the end of the century there were over thirty resident companies in permanent theaters throughout Germany. Among them was the Weimar Court Theatre under the direction of Johann Wolfgang von Goethe.

Goethe's genius manifested itself in many diverse fields throughout his lifetime. Born in 1749 into a middle-class Frankfurt home, he was able to write in five languages by the age of eight, adding two more when he was eleven. His fascination for Shakespeare began during his student days in Leipzig and was reinforced by his friendship with Herder. The celebrity he gained with *Götz von Berlichingen* was quickly augmented by the publication of his novel *Die Leiden des jungen Werthers* (The Suffering of Young Werther, 1774). Based upon one of the numerous and passionate love affairs that Goethe carried on even into his old age, *Werther* gave currency to the concept of *Weltschmerz* (literally, "world pain," the melancholy of deep feelings) for a generation of German youth. In 1775 the eighteen-year-old duke of Saxe-Weimar invited the twenty-six-year-old Goethe to take up residency there and by his presence make of the tiny duchy (population six thousand) a "German Athens." Over the years, Goethe not only wrote plays, poetry, novels, theoretical and scientific treatises, love letters, and journals, but he also conducted experiments in botany and optics, supervised the duchy's army and its roads, served on the privy council, and presided over a commission for architecture. A two-year trip to Italy, 1786–88, gave him a new appreciation for classical art; his subsequent writing reveals his rejection of the excesses of *Sturm und Drang*. Indeed, there was a current of revived interest in classicism running alongside the romantic impulses of the end of the eighteenth century, and it owed much to the art historian Johann Winckelmann, whose *History of Ancient Art among the Greeks* (1764) stressed the "noble simplicity and quiet grandeur" of Greek art.

Goethe had also participated sporadically in the private theatricals at the Weimar court. Most notably, he played Orestes—looking quite "Apollonian" in his Greek costume—in the early prose version of his own *Iphigenia in Tauris* (1779) opposite the celebrated actress-singer Corona Schröter, who had been invited to Weimar to play the title role. In 1791 the Weimar Court Theatre was put on a professional basis under Goethe's supervision. He faced a difficult task, as his actors were a mediocre lot, given to "slovenly droning," posturing, and vying for center stage. A turning point came in 1796 with the one-month residency of August Wilhelm Iffland, the leading actor of the day. Iffland had trained under Ekhof at Gotha, then joined Dalberg's company at Mannheim, where his rapid rise to prominence led to numerous guest appearances in other cities. Iffland's discipline and his harmony of conception for each of the fourteen roles he played at Weimar inspired both Goethe and his company to better results. Goethe was also aided by his close association with Friedrich Schiller, especially after the remodel-

Above, left, Corona Schröter and Goethe (1749–1832) performed together as Iphigenia and Orestes in Goethe's Iphigenia in Tauris *(1779) on a temporary outdoor stage for the court at Weimar. The painting is by Georg Melchior Kraus. Courtesy of the Goethe-Nationalmuseum, Weimar.*

Above, right, Wilhelm August Iffland (1759–1814), shown here as King Lear in 1812, began his career under Ekhof at Gotha and went on to perform successfully at Mannheim, Hamburg, Weimar, and Berlin. He was also a popular playwright. Kostüme auf dem Kgl. Nationaltheater in Berlin *(1812).*

This ground plan of the Weimar Court Theatre (below) shows how the 1798 remodeling of the facility reduced the depth of the stage. A. Doebber, Lauchstädt und Weimar *(1908).*

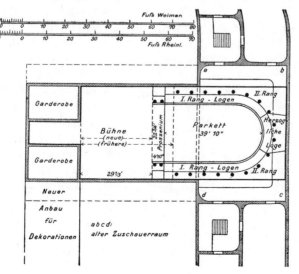

ing of the theater in 1798. Enhanced by a more comfortable auditorium with an enlarged capacity, a proscenium arch decorated with classical motifs, and Argand lamps instead of tallow candles, Weimar Court Theatre reopened with the premiere of Schiller's *Wallenstein* (1798). Thereafter, until Schiller's untimely death in 1805, the repertoire bene- fited much from his advice and contributions of new plays and transla- tions, while Goethe attempted to achieve a balance between his own literary tastes and the popular appeals of opera, operetta, and plays by Iffland and August von Kotzebue. During Goethe's quarter-century as theater director, the repertoire included eighty-seven plays by Kotzebue, thirty-one by Iffland, nineteen by Goethe, eighteen by Schiller, and eight by Shakespeare.

Although the list of produced plays suggests considerable compro- mise on his part, Goethe's taste made a greater impact on his company's style of acting, which became known as "Weimar classicism" (in contrast to "Hamburg realism"). The Weimar style drew heavily from the idealism of the "Mannheim school" as embodied in Iffland's approach. That ideal placed Beauty once more ahead of Nature; that is, artistic truth was to take precedence over strict imitation of reality. Schiller wrote several essays on the subject. In the preface to his play *The Bride of Messina* ("On the Use of the Chorus in Tragedy," 1803), for example, he analyzed the interrelationship of truth to nature and to the ideal: Art "rears its ideal edifice on truth itself—on the solid and deep foundations of Nature . . . [but] art is only true insomuch as it altogether forsakes the actual and becomes purely ideal." In the course of his practical work with actors, Goethe jotted down random notes covering such topics as enunci- ation, positions and movements of the hands and arms, observations for rehearsals, and conduct of the actor in private life. His secretary Ecker- mann later organized these notes into ninety-one "Rules for Actors." For example, in the section on "Placement and Movement of the Body on Stage," rule 35 states: "First the actor must consider that he should not only imitate nature but present it in an idealized form, and thus unite the true with the beautiful in his presentation." Rule 74 in the section on "Avoiding Bad Habits" suggests the kinds of concerns that stood in the way of achieving an ideal of beauty on the stage: "The actor should never allow his handkerchief to be seen on the stage, still less should he blow his nose, still less spit. It is terrible to be reminded of these physical necessities within a work of art." The standard of beauty to which Goethe aspired for his stage was elusive. A source of many of his problems was the popular leading actress Caroline Jagemann, Duke Karl August's mistress. A showdown occurred in 1817 when Goethe tried to block a scheduled performance by a touring actor named Karsten and his trained poodle in *Der Hund des Aubry de Mont-Didier* (a version of the

French melodrama *Le Chien de Montargis*). Karsten's dog had won acclaim throughout Germany for its performance of the title role, but Goethe saw its featured appearance on the classical stage of Weimar as a violation of taste. Jagemann appealed to the duke, who ruled in favor of the dog, and Goethe took advantage of the occasion to end his twenty-six-year directorship of the theater.

Given his attitude, it is interesting that Goethe wrote a poodle into scenes two and three of the first act of *Faust, Part I* (1808). Scene three is clearly intended to be done with a performing dog that follows Faust into his study and then disappears behind the stove whence Mephistopheles materializes. The explanation lies in the play's "Prelude on the Stage," in which the Director, the Dramatic Poet, and the Performer discuss their aims in art. While the Poet expresses lofty sentiments and writes for posterity, the Director's concern is to attract and hold an audience. The Director tells the Poet, in Robert David MacDonald's translation:

> Pack your plays tight, my dear, and when you've packed them
> with incident and wit enough, we'll act them.
> Variety insures the house is full.
> The most the best of us can do's distract them.
>
> . . . .
>
> Don't spare me in the matter of machinery,
> have backdrops, trapdoors, all you want of scenery,
> sun, moon and stars, mountains, water, fire,
> and all the birds and beasts you could desire.

Goethe's masterpiece accordingly contains something for everyone: humor, pathos, irony, spectacular stage effects, poetry, philosophy—and a performing dog to please the masses.

Goethe had been working on *Faust* at various times since the 1770s. An unpublished early version now known as the *Urfaust* (probably composed in 1773–74) was discovered long after his death. His publication of *Faust; A Fragment* in 1790 suggests, according to Charles E. Passage, that Goethe already saw his work-in-progress outgrowing the limitations of the stage. *Part I*, published in 1808, was first performed in an abridged version in 1819. That performance in Prince Radziwill's private theater in Berlin was staged by Count Karl von Brühl, director of the Berlin Nationaltheater. Instead of following Goethe's sketch of a Jupiter-like apparition for the Earth Spirit in Faust's study, Brühl suddenly illuminated a huge bust of Goethe. Fuller texts were used for the 1828 Paris production in French and the 1829 Braunschweig public theater production, which also toured to Dresden, Leipzig, and Frankfurt. Later in 1829, Goethe directed a rather static production of *Part I* at Weimar to

This is Goethe's sketch for the apparition of the Earth Spirit in Faust's study in act 1 of his great tragedy, Faust, Part I *(1808). Courtesy of the Goethe-Nationalmuseum, Weimar.*

Goethe's sketch for the Walpurgis Night scene in Faust, Part I. *Courtesy of the Goethe-Nationalmuseum, Weimar.*

Left, Karoline Jagemann at center played Thekla to Heinrich Vohs's Max in Wallenstein's Death *by Friedrich von Schiller at Weimar in 1799. Johann Graff, in the hat and cape, played the title role. From Ludwig Bellerman,* Schiller *(1901).*

Right, Schiller's Intrigue and Love (Kabale and Liebe) *was revived at the Vienna Burgtheater in 1808. Betty Koberwein played Luisa Miller. Engraving by F. Weber. From* Wiener Nachdrucks *(1808).*

celebrate his eightieth birthday. Upon completing *Part II* in 1831, Goethe locked it away, forbidding publication until after his death. Having worked on *Faust* during a period of about sixty years, he synthesized in it his youthful *Sturm und Drang* affiliation, his Weimar classicism, and the reflections of his old age. Goethe died and *Part II* was published in 1832, but not performed until 1854. The first production of the entire work was in 1876 at Weimar. Although too seldom presented in its entirety outside Germany, the stageworthiness of *Faust I* and *II* has been demonstrated, and it remains a pinnacle of dramatic literature.

Like Goethe, Friedrich Schiller started out as a *Sturm und Drang* writer. His first play, *The Robbers,* was produced at the Mannheim National Theatre in 1782; still in military school, Schiller went AWOL to see it. The strict discipline of his school as well as the repressive policies of the local duke fueled the passionate spirit of rebellion against unjust authority that permeates his early work. *Kabale und Liebe* was also tremendously popular, but drew the wrath of the duke, and Schiller was

forced to flee. After *Don Carlos* (1787), his first play in verse, he abandoned playwriting for over a decade. He taught at the University of
Jena, wrote historical and philosophical treatises, and began his close
association with Goethe. Although very different in temperament, each
provided the stimulus that the other needed for his writing: Goethe
owed his return to work on *Faust* to Schiller, and Schiller owed his
renewed interest in the drama to Goethe. Before he died at the age of
forty-five, Schiller completed several more historical dramas in verse:
Wallenstein (a trilogy, 1797), *Maria Stuart* (1800), *Die Jungfrau von Orleans*
(The Maid of Orleans, 1801), and *Wilhelm Tell* (1804). In those works he
was moving toward the synthesis of romantic and classical elements that
was soon to bring universal recognition to Germany's new position in the
forefront of world literature.

THEATER AND DRAMA IN NORTH AMERICA

The history of American theater is traditionally begun with such
isolated events as the performance of a Spanish *comedia* by Capitán
Marcos Farfán de los Godos on the banks of the Rio Grande in 1598, and
a 1606 performance in canoes on what is now the Annapolis River in
Nova Scotia. The latter consisted of humorous French verses composed
by Marc Lescarbot to greet an exploratory party upon its safe return to
base camp. The text of *Le Théâtre de Neptune en la Nouvelle France,* which
Lescarbot later included in his history of New France published in Paris,
indicates that Frenchmen costumed as Micmac Indians, Neptune, and
his attending Tritons rowed out to meet the overdue ship, and after
declaiming their verses interspersed with trumpet fanfares, invited
everybody to a feast. It was thirty-four years before the next known
performance, a Jesuit school drama, which was given to commemorate
the second birthday of the future Louis XIV and to provide religious
instruction for the Indians in attendance.

There are, however, accounts of even earlier dramatic enactments
by North American Indians in territories that are now Mexico, Canada,
and the United States. The Spanish *conquistadores* arriving in Mexico in
1519 reported that the Aztecs built elevated earthen platforms for performances that blended song, dance, animal imitations, and buffoonery.
These "farces" were apparently quite distinct from the ritual enactments
in honor of the Aztec deities. It was not long before Spanish missionaries
were translating *autos sacramentales* into the various Indian languages
and acting in them alongside the natives, as in the Nahuatl-language
performance of *The Last Judgment* in 1533. Four such religious playlets

were presented in Tlaxcala at Corpus Christi in 1538, followed by baptisms of the converted. The warlike tribes of the northern Atlantic seaboard were less inclined to formal theatricals, but Thomas Morton, a Massachusetts trader, described some local Indian festivities in the 1620s: "They exercise themselves in gaminge, and playinge of juglinge tricks, and all manner of Revelles, which they are delighted in, that it is admirable to behould, what pasttime they use, of several kinds, every one striving to surpasse the other." In the Pacific northwest, the Nootka and Kwakiutl Indians created elaborate stage effects—using tunnels, trapdoors, rigging for flying fanciful creatures overhead, and disembodied voices—for their dramatizations of tribal mythology.

During the first century of settlement of Mexico by the Spaniards and of Canada by the French, the theater of the colonists adhered closely to that of their mother country. Mexican theater and drama then is most conveniently traced within the Hispanic context of Latin America. Canadian theater, after the mid-eighteenth century, comprised two parallel traditions, one French and one English. In the latter tradition, there has often been an overlapping of elements with American theater. In what was to become the United States, the dominant influence was English. Pre-revolutionary dramatic art in the colonies, however, was not merely a distant reflection of a British prototype. Such factors as the geographical distance between population centers and a relative lack of continuity of theatrical enterprise in any given locale ensured an independent history for American theatrical entertainment almost from the beginning. One way in which it differed from the mother country during the colonial period was that American theater developed virtually independently of American dramatic literature. The earliest known theatrical performances were based upon texts that have not survived or, later, upon imported English plays. The earliest plays written by American settlers, on the other hand, were generally published but not performed. Not until after the Revolution, with performances of *The Contrast* beginning in 1787, did the theater and the drama begin to intertwine. Another factor that immediately distinguished American theater from its British prototype was the vehemence of attempts to suppress it.

The earliest known English-language play in America was William Darby's *Ye Bare and Ye Cubb,* which Darby and two other men presented in Acomac County, Virginia, in 1665. Although the text has not survived, the activity is documented in court records that show charges brought against the three. Ordered to repeat their performance, in costume, for the court, Darby and friends complied and were found "not guilty of fault." Indeed, Virginia and Maryland were the only two colonies where theatrical performances were never prohibited by law. Prejudice against theater came to America with the Puritans, who left England to escape religious persecution in the decades before the Commonwealth and settled mostly in the northern colonies. Although they prized books (a printing press was brought over in 1638, and Boston had a bookstore by 1645), the Puritans regarded theater—like Christmas merrymaking—as frivolity that was harmful to the spirit. To the Dutch in New York and the Quakers in Pennsylvania, theater was an expensive endeavor that would only encourage vagabondage. Such prejudices lingered among New England colonists long after the Restoration of a king and legal theater to the mother country. While licentiousness reigned on the English stage, a Boston tavernkeeper, John Wing, in 1687 was talked out of his "unseemly" plan to present magic shows in a separate room.

In 1690 Harvard College students apparently gave one performance of a play entitled *Gustavus Vasa*, written by their classmate Benjamin Coleman. Students at William and Mary College recited a "pastoral colloquy" in 1702, and there are a number of other such instances of "dramatic dialogues" presented in academic settings throughout the eighteenth century. But, apart from academe, the obstacles were formidable: William Penn promoted laws against theater in Pennsylvania from 1699, and New York forbade playacting in 1709. Justice Samuel Sewell, who had taken part in the Salem Witchcraft trials, fulminated against "the practice of Shamefull vanities" in Boston in 1714.

In Canada it was the Catholic clergy that put an end to theatrical performances in French after thirty years of lively Jesuit school drama. Matters came to a head in 1694 when a Quebec troupe sponsored by Governor Frontenac planned to follow up their successful presentations of plays by Corneille and Racine with Molière's *Tartuffe*. Bishop Saint-Vallier reacted by excommunicating and imprisoning for blasphemy Lieutenant Mareuil, who was to have played the title role and directed. Saint-Vallier also issued *Instructions for the Enlightenment of Consciences Regarding Comedies* condemning plays as "a criminal or dangerous thing, a sin, or an invitation to sin." Frontenac canceled the production, but the damage done by "the *Tartuffe* affair" virtually annihilated French Canadian theater for two hundred years. Besides banning public playacting, Saint-Vallier in 1699 extended his prohibition to cover Jesuit school drama. After the formal cession of New France to Britain in 1763, English-language theater gained the ascendancy, especially as "garrison theatre" performed by British soldiers for their own diversion launched a strong amateur stage tradition in Canada.

Another part of the New World that followed Restoration England's example in the pursuit of pleasure was Jamaica. The island had first been settled by Spaniards, but was ceded to the English in 1670. A public theater was listed in a 1682 account of the attractions there: "Horse Racing, Bowls, Dancing, Musick, Plays at a Publick Theatre, etc." Jamaica was a preliminary stop for Anthony Aston, the first professional actor to perform in America. At sixteen he was a strolling player in England, but, seeking adventure, he made the eleven-week crossing to Jamaica in 1701. A year or so later he caught a ship to Charleston. He later recalled that journey in an autobiographical sketch prefacing his play *The Fool's Opera* (1731): "After many vicissitudes I arrived at Charles-Towne full of Lice, Shame, Poverty, and Hunger:—I turned Player and Poet, and wrote one Play on the Subject of the Country." The play is lost and the circumstances of his performances are not known, except that he made his way to New York and spent the winter "acting, writing, courting, fighting." Returning to London, he enjoyed a successful career performing original variety material under the stage name Matt Medley.

Williamsburg, Virginia, was strongly oriented to London fashions, and thus it was fertile ground for adoption of the theatergoing habit. An enterprising merchant, William Levingston, with the assistance of his indentured servants Charles and Mary Stagg, began offering entertainments there in 1716. Sometime within the next two years, Levingston built the first theater in America. Little is known about the building except the rough dimensions, thirty feet wide and eighty-six feet long. Although Levingston did not long remain in charge of it, the Williamsburg theater continued to be used for amateur productions of Restoration plays like *The Recruiting Officer* until about 1736. Farquahar's comedy was also the earliest recorded play to be performed in New York, in December 1732. The New York actors, who were probably amateurs, performed three times a week until February 1734 in Rip Van Dam's "New Theatre," which was apparently a second-floor facility in a warehouse. *The Recruiting Officer* was also chosen to open Charleston's Dock Street Theatre in 1736. Charleston had already entered the annals of American theater history with the first musical play produced in America, the English ballad opera *Flora; or, the Hob in the Well,* in 1735. The colonies echoed London's vogue for the genre, especially in the less expensively produced short versions that often served as "ballad afterpieces." By the latter half of the eighteenth century, however, the most frequently produced author in America was Shakespeare; by all indications, his plays comprised a greater share of the colonial repertoire than that of England.

America's first published play was actually a pointed, and even ribald, political satire in dialogue form. Written in 1714 by Robert Hunter, who was then governor of New York, and entitled *Androboros*, or Man-Eater, the three-act "Biographical Farce" apparently achieved its purpose of discrediting Hunter's obstructionist lieutenant governor. It was fifty years before the next play appeared in print. The anonymous author of *The Paxton Boys* (1764) satirized Presbyterians as well as the gang of frontiersmen named in the play's title who bungled relations with Indians on the Pennsylvania border. There is no indication that either of these plays was produced.

Despite its early antipathy toward theater, Philadelphia gradually emerged as the leading American city for theater until the end of the eighteenth century. Strolling players were performing there by 1723, and, in 1724, what was probably a fairground booth type of theater—"the New Booth on Society Hill"—was offering "Roap Dancing" and "your old friend Pickle Herring." It was in Philadelphia that the Murray and Kean company is first known to have performed. This "Company of Comedians" presented Addison's *Cato* in Plumstead's warehouse in 1749, but left for New York six months later, discouraged by the Common Council's concern that "weak and inconsiderate persons" would squander their money, "though the performance be ever so mean and contemptible." In New York, Walter Murray and Thomas Kean's company presented twenty-four plays in little over a year in a three-hundred-seat room on Nassau Street, and then moved on to Williamsburg. Their twenty or so years of touring gave many Americans a first exposure to theater, and this paved the way for acceptance of a far more important troupe, the Hallams, who were to arrive in 1752. Meanwhile, theater was thriving in Jamaica where a Shakespearean actor named John Moody had been playing to enthusiastic audiences since 1745. On return visits to England to recruit additional actors, Moody gave glowing reports of the opportunities in the New World. Moody monopolized theater in Jamaica until he finally returned to England for good, giving over his theater company to an actor, David Douglass. However, Moody's account of entertainment-starved audiences on the American mainland was a strong incentive to William Hallam, the manager of Goodman's Fields Theatre in London, when his theater went bankrupt. He organized and backed a company—establishing a commonwealth scheme for sharing responsibilities and profits—under the leadership of his brother Lewis Hallam, to brave the uncivilized wilds of America. The Hallams' only mistake was to send Robert Upton as an advance man to obtain permissions and build a theater in New York. Neglecting his employers' interests, Upton performed for a season with the Murray and Kean company, whose repertoire thereafter featured seven new plays and four new farces, all taken from the repertoire that the Hallams were preparing to bring to America. Upton returned to England just in time to avoid the Hallams when they arrived.

Lewis Hallam, his wife, their three children, and ten other adult actors landed in Yorktown, Virginia, on June 2, 1752. They traveled to Williamsburg, obtained the governor's permission to perform, purchased a warehouse on the edge of town, and spent the summer putting

in boxes, galleries, and some sort of "balconies," perhaps over the proscenium doors. Having set the desired tone in an announcement in the
Virginia *Gazette* ("Ladies and Gentlemen may depend upon being entertain'd in as polite a Manner as at the Theatres in London, the Company
being perfect in all the best Plays, Operas, Farces, and Pantomimes that
have been exhibited in any of the Theatres for these ten years past"), the
Hallam Company opened on September 15 with *The Merchant of Venice*
and a farcical afterpiece, *The Anatomist*. They were received, the *Gazette*
reported, by "a numerous and polite audience, with great Applause."
The Hallams remained in Williamsburg for eleven months, performing
two or three times a week. In November the "Emperor and Empress" of
the Cherokee nation with their son and several warriors called upon
Governor Dinwiddie, and he took them to the theater to see *Othello,*
followed by a pantomime. The "fighting with naked Swords on the
Stage" in the afterpiece so alarmed the Empress that she ordered "some
about her to go and prevent them killing one another."

Arriving in New York with a certificate of good behavior from
Governor Dinwiddie, the Hallams encountered unexpected difficulty
obtaining permission to perform, in part because the "roystering young
men" of the Murray and Kean Company had generated bad feelings
with their "tricks and mischief." After building a new theater, the Hallams presented a season of twenty-one plays in six months. In 1754 they
moved on to Philadelphia, again facing opposition but guaranteeing that
nothing indecent would be performed, tendering security for any debts,
and offering one of their twenty-four performances for the benefit of
the poor. Given the troupe's stimulus to the economy (through the
hiring of local hairdressers, play copyists, musicians to accompany performances; printing of handbills, tickets, advertisements; purchase of
candles, etc.), the city's continuing resistance to the theater suggests how
deeply entrenched were the moral concerns. Some even saw theater as
detrimental to trade because it would "encourage idleness." After a
Charleston engagement, the company sailed for Jamaica. There in 1755
Lewis Hallam died. David Douglass soon merged John Moody's former
company with the Hallams, and the combined troupe played several
seasons in the West Indies. In 1758 Douglass married the widowed Mrs.
Hallam and took the company back to the mainland.

With Mrs. Hallam as leading lady and her son Lewis Hallam, Jr., as
leading man, the Company of Comedians from London played New
York, Philadelphia, Annapolis, Williamsburg (where the young planter
George Washington was frequently in the audience), and finally they
tackled New England, where they met with considerable hardship. Accused of peddling "Vice, Impiety, and Immorality," they hit upon a
successful advertising strategy: the plays were touted as "moral dia-

logues." *Othello,* for example, was described as "a Series of MORAL DIA-LOGUES in five parts / Depicting the evil effects of Jealousy and other Bad Passions, and Proving that Happiness can only Spring from the Pursuit of Virtue." In 1763 Douglass responded to the drift of public opinion by renaming his troupe "The American Company." In 1766 Douglass constructed, with the approval of the governor and against vigorous protests by the Quakers, the Southwark Theatre in Philadelphia. Since the first story was of brick, the Southwark is considered to be the first permanent theater in America. It was a leaky building with poor sightlines, but it had oil lamps over the stage area. (Earlier American theaters used spermaceti candles over the stage and tallow candles in the auditorium.) Douglass constructed a similar brick building in New York, the John Street Theatre, in 1767. That same year saw the American debut of a new leading man in the company, the handsome, Irish-born John Henry, who had performed at Covent Garden, but chose to make his career in the colonies. At about that time also, Nancy Hallam rejoined the company as its leading actress. A cousin of Louis Hallam, Jr., she had earlier been a child performer with the Company of Comedians, but apparently went to England for voice training. Typical of the encomia that appeared in the *Maryland Gazette* between 1770–72, often with reference to her portrayal of Imogen in Shakespeare's *Cymbeline,* was this: "Such delicacy of Manner! Such classical Strictures of Expression! The Musick of her Tongue! The *vox liquida,* how melting! . . . How true and thorough her Knowledge of the Character she personated!"

A notable event in the opening season of the Southwark Theatre was the first professional production of a play by an American author. Thomas Godfrey, born in Philadelphia, was a promising poet who had died suddenly at twenty-seven. In order to preserve the memory of his genius, his friends published his only play, a five-act heroic verse tragedy, *The Prince of Parthia.* (Benjamin Franklin reportedly bought twelve copies.) The American Company hoped the production would ingratiate them with the difficult Philadelphia critics, but it was not successful and was not given a second performance. Actually, they had previously announced and begun to rehearse another work by an American author, Colonel Thomas Forrest's comic opera *The Disappointment* (1767). That pointed topical satire—which included the first Negro character in American drama—was withdrawn, as its "personal reflections" were deemed "unfit for the stage." One of the most interesting plays of this period—though not produced in the author's lifetime—was *Ponteach; or, The Savages of America* (1766), a sympathetic portrayal of the tragic-heroic Native American title character (pronounced Pontiac). The author, Major Robert Rogers, commanded "Rogers's Rangers" in the

"When Hallam as Fedele comes distress'd, / Tears fill each Eye, and Passion heaves each breast," wrote Jonathan Boucher in a poem of tribute to Nancy Hallam. It was inspired by Charles Willson Peale's 1771 painting of her in Shakespeare's Cymbeline *as Imogen in the disguise of the boy Fidele. Colonial Williamsburg Foundation.*

French and Indian War. His play was one of dozens of dramas on Indian themes that were to appear over the next century.

Among the numerous theaters that Douglass scattered up and down the colonies were two in Annapolis: a small wooden structure in 1760 and an impressive six-hundred-seat brick theater in 1771. Brooks McNamara cites this pattern as the standard process for overcoming opposition to theater. The earliest facility built for theater in any town would be a temporary structure. After a community had got used to the idea of theater, a more elaborate, permanent building could be erected.

As friction between England and its colonies increased, the Continental Congress—during its meeting in Philadelphia in 1774, in order to "encourage frugality, economy, and industry"—passed a resolution recommending the suspension of "every species of extravagance and dissipation, especially all horse-racing, and all kinds of gaming, cock-fighting, exhibitions of shows, plays, and other expensive diversions and entertainments." The American Company departed for Jamaica in February 1775 and remained there until 1785. In 1778 Congress severely strengthened its earlier edict. Throughout the revolutionary period, theatricals were almost exclusively done by British soldiers who occupied the existing theaters. However, this did not prevent American patriots from writing "pamphlet plays" for publication but not performance. Two of the best were written by Mercy Otis Warren, the wife of a general in Washington's army and the close friend of John and Abigail Adams. *The Adulateur* (1772) and *The Group* (1775) are both vehemently patriotic, satiric attacks in verse on Tories like Massachusetts Governor Hutchinson, who is lampooned in the former play as the villainous Rapatio. That character appears also in *The Defeat* (1773), which is sometimes attributed to Mrs. Warren. In response to *The Blockade of Boston* (1775), a play by General Burgoyne that mocked Americans, an anonymous patriot published *The Blockheads; or, The Affrighted Officers* (1776). John Leacock served the cause of Liberty with *The Fall of British Tyranny; or, America Triumphant, the First Campaign,* "a tragicomedy of five acts" (1776). Tracing the Revolution from its origins in England to the events of 1776, this immensely popular work is said to be America's first chronicle play. It is also the first of many plays in which George Washington appears as a character. Although several editions were published within the year, there is no evidence that it was produced. Hugh Henry Brackenridge's *The Battle of Bunker's Hill* (1776) and *The Death of General Montgomery* (1777) are unusual in that seriousness of tone and historical accuracy take precedence over satire and propaganda values. Colonel Robert Munford fought on the American side, but took a strictly nonpartisan view of events in his two comedies, *The Candidates* and *The Patriots*, both written in the 1770s and published in 1798.

When John Henry and Lewis Hallam, Jr., reassembled the American Company on the mainland in 1785 (David Douglass having retired in Jamaica), they used patriotic songs and recitations on American themes as an entering wedge against antitheatrical prejudices in Philadelphia and New York. One perennially popular piece that often managed to skirt the laws against theater was George Alexander Stevens's *Lecture on Heads,* a satiric one-man show that could easily be adapted in length and topicality; Douglass had performed it before the war, and John Henry was among those who revived it afterward. Yet the theater was actually encountering greater obstacles following the War for Independence than it had before. If moral superiority had helped Americans to achieve their victory, then the strength of the young republic depended upon maintaining such moral discipline. In view of the country's serious postwar economic difficulties, theater seemed frivolous to many. Thus many states and municipalities hesitated to repeal their wartime antitheater laws, and some were toughened. In 1786 the Pennsylvania legislature passed a sweeping Act for the Prevention of Vice and Immorality, to take effect at the end of August 1787. Until then, Hallam and Henry offered varied but relatively sober fare at the Southwark to entertain delegates to the Constitutional Convention in Philadelphia, and George Washington was among those who attended several times. When the law took effect, the company flouted it, all the while currying public favor by contributing to charitable causes. Finally, in 1789 Pennsylvania repealed its standing antitheater laws, thus leading the way to legal theater everywhere. The process of legalizing theater was not without dissension and backsliding, but a national affirmation of identity through culture was the overriding need.

Three actors left Hallam and Henry in 1785 to try their fortunes in Canada, where the economy was expanding and English-language entertainment was largely limited to garrison theater. Edward Allen, John Bentley, and William Moore, along with other actors they recruited en route, leased an assembly room in Montreal and won a warm welcome with the thirty or so plays and farces they presented in their four months there. Thus they established themselves as the first professional company in Canada. In the summer of 1786 the company moved on to Quebec City, where Bentley and Moore settled for many years, enthusiastically supported by their audiences and winning prominence in the community by their involvement in civic affairs.

Meanwhile, Henry and Hallam's troupe, now known as the Old American Company, acquired a new leading man whose strong suit was comedy; Thomas Wignell originated the role of Jonathan in Royall Tyler's comedy *The Contrast,* which opened at the John Street Theatre in 1787. This play may be credited with several firsts: it was the first professionally produced play on an American subject, the first produced comedy by a native-born American, the first American play reviewed in the press, the first play to feature a "stage Yankee" character (Jonathan), and the first wholly successful, long-running (five consecutive performances) American play. Perhaps most significantly, it is the earliest American play that still frequently finds a place in today's repertoire. And Walter Meserve signals it as the one literary work that, more than any other, helped to unify the new American nation in the difficult post-Revolutionary years. It did this by pointing up, in humorous dialogue, clever twists of plot, and believable characterizations, the "contrast" between the pretentious affectations of Europeans and the straightforward honesty of Americans. The texts of Tyler's three other produced plays have not survived, while none of his four other extant plays was produced.

By one report (the *Daily Advertiser*), the Old American Company's scenery and management at that time left much to be desired: "Frequently where the author intended a handsome street or a beautiful landscape, we only see a dirty piece of canvas; what else can we call a scene in which the colors are defaced and obliterated? Nor is it uncommon to see the back of the stage represent a street, while the side scenes represent a wood. . . . The musicians too instead of performing between the play and the farce, are suffered to leave the orchestra to pay a visit to the tippling houses, and the ladies in the meantime, must amuse themselves by looking at the candles and empty benches." It was inevitable that rival companies would challenge the Old American Company's virtual monopoly on professional theater from New York to Charleston. Wignell left Henry and Hallam in 1791 and went to England to recruit actors for a company he formed with Alexander Reinagle.

Wignell and Reinagle leased the elegant Chestnut Street Theatre, the construction of which was underwritten by some prominent Philadelphians to replace the deteriorating Southwark. Opening in 1794, the Chestnut Street Theatre, modeled after England's Theatre Royal in Bath, seated two thousand in a semi-elliptical configuration and boasted a stage thirty-six feet wide by seventy-one feet deep. With performances six nights a week in scenery imported from England, Wignell and Reinagle's productions easily outclassed those of the Old American Company. John Henry and Hallam, Jr., kept their focus on New York and upgraded their company with a new leading actor from England, John Hodgkinson. Still they experienced extreme financial difficulties, especially as actors and audiences succumbed to the yellow fever epidemic of 1792–93. Hallam and Hodgkinson were not successful in managing the troupe after Henry retired. Over the next few years they sold out more and more of their interest in the Old American Company to a young painter-playwright, William Dunlap. By 1798 Dunlap was sole manager. That same year the company moved into the new Park Street Theatre. Although less impressive than Philadelphia's Chestnut Street, the Park was to become America's leading theater of the early nineteenth century when New York surpassed Philadelphia as a theater center.

As the first professional playwright in America, William Dunlap earned the epithet "father of American drama." He wrote twenty-nine original plays and did translation/adaptations of about thirty others from French and German sources. When Dunlap was eighteen, his father sent him to London to study painting, but he became more strongly attracted to the theater. After three years abroad, he returned to New York just in time to see *The Contrast,* and this inspired him to try playwriting himself. His second play, *The Father; or, American Shandyism* was produced in New York in 1789, and was soon followed by his comic Irish-character sketch, *Darby's Return.* George Washington, a frequent theatergoer, attended the premiere of the latter and laughed heartily at a joke about himself. Dunlap greatly admired Washington and once painted his portrait.

Dunlap's best-known play, which exists in two distinct versions, drew upon an actual event during the Revolutionary War: Major André, an honorable young British officer sent on a mission to Benedict Arnold, was caught out of uniform and sentenced to be executed for spying. Dunlap's first treatment, a five-act tragedy entitled *André* (1798), weighs the Enlightenment values of reason and emotion. Emotionally, the Americans want to spare the life of the gentleman who has impressed them so profoundly by his virtue. But reason calls for adherence to a principle, even to the extent of hanging André as a spy instead of acceding to his plea that he be shot as a soldier. A featured role in the production was played by Thomas Abthorpe Cooper, whom Dunlap had recently lured away from Wignell and Reinagle. The British-born Cooper, who was to become a naturalized citizen and the first "star" of the American stage, could not redeem *André* for the public. Perhaps the appeals were too mixed for an audience whose memories of the war were still vivid. In any case, Dunlap rewrote *André* in 1803, making it into a flimsily plotted comic pageant with songs and fireworks. Retitled *The Glory of Columbia: Her Yeomanry!,* it was often revived over the years as a Fourth of July spectacle, thus provoking Dunlap's remark that history was "occasionally murdered for the amusement of holiday fools."

Dunlap's career as a theater manager peaked in the 1800–1801 season, but his financial situation worsened thereafter. Attendance may have been hurt somewhat by a series of critical letters published in the New York *Morning Chronicle* by Washington Irving under the pen name Jonathan Oldstyle. The loss of several of the best company members was another blow. Dunlap mortgaged his farm to keep the theater going, but he was finally forced into bankruptcy in 1805. A year later, Thomas A. Cooper revived the company, and Dunlap became his assistant manager. From 1812 until his death in 1839, Dunlap devoted himself largely to painting and writing books on historical subjects. Among them was his

History of the American Theatre (1832), which, despite its inaccuracies, flavorfully records events from eyewitness accounts of the previous generation's theater. He was also a founder and vice president of the National Academy of Design, and director of the American Academy of Fine Arts. In 1828 he wrote one last play, *A Trip to Niagara; or, Travellers in America,* which turned out to be his greatest box-office success. Dunlap described this comedy-travelogue with stock ethnic characters as "a kind of running accompaniment to the more important product of the Scene-painter." It featured a diorama: twenty-five thousand feet of moving scenery depicting the landscape along the Hudson River and Erie Canal from New York to Buffalo.

New York's Park Street Theatre and Philadelphia's Chestnut Street Theatre were part of a larger trend toward building permanent theaters in the 1790s. Even Boston, the last Puritan stronghold, opened its Federal Street Theatre in 1794. Brooks McNamara has described an architecturally imaginative theater designed in 1798 by Benjamin Latrobe for Richmond; it is unfortunate that this theater was never built, because its continental European features (a domed ceiling, semi-circular galleries, a featured staircase from the lobby, and the suppression of proscenium doors) might have contributed some healthy diversity to the English architectural tradition that was otherwise so firmly entrenched. Charleston opened two theaters in the 1790s: the Charleston Theatre and Alexander Placide's French Theatre in the existing Harmony Hall. Placide was a French rope-dancer who came to America in 1791 and progressed from his feats of "agility and pantimime" on the tightrope to producing a long series of patriotic pageants at the French Theatre and later at the Charleston Theatre when he took over that management. Several of Alexander Placide's children went on to distinguished careers in theater, most notably his son Henry Placide, who made his adult debut in 1823.

Another trend in the 1790s was a more favorable hearing—that is, production opportunities—for plays by American authors. Many of these plays developed the theme of what it meant to be an American. Susanna Rowson's four plays included *Slaves in Algiers; or, A Struggle for Freedom* (1794) and *The Female Patriot* (1795). The former, a melodrama with songs, about American captives in Algiers, illustrates the thesis that "No man should be a slave." Irish-born John Daly Burk contributed *Bunker Hill; or, The Death of General Burgoyne* (1797), a patriotic play renowned for the staging of its spectacular fifteen-minute battle scene without dialogue. Other playwrights of the decade include Margaretta Bleecker Faugères, John Murdock, John Blair Linn, David Everett, and Judith Sargent Murray. Many of their plays exhibit some characteristic features of nineteenth-century melodrama: national spirit, exotic settings, emphasis on action and spectacle. American drama was ready to hold its own against British imports in the popular favor.

BEAUMARCHAIS AND THE FRENCH REVOLUTION

Rarely does one find two such momentous events so close in time, with so many interconnecting links, leading whole nations down such different roads, as the American and French Revolutions. Both may be seen to have been generated in part by Enlightenment philosophy, a significant factor also in the American leaders' shaping of a new nation. The American War for Independence could not have been won without France's material aid, much of which came at the instigation of the greatest French playwright of the period, Beaumarchais. Nor perhaps might the French Revolution have happened without the inspiration of the American model. American statesmen were extremely visible in Paris during the years following the declaration of their new nation: Benjamin Franklin had an emotionally charged meeting with Voltaire before twenty witnesses in 1778; Thomas Jefferson resided in Paris from August 1784 to September 1789 and frequented all the major French theaters. Although Jefferson—as American minister to Paris—maintained a diplomatic neutrality during the tumultuous summer of 1789, he was often called upon to consult with those attempting to draft a new constitution for France, and he wrote optimistically in August 1789: "Here is but the first chapter of the history of European liberty." The early idealism of the French Revolution was unfortunately subverted by the Reign of Terror, Napoleon's rise to power, and the restoration of the monarchy, a chain of events that only engendered more revolution in 1830, 1848, and 1871. The greater success of the American experiment in democracy was due to many factors, including the colonists' familiarity, through their largely British lineage, with a tradition of representative government. In addition and perhaps even more fundamentally, the framers of the American constitution were influenced by the Iroquois Confederacy's Great Law of Peace, with which Benjamin Franklin, Thomas Jefferson, and others were known to have been acquainted. The Indians' constitution, "by the people, for the people, of the people and for those yet unborn," provided for each of the Five Nations to govern its affairs independently while binding them all together against outside enemies. No such unity could be achieved in France while the emphasis of the revolutionary leaders was upon the differences among the three estates of French society.

The divergent approaches to revolution and its aftermath were echoed in the theater of the period in the United States and France. Despite the suspension of theater during the War for Independence, there was in general a continuity of tradition in American theatrical practice that gradually effected a broadening of the audience base. Trying out their freedoms little by little, Americans assimilated the idea that theater could well be "a rational amusement to an enlightened community" and that it was "contrary to the principles of a free government to deprive any of its citizens of a rational and innocent entertainment." For rough-and-ready American audiences, the key word was "rational." In contrast, France—the home of neoclassical "regularity" in art, rational philosophy, and a well-defined social order—fell prey to extremism. There, theaters served as battlegrounds for the conflicting views of royalists and republicans who regularly disrupted performances in the early years of the revolution. The law of January 13, 1791, that abolished all restrictions on theater led to a frenzy of activity: dozens of theaters opened and closed, experimenting with every variety of entertainment. Suddenly there was a greater quantity and variety of theater in Paris than at any other time in the city's history. But with the Reign of Terror, beginning in 1793, came new regulations imposed by Jacobin fanatics. Theaters were closed for a time, then reopened with the proviso that the repertoire include regular performances of certain plays that offered a correct interpretation of the revolutionary cause; the classics were banned or altered to reflect orthodox patriotic sentiments. Finally, although order was restored to daily life and the classics to the stage, the French theater and its public had been irrevocably altered by the harrowing experience of revolution. Amid the chaos of those years, the important events in the theater might be best traced through certain individuals: the playwright-diplomat-adventurer Beaumarchais, the actor François-Joseph Talma, the theater manageress Mademoiselle Montansier, and the painter-impresario Jacques-Louis David.

Beaumarchais, born Pierre-Augustin Caron, was an extraordinary figure in eighteenth-century arts and politics. The son of a watchmaker, he entered the ranks of the landed gentry in 1757 at the age of twenty-five, and the nobility in 1758, through a combination of ingenuity and a fortunate first marriage. No fortune accompanied the titled name of Beaumarchais when his wife died, but neither could a nobleman practice the watchmaking trade that had brought him into contact with the royal household; (his invention of a certain escapement allowed watches to be made smaller, flatter, and more accurate than ever before). Beaumarchais thus went into financial speculation with an older gentleman, M. Pâris-Duvernoy. He also wrote at least five *parades* that were performed as titillating *théâtre de société* between 1757–63 at the chateau of Madame de Pompadour's husband. On a 1764 business trip to Madrid, Beaumarchais became embroiled in a series of adventures in defense of

Eugénie (1767) was Beaumarchais's attempt to write a drame *in accord with Diderot's precepts for the new genre. It was not particularly successful, in part because the treatment of the young woman lured into a mock marriage by an unscrupulous aristocrat was thought indelicate. From Felix Gaiffe,* Le Drame en France au XVIIIe siècle.

his sister's honor against a scoundrel named Clavijo, a story that became the basis for Goethe's play *Clavigo* (1779). Beaumarchais's first two full-length plays were both imitative of Diderot. *Eugénie* (1767), generally considered a mediocre effort although it achieved an initial run of seven performances, was criticized in that the title character did not come to a bad end after having been seduced by an aristocrat through a false marriage; moreover, the censor insisted that Beaumarchais change the setting to England on the grounds that such scandalous doings could never occur in France. Beaumarchais's prefatory *Essay on the Serious Dramatic Genre* served as his defense of the play. *Les Deux amis; ou le Négociant de Lyon* (The Two Friends; or, The Merchant of Lyon, 1770); portrays a commercial milieu from an insider's point of view and makes a case for the virtuous businessman's contribution toward the good of the nation; although it failed in Paris, the play was popular in provincial cities like Lyons.

The death of Pâris-Duvernoy in 1770 launched Beaumarchais into several years of legal imbroglios that were complicated by Louis XV's dissolution of Parliament that year. Beaumarchais found himself slandered, then imprisoned on a *lettre de cachet,* and finally stripped of his civil rights. He swayed public opinion to his side by recounting his story in a series of witty, best-selling pamphlets, and in order to earn back his legal identity, he carried out a series of secret diplomatic missions abroad for the king. Even before his official rehabilitation in 1776, Beaumarchais succeeded in getting his *Le Barbier de Séville* (Barber of Seville, 1775) produced at the Comédie Française. After an unsuccessful opening, he reduced the five acts to four; two days later the play was a phenomenal success. Its popularity was due in large measure to the recognizable portrait of the author himself in the character of the valet Figaro (whose name in French sounds like "*fils* Caron" or "son of Caron"). In act 1 Figaro tells Count Almaviva about his adventures: "welcomed in one town, imprisoned in the next, and everywhere I rise above my problems; praised by some, blamed by others; doing some good in fair weather, putting up with the foul; making fun of fools, standing up to bad guys; laughing off my poverty, and ready to shave anyone." Although the servant is certainly more nimble-minded than the nobleman, the play had no particular problem with the censors, for there is a long tradition of clever servant characters in French drama. Perhaps the most tendentious line is Figaro's comment to Almaviva: "Given the fine qualities expected in a servant, do you know many masters who have the right stuff to be a valet?" Still, this comedy of intrigue shows the two estates working together to achieve a common goal.

That same year, undaunted by the reverses he had suffered under the corrupt judicial system, Beaumarchais spoke out for the American cause, writing letters to Louis XVI that advocated French support for the American colonies in their revolt against England. Beaumarchais himself took the financial risk of secretly and privately shipping arms to America. His motives were altruistic ones; he was enthusiastic about the cause of liberty, and he took a serious financial loss for his significant efforts. In an autobiographical summary he wrote toward the end of his life, he truthfully claimed: "I did more than any other Frenchman, whoever they may be, for the freedom of America, that freedom which gave birth to ours, which I alone dared to conceive and begin to nurture despite England, Spain, and France herself."

On July 3, 1777, twenty-two playwrights came at Beaumarchais's invitation to his house for dinner. Each had some story to tell about having been mistreated by the theaters and habitually receiving less than the one-ninth of the profits that were due to the dramatist. Beau-

Left, a modern production of The Barber of Seville *by Beaumarchais at the Comédie Française featured Raymond Acquaviva as Count Almaviva and François Chaumette as Bartholo. Michel Etcheverry directed, and Olivier Etcheverry designed the sets and costumes. Courtesy of French Cultural Services.*

Right, Beaumarchais's Marriage of Figaro *was produced at the Théâtre National Populaire in 1957 with Sylvia Montfort, Catherine Le Couey, and Yves Gass. Courtesy of French Cultural Services.*

A 1977 production of The Marriage of Figaro *at the Comédie Française was directed by Jacques Rosner. Pictured are Alain Pralon, Paule Noëlle, and Jacques Toja. Courtesy of French Cultural Services.*

marchais rallied them to found the world's first dramatists' guild, the Société des Auteurs et Compositeurs Dramatiques, which still functions under articles much like those drawn up at that time. It was a long struggle for Beaumarchais, but the 1791 liberation of the theaters also brought copyright protection for dramatic authors. In another service to French literature, he undertook shortly after Voltaire's death to publish the great philosopher's complete works, even though two-thirds of Voltaire's books were still banned in France. The challenges were enormous, but Beaumarchais set up a press in Kehl, just across the French border, to circumvent censorship, and bought up the rights that were held by various European publishers. He sank his fortune into the publication of 162 deluxe volumes, annotated by the Marquis de Condorcet, that appeared between 1783 and 1790.

Beaumarchais's own dramatic masterpiece reflects the changing political climate on the eve of the revolution. He had probably completed *The Marriage of Figaro* (whose correct French title, *La Folle journée; ou le mariage de Figaro* might be interpreted as a metaphor for the follies of the epoch) as early as 1778, and it was accepted by the Comédie Française in 1781, but its performance was prohibited until 1784 by censors and by the king himself, who recognized the political satire in it. Beaumarchais stirred up public interest in the play by making it available for private readings. At one point the king's brother, the Comte d'Artois, arranged for a private performance by members of the Comédie Française in the theater of the Menus Plaisirs at Versailles. Beaumarchais had conducted a month of rehearsals. The guests were already seated for the opening curtain, when word arrived from the king that the performance was forbidden. In response to the courtly audience's outrage, a single performance was allowed at a private residence in a suburb of Paris. Finally, after six different censors failed to reach a consensus, a hearing took place at which Beaumarchais countered all objections with such wit and charm that the work was approved. Although the action of the play was transferred to Spain, the references to social and political conditions in France are obvious. In this sequel to *The Barber of Seville*, Count Almaviva and Figaro find themselves at cross-purposes. Having helped bring together the count and his countess and having served faithfully for some time, Figaro finds himself a victim of the entrenched privileges of the nobility: the jaded Almaviva intends to invoke *le droit du seigneur,* that is, the old feudal practice of "first-night rights" to the bride when any of his servants marry. The frustrations of a talented individual in the face of a system that blocked advancement on merit are expressed in Figaro's fifth-act monologue, a daring speech not only for its excessive length but also for the serious tone it takes within the context of a comedy—by a valet commenting on social conditions. This was the voice of the coming revolution, although Beaumarchais himself would have preferred rational reform leading to the establishment of a stable constitutional monarchy.

The Marriage of Figaro premiered on April 27, 1784, at the Comédie Française, which was then housed in Peyre and Wailly's left-bank theater. It was one of the most celebrated opening nights in French theater history. The applause that greeted many lines extended the performance time of this exceptionally long play to five hours. The sixty-eight consecutive performances made Beaumarchais wealthy once again. However, one of his clever but careless remarks provided an opportunity for the king to get back at him by having him arrested and humiliatingly imprisoned in a juvenile detention home. When friends intervened and obtained a royal pardon, Beaumarchais refused to leave his cell until the king apologized publicly. The matter was resolved when Louis XVI and his entire cabinet attended a public performance of *The Marriage of Figaro*. Mozart's opera version appeared just two years after the premiere of the play.

Beaumarchais wrote two more works for the stage: *Tarare* (1787), an opera composed by Salieri, and *La Mère coupable* (The Guilty Mother, 1792), a return to the *drame,* which failed. The ostentatious house he built—on an innovative semicircular plan with a central salon, for play readings, that overlooked the gardens—was close enough to the Bastille that he watched its fall on July 14, 1789, from his windows. During that year of terrible privations due to the severe winter of 1788–89 and ensuing food shortages, his ownership of a house with two hundred windows undermined his constant pleas for moderation. The fact that he had built such a mansion on sound business principles, renting out most of it to pay for his own apartments on one side and the upkeep of the luxurious garden they faced, was lost on the public. While he was out of the country on another patriotic venture, the Revolutionary Convention declared him an émigré. To return to France, as he wished to do, would have meant the guillotine. Living in exile in Hamburg for two years, growing increasingly deaf, he was reduced to extreme poverty. But in 1796 he was able to return to Paris, where he spent his last years studying aviation.

One of Beaumarchais's innovations as a playwright was to include with the texts of his plays a detailed description of the costume that should be worn by each character as indicative of personality, social position, and geographical milieu. Although his characters often fall into traditional categories of dramatic functions, the costume indications reveal a sense of them as individuals. This approach is reified by Beaumarchais's lifelong assertion of himself as an individual (to the extent that he deliberately forfeited his title of nobility in 1783, but made a

point of retaining the name Beaumarchais). A similar assertion of individuality is evident throughout the career of the great actor François-
Joseph Talma, who was also a revolutionary in the area of stage costume.
Growing up in both London and Paris, Talma was acquainted with the
theater and the philosophical thought of both countries. The relatively
"natural" acting and authenticity of costume he saw in performances by
Charles Macklin and John Philip Kemble were to have a profound
influence on his own work. After his expulsion from a suburban Paris
boarding school for promoting atheism among the students, he returned to London and joined Jean Monnet in organizing productions of
plays in French, which gained a following among the English aristocracy.
Talma would probably have gone on to become a Shakespearean actor in
English if his father had not sent him back to Paris, where he was
encouraged in his theatrical inclinations by François-René Molé. Molé,
who had been the first French Hamlet in Jean-François Ducis's 1769
adaptation from Shakespeare, had recently triumphed as Almaviva in
The Marriage of Figaro, and he got Talma admitted to the Comédie
Française's newly established speech-training institute.

Talma made his professional debut in 1787 at the Comédie Française in a small role in Voltaire's *Mahomet.* Although praised for the
emotional variety he achieved, he was trapped in minor roles by the
theater's system of seniority. In one of the boldest moves of his career, in
1789, he asked the painter Jacques-Louis David to design an authentic
Roman costume for his seventeen-line role as the tribune Proculus in
Voltaire's *Brutus.* His fellow actors, periwigged and costumed in the
traditional silk coats and breeches, were shocked by his short haircut and
the short tunic that revealed bare arms and legs. "He looks like a statue!"
one of them exclaimed, but the audience readily accepted it, and Talma
was later able to use the costume for the larger role of Titus in the same
play. Politically as well as artistically, Talma was on the side of revolution.
His inclinations in both regards found simultaneous expression when he
was cast in the title role of M. J. Chénier's historical drama *Charles IX*
(1788). Chénier, a former aristocrat who was unsuccessful in getting his
plays accepted on literary merit, had decided to harness his ambition to
the prevailing political current; his strongly anticlerical play called attention to the responsibilities of monarchy by placing the blame for the
infamous St. Bartholomew's Day massacre of 1574 directly on the king.
At about the time that the National Assembly passed the Declaration of
the Rights of Man, Danton and other patriots began demanding that the
Comédie Française produce the play. Thus Talma won his first major
role because the older, conservative actors in the company hesitated to
contribute to antiroyalist sentiments by portraying the unsympathetic
king. The premiere of *Charles IX* on November 4, 1789, was a triumph

When François Joseph Talma (1763–1826) (left) first appeared in Voltaire's Brutus *at the Comédie Française, it was in the minor role of Proculus, but his authentic Roman costume won him overnight fame. Later he played the title role, as shown here. Karl Mantzius,* A History of Theatrical Art, 6.

André Chénier's Charles IX *(right) stirred up antimonarchical and anticlerical fervor when the Comédie Française presented it in 1789. Twenty-six-year-old Talma, at center, played the title role. He is flanked by Madame Vestris and Saint-Prix in this scene from act 2.*

for Talma and for the revolutionary cause. The play soon acquired a subtitle, *The School for Kings.* Danton commented, "If *Figaro* killed the aristocracy, *Charles IX* will kill the royalty." After twenty-three performances, however, the clergy succeeded in getting the play removed from the repertoire, a serious blow to Talma, who had been assigned no other major role. Reinstatement of *Charles IX* to the repertoire became a *cause célèbre* for liberals, and Talma did his share to rally public sentiment behind it.

During the course of the following year, Talma's outspokenness on various matters created the public impression that he was a man of the people within a nest of reactionaries. This, of course, earned him the resentment of many of his fellow actors at the Comédie Française. His call for abolishing the restrictions on theater was naturally opposed by actors who relished the security of their positions in the privileged company. Not long after the January 1791 liberation of the theaters,

The final scene from Charles IX *includes a line that made a great impact during the Revolutionary period: "Heaven strikes me down as an example to kings."*

Talma and several other antiroyalists (Dugazon, Grandmesnil, Madame Vestris, Madame Desgarcins, Mademoiselle Simon, and Mademoiselle Lange) seceded from the Comédie Française and premiered a new tragedy by Chénier, *Henry VIII and Anne Boleyn,* at the theater designed by Victor Louis that had recently opened as the Variétés Amusantes. That theater now took the name Théâtre Français, which was soon changed to Théâtre de la République. Gaillard and Dorfeuil, the producers of the Variétés Amusantes, wanted to take advantage of their upscale location at the Palais Royal now that the law allowed any producer to present any kind of play. The actors were motivated only partially by their political differences with those who remained at the Comédie Française (including such illustrious names as Molé, Saint-Prix, Dazincourt, Mademoiselle Contat, and Mademoiselle Raucourt). The primary goal of the splinter group led by Talma was to play the great classical roles that had hitherto been unavailable to them.

Among the provisions of the National Assembly's decree of January 13, 1791, several of which were set forth in response to demands made by the playwrights who rallied behind Beaumarchais, were the following:

Any citizen has the right to set up a public theatre and present in it any genre of play, as long as a declaration of intention is first presented to the municipality.

The works of authors dead for five years or more are public property and may, without regard to any previously held privileges (which are now abolished) be presented in any theatre without restriction.

The works of living authors may not be presented on any public stage without the formal, written consent of the authors, under penalty of confiscation of the total receipts from such presentations, which shall be turned over to the author.

Producers and company members of the various theatres will be, by reason of their position, subject to municipal jurisdiction. They will be regulated only by municipal officials who will have no authority to stop or prohibit the performance of any play except at the request of authors or actors, and who shall make no requirements that do not conform to the law or to police regulations.

Having lost its monopoly on spoken drama, the Comédie Française faced the competition by attempting to define itself in terms of taking a stance for moderation. In January 1793, the company, now calling itself the Théâtre de la Nation, premiered a specially written play by Jean Louis Laya, an early supporter of the revolution, who now deplored its excesses. *L'Ami des lois* (The Friend of Laws) recognizably caricatured Robespierre and Marat, and it pleased the company's coterie audience. But the production became a focal point in the rivalry between the municipal government (the Commune de Paris), which decreed that the play be removed from the repertoire, and the National Convention (the extremist body that replaced the National Assembly), which invoked the law of January 13, 1791. The commune reacted by closing all theaters on the pretext of preserving public order. The convention reopened them. The Comédie Française then chose to mount a presumably safe play, François de Neufchâteau's *Pamela* (1788), based upon the English novel. However, a couplet in the fourth act preaching tolerance was denounced as royalist sentiment by the Jacobins. Within twenty-four hours, on September 3, 1793, all but three members of the Comédie Française (a total of about forty people) were arrested. They remained in prison throughout the Reign of Terror, only narrowly escaping the guillotine through the dangerous disposal of their documents by Charles de Labussière, a courageous, theater-smitten clerk in the Bureau des Pièces Accusatives.

At the height of the Terror, although dozens of theaters were active, the material of the stage was at a low ebb as the Jacobins imposed patriotic rather than artistic standards. Classics and new plays alike could be presented only if granted a certificate of "civism." Most productions were geared to arousing their audiences of *sans-culottes* to a state of revolutionary ardor, which often had them singing along or dancing on the theater seats. Unruly audiences altered the course of performances capriciously, calling out instructions to actors to repeat or change their lines, or engaging them in dialogue about the patriotic import of a scene. Jean-François Ducis, best known as France's first important translator/adapter of Shakespeare, commented in a letter upon the impossibility of sustaining a noble genre like tragedy in such an atmosphere:

> Tragedy takes to the streets. If I set foot outside my door, I wade in blood up to my ankles. It's no use wiping the dust from my shoes when I return home; like Macbeth I say: "This blood will never be wiped away!" So goodbye to tragedy. I've seen too many Atreuses in peasant clogs ever to dare put one on stage. It's a crude drama when the people play the tyrant. My friend, the only possible resolution to this drama is Hell.

Talma and his colleagues at the Théâtre de la République, however, somehow remained above suspicion while indulging in a repertoire that gave him such great roles as Rodrigue in Corneille's *The Cid* and Othello. One of their most successful productions was M. J. Chénier's *Caius Gracchus* (1792), which used a classical setting as a context for a plethora of contemporary references and gave the moderates their slogan: "Laws, not blood."

The Reign of Terror (during which about seventeen-thousand people from all stations in life were guillotined) ended with the execution of Robespierre in July 1794. One of its last victims was the brilliant lyrical poet André Chénier, older brother of the author of *Charles IX*. Only thirty-one when he was guillotined for being a revolutionary moderate, André Chénier left a substantial body of work, the best French poetry of the eighteenth century and an important influence on the romantic sensibilities of the succeeding generation. After the revolution, M. J. Chénier was stigmatized for an apparent lack of effort to save his brother. Released from prison, the members of the former Comédie Française returned to their old left-bank theater, which had been stripped of its boxes (since they signified class distinction) and renamed the Théâtre de l'Egalité. That company and Talma's troupe both experienced vicissitudes and moves from one theater to another during the aftermath of revolution. Finally, some delicate negotiations reunited both groups of players in the Théâtre Français at the Palais Royal on the site of today's Comédie Française. On May 30, 1799, they opened with *The Cid* and Molière's *School for Husbands*. Five years later the company, with Talma as its leading man, once again took the name Comédie Française.

Talma continued acting until the year of his death, 1826, often leaving the Comédie Française to tour abroad. As Napoleon's favorite actor, he was invited to the Congress of Erfurt in 1808 to perform before five crowned heads. He performed opposite Mademoiselle George at Covent Garden in London in 1817. His ever-evolving style of acting was always in the forefront of his time. At the outset of his career, he brought a relatively "natural" manner to the school of classical declamation. For a time, his acting became extremely frenzied and exhibitionistic, yet he had moments of touching depth of emotion. In his last decade, he achieved a more concentrated and focused expressiveness coupled with an increasingly subtle use of pantomimic gesture and business.

Another outstanding figure whose theatrical career closely intertwined with events of the revolution was Mademoiselle Montansier, born Marguerite Brunot, in 1730. At fifteen she went to Paris to live with her aunt, Madame Montansier, a vendor of toiletries and personal favors; she soon adopted both her aunt's name and lifestyle. One of her protectors took her to Martinique for four years. At thirty-three she decided to go into the theater and charmed the eighteen-year-old Marquis de Saint-Contest into obtaining for her the exclusive right to present plays in Nantes. After falling in love with Honoré Bourdon-Noeuville, an actor six years her junior, she became intensely involved in building up a network of provincial theaters and touring companies. With Bourdon-Noeuville serving as her business manager, she added cities like Amiens, Angers, Caen, and Le Havre to her circuit. In 1768 she established her headquarters in the town of Versailles, first renting a small theater there, and later, in 1777, building the imposing theater that still bears her name. She soon developed a close friendship with Marie-Antoinette and obtained the title *Directrice des Spectacles à la suite de la Cour;* this put her in charge of the entertainment at such royal residences as Marly and Fontainebleau. She then had the audacity to request control of every theater in the kingdom, but the king turned her down.

In 1789, when the royal family was brought to live in the Tuileries in Paris, Montansier transferred her base of operations to the capital. She had already begun buying up arcades at the Palais Royal, so she was immediately in a position to take over the debt-ridden Théâtre Beaujolais. (Delomel and Gardeur had been struggling to keep the Beaujolais going as a regular variety theater after the lieutenant general of police shut down their lucrative spectacles performed by *bamboches* [marionettes] and children.) It reopened as the Théâtre Montansier in April 1790 with a comic opera and a comedy, both of which were extremely popular. The unstoppable Montansier won a special following when she presented French versions of the works being sung in Italian at the Opera. She was not alone in ignoring the monopolies of the licensed theaters even before the 1791 abolition of theatrical privileges. However,

Left, Mademoiselle Montansier (1730–1820) was one of the most successful women entrepreneurs of all time, despite the chaotic era during which she lived. Théâtre Palais Royal (Photograph: G. Neveu).

Right, during the eighteenth century, fair entertainments turned into year-round attractions on the boulevard du Temple. The parades, short, bawdy sketches performed on elevated platforms or theater balconies remained virtually unchanged. From Louis-Sébastien Mercier, Tableau de Paris.

most of such activity was at that time concentrated on the Boulevard du Temple, which had developed into a lively entertainment center for all social classes. There, an old-fashioned fairground comedy might be seen alongside a demonstration of electricity. Even the displaced Beaujolais company turned up on the boulevard. Any entertainment entrepreneur with a good idea could enjoy a moment in the sun. One of these was a secondary-school teacher, Beffroy de Reigny, who used the pseudonym Cousin Jacques on his comic extravagances as well as the humorous literary periodical he edited. After several years of writing popular libretti for the Comédie Italienne, he was inspired by the fall of the Bastille to write patriotic spectacles celebrating the people's sense of unity in comedy, song, action, tableaux scenes, politics, morality, and humanity. The peak of his success came in 1790 with *Nicodème dans la lune, ou la Révolution pacifique* (Nicodemus on the Moon; or, the Peaceful Revolution), which ran for 150 consecutive performances at one of the boulevard theaters. The satire on rank and privilege is good-natured but unmistakable. Within the space of only three years, the fickle public was to turn from buying eighteen-inch reproductions of Cousin Jacques's bust to excoriating him for his moderation.

It was Montansier who commissioned Victor Louis in 1791 to enlarge the theater that is today the Théâtre du Palais Royal, and then to build the magnificent Théâtre National de Montansier opposite the Bibliothèque Nationale. The salon of her apartment adjoining the earlier theater became a gathering place for political and artistic celebrities. When suspected of unpatriotic activities, she mobilized eighty-five members of her company as a volunteer force in the French campaign against Austria. While they were in Belgium, from September 1792 to March 1793, she gained the controlling interest in a theater in Brussels and imposed an ultrapatriotic, anticlerical repertoire that was not to the taste of the local theatergoers. Despite such efforts, Montansier and Bourdon-Noeuville were both arrested in November 1793. Although the name of her Palais Royal theater was changed—first to Théâtre du Péristyle Jardin Egalité, then to Théâtre de la Montagne—she continued to run it from prison through intermediaries who came there to receive her instructions. She also wrote a long defense of her patriotism, which undoubtedly kept her from the guillotine. Released from prison on September 16, 1794, she learned that her Théâtre National had been given to the Opéra. While agitating for reparations, which she eventually won, Montansier made her first theater, now the Montansier Variétés, into a fashionable hub for the *jeunesse dorée*. These "gilded youths" disassociated themselves from their all-too-vivid memories of the Terror by assuming an excessive daintiness of speech and dress, by living for the moment, in pursuit of empty glamour. Every evening, young ladies in daringly low-cut gowns paraded their charms about in La Montansier's foyer.

In 1798, Montansier retired from the direction of the Montansier Variétés. The following year, at sixty-nine, she married Bourdon-Noeuville. In the Napoleonic period, she opened and managed a succession of small variety theaters, all against the grain of the grand style that Napoleon deemed appropriate to his vision of French culture. When Montansier died in 1820 at the age of ninety, she had constructed four theaters and directed twenty. Her unjust neglect in theater history may derive from the fact that her work was never associated with a strong dramatic literature. However, she set a standard of theater management that would have been exemplary even in settled times but, given the hardships she faced, was close to miraculous.

Whereas Montansier carried the burden of her royalist associations throughout the revolutionary period, Jacques-Louis David seemed to incarnate revolutionary ideals in his work even before the fall of the Bastille. His 1784 painting, "The Oath of the Horatii," demonstrates his affinity for the heroic Roman neoclassic mode that appealed to the republicans, as opposed to the *ancien régime*'s preference for the relative serenity of Greek neoclassicism. For David, painting was a medium for transmitting a social and political message; the clarity, directness, and idealism of his style was intended to appeal to the Third Estate to which he belonged. David belongs also to the history of the theater for his role as organizer of the government-sponsored revolutionary festivals in Paris.

The ten festivals held between 1790 and 1794 were designed to function almost as religious rites in unifying popular sentiment. The first of these, the *Fête de la Fédération,* held on July 14, 1790, commemorated the first anniversary of the fall of the Bastille and celebrated the federative pacts made by the French citizenry all over France during the previous winter. A procession of uniformed soldiers, musicians, and eighteen thousand federal deputies culminated in ceremonies on the Champ de Mars surrounding an "altar of the Nation." There Talleyrand said Mass accompanied by the hymns of four hundred children. An oath of federation was sworn by the king, the national hero Lafayette, the National Guard, and the deputies. Despite the municipality's failure to lift the ban on *Charles IX* at the Comédie Française so that the visiting deputies might see it, the event generated tremendous good feelings and hope for a future of peace and brotherhood. Indeed, the *Fête de la Fédération* inspired two patriotic revues by Cousin Jacques: *The Federation of Parnassus* and *Return to the Champ de Mars.*

David's direct involvement in planning the festivals began with the ceremonial reinterment of Voltaire in the Pantheon in Paris in July 1791. This event incorporated elements of the previous festival that were to become standard: a procession, an oath, and symbolic props. In this case, the sarcophagus containing Voltaire's remains was surmounted by a plaster effigy on a classical bed with a perfume-burning candelabrum at each corner; the chariot was pulled by twelve white horses. At one stop in the procession, actors costumed as characters from Voltaire's plays laid wreaths at the foot of his statue. M. J. Chénier wrote the lyrics for specially composed music by François-Joseph Gossec.

By 1792 David had been appointed official director of festivals. The *Fête des Suisses de Châteauvieux* in April 1792 emphasized the participation of workers and students with a great deal of dancing in the streets en route to the Champ de Mars. A series of funerary festivals occurred in 1792 and 1793; these made important use of the icons of revolution: the sword of justice, the *fasces* (a bundle of sticks with an axe), statues of liberty. The procession for the *Fête de l'unité et de l'indivisibilité* (or *Fête de la fraternité*) on August 10, 1793, assembled amid the rubble of the Bastille where, according to the plan presented to the convention by David, a fountain of regeneration would be raised: "When she presses her fruitful breasts with her hands, pure and healthful water will gush forth. Eighty-six deputies from the delegations of the Primary Assemblies— that is, one for each department—will drink of it. The oldest will drink first, and all will use the same cup." After all had drunk and exchanged a kiss of brotherhood, they would proceed to the next of the five designated stations for another ceremony.

The *Fête de la raison* on November 10, 1793, focused upon an actress playing the Goddess of Reason in the Notre Dame Cathedral. This renunciation of Christianity in favor of the abstract ideal of the Enlightenment was the signal for the closing of churches, many of which were subsequently converted to Temples of Reason. However, the last and most ambitious festival staged by David came as a result of Robespierre's rejection of the Cult of Reason; "The Incorruptible" proposed instead a Cult of the Supreme Being and put David in charge of a *Fête de l'Etre Suprême* celebrated on June 8, 1794. Drums, cannons, and church bells summoned Parisians to the Jardin des Tuileries in the morning, and garlands were distributed to the multitude. Robespierre gave an oration, then took up the "torch of Truth" and set fire to the cardboard statue of Atheism, which burned away to reveal a white plaster statue of Wisdom. Then the throngs marched in procession to the Champ de Mars where an artificial mountain had been erected. Several thousand people ascended to various levels on the mountain, and a tricolor flame was ignited at the summit to the accompaniment of twenty-four hundred singers. Robespierre, as the people's Moral Tutor, pronounced the republican oath. Within two months, Robespierre was sent to the guillotine, and the Reign of Terror ended.

David had often behaved as a hothead in the National Convention. It was he who called for the dissolution of the Royal Academy of Painting and Sculpture, to which he had been elected; all of the academies of arts and letters were, in his view, "the last refuge of all aristocracies." In 1794 he was arrested and spent four months in prison, but lived to become First Painter to the Emperor. Under Napoleon, David turned once again to classical subjects in the grand style. This was to be Napoleon's program for the theater as well, but the people who had lived through the Terror needed a theater of more direct impact. Once again, there was to be a gulf between literary and nonliterary theater in France.

The Romantic Impulse and Popular Offshoots

ALTERNATIVES TO NEOCLASSICISM

Challenges to the neoclassical ideal in art became insistent as early as the mid-eighteenth century. Diderot's *drame*, with its mix of tears and laughter, defied the classical notion of "purity of genre," although his new genre usually conformed to the traditional French unities of time, place, and action. Perhaps even more significant than the move toward a break with classical form were the new emphases in content introduced by Jean-Jacques Rousseau. In works like his novel of sensibility *La Nouvelle Héloïse* (1761), his educational treatise *Emile* (1762), and his pastoral operetta *Le Devin du village* (The Village Soothsayer, 1752), he dwelt upon feelings as opposed to reason, the simple pleasures of living close to nature, and freedom from the social and political constraints of overdeveloped civilization. Those tenets, like the ideas in his long-ignored political philosophy, *The Social Contract* (1762), which proclaimed the sovereignty of the people, took on new relevance after 1789. At the same time, the vision of classical Greek democracy that helped to fuel the yearnings of the people was undermined by the failure of the French Revolution. What remained was the citizenry's strong sense of national identity, which Napoleon was able to exploit in consolidating his dictatorship. That consciousness of a common heritage binding together all levels of society—in fact, deriving essentially from those closest to the land, like the French peasantry or the German *Volk*—was to become a central feature of the new aesthetic.

Besides the American and French Revolutions, there were violent attempts at revolution in Geneva in 1782, the Netherlands and Poland in 1794, Ireland in 1798, and Naples in 1799. Napoleon's wars further unsettled matters for another fifteen years. This pan-European instability and focus of energies on the possibility of change permeated the arts, with freedom as a recurring theme. The opposition between classicism and romanticism was enunciated as early as 1798–1800 by the German critic-translator A. W. von Schlegel and his brother Friedrich, who gathered a literary following at Jena to formulate the doctrine of artistic revolution against the received rules. Shakespeare was upheld as an example; the translations of seventeen of his plays into German by A. W. von Schlegel and Ludwig Tieck have remained a staple of the German stage since then. Even Weimar classicism was shaken by events like Napoleon's victory at Austerlitz in 1805, his reorganization of the German states, and his 1806 victory at nearby Jena, which opened his way to Berlin. With audiences becoming too restive for the classical repertoire, Goethe gratified them by producing eighty-seven of Kotzebue's plays of sentiment and intrigue as well as eight plays by Shakespeare.

Kotzebue's plays, like many others of the period of *Sturm und Drang* and after, often placed the action in a historical epoch. This fueled a production trend featuring "historical" sets and costumes. Most prominent in that effort was the Berlin Royal Theatre under the direction of August Wilhelm Iffland (from 1798 to 1814) and his successor Count Karl von Brühl. Iffland tended to emphasize spectacle at the expense of

Karl Friedrich Schinkel (1781–1841) designed this setting, left, of a Gothic hall with a view of the cathedral of Rheims for an 1817 production of Schiller's Maid of Orleans *at the Berlin National Theater. Schinkel,* Dekorationen an den beiden Königlichen Theatern in Berlin *(1819–1824).*

Ludwig Devrient (1784–1832), right, the greatest German Romantic actor, was renowned for passionate portrayals of the great roles in Schiller and Shakespeare. He is shown here as King Lear. Courtesy of Museum der Berliner Staatstheater.

accuracy; the best known example is his 1801 production of Schiller's *Maid of Orleans*, which included over 250 people on stage for the coronation procession scene, in "historical" costumes ranging from medieval armor to seventeenth-century ruffs at the neck. Accuracy was more important to Brühl, who directed the Berlin Royal Theatre from 1814 to 1828 and carried out his own research on historical architecture and dress. He also hired Karl Friedrich Schinkel, the finest German stage designer of the century, a romantic in his ability to evoke atmospherically the essence of a historical period and place. His most famous designs were for the Berlin Royal Theatre's 1816 production of Mozart's *The Magic Flute*.

The tension between Weimar classicism and the iconoclastic tendencies that opposed it was evident in the contrasting styles of the two leading actors at the Berlin Royal Theatre in Brühl's era. Pius Alexander Wolff had performed at Weimar from 1803 to 1816, working closely with Goethe, whose "Rules for Actors" drew upon Wolff's "idealist" approach. At Berlin from 1816 until 1828, Wolff played great tragic roles, such as Hamlet, with methodical attention to achieving aesthetic harmony and clarity. At the same time, Ludwig Devrient's exploitation of idiosyncrasies of character proved far more fascinating to audiences, despite such handicaps as his increasing alcoholism and Brühl's relegating of him primarily to the comic repertoire. Each of the five hundred roles Devrient played in his lifetime—at Breslau 1809–14, on his tours of Germany, in guest appearances like his triumphal residency at the Vienna Burgtheater in 1828, and at Berlin from 1815 until his death at forty-eight in 1832—was a distinct individual in whom a complex interplay of emotions worked just beneath the surface, occasionally to break forth in externalized passion. Devrient's great roles included Franz Moor in Schiller's *The Robbers*, Falstaff, Shylock, and King Lear. There was an unsettling quality about Devrient's anti-Weimar style, which led his admirers to describe it as "demonic" or possessed.

Rebellion against classical convention is evident in the work of the two major German playwrights of the Napoleonic period. Besides translating—and later directing—Shakespeare, Ludwig Tieck wrote loosely constructed fairy-tale plays and historical tragedies employing "romantic irony," that is, revealing the discrepancy between the ideal and the real by commenting upon, and thus destroying, the illusion of reality that the work has established. Even more successful at that technique—perhaps in part because he was more bitterly disillusioned with reality—was Heinrich von Kleist in his dramatic masterpiece, *Prinz Friedrich von Homburg* (The Prince of Homburg, 1810). Deeply troubled by political events that seemed to negate the Enlightenment's faith in reason and human perfectibility, Kleist wrote a number of plays and stories depicting aberrant personalities in an unpredictable world. His comedy *Der zerbrochene Krug* (The Broken Jug, 1805), now recognized as one of the best in the German language, failed disastrously in Goethe's production of it. Indeed, his only successfully produced play during his lifetime was *Käthchen von Heilbronn* (1808). Kleist shot himself in 1811 at the age of thirty-four.

Britain also had to mobilize against Napoleon, but a more drastic social upheaval, lasting from the 1780s to the 1830s, was brought about by the Industrial Revolution. England's unprecedented, rapid growth of an urban population led to a variety of social problems that could only gradually be addressed. Meanwhile, art could serve as an escape mechanism by expressing nostalgia for the countryside. The poetry of William Wordsworth distilled the essence of the changing times in its rejection of classical rules, its focus on "humble and rustic life" (preface to the *Lyrical Ballads*, 1798), and its outpouring of romantic feeling. Wordsworth attended the *Fête de la Fédération* in Paris in 1790 and, in his autobiographical poem *The Prelude*, expressed the rapture he had felt:

Bliss was it in that dawn to be alive,
But to be young was very Heaven!

Later he observed the process of urbanization:

At social Industry's command,
How quick, how vast an increase! From the germ
Of some poor hamlet, rapidly produced
Here a huge town.

And "oft in lonely rooms, and 'mid the din / Of towns and cities," he recalled "sensations sweet, / Felt in the blood," of simple pleasures derived from nature. Neoclassicism had never been as firmly entrenched in England as on the Continent; thus, between 1793 and 1815, when England was almost constantly at war with France, it was all the easier to turn away from the "French" aesthetic.

Also contributing to the demise of neoclassicism in England was the rise of popular literature, most notably the vogue for "Gothick romance." Horace Walpole's *The Castle of Otranto* (1764) exercised a lingering influence on the novel, poetry, and plays. Supernatural elements, gloomy castles, uncontrollable passions, and historical or geographical local color became standard features of the genre. Among the best-known examples were novels like William Beckford's *Vathek* (1786), "Monk" Lewis's *The Monk* (1796), Mary Shelley's *Frankenstein* (1818), and Sir Walter Scott's historical romances. Scott also translated Goethe's early

Sturm und Drang play *Goetz von Berlichingen* into English, and Scott's novels in turn were translated into French beginning around 1816, thus helping to prepare the public for French Romantic drama. The English fad for Gothic romance merged seamlessly with imported melodramas from Germany and France.

Popular entertainment for the urban English working-class expanded considerably in the 1800s and 1810s. A liberal interpretation of the Licensing Act of 1737 allowed new theaters to open, even in the center of London—as long as they did not encroach upon the privileges of the patent theaters, Drury Lane and Covent Garden (and, in summer, the Haymarket). However, the distinction was soon blurred between "legitimate" spoken drama (tragedy, comedy, and farce) and various "illegitimate" forms (pantomime, musical spectacles, equestrian shows like Astley's, burlesque, dumbshow melodrama, "scientific" diversions). Under the all-purpose term "burletta," minor theaters discovered that they could get away with appropriating the plots of classic plays and setting them to music, or merely adding a few songs and some scenic

Variety entertainment flourished as "illegitimate" theater in small London playhouses like this one, as illustrated by George Cruickshank in 1811.

spectacle. For the most part, however, the influence went the other way: the patent theaters lowered their standards—shifting their emphasis from dialogue to visual effects—to meet the competition. For two seasons, 1804–5, first at Covent Garden and then Drury Lane, the boy actor Master Betty took London by storm with his renditions of Hamlet, Romeo, Richard III, and other roles. His engagement at Drury Lane is said to have saved the theater from bankruptcy, but then, almost as suddenly as he had risen to fame, the "young Roscius" was a has-been at fourteen. Although such novelty seeking provided little incentive for serious authors to turn their talents to dramatic literature, the payoff was a lively, imaginative, varied theater attracting audiences from the most rapidly increasing segment of the population. This situation lasted long beyond the Regency period (1811–20) and persisted even after the Theatre Regulation Act of 1843 made it possible for any theater to present any kind of play, subject only to the lord chamberlain's censorship authority.

A similarly varied, popular theater enlivened the Boulevard du Temple and the adjoining Boulevard Saint-Martin in Paris. The entertainments there had long thrived as an alternative to "classical France" and the privileged theaters that the public jokingly called "the Romans." Within a few years after the 1791 liberation of theaters, at least twenty-three new theaters had opened on the boulevards, some venturing to tackle the long-forbidden classics, but most continuing to serve the populace with propagandistic pantomime and patriotic spectacles. When Napoleon began his rise to power in 1795, he recognized the "safety valve" function of boulevard entertainment, although his own tastes were much loftier. At first, his only restriction was to ban propaganda plays, which he thought perpetuated a spirit of factionalism. His more serious concern was to revive the classical repertoire as an emblem of France's glory—and his own. In addition, he saw classical theater as the best means of showcasing the talents of his favorite actor Talma and a young (sixteen at her debut in 1802) actress of majestic bearing, Mademoiselle George, whom he took as his mistress. After the Comédie Française was reintegrated in 1799, Napoleon reinstated its state subsidy and pensions. He took the time during his 1812 Russian campaign to review and sign the "Decree of Moscow," which still serves as that theater's basic governing document. Despite his encouragement, the classics lost audiences to the boulevard. Even Empress Josephine had to be reprimanded for attending the popular theater while he was away from Paris. After receiving the report on her activities, Napoleon wrote to her: "My dear, you must not go to the minor theaters and sit in private boxes. It is not appropriate to your rank. You must attend only the four big theaters, and always occupy the Imperial box."

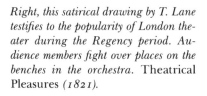

Right, this satirical drawing by T. Lane testifies to the popularity of London theater during the Regency period. Audience members fight over places on the benches in the orchestra. Theatrical Pleasures (*1821*).

This watercolor (above) from Pierce Egan's Life of an Actor (*1825*) *not only captures the dispiriting atmosphere of a sparse audience in a small provincial English theater, but also demonstrates the persistence of the eighteenth-century architectural model albeit on a small scale. Egan also wrote the book on which W. J. Moncrieff based his popular contemporary melodrama,* Tom and Jerry: or Life in London (*1821*).

Below, the importance of visual effects on the early nineteenth-century English stage is suggested by this watercolor of a backstage auction of theatrical property. Pierce Egan, The Life of an Actor (*1825*).

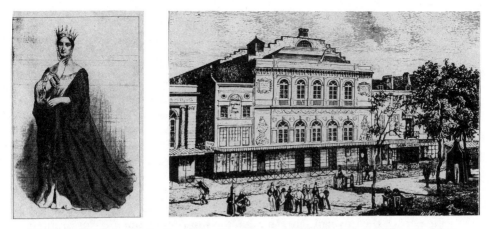

Above, left, Mademoiselle George (1787–1867), born Marguerite-Joséphine Weymer, sustained her career throughout the Napoleonic and Romantic periods. Her statuesque presence and majestic bearing were especially suited to the classical roles she played in the 1810s–20s. She is shown here in Corneille's Rodogune. Mantzius, A History of Theatrical Art, 4.

Above, right, the Théâtre de la Gaité was long a mecca of variety entertainment on the boulevard du Temple. This is its facade from 1837 to 1862. Donnet, Architectonographie des théâtres de Paris (1840).

Left, designer-machinist Chéret (1820–82) created this dazzling apotheosis for a production entitled The Aquarium *at the Théâtre de la Gaité. About twenty characters were raised up through traps in the floor while colored lights enhanced the effect. Reynaud,* Musée rétrospectif de théâtre à l'Exposition universelle international de 1900 (1900).

Right, the Odéon, built by Peyre and Wailly in 1782, burned in 1818, but was quickly reconstructed—but without the bridges on either side that had joined the theater to nearby buildings. During the Napoleonic period, the Odéon was one of the so-called "Roman" theaters. Bapst, Essai sur l'histoire du théâtre (1893).

The four big or "first class" theaters authorized by Napoleon's decree of 1807 were the Comédie Française (renamed Théâtre de l'Empéreur), the Odéon (Théâtre de l'Empératrice), the Opéra, and the Opéra Comique. By the same decree, Napoleon abolished all but four of the secondary theaters. Each of these theaters—the Ambigu Comique, Théâtre de la Gaité, Vaudeville, and Variétés—was restricted to a specific category of light entertainment. But the Théâtre de la Porte Saint-Martin, the large theater that had housed the Opéra until 1794, pleaded a special case: When the Opéra moved out, the state had sold the building at a price based upon its value as a theater property; closing it and bringing financial ruin to its owners would be an act of bad faith on the part of the government. In 1809 the minister of the interior granted it the right to reopen with a repertoire restricted to gymnastic demonstrations (rope-dancing, gladitorial combat, jousting), historical tableaux presenting great events in elaborate settings "in the manner of Servandoni," military choreography, and prologues spoken by no more than two persons. In addition, it could no longer be called a theater, but had to change its name to Les Jeux Gymnastiques. One of its first productions was *The Crossing of the Saint-Bernard Pass* with a tableau scene of Napoleon on the icy summit of a mountain, wearing his gray *redingote* and his "little corporal" hat. The public's response to this scene was overwhelmingly enthusiastic, and the piece played to full houses for four months.

The fall of Napoleon and the restoration of the Bourbon monarchy in 1815 once again freed the theaters from most restrictions. Still the Boulevard du Temple remained the popular entertainment mecca of Paris. Besides the ever-appealing melodrama, there were fairy spectacles, ballet-pantomimes, prologues, historical tableaux, equestrian dramas, optical spectacles created with panoramas and dioramas, staged combats, pyrotechnical displays, and performing animals. The atmosphere was further enlivened by street vendors and hawkers, *parades* on the front balconies of the theaters giving a taste of the pleasures that awaited inside, and a plethora of cafés. It would all come to an end in 1862 when the theaters were demolished and the boulevard redesigned as part of Georges Haussmann's urban renewal project for Napoleon III.

PANORAMAS

Among the interesting English and French alternatives to "regular" tragedy or comedy was the panorama. The idea for the panorama, a seamless landscape picture that would completely surround the viewer, was patented by an Irishman, Robert Barker, in 1787. In 1792 he opened the Panorama in London. The popularity of the series of 360-degree vistas that he exhibited there (a view of London, a view of the British fleet between Portsmouth and the Isle of Wight, etc.) launched a fad that lasted a century and spawned such variations as the diorama, neorama, cosmorama, mareorama, and stereorama. Paris got its first panorama thanks to the American engineer and inventor Robert Fulton, who was granted a license in 1799. Like Barker's panorama, Fulton's "Vista of Paris as seen from the terrace of the Tuileries Palace" was viewed from a central platform reached by a spiral stair from below. The top of the vast circular canvas was masked by a kind of parasol above the platform that let natural light fall only on the painting. To mask the bottom of the painting, Fulton improved upon Barker by placing real objects in front of it, and this also enhanced the illusion. The one-and-a-half franc entrance fee was easily afforded by the general public, and the Panorama was open continuously during daylight hours. Eventually, Paris boasted thirteen panoramas in operation at one time. Theater designer Johan Breysig opened a panorama in Berlin in 1800, and another, painted by Karl Friedrich Schinkel, opened in 1808. By catering to the nineteenth-century "appetite for visual information," simultaneously fulfilling an educational and an entertainment function, panoramas quickly became an international phenomenon.

A tourist guidebook to Paris noted that patrons of the panorama "become so absorbed in the view that they forget it is a mere illusion." This illusionistic quality appealed to the theatergoing public as an alternative to the symmetry of traditional Italian-style stage settings for plays in the classical mode. In 1822 Louis Daguerre and his assistant Charles-Marie Bouton invented the diorama, which used more than one painted canvas, those in the foreground having transparent areas backlit in various colors to project a variety of atmospheric effects. Furthermore, the auditorium could be rotated to give the illusion of movement. The logical next step—combining a panoramic setting with theatrical performance—occurred when Baron Taylor and designer Jean-Pierre Alaux opened the Panorama Dramatique on the Boulevard du Temple in 1822. They were licensed to present dramas, comedies, and vaudevilles as long as no more than two actors appeared on the stage. Although that enterprise lasted only a year, such endeavors made a lasting impact on the theater in the area of stage design. One of Pierre Ciceri's early designs for the Opéra (Auber's *La Muette de Portici*, 1828) incorporated an effect that had caused a great deal of excitement at Daguerre's Panorama in 1827: an eruption of Vesuvius. Although volcanoes had been erupting on French stages since Rameau's *Les Indes galantes* (Seduc-

This cross section of a panorama shows the viewing platform and the "umbrella" that masks the top of the circular painting from view while allowing natural light from windows in the ceiling to fall upon the panoramic vista. Hopkins, Magic, Stage Illusions and Scientific Diversions *(1897).*

Pierre-Luc-Charles Cicéri (1782–1866) established himself as the leading French scene designer by the 1810s. Most of his innovative and beautifully rendered stage settings were done for the Paris Opera. This sketch by Cicéri, with its classical architecture falling into ruin and overcome by nature, suggests the triumph of romanticism over neoclassicism. Reynaud, Musée rétrospectif de théâtre à l'Exposition universelle internationale de 1900 *(1900).*

tive India, 1735), the melodrama theaters' readiness to employ such effects added a competitive edge. Reports reached Paris that the great Italian designer Alessandro Sanquirico had achieved the most magnificent eruption of all in Pacini's *Last Day of Pompeii* (1825) at Milan's La Scala. Ciceri traveled to Italy to study the volcanic effect later described by the *Revue de Théâtre:* "Sanquirico, a man of genius, represented Vesuvius with a frightful truth and a grandeur unthinkable in France. Ingenious machinery simulated naturally the flow of the lava and the explosions of the crater, and all combined to make the scene sublime." Ciceri's eruption combined elements from both Sanquirico and Daguerre. Whether or not it equaled Sanquirico's, it "threw young ladies, children, and many journalists into ecstasy."

The work of nineteenth-century scene designers like Gué, Ciceri, Cambon, and Rubé and Chaperon shows how Italian perspective scenery's illusion of depth was replaced by a vaster "panoramic vision" based upon the sky effects achieved in the "rotundas of illusion." In the 1820s, as flat wings began to be replaced by an enclosed stage space, the traditional *bandes d'air* (cloud borders) became unacceptable. The theaters built by the earlier French "visionary architects" (Louis, Ledoux, Boullée, Lequeu, and others) had incorporated domes painted with clouds and stars to create an interior illusion of celestial spaciousness—in contrast to the flat ceilings of most English theaters of that period. Now French scene designers wanted to echo on stage the spherical shape of the theater auditorium. Thus, the sky is a prominent feature in many of their settings. Gradually the traditional painted backdrops were replaced by immense concave panoramic backcloths, forerunners of the modern sky cyclorama.

MELODRAMA

Undoubtedly the dominant form of theater throughout the nineteenth century was melodrama. Although its origins extend back to *le drame,* August von Kotzebue is usually named as the founder of the genre. Beginning with his tremendously successful *Menschenhass und Reue* (Misanthropy and Repentence, 1789), produced in 1798 at Drury Lane as *The Stranger,* he combined such popular appeals as thrilling action, sensationalistic stage effects, sentimentality, and historical and geographical exoticism. Following that first international success (*Menschenhass und Reue* was translated into ten languages; Paris alone saw 172 performances of it in six years), Kotzebue remained for at least two decades the most produced playwright in the world. Twenty-two of his plays were presented in English translation in London between 1790 and 1800, and over seventy in Copenhagen between 1801 and 1825. It is estimated that as many as half of all plays performed during most of the Moscow and St. Petersburg theater seasons from the late 1790s until 1820 were by Kotzebue; certainly his impact on Russian culture was enormous and inspired many imitators. A facile writer, Kotzebue took a variety of approaches (comedy, parody, tear-jerking bourgeois drama, patriotic spectacle), but most of his over two hundred plays can be broadly classified as melodrama. Among his most renowned were *Der Indianer in England* (The Indians in England, 1789), *Die Spanier in Peru oder Rollas Tod* (The Spaniards in Peru; or, the Death of Rolla, 1794; adapted by R. B. Sheridan as *Pizarro*, 1799), *Die Sonnenjungfrau* (The Virgin of the Sun, 1789), *Die beiden Klingsberg*, (The Two Klingsbergs, 1799), and *Die deutschen Kleinstädter* (The Small-Town Germans, 1802). Kotzebue's life was almost as colorful as his plays. At twenty he gave up his German law practice to take a civil service position in St. Petersburg, Russia. Drawn to the German-language theater there, he tried his hand, unsuccessfully—at playwriting. After discovering his dramatic formulae, he was associated at various times with the theaters in Berlin, Vienna, and Weimar. Returning to Russia in 1800, Kotzebue was mistakenly arrested and sent to Siberia for four months; he was released when the tsar appointed him director of the German Theatre in St. Petersburg. Kotzebue's hatred of Napoleon found an outlet in a succession of literary journals he founded and edited, but his increasingly reactionary political views, especially after he returned to Germany on commission for the tsar, led to his assassination by a student zealot in 1819.

A second playwright who contributed to the entrenchment of melodrama in nineteenth-century theater was René-Charles Guilbert de Pixérécourt. His family's noble status was of a fairly recent vintage when the revolution nullified it. Moreover, Pixérécourt had just completed his law studies when all the laws of the *ancien régime* were repealed. He emigrated briefly to Coblenz where he fell in love with an orphaned heiress who died at sixteen; she was to become the model for his melodramatic heroines. He based his villains upon Marat Maugier, a Jacobin opportunist in his hometown of Nancy, who used his power of life or death over local prisoners to terrorize their wives and daughters into submitting to him. Pixérécourt's early melodrama *Marat Mauger; or, The Jacobin on Mission* (1793) brought a warrant for his execution, but he escaped to Paris, the eye of the storm, and found an inconspicuous post as a clerk. As a witness to the Terror, he understood that it would take strong dramatic action and sensational effects to arouse the jaded sensibilities of the plebeian theatergoer. His career as a writer of melodrama got under way with *Victor; or, The Child of the Forest (Victor, ou l'enfant de la forêt)*, produced in 1798 at the Théâtre de l'Ambigu-Comique; but it was his seventh produced play, the long-running *Coelina, ou l'enfant du mystère* (Coelina; or, The Child of Mystery, 1800), that established his pre-eminence on the boulevard as well as that of the genre itself. "I write for those who cannot read," declared Pixérécourt. He had tapped a boundless market that soon attracted numerous other writers, the best known of whom were Louis Caigniez and Victor Ducange.

Melodrama (*mélo-drame* meaning "drama with melody") evolved out of the so-called *pantomimes dialoguées,* one of the forms of boulevard entertainment devised to circumvent the prerevolutionary restrictions on spoken drama. Those were plays of exaggerated physical action performed to musical accompaniment with only an occasional line of dialogue as needed to clarify the plot. Thus melodrama was characterized by a strong, clear-cut line of action, ordinary (nonliterary) speech, emotional variety and intensity, uncomplicated character types, comic relief, spectacular visual effects, and a morally satisfying conclusion. Melodramas were also heavily populated with piteous, innocent victims: the war-wounded, the poverty-stricken, the orphaned, and, as in *Coelina,*—subtextually recalling a time when the theater had no voice—the mute. Crime was rampant in the melodrama theater, which was sometimes referred to as "tragedy of the masses." One tabulation of the violent actions committed on the stages of the various boulevard theaters during a one-year period in the 1820s yielded the following totals: 150 suicides, 353 poisonings, 390 murders by other methods, and 491 arson attempts. The Boulevard du Temple soon earned its nickname "Boulevard of Crime."

Pixérécourt wrote about 120 plays and soon equaled Kotzebue in popularity. He also designed much of his own scenery and machinery to create such effects as an erupting volcano in *The Belvedere; or, The Valley of Etna* (1818), a flood in *Charles le Téméraire* (Charles the Bold; or, The Siege of Nancy, 1814), a forest fire in *Margaret d'Anjou* (1810), and a two-deck ship in *Christopher Columbus* (1815). His *Le Chien de Montargis* (Dog of Montargis; or, The Forest of Bondy, 1814), featured both a mute boy and a performing dog. Parisian audiences so thrilled to the animal's exploits that the ubiquitous question after the play's premiere was "Have you seen the dog?" By 1816 it had been adapted for the London and New York stages, and it spawned a host of melodramas in which an animal—for example, a magpie, a monkey, a horse, or even a pride of lions—figures in the action. London was especially receptive to "dog dramas." As early as 1803, Drury Lane had profited immensely from Frederic Reynolds's *The Caravan; or, The Driver and His Dog,* in which Carlo the dog leapt into a tub of water to save a child. A revival of such melodramas occurred in the 1850s–60s at the Bower Saloon, whose playbills carried the slogan "Everybody Going to the Dogs." There was even a production of *Hamlet* in which the prince's faithful dog killed Claudius at the end.

The first English play specifically tagged as a "Melo-Drame" was Thomas Holcroft's *A Tale of Mystery* at Covent Garden in 1802. Closely based upon Pixérécourt's *Coelina,* which Holcroft had seen in Paris, it also borrowed the French practice of using music as an emotional commentary upon the action. Holcroft's stage directions specify, for example, "Music of doubt and terror" and "Soft music but expressing first pain and alarm, then the successive feelings of the scene." This kind of orchestral accompaniment, as opposed to incidental songs, was a defining feature of early English melodrama, which soon merged with imitations of Kotzebue and Gothic romances. Holcroft's helping himself to the biggest crowd-pleaser he had seen on a trip to Paris became typical practice throughout the century, as copyright protection did not extend beyond national borders. Hundreds of examples may be found in the annals of English, American, French, German, Russian, Hungarian, Spanish, and other theaters of plays roughly translated from another language, with the names and cultural referents changed, and presented as original work.

Ironically, the two London theaters patented for legitimate drama, because of their size, were better suited to the broad gestures and spectacular effects of melodrama and pantomime. This was especially true after both burned down and were rebuilt—Covent Garden in 1809 and Drury Lane in 1812—on an even larger scale than before. They tended to use melodramas as afterpieces to the main bill. Meanwhile, the numerous minor theaters that appeared and disappeared over the years were physically suited to the spoken drama, but—until 1843—were restricted to variety entertainment. However, since melodrama was not legitimate drama, it became the staple of minor theaters like the Surrey (1809), the Royal Coburg (1818), the Adelphi (1819), the Strand (1832), and many others. Each developed a clientele for a particular kind of melodrama. In general, the minor theaters' audiences were the working poor who craved the color and excitement that was missing from their squalid lives. For them, the best melodramas mingled comedy, sentiment, and horror. The crudest offerings, mostly concentrated in London's East End, were those of the small, makeshift theaters called "penny gaffs" or "blood tubs," specializing in horrific effects.

The earliest of the many varieties of melodrama that came and went during the century were Gothick melodramas like "Monk" Lewis's *The Castle Spectre* (1797), George Colman the Younger's *Blue Beard* (1798), and James Robinson Planché's *The Vampire; or, The Bride of the Isles* (1820). Isaac Pocock's *The Miller and His Men* (1813) was the longest-running of the "bandit melodramas." James Sheridan Knowles pitched his blank-verse melodramas like *Virginius* (1820) and *The Hunchback* (1832) to a middle-class audience, but they succeeded largely as vehicles for the actor William Macready. Later in the century, Charles Kean geared the Princess Theatre toward that audience by offering "gentlemanly melo-dramas" like Dion Boucicault's *The Corsican Brothers* (1852). Douglas William Jerrold's *Black-Eye'd Susan* (1829) was a favorite among the so-called "nautical melodramas" that featured sailors, pirates, hornpipes, and patriotic sentiment. Sadler's Wells Theatre became a headquarters for nautical melodrama, as·well as other "aquatic spectacles," after Charles Dibdin the Younger installed a mammoth water tank on its stage in 1804. Closely related to the nautical melodramas were "military melo-dramas" whose titles bore the names of famous battles. Melodramas based upon actual crimes were a specialty of Edward Fitzball, who also dramatized Sir Walter Scott's novels. "Factory melodramas" like John Walker's *The Factory Lad* (1834) paralleled workers' reform movements in the 1830s–40s. The low comedian John Baldwin Buckstone wrote over 150 short plays and initiated the trend toward "domestic melodrama" with his *Luke the Labourer* (1829). This latter category extended to such midcentury melodramas as Tom Taylor's *The Ticket-of-Leave Man* (1863) and even fed into late Victorian and Edwardian plays like Henry Arthur Jones's *Mrs Dane's Defence* (1900) or Arthur Wing Pinero's *Mid-Channel* (1909). The broad range of domestic melodrama also embraced tem-perance dramas like Jerrold's *Fifteen Years of a Drunkard's Life* (1828). The latter half of the century saw a renewed proclivity for strong effects in what were now called "sensation dramas," often featuring fiendish women glorying in their villainous deeds, as in Lady Clara Cavendish's *A Woman of the World* (1858) and in the various dramatizations of Angela Braddon's novel *Lady Audley's Secret* (1863).

The stage directions of many of these melodramas testify to an energetic, larger-than-life style of acting. Actors were constantly called upon to show consternation, agitation, distress, alarm, agony, horror, astonishment, importunity, impetuousness, tremulousness, contrition, hysteria, grief, rage, delirium, and excess of joy. They fainted, writhed, recoiled, trembled, collapsed, glared, laughed wildly, gesticulated vio-lently, knelt, shrieked, shuddered, groaned, and were overcome with emotion. Similarly, the scene designer was expected to produce a variety of effects having clear and immediate impact. By midcentury it was standard practice to alternate flat painted scenes and scenes composed of practical set pieces in the same production. The flat scenes were easily shifted in view of the audience, but the scenes "in relief" had to be changed behind a curtain. This accounted for the practice of writing strong final lines on which to ring down the curtain at the end of an act.

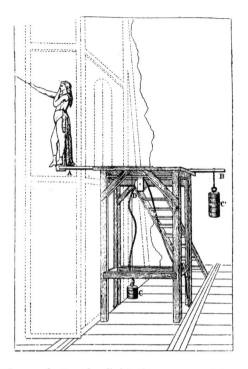

The "vampire trap" or, as the French called it, the trappe anglaise, *was a double shutter with spring hinges that was set in an apparently solid wall. If an actor pushed through quickly enough, spectators would not notice the opening of the shutters.* Moynet, Trucs et décors (*1885*).

Among the many mechanical devices invented to enhance the melodrama were various kinds of traps: The "Vampire trap," developed for Planché's *The Vampire,* consisted of two flaps on springs in a piece of scenery, making it appear that the actor had walked through a solid wall. The "Corsican trap" or "ghost glide," first used in *The Corsican Brothers,* was a concealed slot in the stage floor through which an actor rose while crossing on a wheeled platform. Elevators, treadmills, scrims, and, by midcentury, gas lighting and limelights added to the stage technician's bag of tricks.

AMERICAN MELODRAMA

Although the heyday of American melodrama was the second half of the nineteenth century, it is possible to class virtually all American drama of the century as melodrama. Kotzebue's plays were known to

American audiences, beginning with William Dunlap's enthusiastically received adaptation of *The Stranger* at the Park Theatre in 1798. Within two seasons, Dunlap had adapted and produced eighteen plays by Kotzebue, winning special favor with *False Shame; or, The American Orphan in Germany* (1799). Putting the word *American* into the title of Kotzebue's *Falsche Scham* (1796) was also astute on Dunlap's part, as the romantic spirit that made Americans so receptive to melodrama derived in large measure from a desire to define a distinctive American cultural identity. Although some have thought that the development of the arts in the United States was retarded by a national inferiority complex, a tacit acknowledgment of the cultural superiority of anything British, there was at the same time a plethora of plays featuring "Yankee" characters and even actors like James Henry Hackett who specialized in portraying the stage Yankee. Other popular subjects for plays in the 1810s to 1840s included the American Revolution, the War of 1812, Native American Indians, and the opening up of the American frontier. The form may have followed European models, but the content certainly reflected interest in the self-made man, transcending social and political restraints, and seeking adventure in unexplored territory. This was the stuff of early American romantic melodrama.

Pizarro, Sheridan's adaptation of Kotzebue, figured prominently in the repertoire of the first important touring company on the American frontier, that of Samuel Drake. (Indeed, David Grimsted's statistical ranking of plays performed in the major American cities shows *Pizarro* in first place from 1800 to 1816, and in second place from 1816 to 1831.) In 1815 Drake's company made the six-month journey (including three months in Pittsburgh to earn money for the rest of the trip) from Albany to Kentucky by horse-drawn wagon, flatboat, and on foot. The scenery they transported consisted of six roll drops (woods, street, parlor, kitchen, palace, garden), three sets of wings (exterior, fancy interior, plain interior), a painted drapery that could serve as a proscenium in any size of hall, and a green baize carpet. They found a receptive market. Lexington's amateur theatricals had already prompted that city to call itself "the Athens of the West." Louisville's population of three thousand sustained the company through ten weeks of full-house performances. Drake spent the next fifteen years building up his theatrical circuit in the Ohio Valley. A member of "Old Sam" Drake's original troupe, Noah Ludlow, left in 1817 to form his own company. Ludlow's was the first English-language company in predominantly French-speaking New Orleans. He opened up remote areas of the west and south to theater. In partnership with Sol Smith, Ludlow built a 1,000-seat "Temple of the Muses" (1837) in the rugged frontier town of St. Louis. According to the moral code announced by Ludlow and Smith, they would "refuse admit-

John Searle's 1822 watercolor of the interior of the Park Theatre includes portraits of fashionable New Yorkers in the audience, all of whom can be identified. The original Park Theatre, built in 1798, burned in 1820, but was quickly rebuilt as shown here, with the proscenium doors fitted into the elegant curve of the proscenium arch. Stars of the English and American stage performed here, giving the Park its reputation as the leading American theater of the 1820s and 1830s. Destroyed by fire in 1848, it was not replaced. Courtesy of the New-York Historical Society, New York City.

tance to any female who did not come attended by a gentleman, or someone having the appearance of a man of respectability, not even in the third tier."

Another pioneering theatrical entrepreneur, James H. Caldwell, took it upon himself to organize a municipal gas company for New Orleans so that he could build the first gas-illuminated theater in America, the Camp Street Theatre (1824). He also built the St. Charles Theatre of New Orleans (1835), by far the most luxurious theater anywhere in America. William Chapman's Floating Theatre was a flatboat that docked for nightly performances of Kotzebue or Shakespeare as it floated downriver from Pittsburgh to New Orleans. At the end of the line, Chapman would sell the boat for firewood, take a steamboat back upriver, build another flatboat, and start the cycle again. He did this from 1831 to 1835, when he could finally afford to buy a steamboat with a twenty-foot-wide stage, so he could ply the river in both directions. This was the prototype for the Mississippi showboats that flourished after the Civil War.

Among the best of the early American melodramas, *She Would Be a Soldier; or, The Plains of Chippewa* (1819) by Mordecai M. Noah brings together in a tightly plotted piece a spirited heroine who disguises herself as a soldier, a noble Indian chief, and caricatures of a Frenchman, a foppish Englishman, and an American yokel. Capitalizing on public interest in the War of 1812, it used songs, dances, a military display, and a last-minute rescue to good effect. In his preface, Noah deplored "prejudices against native productions," and predicted: "We will succeed in time, as well as the English, because we have the same language, and equal intellect." Although John Howard Payne chose a classical subject for his *Brutus; or, The Fall of Tarquin* (1818), its sensationalism places it squarely in the category of melodrama. It first won acclaim in a Drury Lane production, opened in New York several months later, and remained an American favorite for the rest of the century. Payne's effort to promote American drama began with his publication of a journal, *The Thespian Mirror* in 1805, when he was fourteen, the same year that he made his acting debut at New York's Park Theatre. He wrote fifty or sixty plays, many of them adapted from French originals by Pixérécourt and Scribe. Another successful author of melodrama was James Nelson Barker, who wrote *The Indian Princess* (1808), a musical treatment of the Pocahontas legend; *Marmion* (1812), a focus for anti-British sentiment during the War of 1812; and *Superstition; or, The Fanatic Father* (1824), with its masterfully portrayed eloquent villain, Reverend Ravensworth.

Two especially capable authors of melodrama came to the fore when they won prizes in the series of nine playwriting contests sponsored by the actor Edwin Forrest, who was seeking new American plays to suit his passionate, energetic acting style. The first contest was announced in 1828: "To the author of the best Tragedy in Five Acts, of which the hero or principal character shall be an aboriginal of this country, the sum of five hundred dollars and half of the proceeds of the third representation, with my own gratuitous services on that occasion. The award to be made by a committee of literary and theatrical gentlemen." John Augustus Stone's *Metamora; or The Last of the Wampanoags* (1829), the first prize winner, gave Forrest, in the title role of the "noble savage" who lives and dies free of the "white man's bondage," one of the great roles of his career. Stone won the competition again in 1833 with *The Ancient Briton*. The second most successful play to come out of Forrest's competition was *The Gladiator* (1831), dramatizing the story of the slave uprising led by Spartacus against the Romans, by Robert Montgomery Bird. Bird also garnered prizes with *Oraloosa: Son of the Incas* (1832) and *The Broker of Bogota* (1834), but apart from the prize money he got no share of the fortune Forrest made on the plays, nor would Forrest allow Bird to publish his plays. Bird later commented that it was the inadequate copyright protection that stopped him from further pursuing his promising career as a dramatist.

James K. Paulding made a name for himself as a defender of

One of the great roles of Edwin Forrest (1806–72), left, was that of the noble American Indian chief Metamora in the 1829 play of that title by John Augustus Stone (1800–1834). Engraving by T. Johnson from the Brady photograph, in The Autobiography of Joseph Jefferson.

James Henry Hackett (1800–1871), right, won renown for his Yankee characters as well as frontiersmen like this one, Nimrod Wildfire in The Lion of the West *(1831) by James K. Paulding (1778–1860). Scribner's Monthly (July 1879).*

Davy Crockett (*1872*), *a frontier melodrama by Frank Murdoch, was performed over two thousand times by Frank Mayo (1839–96). The high point of the action occurred when wolves were heard outside the cabin where Crockett was sheltering the heroine. Having burned the door's wooden bar to warm her, he uses his arm as a door latch throughout the night while the wolves howl and thrust their heads through openings in the cabin walls.* Scribner's Monthly (*July 1789*).

American intellectual independence in the *Salmagundi* papers (1807), witty commentaries on New York fads and foibles, which he coauthored with Washington Irving. His 1831 comic melodrama *The Lion of the West* introduced a backwoodsman as hero. The role of Colonel Nimrod Wildfire, based upon the character and exploits of Davy Crockett, stood for the self-taught, uncorrupted, free-spirited American individualist, and provided James Henry Hackett with one of his best roles. Another successful realization of an American type was Jonathan Ploughboy in Samuel Woodworth's *The Forest Rose; or American Farmers* (1825). Louisa Medina's *Nick of the Woods* (1838) achieved the longest run of the many profitable adventure-melodramas she wrote for New York's Bowery Theatre under the management of Thomas S. Hamblin in the 1830s. Anna Cora Mowatt's *Fashion* (1845) twined a melodramatic subplot into its social satire; the timelessness of her good-natured mockery of social pretensions made this, in the twentieth century, the most frequently revived pre–Civil War American play.

Melodrama came into its own with the phenomenal success of *Uncle Tom's Cabin* (1853). The earlier American plays had not been particularly identified with the facile popular appeals of the genre, but an increasing appetite for entertainment across the country and a growing number of troupes on the road unabashedly established melodrama as the dominant genre. From Harriet Beecher Stowe's sincere effort "to awaken sympathy and feeling for the African race as they exist among us, to show their wrongs and sorrows, under a system so necessarily cruel and unjust," dozens of dramatizations were made. She had argued against her novel's dramatization on the basis that theater was held in such low regard that it would negate the moral purpose of her work. In actuality, according to the approbatory reviews of the George L. Aiken dramatization that opened in New York on July 18, 1853, *Uncle Tom's Cabin* not only made the stage "an agent for the cause of abolition," but contributed to making the theater itself respectable, as Quakers, Baptists, and others "of the straight-laced school" were glimpsed among the audiences that cheered and wept in alternation.

The first stage version of *Uncle Tom's Cabin* that opened in New York in 1852 was disparaged for its "overdrawn caricatures" and "bad taste," but Aiken's sensitive shaping of the complex, episodic work maintained its moral integrity as it drew together the basic appeals of melodrama: an archvillain in the brutal Simon Legree, suffering of the innocent as represented by Little Eva and Uncle Tom, the thrill of the chase in Eliza's desperate flight carrying her baby across the ice floes on the Ohio River while pursued by dogs, comic relief provided by the lovable Topsy, and poetic justice in the death of Legree and the apotheosis of Uncle Tom. Aiken's dramatization was soon given three performances a day, eighteen performances a week, while competing versions were also filling four other theaters in New York. The superiority of Aiken's version was augmented by the Howard family's performance of it; five-year-old Cordelia Howard's touching portrayal of Little Eva made her an overnight star. Cordelia's mother, Mrs. George C. Howard, played Topsy. At that time, black characters were always played by whites in blackface. However, Errol Hill sees the play as an agent for the admission of black performers to mainstream theater in that some post–Civil War touring companies of *Uncle Tom's Cabin* employed blacks as chorus members to sing and dance plantation songs. With so many "Tommers" touring various versions of the play at any given time, it may be said to have had a continuous stage life of ninety years, that is, until World War II. In the 1890s there were reportedly up to five hundred companies of Tommers playing towns of all sizes, perhaps borrowing the local mongrels to chase an Eliza who clutched a piece of meat wrapped in a blanket to draw them after her as she traversed the ice floes represented by soapboxes painted white.

A leading figure in American melodrama was the Irish-born Dion Boucicault. His first play, *London Assurance* (1841), written when he was nineteen, premiered successfully at London's Covent Garden. He also resided for a time in France, and the French melodrama became a source of quite a few of the four hundred plays he wrote. In 1853 he came to America, managed a company, and wrote his most popular melodramas: *The Poor of New York* (1857), *The Octoroon* (1859), *The Colleen Bawn* (1860), and *The Shaughraun* (1874). He had a highly developed theatrical sensibility that balanced clever twists of plot with spectacular scenic effects and, especially in his "Irish" plays, atmospheric details of local color. Despite his proclivity for borrowing from other sources, Boucicault worked hard to win passage of an American copyright law in 1865.

Certain melodramas held the stage through their close identification with particular performers. This was the case with Adah Isaacs Menken in *Mazeppa,* an equestrian melodrama that had premiered in London in 1823. Menken caused a sensation in 1861 when she first appeared in the male role of Mazeppa, exposing more of a woman's body than had ever been publicly seen in San Francisco. In the big scene, Mazeppa is stripped naked and tied to the back of a horse that gallops wildly through storms, menaced by vultures and wolves, before Mazeppa is rescued by his fellow countrymen of Tatary. Everywhere she toured in the role, including London and Paris, Menken's flesh-colored tights and bit of drapery proved even more of an attraction than the live horse galloping on a treadmill.

Dion Boucicault's dramatization of *Rip Van Winkle* (1865) became a star vehicle for Joseph Jefferson III, who fleshed out the bare-bones script with humorous business. In 1881 Jefferson estimated that he had played the role 2,500 times and was still discovering new "character" touches; it remained the centerpiece of his repertoire until his retirement in 1904. James O'Neill began playing Edmond Dantès in Charles Fechter's dramatization of *The Count of Monte Cristo* in 1883 and it took over his life, as public demand kept him in the role for thirty years.

As the American theater embraced an ideal of greater realism on the stage in the 1870s and after, it becomes difficult—especially from a twentieth-century perspective—to make a distinction between serious drama and melodrama. Augustin Daly produced a variety of comedies and dramas in New York, but as a playwright he is best remembered for his melodrama *Under the Gaslight* (1867). James A. Herne's 1890 masterpiece of social realism, *Margaret Fleming,* is not far from sentimental melodrama. *Hazel Kirke* (1878), Steele MacKaye's tale of a virtuous woman duped into a false marriage, was echoed in Lottie Blair Parker's *Way Down East* (1897). Actor William Gillette wrote much of his own material, most notably the Civil War spy melodrama *Secret Service* (1895) and his melodramatic signature piece *Sherlock Holmes* (1899). The leading turn-of-the-century producer David Belasco was an unabashed seeker of sentiment and sensation in his plays like *The Heart of Maryland* (1895) and *The Girl of the Golden West* (1905). Outstanding dramatists like Bronson Howard, Clyde Fitch, and William Vaughn Moody must be said to have at least flirted with melodrama even if they did not go to the extremes of Owen Davis's *Nellie, the Beautiful Cloak Model* or Theodore Kremer's *Bertha, the Sewing Machine Girl*. Actress-manager-playwright Lillian Mortimer gave herself the mission of reviving old-fashioned moral melodrama in the early decades of the twentieth century, but she never surpassed her 1905 success, *No Mother to Guide Her*. Although little of timeless value remains from the golden age of American melodrama, it must be credited with broadening the base of the American theatergoing public at a crucial time in the nation's cultural development.

ROMANTICISM IN THE THEATER

In many respects, melodrama and romantic drama were two sides of the same coin. Romantic drama was melodrama disguised as literature. Melodrama prepared the way for romantic drama, which set itself apart from the lower form largely by its use of more elevated language and by its adherence to the classical five-act structure as opposed to melodrama's one to three acts. Because of its literary pretensions, romantic drama could not flower until it had a theoretical basis. This may explain why the English Romantic drama seems less "romantic" than what came later on the Continent. When the English romantic poets wrote their plays, they were distilling impulses that were as yet unrefined by extensive discussion and debate.

Friedrich Schlegel's use of the term "romantic" around 1800 conveniently embraced whatever was the opposite of "classical." If neoclassicism meant regularity, objectivity, emotion controlled by reason, tightness of literary construction or pictorial composition, purity of genre, and aesthetic discipline, then the romantic artist's rebellion expressed itself in freedom from established convention, subjectivity, emotion overruling reason, episodic or sprawling configurations, abrupt shifts of mood and tone, and unfettered imagination. Given those parameters, melodrama and Shakespeare's plays alike are romantic. But the term gained currency more and more with reference to the self-conscious artistic revolution that swept Europe in the early decades of the nineteenth century. The French writer Charles Nodier had picked it up by 1820: "Romantic poetry springs from our agony and our despair. This is not a fault in our art, but a necessary consequence of the advances made in our progressive society." When the term acquired a capital *R*, it applied specifically to the artistic movement that began in Germany with A. W. Schlegel's Jena circle and ended—at least in literature and the fine arts, if not in music—in the 1840s.

Goethe's *Faust, Part I* and several of Schiller's historical tragedies, especially *Don Carlos* and *Maria Stuart,* served as early models for literary Romantic drama as the concept spread across Europe. But perhaps the single most important German romantic work for the theater was the opera *Der Freischütz* (1821) by Carl Maria von Weber. The title refers to the "free-shooter" Max, who goes at midnight to the eerie Wolf's Glen to mold seven magic bullets. The demon Zamiel guarantees that those bullets will always hit their mark, thus enabling Max to win the shooting match and claim his bride Agathe. The sinister musical evocation of the supernatural element in the Wolf's Glen dramatically extended the range of operatic music. This, combined with the romantic love interest, the comic folk elements, and the visual power of the moonlit forest scene, made of *Der Freischütz* a virtual compendium of major romantic motifs, and it was the first such work that truly succeeded on the stage. The enthusiasm that greeted its premiere in 1821 at the Berlin Royal Theater brought an end to the German musical stage's long domination by Italian opera. Although *Der Freischütz* failed in Paris in 1824, it quickly established itself in the repertoires of Nordic countries. It premiered in Copenhagen in 1822, for example, and Hans Christian Andersen's theater diary shows that he attended a number of productions of it.

Romanticism came easily to Denmark, championed by the great poet-playwright Adam Oehlenschläger. By 1802 Oehlenschläger had fallen under the influence of Goethe and the Jena Romantics in addition to that of the leading Danish dramatic poet of the previous generation, Johannes Ewald. Although molded by French neoclassicism, Ewald gave free rein to the emotions in his lyric poetry; his study of Shakespeare informed his plays thematically. Ewald's heroic verse tragedy *Balders Død,* (Balder's Death, 1778), with its atmospheric mountain setting, initiated a Nordic Gothic tradition in Danish drama which Oehlenschläger would inherit. Oehlenschläger wrote over thirty plays between 1802 and 1845, but one play above all established his important place in Danish romantic drama: *Hakon Jarl* (1808). This five-act patriotic tragedy pitted the larger-than-life Viking-age title character against Christian invaders who arrive in a boat that glides onstage through a painted sea. The verbal power and savage pictorial beauty of his Nordic sagas established Oehlenschläger as second only to Holberg in his importance to Danish drama.

More varied in his dramatic style was Hans Christian Andersen, who remains best known for his fairy tales despite his overwhelming commitment to theater both as a playgoer and playwright, and later as drama-turg for Copenhagen's first authorized private theater, the Casino (1848). Besides his early tragedies, vaudevilles, operas, singspiels, fairy plays, and comedies, Andersen wrote several Romantic dramas. Whereas Oehlenschläger had been formed by the German Romantics and even visited Goethe in Weimar, Andersen inclined toward French Roman-ticism and became a friend of Victor Hugo. His greatest success in that vein was *Mulatten* (The Mulatto, 1840). The exotic local color of the Martinique setting—with scenes in a tropical jungle, a prison, a ball-room, and at an emotion-packed slave auction—was somewhat haphaz-ardly suggested by the mix of painted and practical scenery, old stock and new scenic units, brought together for the production, according to the standard practice of the day.

After Germany and Denmark, the earliest artists who can be called Romantic surfaced in England, and they were primarily poets. William Blake and Robert Burns ran interference for the movement, followed by first-generation Romantics William Wordsworth, Sir Walter Scott, and Samuel Taylor Coleridge. The *Oxford English Dictionary* records that in 1812 Coleridge spoke of classifying poetry into ancient and romantic, and in 1814 *The Monthly Review* divided European poetry into two schools, the classical and the romantic. The second generation of Ro-mantics, Lord Byron, Percy Bysshe Shelley, and John Keats—reached their peak of activity by the early 1820s, a decade before the triumph of Romanticism in France. Unlike the major Romantic writers of France, Spain, and Russia, the English poets did not contribute significantly to the stage. It was long traditional to attribute this to a lack of interest on their part, but some evidence suggests that they would have welcomed the kinds of opportunities and more favorable theatrical conditions that allowed their continental contemporaries to develop their dramatic craftsmanship through practice. The fact that London's patent theaters were abnegating their responsibility to provide a high standard of legiti-mate theater must surely have contributed to this unfortunate gap in English dramatic literature.

Wordsworth's *Lyrical Ballads* is usually signaled as English Roman-ticism's initial publication. To Wordsworth's emphasis on feelings and nature, Coleridge added, in his poem *The Rime of the Ancient Mariner,* the theme of society's outcast and an element of the supernatural. With Robert Southey, Coleridge wrote a historical drama *The Fall of Robespierre* (1794) as a study of the French Revolution's orators, whom he called its "chief actors on a vast stage of horrors." It did not get produced, but Coleridge tried again with *Osorio* (1797), which Drury Lane at first rejected, but later staged—for a run of twenty performances, and an 1817 revival—in a revised version entitled *Remorse* (1813). In 1800 Coleridge translated Schiller's *The Piccolomini* and *The Death of Wallenstein.* His last play, *Zapolya* (1815), based upon *The Winter's Tale,* was rejected by both Drury Lane and Covent Garden. According to Coleridge: "I was informed that it would not do as a Play; but that it would answer very well as a Melodrama with some slight alteration. That this slight alteration consisted in omitting all that was of any value in the Piece did not give me a moment's concern." Even though his willingness to cut and revise *Remorse* for the Drury Lane production had earned him the epithet "the amenable Author," Coleridge was given no such opportunity with *Zapolya.* It was made into a melodrama by another hand and presented at the Royal Circus and Surrey Theatre in 1817.

Wordsworth showed no interest in writing for the stage after Covent Garden *"judiciously* returned" his only play, *The Borderers* (1796). Certainly his French-Revolution-inspired attempt in dramatic verse to examine the qualities in human nature that cause men of good intentions to commit evil deeds offered little that was stageworthy. Sir Walter Scott simply refused to write for the theater, despite Lord Byron's invitation to him on behalf of Drury Lane. Scott's reasons, as expressed in a 1819 letter to Southey, included his unwillingness to put himself at the mercy of "low, ill-informed and conceited actors," and his indifference to the kind of people who comprised the London theater audience: "One half come to prosecute their debaucheries so openly that it would degrade a bagnio. Another set snooze off their beef-steaks and port wine; a third are critics of the fourth column of the newspaper; fashion, wit and literature there is not."

Lord Byron, in contrast, loved the theater. He organized and acted in amateur theatricals all his life, and read about five hundred plays while serving on Drury Lane's Committee of Management from 1812 until his final departure from England in 1816. But it was only in exile that he began writing his own historical dramas: *Manfred* (1817), *Cain* (1821), *Marino Faliero* (1821), *Sardanapalus* (1821), *The Two Foscari* (1821), and the melodrama *Werner* (1821). He deliberately flouted theatrical techniques, although he understood them well, preferring to write what he called "mental theatre" for the reader. Of *Manfred* he commented: "I have at least rendered it *quite impossible* for the stage." And in his preface to *Marino Faliero,* he wrote: "I have had no view to the stage; in its present state it is, perhaps, not a very exalted object of ambition." But in 1820 Drury Lane presented an unauthorized and heavily adapted *Marino Faliero,* the only one of his plays performed during his lifetime. Three others met the test of the stage in the 1830s when William Charles Macready performed them. *Werner* proved especially gratifying in its scope for Macready's ability to communicate shades of emotion. *Sardanapalus* had several nineteenth- and twentieth-century revivals.

Karl Maria von Weber's Romantic opera Der Freischutz *(1821) exercised its visual and musical influence all over Europe as suggested by this atmospheric setting for the Wolf's Glen scene in the 1851 London production.* Illustrated London News *(1850).*

Right, the eminent tragedian William Charles Macready (1793–1873) made a success of three of Lord Byron's rather static but atmospherically romantic plays. Macready is shown here in the title role of Werner *(1821). The Victoria and Albert Museum Picture Library.*

Greatly influenced by Shakespeare and daring in its use of the theme of incest, *The Cenci* (1819) by Percy Bysshe Shelley was not produced until 1886. Shelley had pinned his best hopes for production on that play, calling it "expressly written for theatrical exhibition" and "singularly fitted for the stage." Indeed, *The Cenci* has had a number of revivals and is thought by some to be the best of the English Romantic dramas. Shelley also wrote two political satires, translated plays by Euripides, Calderón, and Goethe, and wrote two "lyrical dramas" on classical themes, *Prometheus Unbound* (1820) and *Hellas* (1821), but received no encouragement from the theater for any of these endeavors. John Keats completed only one play, a historical drama *Otho the Great* (1819), which at least piqued the interest of Drury Lane, but was not performed in his lifetime.

Whether it was the fault of poets who took themselves too seriously or of a theater that did not take itself seriously enough, the romantic aesthetic did not produce a drama that was both literary and stageworthy. It did, however, contribute to a strong nineteenth-century revival of Shakespeare production, which—along with melodrama—provided a base for Romantic acting. Edmund Kean embodied the passion and unpredictability of romanticism in both his private and stage lives. He had grown up in the theater, performing as an acrobat, singer, dancer, and mime, under the name Master Carey. At his adult debut in 1814 at Drury Lane, he broke with convention by portraying a suave black-bearded Shylock as opposed to the traditional figure of fun in a red Judas wig. The box office soon reflected his triumph in that role as well as others like Richard III, Othello, Iago, and, perhaps best of all, Macbeth. Kean was always to excel as villains who give way to maniacal passions. He threw himself without restraint into such roles, using rapid emotional transitions and vivid facial expressions to achieve an effect that Coleridge likened to "reading Shakespeare by flashes of lightning." The two great theater critics of the period, William Hazlitt and Leigh Hunt, both extolled Kean's intensity and declared him superior to all other tragedians. Hazlitt wrote of Kean's Macbeth after the murder of Duncan: "The hesitation, the bewildered look, the coming to himself when he sees his hands bloody, the manner in which his voice clung to his throat and choked his utterance, his agony and tears, the force of nature overcome by passion—beggared description. It was a scene which no one who saw it can ever efface from his memory." But the emotionally unstable Kean was ill-equipped to handle his success, and his heavy drinking took its toll within a few years. In 1825, he suffered the humiliation of a sensational trial when the most serious of his numerous affairs—with Charlotte Cox, wife of a city alderman who was also a member of the Drury Lane committee—ended with her husband's dis-

The dramatic intensity of Edmund Kean's romantic acting is suggested in this portrait of him as Coriolanus. Mantzius, A History of Theatrical Art, 4.

Right, Kean's passionate acting of roles like Othello promoted the Shakespeare revival in England. Century Magazine *(August 1911).*

covery of Kean's love letters, all of which were read in court to the public's delectation. In 1833 Kean collapsed during the third act of his performance of Othello opposite his son Charles Kean's Iago; after lingering near death for seven weeks, his brandy ever at his bedside, he died at forty-four.

Kean was briefly rivaled in the Romantic style of acting by Junius Brutus Booth, who made his debut at Covent Garden in 1817. The suggestion that he might be imitating Kean long rankled with Booth, although he held his own in performances opposite Kean at Drury Lane in 1820. John Howard Payne saw Booth play Iago to Kean's Othello and described it as an extraordinary trial of skill. In 1821, with no advance preparation, Booth sailed for the United States, which became his permanent home. For his American debut, he announced that he would play Richard III on alternate nights in his own style and in Kean's style. This romantic individualism pleased American audiences. Booth was truly an original and compelling actor, but frequently subject toward the end of his career to fits of erratic, even manic, behavior both on stage and off. He died in 1852, leaving three sons to carry on the Booth name in American theater.

Above, left, Junius Brutus Booth (1796–1852) was Kean's closest rival in the energetic Romantic acting style. He is shown here as the comic villain Sir Giles Overreach in Phillip Massinger's A New Way to Pay Old Debts. Century Magazine *(January 1890).*

Above, right, following his 1821 American debut as Richard III, Junius Brutus Booth devoted the rest of his career to the American stage. Three of his sons—Junius Brutus, Jr., Edwin, and John Wilkes—became important actors. Century Magazine *(November 1889).*

Fanny Kemble (1809–93), shown here as Juliet, enchanted audiences in her native England and on tour in America in the 1830s. Mantzius, A History of Theatrical Art, 6.

Fanny Kemble, a niece of Sarah Kemble Siddons and John Philip Kemble, also developed a passionate romantic style of acting in contrast to the classical style of the other Kembles. She made her debut at Covent Garden as Juliet in 1829 and toured to America with her father, Charles Kemble, in 1832. Her marriage to Pierce Butler, a handsome, wealthy American, proved disappointing; the *Journal* she later published reveals her shock at the poor treatment of the slaves on his plantation. After her divorce, she supported herself in England and America by her public readings of Shakespeare.

Although lacking Kean's charismatic presence and always resentful that he had been forced by economic necessity into the theatrical profession against his inclinations, William Charles Macready gained a strong following by the high standards he upheld in his own performances and in the productions under his management at Covent Garden, 1837–39, and at Drury Lane, 1841–43. He rivaled Kean in tragic roles like Hamlet, Macbeth, and Lear; he pointed the way back to Shakespeare's

William Charles Macready always resented having been forced into theater by economic necessity, but he contributed much to the art of the stage and was an excellent actor. Here he appears as Rob Roy. Mantzius, A History of Theatrical Art, 6.

original texts, purging them of two centuries' tampering; and he promoted historical accuracy in sets and costumes. His interest in the scenic evocation of historical period, geographical locale, and poetic mood exemplified the strongly visual orientation of the Romantic aesthetic in English theater. It was manifested especially in the work of scene designers like the Grieve family or Clarkson Stanfield, who excelled at painting the romantic picturesque or dramatic landscapes and seascapes. That influence would continue in efforts like the "antiquarian" productions of Charles Kean at the Princess Theatre in the 1850s, showing the same concern for historical accuracy that Count von Brühl had pioneered in Berlin in the 1820s.

Both Edmund Kean and William Charles Macready toured to

America in the 1820s, both with unfortunate results. In 1820–21 Kean performed to sellout houses in New York, Philadelphia, Boston, and Baltimore. His success prompted him to book a return engagement in Boston in May, when the season was virtually over. Seeing only a handful of people in the house for his third performance there, he refused to go on. Bostonians were insulted, especially after Kean published an "apology" implying that American audiences could not appreciate his art. The resentment lingered to cloud the beginning of a second American tour four years later, but gradually Kean regained theatergoers' good will—except in Boston. In Albany, Kean's expressed admiration for the nineteen-year-old local actor assigned to play Iago opposite his Othello launched the career of the great American Romantic actor Edwin Forrest.

Macready made three tours to the United States between 1826 and 1849. His American debut at New York's Park Theatre happened to coincide with Edwin Forrest's engagement at the Bowery Theatre in many of the same roles, which led to the press's manufacture of a bitter rivalry between the two actors. Hostilities erupted during Macready's third tour twenty-three years later, when again both actors were performing in New York, Macready at the Astor Place Opera House and Forrest at the Broadway Theatre. In a series of letters to the newspaper, Forrest had attempted to stir up antipathy toward Macready, and theatergoers tended to divide along class lines into two opposing camps: those who rallied behind Forrest out of patriotic sentiment versus genteel New Yorkers who deplored the display of bad manners toward a distinguished foreign guest. The New York *Herald* commented that "as Americans, we prefer the unsophisticated energy of the daring child of nature to the more glossy polish of the artificial European civilization." Macready's opening performance of *Macbeth* was disrupted by fifty or so organized rioters who shouted and threw eggs, potatoes, and other items while Macready, maintaining his dignity, gave a virtually inaudible performance of the first two acts. When the mob began throwing chairs in the third act, Macready canceled the rest of the performance. He intended to cancel his engagement, but gave in to a written appeal signed by forty-seven prominent New Yorkers, and offered *Macbeth* again on May 10, 1849. During that performance, a mob of several thousand—largely composed of Bowery Boys and other toughs, drawn by handbills challenging "workingmen" to "express their opinion this night at the English Aristocratic Opera House"—gathered on Astor Place. Some began throwing stones to break the windows of the opera house. The militia first fired above the crowd's heads, but when attacked with paving stones, they fired into the crowd. Thirty-one were killed and about 150 wounded. Macready escaped and returned by the next steamer to England.

Bowery Boys or "soap-lorks" loiter in front of a profusion of theatrical advertisements in this 1847 watercolor by Nicolino Calyo. The area around New York's Bowery gained a reputation as a "tough" neighborhood with successive waves of immigrants settling there. Courtesy of the New-York Historical Society, New York City.

Edwin Forrest had grown up in a tough neighborhood of Philadelphia. His schooling ended when he was ten, as he had to take various odd jobs to help support his family. Attending his first play at thirteen, at the old Southwark Theatre, he knew he had found his calling. He hung about theaters, gaining whatever experience he could. A frontier circuit tour took him to New Orleans in 1824 when he was eighteen, and he was hired by James H. Caldwell. Forrest's muscular physique, powerful voice, unflagging energy, and intuitive line readings served him well with the public, but he soon quarreled with Caldwell and retreated from civilization to live in a teepee for a time with his Indian friend Pushmataha. By the fall of 1825, he had returned to the east coast where his appearance opposite Kean launched him to stardom. He stirred American and London audiences alike with his vocal resonance and variety in roles like Metamora, Spartacus, King Lear, and Macbeth. But he responded to an imagined slight on his second London tour, in 1845, by nurturing feelings of enmity toward Macready. Forrest's turbulent nature was not only a contributing factor toward the tragic Astor Place riot, but also led to his scandalously publicized divorce. He continued to act until his death in 1872, although his romantic style had long been out of fashion.

Other prominent American actors of the Romantic period include

James Henry Hackett and George Handel Hill, both of whom specialized in stage Yankees. Charlotte Cushman became the first internationally renowned American actress. At various times she acted opposite both Forrest and Macready. She often played breeches roles, one of her most successful being Romeo to her younger sister Susan Cushman's Juliet on an 1845 tour to London. Thus the American stage, like England's, manifested the romantic impulse better in a generation of outstanding actors than in a strong dramatic literature. However, the American theater does boast one triumph of Romantic literature for the stage: George Henry Boker's verse tragedy, *Francesca da Rimini* (1855). Like the English romantics, Boker defined himself as a poet and not as a playwright, but his fusion of playable poetic dialogue with character psychology and the pictorial values of the historical setting demonstrate that Romantic drama in the English language was not an impossible proposition.

The Italian-language theater deviated from its Latinate tradition long enough to indulge another of the smaller-scoped romantic movements. Although the unification of the numerous independent states of the Italian peninsula was not achieved until 1871, that goal was a dominant preoccupation of writers and artists beginning in the latter half of the eighteenth century and especially after the Napoleonic Wars. The dramatist who best captured the nationalistic spirit that later became the Risorgimento is generally classed as a pre-Romantic. Count Vittorio Alfieri set out to give Italian literature a body of verse tragedy to balance the great storehouse of Italian comedy accumulated from the Romans to Goldoni and Gozzi. From his first effort, *Cleopatra* (1775), to the more political tragedies like *Saul* (1783) and *Myrrha* (1786), Alfieri maintained high literary ideals, confining his passions to neoclassical structure, but he could not succeed in elevating the taste of his audiences. Nevertheless, his lofty themes paved the way for the leading Italian Romantic dramatist, Alessandro Manzoni. Besides his famous novel *I promessi sposi* and his two now-forgotten Romantic plays, *The Count of Carmagnola* (1820) and *Adelchi* (1822), Manzoni wrote two early treatises on Romanticism, and he was instrumental in bringing Shakespeare to the Italian stage.

On the whole, Italian Romanticism may have been better served by its operatic stage designers than by its dramatists. Other countries were still using stock settings long after this period, while Italian theaters regularly featured explicitly-designed new scenery for the particularized locales that are called for in romantic drama and opera. Alessandro Sanquirico at Milan's La Scala was acknowledged as the leading Italian designer. Another was Francesco Bagnara, resident designer at Venice's La Fenice for twenty-five years and guest designer at many other theaters. Their supremacy lay in their painterly skill and eye for detail as well as their ability to create mechanical effects.

French Romantic Drama

Finally, Romantic drama penetrated France, the bastion of neo-classicism. Romanticism's conquest of French theater was considered decisive after "the battle of *Hernani*" at the Comédie Française in 1830. It took thirty years to reach that point. The campaign to establish Romanticism in France began with the efforts of Madame de Staël, a cultivated woman, daughter of the great finance director Jacques Necker. Her romantic outlook manifested itself as early as her 1796 treatise *On the Influence of the Passions on the Happiness of Individuals and of Nations* as well as in the more important *Consideration of Literature in Relation to Social Institutions* (1800). Her most influential work, *De l'Allemagne* (About Germany, 1810), described the new movement in German art, which she had often discussed with A. W. Schlegel. Using examples from Schiller and Shakespeare, she exalted a Nordic spirit of idealism, Christian mysticism and chivalry, individualism and the romantic soul. On its first publication, *About Germany* was seized and destroyed by order of Napoleon, but it was republished after his fall in 1814. Madame de Staël's recommendation that the medieval period in Christian countries replace classical Greece and Rome as a source of artistic inspiration proved a timely complement to the novels of Sir Walter Scott in translation. Another early exemplar of the romantic impulse, François-Auguste-René de Chateaubriand, gratified the ideology-weary public with an emotional treatment of religion in *The Genius of Christianity* (1802). He was also the progenitor of the wave of Romantic melancholia, or *le mal du siècle*, that overtook French youth, in the same way that Germans of the previous generation had succumbed to Werther-like *Weltschmerz*.

Romanticism seemed to have arrived in poetry and painting long before it passed the official test of the theater. In 1819 André Chénier's poems were rediscovered and published; from there it was but a short step to the lyrical poetry of the early 1820s by Alphonse Lamartine and Alfred de Vigny. Théodore Géricault exhibited his epochal *Raft of the Medusa* (1819) and Eugène Delacroix his *Dante and Virgil in Hell* (1822), both of which shocked the neoclassicists with their sensational subject matter and rebellious form. But the London press reported in 1823 that the Académie Française had "determined never to receive within its bosom any one polluted by the *dramatic* heresy of romanticism." Philippe Van Tieghem offers several reasons for the importance of theater as the ultimate testing ground of French Romanticism. First, the theater was stagnating under the burden of a form that had reached its apex in the seventeenth century, while calls for reassessment had been voiced since the time of Voltaire. Second, the theater stood as a symbol for all of French literature, incorporating as it did both the lyric and the epic. Third, foreign models for the new aesthetic were mostly in the dramatic mode. And, finally, the theater, with its large audience, would be an author's shortest road to glory. Thus there were a number of authors who made tentative forays into the field: Benjamin Constant adapted Schiller's *Wallenstein* as *Wallstein* (1809), but it remained classical in form and tone. Népomucène Lemercier's abandonment of the unities and mingling of ordinary and noble characters in *Christopher Columbus* (1809) incited a riot in the theater in which one person was killed and several were wounded, so the play was banned. Pierre Lebrun's *Mary Stuart* (1820) bleached all the Romantic coloration out of Schiller's tragedy from which it was adapted. Casimir Delavigne's *Les Vêpres siciliennes* (Sicilian Vespers, 1819), and *Marino Faliero* (1829) were colorful but classical in their regular verse and restricted scope. For all his local color in the six plays that made up his collection published under the pseudonym Clara Gazul (1825), Prosper Mérimée avoided identification with the Romantics; he was later to define Romantic drama as follows: "Bam, bam, bam. *Les trois coups.* Curtain up. Laugh, suffer, weep, kill. He is killed, she is dead. The end."

Another step toward a Romantic drama in France was François Guizot's 1821 publication of a new edition of Shakespeare's plays in freshened-up translations with a prefatory essay, "In Praise of Shakespeare." The general theatergoing public, however, was not yet prepared to accept Shakespeare on the stage, as evidenced by the hostile reaction to a company of English actors that attempted to present Shakespeare in English at the Porte Saint-Martin in 1822. Pelted with vegetables and hooted down, the actors could not complete their opening performance, but they fared better when quietly moved to a small theater for the *cognoscenti*. Only five years later, the same English company again brought Shakespeare to Paris and won the accolades of the press and public. Several factors contributed to this total about-face. One was that the timing of the earlier visit had been premature, as the French still resented their defeat by the English at Waterloo in 1815. Another factor was the 1823 publication of Stendhal's *Racine and Shakespeare,* a hard-hitting polemic that extolled Shakespeare's freedom of imagination over the polished perfection of France's greatest tragic poet. And 1824 saw the founding of a literary journal, *The Globe,* devoted to Shakespeare and Romanticism. Perhaps the most significant factor was the improved quality of the English troupe on its second visit, enhanced by the guest appearance of Charles Kemble as Hamlet in the opening performance and in *Romeo and Juliet* and *Othello* on subsequent nights. The emotional power of Ophelia's mad scene as played by Harriet Smithson, with bits of straw in her loose hair, caused a sensation. She became the darling of Paris, and Hector Berlioz married her in 1833. Even the staging was a revelation; the actors moved about and handled props instead of standing in a semicircle around the prompter's box.

Charles Kemble as Hamlet and Miss Smithson as Ophelia, on the left, watch the play-within-the-play in act 3 of Hamlet, *as performed by the English players in Paris in 1827. L. Boulanger and A. Devéria,* Souvenirs du Théâtre-Anglais à Paris.

The English players' four-month engagement was extended to a year; Edmund Kean and William Charles Macready came to Paris to perform with them. Something of the impact that was made on the Parisian theater public comes across in Alexandre Dumas *père*'s recollection from "How I Became a Playwright":

> Imagine someone blind from birth suddenly given sight, who discovers a whole new world about which he had no idea. . . . The performance opened a door for me onto the enchanted garden of Eden. Oh! this is what I had been seeking, what I had been missing, what had to come to me. It was theatre professionals forgetting they were on a stage. It was fictitious life springing fully to life through art. It was the reality of the words and gestures that made, of these actors, God's creatures with all their virtues, passions, and weaknesses, instead of stilted, expressionless, one-note declamatory heros. O Shakespeare, thank you! O Kemble and Smithson, thank you! Thanks be to God! Thanks be to my poetic muses!

Not only was French acting influenced by the actors' energetic expressiveness, but the need was brought home for more faithful translations of Shakespeare into French.

A second pivotal event occurred in 1827: Victor Hugo published his play *Cromwell* along with a preface that set forth the major characteristics of the romantic aesthetic. The play itself was too unwieldy for performance, far too long, with too many characters; but the "Preface to *Cromwell*" became the manifesto of Romanticism. In elegant prose, Hugo declared that rules for art were obsolete, as thoughts should be no more fettered than people in an era of hard-won liberty. He ridiculed the unities of time and place, but redefined unity of action in terms of its relationship to nature. In the most original section, he championed the mixing of genres. To separate tragedy and comedy into two distinct genres seemed to him a betrayal of nature. In nature, furthermore, beauty and ugliness coexist. The neoclassical focus exclusively on beauty produced only monotony. In order for beauty to attain its full value in art, it must be juxtaposed—as it is in nature—with the ugly. Similarly, he called for the juxtaposition of light and shadow, humble and royal, flesh and spirit, and—in the most famous phrase from the preface—"the grotesque and the sublime." Hugo followed these precepts in his own Romantic dramas, but perhaps nowhere are they better illustrated than in his 1831 novel *Notre Dame de Paris*. The backdrop for the story is the sublime medieval Gothic architecture of the cathedral of Notre Dame with the heavenward thrust of its tall slender columns, vaulted arches, and soaring spires. But sculpted on the facade of the cathedral are the grotesque figures of the gargoyles. Similarly, the hunchbacked Quasimodo who inhabits the cathedral is beastly in his external appearance, especially next to the beautiful gypsy Esmeralda, but his capacity for love and self-sacrifice reflects the magnificence of his immortal soul.

Victor Hugo had long aspired to recognition as the foremost man of letters of the new movement. In 1816, when he was fourteen, he declared: "I want to be Chateaubriand or nothing." Ultimately, he far surpassed Chateaubriand to become, in some estimations, the greatest French poet of all time, as well as a major novelist, a playwright, pen-and-ink artist, and political voice. By 1824, when he was twenty-two, he had founded a literary journal, married his childhood sweetheart Adèle Foucher, and published his first novel and two volumes of poetry. He also emerged as a leading light in the Cénacle, the first Romantic literary *salon*, which was founded that year by Charles Nodier, librarian at the Bibliothèque de l'Arsenal. It only remained for Hugo to triumph in the theater, and that proved more problematic. Romanticism had for all practical purposes been accepted everywhere except at the Comédie Française, but until it breached that fortress of official theater it could not truly claim victory. However, in 1825 Baron Taylor, a man of liberal artistic views, was appointed chief administrator of the Comédie Française. He was receptive to the idea of producing a Romantic drama, but *Cromwell* was unstageable and Hugo's next submission, *Marion de Lorme* (1829), was rejected by the censors as antimonarchist. Thus it was that two other quasi-romantic productions preceded Hugo's *Hernani*.

In February 1829 the Comédie Française produced *Henri III et sa cour* (Henry III and His Court) by the twenty-five-year-old Alexandre Dumas *père*. Audiences thrilled to the blend of passion, suspense, violence and historical color that clearly placed it in the romantic mode. It also featured a daring breach of taste: the brutal Duc de Guise, jealous of his wife's hitherto-innocent affection for a young courtier, forces her to write a fatal letter by crushing her arm with his fist in an iron glove; such violent acts had long been commonplace on the English stage, but this was shocking to a French audience. However, *Henry III and His Court* aroused no polemic and was not thought to be the true test case for Romantic drama, because it was in prose rather than verse. The next challenge came in October of that year when the Comédie Française produced poet Alfred de Vigny's translation/adaptation of Shakespeare's *Othello*, entitled *Le More de Venise* (The Moor of Venice). Vigny had assembled a large claque of personal friends to support the play, but the performance was disrupted in several places by the whistles and catcalls of thirty or so neoclassicists. One journal reported that "Sometimes the orchestra applauded while the boxes laughed and the gallery whistled." Most of the audience responded warmly to the lush costumes and the seven settings designed by Ciceri and Labe-Gigun, as well as to "Shakespeare, no longer compressed into classicism, twisted, travestied, but finally given a faithful translation!" The unfavorable reactions tended to focus upon moments of questionable taste: Cassio's drunk scene, the use of the vulgar word *mouchoir* (handkerchief) in spoken dialogue, Desdemona's undressing for bed, and the violence of her death by suffocation with a pillow. Of these, the most infamous was the mention of an intimate article, *mouchoir*. With a total of seventeen performances, *The Moor of Venice* could be called a modest success.

Meanwhile, Victor Hugo had written another play. Despite changes demanded by the censors and reservations expressed by some of the actors in rehearsal, *Hernani* premiered at the Comédie Française on February 25, 1830. Instead of relying on the Comédie Française's usual hired *claqueurs*, Hugo obtained a great number of tickets in every part of the auditorium for young supporters of his cause. Among them was a nineteen-year-old art student, Théophile Gautier (later an important poet-critic), who flaunted his rebellion by wearing a bright pink doublet with pale green pants and a velvet-collared jacket, an effect calculated to shock the conservatives in the audience, as it had his tailor when he ordered it. The disturbances began virtually with the first lines of the play. In the neoclassical theater, royal figures had always struck noble poses and declaimed their lines without moving from their positions on stage. If audiences were now growing accustomed to lively action (climbing through windows, breaking down doors, sword fighting) such as Alexandre Dumas and the influence of the melodrama were bringing to "the Romans," they were scarcely prepared for the shock of seeing a king make a very unroyal entrance through a secret panel in the wall. And a few moments later the king climbed into a cupboard to hide! Even so, it was not that kind of lapse in taste that upset the classicists so much as what Hugo did with the language. Like any serious French tragedy, *Hernani* was written in alexandrines. Hugo's audacity was to break up the rhythmical regularity of those twelve-syllable rhymed couplets by punctuating them at odd intervals; he even used enjambments, that is, finishing a breath group at the beginning of a new line instead of on the rhyming word. The playful and intentionally provocative opening lines of the play, spoken by the heroine's *confidante* and interrupted by pounding on the door, will illustrate:

> *(Someone knocks at the small door concealed at right. She listens.*
> *A second knock.)*
> > Serait-ce déjà lui?
> *(Another knock.)*
> > > C'est bien à l'escalier
> > Dérobé.
> *(A fourth knock.)*
> > > Vite, ouvrons.
> *(She opens the hidden door. Enter Don Carlos, his cloak pulled up to*
> *his nose and his hat pulled down over his eyes.)*
> > > Bonjour, beau cavalier.

Furthermore, the lines were full of more concrete images and richer metaphors than had ever been heard in neoclassical tragedy, which had always scrupulously avoided naming mundane items from daily life or parts of the body, except metonymically, like the "forehead" or the "eyes." Mademoiselle Mars, the fifty-two-year-old actress who created the role of the seventeen-year-old heroine Doña Sol, warned Hugo in rehearsal that a line like *"Vous êtes mon lion, superbe et généreux"* would be difficult to get away with. She was right; referring to her beloved Hernani as an animal—even if it was the king of the beasts—was a daring choice, and it was one that provoked whistling, jeering, and derisory laughter from some quarters, cheers and applause from others. The "battle of *Hernani*" escalated into physical fighting. One engraving of the period shows Romantic youth and older neoclassicists literally at each others' throats. The Romantics won.

Although Hugo and his friends declared the opening performance

One of the most famous of all French opening-night riots in the theater occurred at the premiere of Hernani *(1830) by Victor Hugo (1802–85) when romantic youth defended the play's outrageous features against the older spectators who were called "Romans" because they preferred neoclassicism. Grand Carteret,* XIXe Siècle *(1892).*

Act 2 of Hernani *is set in a square outside the palace of Silva in Zaragossa. Boulanger's engraving from Hugo's* Oeuvres complètes *(1857–60) is based upon the original production.*

a triumph for the play, the press waged a polemic that lasted all during the thirty-nine performance run. The excitement of the romantic rebellion in the theater was soon matched by the political excitement of the July Revolution of 1830. Censorship had been a serious problem under Charles X, but his five ordinances issued on July 26, 1830, were intolerable. He seized control of the press, dissolved the newly elected Chamber of Deputies, and changed the electoral system to strip the wealthy middle class of their voting rights. With thirty thousand printers and news vendors suddenly thrown out of work, the streets were quickly filled with rioters building barricades. The romantics were ready to join battle here too. That generation of *bourgeoisie*—like Dumas, Vigny, and Hugo, born around 1800—had missed participating in the great events marshaled by Napoleon; their restlessness and nostalgia for France's lost glory accounted in part for their proneness to *le mal du siècle*. Now the real-life drama of the barricades equaled the vicarious excitement they had been seeking in the theater. After "three glorious days," Charles X was deposed. Louis Philippe, Duke of Orleans, son of Philippe Egalité, was chosen to continue the constitutional monarchy. Carrying an umbrella, symbol of the middle class, Louis Philippe styled himself as the "*bourgeois* king of the French people," and enjoyed a relatively stable eighteen-year reign. Thus the triumph of Romantic drama virtually coincided with the lifting of the censorship restrictions that had so hampered writers under Charles X.

The public craved what had previously been denied them, historical dramas with political overtones. There was a great vogue for plays about Napoleon fueled by the popularity of numerous songs by Pierre-Jean Bérenger, which had already been promoting Romanticism's "Napoleonic legend" for many years. Several boulevard theaters employed actors who specialized in impersonations of Napoleon. Perhaps as a publicity stunt or perhaps in self-defense, theaters that regularly produced plays about Napoleon hired as technical advisors old soldiers who had served under him. Dumas succumbed to the plea of Charles-Jean Harel, manager of the Odéon, to write *Napoleon Bonaparte,* a popular spectacle, but at the same time he bucked the trend to historical drama with his dramatic masterpiece *Antony* (1931), produced at the Porte Saint-Martin.

Antony marked the first time in French theater that a tragedy was set in the contemporary period instead of in the historical past. Inspired in part by Dumas's own affair with a married woman, *Antony* is the story of a passionate young man unable to marry the woman he loves because of his illegitimate birth. Adèle marries another, but Antony cannot resist pursuing her. She succumbs. In the final scene, Antony and Adèle are alone together in her room when her husband unexpectedly returns from his military duty. As they hear him mount the stairs, Adèle asks Antony to kill her in order to save her honor and that of her baby daughter. Antony kisses her and stabs her. The door bursts open. Antony flings the dagger at the colonel's feet and speaks the immortal curtain line: "Yes! dead! She resisted me, so I killed her!" Gautier recorded the opening-night response: "The audience went wild; they applauded, sobbed, wept, screamed. The burning passion of the play had inflamed their hearts." Deliriously, they tore at Dumas's coat and took away pieces of it for souvenirs. Antony's act 5 curtain line never failed to achieve its emotional impact, even on one occasion when the curtain was mistakenly rung down too soon. There was an uproar in the audience; they demanded to hear the line they already knew by heart. Bocage, as Antony, refused to return to the stage, but the curtain was raised on Marie Dorval in Adèle's final posture of death. She rose from the dead and addressed the audience: "As you see, ladies and gentlemen, I resisted him, so he killed me." She fell back dead again, and the audience left satisfied. *Antony*'s success was a product not only of Dumas's theatrical acumen, but also of its simultaneous appeals to romantic rebelliousness (romantic passion between the social outcast and the virtuous wife sweeping aside all social constraints) and to conservative morality (Adèle's death as the wages of sin, even as it served as the means of restoring her honor).

Dumas continued to write voluminously. Among his crowd-pleasers were *Richard Darlington* (1831), in which the title character murders his wife by defenestration; *La Tour de Nesle* (The Tower of Nesle, 1832), the most frequently performed play of the century in France, about a nymphomaniac queen who indulges in licentious orgies in the tower and then disposes of her lovers by tossing them into the Seine; and *Kean; or, Disorder and Genius* (1836), based upon the life of the celebrated English actor who had died only three years earlier. Dumas's dramatizations of novels he wrote for serial publication included *The Count of Monte Cristo* (novel, 1844; play, 1848), the first French play to be performed in two parts on successive evenings. It was produced at Dumas's own Théâtre Historique, which he opened in 1847 on the Boulevard du Temple, with an excellent company of actors to perform a repertoire composed largely of his historical romances. The enterprise was quite successful until the February Revolution of 1848 cut Parisian theater attendance almost in half; he closed it in 1851. The prodigious Dumas made and lost a great deal of money, as well as many mistresses, during his colorful life. Grandson of a San Domingo plantation owner and his black mistress, and son of a famous general under Napoleon, Alexandre Dumas *père* cut a flamboyant figure. His ready wit and affable manner coupled with the popularity of the flow of works from his pen earned him the nickname "King of Paris." The scantily educated writer was hampered only by his clumsiness with language. His own consciousness of this shortcoming is evident in his reaction after hearing a reading of Victor Hugo's *Marion de Lorme:* "I—lacking style above all else—was overcome by the magnificence of that style. I would have given ten years of my life without hesitation if I could have had in return the promise of someday attaining that. Ah, if only I were capable of writing such verse—knowing as I do how to craft a play!" In Lucien Dubech's assessment, the "Great French Romantic Dramatist" was unfortunately divided into two people, one who could write lines and one who could write action.

Hugo's long career was equally colorful. Whereas Dumas *père* got away with flaunting his improprieties, Hugo managed to project a public image of bourgeois morality, even when taking subscriptions from his friends to support Juliette Drouet, who remained his mistress for fifty years, 1833–83. He was the dominant figure in French romantic drama, even though few of his plays were particularly successful. *Le Roi s'amuse* (1832) failed in the Comédie Française production, and is better known in its operatic version *Rigoletto. Lucretia Borgia* (1833) succeeded at the Porte Saint-Martin as much for the performances of Mademoiselle George and Frédérick Lemaître as on its own merit. *Mary Tudor* (1833) was excoriated by the press, which was uncertain about its political subtext. *Angelo, Tyrant of Padua* (1835) was received with virtual indifference despite the opportunity to see the two great actresses of the age—Mademoiselle Mars, beloved of the Comédie Française's élitest audience, and Marie Dorval, freshly hired away from the Boulevard— together for the first time in the same play.

One play by Hugo, however, outshines all the others in its poetic brilliance and theatricality: *Ruy Blas* (1838). With it Hugo hoped to realize his dream of uniting the élitest and popular theater audiences. Thus he took his play neither to the Comédie Française nor to the Porte Saint-Martin. Encouraged by Hugo and Dumas, Anténor Joly acquired the former Salle Ventadour, remodeled it, and renamed it Théâtre de la Renaissance with a vision of making it a theater that would draw from all segments of the theatergoing public. *Ruy Blas* (1838) was its inaugural production. With Frédérick Lemaître in the title role, one of the best of his career, it ran forty-eight performances and was revived three years later for an even longer run. The action occurs in seventeenth-century Spain. Ruy Blas is a humbly born but noble-minded lackey, prevented by a rigid social order from fulfilling his potential. He becomes an unwitting pawn in the evil Don Salluste's machinations to dishonor the Queen, who has exiled Don Salluste for refusing to marry the lady-in-waiting he seduced. Don Salluste concocts a scheme whereby Ruy Blas is thrust into the role of Don César, a down-on-his-luck nobleman who has long been

Antony (1831) by Alexandre Dumas père *(1802–70) culminated in the immortal act 5 curtain line: "She resisted me, so I killed her," spoken by Bocage (1797–1893) in the title role.* L'Artiste *(1831).*

Victor Hugo's dramatic masterpiece Ruy Blas *(1838) inaugurated the Théâtre de la Renaissance. Shown here in act 5 are Frédérick Lemaître as Ruy Blas, Mauzin as Don Salluste, and Mademoiselle Baudoin as the Queen.* Monde dramatique *(1838).*

absent from court. Under the assumed identity, Ruy Blas rises to the position of first minister and in a famous, stirring speech *(O ministres intègres!)* rebukes the corrupt ministers who do not have their country's best interests at heart. The melancholy queen discovers Ruy Blas's secret passionate love for her and confides her love for him. However, at this moment of sublime happiness for the "earthworm in love with a star," Don Salluste returns to claim Ruy Blas's pledge of servitude. Act 4 takes a comic turn with the unexpected appearance of the real Don César, who enters down the chimney of his house, where Don Salluste has laid his trap. One by one, Don César dispatches the various emissaries who arrive for Ruy Blas. In act 5, Ruy Blas believes that he has succeeded in saving the queen from danger, but her sudden arrival, and the threat posed to her by Don Salluste, cause Ruy Blas to confess his humble status. He takes poison in order to save the queen's honor by his death, but he dies satisfied in the knowledge that she loves him for himself, even without rank.

In his preface to *Ruy Blas,* Hugo claimed that his aim was to please all three kinds of spectators that make up the general public: First, women want passion to arouse the emotions; their preferred genre is tragedy. Second, thinkers want characters to stimulate their minds; they like comedy. Third, the masses want action to arouse the senses, preferably through melodrama. According to Hugo, romantic drama should satisfy all of these needs. Each act of *Ruy Blas* has its own style and mood, intrigue in act 1, romantic lyricism in act 2, historical and political content in act 3, comedy in act 4, and a synthesis of all styles in the final act. The play has retained its power through numerous revivals. In 1872 Emile Zola said of it: "Of all of Victor Hugo's dramas, *Ruy Blas* is the most scenic, the most human, the most dynamic. . . . Yes, music, light, color, perfume, it's all there. Hugo's poetry smells good, has crystal voices, gleams with purple and gold. Never has the human tongue spoken such lively and passionate language." Notable among its twentieth-century revivals were the Théâtre National Populaire's 1954 production starring Gérard Philipe, and Denis Llorca's stunning staging of it in 1985, to commemorate the centenary of Hugo's death, at the Théâtre de la Renaissance, the same theater where the play had premiered.

Frédérick Lemaître, known to his public simply as Frédérick, was the French Romantic actor *par excellence,* as—in accordance with Hugo's precept—he could incorporate a touch of the grotesque along with the sublime aspects of his romantic heroes. Hugo described Frédérick's juxtaposition of opposite traits: "M. Frédérick is elegant yet unpretentious, he is brooding yet graceful, he is fearsome yet tender, he is both child and man, he charms and he horrifies, he is modest, stern, and awesome." Frédérick Lemaître began his career as a variety performer,

Frédérick Lemaître (1800–1876), left, France's great Romantic actor, was equally at home in melodrama on the boulevard of Crime as in the verse dramas of Victor Hugo. Cain, Anciens Théâtres de Paris *(1920).*

Right, Frédérick Lemaître's most famous role was that of the comic brigand Robert Macaire in L'Auberge des Adrets *(1824) and its sequel* Robert Macaire *(1834).* Encyclopédie du théâtre contemporain.

including a stint at the Funambules, finally moving on to melodramas on the Boulevard of Crime. He gained overnight fame in 1824 when he guyed the role of the melodramatic brigand Robert Macaire in *L'Auberge des Adrets* (The Inn of the Adrets), wearing a ragged costume he had cobbled together and improvising a hilarious antihero. The role—which in that play and in a sequel, *Robert Macaire* (1834), remained identified with Frédérick for over a quarter of a century—acquired legendary status as a vicarious means of thumbing one's nose at authority. The triumph of Romantic drama gave him an avenue of escape from melodrama, beginning with his creation of the role of Gennaro in Hugo's *Lucretia Borgia*. With the fall of Romantic drama, Frédérick returned to the Boulevard, where until his death in 1876 he maintained his old flamboyance in revivals of *Robert Macaire* and other past successes like Victor Ducange's *Trente ans de la vie d'un joueur* (Thirty Years in the Life of a Gambler, 1827).

Playing opposite Frédérick in the latter melodrama as well as in a number of other important productions was the outstanding Romantic actress, Marie Dorval. Like him, she was a product of the Boulevard, where she learned to make the most extreme paroxysms of emotion seem "natural." She used to full advantage that most-prized asset of the French actor, a well-placed, expressive voice. According to Gautier, her voice produced "cries of poignant truthfulness, heartbreaking sobs, intonations so natural and tears so sincere that one forgot it was theatre." Frédérick's closest rival was Bocage, who excelled in the title role of Dumas's *Antony*, opposite Marie Dorval's Adèle. His feverish intensity often manifested itself in a nervous trembling that became a hallmark of his romantic style. In spite of his physical shortcomings, Bocage managed to project a darkly attractive complexity that worked well for characters like Antony, Shylock, and Buridan in Dumas's *Tower of Nesle*.

The failure of Hugo's *Les Burgraves* at the Comédie Française in 1843 is usually taken to mark the end of the Romantic movement in French theater. Romanticism's demise might be attributed not only to a general satiety with its overblown rhetoric and theatrical claptrap, but also to the tremendous impact of what was virtually a one-woman revival of neoclassicism. Rachel (born Elisa Félix) made her Comédie Française debut in Corneille's *Horace* in 1838. The melodic clarity of her voice, which infused the seventeenth-century rhetoric with emotional truth, reawakened the public's appreciation of the classics. In same year that *Les Burgraves* failed, Rachel gave an unprecedented seventy-four consecutive performances in the title role of Racine's *Phèdre* (Phaedra, 1667). Hugo turned away from the theater to devote himself to politics, poetry, and the novel. From 1851 to 1870 he lived in self-imposed exile on the islands of Jersey and Guernsey. During that period he did write a number of whimsical miniplays not intended for the stage, which were published posthumously under the title *Théâtre en liberté*. Before Romanticism ended, however, it produced important plays by two other dramatists, Alfred de Vigny and Alfred de Musset.

Besides *The Moor of Venice*, the poet Vigny achieved one other major triumph in the theater: *Chatterton* (1835). He wrote it for his mistress of six years, the great romantic actress Marie Dorval, whose utterly moving performance reduced strong women like George Sand to tears. Set in middle-class eighteenth-century England and written in prose, *Chatterton* was based upon the true story of the misunderstood poet who committed suicide at eighteen. Vigny's play explores the theme of unappreciated genius and society's failure to recognize the exceptional needs of the artist. That romantic theme, however, is compressed within a classical structure and a plot composed of more talk than action. What saved the play for the Romantics was the clarity with which it communicates the intense love that Chatterton and his landlord's wife Kitty Bell feel for each other, although they never express it in words. And the play ends

Rachel (1820–58) almost singlehandedly launched a revival of interest in the classics during the heydey of French Romanticism. This widely published contemporary lithograph shows her in the title role of Racine's Phaedra.

The captivating Marie Dorval (1798–1849), right, was utterly moving in the leading roles of Romantic dramas like Hugo's Marion De Lorme *(shown here), Dumas père's* Antony, *and Vigny's* Chatterton. *It was during the period of their romantic liaison that Vigny wrote the latter with the role of Kitty Bell for Dorval. Engraving by A. Devéria.*

upon the romantic conceit that one can die instantly of love. Upon learning that Chatterton is dead, Kitty Bell herself falls dead on the stairs. For this final moment, Marie Dorval devised a dramatic fall during which she slid backward along the bannister to die with her head on the bottom step. The effect produced by this grand romantic gesture of the Boulevard-trained actress in a Comédie Française production was recorded by Gautier: "And what a piercing cry at the end, what forgetting of herself, what abandonment to the moment when she rolled, stricken with grief, to the bottom of the stairs she had climbed in hysterical spurts, in crazed jerks, almost on her knees, her feet catching in her hem, her arms outstretched, her soul darting forth from the body that could not keep up with it!"

Alfred de Musset was the *enfant terrible* of French Romanticism. Introduced into Nodier's Cénacle at eighteen in 1828, he charmed the movement's leaders with his graceful wit. By the time he published his first collection of poetry in 1830, he was already tending to mock Romanticism's excesses. Later that year, his first play was produced and whistled off the stage after only two performances at the Odéon. The gossamer moonlit whimsy of *The Venetian Night* was undercut at its opening performance when one of the actresses in a white gown backed against a freshly painted trellis and came away with a green pattern on her skirt. Musset vowed never to write for the theater again. But he did continue to write plays without regard for the demands of the stage, the earliest group of which he published as *Spectacle dans un fauteuil* (Armchair Theatre) in 1832. Unlike Lord Byron's "mental theatre" or Hugo's *Théâtre en liberté,* Musset's plays of unfettered imagination are inherently dramatic without making impossible demands on the resources of the stage. Unfortunately, this was not discovered until 1847, after Musset's heavy drinking and dissipated lifestyle had taken a serious toll on him. The women who loved him at various times in his life—including George Sand, whose famous two-year liaison with him began when he was twenty-three and she was twenty-nine—often commented that he was like two separate personalities in one: he could be a socially polished, elegantly witty man of the world or an irrational, ill-tempered child. His plays and his poetry often show the two sides of the romantic hero, one suffering with *le mal du siècle,* the other adventuring forth, sword in hand, to do great deeds. In *Les Caprices de Marianne* (Marianne's Caprices, 1833), Musset opposes the melancholy lovestruck poet Célio and the debauched, rakish Octave. The title character of *Fantasio* (1834), a disaffected carouser and debtor (he has "the month of May on his cheeks, the month of January in his heart"), decides on a whim that he will impersonate the court jester; by the end of the play he has brought two countries to the brink of war, but he has accomplished the essential: saving the princess from an unhappy marriage. In Musset's masterpiece, *Lorenzaccio* (1834), the effeminate and idealistic title character makes himself the accomplice of the vice-ridden duke, planning to kill the duke and save Florence from his despotism; but Lorenzaccio's own loss of purity is irrevocable.

These and other dramatic gems by Musset were not considered for production until a French actress, Madame Allan-Despréaux, performing in St. Petersburg, saw Musset's *Un Caprice* (1837) presented there in Russian. Charmed by the delightful and psychologically penetrating three-character play, she took it to the Comédie Française, performed it there with great success, and became Musset's mistress. The production brought attention to Musset's other plays, most of which finally reached the stage before his premature death in 1857. But *Lorenzaccio,* his only five-act play, remained unproduced until 1896, when Sarah Bernhardt triumphed in the male role, although the text was badly cut and rear-

Romantics were fascinated by historical or fanciful costumes. Left, the young poet–playwright Alfred de Musset (1810–57) wears a Renaissance costume. Engraving by Devéria.

Above, right, Mlle Allan-Despréaux was the actress who brought Alfred de Musset's plays back to the theater. She is shown here in the role of Mme de Léry in Musset's Un Caprice *at the Comédie Française in 1847. Courtesy of French Cultural Services.*

Below, Musset's Lorenzaccio *was directed by Franco Zeffirelli at the Comédie Française in 1976 with costumes by Marcel Escoffier. Jean-Luc Boutte, at right, played the corrupt Alexandre de Medici. Courtesy of French Cultural Services.*

ranged. Because of its complex title character, its scenic scope, and its blend of poetry, intrigue, love, political subtext, and local color, *Lorenzaccio* is sometimes referred to as "the French *Hamlet*." What distinguished Musset from the other Romantics was his light touch, often extending to a wry self-mockery for his extremes of emotion. There is more psychological truth in his plays than in those of any other Romantic dramatist, and he was particularly skillful in his portrayal of women. Musset's plays are today the most frequently produced of the French Romantics, and during the 1930s he surpassed even Molière and Marivaux as the most produced dramatist in France.

The Romantic Period in Spain

French romantic drama helped to prepare Spanish audiences for a romantic drama of their own beginning around 1834; but a more significant factor was the political situation in Spain. Napoleon's 1808 invasion and subsequent placement of his brother Joseph on the Spanish throne set off a grass-roots War for Independence. The concept of "guerrilla" warfare arose from the many isolated patriotic deeds of heroism among small bands of peasants. Such episodes, quickly mythologized, fed into Spain's earliest romantic impulses. In 1812 a group met in Cádiz and drew up a liberal constitution that, among other things, provided for the separation of church and state and an end to abuses against American Indians by the Spanish colonists. Fernando VII promised to uphold this constitution when he was restored to the throne in 1814, but he soon reneged, renewing the Inquisition and closing universities. His repressive constitution of 1823 drove many liberals into exile. Among the writers who took refuge in England were Duque de Rivas and José de Espronceda, while others like Martínez de la Rosa went to Paris. One Spanish exile's work, published in English, had a particularly strong influence on proto-romantics all over the Continent; this was *Letters from Spain* (1822) by the Seville poet Blanco White (José Blanco Crespo). The exiled Spanish liberals in turn were exposed to Romantic currents abroad and brought an enthusiasm for the new literary movement when they returned to Spain in 1834, after the accession of Isabella II. Even before that, however, Sir Walter Scott—dubbed "the Cervantes of Scotland"—was widely read in Spanish translation, and a Barcelona periodical of the arts, *Europeo* (1823–24) was purveying an awareness of romantic works in other countries. In his *Discourse* (1828), Augustín Durán, director of the Biblioteca Nacional, propounded the intrinsic merit of Spanish poetry, arguing that it could again achieve greatness if it would not remain subservient to foreign models.

The turning point toward general acceptance of Romanticism in Spain was 1834, the year of the exiles' return. At the same time, adaptations of plays by Hugo and Dumas began to enjoy a great vogue, and three Spanish plays set the course of the theater generally in that direction. Francisco Martínez de la Rosa wrote what is considered to be the first Spanish Romantic drama, *La Conjuración de Venezia* (The Conspiracy of Venice, 1834). Its melodramatic action, set against a carnival backdrop, disregarded the unities and mingled prose and verse dialogue; however, it was not particularly successful. Six months later came *Macías*, a classically structured study of unbridled passion, by Mariano José de Larra, the greatest essayist and satirist of the century. More important than his play were his *Artículos de costumbres* (Essays on Customs, 1832–36), published under the pen name Figaro. Larra's *costumbrismo*—commentary on manners and morals, using picturesque details, local color, and amusing anecdotes—was often directed toward raising the standards of Madrid theater, which had long been mired in tasteless spectacle and abominable acting. A third "pre-Romantic" play in 1834 was Manuel Bretón de los Herreros's *Elena*. Although the plays of Bretón de los Herreros were predominantly neoclassical, a surge of passion in the last act of *Elena* made it seem to support the romantic cause. By the following season, however, Bretón was finding box-office success with a satire of Romantic drama entitled *Todo es farso en este mundo* (All the World's a Farce, 1835).

Spanish Romantic drama is said to have triumphed with the 1835 production of *Don Alvaro; or, The Force of Destiny* by Angel de Saavedra, a liberal aristocrat who wrote under the name Duque de Rivas. Mingling tragedy and comedy, prose and verse, love and violence, pathos and vulgarity, folk elements and fate, thunder and lightning, it was advertised as *románticamente romántico*. That play and another 1835 hit—Antonio García Gutiérrez's *The Troubador*—later served as plots for Verdi's operas *La Forza del Destino* (1862) and *Il Trovatore* (1853). The last year of Romanticism's tenuous reign in Spanish theater was 1837. Ten new Romantic plays premiered that year, garnering a total of over one hundred performances. The best of these was *The Lovers of Teruel* by Juan Eugenio Hartzenbusch. But signs of the movement's collapse were already evident. Among them was Ramón de Mesonero Romanos's satirical tract "Romanticism and the Romantics," which brought laughter even to the romantics in the newly formed literary circle, the Liceo, where Mesonero Romanos read it. In a sense, Romanticism had never fully swept the stage in Spain as it had in France. Nor could Spain boast a great romantic actor; Isidoro Maíquez made heroic efforts to raise the standards of acting and of Spanish theater in general, but his approach was formed by the more classical idea of "natural" acting that he had assimilated during two years of study under Talma in Paris. Despite the work of Maíquez and of the impresario José de Grimaldi, Spanish theater audiences were so avid for the lowest forms of dramatic entertainment that a Romantic drama of literary pretensions could easily be ignored.

The great exception to that attitude, the one sublimely poetic Romantic drama that captured Spanish-speaking audiences everywhere, came a few years later. It was José Zorrilla's *Don Juan Tenorio* (1844). In an indirect way, Zorrilla owed his career and his very life to Larra. In 1837, at age twenty-eight, Larra committed suicide. His essays testify to his growing anguish over Spain's political problems, and his romantic *weltschmerz* or *mal du siècle* was brought to a head by the end of his affair with a married woman. On February 13, 1837, he looked forward to a meeting with her, but her purpose was to take back her love letters. She heard the shot as she was leaving with the letters in hand, but hurried away; sailing to join her husband in the Philippines, she went down with the ship in a storm. Larra's funeral attracted all the *literati* of Madrid; their public homage to a suicide served also as a demonstration of anticlerical feeling. At the graveside, the unknown, nineteen-year-old, ragged, starving poet Zorrilla emerged from the crowd of eulogists to read his ode to Larra. The sonorous melodic beauty of his lines was a revelation to his listeners. Overcome by emotion and hunger, Zorrilla fainted before he could finish. Had Larra not died, Zorrilla would certainly have starved to death before gaining any notice for his poetry; instead he achieved overnight fame.

Zorrilla's first produced play, *Juan Dandolo* (1839), was a collaboration with Gutierrez. By 1840 he had written eight volumes of poetry and won his first success as a playwright with *El zapatero y el rey* (The Cobbler and the King, 1840). Of his approximately forty plays, *Don Juan Tenorio* is the one that has held the stage; it is still performed annually in Spanish-speaking countries on All Souls' Day. Based upon the Don Juan legend that goes back to Tirso de Molina's Golden Age play *El burlador de Sevilla* (The Trickster of Seville, ca. 1630). Zorrilla's play captures the spirit of Spanish folklife in its local color, its treatment of the traditional theme of honor, and its fast-paced action. *Don Juan Tenorio* differs from its predecessors in the romantic conception that allows Don Juan's soul to be redeemed at the moment of death by the love of a pure woman. The action is melodrama, but on the strength of Zorrilla's gorgeous lyrical poetry it soars to the sublime. Zorrilla unfortunately sold the rights to his play before the premiere, so he gained nothing from the vast fortunes it earned all over the world in his lifetime. He went to Mexico in 1855; after serving for a time as director of the Mexican National Theatre, he returned to Spain to live out his life in fame and poverty. E. Allison Peers notes that the immediate success of *Don Juan Tenorio* when the Romantic movement was virtually dead attests that with the proper leadership Romanticism could have had a longer life in Spain.

Russian Romanticism

Like Spain, Russia owed its short fling with Romantic drama more to political events than to any organized artistic program. The roots of Russian Romanticism, as in western Europe, can be traced back to sentimental literature of the late eighteenth century. However, the tragically romantic Decembrist uprising of 1825 serves as a landmark to which a distinctive Russian Romantic literature can be tied. In November 1825, Tsar Alexander I died without an heir. Of his three younger brothers, the next in line, Constantine, secretly renounced his claim in favor of the next brother, Nicholas. During the period of public confusion about the succession, some idealistic young army officers hastily decided to take advantage of the uncertainty to stage a coup. Such projects had been frequently discussed in various secret societies ever since the Russian campaigns against Napoleon had taken many Russians to Europe and awakened them to the possibilities of republican forms of government. On December 14, 1825, the liberal-minded officers assembled their troops on the square in front of the Winter Palace and instructed them to shout for "Constantine and Constitution!" The failure of the starry-eyed rebels to prepare a mass following is exemplified by the fact that most of the soldiers did not know why they were there and simply assumed that "Constitution" was the name of Constantine's wife. When the troops would not disperse, Nicholas I sent a cavalry charge. The chaos caused by the horses slipping on the ice led to shooting. Many were killed both on the square and on the frozen River Neva when cannonballs broke the ice across which the men were escaping, but Nicholas ordered all traces obliterated overnight so that the general public would remain ignorant of the failed revolt. Hundreds of Decembrist leaders and sympathizers were arrested and questioned. The five who were hanged are yet today remembered as the first martyrs to the cause of Russian revolution. With so many others sent into exile in Siberia, their wives often following voluntarily on foot, the cream of Russia's intelligentsia was wasted. The reign of Nicholas I, 1825–55, is considered the most repressive of the nineteenth century, with severe literary censorship; and yet, ironically, it somehow inaugurated a golden age in Russian literature.

"Literary Decembrism" was one aspect of Russian Romanticism; it was informed by a self-consciousness about western Europe's ignorance of Russian culture, although the Russians were well acquainted with the work of Schiller, Scott, Hugo, and others. In addition, the Russian stage was overflowing with adaptations of German melodramas and French vaudevilles. Thus, the focus of these romantics was on creating a distinctive national literature based upon Russian folklore and history, rather than merely grafting their work onto European Romanticism. Furthermore, literature was assumed to have political content no matter what censorship might do to it. Aleksandr Sergeyevich Griboyedov's great play *Gore ot uma* (Wit Works Woe, 1823), despite its neoclassical structure, is tied to this streak of romanticism in that it was circulated as antiestablishment propaganda after being banned from production and publication. Although Griboyedov was in the Caucasus in 1825 and could not have been part of the Decembrist conspiracy, he was arrested and imprisoned for four months on the basis of his friendships with certain Decembrists. Griboyedov had begun writing the play in 1816 and continued polishing its verse until his death at thirty-four (he was killed when a Persian mob attacked the Russian embassy in Teheran, where he was stationed) in 1829.

Wit Works Woe, also known as *The Trouble with Reason* or *The Misfortune of Being Clever,* centers upon Chatsky, an intelligent young gentleman whose very potential for doing something worthwhile makes him a misfit in the shallow, favor-currying Moscow social milieu. Returning to Russia after an extended tour abroad, he sees with fresh perspective the uselessness of the lives of the nobility, the vapidity of his former sweetheart, the hollow braggadocio of his friend Repetilov (a compulsive joiner of secret societies, whose "progressive" thought is clouded by alcohol), and a host of other sharply etched portraits assembled at an evening party in act 3. Some saw Chatsky as the portrait of a Decembrist, but in the play he remains a passive rebel. His inability to move beyond a detached critical stance to taking an active role in improving the conditions he deplores established Chatsky as the prototype of a recurring figure in Russian literature, later to be called the "superfluous man." Many lines from the play's sparkling verse dialogue have passed into everyday Russian usage as proverbs and aphorisms. When first performed in 1830, act 3 was entirely excised along with other substantial cuts. It was not published in its entirety until 1861 and produced in 1869.

Like Griboyedov, Aleksandr Sergeyevich Pushkin missed participating in the Decembrist uprising because he was away from St. Petersburg at the time, exiled from 1820 to 1826 for his "subversive" early poetry. Under interrogation, many of the Decembrists cited the influence of Pushkin's poems like "Ode to Liberty" (1817), which the prodigious poet had written at eighteen, shortly after completion of his secondary schooling at the Imperial Lyceum of Tsarskoe Tselo. A voracious reader of

Act 3 of Wit Works Woe *(1823) by Alexander Griboyedov (1794–1829) was omitted from the original production, because the evening-party scene satirized so many recognizable types in Moscow society. This 1914 revival at the Moscow Art Theatre was designed by Douboujinsky.*

Below, the setting for act 4 of Wit Works Woe *is the ground-level entrance hall of Famusov's house, where guests await their carriages. Door to servants' rooms are located on either side. Guests are descending from the ballroom-level in this production photo from the Maly Theatre in 1938.*

French literature, Pushkin had made a name for himself as a poet even before graduation from that prestigious academy, but he became equally known in St. Petersburg for his frenzied life of dissipation, and lived most of his thirty-eight years (1799–1837) as a romantic rebel. De-

Alexander Pushkin (1799–1837) was painted in romantic style by Orest Kiprensky in 1827, two years after Pushkin wrote his major play, Boris Godunov. *Tretyakov Gallery, Moscow.*

scended from centuries-old nobility on the Pushkin side and from the black Abyssinian emperor Hannibal on his mother's side, his dark complexion and exotic features reified his strongly individualistic personality. Besides the usual gentlemanly indulgence in drinking and gambling, he attended the theater or ballet almost nightly and often disrupted performances by his loud comments, but his intimate acquaintances with actresses and ballerinas earned him the epithet "honorary citizen of the backstage." He kept a "Don Juan list" of his numerous love affairs and duels. As a member of the Arzamas and Green Lamp societies, he engaged in passionate political discussions. Exile to the provinces did not curtail his amorous adventures, but at least it forced a literary productivity that might not have come about if there had been more available distractions. It was during his exile that he came under the literary influence first of Lord Byron and then of Shakespeare, and wrote his "Shakespearean" historical drama *Boris Godunov* (1825).

Much of Pushkin's poetry and fiction is inherently dramatic, and many of his works have been dramatized or made into operas, including the long poems *Bakhchisaray Fountain, Ruslan and Ludmila,* and *Eugene Onegin,* and such stories as *Queen of Spades* and *The Golden Cockerel. Boris Godunov* was his only full-length play and one of the supreme achievements of Russian Romanticism. Writing in conscious imitation of Shakespeare, Pushkin varied the form and vocabulary of his blank verse from coarse vulgarity to the lyricism of a romantic moonlit tryst. The twenty-three scenes range in local color from the monastic cell in which Father Pimen writes his chronicles by the light of an icon lamp to a rough inn on the Lithuanian border, from the Tsar's stately council chamber in the Kremlin palace to the confusion of the battlefield. The play also launched the Russian literary tradition of emphasizing the role of "the people," the Russian masses, as agent or victim of historical change. Because Pushkin's choice of historical subject (the "Time of Troubles," 1598–1605) implied a political analogy with contemporary events, the play was banned from publication until 1830 and not performed until 1870.

Pushkin's dramatic writing also includes the unfinished folk-fantasy play *Rusalka* (The Water Nymph, 1832) and the four *Little Tragedies,* three of them dramatizing particular vices: *Mozart and Salieri* (envy), *The Covetous Knight* (greed), *The Stone Guest* (lust), and the unfinished *Feast during the Plague.* His marriage in 1831 to the beautiful, coquettish Natalia Goncharova led to his untimely death following a duel with Georges d'Anthès, whom gossips had linked with his wife's name. Pushkin was not only the supreme embodiment of Russian Romanticism but is still revered as the great "national poet" of the Russian language. His contemporary, Nikolai Gogol, stated: "In him, as if in a lexicon, have been included all of the wealth, strength, and flexibility of our language. More than all the others, he has pushed back its boundaries and showed all of its spaciousness."

Shortly after Pushkin's death, a poem entitled "The Death of a Poet" began circulating in handwritten copies; it blamed the court and St. Petersburg society for creating the conditions that allowed Pushkin's death to occur. The discovery of the author, Mikhail Lermontov, brought him instant fame and a year's imprisonment. His romanticism was of the dark, brooding, even demonic variety. He wrote his first play at fifteen, *Ispantsy* (The Spaniards, 1830), and followed it with *Lyudi i strasti* (Men and Passions, 1830), *Staranny chelovek* (The Strange One, 1831), and *Dva brata* (Two Brothers, 1834), making no attempt to have them published or performed. His best play, however, was weakened by his constant revisions in hopes of getting it past the censors; not until 1852 was a severely cut version of *Maskarad* (Masquerade, 1836) staged, and its first complete production was the famous one by Meyerhold in 1917. Unmistakably influenced by both *Wit Works Woe* and *Othello,* Lermontov's verse drama traces the psychotic progression of Arbenin's morbidly jealous suspicion of infidelity by his innocent wife. The pivotal scene occurs at a masquerade ball, which serves as a metaphor for the corrupt, hypocritical, debauched aristocratic society of St. Petersburg. There Arbenin gives his wife a dish of poisoned ice cream; when they return home, he coldly watches her die. Lermontov's novels and poetry were more successful than his plays. Like Pechorin, the intensely individualistic "superfluous hero" of his best novel *A Hero of Our Time* (1840), Lermontov was killed in a duel; he was twenty-seven years old.

The Romantic Drama in Poland

Russia's political hegemony was a major impetus behind one of the most vital and distinctive manifestations of Romantic drama in Europe: that of the Polish émigré poets between 1822 and 1863. The appeal of romanticism in a period of political unrest is clear, but it should be noted that the theater in Poland had traditionally served as an outlet for political expression from as early as the sixteenth century. Jan Kochanowski's 600-line play *The Dismissal of the Grecian Envoys* (1578) used a classical subject—Greek messengers on a diplomatic mission to Troy to negotiate the release of Helen—as a pretext for exploring questions of national identity and destiny.

Under Stanislaw Augustus Poniatowski, the last Polish king (reigned 1764–95), playwrights were especially encouraged to use the stage to air proposed reforms that might have saved the crumbling Polish state. Poland's first public theater, Teatr Narodowy, opened in 1765 with *Natręci* (*Intruders,* an adaptation by Bielawski of Molière's *Les Facheux*), an allegorical reference to problems on Poland's borders. Such initiatives were to no avail; in 1772 Poland was partitioned by Russia, Prussia, and Austria, losing about one-third of its territory and half of its population. The Polish theater continued to keep alive questions of reform. One play, *Powrót posła* (The Return of the Deputy, 1791), by Julian Niemcewicz, actually achieved its political end. Through the characters of an empty chatterer and a slavish follower of foreign fashions, the comedy exposed the foibles of conservative deputies in the Four Year Diet. The Warsaw public laughed heartily at the portraits and then brought pressure upon the Diet to vote a new constitution. It seemed as if life imitated art when one deputy reacted to *The Return of the Deputy* by filibustering

Pushkin's full-length dramatic masterpiece Boris Godunov *(1825) was the poet's attempt to write the Russian equivalent of Shakespeare. No single character emerges as a protagonist, but "the people" constitute a powerful presence in the sweep of historical events. This engraving shows the setting for the 1878 production of the Alexandrinsky Theatre in St Petersburg.*

A. J. Golovin designed sumptuous settings for Vsevolod Meyerhold's production of Mikhail Lermontov's Masquerade *at the Alexandrinsky Theatre of St. Petersburg in 1917. In this bedroom setting, the jealous husband Arbenin admits to his wife Nina that the ice cream he gave her at the masquerade ball was poisoned, and she dies.*

against subversive plays, making himself more and more ridiculous as he called for reprisals against Niemcewicz and his comedy. The divisive intriguing of the Polish gentry, who were unwilling to countenance the 1791 constitution's inchoate steps toward democracy, invited Russian intervention, and the Second Partition of Poland brought the loss of additional territory to Russia and Prussia in 1793.

It was during this period that another of Poland's major plays with political significance appeared: *Krakowiacy i Górale* (The Krakovians and the Mountaineers, 1794) by Wojciech Bogusławski. Often called "the father of Polish theater," Bogusławski was nobly born but gave up every advantage to work in the theater. After acting at the Narodowy for five years, he became its artistic director in 1783 and held that post for thirty years. Founding an actor training school, he made acting a respectable profession in Poland, and his tours to various Polish cities prepared the way for additional permanent theaters. Among the eighty or so plays he wrote and translated, *The Cracovians and the Mountaineers* was best loved for its fast-paced comic action, its colorful peasant types, and its incorporation of patriotic songs. Furthermore, it premiered shortly after the beginning of the popular Insurrection of Poles led by Tadeusz Kościuszko against the Russians. Poland might have liberated itself from the Russians if Austria had not joined the battle. In 1795 the Third Partition of Poland brought the end of the Polish state, as all of its former land was swallowed up by Russia, Prussia, and Austria, with over half of it going to Russia. Under Russian censorship, *The Cracovians and the Mountaineers* and other such plays were banned.

At the beginning of the nineteenth century, many Poles saw Napoleon as a possible deliverer of their country and flocked to join his army, but that hope had to be abandoned after Waterloo. Despite the enmity that the Polish people felt toward Tsarist Russia, a bond was forged between those Russians who were soon to be known as Decembrists and many young Polish officers who shared similar ideals. An especially close friendship developed between the two greatest poets of all time in the Russian and Polish languages, Aleksandr Pushkin and Adam Mickiewicz; each translated the other's poetry into his own language. A captivating personality, Mickiewicz formed many warm, lasting friendships during his years in Russia, 1824–29. He had already established his reputation as "the Polish national poet" on the basis of his early poetry. The publication of the first volume of Mickiewicz's *Poems* in 1822 is often taken as the beginning of Polish romanticism. However, it was another political event that accelerated the movement and gave Polish Romantic drama its distinctive character. The November Insurrection of 1830 launched a year of patriotic struggles to expel the Russian occupiers from Poland. When the effort failed in 1831, thousands of Poles had to flee into exile.

The Great Emigration included most of the Polish intelligentsia and virtually every important writer of the period. It meant that for an entire generation Polish culture would flourish only in alien surroundings. As Harold B. Segal points out, up until 1831 Polish Romanticism was developing along the lines of the European Romantic movement in general, broadly influenced by Schiller and Lord Byron; but after the Great Emigration separated the writers from their roots, paradoxically, Polish Romanticism became intensely nationalistic and, by the same token, relatively inaccessible to the foreign reader, even in translation. Thus the great Polish Romantic dramas could neither be performed inside Poland because of censorship, nor in countries of exile because of language and cultural barriers. Of the many Polish émigré enclaves all over Europe and in America, by far the most important was Paris, and that was where Mickiewicz settled. Although Mickiewicz, to his everlasting regret, had been outside the country in 1830–31 and did not participate in the November Insurrection, he emerged as a rallying figure for Polish émigré spirit. Like other émigrés, he at first believed that the period of exile would be short, that other countries imbued with the romantic spirit of freedom would join together to help Poland throw off its yoke of tyranny. The exiled writers kept this vision alive for about ten years, but gradually disillusionment set in. Around 1840 their work began to reflect the change from a unified sense of militant struggle to a range of attitudes that could be roughly grouped under the rubric of "Polish Messianism." They sought spiritual sustenance in mystical visions such as the belief that Poland's Christlike suffering must have some redemptive purpose—perhaps even the re-Christianization of a jaded Europe that had allowed foreign nations to help themselves to a once-proud country. Polish Romanticism peaked in 1848, at the time of the various uprisings known as the Spring of Nations. The failure of those revolutions brought new disillusionment to the émigrés. Finally, with the collapse of the January Insurrection of 1863 (the last of the many nineteenth-century revolutions inspired by the French), Poland found itself more harshly repressed than ever. The blame was shifted to the émigrés—and their Romantic vision—for having promulgated such false hopes.

These transformations in the Polish émigré spirit were all part of the fabric of their artistic creativity. The three greatest Polish Romantic poets were also the authors of the three landmark Polish Romantic plays: *Dziady* (Forefathers' Eve, 1823, 1832), by Adam Mickiewicz, *Kordian* (1834) by Juliusz Słowacki, and *Nieboska Komedia* (The Un-Divine Comedy, 1833), by Zygmunt Krasiński. Mickiewicz's multifaceted dramatic poem *Forefathers' Eve*, the national sacred drama of Poland, is a complex amalgam of patriotic, folkloric, and philosophical material written in different times and places, but unified by its pervading national spirit.

That nationalism is expressed metaphorically through the *dziady,* a twice-annual folk ritual synthesizing pagan mysticism and Catholicism's All Souls' Day, when peasants would gather in the graveyard and offer a banquet for the spirits of their departed forefathers. In 1823 Mickiewicz published what he called *Forefathers' Eve, Parts II and IV;* the apparently capricious numbering of the parts may have been intended to tantalize readers by provoking their curiosity about the missing parts. A fragment of *Part I* was eventually found and published posthumously. Drawing upon his own experiences (prison in Wilno, his Russian sojourn, his religious doubts, and, above all, his failure to return to Warsaw during the November Insurrection) and upon the disastrous course of events in Poland, Mickiewicz hastily wrote and published what he called *Part III* in 1832. Chronologically, the events in *Part III* occur after *Part IV,* but the entire work, with its unconventional jumble of dreams, visions, and reality, seems to be open-ended. For theatrical purposes, some see *Part III*—the dramatic heart of the work—as a self-contained play. However, when *Forefathers' Eve* finally reached the stage in 1901 as a full evening of theater, that production's text was composed of seven scenes taken from all four parts of the work. *Forefathers' Eve* dwells considerably upon the sufferings of Poland, with which the hero comes to identify. His transformation from a young man wounded by love to a potential leader who has transcended his personal problems (indeed, one scene shows angels and demons at war over his psyche as he sleeps) is reified in his change of name from Gustave to Konrad at the beginning of *Part III.* Depicting Poland as a victim by divine ordination, Mickiewicz could offer only a mystical vision of a savior as the solution to Poland's problems.

Although Słowacki eventually also went through a mystical phase, he conceived his dramatic masterpiece, *Kordian,* as a rebuttal of Mickiewicz's view. The "Hamletlike" Kordian emerges as a would-be Romantic hero full of grand gestures and rhetoric, but unable to act. A high point of the play occurs in a scene outside the door of the bedroom where the tsar is sleeping. Standing guard there, Kordian has his opportunity to kill the tsar, but instead he wrestles with the personifications of his fear and his imagination, and faints without having accomplished anything. Metaphorically, Słowacki was blaming the Polish people themselves, especially the "leaders," for their inaction as the cause of the nation's predicament. Słowacki's deep love for the Polish language made his exile particularly painful for him, and his writing became a way of reentering his native realm. The most prolific of the Polish Romantic dramatists, Słowacki wrote twenty-six plays comprising over half of his verse; yet only one of his plays, *Mazeppa,* was performed during his lifetime, and that production was in Hungary. Besides *Kordian,* his outstanding plays are *Balladyna* (1839), *Lilla Weneda* (1840), *Fantazy* (1841), and *Father Marek* (1843).

The third great Polish Romantic dramatist, Zygmunt Krasiński, was a spiritual exile even though he was free to travel into and out of Poland. The son of a reactionary general who acted opportunistically to retain his aristocratic social position after the Russian occupation, Krasiński was psychologically torn between respect for his father and his own intuitive patriotic idealism. For a long time, the work he published was attributed only to "the anonymous poet," because to use his family name would have brought reprisals against his parents, and yet his authorship was generally known to the émigré community. At twenty-one he wrote his remarkable poetic drama in prose. Like the great plays of Mickiewicz and Słowacki, *The Un-Divine Comedy* traces its hero's evolution from personal problems to political commitment, using an interplay of scenes—often fragmented—between reality and supernatural elements. Krasiński's romanticism differed from that of his compatriots in that he looked at Polish history from the broader perspective of an international class struggle that was bound to culminate in revolution. The dialectical opposition between the Christian, aristocratic Count Henryk and the atheistic Pancras, a professional revolutionary, culminates in Pancras's vision of Christ: "Like a column of snowy brightness He stands above the precipices, both hands on the cross, like an avenger on his sword. His crown of thorns is woven of thunderbolts." *The Un-Divine Comedy* did not reach the stage until 1902; Krasiński's other play *Irydion* (1836) had its first production when it inaugurated the Teatr Polski in Warsaw in 1913.

Although the comedy writer Aleksandr Fredro and the enigmatic poet-playwright Cyprian Norwid also lived and wrote during the Romantic period, their work is more appropriately interpreted in the context of the generation after the "Great Romantics." When the plays of Mickiewicz, Słowacki, and Krasiński finally began to be staged in Poland, to powerful emotional effect, they launched a so-called neo-romanticism in Polish theater that was actually closely akin to the symbolist movement in the arts at that time. Indeed, although the entire turn-of-the-century symbolist movement—which was centered first in France and later Russia—might be seen as a kind of neoromanticism, it will be treated as a distinctive avant-garde phenomenon in chapter 5. One French play of the period, however, does stand apart from all others as a self-contained exponent of neo-romanticism: Edmond Rostand's *Cyrano de Bergerac*.

A Romantic Postscript

When *Cyrano de Bergerac* opened at the Porte Saint-Martin on December 28, 1897, mainstream or "boulevard" theater consisted entirely of light comedies or farces and serious psychological dramas. Efforts to blaze new artistic trails were fragmented into coexisting movements as

Left, Constant Coquelin (1841–1909) created the role of Cyrano de Bergerac in the great neo-Romantic play by Edmond Rostand (1868–1918). Le Théâtre (1898).

Right, Jean Piat in the role of Cyrano and Geneviève Casile as Roxanne in this 1964 production of Cyrano de Bergerac. *Courtesy of French Cultural Services.*

polarized as symbolism and naturalism, and supported mostly by coterie audiences. Bursting onto this scene, Rostand's unabashedly romantic verse drama took jaded Parisian audiences by storm, tapping latent yearnings for an almost-forgotten idealism. With its verbal virtuosity, its compelling tale of heroism and self-abnegation for love, and its exuberant theatricality, this brilliant drama offered something for popular audiences, middle-class theatergoers, and intellectuals alike. "You're transported back to the most beautiful moments of Romanticism," rhapsodized critic Paul Meurice. After the opening performance, according to one report, "People who had been enemies for years were embracing each other. Two writers scheduled to meet in a duel the next morning shook hands and wept. Others sang the *Marseillaise* at the top of their lungs. At one o'clock in the morning, not a single audience member had gone home. Gentlemen in black tie stood on their seats clapping their hands and calling for the author. After forty curtain calls, the curtain finally remained raised. At two o'clock in the morning, the audience was still shouting, laughing, weeping, applauding, and didn't want to leave." The play's flamboyant yet sensitive title character, with his outsized nose and magnificent soul, was the ultimate embodiment of Hugo's "grotesque and the sublime." The role of Cyrano was created by Constant Coquelin, who had made his reputation in comic roles like Don César in *Ruy Blas* and Tartuffe. Rostand wrote *Cyrano de Bergerac* with Coquelin in mind, but the play would not have reached the stage at all if Coquelin had not assumed most of the financial risk for the expensive production. His unwavering faith in the play in the face of universal skepticism, including the author's own last-minute doubts, paid off in a run of over four hundred performances and posterity's association of his name with one of the greatest roles ever written.

Edmond Rostand wrote other plays, most notably *The Romancers* (produced in 1894 it became the basis for the long-running American hit, *The Fantasticks,* in 1960), *L'Aiglon* (1900), and *Chanticleer* (1910), but he never again found the formula that had propelled his masterpiece to such heights. Nor did the success of *Cyrano de Bergerac* launch a full-scale neo-romantic movement. It remained an exceptional phenomenon. Thus, the supreme exemplar of the Romantic drama arrived fifty years after the movement itself had died.

THE VAUDEVILLE AND OTHER PLEASURES

Even before romanticism came to France and long after it was gone, one French writer was drawing middle-class audiences in droves to the theater, and making himself fabulously wealthy. His preferred medium was the vaudeville, which was to comedy what melodrama was to tragedy. Author of an estimated 250 of these superficial and amusing comic intrigues in one to three acts, Eugène Scribe found a formula that worked to seize and hold an audience's attention. The formula, now referred to as that of the *pièce bien faite* (well-made play), could also be applied to comedies, melodramas, tragedies, and opera libretti, all of which comprised an additional two hundred or so works by Scribe and his various collaborators. Hack writer though he may have been, he was also one of the most influential figures of the century, for the techniques he perfected were ultimately incorporated into the work of dramatists from England's Tom Robertson to Norway's Ibsen.

Scribe tried to break into the theater for about five years before he achieved overnight success in 1815 with *Une Nuit de la Garde Nationale* (A National Guard Night). In 1821 he became resident dramatist at the Théâtre du Gymnase (a fashionable boulevard theater originally called Théâtre de Madame) and supplied it with over a dozen plays a year for the next decade. Whether using a contemporary or a historical setting, he wrote only to entertain, never to instruct. He had no sense of literary

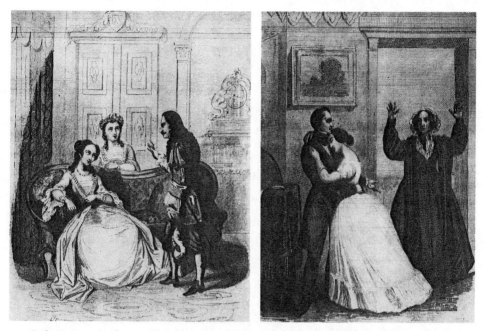

Left, Eugène Scribe (1791–1861), a prolific author of vaudevilles *as well as historical dramas and opera libretti, employed a formula for so-called "well-made plays." His historical comedy of intrigue* A Glass of Water *(1840) was set in eighteenth-century England. Engraving by L. Marcki from Scribe,* Oeuvres complètes *(1858).*

Right, La Calomnie (Slander), a five-act comedy-drama by Scribe, was produced at the Théâtre Français in 1840. Engraving by L. Marcki from Scribe, Oeuvres complètes *(1858).*

style and took no interest in the polemics over aesthetic theory that went on during the heyday of Romanticism, but he was elected to the French Academy five years ahead of Victor Hugo! Several of his plays, including *Le Verre d'eau* (The Glass of Water, 1840) and *Adrienne Lecouvreur* (1849), even premiered at the Comédie Française. The latter play, about the eighteenth-century French actress, was written for Rachel and later served as a vehicle for many of the great international actresses of the century. Best known among his twenty-eight opera libretti are Giacomo Meyerbeer's *Robert le diable* (Robert the Devil, 1831), and *The Huguenots* (1836), and Fromental Halévy's *La Juive* (The Jewess, 1835).

The interest of the well-made play lies in an intricately plotted action that encompasses suspense, reversals, and *coups de théâtre*, all seamlessly blended in a logical sequence of events. A basic device is to let the audience in on some crucial information while the major characters remain ignorant of it; the revelation of this secret late in the play precipitates the *peripeteia*, or change of fortune, for the hero and the antagonist. Up to that point the action follows a seesaw pattern as hero and adversary alternately get the upper hand. Scribe was a master at preparing the *scène à faire,* or obligatory scene, a climactic showdown toward which the action has been pointing. The *dénouement,* or resolution, leaves no strand of plot untied. In Scribe's plays, no time was wasted on social problems, moral questions, character psychology, or establishing an atmosphere, although these might be touched upon incidentally. The action often turned upon such middle-class preoccupations as money, social standing, politics, marriage, and other relations between the sexes, as long as the complications could be neatly resolved to the satisfaction of all.

Scribe's techniques were disparaged from the beginning—dismissed with epithets like "bastard Romanticism" or "patent-leather themes"—by writers with loftier ideals than making money. However, in the hands of a master like Henrik Ibsen, the bones of the well-made plot's skeleton can be fleshed out with characterization and ideas substantial enough to elevate it to a level of artistry. Certainly, some major French dramatists of the succeeding generation—Eugène Labiche, Alexandre Dumas *fils,* and others—would benefit from the methods that Scribe elucidated. The playwright who most closely followed in Scribe's footsteps was Victorien Sardou, who is probably best remembered for George Bernard Shaw's one-word description of his work: "Sardoodledum." His most frequently performed plays are social comedies like *Les Pattes de mouche* (A Scrap of Paper, 1860), and *Divorçons!* (Let's Get a Divorce!, 1880). Among the vehicles he wrote for Sarah Bernhardt are *Fédora* (1882), *Théodora* (1884), and *La Tosca* (1887). He was also good at superficial historical comedies like *Madame Sans-Gêne* (1893) and patriotic spectaculars like *Patrie* (Fatherland, 1869).

Among the countless writers who undertook to supply the inexhaustible market for vaudevilles, Eugène Labiche achieved lasting recognition for his comic finesse that transcended the shallow appeals of the form. His frequently revived tour de force, *Un Chapeau de paille d'Italie* (An Italian Straw Hat, 1851), a five-act chase with vaudeville songs, made it to Broadway in 1936 in an adaptation entitled *Horse Eats Hat.* Of his 172 plays, Labiche chose fifty-seven (thirty-four of these were one-act vaudevilles) for inclusion in the standard edition of his works published in 1879. Writing for and about the middle class, Labiche maintained a generally wholesome tone until late in his career, when works like his *Le Plus heureux des trois* (The Happiest of the Three, 1870) began to point the way toward the French bedroom farce of Georges Feydeau.

French vaudeville was introduced to Russia by Prince Aleksandr Shakhovsky, a descendant of old Moscow aristocracy who went to St. Petersburg for military service and discovered a passion for the theater. Encouraged by the great actor Ivan Dmitryevsky, Shakhovsky began at eighteen to write little comedies in the French manner. After leaving the

An Italian Straw Hat *(1851) remains the best-known work by Eugène Labiche (1815–88), and one of the most popular farces of all time.* Théâtre contemporain illustré.

Labiche's Belle of the Canebière *was produced at the Théâtre de l'Atelier in Paris in 1948. Shown here are Yvonne Clech, Palau, and Madeleine Geoffroy. Courtesy of French Cultural Services.*

military in 1802 to become director of the Imperial theaters, he traveled to Paris to study the French system of actor training; this experience also helped him to formulate regulations for the Imperial theater system, which were approved by Tsar Alexander I in 1825 and remained in effect until 1917. Shakhovsky's *The Cossack Poet* (1812) is considered to be the first Russian vaudeville. Besides satirical comedies, melodramas, and magical comedy-ballets, his one hundred or so plays included many adaptations of French vaudevilles, a form he described as the "bastard child of comedy and comic opera."

From the 1820s to the 1840s, French vaudevilles dominated the Russian stage. Since they had no literary value, any dilettante could translate them rapidly, merely rebaptizing the French characters with Russian names. Since they were simple to produce, a new vaudeville performed as a curtain raiser was a good way to freshen up the bill when a tired mainpiece was offered. Unfortunately, the ubiquitous vaudeville also encouraged superficial acting, as the characters were virtually interchangeable and the simple tunes required no real singing ability. Their blandness may also have contributed to the late development of Russian dramatic criticism, which had already been seriously impeded by an 1815 government ukase: "Opinions concerning the Imperial theatre and the actors in His Majesty's service are taken to be inappropriate in any periodical." Russia's first professional critic, Vissarion Belinsky, whose literary judgments had great influence in the 1830s and 1840s, enjoyed vaudevilles despite the emphasis on content in his literary theory and despite his harsh assessment of French vaudevilles that were "neither translated nor adapted" but "forcibly dragged from the French stage to the Russian" so that they emerged with "dull witticisms, flat jests, and poor verses." He elaborated the point: "Dress a Frenchman in a dark gray tunic, gird him with a belt, put leggings and bast shoes on his legs, tie somebody's bushy beard on his face, and make him even curse in Russian; still he will not be a Russian muzhik, but to his own and your regret will continue to be a Frenchman in the guise of a Russian peasant. Consequently he will be neither a Russian nor a Frenchman, but a caricature of both, with no face of his own." Writing in a more positive vein, Belinsky commented: "The subject of vaudeville: little passions and weaknesses, funny prejudices, amusingly-eccentric characters, anecdotal events of the private and home-life of society. In a word, if the vaudeville does not trespass its frontiers, and does not wander into spheres alien to it; when it is amusing, light, witty, lively, it can give a very great—though momentary—pleasure both when reading it and when seeing it on stage."

Unfortunately, it was this kind of material that predominated during the career of nineteenth-century Russia's greatest actor, Mikhail Semyonovich Shchepkin. Born a serf, he began acting in his teens in Count Volkenstein's private theater. From 1805 to 1821 he toured the provinces with a professional company, finally gaining his freedom in 1821, when he was thirty-three. He made his Moscow debut in 1822 and soon established himself as the leading actor at the Maly Theatre, where his finely tuned characterizations seemingly gave substance to the flimsy vaudevilles that made up the bulk of his repertoire. A dedicated, conscientious actor, Shchepkin constantly worked toward greater naturalness in his own acting and toward welding the Maly company into an ensemble. It was his example and leadership that advanced the Moscow theater's prestige beyond that of the Imperial Theatres of St. Petersburg. His friendships with writers like Gogol, Griboyedov, Pushkin, and Turgenev spurred their writing for the theater, thus beginning an infusion of native Russian material. Besides bringing great warmth and believability to his countless "comic old man" roles in vaudevilles, Shchepkin had the satisfaction of playing two great roles: the jovial but limited father, Famusov, in Griboyedov's *Wit Works Woe* (performed 1831), and the Mayor in Gogol's *The Inspector General* (1836). Shchepkin's great colleague at the Maly, Pavel Stepanovich Mochalov, brought a romantic temperament to the serious roles in which he specialized. In contrast to Shchepkin's disciplined technique for achieving realistic portrayals, Mochalov relied upon inspiration and was often uneven. Although he was called "the Russian Kean," his potential was limited by the material of his repertoire, which consisted largely of German melodramas and Russian translations of French adaptations of Shakespeare.

By the 1840s, the dependence on French sources was decreasing and many Russian authors had begun writing original vaudevilles. Some exploited the form to vent their frustrations with Russian life, since the censors relaxed their vigilance over a genre they regarded as superficial. While—under the strict controls of Nicholas I—serious literary efforts like *Boris Godunov, Wit Works Woe,* and *Masquerade* remained unperformed or produced only in severely cut versions, the vaudevilles were at least reaching an audience. There was a gradual change in the kinds of settings used for the vaudevilles on the Russian stage. Whereas the French-based vaudevilles were set in the drawing rooms of the nobility, the locales of the original Russian ones are suggested in such titles as *The Bakery; or, A Petersburg German* (1843) and *A House in the Petersburg District; or, The Art of How Not to Pay the Rent* (1838), both by P. A. Karatygin, or *St. Petersburg Lodgings: A Vaudeville Comedy in Five Apartments* (1840) by Fyodor Koni. The best Russian author of vaudevilles was Alexander Ivanovich Pisarev, author of twenty-three plays, all written between 1823 and 1828. The title character in his vaudeville *Khlopotun* (The Busybody, 1824)—a bachelor who bustles about his friend's estate, interfering in everything—passed into the permanent gallery of Russia's great stage characters. Vaudevilles remained popular throughout the century in Russia, so that as late as the 1880s Chekhov would embark upon his writing for the theater with, as he wrote to a friend, "a trivial little vaudeville in the French manner, called *The Bear*."

A third great flourishing of the vaudeville occurred in Denmark, largely due to the efforts of Johan Ludwig Heiberg. After studying in France and Germany in the 1820s, he returned to Copenhagen and worked his way up to becoming the country's unofficial arbiter of artistic taste through his literary criticism, his own playwriting, and his directorship of the Danish Royal Theatre on Kongens Nytorv. Copenhagen theater was mired in Kotzebue and his clones in the mid-1820s, with only occasional token performances of the great Danish tragic poet Oehlenschläger; but through Heiberg's leadership, the theater soon became the focus of Danish intellectual life, with celebrities like Hans Christian Andersen and Søren Kierkegaard attending night after night. What is astounding is that he raised production standards and the public's level of taste through the medium of French vaudeville. He began by getting the theater to produce his own play, the first Danish vaudeville, *Kong Salomon og Jorgen Hattemager* (King Solomon and George the Hatter, 1825). To a public long steeped in grand passions and Gothic horror, the pleasure of light comedy came as a revelation. Next Heiberg published his eloquent defense of the genre, *On the Vaudeville as a Dramatic Genre and Its Significance for the Danish Stage* (1826). Using a Hegelian dialectic, he showed that the vaudeville "fills a necessary place in the system of genres, being fully as good and fully as necessary as the others," and that once vaudeville had fulfilled its potential, it would serve as a launching pad for a higher form, a new national comedy. The impact of this essay was immediate and lasting; even thirty years later Henrik Ibsen was to incorporate its ideas into his own early writing.

In 1829 Heiberg was appointed resident playwright and translator for the Danish Royal Theatre. Although his theatrical craftsmanship is undisputed, much of his success was built upon the talents of the lovely actress whom he married in 1831 and for whom he wrote the principal roles in his plays, Johanne Luise Heiberg. Among his original plays, the longtime favorite was *Elverhøj* (Elves' Hill, 1828). Over the years he translated forty foreign comedies, the majority of them by Scribe. But Heiberg eventually tired of the formula that had served his aims so well. One departure from his characteristic manner was his verse satire or "apocalyptic comedy" *En Sjoel efter Døden* (A Soul after Death, 1840). Produced only posthumously, in 1891, it has been called "the wittiest work in Danish literature." From 1849 to 1856, Heiberg held the difficult position of managing director of the Danish Royal Theatre, where, ironically, considering all he had done to raise the theater's standards, he was regarded by the younger members of the company as impossibly reactionary. In the vaudeville tradition, Heiberg's major disciple was Henrik Herz, who devoted himself for forty years to writing plays with fine roles for Johanne Luise Heiberg. Among these were *The Savings Bank* (1936), *Svend Dyring's House* (1837), and *Kong Renés Datter* (King René's Daughter, 1845, upon which Tchaikovsky's *Iolanthe* was later based). The vaudeville also predominated in Hans Christian Andersen's dramatic writing of the 1830s.

Johanne Luise Heiberg captured the hearts of Copenhagen theatergoers and her future husband alike when she made her debut at thirteen under her maiden name, Hanne Pätges, in Heiberg's vaudeville *Aprilsnarrene* (The April Fools, 1826). There was a charming lightness of touch about her portrayals that somehow combined girlishness and womanliness, modesty and coquettishness. Striving for an idealized harmony of form, she moved and gestured with a dancer's grace while her face and voice expressed subtle shades of meaning. Some even saw her as the finest actress anywhere in Europe at the time; in Denmark she won the honor of being billed as "Fru Heiberg" instead of the standard "Madame." In the 1840s she moved into Shakespearean roles, distinguishing herself particularly as a vibrant, electrifying Lady Macbeth. Her outstanding contemporaries at the Danish Royal Theatre included her leading man C. N. Rosenkilde, the sly comedian Ludwig Phister, and serious actors N. P. Nielsen, Anna Nielsen, and Michael Wiehe.

A major appeal of vaudeville was its lack of pretension. Undemanding of its audiences or performers, it adapted easily to small theater facilities that could not compete in the realm of machinery, and it could be targeted to a specific audience by the simple addition of a few topical references in the dialogue. These very features, however, made it somewhat of an anomaly in a century that seemed to prize scenic overkill and mass appeal. Two theatrical elements that gave special pleasure in the nineteenth century were visual effects and musical enhancement in the form of dance, song, or dramatic underscoring. The many possible formats in which visual and aural spectacle could be combined gave rise to such a bewildering variety of theatrical entertainments that it is often difficult to make a clear distinction between, for example, the fairy extravaganza and the ballet-pantomime on an exotic subject, or circus and equestrian drama, or parody and burlesque. Only a few examples of the many combinations can be touched upon here.

The English pantomime that had been popularized by John Rich in the 1720s underwent some modifications in the nineteenth century. The original format, called a Harlequinade, was a series of nonspeaking low-

Johanne Luise Heiberg (1812–90) and Ludwig Phister appear as Helen and Howard in Slaegtningene *(In-Laws), a vaudeville by Henriette Nielsen. Colored drawing by A. H. Harttung. Courtesy of the Teatermuseet, Copenhagen.*

comedy exploits performed by characters borrowed from Italian *commedia dell'arte*. It was prefaced by a short "opening" in verse, based upon a fairy tale or nursery rhyme, which culminated in the transformation of the fairy-tale characters into the energetic pantomime artists (Clown, Harlequin, Pantaloon, Columbine) who would perform the more physical action of the harlequinade or "clown show" portion of the pantomime. The emphasis shifted from the figures of Italian origin to the purely English "Clown," beginning in 1806 with Joseph Grimaldi's *tour de force* performance as Clown in Thomas Dibdin's *Harlequin and Mother Goose; or, The Golden Egg* at Covent Garden. Starting with the white costume and whiteface makeup of the French Pierrot character, Grimaldi painted red half-moons on his cheeks, and added English jester patches to his costume. His comic resources were endless: his entering cry of "Here we are again!," the contortions of his mobile features, his exuberant impudence of gesture and movement, his way of sitting at the front of the stage and selling a song like the woeful tale of "The Oyster Crossed in Love," or "Tippetywichet" (punctuated by staggering, sneezing, yawning, crying, and laughing), or his famous "Hot Codlings." One of his most delightful tricks was to take ordinary items such as broom handles, rolling pins, umbrellas, chains, coal-scuttles, etc., and use them to construct animated figures. In *Harlequin Asmodeus; or Cupid on Crutches* (1810) at Covent Garden, he created a pugilist out of a cabbage, turnips, carrots, parsnips, and radishes; the vegetable man came to life, engaged Grimaldi in a fight, and "beat him off the stage." After Joey Grimaldi's retirement in 1823, Clown was always named Joey, in honor of him. However, as no other Joey could nearly fill Grimaldi's shoes, the Harlequinade portion of the English pantomime decreased in importance while the fairy-tale opening was expanded and enhanced with large-scale scenic transformations. There was, however, an equally legendary American pantomime Clown, George L. Fox, a droll-looking, bald-pated whirlwind of mischievous energy, who could elicit gales of laughter by putting an expression of wounded innocence on his face and winking at the audience. His *Humpty Dumpty* (1867), the first full-length pantomime in America, ran a phenomenal 1,168 performances in New York.

The English pantomime gave rise to a number of related forms. Taking advantage of its right to use speech on stage before the Theatre Regulation Act of 1843, Covent Garden experimented briefly with the "speaking pantomime." The "speaking Harlequinade" did not catch on, but the "speaking opening" did. The latter developed into two different kinds of longer entertainments: the burlesque and the fairy extravaganza. The burlesque was an exaggeration and mockery of any well-known material. Anything ranging from nursery rhymes to classical mythology to currently running plays could become the target of a burlesque. Burlesques were often written in relentless doggerel, as was H. J. Byron's *The Babes in the Wood* (1859), a burlesque of the melodrama *The Children in the Wood* by Thomas Morton. Byron was one of the most prolific Victorian dramatists, but he wrote hastily to satisfy the constant demand for new material, and his work was little remembered beyond his lifetime. In New York, while Edwin Booth was performing his critically acclaimed Hamlet, George L. Fox offered a full-length burlesque *Hamlet* (1870) by Thomas Cooper DeLeon.

England's fairy extravaganza combined aspects of the pantomime and of the French *féerie* that flourished early in the nineteenth century. In France, a specific antecedent for the *féerie* might be seen in the magic shows concocted by a Belgian magician, sometime professor of physics, and balloon ascensionist, Etienne-Gaspard Robert, whose stage name was Robertson. He opened in Paris in 1797 a "chemical and phantasmagorical theatre" of light projections and sounds, aided by a ventriloquist named Fitz-James. With smoke and mirrors and a magic lantern that slid on a track, the secrets of which he revealed in his 1833

Above, the greatest clown on the American stage, George L. Fox (1825–77), achieved his most enduring success in the 1868 pantomime Humpty Dumpty. *From Appelbaum,* Scenes from the Nineteenth-Century Stage in Advertising Woodcuts.

Below, in his studio in the Cour de Capucines in Paris in 1797, the magician Robertson and his assistant Fitz-James created amazing fantasmagoria—projections in midair—like those seen here. From E. G. Robertson, Mémoires, *volume 1 (Paris 1831).*

Right, Robertson's Mémoires *reveals all the secrets of his fantasmagoric art. Diagrammed here is his magic lantern that increased or reduced the size of projected images by sliding backward or forward on a track.*

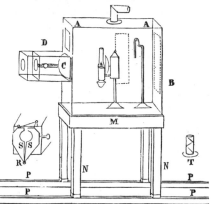

Mémoires, Robertson was able to create multiple projections in midair. The loose narrative of his *Petit répertoire fantasmagorique* served as a pretext for stringing together amazing effects in episodes like the bleeding nun, the tomb with ghostly apparitions, the witches' sabbath, the temptation of Saint Anthony, the maiden restored to life by Cupid, and many others, including impressive patriotic spectacles like the fall of Robespierre. At one performance when he was presenting apparitions like William Tell and Voltaire, an audience member asked to see Louis XVI; Robertson was said to have replied wittily: "I used to have the formula for that, but I've lost it and probably won't ever find it, so we'll never be able to bring kings back to France." Such material, transferred to the live-action stage, was the basis for the early nineteenth-century *féerie.*

Despite the emphasis on spectacular effects along with elaborate dance numbers, the *féerie* usually managed to retain the whimsical charm of such eighteenth-century sources as Charles Perrault or the Comtesse d'Aulnoy. In Merle and Carmouche's *The Marvelous Lamp* (1822), Aladdin is pursued by soldiers, but he rubs his magic lamp and suddenly—by an ingenious trick worked out by the costumer and machinist together—they are all transformed into cooks! It is possible that the earliest representation of a train on stage was in a *féerie,* Laloue's *The Devil's Pills* (1839). Toward the end of the century, the *féerie* turned to science fiction with stage versions of Jules Verne's *A Trip to the Moon* (1875) and *Impossible Voyage* (1882). One of the genre's biggest hits, A. L. D. Martainville's *Le pied de mouton* (Sheep's Foot, 1806), mustered such enchantments as a hat turning into a hot-air balloon and flying away, a banquet table turning into a giant, a wall disappearing so the two lovers could be lifted away on a magnificent cloud, and waves increasing in size until they lapped up against the clouds.

This same *féerie,* adapted by the impresario José de Grimaldi (no relation to the English clown) and retitled *La pata de cabra* (Goat's Foot, 1829), became the most popular play in Spain in the first half of the nineteenth century, far eclipsing in box-office receipts all the great literary dramas of the Spanish romantics. In Spain, the *féerie* was known as *comedia de magia* (magic spectacle). Italian Harlequinades had long been performed in Spain, and the Golden Age *comedias* of Calderón had often called for special effects, but that machinery had been relatively simple. It was Juan Salvo y Vela's five early eighteenth-century plays known by the collective title *El mágico de Salerno* (The Magician of Salerno, published 1733) that truly gave Spanish audiences their taste for spectacle at the expense of literary drama. With each succeeding play, Salvo y Vela's magician Pedro Vayalarde performed ever more extravagant magical feats. The numerous imitations that followed, from the 1730s to the 1830s, retained the central figure of the magician as a distinguishing feature of the Spanish *comedia de magia*. Grimaldi's *Goat's Foot* differed from the norm in that the hero is aided in his amorous conquest by the magic of Cupid himself. In the first scene Cupid gives the hero a goat's foot as a magic talisman, and thence the play proceeds through thirty-five different magical effects. In adapting the French original, Grimaldi tightened the plot, added comic business to make the villain's blundering pawn Simplicio into one of the great character roles of the nineteenth-century Spanish stage, and tailored the dialogue to the Spanish cultural outlook. The eleven different settings (with twelve scene changes) and the complicated magic tricks, all designed by Juan Blanchard, were far more elaborate than anything previously seen on the Spanish stage. Although forty-eight extra stagehands had to be hired for each performance, as well as extra musicians and actors, *Goat's Foot* never failed to recoup its running costs, drawing audiences to Madrid from all over Spain despite the difficulty of travel in that period of political repression. David Gies, author of a study of Grimaldi's seminal place in the development of modern Spanish theater, suggests that it was this *comedia de magia* that kept Madrid's two theaters going financially in a difficult period and also helped to form audiences for the extravagances of Romantic drama.

The English fairy extravaganza did not emerge as a separate genre until the 1830s. The outstanding creator of these was the multitalented James Robinson Planché, author of about 180 plays for a dozen different London theaters, including the two patent theaters. His prodigious career extended to play translation, theater management, costume design, and antiquarian scholarship. His efforts in the latter areas were particularly noteworthy, earning him the respect of professional archaeologists and prompting definite advances in stage costuming for historical accuracy. His partnership with Madame Vestris—who managed three London theaters in succession: the Olympic, Covent Garden, and the Lyceum—from 1831 to 1855 afforded him opportunities to apply his expertise in design history to the stage settings as well as to write in a variety of genres. His first fairy extravaganza, *Riquet with the Tuft* (1836), relied heavily upon a *féerie* he had seen in Paris, *Riquet à la houppe*, but he subsequently worked directly from fairy tales, as in *Puss in Boots* (1837), *Blue Beard* (1839), *Beauty and the Beast* (1841), and many others. Drawing upon the tradition of English pantomime, he provided fine breeches roles for Madame Vestris. As an example of his magical effects, the finale of *Fortunio and his Seven Gifted Servants* (1843) calls for: "Music. The pile of treasure gradually opens, and discovers a magnificent Fairy Chariot, drawn by twenty-four sheep with golden fleeces, in which is the Fairy."

Victorian England indulged in a veritable cult of fairies. Poetry, stories, book illustrations, and paintings give evidence of the obsession, which found expression on the stage not only in fairy extravaganzas but also in fairy ballets incorporated into other kinds of productions as well as in the ubiquitous sylph of the Romantic ballet. Shakespeare's Puck from *A Midsummer Night's Dream* and Ariel from *The Tempest* became frequent subjects of illustrations. Madame Vestris and her husband Charles Mathews produced *A Midsummer Night's Dream* at Covent Garden in 1840, inaugurating a century-long tradition of treating the last act as a shimmering fairy spectacle. Samuel Phelps (who also played Bottom) revived the play at Sadler's Wells in 1853, treating the fairy world in the muted manner of a dream. According to one reviewer: "Over all the fairy portion of the play there is a haze thrown by a curtain of green gauze placed between the actors and audience, and maintained there during the whole of the second, third, and fourth acts. This gauze curtain is so well spread that there are very few parts of the house from which its presence can be detected, but its influence is everywhere felt; it subdues the flesh and blood of the actors into something more nearly resembling dream figures." And according to another: "There is a misty transparency about the figures that gives them the appearance of flitting shadows more than of human beings. You fancy you can see the moon shining through them. There they dance and whirl, and are puffed about first from one side and then to another, like a cloud of silver dust; . . . you may almost imagine, in the dreamy stage which the play engenders, that the little fairies are being tossed in a big sheet of the moon, and that Puck is looking on and enjoying the fun." Only three years later, Charles Kean staged *A Midsummer Night's Dream* at the Princess Theatre in a lavish production that borrowed bits from both the Vestris and Phelps revivals. A chorus of seventy fairies danced around a flower-garlanded maypole as they sang Titania to sleep at the end of act 3. A sidelight of Kean's production was the appearance of nine-year-old Ellen Terry as Puck.

Three important Austrian dramatists wrote fairy plays. The beloved Viennese comedian-dramatist Johan Nestroy began his playwriting career with fairy plays, but his tremendous popularity came to rest more upon the lively satirical comedies of intrigue he wrote to feature himself. A tall, gangling figure, Nestroy played off against the short, fat Wenzel Sholz in some fifty plays like *Lumpazivagabondus* (1833) and *Der Talismann, oder Die Schicksalperüken* (The Talisman; or, The Wigs of Fate, 1840). Ferdinand Raimund acted with the Leopoldstadt Theatre for six years before he began writing its *Zauberspieler,* a traditional Viennese type of musical fairy extravaganza featuring the adventures of ordinary Viennese characters in a world of magic. The best of his nine plays were *Der Alpenkönig und der Menschenfeind* (The King of the Alps and the Misanthrope, 1828), and *Der Verschwender* (The Spendthrift, 1834).

Acting in his own musical-Romantic folk comedy The Spendthrift, *Ferdinand Raimund, on the right, captured all the nuances of Austrian popular character types. Mantzius,* A History of Theatrical Art, 6.

Franz Grillparzer's dramatic work ranged from plays on classical themes, like his trilogy *The Golden Fleece* (1821, *Das golden Vliess*), to historical dramas and translations. He often dealt with sexual relationships, and this brought him into conflict with the censors, which led him to withhold his plays from the stage after 1838. His most popular work, however, was the fairy play *Der Traum ein Leben* (A Dream of Life, 1834), which was loosely inspired by Calderón's *Life Is a Dream*. Although Viennese fairy plays were normally relegated to the popular stage, Grillparzer's elimination of low-comedy clowning made this blend of magic and the supernatural acceptable to the staid Burgtheater, where it premiered.

Romantic Ballet

The nineteenth-century interest in spirits and supernatural elements was reflected also in the ballet and the opera. It was in an opera that the Romantic ballet made its initial impact. Newly appointed to the administration of the Paris Opéra in 1831, Dr. Louis Véron opened the brilliant five-year period of his tenure with Giacomo Meyerbeer's *Robert le diable* (Robert the Devil, 1831), in which the third act was given over to a ballet of dead nuns, who rose from their graves to dance in the moonlit Gothic cloister designed by the inimitable Ciceri. The role of the abbess Helen was danced by Marie Taglioni, a gawky-looking young woman off the stage; but she had been coached by her choreographer father to move with apparently effortless grace, to appear almost weightless. Dancing on *pointe* had been introduced only a decade earlier, and she was the first to base an entirely new style upon it. Opening night was a disaster. A brace of lighted gas lamps with glass shades fell from the flies, narrowly missing a dancer, and a flat nearly dropped onto Taglioni as she lay on her grave, but she moved aside just in time to avoid being hit; the curtain was rung down for a few moments to allow her to compose herself. Finally, the lead male dancer accidentally plunged through an open trapdoor, prompting a dancer waiting below stage to ask: "What the devil are you doing down here? Have they changed the plot?" Nevertheless, Taglioni's ethereal dance and the haunting vision of the *corps de ballet* all in white sinking back into their graves to the ghostly music took Paris by storm.

Taglioni repeated her success in *La Sylphide* (1832), and her lighter-than-air style of movement added a new word to the French language: *taglioniser* meant to move with gossamer grace. Fashionable women adopted the ballerina hairdo and the pale, virginal look of the white gown with flowers. Furthermore, Taglioni's sloping shoulders became a physiognomic ideal during the Romantic period. Many other ballets were created to feature the ethereal ballerina in white, even as late as the turn of the century; for example, *Le Lac des cygnes* (Swan Lake, 1895), and *Les Sylphides* (1909). But one ballet in particular epitomizes the Romantic movement: Adolphe Adam's *Giselle* (1840). Act 1 employs the saturated color and folk motifs of the middle European peasant milieu to which Giselle belongs. In act 2, having gone mad and died for the false love of a duke, Giselle reappears as a ghostly spirit, summoned from her grave in a moonlit forest glade by the Queen of the Willis. The work thus incorporates both local color and the supernatural. It combined a chaste *Weltschmerz* and the hysteria of an energetically danced "mad scene." *Giselle* brought to the fore another of the great romantic ballerinas, Carlotta Grisi.

The ideals of Romantic ballet spread rapidly from Paris to the rest of Europe. One of the greatest exponents of the style was Auguste Bournonville, born in Copenhagen of French and Swedish parentage. After studying in Paris and winning acclaim as a dancer, he chose to return to Denmark. During his forty-seven-year career at the Danish Royal Ballet, 1829–77, he made his name virtually synonymous with that institution. He developed a system of training that yielded early results when his protégée Lucile Grahn won international renown at seventeen. He produced all the great Romantic ballets, but—in the age of dominance by the ballerina—he kept the work of the male dancers up to strength. Furthermore, it is his version of *La Sylphide* that has continued to be revived. Bournonville had the advantage of working with such

Ciceri's romantic moonlit Gothic cloister was the setting for the ballet of dead nuns in the Paris Opera production of Meyerbeer's Robert le diable *(1831). Georges Moynet,* Trucs et décors *(1885).*

Valdemar Gyllich (1836–85) designed this setting for Valdemar, *a ballet by August Bournonville (1805–79), who brought the Danish Royal Ballet to its golden age. Teatermuseet, Copenhagen.*

outstanding designers of the Danish Royal Theatre as Aron Wallich, Troels Lund, C. F. Christensen, and Valdemar Gyllich. Credited with introducing the box set in his ballet *La Sonnambula* (The Sleepwalker, 1829), Bournonville thus predated by several years Madame Vestris's first use of the box set on the London stage.

Russia also proved hospitable to Romantic ballet as developed in France. The Imperial Theatre Ballet School, founded by Catherine the Great in 1779, had followed the French model. A French-Swedish ballet-master, Charles-Louis Didelot, was brought to St. Petersburg in 1801 and, by the time he retired in 1836, the exigent teacher-producer had established a system that earned him the epithet "the father of Russian ballet." The idolatry inspired by his ballerinas—like Marie Danilova and Avdotia Istomina—ultimately made the Russians into more fervid *balletomanes* than the French. It was reported that after Marie Taglioni's 1837 tour to Russia, a pair of her ballet shoes was sold for two hundred rubles to a group of *balletomanes,* who held a banquet at which the cooked shoes were eaten with a sauce. In 1847 the French dancer Marius Petipa joined the Imperial Ballet as *premier danseur.* Soon he began choreographing new ballets and, in 1869, became balletmaster. During his sixty years in Russia, under four tsars, he choreographed forty-six new ballets—including Tchaikovsky's *Sleeping Beauty* (1890) and *The Nutcracker* (1892)—and thirty-four operas, and he added improvements to seventeen ballet revivals. Petipa retired in 1903, knowing that Russian ballet was then unsurpassed in the world.

American Popular Entertainment

One of the most spectacular productions of the century was a ballet extravaganza that combined imported dancers with a forgettable script by American author Charles M. Barras. It was entitled *The Black Crook; An Original Magical and Spectacular Drama in Four Acts* (1866). The production came about partly by chance. William Wheatley, manager of Niblo's Garden Theatre in New York, had already scheduled Barras's fairy melodrama for production, when producers Jarrett and Palmer approached him with the idea of turning it into a musical extravaganza. On a trip to Europe, Jarrett and Palmer had booked a Parisian ballet troupe's production of *La Biche aux bois* (Sleeping Beauty) for New York's Academy of Music that fall, but the theater burned down, leaving Jarrett and Palmer stuck with three ballerinas, a huge *corps de ballet,* and all their sets and costumes. The penniless Barras finally agreed to those embellishments to his script—a reluctant decision that was to earn him over $60,000 in the first six months. The plot of *The Black Crook* was a farrago of ideas taken from various melodramas, fairy extravaganzas, Weber's

Der Freischütz, and Goethe's *Faust.* The "Black Crook" of the title is the sorcerer Herzog, who makes a pact with the archfiend Zamiel, but fails in his machinations against the starving artist Rodolphe and his beloved Amina. The action brings encounters with Immortals (Fairies, Sprites, Naiads, Submarine Monsters, etc.), Amphibea, Gnomes, and Infernals (Skeletons, Apparitions, Demons, Monsters, etc.). The visual effects included transformations, phantasmagoria, displays of fire and water, and more of the female leg than the public was accustomed to seeing. The "indecent and demoralizing exhibition" of a chorus of eighty dancers in flesh-colored tights proved to be one of the major attractions; the more they were denounced from the pulpit, the more the curious flocked to see for themselves. The New York *Tribune* reviewer commented: "The scenery is magnificent, the ballet is beautiful; the drama is—rubbish." It cost an unprecedented $55,000 to open this most spectacular show ever seen in America, but it ran for 474 performances and took in over a million dollars. Revived eight times in New York during the nineteenth century, *The Black Crook* spawned smaller touring companies and such spin-offs as *The Black Crook Burlesque* and *The Black Crook Song Book.* Its place in American theater history seems assured in that it might be considered the first American musical comedy.

Another distinctly American form of entertainment, the minstrel show, flourished from the 1840s to the 1870s. Around 1830 Thomas D. Rice discovered a market for song and dance performed in blackface by a professional white entertainer. The success of his "Jim Crow dance" led him to collect other Negro melodies for performance, and also attracted imitators. In 1843, Dan Emmett and three others calling themselves The Virginia Minstrels worked up a blackface musical entertainment that proved popular enough to tour London. Wearing white trousers, calico shirts, and cutaway swallow-tailed dress coats made of blue calico, they played the fiddle, banjo, bones, and tambourine. Over the years Emmett composed many songs that long remained in the standard repertoire, including "Dixie," "The Blue-Tail Fly," and "Early in the Morning." It was Edwin P. Christy's Christy Minstrels that set the basic pattern for the minstrel show: The first part followed a standard format beginning with the Interlocutor acting as straight man to the patter of the two end men, Mr. Tambo and Mr. Bones. Behind them in a semicircle sat the minstrels who played musical numbers in alternation with the dialogue sequences. The first part ended with a "walk around" or Cake Walk. Olio acts were performed during the break. The second part of the minstrel show was a "free fantasia" composed of variety specialties in a spontaneous manner, as if improvised for each new audience. The 1850s saw so many minstrel companies on the road that legitimate theater could scarcely compete. The first minstrel company

Visual spectacle and dancers in scanty costumes contributed to the success of The Black Crook *(1866) at Niblo's Garden Theatre in New York. Appelbaum,* Scenes from the Nineteenth-Century Stage in Advertising Woodcuts.

Aida Overton Walker and George Walker perform a cakewalk. She toured to London with George Walker and Bert Williams in 1903. Sampson, The Ghost Walks. *Henry T. Sampson Black Theatre and Motion Picture Collection.*

composed of black performers, The Georgia Minstrels, was organized in 1865 by a black showman, Charles B. Hicks. This paved the way for a number of "genuine" or "Simon Pure" black minstrel companies touring in the northern United States, and some achieved highly acclaimed foreign tours in the 1870s. Black comedian Billy Kersands, for example, started out with Hicks and later starred with Haverly's Genuine Colored Minstrels in England; he could put a full-size cup and saucer in his mouth, or do his monologue with a billiard ball in his cheek. But the market for minstrel shows in general declined steadily, leaving only a few companies at the end of the century.

Despite the serious obstacles they had to overcome, many black performers enriched the nineteenth-century American entertainment scene. William Henry Lane, whose professional name was Juba, had a short, brilliant career as a solo dancer in the 1840s. Starting with the Irish jig, he added complex African American rhythms innovatively tapped out with his feet. Juba toured to England in 1848, and a British reviewer marveled at his ability to "tie his legs into such knots, and fling them about so recklessly, or make his feet twinkle until you lose sight of them altogether." As the father of American tap dancing, Juba has been called the "most influential single performer of nineteenth-century American dance." He remained in England until his death in 1852 at age twenty-seven. Another black American who found great favor in England was singer-composer James Bland, author of hundreds of famous songs. Sam Lucas began as a minstrel performer at nineteen in 1869, but his determination as well as his extraordinary talents as a singer, composer, and character actor enabled him to break away from the restricting format and blaze a trail for blacks in other areas of entertainment. He joined black operatic singers Anna and Emma Hyer in several of their productions, beginning with the ground-breaking *Out of Bondage* (1875). As the first black to play the title role in an *Uncle Tom's Cabin* company (in 1878), and the first black to star in a movie (the 1915 version of *Uncle Tom's Cabin*), and an early black performer in the "white" Loew's vaudeville circuit, Lucas earned his title, "The Grand Old Man of the Negro Stage." Among the most acclaimed of the many African-American talents who made names for themselves in show business was the turn-of-the-century song-and-dance team of George Walker and Bert Williams. They struggled for years before finding their comedic formula: Walker portrayed a wisecracking dandy, and Williams, using burnt-cork makeup over his own medium-dark complexion, played the clowning simpleton. They played the top vaudeville houses, the music-hall circuit, and even produced their own musicals, beginning with *A Lucky Coon* (1899) and culminating on Broadway with *In Dahomey* (1903), which also toured to England. Although Walker died in 1911, Bert

Before Tony Pastor made respectable family entertainment of American vaudeville, variety acts were performed in saloons like this one in Cheyenne, Wyoming.

Williams went on to star in the Ziegfeld *Follies* nearly every year until 1919. Remembered especially for his rendering of the song "Nobody," Bert Williams was described by W. C. Fields as "the funniest man I ever saw, and the saddest man I ever knew."

Variety acts grew to make up a large portion of American entertainment in the latter half of the nineteenth century. In the 1850s, minstrel-show specialty acts began to be performed as olios—that is, in front of a painted curtain—in concert saloons for male audiences. While many "captivating young ladies" were employed to sing and dance in concert saloons, no respectable woman would be seen in such places, whether in New York or in a Western frontier town. Variety entertainment's move from the saloon to regular theaters, and its ultimate success in drawing family audiences, came only after twenty years of efforts by Tony Pastor. He was a variety performer who began putting together his own shows in 1865. Besides musical numbers, Zouave drills, and athletic feats, his bill often included short burlesques like *The White Crook* (1867) or his own burlesque of the Edwin Booth *Hamlet* that was running in New York in 1870; playing the title role himself and using a pumpkin for Yorick's skull, Pastor called his version *Hamlet the Second* to avoid confusion with George L. Fox's concurrent burlesque. Pastor's campaign to draw women to his theater included such strategies as selling no drink stronger than ice water, and putting up a major advertising effort behind his Saturday matinees "when Ladies and Children can safely attend without escort." Over the years he moved several times, always opening his theaters further uptown, from the Bowery in 1865 to Tony Pastor's New 14th Street Theatre in 1881. It was in the latter location that he finally succeeded in drawing women to evening performances, and the term "variety" was replaced by the more respectable-sounding "vaudeville."

American vaudeville (which bears little relationship to the French *vaudeville*) flourished from the 1880s to the 1920s. When Benjamin Franklin Keith and Edward Franklin Albee entered the field, building palatial theaters in cities across the country and booking the talent to fill them, family vaudeville rapidly expanded into a big business. Eventually "Big Time" vaudeville was dominated by the Keith circuit in the east and the Orpheum circuit west of Chicago, but they were closely rivaled by Loew's and Pantages. In addition, there were hundreds of "Small Time" and independent vaudeville theaters. In "Small Time," performers were usually subjected to the grueling "continuous showing" format whereby each act on the bill came around several times in the continuous cycle from noon until eleven o'clock at night; spectators could thus "come any time and stay as long as you like." It was the dream of every vaudeville performer to break into the "two-a-day" and, finally, to "play the Palace." New York's Palace Theatre remained the mecca of vaudeville until it became a movie house in 1932. A few headliners missed the Palace, only because they were under contract to producers other than Keith-Albee; these were Al Jolson, the Scottish singing comedian Harry Lauder, and George M. Cohan. Among the brightest stars at the Palace during its glory days were Eva Tanguay, the "I Don't Care" Girl; Nora Bayes, who popularized "Shine On, Harvest Moon"; Lillian Russell, the buxom beauty; Elsie Janis, the Queen of Make-Believe; Sophie Tucker, the Last of the Red-Hot Mamas; Nat Wills, the Happy Tramp; W. C. Fields, the Eccentric Juggler; Harry Houdini; Ed Wynn, the Perfect Fool; Will Rogers; Eddie Foy and the Seven Little Foys; "Banjo Eyes" Eddie Cantor; Ray "Rubberlegs" Bolger; Bill "Bojangles" Robinson; ballroom dancers Vernon and Irene Castle; the female impersonator Julian Eltinge; Gallagher and Shean; Weber and Fields; Willie West and McGinty, the Demon Housewreckers; George Burns and Gracie Allen; the Dolly Sisters; the Marx Brothers; and many more.

Like vaudeville, circus grew into a big business during the century. Beginning with eighteenth-century equestrian exhibitions like those of Philip Astley in London, Antonio Franconi in Paris, and John Bill Ricketts in Philadelphia, the circus little by little drew into its ring such supplementary entertainments as rope-dancers, acrobats, performing menageries, and clowns. One of the most colorful figures in the English circus was Andrew Ducrow, a daring equestrian acrobat who also excelled at pantomime. His management of Astley's Amphitheatre from 1830 to 1841 brought drama on horseback to its apogee. The "Great American Showman" P. T. Barnum not only created "The Greatest Show on Earth" by merging his circus with that of James A. Bailey in 1880, but also demonstrated a genius for publicity. Even misfortune—like the loss of his expensive elephant Jumbo in a train wreck—was turned to financial advantage in the cleverly worded press release: Jumbo had supposedly given his life to save the baby elephant Tom Thumb.

Pleasure Gardens, Parades, and Pantomimes

The nineteenth century also saw the apotheosis and demise of the pleasure garden. Pleasure gardens had been far more numerous in the eighteenth century, as well as more intimate, but they were expensive to maintain, especially when a season was cut short by bad weather. Over sixty different pleasure gardens existed at various times in eighteenth-century London, among which the most prominent were Marylebone (1738–78), Ranelagh (1742–1805), and Vauxhall (1661–1859). Those that survived or opened—like Cremorne Gardens (1846–77)—in the nineteenth century had to be enlarged to accommodate the crowds that paid admission to stroll in the pleasant walks, take refreshments, enjoy the marching band's music, watch a ballet on the outdoor stage, dance under the fairy lights after dark, and conclude the evening with a fireworks display. But more and more variety was required to keep people returning night after night. With the addition of balloon ascensions, wrestling matches, shooting galleries and other tests of skill, the gardens began to be frequented by a rowdy element. A pleasure garden could not remain long in business without the support of the middle classes.

A similar pattern is evident in Paris. Arthur Pougin lists twenty-nine pleasure gardens that opened between 1766 and 1855, the majority of them flourishing in the eighteenth century. The attractions were similar to those of the English pleasure gardens: charming natural settings, pantomime theater, horseracing, hot-air balloons, concerts, dance pavilions, and fireworks. Even the gardens' names were similar. Paris had a Ranelagh (1774–1860?), a Tivoli (1796–1828), a summer Vauxhall (1785–1830), and a winter Vauxhall (1773–85). One interesting feature of certain Parisian pleasure gardens was the so-called "Russian mountain" *(montagne russe)*, a very long wooden incline, the surface of which was made slick with ice; daring young people would climb up into a little car which was then pushed off for a thrilling ride. This amusement can actually be traced back to Russian origins. In 1735 the wife of a British diplomat at the court of St. Petersburg described a wooden slide— "broad enough for a coach" and "covered with ice of a considerable thickness"—built from an upper-story window of the palace down to the courtyard. She noted that ladies and gentlemen of the court got on sledges at the top and went flying down. If the sledge met any resistance, the rider would tumble head over heels. Mrs. Ward avoided participating in the sport, for she had "not only the dread of breaking my neck, but of being exposed to indecency too frightful to think on without horror." An iceless summer version, called the "French mountain" was inaugurated with great fanfare at the Jardin Beaujon in Paris in 1817. Although within a year there were two accidents with overturned cars, and a couple was killed, the French mountain remained fashionable until the land values went up so much that the garden had to be sold.

The most famous pleasure garden of all, Copenhagen's Tivoli, opened in 1843 and remains a public attraction yet today. Its founder Georg Carstensen envisioned it as a place where the various social classes could freely mix, and for that reason, some city leaders opposed it. The public, however, was soon won over by such attractions as the Tivoli Guards, eighty-nine boys between the ages of nine and seventeen, marching about the gardens in their bright uniforms like a "midget military." Each evening a silent *commedia dell'arte* was enacted in the outdoor pantomime theater, the modern incarnation of which has augmented its fanciful elements of *chinoiserie* with a peacock-tail fan-curtain. For much of the nineteenth century, the whiteface clown Pierrot was played by Niels Henrik Volkersen, whose comic legacy colored the interpretation of the role by his successors to the present day.

In Paris, the legendary mime Jean-Baptiste Gaspard Deburau brought pleasure to the masses and fortune to the Théâtre des Funambules on the Boulevard du Temple from 1819 to 1846. The boulevard itself boasted most of the attractions of a pleasure garden, with its shade trees, its street vendors, and its entertainers in the fair tradition: marionettes, peep shows, and, on the balconies outside the smaller theaters, the ever-popular *parades*. Like their eighteenth-century antecedents, the *parades* in the era of Deburau were short bawdy sketches performed by two or three characters as pretexts for a string of heavy-handed puns and *double entendres* enlivened by slaps and punches. Bobêche and Galimafré, the best-loved *parade* characters of this period, typified the standard device of bringing together two opposite character types. The city slicker Bobêche wore the bright colors of Italian *commedia* figures—a red vest, yellow breeches, blue stockings, and a rust-colored wig tied back with a red ribbon—while dull stripes emblematized the simpleminded rube Galimafré. One of the major legacies of the old-time fairs to the boulevard was the *funambule* or rope-dancer. In fact, the Théâtre des Funambules was located next door to the theater where the celebrated rope-dancer Madame Saqui continued performing into her sixties. The competition pushed Michel Bertrand, proprietor of the Funambules, in the

Above, some of the recreational delights available at Copenhagen's Tivoli Garden around 1860 are depicted in this color lithograph by Emilius Baerentson. On the stage of the pantomime theater at center, the whiteface clown Pierrot gazes at the ingenue *in ballerina costume, while Harlequin hovers behind, his slapstick raised. In the lower right corner is a "Russian mountain." Teatermuseet, Copenhagen.*

Below, left, the marquee of the Théâtre des Funambules on the Boulevard of Crime *announces* Le Rameau d'or *(The Golden Bough), one of Deburau's pantomimes. A contemporary illustration.*

Below, right, Charles Deburau (1829–73) succeeded his father, the great Jean-Baptiste Gaspard Deburau (1796–1846), at the Funambules in the mime role of Pierrot. He is shown here with a small statue of his father, whose genius at capturing the emotion of the workingman the son never quite attained. Mantzius, A History of Theatrical Art, 6.

direction of pantomime. As the so-called *pantomimes sautantes*—acrobatic pantomimes, with story line and scenic embellishment—tended more and more to belie the theater's name, the authorities insisted only that each performer prove his tightrope-walking ability at some point in every production.

When Deburau joined the Funambules, he led the pantomime away from its rough–and–tumble Italian origins toward a more subtle poetry of gesture. Nor did French pantomime depend as heavily upon scenic tricks and transformations as English pantomime, although one does find in Duburau's repertoire titles like *Mother Goose and the Golden Egg,* a favorite of both Joseph Grimaldi and George L. Fox. (That scenario was brought to Paris by Philippe Laurent, who had worked at Drury Lane during the Napoleonic period, and later played Harlequin at the Funambules.) Born Jan Kaspar Dvorak, Deburau grew up as the misfit in a family of touring acrobats from Bohemia. Around 1814 they came to Paris and settled into regular engagements at the Funambules. Deburau won little notice in the odd roles assigned to him until 1826 when he persuaded Bertrand to allow him to attempt the role of Pierrot. He discovered the humor in taking the falls and being the butt without ever changing his expression. He worked hard to perfect each nuance in his routines, and he took his inspiration from the working poor who made up the majority of the audience at the Funambules. His Pierrot represented at different times a variety of trades: water carrier, cook, baker's apprentice, shoe repairman, charcoal seller, ragpicker, bricklayer, national guardsman. Certainly Deburau had suffered the same hardships as his audience, but the quality that eyewitnesses most often mention in describing his appeal was his irony. Jules Janin, the leading Paris theater critic, drew the attention of the literary élite to this popular entertainment figure by treating him as a serious artist: "He is Deburau just as Talma was Talma. How he can be what he is, I don't know. The fact is that he has revolutionized his art." George Sand wrote of Deburau in her *Memoirs:* "I have never seen an artist who was more serious, more conscientious, more religious in his art." In 1836, Deburau killed a man who was following and insulting his wife as they walked on the boulevard; his murder trial attracted throngs of people who were intrigued by the idea of hearing Deburau speak. He was acquitted. After his death in 1846, his son Charles Deburau carried on the tradition but without the spark of genius.

The Drama Sobers Up: Realism and Naturalism

MIDDLE-CLASS VALUES

Disenchantment with romantic idealism began to occur in Germany even before Romanticism had fully bloomed elsewhere. The reactionary policies of Prince Metternich, the Austrian foreign minister from 1809 to 1848, dominated not only Austria but also the thirty-seven other independent states, including Prussia, that made up the German Confederation. Metternich's concern with maintaining the European balance of power and the privileges of the aristocracy was challenged by a rising tide of nationalism and liberalism. Those twin agendas—political unification of peoples sharing a common language and cultural heritage, and a representative government with guaranteed individual freedoms—were pursued most ardently by the middle classes, who had great economic and intellectual strength, but were politically disenfranchised. German unrest—especially in the middle-class-dominated universities—was effectively repressed by the opprobrious Carlsbad Decrees of 1819. The ensuing censorship of German-language books and newspapers and the infiltration of universities and liberal societies by a network of informers created an atmosphere of disillusionment. German theaters, now mostly run by bureaucratic appointees of the conservative courts, settled into a kind of lethargy, relying upon the novelty of guest performers to enliven the shallow entertainments they presented. Although Goethe and Schiller continued to be staged, the emphasis was on contemporary plays of broad commercial appeal, which might be called "pseudoromantic" because they reduced the heartfelt impulses of Romanticism to facile sentiment and shopworn stage tricks.

Under such conditions, the best German dramatists rarely saw their

Dietrich Grabbe's play Napoleon; or, The One Hundred Days *was produced at the 1967 Ruhr Festival in Recklinghausen. Pictured are Peter Mosbacher as Fouché and Heinrich Schweiger as Napoleon. Courtesy of the German Information Center.*

work staged at all. The plays of Heinrich von Kleist, Ferdinand Raimund, and Franz Grillparzer, discussed elsewhere in terms of their specialized appeals, were not widely known in their day. Only posthumously did Christian Dietrich Grabbe and Georg Büchner achieve full recognition for plays that were far ahead of their time when written in the 1820s and 1830s. Only one of Grabbe's dozen plays, *Don Juan and Faust* (1829), was performed before his death in 1836 at age thirty-four, although it must be conceded that his difficulties were as much the product of his eccentric personality and heavy drinking as of the unadventurous theatrical climate. For *Scherz, Satire, Ironie und tiefere Bedeutung* (Jest, Satire, Irony, and Deeper Significance, 1827), he borrowed the structure of sentimental comedy to parody every variety of stage literature from Goethe to puppet theater—especially anything of romantic origin—while achieving "deeper significance" in its piercing commentary on man and his social institutions. At the end of the play, Grabbe himself arrives, but the Schoolmaster shuts the door on him. The "heroine" chides: "Schoolmaster, Schoolmaster, how embittered you are against the man who created you!" and she admits Grabbe, who enters with a lighted lantern, as the curtain falls. Such imaginative and provocative metatheatricality was typical of Grabbe's work, but there was no place for it among the formulaic moral comedies that held the stage.

Like Grabbe, Büchner was an iconoclast. The three surviving plays that he wrote in his twenty-three years continued to be overlooked long after his death in 1837; not until the first publication of Büchner's collected works in 1879 did they begin to be known, and it is since the 1920s that his plays—still striking in their modernity—have entered the repertoire of standard German classics. The son of a doctor, Büchner studied medicine at the University of Strasbourg, but became involved with radical politics. His revolutionary pamphlet *The Hessian Courier* (1834), denouncing the economic oppression of the peasantry, brought the arrest of several of his friends. Anticipating his own imminent arrest, Büchner worked feverishly at his father's dissecting table to write a play that would finance his escape to France. Written in five weeks, *Dantons Tod* (Danton's Death, 1835) has been called "the finest first play ever written." This dramatic dissection of events in the French Revolution demonstrates Büchner's disillusioned view that man is powerless to effect social change in the face of what he called "the frightful fatalism of history." The passive "hero" Danton is not only Büchner's closest approach to a self-portrait but also the antithesis of the romantic hero. *Danton's Death* was accepted for publication by the liberal editor Karl Gutzkow, but Büchner died before his next two plays could even reach a reading public. *Leonce and Lena* is a savage political and literary satire under a veneer of Musset-like love comedy. Büchner's incomplete masterpiece *Woyzeck* (1837) is a stark folk tragedy in approximately twenty-eight scenes. Since the manuscript consisted of four revisions totaling forty-nine unnumbered scenes, it is an editor's task to select and arrange those scenes, and various interpretations are possible. *Woyzeck* is based upon an actual event that had occurred in 1821 and led to the widely publicized execution three years later of the peasant soldier Woyzeck. Büchner's treatment of the story was innovative in its unconventional episodic structure, in its focus on a "common man" as a tragic figure, and in its understatement, which invites an assessment of social responsibility for Woyzeck's erratic behavior. If Grabbe's plays anticipated the Theatre of the Absurd by well over a century, those of Büchner contain the seeds of such modern artistic movements as naturalism and expressionism. Although they do not embrace the realistic aesthetic that was soon to replace romanticism, they represent a clear break with the romantic conventions of their time.

Büchner can be loosely identified with a group of writers known as Young Germany *(Das junge Deutschland),* who took inspiration from the July Revolution of 1830 in France and attempted to reconcile social concerns with aesthetic theory. While the French Romantic movement thrived on the spirit of nationalism and liberalism, German national and liberal sentiment was tempered by practical reality. The excellent German university system propagated broad awareness of scientific advances, and scientific methods of inquiry were in turn applied to humanistic subjects. Büchner's Woyzeck, for example, is the victim of a scientific experiment in nutrition. Young Germany placed its emphasis on observation of real life and ordinary people as opposed to the false idealism and bigger-than-life heroes of Romanticism. The death of Goethe in 1832 and the posthumous publication of part 2 of his *Faust* added a sense of finality to the romantic impulse in Germany. Other Young Germany writers included the poet Heinrich Heine and playwrights Heinrich Laube and Karl Gutzkow. Laube, whose highly disciplined management revitalized the Vienna Burgtheater from 1849 to 1867, tended to weight his plays too heavily with political significance, but won audiences with *Die Karlsschüler* (1846), because it depicts Schiller's struggle against the reactionary Duke Karl over his play *The Robbers*. Karl Gutzkow served as dramaturg for the Dresden theater and wrote one of the better plays of the Young Germany movement, *Uriel Acosta* (1847).

One practical man of theater succeeded, at least briefly, in finding his way beyond the commercial fare of the day as well as the heavily propagandistic offerings of Young Germany and—what most appealed to him—the past glories of theater under Goethe and Schiller's influence. In 1832 Karl Immermann took over the artistic direction of the Düsseldorf theater and initiated a subscription series of plays by classic authors like Schiller, Shakespeare, and Calderón. Despite the scenic simplicity of the productions and the lack of celebrity artists, audiences seemed to appreciate Immermann's high artistic standards: actors were disciplined to learn their lines and Immermann worked closely with them on line interpretation; the prompter, when needed, was inaudible to spectators. Immermann's expansion of the concept of rehearsal adumbrated modern directorial methods. His preparation for Schiller's *Emilia Galotti* in 1733, for example, far exceeded standard practice of the day. First, Immermann read the play to his actors, then he worked with individual actors in private sessions, followed by a reading of the play by the entire company. The play then had four so-called "room rehearsals," in which Immermann innovatively worked with actors in a bare room "without any illusionistic props." Only after he was satisfied with the clarity and lack of artifice in their interpretations did Immermann take the cast onto the stage for a final two rehearsals before opening.

For one season, Immermann brought in composer Felix Mendelssohn to direct the operas that made up about one-third of the repertoire. During the four-year existence of the theater in Düsseldorf under Immermann, 355 productions were presented, but the great majority of these were undemanding "filler" offerings such as light commercial comedies, concert and dance programs by guest artists, and *tableaux vivants,* that is, stage pictures posed by actors to recreate famous paintings or illustrate poetry readings. In addition, Immermann tried to encourage new writers. Without going so far as to produce one of Grabbe's plays, he did help Grabbe to make a fresh start at one of the lowest points in Grabbe's unhappy life. It was Immermann who induced Grabbe to write his series of critical essays on "The Theatre in Dusseldorf" and to complete his last important play *Hannibal* (1836).

Immermann hoped that his emphasis on thoughtful presentations of the classics would serve as a model, or *Musterbühne,* for other German theaters, and in this he was disappointed. Although he had proven that theater could survive in Germany without pandering to the lowest level of middle-class tastes, his endeavor remained an isolated bright spot in a cultural wasteland, and his combined administrative and artistic duties took their toll on his energies. He disbanded his company and left the theater in 1837, but came out of retirement in 1840 to stage his most famous production, Shakespeare's *Twelfth Night,* taking advantage of the irresistible opportunity to attempt an archaeological reconstruction of Elizabethan staging as it was then understood. For this one private performance, an architectural facade was constructed to frame a small inner space upstage where scenic units could be changed.

The middle class was, at least temporarily, shaken out of its torpor by the revolutions of 1848 that affected every country in Europe, except England (which was beginning to find solutions to some of the problems caused by its early, rapid industrialization) and Russia (which remained paralyzed under the despotic rule of Nicholas I). The uprisings began in France in February when the middle and working classes together overthrew the constitutional monarchy. Within a few months, however, an ideological split between the classes led to middle-class support for Louis-Napoleon, a nephew of Napoleon Bonaparte who pledged a restoration of law and order. Elected by a landslide to the presidency of the Second French Republic, he molded public opinion and nurtured middle-class prosperity so adroitly that he was able to proclaim himself Emperor Napoleon III in 1852. Meanwhile, uprisings of Hungarian and Czech nationalists, as well as Viennese students, against the Austrian empire succeeded in driving out Metternich, but all of these ultimately suffered defeat by aristocratic reactionary forces that placed Francis Joseph on the throne. Similarly, in Prussia, the middle class, which dominated the Frankfurt National Assembly of 1848, asserted itself in drafting a liberal constitution, but it was quickly cowed by the conservative Frederick William and his prime minister Otto von Bismarck. Thus, in the end, no political gains were achieved for liberalism, but the middle class was placated by the material advantages it enjoyed during the next decade or so of general economic progress.

The triumph of conservatism led to increased censorship of plays, which effectively silenced Young Germany. The theater that served post-1848 middle-class audiences became a reflection of their everyday concerns, which revolved around money, marriage, social status, and family—all neatly packaged in the ubiquitous Scribean well-made-play format. The only important serious German-language playwright of this period had already, before 1848, set his course as a commentator on middle-class values. Friedrich Hebbel overcame thirty years of extreme poverty and other hardships when he finally won recognition for his fourth play, *Maria Magdalena* (1844). This lower-middle-class tragedy elucidates an observation from Hebbel's diary: "There is no worse tyrant than the common man in his family circle." Hebbel's characters are not the victims of cosmic forces or of an oppressor class, but they struggle within a social context that they themselves have created: the necessity of maintaining an appearance of respectability no matter what the personal cost. For this innovation Hebbel is signaled as an important precursor of Ibsen. Luckily, Hebbel found a director who was sympathetic to his work. Franz von Dingelstedt brought the Munich theater into prominence from 1851 to 1856, premiering Hebbel's *Agnes Bernauer* in 1852. In 1856 Dingelstedt transferred to the Weimar theater, where he continued to produce Hebbel's plays, but the peak of his career may have been his week-long cycle of Shakespeare history plays in 1864. That event, attended by theatrical leaders from all over Germany, gave impetus to the founding of the German Shakespeare Society. In 1867 Dingelstedt succeeded Heinrich Laube as director of the Vienna Burgtheater.

The unprecedented prosperity of the French middle class during the 1850s and 1860s gave rise to two intertwining trends in the booming Parisian commercial theater. On the one hand, this *nouveau riche* audience of bankers, lawyers, and businessmen with pretenses to high society craved displays of luxury. Napoleon III and Empress Eugénie set the tone of conspicuous consumption, and the bourgeoisie aped them by filling their homes with decorative objects and heavy furniture, including chairs large enough to accommodate the voluminous crinolines that came into fashion largely because Empress Eugénie admired Marie-Antoinette. Stage settings were expected to serve as examples of the latest styles in interior decoration, which ran to eighteenth-century salons and Renaissance dining rooms. Along these lines, the theater also offered titillating glimpses of the licentious behavior of a decadent aristocracy. At the same time, however, the theater was expected to reaffirm middle-class moral and social values. The flourishing genre known as the *pièce à thèse,* or social problem play, did not raise provocative questions about social issues so much as it preached to the converted. Since most plays dealt with contemporary subjects, the censors exercised

Chaperon's design for Victorien Sardou's Les Pattes de mouche (A Scrap of Paper, *1884) at the Comédie Française was clearly intended to appeal to the theater's middle-class audiences; they wanted to see the kind of elegant interior decor that they might aspire to afford for themselves. Courtesy of Collections de la Comédie-Française.*

In 1847 Alexandre Dumas père *(1802–70) opened his Théâtre Historique on the Boulevard du Temple as a venue for his own plays. Shown here is the inaugural production, a dramatization of his own serial novel* La Reine Margot, *which lasted from 6:30* P.M. *to 3:00* A.M. *on opening night.* Illustrated London News.

special vigilance, but their main concern was to repress any expression of political dissatisfaction that might well up from the lower orders. The flagrant affronts to middle-class morality depicted in the plays of Dumas *fils* and Émile Augier could be tolerated as long as the virtues of marriage, family, and financial stability were reasserted in the end.

Alexander Dumas *fils*, the illegitimate son of Dumas *père*, may have acquired his zeal for social justice when he was taunted in school for his illegitimacy. The serious-minded Dumas *fils* once said of the flamboyant, profligate elder Dumas: "My father was a great baby I had when I was very young." When he was twenty, Dumas *fils* fell in love with Marie Duplessis, who was a courtesan, one of countless attractive young women who flocked to Paris during the Second Empire to be supported in style by the well-to-do gentlemen upon whom these women bestowed their favors. She died of tuberculosis two years later, and Dumas *fils* wrote a novel based upon their affair. Its success prompted him to dramatize the story for production in his father's Théâtre Historique. But that theater went bankrupt, and Dumas had to wait until 1852 to see the play staged. *La Dame aux camélias* (The Lady of the Camelias) opened at the Théâtre du Vaudeville, one of several theaters that were restricted to plays in prose with musical couplets; the author obligingly added a snatch of song to the midnight supper scene in the apartment of the lovely courtesan Marguerite Gautier. Marguerite readily gives up all she has acquired in order to live for the love of one man, Armand Duval. But she succumbs to the pleas of Armand's father, the voice of bourgeois morality, who convinces her that a fallen woman can never be redeemed in the eyes of society and that the liaison can only bring shame to Armand's family. She allows Armand to think that she could not renounce her life of pleasure in Paris. It is only on her deathbed that a last-minute reconciliation is effected. The melodramatic story successfully synthesized romantic idealism and socially conscious realism. The idealized portrayal of a notorious real-life courtesan shocked even as it fascinated theatergoers. The father's moralizing helped to make palatable the thesis that a courtesan could have noble feelings. Despite some outrage, the play had an initial run of over two hundred performances.

After *The Lady of the Camelias*, his first play, Dumas *fils* adopted a more didactic approach. Most of his plays deal with sexual morality. *Le Demi-monde* (Not Quite Society; or, Half-World, 1855), for example, unsympathetically depicts women with social pretensions whose life-style has compromised them so that they can no longer be admitted to the society of good women. They can, however, interact freely with the male half of polite society, and they exploit this advantage by conniving to marry a man whose good name would allow passage out of the confining "half-world." In addition to its perorations on the situation of these

Francillon *(1887)*, *one of the more popular plays by the prolific Dumas* fils, *premiered at the Comédie Française, with Julia Bartet (standing, at center) in the leading role. Courtesy of Collections de la Comédie-Française.*

The Prodigal Father *(Le Père prodigue) was another of Dumas* fils*'s moralizing melodramas, shown here as it was presented at the Théâtre du Gymnase in Paris in 1859.* L'Illustration *(1859)*.

women—and "the social law which requires that an honest man marry none but an honest woman"—the play includes frequent discussions of financial transactions and a meticulous portrayal of the etiquette of preparations for a duel between middle-class men of honor. *La Question d'argent* (A Question of Money, 1857) deals more specifically with money as a social instrument; *Le Fils naturel* (The Illegitimate Son, 1858), with the problem of illegitimate children. The complete plays of Dumas *fils* were published in seven volumes.

Emile Augier surpassed even Dumas *fils* in his use of the stage as a pulpit from which to expound in favor of—in Eugène Brieux's words—"order and regularity, justice, the family and the fireside." After mastering his craft with eleven plays in verse, Augier hit his stride in the 1850s with his realistic prose dramas that skillfully employ Scribe's well-made-play formula. Undistinguished in style, these antiromantic plays are redeemed by a dash of humor and by the theatrical interest of his bad characters, the ones who threaten the ideal of domestic bliss. Like the plays of Dumas *fils*, Augier's *pièces à thèse* are set in elegantly appointed drawing rooms. In *Le Gendre de M. Poirier* (Poirier's Son-in-Law, 1854), a *parvenu* businessman marries his daughter to an impoverished nobleman whose amorous and financial indiscretions threaten to dishonor him, but the wayward duke is saved by his virtuous wife, thus establishing a solid union of aristocrat and bourgeois. Augier apparently conceived *Le Mariage d'Olympe* (Olympe's Marriage, 1855), as a reply to Dumas *fils*'s *Lady of the Camelias*. This alternate point of view on the fallen woman, devoid of romantic compassion, shows a well-meaning but weak young gentleman who is almost brought to ruin by a former courtesan who succeeds in passing herself off as a lady. However, she is responsible for her own undoing, as she cannot overcome *la nostalgie de la boue*, her gutter-level tastes. According to Augier, a woman who has lost her purity can have no hope of regaining it, no matter how many opportunities decent people may offer her. In the wealthy bourgeois milieu that Augier most often depicted, the characters are motivated by money more than love. Indeed, a number of his plays fall into a category known as *drames de l'agio*, plays about financial speculation.

Despite his facile manner, Victorien Sardou must also figure among the authors of popular social problem plays. Others included Octave Feuillet, Edouard Pailleron, and the Goncourt brothers. Such dramatists benefited especially from the encouragement of Adolphe Montigny, an actor-playwright who, beginning in 1844, successfully managed the Théâtre du Gymnase for over thirty years. Although his own plays were featherweight vaudevilles, Montigny devoted himself to the realistic staging of serious drama. Like Immermann in Düsseldorf, he increased the amount of rehearsal for each production. Like Madame Vestris in London, he incorporated real furniture and hand props into his draw-

Even Victorien Sardou (1831–1908) turned to contemporary themes of marriage, money, and family, as in his comedy– melodrama The Benoiton Family *(1865).* Univers illustré *(1865).*

This late-nineteenth-century production of Shakespeare's The Merchant of Venice *at the Comédie Française illustrates an aesthetic approach to historical period with detailed scene painting, heavy draperies, and realistic set props. From Sheldon Cheney,* Stage Decoration.

A pupil of Ciceri, Auguste-Alfred Rubé (1818–99) ran a Parisian sceneshop with designer Philippe-Marie Chaperon, as depicted in Chaperon's watercolor. Their grandiose settings for operas and ballets combined romantic picturesqueness with realistic architectural and geographical detail. Reynaud, Musée rétrospectif de théâtre à l'exposition internationale de 1900 *(1900).*

The exterior of the Paris Opéra, built between 1861 and 1874, designed by Beaux Arts architect Charles Garnier (1825–98), flaunts a neo-baroque facade calculated to impress upwardly mobile opera patrons. Scribner's Monthly (May 1875).

Below, left, one of the most striking features of the Paris Opéra is its Grand Staircase, which functions as part of the spectacle of an evening at the opera. Scribner's Monthly (May 1875).

Below, right, the Grand Foyer of the Paris Opéra, reminiscent of the Hall of Mirrors at Versailles, offers a luxurious intermission promenade for operagoers. Scribner's Monthly (May 1875).

ing-room settings. By guiding his actors in the use of these items, he broke up the traditional semicircle of actors addressing the audience and facilitated their more natural interaction. By now, it was *de rigueur* that a new setting be designed for each play. As Becq de Fouquières noted in his *Art de la Mise en Scène* (1884), "A financier's study does not resemble that of a diplomat. A society woman's drawing room is not at all like that of a *demi-mondaine*, whose salon in turn looks nothing like that of a courtesan." These Second Empire salons were represented by box settings, that is, enclosed spaces with practical doors, as opposed to the old wing and drop settings. But even after Montigny began filling up the space with everyday objects and hanging thick draperies on the drawing-room windows, the canvas walls of the set were painted with *trompe l'oeil* mirrors, sconces, and a profusion of framed pictures. Scene design had less in common with art than with interior decoration, for the painter's tricks were the product of large commercial studios, several of them founded by disciples of Ciceri. The best known of those "factories" for the creation of meticulously detailed illusionistic painted settings in the tradition of Ciceri was that of Charles Cambon, who later was affiliated with Philastre. Their hallmark was a downstage arch or drapery framing an angled setting that gave an illusion of great depth. The studio of Rubé and Chaperon supplied its share of realistic interiors, but also excelled at archaeological evocations of historic periods for the Opéra or for Sardou's exotic dramas. Other successful scene painters of the period included Charles Séchan, Edouard Despléchin, and Jules Dieterle, all of whom designed for the Paris Opéra as well as for various provincial theaters.

Napoleon III's projects with Baron Haussmann for the beautification of Paris included both a terrible disservice and a splendid boon to the theater. The worst of Haussmann's "improvements" was the previously described destruction of the Boulevard du Temple. The best was the new Paris Opéra, which reflected upper-middle-class inclinations in its monumental scale, its decorative sumptuousness, and in the choice of location, near the stock exchange. A design competition announced in 1860 was won by the unknown thirty-one-year-old architect Charles Garnier. Construction began at once, but only the exterior was completed before the Franco-Prussian War brought an end to the Second Empire in 1870. Used as a warehouse during the war, the unfinished building was further delayed from completion by the chaotic days of civil war leading to the two-month Paris Commune and its Terror in 1871. With the foundation of the Third French Republic in July 1871, work resumed on the Opéra, and it was finished in January 1875. This opulent architectural monument to middle-class taste and financial clout, with its magnificent grand staircase leading up to the palatial foyer extending across the front facade, is also a supremely functional building. It reaffirmed the bourgeois dominance of the arts throughout the 1870s and 1880s.

While the middle class retained its economic and cultural hegemony after the Franco-Prussian War and the Commune, it could not ignore pressure from below. As the upper levels of the working class moved into the lower middle class, they too became theatergoers. The period between 1871 and 1885, according to Michael Hays, marks a concerted effort by the old bourgeoisie to cling to and impose its concept of social order. It was marked by constant revivals of the plays of Dumas *fils,* Augier, and Sardou, as well as revivals of serious Romantic plays like *Hernani* and *Ruy Blas.* The only new plays admitted were comedies.

In England the evolution of the theater audience composition was almost the reverse of that in France. During the first half of the century, it was largely the working class and lower middle classes that supported London's wealth of nonliterary variety entertainment. By midcentury the gradual process of luring polite society back to the theater had begun. The Shakespeare productions of Samuel Phelps at Sadler's Wells Theatre and those of Charles Kean at the Princess Theatre in the 1850s were financially risky ventures that paid off primarily in the long-term effect of building audiences for a theater of substance. Another factor contributing to a revival of legitimate drama in the 1860s was the example of Queen Victoria's frequent attendance of the theater, as well as her command performances at Windsor Castle under Charles Kean's stewardship. As working-class audiences gravitated from the variety theaters to the music halls, where drinking and entertainment could be combined, theater managers were obliged to seek, and tailor their repertoires to, a more fashionable clientele. The ascendancy of "gentlemanly melodrama" over the more sensational varieties was accelerated by the French actor Charles Albert Fechter, the original Armand Duval in *La Dame aux camélias,* who moved to London in 1860 and won a substantial female following for his dashing melodramatic heroes as well as his elegant Hamlet, all performed in an alluring French-accented English. The 1860s also saw a boom in new theater construction in London after a twenty-year hiatus. The trend was to smaller theaters with balconies projecting forward over the pit, instead of the old horseshoe-shaped galleries. The added intimacy between actors and audiences allowed the development of the more subtle acting that suited the realistic dramas of Robertson, Jones, and Pinero.

Subtlety in acting was also encouraged by the installation of gas lighting in theaters. The broad gestures, exaggerated facial expressions, and pronounced makeup that had been appropriate by candlelight and oil lamp seemed grotesque when subjected to the comparatively brilliant illumination by gas, which became standard in theaters by 1850. Further-

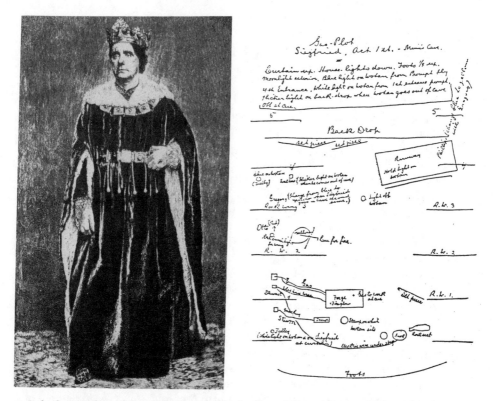

Left, the "gentlemanly" actor–manager Charles Kean (1811–68), son of Edmund Kean, produced a number of Shakespeare plays at his Princess Theatre. He is shown here in the title role of Shakespeare's King John. *The Autobiography of Joseph Jefferson.*

Right, the installation of gas lighting in theaters allowed for an increased variety and subtlety of effects. This is a page from the complex "gas plot" for Wagner's Siegfried *at New York's Metropolitan Opera House in the 1880s.* Scribner's Magazine *(October 1889).*

more, the possibility of distributing directional light within a stage set-ting contributed to the suppression of the lineup of actors before the footlights in favor of opportunities for "natural" movement behind the proscenium. Gas lighting had been introduced in certain public areas of Covent Garden and in the auditorium of the Olympic Theatre in 1815. London's Lyceum Theatre boasted the world's first gaslit stage in 1817, and a month later Drury Lane became the first theater lit entirely by gas. Gas lighting was installed at the Paris Opéra in 1822 and at the Comédie Française ten years later, except that the latter retained its oil bor-derlights in order not to tire the actors' eyes. Besides its increased brightness, gas afforded the advantage of central control; the gas table for the elaborate system at the Paris Opéra eventually comprised eighty-eight valves governing 960 gas jets. In the early days of gas, the number of fires in theaters was almost double what it had been, but refinements—both for safety and artistic effect—were steadily made. By the 1880s most theaters were following Henry Irving's practice of darkening the auditorium during the performance. The high intensity white light produced by the limelight was put to various uses in combination with gas during the latter half of the century, and later, with electricity. In 1881 D'Oyly Carte's Savoy Theatre became the world's first public building entirely illuminated by electricity. Thus, within the century theaters all over Europe and North America progressed from candles and oil lamps to gas to electric lighting.

Tom Taylor, a professor of English, editor of *Punch,* practicing barrister, sometime actor, and prolific author of melodramas, took some preliminary steps toward realism in his plays by introducing contemporary social themes. He borrowed heavily from the French, but his sure sense of stagecraft gave his seventy or so plays an ephemeral popularity; the best were *Our American Cousin* (1855) and *The Ticket-of-Leave Man* (1863). Another precursor of middle-class drama, John Maddison Morton, wrote one of the most popular midcentury farces, *Box and Cox.* It began as his one-act farce entitled *The Double-Bedded Room* (1843). Three years later it appeared on the Paris stage in a French adaptation, *Une Chambre à deux lits,* which Morton drew upon in turn, along with Labiche's *Frizette,* to create his full-length *Box and Cox* (1847). The eponymous heroes, serious middle-class gentlemen with typical middle-class concerns like food and money, are caught up in comic complications arising from the fact that—unknown to them—their landlady rents the same room to one of them by day and to the other by night. Not only was the play translated into virtually every European language (becoming *Dumont et Dupont* in French, for example), but it also spawned several sequels as well as the comic opera *Cox and Box* by F. C. Burnand and Arthur S. Sullivan. This was Sullivan's first musical composition for the stage, ten years before he teamed up with W. S. Gilbert.

The trend toward realism in staging in England had precursors in the efforts of William Charles Macready and James Robinson Planché to achieve historical accuracy in costuming. Macready had also been a leader in the invention of lifelike stage business and the use of hand props to enhance a performance. Further advances may be credited to Madame Vestris, *née* Lucia Bartolozzi, who gave up her career as a musical performer in Paris and London to manage London's Olympic Theatre from 1831 to 1839. There, as early as 1832, she was using box sets with practical doors and windows, carpets on the floor, and other realistic details. Finally, realism was truly established as the dominant mode through the long, successful collaboration of playwright T. W.

Robertson with the husband-and-wife theater management team of Squire and Marie (Wilton) Bancroft.

Marie Wilton had acted since childhood, but at twenty-six she decided to go into theater management, rented a rundown theater known as the "Dusthole," renovated it inexpensively but tastefully, and got permission to call it the Prince of Wales Theatre. She opened it in 1865 with a burlesque by H. J. Byron, but with the production of T. W. Robertson's *Society* in 1865, she established the style that was to be identified with her. *Society* also marked the London debut of the comic actor Squire Bancroft, who married Marie Wilton in 1867 and became her co-manager. They ran the Prince of Wales until 1879, then managed the Haymarket Theatre until 1885, when they retired in great wealth, owing much of their success to Robertson's plays. During their two decades of theater management, the Bancrofts offered about three-thousand performances of his plays, that is, an average of one hundred fifty performances a year. T. W. Robertson's social comedies were distinctive not only for their one-word titles—for example, *Ours* (1866), *Caste* (1867), *Play* (1868), *School* (1869), *Progress* (1869), *Birth* (1870), *War* (1872)—but also for their emphasis on character psychology. Even the eccentric comic figures had an amusing credibility when placed in the middle-class milieux that the Bancrofts so meticulously created on the stage. Robertson's masterpiece *Caste* became the prototype for an abundance of "cup-and-saucer" comedies in succeeding decades.

Robertson undoubtedly owed his success to the Bancrofts as much as they relied on him. They afforded him the opportunity to supervise rehearsals and to exercise authority over details of staging his plays, which contain unusually precise stage directions. The careful working out of lifelike activity within realistic box sets brought the Robertson-Bancroft productions to a level of realism hitherto unknown on the London stage. The Bancrofts also maintained an excellent company of actors, paying them generously enough to keep up their morale as well as to grant them a measure of social respectability. Their management innovations included the single-play bill (no curtain raiser, afterpiece, or olios), the matinee performance (not particularly successful), the long-running production (they presented only about thirty plays in twenty years), and the full-company tour to provincial theaters with all of the original sets and props transported by railroad. Under Bancroft, the Haymarket was the first theater to eliminate benches in the pit, moving all the low-priced seating to the less-visible upper galleries. Clearly, the Bancrofts must be credited more than any others with making theater fashionable again for the upper middle class.

As the long-running play became the goal of other managers, actors began to be cast by the play in London theaters, while the old resident stock companies were transformed into touring companies. The Bancrofts stood at the head of a long line of distinguished actor-managers: Sir Charles Wyndham, Sir Henry Irving, Sir Herbert Beerbohm Tree, Sir Johnston Forbes-Robertson, Sir George Alexander, Sir Frank Benson, Lewis Waller, Sir John Martin-Harvey, Sir Gerald du Maurier, and many others. Similarly, T. W. Robertson could be seen as a model for playwright-"directors" like W. S. Gilbert, Sir Arthur Wing Pinero, and Bernard Shaw. Not until the 1890s could British social comedies and melodramas be called social problem plays in the French sense, although quite a few earlier ones focused upon a "woman with a past." Fashionable audiences had not returned to the theater only to have their noses rubbed in unpleasant concerns, but they did not mind being titillated. Their preferred fare was broadly termed "society drama," which amalgamated features of the French well-made play, the gentlemanly melodrama, the cup-and-saucer domesticity of Robertson, and, very gradually, the almost-imperceptible influence of the shocking plays of Henrik Ibsen. The best author of society dramas, Sir Arthur Wing Pinero, systematically studied the well-made-play formula and applied it to achieve a chain of successes beginning with *The Money-Spinner* (1880). His farce *The Magistrate* (1885) launched a very successful series of farces at the first Royal Court Theatre. Sensitive to subtle changes of taste over the years, he eventually toned down his sentimentality and wrote the first important English social problem plays: *The Profligate* (1889), his controversial masterpiece *The Second Mrs Tanqueray* (1891), *The Notorious Mrs Ebbsmith* (1895), and *Mid-Channel* (1909). He also wrote a brilliant comedy about theater people—*Trelawney of the Wells* (1898). Henry Arthur Jones tended to allow his melodramatic plots to overshadow his social commentary, but he made an impact with *Michael and His Lost Angel* (1896) and *Mrs Dane's Defense* (1900).

If any country had serious social problems in the nineteenth century, it was Russia under Nicholas I. His reactionary regime (1825–55) was marked by a corrupt judicial system, a vast network of secret police, an ignorant and self-serving bureaucracy, continuing serfdom, and censorship. It was also the "golden age of Russian literature." This might be attributed to the stimulus of the challenge of finding ways to write compellingly about life without running afoul of the censor. Unable to comment directly upon social ills, writers concentrated upon the inner man, on introspective psychological character studies, and upon closely observed descriptions of a character's immediate environment. This realistic approach seemed better suited to the Russian language and mentality than the Romantic movement had been. Another factor goading Russian realistic literature to greater heights was the self-awareness that grew out of the 1840s debate between the Slavophiles and the

Westernizers, a polemic in which every writer was caught up. Slavo-philism began in the 1830s as an affirmation of the folk heritage and traditional values of Holy Russia in reaction against the perception that the state was driving Russia to catch up with and be integrated into Western European culture. Although Westernizers also came out in opposition to the authority of the state, they disagreed with the Slavophiles' clinging to the past and preferred to seek recognition for Russia as an equal partner in the progress of Western civilization. West-ernizers, or *Zapadniks,* also differed from the Slavophiles in their anti-clericalism and their political liberalism. The critic Vissarion Belinsky saw important social significance in both westernization and realism, and was a prominent promoter of both.

Nikolai Vasilievich Gogol has sometimes been called the father of Russian realism, although it is difficult to pin this enigmatic figure down to any category. His literary apprenticeship took place during the Ro-mantic period, and Pushkin was his ideal. The idea for Gogol's comic masterpiece *Revisor* (The Government Inspector, 1835) was given to him by Pushkin, who had once in his travels been mistaken for a government inspector. In Gogol's treatment, the passive imposter Khlestakov merely follows the line of least resistance when he courts the general's wife and takes bribes from the provincial town's time-serving bureaucrats. The play was seen by "simple minds," according to Vladimir Nabokov, as "a social satire violently volleyed at the idyllic system of official corruption in Russia." But the Tsar himself watched a special performance and inexplicably passed the play for public viewing. Gogol was taken as a hero by Russian liberals, although he was a conservative at heart. His intended target was corruption as a moral problem rather than the system as a political problem, and he was taking a comic jab on the side at the shallow romantic intrigues of the vaudevilles. Gogol saw himself as a moralist whose instrument was laughter, but he invariably sent ambigu-ous signals. Certainly he was a close observer of reality; but reality, filtered through his bizarre sensibilities, took a grotesque turn. In addi-tion to several other plays—most notably *Marriage* (1833) and *Gamblers* (1842)—there are numerous dramatizations of his novels like *Dead Souls* and stories like *The Overcoat* and *The Nose.* He also wrote, in the form of a playlet, *Leaving the Theatre after the Performance of a New Comedy* (1836), an amusing compendium of audience responses to *The Inspector General,* which gives the last word—a lengthy monologue—to the Play's Author.

Realism asserted itself more slowly in the theater than in prose fiction, partly because melodrama and vaudeville still held the stage and also because Gogol was viewed as the model for theatrical realism, and Gogol was inimitable. Most of the dramatists before Aleksandr Os-trovsky who aimed for realism were primarily prose writers who merely dabbled in the theater. Novelist Aleksey Pisemsky's best play, *Gorkaya Sudbina* (A Bitter Fate, 1859), is a realistic tragedy of peasant life. Equally pessimistic in a comic vein is *Smert Pazukhina* (Pazukhin's Death, 1857), by Mikhail Saltykov-Shchedrin. Ivan Sergeyevich Turgenev, an ardent Westernizer, spent much of his life in France, and several of his one-act comedies have a delicate Musset-like quality. His first stage success, *Kholostyak* (The Bachelor, 1848), showed the influence of Gogol, but Turgenev's realism was most effectively based in character psychology. Like much of his prose fiction, his best play *Mesyats v derevne* (A Month in the Country, 1850) offers a tender emotional study of women in love. Another contemporary, the well-educated and well-traveled Aleksandr Sukhovo-Kobylin had no thought of writing plays until he found himself imprisoned for the unsolved murder of the French mistress he had brought back to Moscow. His tortured path through the corrupt Russian judicial system to his acquittal took seven years, 1850–57, and inspired him to write a trilogy based upon the experience. *Svadba Krechinskogo* (Krechinsky's Wedding, 1855) incorporates Gogolian elements into a fairly realistic well-made play. *Delo* (The Case, 1862) takes an embittered view of a corrupt bureaucracy, and *Smert Tarelkina* (The Death of Tarelkin, 1869), pushes the macabre elements to grotesque extremes. Count Aleksey Konstantinovich Tolstoy might have fit more comfortably in the Romantic period, but he endeavored to give his historical dramas the psychological credibility and archaeological accuracy of realism. His trilogy comprised *The Death of Ivan the Terrible* (1863), *Tsar Fyodor Ivanovich* (1868), and *Tsar Boris* (1869).

Aleksandr Nikolayevich Ostrovsky not only towers above all other realistic dramatists during the half-century between Gogol and Chekhov, but he, more than any other individual, influenced the course of Russian stage history in the latter half of the nineteenth century. The first Russian to earn his living by playwriting, Ostrovsky wrote forty-seven original plays, twenty-two translations, and seven plays in collaboration. His dramas—like *Groza* (The Thunderstorm, 1859), *Na vsyakogo mudretsa dovolno prostoty* (The Diary of a Scoundrel, 1868), *Les* (The Forest, 1871), and many others that have entered the standard repertoire—recreated the lives, manners, habits of thought, and characteristic speech of the Russian middle classes of his day. In fact, Ostrovsky's plays have preserved for posterity the period slang of bureaucrats and shopkeepers that he constantly overheard when they came to the family's Moscow home on business with Ostrovsky's father, who had a private law practice. Turgenev called Ostrovsky "the Shakespeare of the merchant class." Ostrovsky entered law school, but spent most evenings at Moscow's Maly Theatre, which was then nicknamed "the second Moscow University."

Samoilov's engraving depicts the last scene of The Inspector General *by Nikolai Gogol (1809–52), in its premiere production at the Alexandrinsky Theater of St. Petersburg in 1836.*

Aleksandr Ostrovsky (1823–86) exposed the pettiness and backwardness of provincial Russians in plays like Thunderstorm *(1859). The scene of the storm, shown here, is set in an architecturally interesting passageway, which the townspeople, in their lack of civic pride, have allowed to deteriorate.*

Without completing his studies, he held various civil service jobs for eight years while struggling to get his break as a writer. This came with a reading of his second play, *Svoi lyudi—sochtemsya!* (It's a Family Affair—We'll Settle It Ourselves, 1849), in the home of the editor of the leading Slavophile journal, *Moskvityanin* (The Muscovite), which led to nightly readings in other private homes, although the censor forbade production. "All the characters in the play—the merchant, his daughter, the lawyer, the clerk, and the matchmaker—are first-rate villains," said the report. "The dialogue is filthy. The entire play is an insult to the Russian merchant class."

Ostrovsky's first produced play, *Ne v svoi sani ne sadis* (Don't Sit in Someone Else's Sleigh, 1853), was chosen by the beautiful serf-born actress Lyubov Nikulina-Kositskaya for her benefit at Moscow's Maly Theatre. She went on to create the leading roles in many of Ostrovsky's plays, for which she and the Maly company developed a more realistic style of acting. That same season brought an equally successful St. Petersburg production of the play. Throughout his career, Ostrovsky worked closely with Moscow's Maly Theatre, which has since acquired the epithet "the House of Ostrovsky." One of his major projects was to establish an actor-training program as a means of raising the notoriously poor artistic standards of the Russian theater. Lack of competition was another factor that produced theatrical stagnation, as the Imperial Theatres held a monopoly in the capitol cities until 1882. Despite his affiliation with the state-subsidized Maly, Ostrovsky was instrumental in getting that monopoly abolished. He also spoke out against censorship, organized an Association of Russian Dramatists in 1870, and obtained for them a measure of copyright protection.

In 1856 Ostrovsky participated in a Ministry of the Navy project, which sent writers to explore and report on the lives and folk customs of provincial peoples. Ostrovsky's trip along the upper Volga influenced such portrayals of backward, small-minded townspeople as those in *Groza* (Thunderstorm), and also his rendering of the simple charm of native traditions in his only folk-fantasy play *Snegurochka* (The Snowmaiden, 1873). Although he was usually identified with the Slavophiles, Ostrovsky's realistic plays were championed by Nikolai Dobrolyubov, a socio-utilitarian literary critic who wrote for the leading Westernizer journal, *Sovremennik* (The Contemporary). His influential essays on Ostrovsky, "The Kingdom of Darkness" (1859) and "A Ray of Light in the Kingdom of Darkness" (1860), extolled Ostrovsky's realistic truthfulness in depicting the superstition and cruelty of the *samodurs,* domestic tyrants who victimized their families in the home and their subordinates at work. Unfortunately, Ostrovsky died only a few months after his appointment in 1886 as director of Moscow Imperial Theatres, a position that would have enabled him to carry out many of the theatrical reforms toward which he had been working.

During most of Ostrovsky's career, theater in Moscow and St. Petersburg was the sole province of the Imperial Theatre system, following the regulations established by Prince Shakhovsky in 1825; the actor in this system held a civil service status. Each city had a Bolshoi (Big) Theatre for opera and ballet and a Maly (Small) Theatre for legitimate drama. St. Petersburg's Bolshoi company moved into the Maryinsky Theatre in 1860. The Maly company acquired the Alexandrinsky Theatre in 1832; that building is now the Pushkin Theatre. In 1833, a third St. Petersburg theater, the Mikhailovsky, opened to serve as a venue for foreign companies. The Moscow Maly Theatre was universally recognized as the leading dramatic theater of the entire century, first enhanced by the brilliant actor Mikhail Shchepkin, then the unflagging behind-the-scenes efforts of Ostrovsky, and finally by the example of the outstanding actress Maria Ermolova. Founded in 1806, the company moved into its permanent theater next door to Moscow's Bolshoi in 1824; that building, thoroughly renovated in 1873 and 1989, still houses the Maly. Moscow's impressive and world-renowned Bolshoi Theatre for Opera and Ballet moved into its first theater in 1825, but it burned down in 1853. It has occupied its present facility since 1856. Although private theaters were banned in the two cities, there were many privately owned touring companies performing in other towns of all sizes. By the 1870s some private theaters were opened just outside the city limits of Moscow and St. Petersburg. In addition, some wealthy citizens in the capitals started amateur drama circles in their mansions for invited audiences. Thus the abolition of the Imperial Theatre monopoly in 1882 served in one sense merely to legitimize existing conditions. In a larger sense, it created an atmosphere of healthy competition, as many new theaters opened within a few years. One of the best was Korsh's Theatre in Moscow (1882–1932), which was to premiere some of Chekhov's early plays. With such stimulus, more training schools were opened, the quality of sets and costumes improved rapidly at all theaters, and in 1894 the Imperial Theatres began to hold dress rehearsals before opening. The two Russian tours of the excellent German company, the Meininger, in 1885 and 1890, also inspired the raising of standards for Russian theater. Fortunately, a generation of wealthy capitalists—most of whom made their money in railroads or textile factories—was ready to support the arts. Two of those businessmen devoted their attention particularly to theater. Saava Mamontov founded a private opera company and later opened the commercial Mamontov Opera Theatre. In nearly two decades he produced forty-three Russian and nineteen foreign operas, advancing the careers of many outstanding singers, composers, and scene designers. Among the latter was Viktor Vasnetsov, one of the great set and costume designers of the turn-of-the-century. The other leading philanthropist in theater, Saava Morozov, was to become the major financial backer of the Moscow Art Theatre.

In Italy, the spoken drama was still overshadowed by opera, but by midcentury there were over fifty itinerant theater companies crisscrossing the Italian peninsula, carrying their stock of rudimentary scenery with them. In most cases, their repertoires were no more impressive than their staging. It was in the area of performance that Italian theater excelled, and realism came to the Italian theater most successfully through its actors. The Italian actors who toured abroad during the latter half of the century, gaining international reputations for the truthfulness and emotionalism of their performances, was part of the legacy of Gustavo Modena. A political activist for the cause of Italian unification, Modena's theatrical career was periodically interrupted by exile or other efforts on behalf of the unified state that he would not live to see completed. (The ten-year process culminated in 1870, when Rome joined the kingdom of Italy.) When he could devote himself to theater, Modena managed a company and coached the actors to discover for themselves the varied possibilities of truthful interpretation. Tommaso Salvini, Ernesto Rossi, and Luigi Bellotti-Bon were among those who worked with him in their youth and disseminated his teachings. Modena also wrote *Teatro educatore* (1836), an idealistic treatise on the educational value of theater.

The finest Italian company of the century, the Reale Sarda, launched the adult career of Adelaide Ristori, Italy's first international star. After a successful tour to Paris in 1855, she toured almost constantly—all over Europe, to Russia, the United States, and Latin America—until her retirement in 1885. Not only did she demonstrate an apparent spontaneousness and freedom from artifice in her acting, but also she was hailed as an ambassadress of Italian nationalism. She even learned English in order to perform Lady Macbeth in London and, later, on her final American tour, opposite Edwin Booth. Ernesto Rossi performed opposite Ristori on her first Paris engagement, but thereafter concentrated on Shakespearean roles. Tommaso Salvini, another Modena product who worked with Ristori, won his greatest international renown for his powerful interpretation of Othello. A strong, musical voice, muscular build, and graceful movements enhanced his careful conception of the role, which balanced quiet moments against eruptions of frenzied passion. Some British critics found the realism of his violence in the last act "excessive," but his astonishing truthfulness was seen as the way of the future by such varied witnesses as Edwin Booth, Emile Zola, and Konstantin Stanislavsky.

Italy's first international star, Adelaide Ristori (1822–1906), performed the title role in Francesca da Rimini *with Ernesto Rossi (1827–96) as Paolo, Pasquale Tessero as Guido, and Pietro Boccomini as Lanciotto.* L'Illustration *(1855).*

Tommaso Salvini (1829–1915), right, the great Italian Shakespearean actor, used his rich voice, powerful physique, and passionate energies to best advantage in the role of Othello. Theatre Arts Monthly.

Realism took two forms in Italian drama, and neither produced a great playwright despite the encouragement of an excellent company headed by Luigi Bellotti-Bon from 1859 until his shocking suicide in 1883. The first was the movement known as *verismo*, which took inspiration from the Russian realist novelists and Zola's incipient naturalism. Its outstanding play, Giovanni Verga's *Cavalleria rusticana* (*Rustic Chivalry*, 1884), a sordid vignette of peasant life, was soon eclipsed by its operatic version. The second realistic trend was the dialect drama of writers like Luigi Capuana and Carlo Bertolazzi for theaters that specialized in performances in Italy's various regional dialects. Ironically, these dialect theaters blossomed most fully in the decades after unification. Their comic treatment of local customs appealed to a more popular audience than did the depressing drama of *verismo*.

In Spain, realism was not to produce any major plays until the early twentieth century. Theaters proliferated there in the latter half of the century, but three-quarters of them were devoted to variety and musical entertainments. Only the upper middle class patronized the legitimate theaters where the preeminence of authors like José Echegaray testifies to the low standards of taste. Summing up the approach he took in his domestic melodramas like *El gran Galeoto* (Great Galeoto, 1881), Echegaray commented: "The sublime in art is found in tears, sorrow, and death." Even Spaniards were nonplussed when he won the Nobel Prize for Literature in 1904. Better representatives of Spanish dramatic realism were novelist Benito Pérez Galdós, who also wrote about twenty plays in reaction against Echegaray's false realism; the Catalan regionalist Angel Guimerà; and, above all, Adelardo López de Ayala and Manuel Tamayo y Baus. Although the latter earned his reputation as an author of realistic social problem plays, his best work, *Un drama nuevo* (A New Play, 1867), is set in the Elizabethan period.

The theaters of Bulgaria, Czechoslovakia, Hungary, and Romania all achieved their national identities in the nineteenth century. Czechoslovakian theater was the earliest to emerge, that of the Czech language far outstripping the Slovak. Plays in Czech were performed in Prague and Brno from the 1760s, and a permanent theater was built in Prague in 1783; it was there that Mozart conducted the premiere of his *Don Giovanni* in 1786. That theater was later named after Josef Kajetán Tyl, a major figure in Czech theater history. Tyl directed his own company, the Kajetán, but worked toward the establishment of a Czech National Theatre, which was finally achieved in 1881. Tyl was also an actor, playwright, translator of foreign plays, and a government representative. Although his plays range from fairytales to serious historical dramas, most are strongly patriotic. Indeed, a song from his first play, *The Fair* (1834), became the Czech national anthem. A considerable number of Czech playwrights supplied a steady stream of realistic dramas in the 1880s and 1890s.

Although German theater dominated in Buda and Pest well into the nineteenth century, a Hungarian theater company established itself in Kolozsvár in 1792 and toured Transylvania, finally acquiring a permanent theater in 1821. This stimulated Hungarian playwriting, including such important plays as *Bánk Bán* (The Viceroy, 1814), by József Katona and *Csongor and Tünde* (1831) by Mihály Vörösmarty. A permanent Hungarian theater opened in Pest in 1837 and three years later became the National Theatre. German-language theater declined in the 1840s as Hungarians looked to the vernacular theater for plays that commented upon current social and political concerns. Among these were the *népszinmú,* or folk plays with song and dance featuring romanticized peasants, by the prolific Ede Szigligeti, whose entire professional career was tied to the National Theatre. Imre Madách's *Az ember tragédiája* (The Tragedy of Man, 1860), a despairing epic poem not staged until 1883, became one of the most frequently produced and internationally renowned of all Hungarian dramas. In the 1880s Gergely Csiky emerged as the leading exponent of realism, albeit in the manner of Sardou, with his sharply observed depictions of money, marriage, and business concerns among the Hungarian middle class.

The earliest known performance in the Romanian language did not occur until 1816, and not until 1834 in Moldavian, as the land had long been a crossroads for touring French, German, Italian, Russian, and Polish companies. The first generation of Romanian playwrights emerged in the 1830s–40s; one of these, Ion Heliade Radulescu, also worked toward the establishment of a national theater with an actor training school. A permanent, state-subsidized, 1,000-seat theater opened in 1852 in Bucharest, which became the capital of the country formed by the union of Wallachia and Moldavia in 1859. This National Theatre was eventually named after Romania's greatest playwright, Ion Luca Caragiale, whose well-crafted, sarcastic comedies like *Stormy Night* (1879) and *The Lost Letter* (1884) satirize provincial government and lower-middle-class society.

The development of Bulgarian theater was retarded by Turkish rule that lasted from 1396 to 1878. The first Bulgarian-language theater was founded in Romania in 1865. Dobri Voinikov, its director until 1871, wrote one of the best preliberation Bulgarian plays, *Civilization Misunderstood* (1871). The other outstanding work, also by a Bulgarian in exile, Vasil Drumen, was a historical play of intrigue, *Ivanko, the Assassin of Asen I* (1872), which is still seen in revivals. Bulgarian theater increased rapidly from the 1880s. With its move into a new building in 1907, the National Theatre in Sofia became an important artistic focal point.

ACTING: AN INTERNATIONAL ART

In the wake of Adelaide Ristori, the last two decades of the nineteenth century marked the rise of the international star actor. Tours of
Europe and the Americas provided the ultimate litmus test of an actor or
actress's talent: the ability to captivate an audience for an entire performance in a foreign language. Certainly, international touring had long
been a source of extra income and status. A leading British actor, George
Frederick Cooke, astonished his contemporaries by lavishing his considerable talent on uncultivated American audiences as early as 1810.
Mademoiselle George became a cult figure for St. Petersburg theatergoers not long before Napoleon's 1812 invasion of Russia. Rachel enhanced her prestige in Paris by the acclaim she won abroad, beginning
with an 1841 London engagement and taking her over the next fifteen
years to cities like Warsaw, Moscow, St. Petersburg, Budapest, Prague,
Vienna, Berlin, Amsterdam, and The Hague.

One of the most remarkable midcentury trailblazers on the international circuit, the American-born Ira Aldridge, ironically never won
general recognition in his own country. He made his debut in his mid-
teens, around 1821, as Rolla in Sheridan's *Pizarro,* produced by the
African Company, the earliest known black theater company in America.
Founded in 1821 by William Henry Brown following the success of an
earlier tea-garden entertainment enterprise, the African Company
lasted only three years. Its demise resulted from its success, as an increasing white patronage led Brown to move his company to a hotel next door
to the 2,500-seat Park Theatre; the Park's management could not brook
the rivalry and caused disruption of the African Company's performances. Aldridge's brief acting experience with the African Company was
enhanced by the example of the company's leading actor, the West
Indian James Hewlett, whose Richard III and other Shakespearean
interpretations revealed, according to the New York *American* (April 27,
1825), a "natural genius" and could be favorably compared with "some of
the first actors of the day." Aldridge also had the opportunity to see
performances by major British actors on tour, since the gallery of the
Park Theatre was reserved for blacks.

In 1824, seventeen-year-old Ira Aldridge sailed for England in
hopes of finding there the opportunity to perform the great Shakespearean roles that were unavailable to him at home. There Aldridge
spent nearly three decades developing his skills on provincial tours. A
signal event during that period was his taking over the role of Othello
from Edmund Kean at Covent Garden after Kean fell mortally ill in
1833. Beginning his tours of continental Europe and Russia in 1852,

"The African Roscius" quickly won international renown. His repertoire of over forty roles included Othello, Richard III, Shylock, and King Lear as well as the singing lead in Bickerstaffe's *The Padlock* and various melodramatic characters like the title role in R. C. Maturin's *Bertram; or the Castle of St Aldobrand,* which he created in 1831. His successes won him the Prussian Gold Medal for Arts and Science from King Frederick IV, the Medal of Ferdinand from Emperor Franz Joseph of Austria, and many other awards. On his first tour to Russia, in 1858, Aldridge performed Othello and Shylock in English with a German troupe playing all the other roles in their language. On an 1860s tour to many provincial Russian towns, he played in English to the Russian of local amateur actors. The French critic Théophile Gautier saw Aldridge's Othello in Russia and commented on his "majestically classical style." Russian critics were impressed by his "inner flame" and his apparently total identification with Othello, Lear, and Shylock: "You see how feelings come to birth in his heart, how the words are sought for in his mind." Aldridge was instrumental in bringing about a revival of interest in Shakespeare on the Russian stage, which had been so long dominated by melodrama and vaudeville. Although he had planned a tour to America, he died in Poland in 1867 without ever returning to his homeland.

Polyglot productions like those of Aldridge were not uncommon. In Aldridge's case, it was a necessity, since no other actors were available. When the greatest American actor of his time did it, he was fulfilling his desire to play opposite the best talent available anywhere on the world stage. Edwin Booth, the son of Junius Brutus Booth, reveled in the opportunity to perform his favorite role, Iago, opposite the Othello of Germany's international star actor, Bogumil Dawison. The Polish-born Dawison had been performing in Germany since 1847, and in the 1850s he began touring abroad, playing in Amsterdam, Paris, Warsaw, St. Petersburg, and finally, in 1866, in the United States. Booth and Dawison performed *Othello* three times together in New York and once, in May 1867, in Boston. Dawison spoke German, Booth English, and Marie Methua-Scheller as Desdemona alternated German and English depending upon which actor she was addressing. Conscientious as both Dawison and Booth were about their craft, the production was quite smooth, although the two styles did not entirely mesh. According to Daniel Watermeier and Ron Engle, Dawison seemed to dominate his character whereas Booth was absorbed into his. After the New York engagement, Dawison toured to other American cities. Although he expressed a low opinion of American acting in the provinces, he said of the New York performances that "those three evenings belong to the greatest events in my artistic life." Booth found the experience rewarding enough to undertake other bilingual productions: he played Macbeth opposite a

The American-born actor Ira Aldridge (1807–67) performed only briefly in the United States, at New York's African Theatre, before winning recognition in England and on tours of continental Europe. Among the finest of his forty or more roles, black and white, was his Othello. This portrait by an unknown Russian artist is in the Bakhrushin Theatre Museum, Moscow.

Arguably the greatest American actor of all time (right), Edwin Booth (1833–93) performed opposite most of the international stars of his day. He is shown here as Iago in Shakespeare's Othello. The Century Magazine *(August 1911).*

German Lady Macbeth (Fanny Janauschek) and an Italian one (Adelaide Ristori), and Iago to Tommaso Salvini's Italian Othello as well as Hamlet to Salvini's Ghost.

Edwin Booth's theatrical apprenticeship came when he accompanied his father on cross-country tours. On his own from the age of nineteen, he played California mining camps, and soon embarked upon his first international tour, with Laura Keene's company, to Australia in 1854–55. He began playing Hamlet in 1854, Iago in 1856, and eventually settled on a standard repertoire of eleven Shakespearean roles plus five others including his especially popular title role in Edward Bulwer-Lytton's *Richelieu; or, The Conspiracy* (1839). Various studies by Charles Shattuck and Daniel Watermeier have shown how Booth was constantly refining his Shakespearean interpretations. In contrast to his

Darkly handsome, with expressive eyes, Edwin Booth (above) was a compellingly melan-choly Romantic Hamlet. Crawford, The Romance of the American Stage.

The elaborate facade of Booth's Theatre (1869) in New York (below) was matched by the high standards of production for the plays presented there.

father's undisciplined romantic passion, Booth's style had an intense but cleanly delineated naturalness. According to Otis Skinner, for example, "No actor of his time so completely filled the eye, the ear, and the mind with an ideal of romantic tragedy. Extravagance never marred his work." One of his most compelling features was his dark, expressive eyes, so changeable that Charles W. Clarke observed during a performance of *Hamlet*: "His eyes, normally jet black, were almost white with light." In 1864, Edwin Booth and his two brothers appeared for the only time in a production together, in Shakespeare's *Julius Caesar*. Junius Brutus, Jr., played Cassius, Edwin played Brutus, and John Wilkes played Mark Anthony. John Wilkes Booth's assassination of President Abraham Lincoln on April 14, 1865, occurred less than a month after Edwin Booth completed his phenomenal one hundred consecutive performances of *Hamlet*, an interpretation that William Winter described as "dark, mysterious, afflicted, melancholy."

It was only economic necessity that forced Booth's return to the stage nine months after his brother's shameful crime. Booth also turned his energies to constructing a magnificent new theater at 23rd Street and Sixth Avenue in New York, which opened in 1869. There he mounted a series of visually dazzling productions, even bringing Charlotte Cushman out of retirement to play several roles. Booth had proven his management abilities at several theaters—the Boston, the Walnut Street, and the Winter Garden—but the mortgage payments for Booth's Theatre were exceptionally high and the lavish productions were not making enough profit, especially when theater attendance dropped drastically during the economic depression of 1873. Booth's loss of the theater freed him from management to concentrate on acting, including several tours abroad. In 1881 at London's Lyceum Theatre, Booth and Henry Irving alternated the roles of Othello and Iago, with Ellen Terry as Desdemona. Booth toured to Germany in 1883. In the final stage of his career, 1887–91, he formed a partnership with Lawrence Barrett and they toured together all over the United States. One of their 1887 engagements was to inaugurate the new Warder Grand Opera House in Kansas City. Construction work on the 3,046-seat theater had not been completed by the scheduled opening date, but the show went on despite the absence of auditorium seating or a roof. Temporary camp stools were set up for the audience along with four large stoves to compensate for a heating system that was not yet installed. A snowfall on the day before the opening left an inch of snow in the roofless theater, but a tarpaulin was rigged the next day. For the opening-night performance of *Othello*, Booth played Iago wearing the heaviest costume in his stock, a robe from *Richelieu*, and Lawrence Barrett played Othello in a long quilted robe from *Francesca da Rimini*. They gave a superb performance. But the high point came during the third evening of the week-long

Booth's Theatre opened on February 3, 1869, with Romeo and Juliet. *The stage setting as well as the architectural style and decor of the theater were a Victorian interpretation of the Italian Renaissance.* Frank Leslie's Illustrated Newspaper (27 February 1869).

Sir Henry Irving's bony, long-limbed physique—which he used to great dramatic effect—was easily caricatured. From William Archer and Robert Lowe, The Fashionable Tragedian (1877).

engagement; *Macbeth's* drunken Porter brought down the house with his line, "This place is too cold for hell." On the whole, the Booth-Barrett tours probably did more than any other endeavor of the century to familiarize American audiences with Shakespeare's plays. Upon his death in 1893, Booth left his library and a grant of money to The

Left, "plasticity" as an admired attribute of nineteenth-century acting is evident in this pose by Ellen Terry (1847–1928) as Marguerite in the dungeon scene of Faust. *Pen and Pencil.*

Right, Eleonora Duse (1858–1924) played a blind woman in The Dead City *(1898) by Gabriele D'Annunzio (1863–1938).* Theatre Arts Monthly *(1931).*

In the latter part of her career, Duse became known as a leading exponent of Ibsen's heroines. Below, she appears as Rebecca West in Rosmersholm.

This portrait of Sarah Bernhardt (1844–1923) reveals her characteristically heavy use of stage makeup. Courtesy of French Cultural Services.

Players, a club for theater people on Gramercy Park in New York.

Two years after Booth appeared with Henry Irving at the Lyceum, Irving made his first of eight tours to the United States. As an actor, and as manager of the Lyceum Theatre from 1878 to 1899, Henry Irving (born John Henry Brodribb) dominated the London stage even though he was swimming against the tide: in the age of realism, he produced melodramas and performed them in the romantic manner. A gangly, eccentric-looking figure, Irving used his physical idiosyncrasies—his spindly legs and long fingers—to fascinating effect. Not until he was thirty-three did he achieve his first major triumph, when in 1871 he was hired to act at the Lyceum and persuaded its manager, H. C. Bateman, to stage Leopold Lewis's *The Bells,* a free adaptation of the French melodrama *Le Juif polonais (The Polish Jew).* Although romantic in its early nineteenth-century Alsatian village setting, *The Bells* is a psychological study of Mathias, a burgomaster tormented by guilt for his robbery and murder fifteen years earlier of a traveler in the snow. Throughout the play, Mathias hears the sleigh bells in his mind, and in a dramatic ending to act 1, he sees through the upstage wall of the room a vision of the murder. Henry Irving brought hypnotic energy and credibility to his long monologue sequences, which built climactically to his vivid imagination-induced death throes. The role remained a staple of Irving's repertoire until his death in 1905. Irving's Hamlet, which he first performed in 1874, established the Lyceum as the leading theater of its day.

As soon as Irving bought out Bateman's widow in 1878 and took full charge of the Lyceum, he hired Ellen Terry, a thirty-one-year-old actress making a comeback after a six-year hiatus during which she had lived in the country with the architect E. W. Godwin, by whom she bore two illegitimate children, Edith Craig and Edward Gordon Craig. Irving and Terry's stage partnership, an artistic triumph that included many Shakespearean productions, lasted until 1902. Her indefinable charm made her an exquisite foil to his theatricality. Her long correspondence with Bernard Shaw, published in 1931, reveals that Shaw thought she allowed Irving to overshadow her, but Terry's loyalty to Irving was legendary. Bryan Forbes described "the exquisite and beloved Ellen Terry" as something between Irving's romantic realism and Shaw's social realism. In any case, the public loved Ellen Terry overwhelmingly, and her appeal was both physical and spiritual; Oscar Wilde dubbed her "Our Lady of the Lyceum."

Irving spared no expense on production and on redecorating the Lyceum, but he always preferred gas lighting to electricity. As Terry recollected in her *Memoirs,* "The thick softness of gaslight, with the lovely specks and motes in it, so like *natural* light, gave illusion to many a scene which is now revealed in all its naked trashiness." Irving strove for a painterly quality with his elaborately conceived light-and-dark effects, splendid three-dimensional scenery, and hundreds of extras in lavish costumes for processions and tableaux. He proceeded from careful study of the text to thorough rehearsal. His production of an abridged version of Goethe's *Faust,* in which he played Mephistopheles, one of his great roles, was five years in the planning. Opened in 1885, it was revived several times and taken on two of the American tours. His was the first English company to bring all of its own scenery on tour to America. In addition to the six hundred or so on the Lyceum Theatre payroll for major productions like *Faust* or *Robespierre* (1899)—including approximately 250 performers, 40 musicians, 40 singers in the offstage chorus, 48 administrators and assistants, 60 gas and limelight men, 60 carpenters, 40 proproom assistants—outside specialists like wigmakers and armorers were often employed. Furthermore, Irving worked tirelessly to win respect for theater professionals in society. His efforts paid off in 1895 when he became the first actor to be knighted.

Ellen Terry was one of a triumvirate of internationally renowned actresses who were constantly compared with one another during the last decades of the century. The press fomented a spirit of rivalry among them, especially between Sarah Bernhardt and Eleonora Duse; Ellen Terry was able to get along well with both Berⁿ ıardt and Duse. Another actress, Maria Ermolova, would certainly have rivaled the others if only she had toured outside Russia. In terms of the legends that surround her, the unfashionably thin, redheaded French actress Sarah Bernhardt stood in a class by herself. Born in 1844 (three years older than Terry, nine years older than Ermolova, and fourteen years older than Duse), Bernhardt had established herself as an international star while the others were still struggling for recognition. Shortly after her 1862 debut at the Comédie Française, she was dismissed for slapping one of the company's entrenched actresses. This was Bernhardt's first display of the flamboyant individualism that made for an endlessly lively press throughout her sixty-one-year career on the stage. Despite the theatricality of her private life, she was a conscientious artist, a superb interpreter of roles ranging from Racine's Phaedra to Meilhac and Halévy's Froufrou, from Dumas *fils*'s Marguerite Gautier (*The Lady of the Camelias*) to breeches parts like Hamlet and Musset's Lorenzaccio. The "Divine Sarah" won renown not only for her charismatic presence, but also for her *voix d'or,* her "golden voice" with its clarity of diction, melodiousness, and ability to convey emotion so compellingly as to provoke tears or laughter from the most innocuous lines.

Bernhardt toured frequently to London and America, as well as cities all over Europe. Her return to the Comédie Française in the 1870s was marked by the opportunity to play opposite Jean Mounet-Sully, one of the finest actors of the classics of the century, and it added Victor Hugo's *Ruy Blas* and *Hernani* to her repertoire. She managed four different Paris theaters at various times: the Ambigu, the Porte Saint-Martin, the Théâtre de la Renaissance, and the Théâtre Sarah Bernhardt. At least five of her American tours were billed as "farewell tours"; she kept going back, because it was the best source of income to pay off her continually mounting debts. When the Theatrical Syndicate controlled American theater between 1896 and 1906, she joined many American performers in attempting to break that stranglehold by refusing to appear in Syndicate theaters; she performed in skating rinks and tents, and even went on the vaudeville circuit with one-act plays. On her return from a South American tour in 1886, she suffered a knee injury that was to result, twenty years later, in the amputation of her leg. This did not deter her from offering morale-building readings for the French troops at the front lines in World War I, and she continued to tour (using a wooden leg) until her death in 1923.

It was the dazzling artistry of Sarah Bernhardt on tour in Turin in

1882 that impelled Eleonora Duse to persevere in her acting career. Duse had endured an unhappy childhood as the daughter of itinerant Italian actors and had shown early promise when she played Juliet at fourteen in the amphitheater of Verona, creating some effective stage business with roses she had bought in the marketplace. By the time she saw Bernhardt perform, however, Duse had reached a plateau and was discouraged enough to consider giving up her profession. Within a few years, Duse made her first international tour—to South America in 1885, formed a company in partnership with actor Flavio Andó, and became the lover of Verdi's librettist Arrigo Boito, whose cultivated guidance soon compensated for the education she had missed. While her career progressed through triumphal tours to Russia, America, and even Bernhardt's Paris, Duse's private life (which, in contrast to Bernhardt, she always tried to keep private) became an emotional roller coaster as she carried on a ten-year affair, 1894–1904, with the vainglorious poet-playwright Gabriele D'Annunzio. They dreamed of revitalizing Italian art through her performances of his decadent poetic dramas like *La Città morta* (The Dead City, 1898), *La Gioconda* (1898), and *La Figlia di Iorio* (The Daughter of Jorio, 1904), but his works never appealed to the public as much as the Dumas *fils* and Sardou plays that formed the basis of her repertoire. Later in her career, she discovered the plays of Ibsen, and *The Lady from the Sea* became one of her great vehicles.

Duse was the antithesis of Bernhardt onstage and off. She was utter simplicity in everyday life. On stage she did not so much act as become the character. Her identification with a role affected her facial expressions, posture, and movement so completely that she could project old age without makeup, and at the end of her career, at sixty-five, the white-haired actress could make an audience believe she was in her teens. Bernard Shaw rhapsodically described the transcendental quality she brought to a role, the naturalness of her blush, and her "dance with the arms" (Duse was especially known for her beautiful, expressive hands). Stark Young observed: "She had no tricks, no efforts to attract or pique or impress, but only the desire to convey to us and to confirm for herself the infinity of living within the woman she portrayed there." He extolled "the quiver and directness" of her playing, an art in which "feeling becomes plastic"; (plasticity, a graceful, sculptural quality of movement, was a much valued asset of the nineteenth-century actress). Duse died in Pittsburgh in 1924 on her fourth American tour.

The Russian actress Maria Ermolova's approach to a role was comparable to that of Duse. In fact, throughout his book *My Life in Art*, whenever Konstantin Stanislavsky wanted to cite the highest attainment of the actor's art, he mentioned "Duse, Ermolova, and Salvini." What

they had in common, he noted, was "their physical freedom, . . . the lack
of all strain. Their bodies were at the call and beck of the inner demands
of their wills." Ermolova longed from childhood to be an actress, but was
sent instead to ballet school. Even after she succeeded in entering the
Maly Theatre company in 1870 at seventeen, her talents were not understood and she was confined to vaudevilles. When she got her first benefit
in 1876, she chose the role of Laurencia in Lope de Vega's *Fuenteovejuna,*
which was then staged over the protests of some company members. Her
stirring portrayal inspired liberal political demonstrations, and the show
was closed by censors after a few performances, but she was launched at
last on a long series of interpretations of "heroic women." She continued
to act after the 1917 Revolution, and was the first actress to receive the
honorary title "People's Artist of the USSR."

Like Duse and Ermolova, Norway's Johanne Dybwad was noted for
her simplicity and naturalness, especially early in her career, which
lasted from 1887 to World War II. Norway had established its independence from Denmark in 1814, and there had been several attempts in
Christiania (today's Oslo) since 1827 to establish a theater for Norwegian
plays performed in the Norwegian language as opposed to Danish. The
struggle between Danish and Norwegian factions became particularly
intense around midcentury, but several outstanding figures emerged to
promote Norwegian theater in Bergen, where Ole Bull opened a theater
in 1852, and in Christiania, where Ibsen ran the Norwegian-language
theater for several years in competition with the Danish-oriented Christiania Theatre. The two Christiania theaters merged in 1863, and the
nationalist Bjørnstjerne Bjørnson became director in 1865. That same
year brought the simultaneous performances of Bjørnson's contemporary problem play *De Nygifte* (The Newly Married, 1865), in Christiania,
Stockholm, and Copenhagen. The range of plays that Bjørnson produced, from Shakespeare to early Ibsen, established the theater's
cultural leadership in Norway. With both Bjørnson and Ibsen writing
realistic plays, the old declamatory style of acting seemed inappropriate.
Johanne Dybwad's appearance was well-timed to lead the way toward
realism in acting. Among her great roles were the self-sacrificing wife in
Bjørnson's *Over Aevne I* (Beyond Human Power I, 1883), and Hilda in
Ibsen's *The Master Builder.* Bjørnstjerne Bjørnson's son, Bjørne Bjørnson,
became director of the Christiania Theatre in 1885 and worked closely
with Dybwad over the years. He also campaigned vigorously for a new
National Theatre, which finally opened in 1899, an impressive building
with statues of Ibsen and Bjørnstjerne Bjørnson in front. Dybwad performed on the first night (a Holberg comedy) and the third night
(Bjørnstjerne Bjørnson's patriotic saga *Sigurd the Crusader*) of the inaugural festivities. Ibsen's *An Enemy of the People* was performed the second

Johanne Dybwad (1867–1950), at center, played Hilde Wrangel in the 1910 production of Ibsen's The Master Builder *at Norway's Nationalteatret. The act 1 setting, shown here, is the architect's studio. Courtesy of Universitetsbiblioteket i Oslo.*

Bjørnstjerne Bjørnson's Beyond Human Power I *(Over Ævne I) was toured to small towns and villages of Norway by a remarkable Danish actress–manager, Ludovica Levy (1856–1922), lying at center. Such productions by her Nationalturnèen ensemble earned her the epithet "queen of Norway's long coast." Courtesy of Universitetsbiblioteket i Oslo.*

Right, the great Polish-born actress Helena Modjeska (1840–1909) made a successful career on the American stage, especially in Shakespearean roles like Juliet, as shown here. Scribner's Monthly *(March 1879).*

night. Celebrated especially for her twenty Ibsen roles, Dybwad toured frequently to Sweden and Denmark as well as to Germany and France. After the turn of the century, she became quite assertive and often directed the plays in which she appeared. It was sometimes said that Johanne Dybwad was really more the Nationalteatret's director than Bjørne Bjørnson.

Another outstanding international actress was Helena Modjeska (born Modrzejewska), who acted with the Warsaw Theatre from 1869 to 1876 and then emigrated to the United States. She acted in Polish until she mastered enough English, eventually building up her repertoire to two-hundred-sixty roles, including fourteen by Shakespeare. Her tragic interpretations were deeply moving to audiences. Similarly, Czechoslovakian-born Fanny Janauschek made her debut at the Royal Theatre of Prague, toured the Continent, made her New York debut in German, took a year off to learn English, and launched her English-speaking stage career in 1870. She continued to perform in the grand tragic manner even after Duse had ushered in a more subdued and natural style.

Besides those international stars, a host of other outstanding actors and actresses made bright careers on both sides of the Atlantic. In 1875 sixteen-year-old Mary Anderson made her debut as Juliet in Louisville, rose to stardom, and, at London's Lyceum in 1887, became the first actress to double the roles of Hermione and Perdita in *The Winter's Tale*. A statuesque beauty of youthful charm with a rich, contralto voice, Anderson was considered to be, according to critic J. Ranken Towse, "the representative American actress of her time." Other leading actors and actresses from the 1870s through the 1890s included Americans Clara Morris, Viola Allen, Fanny Davenport, Rose Coghlan, Mrs. John Drew, Minnie Maddern, Ada Rehan, Lotta Crabtree, John Drew, E. A. Sothern, E. L. Davenport, John McCullough, Richard Mansfield, and British Madge Kendal, Emma Waller, Adelaide Nielson, Beerbohm Tree, Ellen Tree, Mrs. Patrick Campbell, Johnston Forbes-Robertson, and John Martin-Harvey.

For those actors and actresses who did not achieve international stardom or at least some local renown, the profession could be a harsh way to make a living. Still, the acting profession was expanding rapidly at the end of the century. A. M. Palmer's count of American actors and actresses in the legitimate theater was fewer than 800 in 1860, about 4,500 in 1888, and 7,000 by 1895. Better wages, increasing social respectability, and the example of celebrity attained by a few were the attractions drawing people of ever higher levels of education into the theater. At the same time, acting was becoming a professionalized occupation, as Benjamin McArthur has shown in his study of the period between 1880 and

1920. Actor training schools were established, and an early professional organization, the Actors' Society of America, was activated in 1896. Perhaps the most remarkable phenomenon was the rapid influx of great numbers of women into the theater. In Europe as in America, women in theater enjoyed certain freedoms not otherwise available to their sex. Since the theater was generally regarded as a world apart, actresses like Bernhardt, Duse, Terry, Lily Langtry, and Mrs. Patrick Campbell could flout moral and social conventions while the public continued to idolize them. The price they paid, according to Claudia D. Johnson, was the loss of opportunity for domestic happiness in marriage.

INNOVATORS AND THEIR INFLUENCE

The seeds of modern theatrical practice were planted in the latter half of the nineteenth century by a number of outstanding individuals. The first among these, and the one whose work had perhaps the farthest-reaching effects, was the ruler of the tiny German duchy of Saxe-Meiningen. When Georg II came to the throne in 1866 at the age of forty, he had traveled widely and attended professional theaters all over Europe. He inherited not only the day-to-day administrative duties of overseeing the welfare of his subjects, but also Meiningen castle where a third-floor ballroom stage built by his great-grandfather in 1776 had accommodated J. F. Schönemann's company in 1785. In addition, there was a permanent theater built by his father in 1831 through a public sale of stock; over the years it had offered a varied fare of opera, operetta, and drama, including a visit by Ira Aldridge in 1857. On the whole, that theater had offered nothing remarkable until the new duke was able to impose his vision of what a theater should be. Perhaps the idea that had most taken root during his years of theatergoing in London and Paris was that a production should have artistic unity: sets, costumes, pictorial composition of the actors on stage, and all other elements working together in service to the text. As a focus for his own artistic efforts, he decided to limit his resident company to legitimate drama. The 1866 season opened with *Hamlet,* setting a pattern of Shakespearean production as a major component of the Meiningen repertoire. Indeed, when asked years later why he had involved himself directly in theatrical production, Georg II, duke of Saxe-Meiningen, replied: "I was annoyed that Shakespeare was so badly played on the German stage."

The Meiningen company was blessed with a well-balanced, dedicated, and compatible artistic team from 1873. In that year, the duke married Ellen Franz, a cultivated young woman who had been an actress with the company for six years and demonstrated excellent artistic judgment concerning the productions as a whole. Upon her marriage, she was given the title baroness and could no longer act before the public; instead she worked closely with the company as dramaturg or literary advisor. She also eventually edited the play texts for publication as *Plays from the Meininger.*Besides Georg II and his wife, a third, indispensable member of the artistic staff was Ludwig Chronegk. He had joined the company in 1866 as a comic character actor, and in his first season had given fifty-three performances in forty different roles. Around the time of the duke's marriage to Ellen Franz, Chronegk was appointed production manager of the Meininger. Chronegk understood the duke's desired reforms and worked hard to help put them into practice. One of their innovations was to cast intuitively instead of according to the traditional German *Fach*. The *Fach* was a system of categorizing actors according to character type; each theater had a *Fach* book listing all roles by category, so that an actress categorized for her physique and vocal quality as "the Sentimental," for example, would automatically be assigned to play Juliet, Ophelia, Gretchen in *Faust,* and Luisa in *Kabale und Liebe.* In addition to ignoring the *Fach* system, Georg II and Chronegk treated the company as an ensemble; a company member might play the lead in one production and a walk-on in the next. The duke loved to stage the crowd scenes—and especially battle scenes—himself; he adopted Charles Kean's method of dividing the extras into smaller units under separate leaders. The artfully prepared yet believable crowd scenes became a hallmark of Meininger productions. As a skilled draftsman, the duke worked for aesthetically pleasing stage pictures with actors arranged asymmetrically for conscious effects of line and mass. He sketched stage compositions, blocking diagrams, and set and costume designs. The Meiningers' claim of historically accurate sets and costumes was far more substantial than that of previous theaters; some scenery was based upon actual reproductions of period engravings and paintings; weapons and armor were made to order, according to the duke's designs, by a Parisian craftsman. Above all, there were the long, disciplined rehearsals after Georg II finished his ducal administrative duties: scenes would be tried according to a variety of interpretations until the artistically correct one had been found; actors were coached on the emphasis or volume of single lines and words; props were used from the first rehearsals.

In 1874 the Meininger made their first tour, taking six productions to Berlin. Their opening performance of Shakespeare's *Julius Caesar* has been credited with changing the course of German theater history. The forty-seven performances in Berlin that season drew a total attendance of thirty-seven thousand, and made a deep impression. For the next

Georg II, duke of Saxe-Meiningen (1826–1914) often sketched the stage compositions he wanted, as in this one for Pope Sixtus V, *a play by Julius Winding that was given only four performances, all in Berlin. Courtesy of the Deutsches Theatermuseum, Munich.*

This illustration reveals the behind-the-scenes trick used at New York's Metropolitan Opera for the Rhinemaidens' swimming effect. Hopkins, Magic, Stage Illusions and Scientific Diversions *(1897).*

fifteen years, the Meininger rehearsed and performed in their home theater during the winter and toured the capitals of Europe during the spring and summer. Between 1874 and 1890 they gave 2,591 performances in thirty-eight different cities. *Julius Caesar* was the most frequently performed play with 330 performances, followed by *The Winter's Tale* (233 performances), Schiller's *William Tell* (223), and *The Maid of Orleans* (194). The duke did not travel with the company, but kept in contact through daily telegrams to and from Chronegk. Chronegk's herculean tasks included arranging the train transportation for the traveling company of about ninety along with their sets, costumes, and props—usually filling about sixteen railway cars; training the local extras in each city; supervising setups; and handling all local arrangements and personnel problems. The tours ended in 1890 when Chronegk became too ill to continue. Among the Meininger actors, Austrian-born Josef Kainz went on to become the leading actor at the Vienna Burgtheatre from 1899 until his death in 1910. Ludwig Barnay moved from the Meininger to touring as an international star. Max Grube joined the company as a nineteen-year-old actor in 1873 and became its historian. Bjørn Bjørnson acted with the Meininger—which also produced two plays by his father, Bjørnestjerne Bjørnson—before returning to Norway to join the Christiania Theatre. The influence of the Meininger on European theater development can scarcely be overstated. It was a seminal factor in the foundation of the Moscow Art Theatre, for example. While not all of Georg II's reforms were completely innovative, they were so expertly handled and exposed to so wide an audience that he can truly be credited with setting the course of the modern theater.

Although Richard Wagner is best known as an operatic composer, his impact on theater was also profound. He was taken to the theater often in childhood, but received no formal training in music until he was eighteen. He lived in extreme poverty for years while composing his early operas. Finally he obtained an excellent position as *Kapellmeister* at the court of Dresden, where three of his operas were produced: *Rienzi* in 1842, *The Flying Dutchman* in 1843, and *Tannhäuser* in 1845. However, his revolutionary activities during the 1848 uprisings forced him into exile. Settling in Zurich, he devoted himself to writing works of aesthetic theory, including such essays as "Art and Revolution" (1849), "The Art-Work of the Future" (1849), and "Opera and Drama" (1851). Taking as his ideal the *Gesammtkunstwerk,* a synthesis of many arts to form a unified whole, he saw the music of the future not in terms of opera but as a union of music and poetry, of Beethoven and Shakespeare, which he called "music-drama." He also felt that art should express the spirit of the community as Greek tragedy had done, and therefore he chose to base his work in the folk roots, the Nordic mythology, of the German people. In keeping with his idea of music-drama as a total work of art, he not only composed the music for his operas, but also wrote the libretti and designed the scenery. His musical innovations included development of the *leitmotiv,* a brief musical phrase that returns periodically with variations throughout the work to evoke a particular character, idea, or emotion. He also wrote continuous music with the overture, arias, and other traditional set pieces embedded in the musical flow. The libretti for the four full-length operas that make up the cycle known as *The Ring of the Niebelung—The Rhinegold* (1854), *The Valkyrie* (1856), *Siegfried* (1871), and *Die Götterdämmerung* (The Twilight of the Gods, 1874)—form a long dramatic poem to which the music adds a complex aural symbolism. Indeed, Wagner's use of both literary symbols and musical leitmotivs was to be a major influence on the French symbolists of the next generation.

Wagner was also to have an influence on theater architecture. He had long wanted his own theater, and finally obtained both an appropriate site and, largely from his admirer King Ludwig II of Bavaria, the financing. The cornerstone for the Wagner Festspielhaus in Bayreuth was laid in 1872, and it opened four years later with the first performance of *The Ring of the Niebelung* as a complete cycle. Without boxes or galleries, the theater structure neither promoted socializing during performances nor reflected class hierarchies. The fan-shaped, raked auditorium also featured continental seating; that is, rows of seats set far enough apart that they could be accessed from side doors, thus obviating the need for aisles. Another innovation was the sunken orchestra pit, so that the musicians were invisible to the audience. A double proscenium, one before and one behind the *mystische Abgrund* (mystic chasm) of the orchestra, contributed to the apparent separation of "the ideal and the real" without adding any spatial distance between spectators and the stage.

Wagner's efforts to integrate all the arts into a *Gesammtkunstwerk* were to be continued at the turn of the century by various theater artists seeking a synthesis of the arts, perhaps most notably by Serge Diaghilev. During his lifetime, however, Wagner also inspired the first major work by the philosopher Friedrich Nietzsche: *The Birth of Tragedy from the Spirit of Music* (1872). Conceiving his work as a manifesto in support of Wagner's music-drama, Nietzsche argued that art owes its continuing evolution to the Apollonian-Dionysian duality. The Apollo of the classical Greeks represented reason, serene lucidity, while Dionysus encouraged ecstatic forgetfulness, irrationality. To repudiate either one is to negate art, whereas the folk song is the joyous union of both. Later, when Nietzsche rejected Christianity, he also renounced his former admiration of Wagner.

Wagner's theater in Bayreuth, inaugurated in 1876, pioneered several innovations in theater architecture, including continental seating and the double proscenium separated by the "mystic chasm" of the orchestra pit.

The exterior of Wagner's Festpielhaus in Bayreuth offers no hint of the advanced design of the interior. Scribner's Monthly (*July 1876*).

Adolphe Appia (1862–1928) designed this setting for Wagner's Parsifal *in 1899. This evocation of the sacred forest through the simplicity of line and mass might be contrasted with the painted realism that was current at the time.* Cheney, Stage Decoration.

This forest setting for Wagner's Twilight of the Gods *at Bayreuth illustrates the norm for operatic stage scenery when Appia began to conceive of an approach to design based upon light and space.* Scribner's Magazine *(November 1887).*

Wagner's influence, however, extended to yet another individual who was himself one of the great innovators of the modern theater, Adolphe Appia. As a student in Germany, the Swiss designer and theorist Appia realized the inadequacy of contemporary production methods by comparison with the staging possibilities that Wagner's music-dramas stimulated in his imagination. He set himself the mission of discovering a stagecraft that would do justice to Wagner's music, and he published his early theories in *La Mise-en-scène du drame wagnérien* (The Staging of Wagnerian Drama, 1895). From that point of departure, his theories evolved into principles for the reform of staging practice in general, as expounded in his major work, *Die Musik und die Inszenierung* (Music and the Art of the Stage, 1899). Still drawing his examples from Wagner, Appia referred to the combination of text and music as a "word-tone poem," which is entrusted to the actor to translate for the audience. The living, three-dimensional actor serves as an expressive intermediary between the poetic-musical text and the elements of visual expression, which are the spatial arrangement of three-dimensional scenery, lighting, and painting. The incongruous element here is painting, a convention of Western theater's false search for scenic illusion. There can be no organic relationship between the three-dimensional actor and flat painted scenery. The stage is a volume of space in which the elements are fused by light. "Light is to production what music is to the score," wrote Appia, "the expressive element in opposition to literal signs; and, like music, light can express only what belongs to the 'inner essence of all vision.'"

Appia's first opportunity to try his theories in production—three performances of scenes from *Carmen* and *Manfred* in a private theater in Paris in 1902—won him praise from leading theater artists, but no commissions for more designs. In 1906 Appia met Emile Jaques-Dalcroze, a pioneer in the study of the expression of an individual's inner being through rhythmical movement, which Dalcroze called eurythmics. The two became close collaborators for the next decade, Appia designing many "rhythmic spaces" for Dalcroze's dance students. One of their major projects was the establishment of an institute for eurythmics at Hellerau, a utopian community near Dresden. The Hellerau summer festivals of 1912 and 1913 gave Appia excellent opportunities to test his concepts of stage lighting. At last Appia's long efforts were paying off in favorable recognition of the new stagecraft he demonstrated: "the stylised simplification of theatrical production, the integration of light and scenery." These triumphant events provided the basis for his mature theory, *L'Oeuvre de l'art vivant* (The Work of Living Art, 1921). Appia died in 1928, leaving designs for dozens of works that had never reached the stage. Yet his influence on modern stage design and stage lighting is

By 1920 Appia had eliminated all suggestively representational elements. This harmonious formal setting was for Echo and Narcissus *at the Dalcroze Institute Theatre. Courtesy of the Deutsches Theatermuseum, Munich.*

equal to that of Georg II, Duke of Saxe-Meiningen on modern stage directing, or of Stanislavski on acting. He must also be credited as one of the great theorists of twentieth-century theater.

The Norwegian dramatist Henrik Ibsen was not so much an innovator as one who used the available tools and materials with exquisite refinement. Nor did success come easily to him; the play that must be considered his breakthrough as a dramatist, *Brand* (1866), was the tenth play he had written over a sixteen-year period. As a child, the withdrawn, bookish, hot-tempered Ibsen heard rumors that he was not the son of the merchant Knud Ibsen, but of the poet Tormod Knudsen, with whom his mother had been friendly before her marriage; this was to be the source of a preoccupation with illegitimacy in many of Ibsen's plays. His father's bankruptcy when he was seven was a humiliation for the family that made home life miserable for Ibsen and his younger siblings. It is possible that Ibsen saw some theater in his youth, for the small timber town of Skien (population three thousand) where he was born frequently received Danish touring companies performing mostly French vaudevilles. At fifteen—his formal education completed—Ibsen was sent to the isolated village of Grimstad, where he lived from 1844 to 1850 as an apothecary's apprentice. So poor that he owned no socks or underwear, Ibsen developed an antipathy toward moneyed society and the church, a hostility that would later show up in his plays. There a servant girl ten years his senior gave birth to his child, for whom Ibsen

Erik Werenskiold's 1895 portrait of Henrik Ibsen (1828–1906) skillfully captures the personality of Norway's greatest dramatist. Photographed by Jacques Lethion, Nasjonalgalleriet, Oslo.

This sketch illustrates the scene set in the Hall of the Mountain King in the original 1876 production of Ibsen's Peer Gynt. *Peer Gynt has a tail because he has agreed to become a troll in order to marry the Troll King's daughter. Courtesy of Universitetsbiblioteket i Oslo.*

Bjørne Bjørnson (1859–1942) played Peer Gynt in the play's 1892 revival at the Christiania Theatre. These photographs, below, show Peer Gynt at the beginning and at the end of the play. Courtesy of Universitetsbiblioteket i Oslo.

Two scenes from a much-acclaimed production of Ibsen's The Pretenders *(1863) at Det Norske Teatret in 1989. Courtesy of Det Norske Teatret, Oslo.*

paid maintenance for fourteen years. In his little spare time, he read voraciously, painted, wrote poems and his first play *Catiline* (1849). He sent the play to the Christiania Theatre, which rejected it, but his friend Ole Schulerud financed the publication of two-hundred-and-fifty copies, only forty of which were sold, the others eventually destroyed.

In 1850 Ibsen went to Christiania to study, but could not pass the university's entrance exams in Greek and mathematics. While eking out an existence by writing articles for student newspapers, he wrote a one-act play, *Kjoempehøjen* (The Warrior's Barrow, 1850), that was much influenced by the romantic patriotic plays of Adam Oehlenschläger. Produced by the Christiania Theatre, it was not particularly successful, but it prepared him for the loosely defined post of resident dramatist/ production manager at Ole Bull's new Norwegian-language theater in Bergen from 1851 to 1857. There, according to Michael Meyer, he was to spend six years, "years of poverty, bitterness, and failure, learning the alphabet of his craft." The theater administration first sent him to Copenhagen, Dresden, and Hamburg to observe theatrical practices. During his tenure in Bergen, Ibsen mounted 145 plays, 75 of which were French. The fact that 21 of those were by Eugène Scribe testifies to Ibsen's working knowledge of the techniques of the *pièce bien faite*. He also staged five of his own plays there. In 1857 he became artistic director of the Norwegian Theatre in Christiania, and this enabled him to marry Susannah Thoresen, to whom he had long been engaged. When the Norwegian Theatre went bankrupt in 1862, Ibsen obtained a small grant to support him on a walking tour of western Norway to collect folklore. This project made an indelible impression on him, just as Ostrovsky's folk studies along the Volga had deeply affected his writing; a folkloric element infuses most of Ibsen's plays, even the late ones. He next served as dramaturg for the Christiania Theatre, which produced his nationalistic historical drama *Kongsemnerne* (The Pretenders, 1863) successfully enough that Ibsen was awarded a grant to study abroad.

Ibsen settled in Rome in 1864 and did not return to live in Norway for twenty-seven years. The change of climate seemed to stimulate him. Without concern for its potential on the stage, he wrote *Brand*, a "dramatic poem" reflecting, in the intransigent title character, his own free-thinking, antiauthoritarian views. The publication in 1866 of this dramatic "gospel of individualism" was hailed throughout Scandinavia as a cultural milestone. According to a Danish reviewer: "It is read with the greatest interest, its praise is in all men's mouths, and its powerful words in all men's thoughts." After that, his great, complex romantic folk drama *Peer Gynt* (1867), his last play in verse, was written quickly. With *Et Dukkehjem* (A Doll's House, 1879), Ibsen began the series of realistic plays for which he remains best known outside Norway: *Gengangere* (Ghosts, 1881), *En Folkefiende* (An Enemy of the People, 1882), *Vildanden* (The Wild Duck, 1884), *Rosmersholm* (1886), *Hedda Gabler* (1890), *Bygmester Solness* (The Master Builder, 1892), and *John Gabriel Borkman* (1896). Throughout this period he became increasingly adept in his use of well-embedded dramatic symbols, and some of his last plays approach symbolist drama: *Fruen fra Havet* (The Lady from the Sea, 1888), *Lille Eyolf* (Little Eyolf, 1894), and *Naar vi døde vaagner* (When We Dead Awaken, 1899). In a sense, the Ibsen canon encompasses the aesthetic progress of the entire century, moving from the neoclassicism of *Catiline* to romanticism to realism and social problems to symbolism. None of these, however, can be so narrowly defined as that; his *Peer Gynt*, for example, is as much a penetrating psychological study as it is an epic folk drama with symbolist sequences and acerbic political commentary. His gallery of insightful portraits of strong-minded women straining against social convention has earned him respect as an early champion of women's rights, but it can also be argued that characters such as Hedda Gabler, Rebecca West, and Hilde Wangel are troll-like creatures bent on the destruction of the hapless men who love them.

Clearly, Henrik Ibsen has left a legacy of dramatic masterpieces, but this alone would not signal him as a trailblazer of the modern theater. In the field of dramaturgy, he showed how techniques borrowed from Scribe could be more than the means to manipulate an audience; used as a skillfully camouflaged framework, they could support the full weight of character, dialogue, and thought to transform craftsmanship into art. He set a new standard for "realistic dialogue," as the concept of subtext for the first time became truly meaningful. His dialogue is rich in its very economy, as every line does double or sometimes triple duty: advancing the action, revealing character, carrying exposition, suggesting atmosphere, exploring an idea. Although Ibsen claimed that he was "more poet and less social philosopher," he certainly provoked audiences and critics to respond to the plays as social documents. He broke new ground for the theater in his handling of themes like power ploys between the sexes, moral and social hypocrisy, altruism overpowered by greed, religious and social conventions that damage the human capacity for self-realization. Indeed, in England in the 1880s and 1890s, the term "new drama" referred specifically to the plays of Ibsen. A small sampling of the critical invective hurled against the 1891 London production of *Ghosts* suggests the extent to which Ibsen was treading on new ground: "unutterably offensive," "morbid, unhealthy, unwholesome and disgusting story," "a piece to bring the stage into disrepute and dishonor with every right-thinking man and woman," "a dirty act done publicly." In the face of that, critic William Archer launched "the Ibsen campaign" to win

This is an example of Ibsen's numerous costume renderings. Courtesy of Universitetsbiblioteket i Oslo.

Ibsen's A Doll's House *premiered in Copenhagen in 1879, but had its first Norwegian production, shown here, the following year at the Christiania Theatre. This sketch of the tarantella scene is by Olaf Jorgensen, who designed the sets. Courtesy of Universitetsbiblioteket i Oslo.*

acceptance for social drama. In the United States also, the Ibsen contro-versy raged for a quarter of a century. Richard Mansfield's 1889 tour of *A Doll's House,* for example, garnered reactions like that of Amy Leslie of the Chicago *Times:* "morbid, forced, repulsive. The world abounds with festers of many kinds, but the way to remedy them is not to smear their horrible oozings over everything else." To give the last word to Ibsen, one can scarcely do better than to quote the final word he spoke on his deathbed in 1906: *Tvertimot!* (On the contrary!).

In the United States, Ibsen's most effective champion was a pert petite redhead who had acted between the ages of three and twenty-five as Minnie Maddern. After her 1890 marriage to Harrison Grey Fiske, editor of the New York *Dramatic Mirror,* she retired from the stage for three years, during which time she wrote sixteen one-act plays. Induced to return to do a hospital benefit in 1894, she chose Ibsen's *A Doll's House* for the single matinee performance. After twenty years of opposition to Ibsen in America, the understated truthfulness of Nora's growth from child to woman in Mrs. Fiske's performance suddenly made his play understandable. The audience's awe and excitement at that matinee impelled Mrs. Fiske to take up her acting career again. With her, the American stage also gained the plays of Henrik Ibsen, as her great roles included Rebecca West in *Rosmersholm,* Mrs. Alving in *Ghosts,* and the title role in *Hedda Gabler.* Often compared to Duse, she based her interpreta-tion of a role in careful preparation that enabled her to project a subtext with utmost clarity and spontaneity. A woman of strong principles, Mrs. Fiske took a stand against the pressures of the Theatrical Syndicate when most actors were capitulating to the demands of that powerful monop-oly. Her successful crusade against the fashion for hats adorned with aigrettes was recognized by the Audubon Society as having saved the South American egret from extinction. Minnie Maddern Fiske was a trailblazer in using the public allure of the actress to rally support on a social issue.

Besides William Archer, Ibsen had a strong British supporter in playwright-critic Bernard Shaw, who was far more actively a social re-former than Ibsen. If Ibsen achieved a seamless fusion of psychological truth and the questioning of traditional social patterns, his admirer Shaw put the emphasis on the latter to the detriment of the former. Shaw's considerable achievement might be said to have been the popu-larization of intellectualism. He showed that ideas could hold the stage even without the support of a realistic plot or characters. Born in Dublin, twenty-year-old Shaw came to London with his mother, a music teacher, in 1876. For eight years he wrote music criticism for the *Star* and the *World,* while educating himself in art and politics, the latter mainly in the reading room of the British Museum where he studied Karl Marx and other political theorists. He also wrote five unsuccessful novels. In 1884 he joined the newly founded, socialist Fabian Society. Through that means, Shaw discovered his abilities as a witty, articulate platform speaker. As drama critic for the *Saturday Review* from 1895 to 1898, he denounced the mediocrity and intellectual emptiness of the general run of London theater and promoted the "new drama" of Ibsen, a position he had already taken with the publication of his extended essay *The Quintessence of Ibsenism* (1891). He also lambasted what he called "bardolatry," the shallow romanticizing of Shakespeare by those who did not really know the works.

Allied by their common interest in Ibsen, Shaw and critic William Archer undertook to collaborate on a play, but the resulting work, *Widowers' Houses* (1892), an attack on slum landlordism, was wholly Shaw's. It was given two performances by Jacob T. Grein's Independent Theatre Club, an organization dedicated to producing the "new drama" for invitational audiences. Shaw improved rapidly in dramatic technique and sparkling dialogue, but he never flinched from controversial subjects in his plays. Among the prolific dramatist's major works are: *Mrs Warren's Profession* (1893), *Arms and the Man* (1894), *Candida* (1897), *The Devil's Disciple* (1897), *Caesar and Cleopatra* (1898), *Man and Superman* (1893), *Major Barbara* (1905), *Androcles and the Lion* (1912), *Pygmalion* (1912), *Heartbreak House* (1916), and *Saint Joan* (1923). But for a long period, the plays were better known through publication (the lengthy stage directions were written as an aid to the reader) than in production. This might be attributed, according to Dennis Kennedy, to the lack of

Minnie Maddern Fiske (1864–1932) did more than any other American performer to promote the plays of Ibsen on the American stage. Mrs. Fiske is shown here as Rebecca West in Ibsen's Rosmersholm *in 1907.*

The plays of George Bernard Shaw (1856–1950) continue to be widely performed. Shaw's Major Barbara *(1905), above, is a lively play of ideas polarized by Barbara Undershaft, a major in the Salvation Army, and her father Andrew Undershaft, a munitions manufacturer. In the Alabama Shakespeare Festival 1990 production, Melody Ryane played Barbara and Kent Gash was Bill Walker. Will York directed. Courtesy of Alabama Shakespeare Festival.*

American actor–manager Lester Wallack (1820–88) played Leon Delmar, who disguises himself as a dumb captain named Zohrab, in his own play The Veteran. *From a crayon drawing by Napoleon Sarony.* Scribner's Magazine *(October 1889).*

Besides his original plays, Augustin Daly (1838–99) adapted works from the European stage. In 1870 he presented Frou-Frou *as illustrated here, based upon the 1869 Parisian success by Henri Meilhac and Ludovic Halévy. Appelbaum,* Scenes from the Nineteenth-Century Stage in Advertising Woodcuts.

"actors of quick intelligence who were capable of understanding how his plays exploded their nineteenth-century models; actors, more importantly, capable of projecting a socially critical attitude inside comic characters." The mischievous intellectualism and irreverent wit of Shavian comedy finally found its appropriate stage realization in the productions of Harley Granville-Barker and J. E. Vedrenne at the Royal Court Theatre from 1904 to 1907, and subsequently at the Savoy. Granville-Barker, an actor, playwright, tireless campaigner for subsidized theater in England, and one of the most important managers of his day, worked closely with Shaw for sixteen years. Kennedy speculates that "without Shaw, Barker would have had insufficient material to base his reforms on; without Barker, Shaw might well have remained unproduced in London until after the war." Shaw's incisive views on acting and production are evident in his dramatic criticism, prefatory essays to his plays, various polemics, and in his voluminous correspondence, most notably with actresses Ellen Terry and Mrs. Patrick Campbell. His contribution to the shaping of modern theater lies not only in his plays of ideas, but also in his influence on the developing art of the director and on the serious consideration of the art of acting.

In the area of theater management, apart from Harley Granville-

Barker, leadership and innovation came from the generation of American producers who flourished in New York from the 1880s to the 1910s. David Belasco's name gained the widest recognition, but many others also built upon P. T. Barnum's innovations in showmanship and Tony Pastor's successful efforts to attract family audiences. One of the first was Lester Wallack, who began as an actor and manager of his father's theater, Wallack's Lyceum. In 1882 he opened his own Wallack's Theatre at 30th and Broadway, where he remained as actor-manager until 1887, the year before his death. Emphasizing a British repertoire, especially the plays of T. W. Robertson, Lester Wallack attracted a fashionable audience with his lavishly mounted genteel comedies and his policy of bringing together the leading actors of the day, stars like Rose Coghlan, E. H. Sothern, and John Broughan.

Augustin Daly achieved success as a playwright (*Under the Gaslight*, 1867), as a drama critic (for five different New York newspapers at one time), and as a press agent (representing Adah Isaacs Mencken, Rose Eytinge, and Kate Bateman) before going into theater management in 1869. Over the next thirty years, at a succession of theaters from the Fifth Avenue to Daly's, he was considered the leading American manager. Whereas Wallack was a star-gatherer, Daly was a star maker. Not content merely to manage a theater (or three, as he did in 1873), he coached his performers in ways that anticipated later directorial practice. Ada Rehan was one of his finest creations, but he also launched the careers of Clara Morris, Fanny Davenport, and about seventy-five others. An idealist and a strict disciplinarian, Augustin Daly achieved an ensemble effect that deeply impressed London audiences when he toured productions there in 1884, 1886, and 1890. One of his innovations, in 1888, was to sell subscriptions for the same seat at all the plays in a series of special performances.

A. M. Palmer, a lawyer with good business sense, set out to rival Wallack's and Daly's Theatres when he opened the Union Square Theatre in 1872. Building audiences with a largely British repertoire of "polite melodrama," he was able to take over Wallack's Theatre in 1888, renaming it Palmer's Theatre. There he made his greatest contribution by switching to a repertoire of new American plays. His encouragement was instrumental in developing such dramatists as Bronson Howard, Clyde Fitch, Augustus Thomas, and James A. Herne. Another manager, James Keteltas Hackett, son of the romantic actor James Henry Hackett, encouraged the development of American scene design, most notably with his 1914 production of *Othello*, designed by Joseph Urban.

Some of the most varied contributions to come from one individual were the work of Steele MacKaye, an actor, playwright, teacher, manager, and inventor. Having studied acting in Paris under François Delsarte, he introduced the Delsarte system of expressive gestures to American acting and elocution. His acting debut in New York in 1871 was followed by an appearance as Hamlet at London's Crystal Palace in 1873. Among the twenty-four plays he wrote, his great hit was the melodrama *Hazel Kirke* (1880); it ran for over a year at the Madison Square Theatre, which MacKaye opened in 1880. There he designed and installed his famous elevator stage, which allowed forty-second scene shifts. It was there that his business manager Daniel Frohman, later an influential producer in his own right, conceived the idea of sending out "auxiliary road companies" while the New York production was still running. MacKaye's next project was the design and construction of his Lyceum Theatre (1885), the first American theater entirely illuminated by electricity—installed under the personal supervision of Thomas Edison. The building also included classrooms where he offered the first actor-training program in America; it later became the American Academy for Dramatic Art. Among MacKaye's inventions were folding theater seats, fireproof scenery, the adjustable proscenium arch, the sliding stage, and heating and ventilation systems. His most grandiose project, the Spectatorium, planned for the Chicago World's Fair of 1893, was never realized due to a financial panic that caused his investors to withdraw their support. It was to have featured *The World-Finder*, a play about Christopher Columbus, on a 150-foot-wide stage with twenty-five revolving units. Steele MacKaye remains one of the great underappreciated geniuses in the annals of American theater, although his son, Percy MacKaye, a playwright, chronicled his father's activities in *Epoch*, a book published in 1927.

David Belasco, the most flamboyant of the playwright-managers, also promoted technical advances in stagecraft. After stage managing at various theaters, he opened his own Belasco Theatre in 1902. At the height of his management career, it was said that he was never too busy to see any inventor with a new kind of lighting instrument to show. In his mania for stage realism, he eliminated footlights as early as 1889. He used lighting to suggest the title character's all-night vigil in his 1900 play *Madame Butterfly* and to create a forty-minute sunrise effect in his *Rose of the Rancho* (1906). Montrose J. Moses commented that no other manager "so profited by the response of the electric switchboard to human psychology." Among the most famous examples of his extreme concern for realistic detail were the live horses in his mammoth production of *Uncle Tom's Cabin*, the imported French tapestries and furniture in his *DuBarry* (1901), and the real Child's Restaurant that had been bought and reassembled at the theater to serve as the setting for the last scene of Alice Bradley's *The Governor's Lady* (1912). Popular favorites among Belasco's own plays included *The Heart of Maryland* (1895), *The Girl of the Golden West* (1905), and *The Return of Peter Grimm* (1911). A self-styled "high

Steele MacKaye (1842–94) opened the Madison Square Theatre in 1880. It boasted the first elevator stage in the United States, and also featured space for the orchestra above the stage, folding theater sets, and a well-designed ventilation system. On the eve of electric lighting in theaters, the Madison Square had state-of-the-art gas lighting. The operator of the gas table may be seen backstage on the main level. Scientific American *(April 1884).*

The Return of Peter Grimm (1911) by David Belasco (1853–1931) and Cecil B. De Mille was a touching fantasy with broad appeal. The extreme naturalism of the setting is typical of Belasco's elaborately mounted productions. Cheney, Stage Decoration.

priest of the theatre," Belasco liked to wear a black suit and clerical collar, but the appeal of his productions was unabashedly commercial. It was said that he practiced the most up-to-date stagecraft on the most out-of-date plays. In defense of his contributions, however, after Belasco's death in 1931, Walter Pritchard Eaton wrote that he "taught our crude theatre the lesson of detailed discipline; he brought to it mood and atmosphere and sensuous beauty; above all he showed us that to achieve a final effectiveness one guiding intelligence must rule the theatre. He taught us how to unify the diversified arts of the modern playhouse and make them one art."

Clearly, Belasco was carrying on the work of Georg II, duke of Saxe-Meiningen. But Belasco can also be credited—along with a few stars like Sarah Bernhardt, Minnie Maddern Fiske, and James O'Neill—with taking a stand against another innovation, that of the ruthless central control of the American theater by the Theatrical Syndicate that formed in 1896. Of the six innovators whose monopolistic enterprise demonstrated that art is most profitably run like a business, only one of them had experience in theater: Charles Frohman, younger brother of Daniel Frohman, so loved the theater that he had started at the bottom, selling programs, and worked his way up to booking touring companies out of New York to play in towns all across America. With the expansion of railroads after the Civil War, the practice of sending entire productions—called "combinations"—on the road had replaced the old system of resident stock companies visited by touring stars. It was simply more economical for local theater managers to bring in touring productions of long-running New York hits for a few performances each than it was for a stock company to add a new play to its repertory every week in order to continue to draw local audiences. Through his work as an advance agent during the 1880s, Charles Frohman claimed to know "every opera house and lodge hall and railroad connection" as well as what kind of audience could be expected in each town; he could book an entire tour without looking at a map. However, the combination system did not always operate so efficiently.

The complexities of the combination system were daunting when theater managers from all over the country converged on New York in the fall to book their seasons. Each manager would have to make individual visits to upwards of forty different New York producers, each of whom was trying to negotiate with numerous provincial managers to achieve the most closely plotted schedule possible. Unscrupulous producers sometimes contracted with two or three different managers for the same date, so the touring company could play the town that best fit the final routing, leaving the other theaters to absorb the loss of income from an unexpected dark night. Some managers then learned to protect themselves by booking two companies for the same dates; the one that arrived first and staked out the dressing rooms would get to perform, while the other would be left stranded, sometimes losing the income needed to get the company to its next engagement. As a partial solution to the problems, the theaters along one railway line began to join together and hire a single agent to negotiate for all of them; at the same time, producers began working through booking agencies that could represent a number of different shows.

In 1896 six businessmen who owned theaters in different parts of the country—Marc Klaw, Abraham Erlanger, Sam Nixon, J. Fred Zimmerman, Al Hayman, and Charles Frohman—pooled their interests in a firm called Klaw and Erlanger, which became better known as the Theatrical Syndicate, to organize the road and control American theater. Frohman joined their ranks by virtue of the fortune he had made through shrewd theatrical investments, which led to his opening New York's Empire Theatre in 1893, as well as his controlling interests in several other New York and London theaters. At first the Syndicate brought welcome relief from chaos. It guaranteed each theater on the road a full season of successful New York productions. The only catch was that the local manager had to sign an exclusive contract with the Syndicate. If the Syndicate could not get control of a theater in a given city, it would build a rival theater and send in top attractions at rock-bottom prices until the original theater went bankrupt. As its power increased, the Syndicate took over the advertising for its shows and charged local managers an extra fee for this obligatory service. The Syndicate's virtual control of theatrical advertising in newspapers gave it a powerful weapon against those artists who tried to avoid booking through it. One newspaper, the *Dramatic Mirror,* under the courageous editorship of Harrison Grey Fiske, held out against the Syndicate despite the loss of advertising and the Syndicate's attempt to forbid its performers to read it.

By 1900 the Theatrical Syndicate controlled five-thousand theaters, including every first-class theater in the United States; it employed 552 railway agents to schedule its touring companies. Having eliminated competition, the Syndicate forgot about quality. The New York *World,* not long before caving in to the Syndicate, accused it of fraud and deceit for sending out "inferior companies, falsely representing them as the original casts of New York successes." The honest businessman Charles Frohman disclaimed active involvement in the Syndicate—indeed, he was spending a great deal of time in London, where he was highly respected for his fair dealings—yet he never formally withdrew from the Syndicate; he died in 1915 in the sinking of the *Lusitania.* Beginning in 1905, three brothers—Sam, Lee, and Jake Shubert—began to build a chain of theaters to rival the Syndicate. One fortuitous event that helped their enterprise was the 1903 fire in one of the Syndicate's major theaters in Chicago, the Iroquois. The deaths of 602 people, either burned or trampled, incited denunciations of the Syndicate for cutting corners with fire regulations. Fire inspections led to the closing of many theaters elsewhere, and when new theaters were built, they joined the Shuberts. The Shuberts were also helped by the publicity generated when Sarah Bernhardt booked her 1906 American tour with them; two-thirds of the million dollars she grossed for her 226 performances went to the Shuberts. The Theatrical Syndicate's power was effectively broken by 1915. Unfortunately, the Shuberts became every bit as dictatorial as their rivals had been. They produced an impressive series of operettas, revues, and other musicals from the 1910s to the 1940s, but a government antitrust suit ended their hegemony in 1956. It is sometimes said that the American public's disaffection with live theater—by contrast with a sizable, dedicated theatergoing population in Europe throughout the twentieth century—might be attributed to these monopolies.

NATURALISM

France, so often in the vanguard of the arts, had allowed its theater to lapse into middle-class complacency in the 1870s. The plays of Dumas *fils*, Augier, and Sardou still reigned supreme, relieved only by occasional revivals of romantic dramas and a rising vogue for operetta: escapist entertainment to blot out memories of France's humiliating defeat in the Franco-Prussian War and the harrowing atrocities committed during the suppression of the Commune of Paris in 1871. However, the theater stood alone in its artifice. Painters like Gustave Courbet, Édouard Manet, and Honoré Daumier, and novelists like Honoré de Balzac and Gustave Flaubert had long evinced the influence of Auguste Comte's positivism, which emphasized the direct observation of social phenomena without metaphysical embellishment. The unromanticized analysis of human behavior in a well-defined physical setting was the hallmark of a number of ground-breaking novels beginning as early as the 1840s with Balzac's long, influential series of fictional commentaries on contemporary society, *La Comédie humaine* (The Human Comedy, 1842–48). Flaubert was brought to trial for offenses against public morals in his novel *Madame Bovary* (1857), a stylistically polished but depressingly realistic depiction of middle-class provincial life. The Goncourt brothers, Jules and Edmond, also interested themselves in the influence of environment upon man, creating their plots to tie together the facts drawn from observation of life; such was their novel *Germinie Lacerteux* (1864), based upon the life of their faithful servant whose secret debaucheries they discovered only after her death. The concerns expressed in that novel's preface reflect those of the arts in general, except—until much later—the theater: "Today when the Novel is expanding and widening its scope, when it is beginning to be a serious, passionate, and lively combination of literary study and social investigation, when it is becoming through analysis and psychological research our contemporary moral History, today when the Novel has appropriated the methods and responsibilities of Science, it can also lay claim to a certain license and liberty."

The application of scientific methodology to literature became an obsession with Emile Zola, who was especially influenced by Claude Bernard's *Introduction to the Study of Experimental Medicine* (1865); Zola believed that the novelist should not only observe humanity as objectively as the scientist sees organisms under a microscope, but should also conduct scientific experiments with his characters by placing them in different relationships and milieux. He took this approach with his twenty-volume cycle of novels covering the "social biology" of a family under the Second Empire, *The Rougon-Macquarts* (1871–93). Zola's theory of literature also borrowed heavily from that of Hippolyte Taine as delineated in the introduction to *The History of English Literature* (1863) and in *De l'intelligence* (On Intelligence, 1870). Taine's determinist philosophy proposed that human development—and, by extension, literature—was a product of interdependent physical and psychological factors: *la race, le milieu, et le moment.* Thus, an author and his fictional characters could both be analyzed in terms of their biologically inherited traits; their physical, political, and social environments; and the driving concerns of the historical moment. It was Zola who popularized Taine's axiom: "Vice and virtue are products, like vitriol and sugar." This view of literature as a kind of scientifically documented case history of human specimens, using the lab techniques of natural scientists to arrive at an accurate depiction of human nature, was called naturalism. Other novelists who were identified with the movement included Alphonse Daudet and Guy de Maupassant.

Emile Zola won a wide following with his literary criticism and his novels of working-class life, but he aspired to success in the theater, which proved difficult to attain. Only one of his original plays, *Thérèse Raquin* (1873), a dramatization of his own 1867 novel of that title, was frequently revived after its initial failure. Still, Zola effectively promoted theatrical reform through the influence of his essays on the theater: "Preface to *Thérèse Raquin*" (1873), "Naturalism on the Stage" from *The Experimental Novel* (1880), and "Naturalism in the Theatre" (1881) from his collection of dramatic criticism also entitled *Le Naturalisme au théâtre*. He called for the abandonment of stale conventions and rigid formulae, focusing instead on life itself, starting from the idea that nature is sufficient—without "artistic" retouching or trimming—to supply its own beginning, middle, and end. "Imagination has no place," he declared. "The work becomes a report," a simple act of recording *un lambeau d'existence* (a fragment of existence). Zola's phrase restated as *une tranche de la vie* (a slice of life) by the minor playwright Jean Jullien became the key idiom associated with the naturalist drama. Since life is not composed of intrigues, reversals, and recognitions, the drama should reject such contrivances. In Zola's view, even the realistic social problem play was too calculated.

Although naturalism might be seen as an extremist tangent of realism, it differed from realism in several essentials: it rejected the notion of artistic selection and arrangement of elements from reality, preferring the untheatricality of ordinary life reproduced in all its formlessness; it allowed no moral dimension in its objective reporting of social phenomena; it gravitated toward subjects in which the effects of heredity and environment could be most tellingly isolated, that is, in the sordid conditions where poverty, alcoholism, and sexual abuse were concentrated. Granted that environment is a strong determinant in the formation of character, the accurate re-creation of a specific environment on stage became an essential feature of naturalist drama; this was considered the stage equivalent of the novelist's minute prose descriptions of environment. Finally, stage language should sound like everyday speech. "If we cannot produce on the stage a conversation with its repetitions, its length, and its useless words, at least the movement and tone of the conversation could be kept; the particular turn of mind of each talker, the reality, in a word, reproduced to the necessary extent." In practice, such tenets led to a characteristic *rosserie* or crudeness in the human behavior depicted on stage and in dialogue realistic enough to include obscenity. Critic Auguste Filon defined *rosserie* as "a sort of vicious ingenuousness, the state of soul of people who never had any moral sense and who live in impurity and injustice, like a fish in water."

Naturalism finally had its day on the French stage not through the offices of Zola or any other literary figure, but through the efforts of a man whose formal education ended at the age of twelve. André Antoine grew up in a working-class milieu in Paris, but was taken by his mother to the low-priced melodrama and vaudeville theaters in his childhood. Forced to go to work to supplement the family income, he was lucky enough to get a job with a publishing house, which enabled him to indulge his inclination for voracious reading. He frequented museums, libraries, and theaters. Hired as a *claqueur* at the Comédie Française,

Antoine attended that theater every evening and eventually learned by heart all the great scenes, an accomplishment often noted by those who worked with him in later years. Later he became an extra for various theaters and further developed his interest in acting by taking a course in diction. Called up for military service, he spent five years with the regiment, including a pleasant tour of duty in Tunisia. He returned to Paris in 1883 and spent the next three years employed as a clerk for the Paris Gas Company. In 1886, when he was twenty-eight, Antoine joined an amateur theater group called the Cercle Gaulois, but quickly became bored with a repertoire that leaned heavily on Scribe. Antoine proposed that the group seek out some original, unproduced plays; but the bill of four one-acts that he put together included one by the controversial writer Emile Zola, which impelled the president of the Cercle Gaulois to withdraw the club's support. Antoine's lively *Memoirs* chronicle his travails in bringing the four plays to the point of performance and luring some theater critics to see them. Antoine set the date of the single performance on his pay day, when he would be able to pay the rental for the hall. To furnish the set, Antoine borrowed his mother's furniture and transported it through the cobbled streets of Montmartre in a borrowed handcart. Of the four short plays presented on March 30, 1887, it was the dramatization of Zola's *Jacques Damour* by Léon Hénnique that won enthusiastic critical acclaim. Antoine played the title role in that piece, incorporating long silences and sometimes even turning his back to the audience; everything about his interpretation was, according to the *Paris* reviewer, "true and striking."

Although that effort had cost him two months' salary at the gas company, André Antoine was encouraged enough to put together a second bill of plays, which—presented on May 30, 1887 under the name Théâtre Libre—drew an overflow crowd, including all the leading theater critics. Soon Antoine was inundated with original playscripts, but his most pressing problem was to raise some money in order to continue. He prepared an announcement of a full season of plays along with a cover letter soliciting subscriptions, 1,300 of which he delivered himself in order to save the postage. Then he impulsively resigned from his job at the Paris Gas Company. Gradually he found the backing he needed as well as a real theater, albeit inconveniently located in Montparnasse. Despite ups and downs on the first three bills of the inaugural season, the Théâtre Libre was the talk of Paris. Since each bill of plays was presented only once, there were more requests for seats than could be filled. In January 1888, Antoine presented a bill of short plays in Brussels, and there he attended performances of the Meininger on tour; the naturalness of their ensemble acting reaffirmed for him that he was on the right track in his own endeavors.

Never narrowly committed to naturalism, Antoine's larger interest was to promote subtlety in acting and to rid the French stage of old-fashioned conventions like multipurpose painted backdrops. His first full season of plays reveals his eclecticism; it even included some one-acts in verse. But the subscription audience and the critics showed a clear preference for naturalism, and the Théâtre Libre became identified in the public mind with that movement, especially after Antoine presented the world premiere of Lev Tolstoy's *The Power of Darkness* (1888) as the fourth evening in his 1888–89 season. Tolstoy's sordid study of moral degeneracy among the serfs, incorporating adultery, murder, and infanticide, had been banned in Russia and was not performed there until 1895. Antoine rejected the existing French translation as too literary and commissioned a more colloquial version. He costumed it with clothes borrowed from political refugees. The single performance for subscribers and critics caused a sensation, which led to the Théâtre Libre's adding their first public performance. Audiences found their way to the suburban theater in spite of a deep snowfall, and the four-hour performance netted four thousand francs. The public's enthusiastic response led Antoine to premiere numerous foreign plays over the years. *Ghosts,* the first Ibsen play produced in France, opened May 29, 1890, to a mixed response, but Antoine immediately made plans to do Ibsen's *The Wild Duck* the following season. Other notable French premieres at the Théâtre Libre included Strindberg's *Miss Julie* in 1893 and Gerhart Hauptmann's *The Weavers* in 1893.

The Swedish playwright August Strindberg, an early proponent of naturalism in the theater, declared in an 1886 interview that he considered Zola to be the literary master of Europe. He credited Zola as the leader in the "war against French comedy, with its Brussels carpets, its patent-leather shoes, its patent-leather themes, and its dialogue, which reminds one of the questions and answers of the catechism." However, whereas Zola emphasized the influence of milieu on extended families, Strindberg preferred to give primacy to psychological factors while focusing on a single individual; thus the germ of Strindberg's later dramatic expressionism already existed within his naturalist work. After reading the manuscript of Strindberg's *Fadren* (The Father, 1887), Zola wrote to him: "Your play is one of the few dramatic works that have deeply moved me," but Zola also prodded Strindberg to ground his work even more solidly in reality. Strindberg complied, subtitling *Fröken Julie* (Miss Julie, 1888), "A Naturalistic Tragedy" and publishing with it a preface that is often cited as the most succinctly stated manifesto of dramatic naturalism. In his preface, Strindberg stressed his characters' "multiplicity of motives" arising from both physiological and psychological circumstances; that is, a combination of heredity and environment.

En famille (*Among the Family, 1887*) *by Oscar Méténier appeared on the second bill of plays presented by André Antoine (1858–1943). Although the one-act's sordid depiction of a low-life family put it into the naturalistic camp, the flat painted portions of the setting tie it to the dominant theatrical mode of the day.* Encyclopédie du théâtre contemporain.

Under the influence of Emile Zola (1840–1902), Swedish dramatist August Strindberg (1849–1912) embraced naturalism early in his career. His first major effort in that vein was The Father *(1887). Shown here is the final scene in a 1908 production at Strindberg's own Chamber Theatre (Intima Teatern). Drottningholms Teatermuseum.*

He explained his suppression of act divisions: "Our capacity for illusion is disturbed by the intervals, during which the audience has time to reflect and escape from the suggestive influence of the author-hypnotist." He confined his action to a single setting to allow greater realism, and he advocated getting rid of footlights in the theater. When Antoine finally produced *Miss Julie* in 1893, translations of the preface were distributed to the audience. Taking the Théâtre Libre as his model, Strindberg opened the Scandinavian Experimental Theatre in Copenhagen in 1889; however, the Danish censor banned his *Miss Julie,* and Strindberg presented only one bill of plays before closing the theater. (It must be noted that the Danish theater boasted an outstanding proponent of naturalistic staging even before Antoine began his work: William Bloch at the Royal Theatre in Copenhagen directed what many claimed were the outstanding productions of Ibsen on any European stage, with special acclaim for his finely detailed *An Enemy of the People* in 1883.)

The Théâtre Libre lasted from 1887 to 1894; after that, the venture could no longer be financially sustained. In its seven-year existence it had offered eighty-four plays on sixty-four bills. Named codirector of the Odéon in 1896, Antoine held the position only seventeen days before resigning over differences with his colleague. He acted with several companies in Paris, then made a South American tour. Upon his return to Paris, he found enough support to open a public theater in 1897, the Théâtre Antoine. During his nine years there, Antoine installed a new lighting system, offered eight productions a year, and continued to produce new French dramatists. Some of those whose works held the stage for several decades were Eugène Brieux, François de Curel, Henry Becque, Georges de Porto-Riche, and Jules Renard. In recent years, Henry Becque has been singled out from among these for revivals of his plays. According to Daniel Lindenberg, his is the only French playwright's name that can be aligned with Shaw's or Strindberg's for the same period. Becque preferred not to be identified with the naturalists, although the public persisted in doing so. His caustic depictions of middle-class corruption, like *Les Corbeaux* (The Vultures, 1882), and *La Parisienne* (Woman of Paris, 1885), might today be called black comedies.

In 1906 Antoine accepted a full appointment as director of the state-subsidized Odéon where he remained until 1914. There, despite bureaucratic constrictions, he continued his reforms in staging; he was the first director in France to eliminate footlights, to use the stage setting and hand props for rehearsals, to stage interior scenes as if there were a "fourth wall" across the proscenium opening, and to darken the auditorium during the performance. His writings suggest that he understood the semiologic value of accumulated details in the stage environment. He also revolutionized French acting—which had always been largely a vocal exercise—by demonstrating the use of pantomimic business and by adopting "conversational" line delivery in place of declamation. He completed the evolution of the French stage director from the function of a production manager to that of the *metteur en scène*, one responsible for the total conception of a production. Building upon Becq de Fouquière's *L'Art de la mise en scène* (Art of Directing, 1884), Antoine developed his theory of directorial art in his *Causerie sur la mise en scène* (Discourse on Directing, 1903), in which he propounded a dialectic between the "tangible" (sets, costumes, blocking of actors, etc.) and "intangible" (tempo, interpretative emphases, etc.) contributions of the director. At the Odéon his eclectic repertoire innovatively juxtaposed new French playwrights, important foreign authors, and the classics. He has been credited as the first French director to take Shakespeare seriously, commissioning new translations and offering plays that were lesser known, like *Troilus and Cressida*. For *Julius Caesar* he traveled to Rome to study the original locale. In his staging of Shakespeare, he experimented with unit settings using a formal—or what he called "decoratively neutral"—stage architecture for productions of *Coriolanus*, *Romeo and Juliet*, and a revival of *King Lear*, which he had previously given a realistic interpretation at the Théâtre Antoine.

Naturalism as an aesthetic movement began losing favor in the 1890s. By scrupulously avoiding the artificial *coups de théâtre* of romantic drama in favor of faithfully reproducing the humdrum existence of ordinary people, and then compensating for the uneventfulness of the material by focusing on lives at the lowest level of the social spectrum, naturalism had settled into monotonous sordidness. It was also undermined by a general renewal of interest in religion and by the incursions of the symbolists, who took a polar opposite approach to drama and theater. However, the example of Antoine's Théâtre Libre spread throughout Europe and generated a number of other small independent theaters that provided opportunities for naturalist dramatists of other countries as well as the plays of Henrik Ibsen, which had not yet won general acceptance. Besides J. T. Grein's Independent Theatre Club in London (founded in 1891) and Strindberg's short-lived theater in Copenhagen, the Théâtre Libre served as a model for the Théâtre de l'Oeuvre (founded in 1893) and the Théâtre du Vieux Colombier (1914) in Paris, the Freie Bühne (1889) in Berlin, the Moscow Art Theatre (1898), the Irish Literary Theatre (1899) in Dublin, the Thália Society (1904) in Budapest, the Scottish Repertory Theatre (1909) in Glasgow, and the little theater movement in the United States in the 1920s.

Of these theaters, the Freie Bühne was most closely identified with naturalist drama. Many German journalists had been calling for a new

German drama to replace the outmoded plays of Dumas *fils*, Augier, and Sardou that had conquered the German stage immediately following Germany's victory over France in the Franco-Prussian War. The Meininger productions of Ibsen seemed to point toward an alternative dramatic style, but during the 1870s and 1880s only one German-language dramatist stood apart from the many imitators of the French models: Ludwig Anzengruber paved the way to naturalism with his dramas of Austrian peasant life that seemed authentic in their use of dialect and in their portrayal of rural customs without the exaggeration that was typical of Viennese comedy. In 1889 a group of young Berlin intellectuals founded an independent theater, which they named the Freie Bühne (Free Stage), with the aim of producing "modern plays of outstanding interest which, because of their nature, might find difficulty in being presented elsewhere." The organizing committee included, among others, a businessman, a bookseller, and a theatrical agent, but they elected the literary man, Otto Brahm, president. Renting the Lessingtheater for a Sunday matinee performance, they opened with Ibsen's *Ghosts*, because they had not yet found the right German play. The right play appeared in time for the Freie Bühne's second production a month later.

Gerhart Hauptmann's *Vor Sonnenaufgang* (Before Sunrise, 1889), opened on October 20, 1889, a landmark date in German theater history. Although much influenced by Tolstoy's *Power of Darkness*, Hauptmann's morbid study of the effects of alcoholism and industrial exploitation in a small Silesian village caused an uproar in the theater: some cheered the play, some hissed it, and some came to blows. The event was significant for several reasons. It launched the playwriting career of Hauptmann, who was to remain the outstanding German dramatist for the next four decades. It gave the Freie Bühne a needed *cachet* for introducing other naturalist playwrights and establishing naturalist production methods during the five years of its existence. And it stirred up the Berlin public, inciting them to discussions of art as well as the subjects examined in the play. As a private subscription theater, the Freie Bühne also provided a venue for plays that were banned from the public stage, as was Hauptmann's fourth and best play, *Die Weber* (The Weavers, 1892). It can be argued that *The Weavers* is the greatest of all naturalist dramas. Based upon an actual event—the revolt of Silesian weavers in 1844—the play focuses on no single character, but adds up to a compelling picture of the life of an entire village. Each of the five acts, using five different settings, reveals a different aspect of their lives, yet the unity of the piece is remarkable. It illustrates, far better than Zola was able to do, the possibilities of the "formless" slice-of-life drama. Hauptmann also succeeded in writing what would seem to be a contradition in terms, a naturalist comedy. *Der Biberpelz* (The Beaver Coat, 1893) pits a lively, thieving washerwoman against uptight Prussian officialdom.

The Freie Bühne closed in 1894 when Otto Brahm was hired away to direct the Deutchestheater. Hauptmann then turned to writing poetic dramas that might be tied to the symbolist movement. Hermann Sudermann's popular dramas like *Heimat* (Magda, 1893), fell midway between Dumas *fils* and the naturalists. Even the influential critic Hermann Bahr, who had helped to introduce naturalism, rejected it as early as 1891, and his own plays moved in the direction of theatricalism and neoromantic decadence. Although naturalism held the stage during no more than a decade, its influence on theatrical practice was seminal and lasting.

THE MOSCOW ART THEATRE

Russian theater had improved considerably since midcentury thanks to the reforms of Ostrovsky, the abolition of the Imperial Theatres' monopoly, and the example of excellent realistic acting by Mikhail Shchepkin, Glikeria Fedotovna, and Maria Ermolova. However, the 1885 and 1890 visits of the Meininger to Moscow and St. Petersburg demonstrated by contrast how far the Russians had yet to go. With a well-entrenched star system, there was no sense of ensemble on the Russian stage. The Imperial Theatre system tended to pour most of its considerable resources into the opera and ballet while neglecting the legitimate theater. The administrative staffs were composed of government appointees, most of whom had little interest in and no understanding of theatrical production. Despite the example set by Saava Mamontov in his support of outstanding new theater designers, there was no effort to harmonize sets and costumes to create a unified impression. The private theaters, concerned only with the box office, offered a steady diet of inconsequential fluff for audiences who expected nothing more from the theater than an evening of amusing distractions. Censorship further dampened many writers' impulse to write for the stage. Provincial theater was the worst of all, as almost daily changes of bill meant underrehearsed and virtually unmemorized performances. The reform of the Russian theater beyond what Ostrovsky had accomplished came about largely through a lucky combination of three major talents: the administrative and dramaturgical skills of Vladimir Nemirovich-Danchenko, the acting and directing techniques advanced by Konstantin Stanislavsky, and the plays and personality of Anton Pavlovich Chekhov. Their efforts conjoined in 1898 to establish an exemplary theater for the twentieth century, the Moscow Art Theatre.

During the preceding decade, all three had experienced both worldly success and artistic frustration. Konstantin Stanislavsky (né Konstantin Sergeyevich Alekseyev), son of a wealthy manufacturer, grew up with every advantage: singing lessons, contact with Russian and foreign artists who toured to Moscow, and unlimited opportunity to participate in amateur theatricals in the little theater on his family's estate only twenty miles from Moscow. From 1877 to 1888, he took charge of the family theater's Alekseyev Circle, producing usually two programs a year, mostly comprised of vaudevilles and operettas. His approach to acting consisted of imitating well-known professional actors. When he got a role in another amateur group's risqué French comedy, he took the name Stanislavski to spare the family reputation. After seeing the piece, his father voiced no objection to Stanislavsky's expanding interest in theater, but advised him not to put his efforts into trashy material. Stanislavsky and several others then founded the Society of Art and Literature, which lasted ten years, 1888–98, and offered plays by authors like Pushkin, Ostrovsky, Molière, Goldoni, Hermann Sudermann, and Reinhold Lenz. After seeing the Meininger productions in 1890, Stanislavsky demanded more disciplined rehearsals. His first major directorial endeavor, Tolstoy's *The Fruits of Enlightenment* in 1891, was well received, but his acting of the role of Othello in 1896, an imitation of Salvini's performance, was an instructive failure. It was at this stage in his development that he received an invitation from Nemirovich-Danchenko to meet and talk about the Russian theater.

By the late 1880s, Vladimir Nemirovich-Danchenko, a nobleman, was widely regarded as Russia's best contemporary playwright. He also wrote drama criticism for several publications and, in 1891, began teaching at the Philharmonic Dramatic School in Moscow. He agitated for improvements—dress rehearsals, new scenery for new plays, historical accuracy of sets and costumes—at the Maly Theatre, which had produced his work. However, it was his winning of the prestigious Griboyedov Prize in 1896 for his play *The Worth of Life* that finally impelled him to seek out a kindred soul who might also envision theater on a higher plane. Nemirovich-Danchenko was angered over winning a prize that he knew should have gone to Anton Chekhov for *The Seagull*, which had premiered under unfortunate circumstances at St. Petersburg's Alexandrinsky Theatre that year. Although he and Stanislavsky had never been introduced, Nemirovich-Danchenko sent him a note suggesting that they meet at the Slavyansky Bazaar Restaurant on June 22, 1897, to discuss "a subject of mutual interest."

Stanislavsky and Nemirovich–Danchenko met for tea, continued talking through dinner, and rode together in the small hours of the next morning to Stanislavsky's villa. In that historic eighteen-hour conversation, they laid down the principles for a new theater that would set an unprecedented standard for dramatic art in Russia. The Moscow Art Theatre was founded with two major aims: to provide training for the actor, and to raise the audience's level of taste and theatergoing behavior. According to Stanislavsky: "Our program was revolutionary. We rebelled against the old way of acting, against affectation and false pathos, against declamation and bohemian exaggeration, against bad conventionality of production and sets, against the star system, which ruined the ensemble." They established their areas of responsibility, Nemirovich-Danchenko in charge of literary matters, while Stanislavsky would have final authority in the artistic realm. From Stanislavsky's Society of Art and Literature and from Nemirovich-Danchenko's Philharmonic Dramatic School they took the most dedicated actors. They spent the following year welding their two groups of actors into an ensemble and raising money. They announced a repertoire of plays by Sophocles, Shakespeare, Aleksey Tolstoy, Aleksey Pisemsky, Hauptmann, Ibsen, and Chekhov. To get the last name on the program, Nemirovich-Danchenko had the difficult task of persuading both Stanislavsky and Chekhov that this would be in their best interests.

Anton Pavlovich Chekhov, descended from serfs, had risen from the poverty of his childhood in the small town of Taganrog to study medicine at the University of Moscow while supporting himself, his parents, and his shiftless older brothers by writing comic fillers for various periodicals. In 1885, Chekhov gained celebrity as a short story writer and also began his medical practice. Having often deplored the stale conventions that held the stage, he wrote a full-length play avoiding stereotypical characters, noting that he had put into it "not one single villain nor one single angel; (buffoons I couldn't avoid)." *Ivanov* (1887) was given four rehearsals before its premiere at Korsh's Theatre in Moscow; it failed. Chekhov turned to writing the one-act farce-vaudevilles that were certain money-makers no matter what he thought of the genre's artistic merit. In 1889, his next full-length play, *Leshi* (The Wood-Demon), was rejected by St. Petersburg's Alexandrinsky Theatre, but produced at Moscow's Abramov Theatre; it failed. Chekhov vowed to write only one-act trifles thenceforth. In 1896, his next full-length play, *Chaika* (The Seagull), was chosen by the popular comic actress Elizaveta Levkeyeva for her twenty-fifth anniversary benefit at the Alexandrinsky. Apparently, she was familiar with Chekhov's one-act farces and with his best-selling humorous stories, so she chose *The Seagull* without reading it, assuming that it would be a comedy. Too late she realized that there was no appropriate role for herself, so she added a comic afterpiece in which to perform. After time lost to cast changes in the roles of Nina and Masha, *The Seagull* had only five rehearsal days. When it opened, the

It seems too good to be true that these three giants of Russian literature—Anton Pavlovich Chekhov (1860–1904), representing the upwardly mobile middle class at the turn of the century, Maxim Gorky (1868–1936), representing the twentieth-century proletariat, and Lev Tolstoy (1828–1910), representing the nineteenth-century aristocracy—should ever have come together in one photograph. Actually the photograph was taken of Chekhov and Tolstoy at Gaspara in the Crimea in 1901, and Gorky later had a photo-montage done to put himself in the picture. Roger-Viollet Documentation Générale Photographique, Paris.

house was packed with theatergoers who had come to see their favorite comedienne in a comedy; soon their displeasure was vocal. Chekhov wrote to his brother: "The play fell flat and flopped with a bang. In the theatre there was an atmosphere of painful tension and bewilderment, as if it were embarrassing to be there. The actors played abominably, stupidly. The moral: one should not write plays." And in another letter: "Never again will I write plays or try to get them produced, not if I live to be seven hundred years old."

Chekhov left St. Petersburg after *The Seagull*'s opening performance, but soon began receiving enthusiastic letters from people who had seen one of the four subsequent performances of the play. They, like Nemirovich-Danchenko, realized that they had heard a compelling new voice for the stage. Chekhov, however, was adamant in turning his back on the theater. He expressed little interest when his *Dyadya Vanya* (Uncle Vanya, 1895), his reworking of *The Wood-Demon,* began to be extensively produced by provincial theater companies. He refused Nemirovich-Danchenko's first request for permission to stage *The Seagull* in the Moscow Art Theatre's inaugural season. Eventually, Chekhov gave in; but Nemirovich-Danchenko had not entirely convinced Stanislavsky of the work's special qualities. The Moscow Art Theatre company spent the summer of 1898 rehearsing several plays in a barn about twenty-three miles from Moscow. Chekhov had a nervous first meeting with Stanislavsky in September before going to Yalta for his health; (the doctor suffered from a number of ailments: chronic coughing caused by his undiagnosed tuberculosis, heart palpitations, migraine, gastritis, hemorrhoids, and defective vision).

For its first four seasons, the Moscow Art Theatre company rented a former variety theater that had been used largely for trained animal acts. Stanislavsky noted that they had to "invent new methods of turning a stable into a temple." The first production, Aleksey Tolstoy's *Tsar Fyodor Ivanovich* opened on October 14, 1898; audiences marveled at the ensemble performances, the atmospheric lighting, and the archaeological detail in the sixteenth-century settings, props, and costumes. It was a success with the public and the press. However, the next two productions failed, putting the entire venture in dire straits. *The Merchant of Venice,* which opened a week after *Tsar Fyodor,* was also produced with naturalistic detail, contrasting the depressing Jewish ghetto with Portia's bright surroundings. The fatal mistake was an excess of zeal for realism: Stanislavsky had coached Shylock to use a Yiddish accent, and this struck theatergoers as inimical to Shakespeare's poetry. The third production was a double bill, Carlo Goldoni's *Mistress of the Inn* and a contemporary play, *Greta's Joy;* this too flopped. Hauptmann's *Hannele* was scheduled as the fourth production, but it was ordered removed from the repertoire on the eve of its final dress rehearsal. The Moscow Art Theatre's translation had passed the censors for both publication and for performance, but the church vetoed the production on the basis of a translation that had not been passed for performance; Stanislavsky and Nemirovich were unable to clear up the misunderstanding. Thus, *The Seagull* was moved up to open on December 17, 1898.

The theater was far from sold out for the premiere of *The Seagull*, and apparently some had come to scoff. According to Nemirovich-Danchenko, the audience was soon won over by the atmospheric beauty of the twilight scene, the simplicity and truthfulness of the acting, and the understated poignancy in the relationships Chekhov had developed by the end of the first act. There was a long silence after the act 1 curtain, "so long indeed that those on the stage decided that the first act had failed," and then came the thunderous storm of applause. The remaining three acts were received with mounting enthusiasm. In Yalta, Chekhov received numerous telegrams congratulating him on his brilliant success. Nemirovich-Danchenko wrote to him: "The actors are in love with the play. With every rehearsal they discovered in it more and more new pearls of art. At the same time they trembled because the public was so unliterary, so poorly developed, spoiled by cheap stage effects, and unready for a higher artistic simplicity, and would therefore be unable to appreciate the beauty of *The Seagull*." He went on to describe how the public not only responded to the mood of the play, but also understood and was possessed by "each separate thought, . . . every psychological movement." For the Moscow Art Theatre company, the theater was truly born at that performance. They had discovered the artistic style that was to remain most closely identified with their work, a style that might best be termed "impressionistic realism." A seagull design was adopted as the theater's logo, which yet today appears on the front curtain, the posters, and the programs.

The Moscow Art Theatre produced *Uncle Vanya* the following season, opening on October 26, 1899. Chekhov longed to go to Moscow, not only for the production, but also to see the company's leading actress, Olga Knipper, with whom he had begun to correspond. An actress of great vitality, strong stage presence, and excellent diction, Knipper in *The Seagull* had been, according to Nemirovich-Danchenko, "an astonishing, an ideal Arkadina. To such a degree has she merged with the role that you cannot tear away from her either her elegance as an actress or her bewitching triviality, *stinginess,* jealousy, etc." Her Elena in *Uncle Vanya* was less successful, but then Chekhov wrote for her the great role of her career, that of Masha in *Tri Sestri* (Three Sisters, 1901). After the close of the 1899–1900 season, the Moscow Art Theatre toured its productions of *The Seagull* and *Uncle Vanya* to Sevastopol in the Crimea, so that Chekhov could see them; it was joked that "the mountain went to Mahomet." Olga Knipper stayed at Chekhov's house; in subsequent

The Moscow Art Theatre opened auspiciously in October 1898 with its meticulously researched and thoroughly rehearsed production of Tsar Fyodor Ivanovich (1868) by Alexei Tolstoy (1817–1875). The production long remained in the repertoire and was toured to the United States in 1922. Shown here are Ivan Moskvin as Fyodor, Vishnievski as Boris, and Olga Knipper as Irina.

V. A. Simov's setting for act 1 of Chekhov's Uncle Vanya at the Moscow Art Theatre in 1899 combined flat painted canvas and three-dimensional elements. This was one of the most successful productions directed by Konstantin Stanislavsky (1863–1938) in the early years of the theater. Courtesy of the USSR Theatre Art Workers' Union.

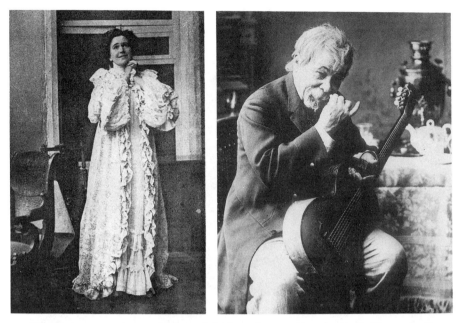

Olga Knipper (1868–1959), above, left, shown here as Elena in Uncle Vanya, *leading actress of the Moscow Art Theatre from its premiere season, married Chekhov in 1901. Courtesy of the USSR Theatre Art Workers' Union.*

Above, right, one of the original Moscow Art Theatre company members, Artiom played Firs in The Cherry Orchard *and, shown here, Telegin in* Uncle Vanya. *Courtesy of the USSR Theatre Art Workers' Union.*

Below, Anatoly Lunacharsky (1875–1933), the most cultivated and tolerant of the Bolsheviks who surrounded Lenin after the October Socialist Revolution, served as People's Commissar for Enlightenment from 1917 to 1929, and thus was in a position to protect and encourage a diversity of theatrical art. Konstantin Stanislavsky, at center, succeeded in keeping his company together throughout the chaotic post-revolutionary years, and he continued his research on a scientific approach to acting. The Irish-born George Bernard Shaw met Lunacharsky and Stanislavsky in 1931.

letters she began proposing marriage to him, and they were wed in a furtive ceremony in May 1901.

Three Sisters was another triumph for playwright and producers. Chekhov's last play, *Vishnevi Sad* (The Cherry Orchard, 1903), opened on January 17, 1904. Chekhov was well enough to attend rehearsals in Moscow, and this brought out the personality differences between the effusive, somewhat pompous Stanislavsky and the retiring, unpretentious Chekhov. Although there were inevitable artistic differences, the good-humored Chekhov was thrilled to work with the company and did not insist that his views be accepted. For example, he saw *The Cherry Orchard* as a comedy, but Stanislavsky imposed what Chekhov called a "cry-baby" interpretation. Chekhov also felt that "realism" could be pushed too far, and remarked: "Listen, I shall write a new play which will open like this: 'How wonderful, how quiet! Not a bird, a dog, a cuckoo, an owl, a nightingale, or clocks, or jingling bells, not even one cricket to be heard.'" On the other hand, Stanislavsky's casting was unerring. Chekhov had intended the role of Lopakhin for him, but Stanislavsky chose to play Gaev, whom he skillfully interpreted as a comic-pathetic overgrown child. Chekhov felt that the character of Carlotta was closest to Knipper's own personality, but she was cast as Ranevskaya, a role that capitalized on her ability to portray "smiling through tears." Opening night, January 17, 1904, coincided with Chekhov's name day; Chekhov was called on stage to hear speeches in his honor, a situation he found extremely discomfiting, and yet he was touched by the outpouring of affection. The play won increasingly enthusiastic notices as the run progressed, especially when it toured to St. Petersburg, but Chekhov persisted in believing that "Stanislavsky massacred my play. But God be with him! I won't hold it against him."

Chekhov died at a health spa in Badenweiler, Germany, in 1904. His writing included ten one-act plays, seven full-length plays, about six hundred short stories, one nonfiction work (*Sakhalin Island*, 1895, his firsthand documentation of conditions in the Russian penal colony), over four thousand surviving letters, several notebooks, and diaries. In addition, he had established four schools, a library, a forest, and two gardens. Not only could it be said that he saved the Moscow Art Theatre from financial ruin, but he gave it the plays that determined its characteristic style of artistry. Stanislavsky had long been experimenting with various techniques of acting; with the production of *The Seagull,* he began to understand that acting did not mean speaking dialogue, but revealing the meaning behind the dialogue. He wrote in 1926: "It was Chekhov who suggested to me the line of intuition and feeling. To reveal the inner contents of his plays it is necessary to delve into the depths of his soul. That, of course, applies to every play with a deep spiritual content, but most of all to Chekhov, for there are no other ways in his case." No theater, he continued, could successfully interpret Chekhov by the old methods of acting. "Chekhov's characters cannot be 'shown';" he noted in 1908, "they can only be *lived*." Chekhov's plays taught Stanislavsky to look for an undercurrent of psychological action beneath the physical action.

Stanislavsky devoted over forty years, until his death in 1938, to his search for scientific principles by which an actor could achieve emotional truth in performance; it was a quest for what he called "conscious means to the unconscious." After the Moscow Art Theatre opened an actor training school in 1901, Stanislavsky worked with the students to explore various approaches to acting. He began on the assumption that the actor was already trained in vocal projection, movement, and other "mechanics" of the craft. His concern was to find a coherent method by which an actor could discover and communicate the inner truth of a character. Stanislavsky's long search led him along several false paths, and he was not satisfied that he had discovered the right answers until shortly before his death, too late to publish his findings. Unfortunately, some of his earlier work had already been widely disseminated, especially in the United States, where the wrongheaded techniques Stanislavsky had been practicing in the 1920s—putting the emphasis on "inner justification"— became known as "method acting." Thanks to the tireless efforts of Sonia Moore, Stanislavsky's final deductions have become available to American actors, as they have long been universally employed in the Russian-language theater. The system that Stanislavsky called the end result of his whole life's work incorporated elements that he had previously discovered: the magic "if," given circumstances, imagination, concentration of attention, truth and belief, communion, adaption, tempo-rhythm, and emotional memory; but the emphasis switched from feelings to physical action as the basis for achieving a truthful performance. Stanislavsky called the system based upon his latest findings "The Method of Physical Action." In line with the Russian scientist Ivan Pavlov's experiments with dogs to study conditioned responses, Stanislavsky understood that a viable approach to acting must be based upon the intrinsic link between the psychological and the physical, that every inner experience has an external physical expression. An actor cannot simply go out on stage and call up an emotion; the only thing an actor can truthfully do on stage is a physical action. It is the physical action, conditioned by the given circumstances, that conjures the emotion.

Although Stanislavsky's importance as one of the most influential figures of the modern theater rests largely upon his development of a system of acting, Stanislavsky also directed and acted in many productions at the Moscow Art Theatre. For much of his career, administrative duties also took a toll on his energies. In 1902 the company moved into a

Vasily Kachalov (1875–1946) joined the Moscow Art Theatre in 1900 and played many major roles, including (shown here) the baron in The Lower Depths, *and the title roles in* Hamlet, *Andreyev's* Anathema, *and Ibsen's* Brand. *His grandson Alexei Bartoshevich is today one of the leading Soviet theater scholars and teachers.*

The Moscow Art Theatre ventured into extreme naturalism with its 1902 production of Gorky's The Lower Depths. *Stanislavsky, seated at the table, played Satan; Olga Knipper played Nastya; Kachalov played the Baron; and Vishnievsky played the Tatar.*

This photograph of Chekhov reading The Seagull *to the Moscow Art Theatre company was posed, but it provides a nonetheless valuable visual record of the illustrious group. Stanislavsky is seated to Chekhov's immediate right, and Olga Knipper is next to Stanislavsky. To Chekhov's left sits Stanislavsky's wife Lilina, and in front of the table on that side is Meyerhold. Nemirovich-Danchenko stands in the upper left corner of the picture.*

Gorky's Enemies *was produced at Moscow's Maly Theatre in 1933. This is the setting for act 2. Courtesy of Jacques Burdick.*

theater on Kamergersky Street, which remained the permanent home of the Moscow Art Theatre until 1974, when a new theater was built on Tverskoi Boulevard. The Kamergersky Street facility was later restored to its original decor and continues in use. The Moscow Art Theatre had opened it with Maksim Gorky's first play, *Meshchaniye* (Petty Bourgeois, 1902). Gorky's introduction to the Moscow Art Theatre had been engineered by Chekhov, who was one of the first to recognize and encourage the young proletarian writer's talent. Heavily cut by the censors, that play was not particularly successful, but the Moscow Art Theatre proceeded with plans to produce his *Na Dne* (Lower Depths, 1902). To prepare themselves for the extreme naturalism of Gorky's depiction of social outcasts occupying a communal basement lodging, the company toured the Khitrov Market area—a Moscow underworld ghetto of tramps and criminals—by night. For Stanislavsky, who played the cynical Satin, the outing enabled him to understand the inner meaning of the play; however, he had not yet learned how to go about translating that feeling into external action. He confesses in *My Life in Art* (1924) that he played not the character but the message, and he overacted badly. The production, however, was a tremendous success and remained in the repertoire indefinitely; by 1938 it had been performed 908 times. Gorky did not long remain associated with the Moscow Art Theatre, but he did write ten more plays before 1913 and a few others in the 1930s; some of his novels have also been dramatized.

After directing three naturalist plays in a row—the two by Gorky and Tolstoy's *The Power of Darkness*—Stanislavsky wanted to experiment with other theatrical styles. Over the next few years he staged some symbolist plays like Maurice Maeterlinck's *The Blind, Interior,* and *The Intruder* in 1904, Leonid Andreyev's *Zhizn cheloveka* (The Life of Man, 1906), and Knut Hamsun's *The Drama of Life* in 1907. Although these fared moderately well with the public, Stanislavsky conceded that "the symbol is a tough nut to crack." He was more successful with fantasy plays like Ostrovsky's *The Snowmaiden* in 1900 and Maeterlinck's *The Blue Bird* in 1908. He also tried his hand at Shakespeare, most notably with the well-documented 1911 production of *Hamlet*, which was designed by Edward Gordon Craig. The first few years after the 1917 revolution were difficult ones for the Moscow Art Theatre, because it was associated with the old prerevolutionary lifestyle. However, it successfully produced some of the requisite propaganda plays like Vsevolod Ivanov's *Armored Train 14-69*, which Stanislavsky directed in 1927. After 1932, when socialist realism began to be imposed as the only acceptable artistic approach, the Moscow Art Theatre was in the advantageous position of being able to show a long commitment to realism. The last years of Stanislavsky's career were primarily devoted to working with students in the Opera-Dramatic Studio he created in 1935. The application of his techniques to operatic performance demonstrated the system's validity not only for the realistic repertoire, but for all production styles.

Mention must be made of some of the outstanding artists associated with the Moscow Art Theatre in its early days. Stanislavsky's wife, Maria Petrovna Lilina, was often cast in ingenue roles. She was good at creating a different kind of movement for each character she played. Some considered her performance as Masha the outstanding one in *The Seagull;* she also played Sonia in *Uncle Vanya,* Natasha in *Three Sisters,* and Anya in *The Cherry Orchard.* Ivan Moskvin, the most gifted actor from Nemirovich-Danchenko's Philharmonic Drama School, played character roles like Epikhodov in *The Cherry Orchard* and Luka in *The Lower Depths.* Vasily Kachalov was a thoughtful, cultivated, attractive young actor, most memorably cast as Hamlet in the 1911 production. Vsevolod Meyerhold worked only a few years with the company—playing Treplev in *The Seagull,* among other roles—before artistic differences sent him off to find his own way and, eventually, to become one of the great twentieth-century directors. His work and that of Stanislavsky's greatest disciple, Evgeny Vakhtangov, will be discussed in chapter 5. One of the most interesting characters associated with the theater was Leopold Sulerzhitsky, a small, sunny-dispositioned jack of many trades; he had been a painter, a disciple of Tolstoy (who called him the three musketeers all rolled into one), an adventurer, and a political prisoner. He assisted Stanislavsky on several productions and was put in charge of the Moscow Art Theatre's First Studio, which Stanislavsky opened in 1912 at his own expense as a workshop for his experiments in techniques of acting. This studio staged a very popular dramatization of Charles Dickens's *Cricket on the Hearth* in 1914. "Suler," as Stanislavsky called him, seems to have been the catalyst who kept the theater going during periods of strained relations between Stanislavsky and Nemirovich-Danchenko. Actors tended to group around the more gregarious Nemirovich-Danchenko when they felt that Stanislavsky was pursuing some ill-defined and elusive goal; at such times, Sulerzhitsky's access to the man who tended to be isolated by his sensitive ego was crucial in preventing a breakup of the entire operation.

During 1923 and 1924, the Moscow Art Theatre toured several productions to New York. There the example of the company's realistic acting and ensemble playing made a lasting impact on American schools of acting and theater organizations. The first such offshoot was the American Laboratory Theatre, founded in 1923 as a theater school by former Moscow Art Theatre actors Richard Boleslavsky and Maria Ouspenskaya; in 1925 it became a producing company. In 1931, Harold Clurman, Cheryl Crawford, and Lee Strasberg founded The Group Theatre, which they modeled after the Moscow Art Theatre. Although it lasted only ten years, The Group Theatre generated a number of out-

The 1908 production by the Moscow Art Theatre of Maurice Maeterlinck's The Blue Bird *remains in the theater's repertoire even today, just as V. E. Egorov designed it. This is the setting for "the land of memory."*

Leonid Andreyev (1871–1919), the outstanding Russian symbolist playwright, wrote a number of plays staged by the Moscow Art Theatre, including The Life of Man *in 1907 and* Anathema *in 1909. Leopold Sulerzhitsky (1872–1916) worked closely with Stanislavsky, often bringing a useful proletarian perspective to the aristocratically inclined director. Maxim Gorky began writing for the theater under the encouragement of Anton Chekhov.*

Armored Train 14–69 (1927) by Vyacheslav Ivanov (1866–1949) typifies the socialist realist fare that was required of all theaters, including the venerable Moscow Art Theatre, from the 1930s. This production was directed by Stanislavsky and designed by Simov.

standing actors and an illustrious record of productions of new American plays. Lee Strasberg studied under Boleslavsky, who—having worked with Stanislavsky during the early years of experimentation with the system—emphasized emotional memory. It was this aspect of Stanislavsky's investigations that Strasberg was to perpetuate at the Actors Studio as "the method." A bitter division occurred within The Group Theatre and among subsequent American actor training methods after 1934, when Stella Adler studied under Stanislavsky in Paris and reported back to her colleagues on Stanislavsky's newer methods, which Strasberg—unfortunately for many of his students—refused to consider. Perhaps the most important Stanislavsky disciple whose subsequent career enriched the American theater was Michael Chekhov (a nephew of the playwright), who worked closely with Sulerzhitsky and Vakhtangov at the Moscow Art Theatre's First Studio. Because of the strong spiritual current in his approach to acting, he was labeled a "mystic" and a "reactionary," and he had to emigrate in 1928 to avoid arrest. Michael Chekhov became a renowned teacher of acting as well as a director and actor of the American stage and screen.

As more documentation on Stanislavsky becomes available in the USSR, his great legacy can be better analyzed and understood.

TURN-OF-THE-CENTURY FRIVOLITY

It was as if the century needed a dessert after its grim diet of urban problems, political instability, and bloodletting through such strife as the Franco-Prussian War and the Paris Commune. Despite continuing international tensions in a period of extreme nationalism, the traditionally conservative middle classes—which formed the bulwark of regimes like France's Third Republic (1871–1940) or the Bismarck government (1871–90) of the German Empire—discovered that upholding the virtues of hard work and education need not negate the right to pleasure. In many instances, the *bourgeoisie*, realizing that the working classes knew better than they how to use their limited leisure time for fun, invaded the proletarian places of entertainment. The British music halls, for example, which had originated as all-male bastions of bawdy song and strong drink, were gradually transformed into luxurious palaces of musical variety entertainment to which ladies were admitted. In Vienna, the intoxicating waltz permeated all levels of society from cheap dance halls to public balls and gardens to select ballrooms like the Sophienbad. A mingling of social classes occurred at public festivals like France's first official celebration of Bastille Day in 1880, and at the great world's fairs of the period: Vienna (1873), Paris (1878, 1889, 1900), Chicago (1893), and St. Louis (1904). Nowhere did the bourgeoisie better assimilate the pleasure-loving spirit of the 1880s, the Gay Nineties, and the Belle Epoque (1900–14) than in Paris. Certainly, much of the French public deplored the rampant anticlericalism, the legalization of divorce in 1884, the increased visibility of the shameless *grandes cocottes*, the greater consumption of alcohol than ever before in French history, and other signs of decadence that accompanied expanding political liberties. But that very unease seemed to serve as an impetus for the middle class to let off steam by joining the throngs in their popular amusements. Such developments led to what Jerrold Seigel calls "a new symbiosis between *la Bohème* and the bourgeoisie."

The publication of Henry Murger's *Scenes from Bohemian Life* in book form in 1851 had given the public an idealized image of the starving artist to counter their impression of the Bohemian milieu as one of depraved criminality. This was an important step in bringing together the raffish art world and the respectable *bourgeoisie* that was to become its main source of support. No longer able to depend upon the patronage of an élite, artists were forced to seek direct access to the public. An example was set by the impressionist painters who, when refused by the official salon, mounted their first independent exhibition in 1874. Since the center of Parisian artistic and intellectual ferment had moved from the private *salons* to the public cafés, it was natural that the café began to serve as a venue for showing off the talents of poets, singers, comedians, and painters. Paris boasted twenty-seven thousand cafés by the turn of the century, but the ones that truly fostered democratic culture and the era's irreverent spirit of gaiety were in Montmartre.

La Butte Montmartre, a hill overlooking Paris, had been a lowlife suburb until it was incorporated into the city in 1860. Untouched by Haussmann's urban renewals, Montmartre retained an appealing rural quaintness, including its windmills, which were to inspire the name of the famous dance hall that opened there in 1889: the Moulin Rouge. It was in Montmartre that the cabaret movement was born. The predecessor of cabaret was the *café-concert,* familiarly known as the *caf'conc'*, where a singer would entertain a large crowd of drinkers. The cabaret— also known as the *cabaret artistique*—geared its more intellectual, satirical, or avant-garde farrago of songs, monologues, poems, and dances to intimate audiences.

The first and best known of the Montmartre cabarets was the Chat Noir (Black Cat), opened in 1881 by Rodolphe Salis and Emile Goudeau. Goudeau had already had three years' experience in running a literary café called the Hydropathes (perhaps a whimsical allusion to the sound of Goudeau's name, *goût d'eau*), and he had published a newspaper under the same name to show off the writing and artwork of his circle of artists. Most of the Hydropathes followed Goudeau to the Chat Noir, which also launched a self-publicizing newspaper, *Le Chat Noir*. Salis's lively sense of fun attracted an ever-growing clientele, so that by 1885 he was able to move to a much larger, three-story facility whose various rooms were given ironically pretentious names. Indeed, the waiters wore green robes like those of the French Academy, and Salis greeted his customers deferentially, addressing them with mock-aristocratic titles. Thus there was a sense of participatory theater about an evening at the Chat Noir. A highlight of the new Chat Noir was the second-floor *Théâtre des ombres* (Shadow Theater) created by Henri Rivière. There, using cutout shadow puppets, a translucent screen, music, sound effects, colored lighting effects, and even different kinds of tobacco smoke for battle scenes, forty-three plays by nineteen different authors were performed between 1887 and 1896. These ranged from biblical stories to parodies and satirical montages of current events. At the Chat Noir one might glimpse the poet Mallarmé or Louis Pasteur or the Prince of Wales. Claude Debussy might appear at the piano. The early years of the Chat Noir also launched the career of the raucous-voiced Aristide Bruant, who flaunted a working-class ethos and composed or improvised his songs in the vulgar language of the streets.

Bruant opened his own cabaret, Le Mirliton, in the premises vacated by Salis in 1885. In contrast to the extreme politeness affected by Salis, Bruant growled insults at his customers. Nor did the populist political stance he vaunted in his songs deter a fashionable clientele, and Le Mirliton soon rivaled Le Chat Noir. Among numerous other Montmartre cabarets, L'Abbaye de Thélème was noteworthy for its Rabelaisian theme, which capitalized on the French public's rediscovery of its Gallic roots, as exemplified in the earthy humor of François Rabelais's novels *Pantagruel* (1532) and *Gargantua* (1534). The *esprit gaulois* projected by that cabaret's Gothic décor with ribald elements was underscored by the costuming of the waiters as monks and nuns. On the Boulevard du Clichy, the Cabaret du Ciel (Heaven) and the Cabaret de l'Enfer (Hell) stood side by side, the one serviced by angels, the other by devils. The entrance to the latter was an *art nouveau* version of a medieval Hell Mouth. Many such "theme cabarets" catered to the *bourgeoisie's* desire for fantasy.

Two outstanding entertainers of the period performed cabaret-type material, but needed much larger premises to accommodate the crowds they drew. One was the red-headed *diseuse* Yvette Guilbert, who half-talked, half-sang Bruant's songs in a manner combining brassiness and sentimentality. The other was Joseph Pujol, whose stage name—Le Pétomane—hinted at his specialty, which might best be described as a "musical *derrière*." According to a medical report cited by Jean Nohain and F. Caradec, Le Pétomane possessed the unique physiological capability of "the absorption and expulsion at will of air and liquid by the rectum." By this means he could produce tunes or sounds like sharp bursts of machine-gun fire or various animal noises, and he could blow out a candle from a distance of one foot. A headliner at the Moulin Rouge from 1892 to 1894 and subsequently at his own Théâtre Pompadour, Le Pétomane elicited unprecedented gales of hysterical laughter among audiences ranging from ordinary people to King Leopold II of Belgium.

The cabaret movement reached Germany around 1900, but faced a less receptive environment due to strict censorship and the moribund state of the arts in general. Otto Julius Bierbaum gave cabaret a strong impetus when, inspired by a visit to Montmartre, he published a best-selling collection of singable German poems. His preface called for a new art built upon the crude variety entertainments pejoratively known as *Tingeltangel*. The following year, 1901, Germany's most famous cabaret, Die Elf Scharfrichter, was founded in Munich. The name, The Eleven Executioners, derived from the group's pronouncement of sentence against reactionary and obscurantist art. Each evening's program opened with the March of the Executioners and proceeded to satirize local politics and official culture. Playwright Frank Wedekind, whose *Frühlings Erwachen* (Spring's Awakening, 1891)—a play about teenage sexuality—had been suppressed, performed the satirical songs he wrote, and part of his play *Der Erdgeist* (Earth Spirit, 1895) premiered there. Despite its claim to be a private club, the Scharfrichter ran afoul of censorship and closed in 1903.

Some artists from the Scharfrichter went to Vienna and opened the Nachtlicht (1906, Night Light), which soon changed its name to the Fledermaus (Bat). This in turn inspired the name of the first Russian cabaret, Letuchaya Mysh (The Bat), founded by Nikita Baliev in 1908. The ebullient Baliev had served as master of ceremonies for the Moscow Art Theatre's in-house variety entertainments when the theaters were closed for Lent, and gradually made an independent enterprise of it. Beginning with evenings of largely improvised comic turns and musical numbers, The Bat eventually produced elaborately staged and costumed parodies of classic Russian plays as well as comic operas and even ballets. In 1920 the company emigrated to Paris, where it became world-famous as Le Chauve-Souris (The Bat). Poland's outstanding cabaret, Zielony Balonik (Green Balloon) was a fount of creativity in Krakow from 1905 to 1912. Its leading light was the talented satirical poet, drama critic, and translator Tadeusz Zeleński.

Another entertainment form much associated with the frivolous decades, the operetta, had actually peaked somewhat earlier. Composer Jacques Offenbach had initiated a remarkable string of operettas in 1855 when he opened his own theater, the Bouffes-Parisiens, with *Ba-ta-clan*, his musical burlesque of the fad for *chinoiserie*. His *Orphée aux enfers* (Orpheus in the Underworld, 1858) became the prototype for the genre: fantastical, funny, innocuous in content, but scintillatingly melodic. Offenbach worked most successfully with the librettist team of Henri Meilhac and Ludovic Halévy; among their hits were *Le Brésilien* (The Brazilian, 1863), *La Belle Hélène* (1864), *Barbe-Bleue* (Blue Beard, 1866), *La Vie parisienne* (1866), *La Grande Duchesse de Gérolstein* (1867), and *La Périchole* (1868). Their leading lady, the magnetic Hortense Schneider, reigned as "Empress of Operetta" in Paris, and won followings in London when the productions toured there. Shortly before his death, Offenbach completed the piano score for an opera, the genre he had so often burlesqued; *Les Contes d'Hoffmann* (Tales of Hoffmann, 1880) had its posthumous premiere in 1881.

The golden ages of operetta in Vienna and London can be credited to the influence of Offenbach. In fact, the greatest of all Viennese waltz-operettas, Johann Strauss II's *Die Fledermaus* (The Bat, 1874), was based upon a three-act comedy by Meilhac and Halévy. *Die Fledermaus* was unusual in its modern dress, although the masquerade scene allowed a fanciful note in the costuming. Its wonderfully tuneful music and champagne spirit spawned a host of other waltz-operettas by various composers, culminating in Franz Léhar's *Die lustige Witwe* (The Merry Widow, 1905).

Londoners came under the spell of Offenbach through both the original productions on tour and English-language adaptations. Those offerings, plus the musical travesties of familiar works presented at John Hollingshead's Gaiety Theatre (better known in the 1890s for its Gaiety Girls), prepared the way for Gilbert and Sullivan. It was Offenbach's *La Périchole* that brought together playwright William S. Gilbert and composer Arthur Sullivan when producer Richard D'Oyly Carte needed a one-act operetta to accompany it on the bill. The result was *Trial by Jury* (1875) and one of the most felicitous combinations of talent in English musical history. Sullivan was clearly influenced by Offenbach's melodic style and orchestration, while Gilbert owed much to Meilhac and Halévy's way with clever lyrics in fanciful plots. Nevertheless, Gilbert later voiced objections to several aspects of French operetta: "We resolved that our plots, however ridiculous, should be coherent, that our dialogue should be void of offence. . . . Finally, we agreed that no lady of the company should be required to wear a dress that she could not wear with absolute propriety at a private fancy ball; and I believe I may say that we proved our case." They proved it with such immortal confections as *H. M. S. Pinafore* (1878), *The Pirates of Penzance* (1879), *The Mikado* (1885), and others, a total of fourteen operettas. The Savoy Theatre—built especially for Gilbert and Sullivan operettas and inaugurated in 1881 with *Patience*—was the first London theater illuminated by electricity. The D'Oyly Carte Company continued to present the Gilbert and Sullivan repertoire until it finally closed down in 1982. Without Gilbert and Sullivan, declares Richard Traubner, American musical comedy would have been impossible.

The spoof of the aesthetic movement in Gilbert and Sullivan's *Patience* (1881) helped to launch the career of England's great apostle of frivolity, playwright Oscar Wilde. The Dublin-born dandy was hired to accompany the production on its American tour as a lecturer and as a living illustration of "the aesthete." Long before his plays were staged, Wilde had won renown for his witty conversation and refined sensibilities. Both are evident in his reply to a wire from the Mayor of Griggsville about whether Wilde would lecture there. Wilde wired back: "Yes, if you'll first change the name of your town." In 1892 Sarah Bernhardt came to London to play the title role in Wilde's decadent poetic drama *Salomé*, which he had written for her in French; but it was banned because of a law against representing biblical characters on the stage. The play was, however, published in English in 1894, with risqué illustrations by Aubrey Beardsley. Although Wilde was not pleased with the drawings, they later contributed toward tainting his public image with an aura of unwholesomeness.

Wilde won his first stage success with *Lady Windermere's Fan* (1892). This and his equally popular *A Woman of No Importance* (1893) and *An Ideal Husband* (1895) were conventionally plotted society melodramas enlivened by the hilariously clever and polished artifice of the dialogue. It is a mark of his rapid rise to celebrity that such leading producers as George Alexander and Beerbohm Tree presented his work. *An Ideal Husband* was still running when Wilde topped it with the brilliant farce *The Importance of Being Earnest* (1895). This play most fully expresses Wilde's philosophy that "we should treat all the trivial things of life very seriously, and all the serious things of life with sincere and studied triviality." As if to mock his words, Wilde's greatest triumph coincided with the beginning of his downfall.

While the public and critics alike (except Bernard Shaw) were acclaiming the English stage's greatest comedy since Sheridan, Wilde received a written insult from the Marquess of Queensberry, father of the young man with whom Wilde had developed an intimate friendship. Urged on by young "Bosie" (Lord Alfred Douglas), who hated his father, Wilde brought a libel suit against Queensberry. The trial was highly publicized, and on the first day the flamboyant Wilde enjoyed making

La Vie parisienne *(Parisian Life)* by Meilhac and Halévy, with music by Jacques Offenbach, was produced at the Théâtre du Palais Royal in 1959. Jean-Louis Barrault directed, and J. D. Maclès designed sets and costumes. This scene features three stars of the Paris stage, Pierre Bertin, Madeleine Renaud, and Jean Desailly. Courtesy of French Cultural Services.

Occupe-toi d'Amélie *(Keep an Eye on Amelia, 1908)* by Georges Feydeau (1862–1921) was produced at the Théâtre Marigny in Paris in 1946, under the direction of Jean-Louis Barrault. Shown here are Madeleine Renaud and Jacques Dacqmine. Courtesy of French Cultural Services.

Some of Feydeau's late plays, like the one-act On purge bébé *(1910), offered darkly comic views of marriage. This modern production, directed by Raymond Gérome and designed by André Levasseur, featured Bernard Blier and Danielle Darrieux in the leading roles. Courtesy of French Cultural Services.*

The situation is typical of Georges Feydeau's Gay 90s bedroom farce: a gentleman stranded in his underwear outside his locked apartment convinces a hapless passerby to surrender his clothes. Un Fil à la patte *has been variously translated as* Strings Attached, Cat Among the Pigeons, Get Out of My Hair! *and* Not by Bed Alone. *This production at the University of Wisconsin–Rock County was directed by Felicia Londré and designed by Gary J. Lenox. John Leon Miller played Bouzin and Tom Warren played Bois d'Enghien.*

amusing quips from the witness stand. But the tide turned, and after his acquittal, Queensberry filed a suit against Wilde, charging him with conspiracy to corrupt the young. Wilde was found guilty and sentenced to two years of hard labor. *The Importance of Being Earnest* continued its run, but Wilde's name was removed from the playbills. Upon his release in 1897, a broken man, he sailed for France and never returned to England. The harsh prison conditions he had experienced gave rise to his best poem, "The Ballad of Reading Gaol."

While events in Oscar Wilde's life served to expose Victorian hypocrisy, certain continental playwrights achieved the same ends with the lightest of touches in their *fin de siècle* comedies and farces. There is no better distillation of the spirit of Gay Nineties and Belle Epoque frivolity than in the French "bedroom farces" that filled Parisian boulevard theaters. Victorien Sardou and Emile de Najac established a model for middle-class farce based upon sexual innuendo with *Divorçons!* (Let's Get a Divorce!, 1880), which was inspired by France's impending legalization of divorce. But it was Georges Feydeau who perfected the genre. Playwright Marcel Achard called him "the greatest French comic dramatist after Molière" and cited the basic premise of all of Feydeau's plays: "When two of my characters should under no circumstances encounter one another, I throw them together as quickly as possible." The preferred milieux for Feydeau's madcap sexual intrigues are those of the upper bourgeoisie: the well-appointed households of professional men—doctors, lawyers, businessmen—whose abundance of money and leisure frees them for the pursuit of pleasure. That weakness sets them off on a frenetic course that may take them to a cabaret singer's apartment or to a hotel room with a revolving bed. Between 1881 and 1908, Feydeau wrote twenty such full-length farces and eleven one-acts in which complex misunderstandings between married couples are somehow resolved to the satisfaction of all. Among the best of these extravagant escapades that unfold with inexorable logic are *Un fil à la patte* (Strings Attached, 1894), *L'Hôtel du Libre-Echange* (Hotel Free-Exchange, 1894), *La Dame de chez Maxim* (The Girl From Maxim's, 1899), and *Une puce à l'oreille* (A Flea in Her Ear, 1907). From a middle-class background himself, Feydeau had married for money, and eventually the marriage turned sour. After 1908, around the time he moved into a hotel and lived alone, his comedy took a darker turn, and many of his later plays— mostly one-acts—featured a shrewish wife who makes life miserable for her ineffectual husband.

The immensely popular Feydeau had many rivals and imitators. One of the bawdiest farcical treatments of suggestive-but-innocent sexual adventurism among the well-to-do, Hennequin and Véber's *Vous n'avez rien à déclarer? (Anything to Declare?)* turns upon a young bridegroom's desperate ploys to overcome his impotence in order not to disgrace his bride's family honor. Flers and Caillavet were another successful team of sophisticated boulevard farce writers. Georges Courteline was less concerned with the battle of the sexes than with the complications of bureaucratic institutions: the law courts, the military, government offices. Among the best of his short comic sketches are *Boubouroche* (1893) and *L'Article 330* (1900).

Arthur Schnitzler's cynical comedies of sexual hypocrisy project a spirit of frivolity because they reflect *fin de siècle* Vienna's image as a place of prosperity, overdecoration, and self-indulgence. That era in the city of pseudobaroque architecture and painting, music everywhere from middle-class drawing rooms to public gardens and stadiums, intellectual ferment and luscious pastries in the famous cafés, and fashionable strollers on the Prater has been called "The Gay Apocalypse," because it all came to an end in 1914. Schnitzler, a doctor whose early interest in psychology anticipated Freud's research, observed the swirling life around him and recaptured it in his plays. Many of them feature a character type known as the *süßes Mädel* or "sweet young thing," an unmarried girl from the suburbs who is easy prey for the heartless playboy of a better social class. The charm and poignance with which Schnitzler depicted the type in *Liebelei* (*Light o' Love,* 1895; adapted by Tom Stoppard as *Dalliance,* 1986) made this one of his most frequently revived plays. Schnitzler's difficulties with censorship of plays like *Anatol* (1891) and *Riegen* (*La Ronde,* 1898) stemmed from the very hypocrisy he intended to expose, as moralists assumed that he was winking at the licentiousness he portrayed. Less provocative in their titillation were the sophisticated light comedies of Budapest's leading dramatist Ferenc Molnár, who won international renown for *Liliom* (1909), *The Guardsman* (1910), *The Swan* (1914), *The Play's the Thing* (1924), and others.

The frothy high spirits of Belle Epoque comedy could not be sustained indefinitely. Even before World War I left its indelible mark upon civilization, an element of decadence had crept into the frivolity. In this respect, it is sometimes difficult to make a clear distinction between the theater that served as an extension of a pleasure-seeking society and the subjective, mystically inclined drama of the symbolists.

Pluralism
and Experimentation

A CHANGING AUDIENCE

Perhaps the most compelling factor in the development of twentieth-century theater was the loss of the mass audience. The motion picture, invented and first commercially exhibited in 1895 by Louis and Auguste Lumière, siphoned off customers, especially when story-telling films like Georges Méliès's *A Trip to the Moon* (1902) or Edwin S. Porter's *The Great Train Robbery* (1903) began to be marketed. The introduction of the "talkies" in 1929 is often blamed for the demise of vaudeville. The widespread availability of radios, phonograph records, cars, and, eventually, television took a further toll on the potential audience pool. As previously indicated, the Theatrical Syndicate and Shubert monopolies in the United States may also have contributed to weakening the general public's loyalty to live theater.

In broadest terms, the result was the hardening into standard practice of a trend that had begun with Antoine's Théâtre Libre. Two kinds of theater coexisted side by side. On one hand, the "boulevard" theater emphasized tried-and-true entertainment values in its constantly embattled efforts to attract and hold the mainstream public on which it depends economically. This kind of theater includes productions on Broadway and in London's West End as well as on the Parisian boulevards: plays that eventually find their way into regional theaters, dinner theaters, and community theater. On the other hand, the "art" theater focused its efforts on small constituencies of adherents, those who cared more for exploring new forms of expression than for mere escapist entertainment. Often allied with the "avant-garde," this kind of inexpensively produced theater has historically been fragmented into numerous short-lived, but often influential, artistic movements. This fragmentation of the serious theatergoing public began to be evident in the last decades of the nineteenth century, when naturalism, symbolism, decadence, and such antiestablishment phenomena as Alfred Jarry's *Ubu roi* (King Ubu, 1896) all found their distinct publics.

The production of *Ubu roi* for two performances at the Théâtre de l'Oeuvre under the direction of Aurélien Lugné-Poe may be seen as a watershed in the development of modern theater art. Although it could be tied to no particular artistic movement, it distilled the "new spirit" of modernism that was in the air, and it has been signaled as the progenitor of many subsequent avant-garde ventures from surrealism to theater of the absurd. The script originated as a schoolboys' satire on a hated physics teacher, the corpulent, incompetent M. Hébert. Fifteen-year-old Jarry and his friend Henri Morin performed the saga of "Père Héb," then entitled *Les Polonais* (The Poles, 1888), in the Morins' attic, and Jarry restaged it as a marionette play. When he moved to Paris in 1891, Jarry quickly found his way into literary circles, forming a close friendship with Alfred Vallette, founder-director of the *Mercure de France,* and his wife, a prolific author of fashionably risqué novels published under the pen name Rachilde. Their regular Tuesday evening receptions brought together the leading symbolist artists, among whom the iconoclastic Jarry made an unsettling impression. The assorted works he published during those years included some dramatic texts based upon the Hébert character, whom he now called Ubu. When Lugné-Poe hired Jarry as administrative assistant at the Théâtre de l'Oeuvre, Jarry seized the opportunity to get his play produced.

The performance on December 10, 1896, provoked the most notorious riot in the French theater since the "battle of *Hernani.*" After Jarry gave a rambling speech, the curtain opened to reveal a composite setting: childlike painting on the walls depicted a sky with a window in it, a fireplace, a bed, palm trees, falling snow, a skeleton on a gallows. To establish the locale for each scene, a gentleman in evening dress tiptoed across the stage and posted a placard. Firmin Gémier played the title role, costumed in a pear-shaped cardboard mask and voluminous padding with a spiral on the belly. His opening line—the single word *"Merdre!,"* shocking in its obscenity, especially within a theatrical tradition that only sixty-seven years earlier had considered the utterance of the word *mouchoir* (handkerchief) inappropriate on the tragic stage—set off fifteen minutes of noisy demonstrations in the audience: shouts, catcalls, whistles, applause. The loosely constructed plot based upon Shakespeare's *Macbeth* centers on the rise to power and despotic rule of Père and Mère Ubu. As King of Poland, Père Ubu wields a toilet brush for a scepter. The dialogue is replete with Jarry's imaginative, quasi-nonsensical scatology.

The battle continued in the press over the next few weeks. Keith Beaumont discerns three main objections to the play: its vulgarity, its

Jarry's own woodcut portrait of Ubu, left, was published in the Livre d'art *(25 April 1896).*

Right, twelve years after its tumultuous premiere, Alfred Jarry's Ubu roi *was revived at the Théâtre Antoine. Firmin Gémier recreated his original role, but the fairy-tale style he imposed upon the scabrous play was not successful. This caricature of Père and Mère Ubu in that production is by de Losques for* Le Figaro *(16 February 1908).*

connotative associations with the threat of political anarchy, and the probability that the author intended it as an elaborate hoax, a mockery of its audience's artistic tastes. Certainly, Jarry succeeded in his desire to *épater le bourgeois,* a class he despised. The Irish poet William Butler Yeats, who happened to be in Paris and was taken to see *Ubu roi,* noted that he and his companion "shouted for the play," but that afterward he became depressed as he realized what this breakdown of conventions and discipline might herald for the future of art: "After us the Savage God."

SYMBOLISM AND DECADENCE

The symbolist movement in the arts can be traced back to midcentury in the poems of Charles Baudelaire. His poem "Correspondences" in the collection *Les Fleurs du mal* (Flowers of Evil, 1857) contains a line that was to become a major tenet of symbolism: *"Les parfums, les couleurs et les sons se répondent"* (Perfumes, colors, and sounds interrelate). The idea was to create a harmony of abstract elements that would evoke an atmosphere, an emotion, an *état d'âme* (soul state), or any such fleeting, indefinable condition that could not be physically represented. Symbolism, like romanticism, is a subjective form of expression. The symbolist poet or painter aimed not to describe objective reality, but to suggest unique, personal impressions of reality, and this could best be accomplished by a complex association of images and other stimuli. Arthur Rimbaud and Paul Verlaine furthered the symbolist movement with their poetry, but it was the poet Stéphane Mallarmé who, inspired by Richard Wagner's writing on the synthesis of the arts, first envisioned the application of that aesthetic to the theater. Mallarmé's theater criticism—beginning with his influential *Notes sur le théâtre*, a series of essays published in the *Revue indépendente* during the 1886–87 theater season—argued against representational theater; he called for an "idealist theater" based upon a fusion of poetic language, gesture, setting, ballet, and musical expression that would celebrate the eternal mysteries of the universe while uniting actors and audience in a kind of spiritual communion. Just as poetry achieves its evocative effect through highly selective use of language, so should the visual elements of theatrical production be reduced to the barest essentials that are thus invested with enhanced evocative power.

The theories were tested in practice when eighteen-year-old Paul Fort founded his Théâtre d'Art in 1890 and committed it to a symbolist production style, largely in reaction against the sordid naturalism that constituted the bulk of the work at Antoine's Théâtre Libre (founded in 1887). Thus, the two opposing aesthetics existed concurrently in Paris, each attracting its own adherents. If the symbolist venture did not last as long or exert as great a long-term influence as the naturalist one did, this may be due not only to the rarified nature of the movement itself, but also to Fort's inexperience in running a theater. Proceeding from the premise that "the text creates the setting as well as all else," Fort's basic agenda was to bring the poet back to playwriting and to restore visual beauty to the stage. He filled out his bills of short plays with recitations of poems accompanied by appropriate lighting and music and sometimes even the display of a painting. In surveying the accomplishments of the symbolists, Edmund Wilson later claimed that their "only originality . . . consisted in reminding people of the true nature and function of words," which are themselves symbols.

The Théâtre d'Art lasted only two seasons. Its major contributions were the first staging of two short plays by Maurice Maeterlinck (*The Intruder* and *The Blind*) and the launching of Aurélien Lugné-Poe's distinguished career. Lugné-Poe had acted at Antoine's Théâtre Libre before joining the Théâtre d'Art. When Fort had to close the Théâtre d'Art in 1892, Lugné-Poe took over the company, renamed it the Théâtre de l'Oeuvre, and presented an acclaimed, if not always financially successful, series of productions until 1929. In its first phase, the Thé-âtre de l'Oeuvre adopted a predominantly symbolist approach to pro-duction: simplified and stylized scenic elements, a dreamlike at-mosphere, and a measured, sonorous intonation of dialogue. However, its offerings were eclectic enough to include Jarry's *Ubu roi* and several productions of Ibsen plays. After 1897, Lugné-Poe gave up on sym-bolism, despairing of its ever generating works whose theatricality matched their poetry. The theater then became known for its produc-tions of foreign authors like Hauptmann, Shaw, Shakespeare, Tolstoy, and Strindberg. Lugné-Poe's 1905 production of Ibsen's *Enemy of the People* caused the police to put him and the theater under surveillance, as fear of anarchist terror lurked just beneath the surface of Belle Epoque gaiety. In that same season, when the theater's finances reached a low point, Eleonora Duse joined the company for a benefit performance of Gorky's *The Lower Depths*. A journal entitled *L'Oeuvre* began publication in 1909, often featuring the work of the Nabis. Two of the Nabi painters, Vuillard and Camille Mauclair, had been Lugné-Poe's cofounders of the theater, a venture undertaken after Lugné-Poe's 1893 success with Maurice Maeterlinck's *Pelléas et Mélisande*.

Before his work had even reached the stage, Belgian playwright Maurice Maeterlinck was hailed by one overenthusiastic critic (Octave Mirbeau) as having written "the greatest work of genius of our time, . . . superior in beauty to what is most beautiful in Shakespeare." This as-tounding remark was occasioned by the 1890 publication of Maeter-linck's play *La Princesse Maleine* (Princess Maleine). Paul Fort's productions of *L'Intruse* (The Intruder, 1890) and *Les Aveugles* (The Blind, 1890; produced 1891) also won critical acclaim for the author. Lugné-Poe produced Maeterlinck's *Pelléas et Mélisande* (1892) in 1893, and played the role of the hunter Golaud who marries the child-woman Mélisande. Although critics complained about the play's episodic con-struction, they acknowledged the effective aura of mystery created by the atmospheric Gothic setting. The play illustrates Maeterlinck's charac-teristic use of understatement, repetition, silences, and simple actions that convey strong dramatic resonances, i.e., maids scrubbing the castle steps, a mysterious lost princess weeping beside a forest pool, a flight of doves just at the moment when Pelléas entangles himself in Mélisande's long hair, a wedding ring lost in a well, and so on. Claude Debussy based his 1902 "impressionistic" opera upon this play.

In addition to plays exhibiting a strong streak of mysticism, such as *La Mort de Tintagiles* (Death of Tintagiles, 1894), *Ariane et Barbe Bleu* (Ariane and Blue Beard, 1901), *L'Oiseau bleu* (The Blue Bird of Hap-piness, 1909), Maeterlinck wrote a number of influential essays. In *"Le Tragique quotidien"* (The Tragical in Daily Life, 1896), he developed the idea of a "static theater." To him, the fullness of life experience that resides invisibly in an old man seated beside his lamp would evoke more powerfully the mysterious forces of the universe than any action-drama hero. Such writing made Maeterlinck enormously influential all over the Continent, with special impact on playwrights like Ramón del Valle-Inclán and Azorín in Spain, Gabriele D'Annunzio in Italy, and Anton Chekhov, Fyodor Sologub, and Alexsandr Blok in Russia. In 1911 Maeterlinck was awarded the Nobel Prize for Literature.

The symbolist movement also brought belated recognition to Philippe Auguste Villiers de l'Isle Adam, a mystical idealist whose posthumous play *Axël* (1890; produced 1894) won the admiration of William Butler Yeats, Paul Claudel, and other important writers of the subsequent generation. Yeats's early Irish folk plays are written in a symbolist vein, as are Claudel's poetic dramas. Other important dramatists who adhered at least briefly around the turn of the century to the symbolist aesthetic included Hugo von Hofmannsthal with plays like *Der Tor und der Tod* (Death and the Fool, 1893; produced 1898), and August Strindberg with *Svanehvit* (Swanwhite, 1901).

After France, the finest flowering of symbolist poetry and drama occurred in Russia, to the extent that the period came to be called the "silver age of Russian literature." The movement was heavily promoted by Zinaida Gippius, a woman poet and social leader, who also published critical essays under male pseudonyms. Her own plays—*Sacred Blood* (1901), *The Red Poppy* (1912), and *The Green Ring* (1914)—reflected her mystical religious inclinations. In general, however, Russian symbolism tended toward deeper gloom and morbidity, as in Andrei Bely's *Past' Nochi* (The Jaws of Night, 1898); Valeri Bryusov's *The Wayfarer* (1910); and Leonid Andreyev's *Zhizn cheloveka* (The Life of Man, 1906), *Anathema* (1909), and *Tot, kto poluchaet poshchechiny* (He Who Gets Slapped, 1915). Playwright-director Nikolai Evreinov worked to develop the affinities between symbolist plays and what he called "monodramas": productions that induce the spectator in the theater to experience the play as if he or she were the chief character in it. Among his own plays, his most original experiment in monodrama was *B kulissakh dushi* (The Theater of the Soul, 1911), which is set inside a human body. Thus, the stage setting represented a gigantic spinal cord along with a pulsating heart and lungs. The man's rational, emotional, and spiritual selves appear as three different characters in the play. Evreinov staged it at St. Petersburg's Crooked Mirror Theatre, a 700-seat cabaret for experimental works, where he served as artistic director from 1910 to 1917.

The greatest of the Russian symbolists was Aleksandr Blok, a poet whose thematic obsession with Russia utilizes the symbol of "the beautiful lady." His short symbolist play *Balaganchik* (Little Fairground Booth,

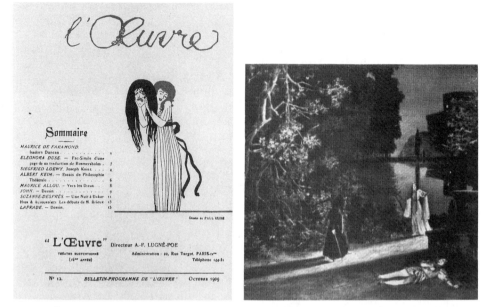

Above, left, ninety issues of the Théâtre de l'Oeuvre's house journal were published between 1909 and 1930, fourteen of them in 1909. This is the cover of one of them, which included a facsimile of a page of Eleonora Duse's translation of Ibsen's Rosmersholm.

Above, right, two designers contributed to the 1902 Opéra-Comique production of Pelléas et Mélisande. *Lucien Jusseaume settings, like this one for the death of Pelléas (act 4, scene 4), tended to be more realistic than those of Eugène Ronsin.* Le Théâtre *(June 1902).*

Below, Debussy's operatic version of Maeterlinck's Pelléas et Mélisande *premiered in Paris in 1902. The opera's demand for sumptuous scenery resulted in settings more realistic than the 1893 production of the play had been, but Eugène Ronsin's design for the grotto (act 2, scene 3) is one of the more evocative scenes.* Le Théâtre *(June 1902).*

The title character in Andreyev's Anathema *represents forces of evil. The premiere of the play at the Moscow Art Theater in 1909 owed much of its success to Vasily Kachalov's performance for which his face and skull were remodeled, changing his appearance beyond recognition.*

Symbolist painter–designer Nikolai Sapunov designed Meyerhold's first production of Balaganchik (Little Fairground Booth) *in 1906. Sapunov's rendering shows the artifice of the stage within the stage. The Mystics seated behind the table used whiteface makeup to suggest the bloodlessness of symbolist art. In the foreground, Pierrot represents the more robust* commedia dell'arte *tradition.*

a.k.a. The Puppet Show, 1906) parodies itself and the symbolist movement alongside its political and autobiographical content. A metatheatrical combination of buffoonery, biting satire, and lyrical poetry,
Little Fairground Booth stands as a seminal work in Russian avant-garde
drama. Vsevolod Meyerhold directed the original 1906 production and
restaged the play twice more in his career. Blok wrote three other
symbolist plays with political overtones: *Korol' na ploshchadi* (The King in
the Square, 1906), *Neznakomka* (The Stranger, a.k.a. The Unknown
Woman, 1906), and *Roza i krest* (The Rose and the Cross, 1913). Censorship kept the first two from the stage despite Meyerhold's interest in
them.

Initially, symbolism was referred to as decadence, but decadence
eventually emerged as a trend only marginally related to symbolism.
Decadent playwriting might be described as that which pushed symbolist
ideas to extremes of self-indulgence, either in terms of an overblown
aestheticism or an unwholesome emphasis on sex, death, and the occult.
Oscar Wilde serves as a prime example of the former tendency, while the
latter is evident in plays by Gabriele D'Annunzio, Arthur Schnitzler, and
Frank Wedekind. Wedekind began his career under the influence of
Hauptmann and other naturalists, but by 1889 he had satirized that
movement in his play *Die junge Welt* (The Young World). There is a
lingering naturalistic quality alongside the morbid supernaturalism of
Wedekind's notorious *Frühlings Erwachen* (Spring's Awakening, 1891), an
episodically structured tale of adolescent sexuality and suicide. It was
banned as pornography until Max Reinhardt staged a bowdlerized version in 1906, and although it still shocks audiences, the play is now
recognized as an important precursor of dramatic expressionism. In his
"Lulu plays," *Der Erdgeist* (Earth Spirit, 1895) and *Die Büchse der Pandora*
(Pandora's Box, 1904), Wedekind further explored the tension between
uninhibited sexual urges and repressive social mores.

FUTURISM, DADA, AND SURREALISM

If symbolism, decadence, futurism, dada, and surrealism had anything in common, it was a rejection of the settled assumptions of the
bourgeois mentality. That rejection could best be expressed by over-
throwing artistic tradition and seeking sources of inspiration apart from
ordinary reality. The symbolists attuned themselves to the ineffable, the
mysterious harmonies of the realm of the spirit, while the decadents
overindulged in whatever quickened their senses. Futurists found excitement in energy, speed, dynamism. Constructivists borrowed industrial
forms in an attempt to amalgamate abstraction and social utility. Dada

merely sanctioned the destruction of the old without proposing anything to replace it. Influenced by Freud's studies, the surrealists delved into the subconscious psyche to seek new realities of the liberated imagination, while the expressionists showed reality distorted by the subjective vision of the observer.

In these twentieth-century avant-garde movements, as always in the arts, it was poets and painters who led the way. Since theater is more expensive to produce, requiring the collaboration of many artists and a large paying audience to support it, the art of the stage is rarely in the vanguard of an artistic movement. However, the small "art theaters" with their coterie audiences were able to assimilate innovations in the other arts quite rapidly. Unlike romanticism or realism, these later isms did not visibly alter the course of commercial, mainstream theater that continued to satisfy its middle-class audiences with traditional fare. As all of the arts became swept up together in revolutionary forms, we see the beginnings of the modernist and postmodernist breakdowns of barriers between the visual and performing arts.

Futurism's earliest adherents were painters, although the movement's founder, Filippo Tommaso Marinetti, was a Milanese poet-playwright-journalist, a man of such boundless energy that he was eventually nicknamed "the caffeine of Europe." To launch the movement, he published his "First Futurist Manifesto" in a Parisian newspaper (*Le Figaro*, February 20, 1909). Two months later, his play *Le Roi Bombance* (a text heavily indebted to Jarry's *Ubu roi*) was produced by Lugné-Poe in Paris in April 1909 and provoked a small riot. In 1911 the wealthy Marinetti financed a trip to Paris for himself and several young Italian painters for the purpose of comparing his futurist agenda with the achievements of the cubist movement in painting. The cubists painted multiple images (for example, depicting a face in profile and full front at the same time) in an effort to convey the pluralism and mobility of objects in reality. The Italian futurists discovered to their satisfaction that their own way of perceiving reality was already far more radical than that of the French cubists. However, the modernist, antibourgeois stance of both groups was closely enough allied that many referred to their works as cubo-futurism.

Some excerpts from Marinetti's "First Futurist Manifesto" suggest why futurism was more suited to live performance than to the immobility of a painting:

We sing the love of danger, the habit of energy and audacity.

. . . .

Until now, literature has glorified pensive immobility, ecstasy, and sleep. We shall exalt aggressive action, feverish insomnia, the quick sprint, the twist in the air, the punch, and the slap.

We declare that the world's splendor has been enriched by a new beauty, the beauty of speed. A racing car adorned with great pipes like serpents with explosive breath—a roaring car that appears to run on bullets—is more beautiful than the *Victory of Samothrace*.

. . . .

No work that is not aggressive in nature can be a masterpiece. Poetry must be generated as a violent attack on forces of the unknown, to diminish and prostrate them before man.

. . . .

We will glorify war.

. . . .

We will destroy the museums, libraries, institutions of every kind. We will struggle against moralism, feminism, every opportunistic or utilitarian evasion.

Evening programs of readings of futurist poetry or artistic and political manifestos were held, always with the hope of provoking a riot or other vociferous audience response. As those performances became more

Umberto Boccioni's caricature of a futurist evening, published in Uno, due e. . .tre *(June 17, 1911), shows Marinetti at center stage. With their paintings behind them, a noisy orchestra in front, and traditionalists underfoot, the futurists on stage are clearly enjoying the chaos.*

elaborate, incorporating costumes, props, and music or sound effects, the constant stream of manifestos issued by Marinetti and his followers focused more and more on the theater. In "The Pleasure of Being Booed" (1911), Marinetti reaffirmed the primacy of theater in the futurist program, but warned against traditional definitions of success and means of achieving it. In the 1913 "Variety Theatre Manifesto," he advocated the kind of surprise and audience involvement that might be achieved by such means as selling the same ticket to ten people, spreading a strong glue on the theater seats, playing a Beethoven symphony backward, reducing all of Shakespeare to a single act, having the singers dye their hair and arms in vivid colors, unifying the atmosphere of stage and auditorium with a haze of cigar smoke, and encouraging the grotesque behavior of eccentric Americans. Emilio Settimelli and Bruno Corra joined with Marinetti in 1915 to issue "The Futurist Synthetic Theater." After eagerly hailing the approach of war, this manifesto laid out some specific proposals for a theater that would be the antithesis of the prolix, psychological, pacifist theater of the bourgeoisie: The ideal theater form would be *sintesi,* plays that could be performed in one minute or less, making a virtue of compression, spontaneity, fragmentation, simultaneous action, and speed. About fifty exemplary *sintesi,* most of them one or two pages, appear in *Futurist Performance* by Michael Kirby. The most famous futurist performance took place in Rome on April 12, 1917: *Fuochi d'artificio* (Fireworks) was a production designed by Giacomo Balla to accompany Igor Stravinsky's short musical composition *Feu d'artifice.* Although it was staged for the Ballets Russes, no dancer or actor appeared in it. The stage was filled with three-dimensional forms in various shapes and colors, all dominated by a kind of pinwheel construction at center. The action consisted of an interplay of lighting effects, with cues on the average every five seconds.

In 1914 Marinetti traveled to Russia, where a futurist movement had already been gathering strength under the leadership of David Burliuk, Velimir Khlebnikov, and Vladimir Mayakovsky. They and others contributed to the manifesto of Russian futurism that was published with some of their poems under the title *A Slap in the Face of Public Taste* (1912). Mayakovsky, a dynamic reciter of his own poetry as well as a bold graphic artist, gained notoriety for the unconventional bright yellow of his long, full cossack shirt and for the wooden spoon he wore in his lapel. His first play, entitled *Vladimir Mayakovsky, A Tragedy,* in which he played the title role, was presented in the Luna Park Theater of St. Petersburg in December 1913. That play, along with its famous companion piece on the same bill, *Victory Over the Sun* by Alexei Kruchenykh, with sets and costumes by Kasimir Malevich, constituted the first Russian cubo-futurist theatrical production. A strong current of cubism manifested itself in the geometrical forms of the setting and the cardboard and papier-mâché costumes. Russian futurism was finding its distinct identity, and Marinetti's poetry readings in Moscow and St. Petersburg were not well received.

Although World War I served to discredit the movement in general, it was carried on into the 1920s by designer-director Enrico Prampolini and scenographer Fortunato Depero. Prampolini's legacy included two manifestos, "Futurist Scenography" (1915) and "Futurist Scenic Atmosphere" (1924). In the latter, he proposed a "polydimensional scenospace" in which every spectacle would be "a *mechanical rite* of eternal transcendence of matter, a magical revelation of a spiritual and scientific mystery." His idea for a "Magnetic Theater" composed of numerous moving parts was never realized in performance, but his model for it won the Grand Prize in theatrical design at the 1925 International Exhibition of Decorative Arts in Paris.

Some aspects of futurism were absorbed into dada: the frequent issuing of manifestos, evenings of readings, aggressive attempts at audience provocation, and unmitigated scorn for the achievements of art of the past. Dada existed for eight years, 1916–24, in Zurich during World War I, and later in Paris and Berlin. It arose out of the desire for expression among a group of bohemian artists of all nationalities who found themselves in neutral Switzerland while the war raged on all sides of that peaceful enclave. From the cacaphony of different languages heard each evening at the Café Voltaire derived the concept of the *poème simultanée*, and this led to regular evenings of cabaret performance. The first simultaneous poem, entitled *"L'Amiral cherche une maison à louer"* (The Admiral Looks for a House to Rent/Praise), was performed for the café's nonplussed patrons on March 30, 1916, by three men shouting whatever words and sounds came into their heads: Richard Huelsenbeck in German, Marcel Janco in English, and Tristan Tzara in French. As Tzara later declared: "Thought is produced in the mouth."

The Romanian poet Tristan Tzara soon emerged as the ringleader of the group. He wrote seven manifestos of dada between 1916 and 1920. Although much of what he wrote reads like nonsense, the movement's basic tenets can be discerned. The impetus for dada grew out of disillusionment with a civilization that could do no better than plunge an entire continent into a terrible, senseless war. The fact that this devastation could be the end product of two thousand years of civilization undermined the significance of all that civilization had produced as art. If art is meaningless, the dadaists argued, it should not be preserved; it should be created and destroyed at the same time. Dada took its cue from a line in *Ubu roi:* "We won't have demolished anything unless we demolish even the ruins." Thus, dada represented anti-art. In his 1918 manifesto, Tzara stated that the word "dada" does not signify anything, but he went on to touch upon some of its meanings: it stands for hobbyhorse in French, mother in Romanian, father in English, a children's nurse and a double affirmative in Russian, a cube in Italian, and the tail of a holy cow in Kroo.

The idea of spontaneous creation of a work that immediately self-destructs took several forms in performance. Bringing together some random *objets trouvés* (found objects) would produce a dada sculpture, as when Marcel Duchamp combined a snowshovel, a typewriter, and a hatrack. Noise concerts might involve jingling keys, pounding the table, ringing cowbells, shaking baby rattles, operating a sewing machine or a fire extinguisher, and rhythmically chanting pseudo-African sounds. Tzara's prescription for making a dadaist poem was to choose a newspaper article of the length wanted for the poem, cut out each word in the article and put them all in a bag, shake the bag, take out the words one by one, and copy them down in that order. The German writer-pianist Hugo Ball, one of the leading figures in the dada movement, recalled the spontaneous effect of the donning of some masks that Marcel Janco made for a dada *soirée:* The masks "dictated a quite particular kind of gesture, full of pathos and bordering on insanity. . . . The motor force of these masks spread through us with an irresistible vigor. . . . The masks simply demanded that their wearers should set in motion a tragi-comic dance."

In 1920 Tzara went to Paris, thus making it the new headquarters of dada. There he formed a new coterie, most of whom were to defect to surrealism within a few years. They presented several dada *manifestations,* evenings of miscellaneous events, often including the performance of short plays, all of which was intended to outrage their curiosity-seeking audiences. In 1921, the American painter-photographer Man Ray came to Paris and fell in with the dadaists, who encouraged his experiments with images produced directly on the photographic plate, which he called "rayographs." Meanwhile, the dada faction that went to Berlin after the war had become politicized. Led by George Grosz and Walter Mehring, the Berlin dada group offered twelve *manifestations* in two years. There, the collage artist Kurt Schwitters sought admission to the dada circle, but was rejected by Huelsenbeck because of his "bourgeois face." However, Annabelle Melzer sees Schwitters's subsequent one-man touring performances as very close to dadaism; his presentations consisted of dancing to his own noisy accompaniment in alternation with dramatic recitations of the alphabet or of phonetic poetry.

Committing plays to paper was perhaps contrary to the prescribed ephemerality of data, but Tzara was soon struggling to sustain a movement that had to destroy itself in order to live up to its purpose. Among

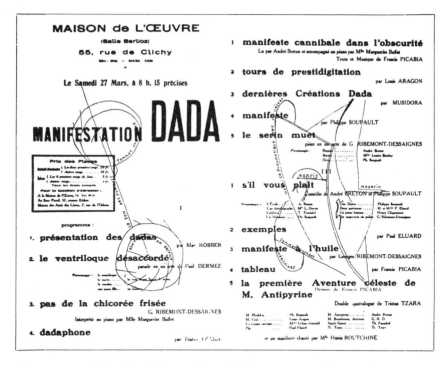

The program of the first dada evening after its move to Paris (March 27, 1920) culminated in the presentation of Tzara's play The First Heavenly Adventure of Mr. Fire-extinguisher. *Several other names on the program later became more strongly identified with surrealism.*

Tzara's plays are *La Première aventure céleste de M. Antipyrine* (The First Heavenly Adventure of Mr. Aspirin/Fire-Extinguisher, 1920), *Le Coeur à gaz* (The Gas Heart, 1921), and *Mouchoir de nuages* (Cloud Handkerchief, 1924). Georges Ribemont-Dessaignes, an unregenerate dadaist, wrote what were perhaps the movement's best plays, most of them after dada was dead. André Breton began challenging Tzara's leadership of the Paris dada group as early as 1921. In 1924 Breton published his "First Manifesto of Surrealism," thus marking his official break with dada and launching a new movement. Dada put on a brave face and conducted its own funeral that year.

"Surrealism devoured and digested Dada," declared the German dada painter Hans Richter. It borrowed such concepts as simultaneity, antirealism, and antiaestheticism. However, the origins of surrealism can be traced back to even before Tzara's arrival in Paris. The word *sur-réalisme* (more than realism) had been coined by the influential poet and art critic Guillaume Apollinaire in his May 1917 essay for the program of the modernist ballet *Parade* (Sideshow), which featured a cubist set and costumes by Pablo Picasso, and Erik Satie's jazz-inspired score that included the sound of clacking typewriters. A month later the word was used again to describe Apollinaire's first play *Les Mamelles de Tirésias* (The Breasts of Tiresias, 1917): *"drame surréaliste en deux actes et un prologue, choeurs, musiques et costumes selon l'esprit nouveau"* (surrealist drama in two acts and a prologue, with choruses, music, and costumes in the modern spirit). The play is an illogical sequence of amusing images and situations spinning off two social concerns of the day, the woman suffrage movement and the need to repopulate a country decimated by war. The setting by Serge Férat was composed of colored paper cut in various shapes and pasted on the wings. An actor covered with current journals played a newspaper kiosk. Another actor represented the People of Zanzibar and provided sound effects using a toy flute, cymbals, broken dishes, and other devices. Musical accompaniment was provided by an onstage piano. After a prologue spoken by the Director, announcing the "new spirit" in the theater, Thérèse renounces her womanhood and turns into Tiresias by releasing the balloons that formed her breasts, while a beard sprouts from the front of her dress to cover her face. The Husband then takes on the sole responsibility of procreating children. The production managed to offend many avant-garde artists as well as traditionalists, because the cubist painters were angered when the critics

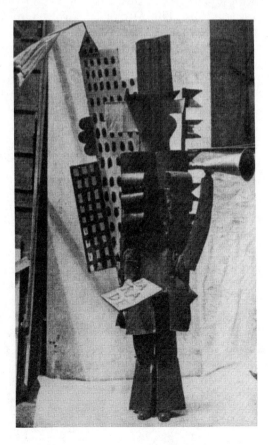

Jean Cocteau wrote the scenario, Erik Satie composed the music, Leonid Massine choreographed, and Pablo Picasso designed sets and costumes for the unconventional ballet Parade *(1917), produced by the Ballets Russes. The ballet featured two sideshow barkers in cubist costumes; the one from New York, shown here, has skyscrapers represented in the construction of the costume.*

applied the term "cubism" to describe what they regarded as a travesty. Floundering for a touchstone, some journalists tied it to Jarry's *Ubu roi* of twenty years earlier, but others saw it as a complete break with the past. André Breton later recalled: "Never again, as at that evening, was I ever so aware of the depth of the gulf that separated the new generation from the preceding one."

It fell to Breton to define the new movement, which he continued to do with periodic modifications even as late as the 1960s. In essence, it was what he called "a certain psychic automatism that corresponds rather closely to the state of dreaming." His preoccupation with Freud impelled him to emphasize the intuitive aspect of artistic creation in order to free the imagination from the dictates of rational thought. Surrealist poems, paintings, and plays thus characteristically juxtapose verbal concepts and visual images that are unrelated by any logic of time or space, as in dreams. In general, there is a cheerful craziness about the work of the French surrealists (as opposed to the darker vision of the later Spanish surrealists like painter Salvador Dalí, filmmaker Luís Buñuel, and, very briefly, poet-playwright Federico García Lorca). Among the major surrealist plays are *Comme il fait beau!* (What Nice Weather!, 1923) by Breton with Robert Desnos and Benjamin Péret, Louis Aragon's *L'Armoire à glace un beau soir* (The Mirror-Wardrobe One Fine Evening, 1924), Roger Daumal's *en gggarrrde!* (1924), Georges Ribemont-Dessaignes's *Le Bourreau de Pérou* (The Peruvian Executioner, 1926), Roger Vitrac's *Les Mystères de l'amour* (Mysteries of Love, 1927) and *Victor; ou, les enfants au pouvoir* (Victor; or, Children Take Over, 1928), Pablo Picasso's *Le Désir attrapé par la queue* (Desire Caught by the Tail, 1941) and *Les Quatre petites filles* (Four Little Girls, 1948). Still more important are the plays of two major figures associated with the surrealist movement in the 1920s: Jean Cocteau and Antonin Artaud.

Jean Cocteau, an extraordinarily multifaceted—if sometimes facile—talent, worked in all of the visual and verbal arts; he was a poet, playwright, ballet scenarist, opera librettist, stage designer, sketch artist, sculptor, novelist, filmmaker, and creator of decorative objects. For him, all of these activities were summed up in the word "poet," and he used Orpheus, the musician of the Greek gods, as the archetypal figure of the poet in both a play and a film entitled *Orpheus* and in other works. Although the surrealists never really welcomed him into their fold, such early works as his ballet *Parade*, his delightful short play *Les Mariés de la tour Eiffel* (The Eiffel Tower Wedding Party, 1921), and his film *Le Sang d'un poète* (Blood of a Poet, 1930) display the same modernist spirit. As his prodigious work evolved over the next forty years until his death in 1963, it relied fairly consistently upon a personal mythology, a repertoire of subjectively generated symbols and allusions, that tie it to the

Jean Cocteau's one-act Eiffel Tower Wedding Party *exemplifies surrealism's cheerful abandonment of logic. This production at the University of Wisconsin–Rock County in 1969 was directed by Felicia Londré and designed by Gary J. Lenox.*

surrealist impulse. He moved easily back and forth between the avant-garde and the mainstream and collaborated with the leading artists in both areas, writing the scenario for Serge Diaghilev's ballet *Le Dieu bleu* (The Blue God, 1912) danced by Vaclav Nijinsky; writing the libretto for Igor Stravinsky's oratorio *Oedipus Rex* (1927); getting music composed by Georges Auric, Arthur Honegger, Darius Milhaud, Francis Poulenc, and Germaine Tailleferre for his *Eiffel Tower Wedding Party;* and working with such major actors as Louis Jouvet, Jean Marais, Maria Casarès, Jean-Pierre Aumont, and designers like Pablo Picasso, Jean Hugo, and Christian Bérard on his plays and films. Cocteau is today best remembered for his one-woman play *La Voix humaine* (The Human Voice, 1930), his best-selling novel of adolescent alienation *Les Enfants terribles* (1930), and his 1945 film *La Belle et la bête* (Beauty and the Beast).

Antonin Artaud was officially affiliated with the surrealists for only two years, 1924–26, but—like Cocteau—all of his subsequent work remained strongly based in that early aesthetic. His break with the movement was precipitated by his refusal to go along with the Marxist politics that Breton and Louis Aragon were injecting into surrealism; in 1927 they would declare surrealism's allegiance to the Communist party. Despite his chronic mental disturbances, Artaud had worked successfully as an actor for several years with such important directors as Lugné-Poe, Charles Dullin, and Georges Pitoëff. By 1926 he was ready to found his own theater, which he and his cofounder Roger Vitrac (who had also been expelled from the surrealist group) named the Théâtre Alfred Jarry. In its financially plagued two-year existence it presented only four productions, including Vitrac's two surrealist plays, which Artaud directed. Artaud also wrote plays that would probably be classed as surrealist: *Ventre brûlé; ou, la mère folle* (Burnt Belly; or, the Crazy Mother, 1927), *Jet de sang* (Spurt of Blood, 1927), and a "talking pantomime," *Le Pierre philosophe* (The Philosopher's Stone, 1931).

Two formative events contributed to the theories that emerge from Artaud's most influential work, the essays collected under the title *Le théâtre et son double* (The Theater and its Double, 1938). Those events were the performances of the Balinese dancers at the Colonial Exposition in Paris in 1931, and his participation in the rituals of the Tarahumara Indians in Mexico in 1936. The highly inflected gestural language of the Balinese dancers impressed him as transcending "the customary limits of feelings and words"—an observation that impelled him to reject contemporary western theater's "dictatorship of speech" and to seek a "pure theatrical language which does without words, a language of signs, gestures, and attitudes having an ideographic value as they exist in certain unpeverted pantomimes." For him, the "language of the *mise en scène*" would also encompass noises, colors, cries, laments, incantations, apparitions, rare notes of music, masks, mannequins, physical action with lights that stimulate heat and cold, and other elements that would carry out an "assault on the senses" of the spectator. The Tarahumara Indians represented, in his view, "a culture whose myths were still animated by the subterranean forces which had engendered them, where a man could rediscover his interior self." Artaud believed that the theater should serve to put spectators in touch with the mysterious and the sublime; he wanted to restore theater to its original function, "to reinstate it in its religious and metaphysical aspect, to reconcile it with the universe." To liberate these repressed tendencies, he proposed a "theater of cruelty." This would be "a theater in which violent physical images crush and hypnotize the sensibility of the spectator seized by the theater as by a whirlwind of higher forces. A theater which, abandoning psychology, recounts the extraordinary, stages natural conflicts. . . . A theater that induces trance."

Artaud's writing was not widely known or seriously regarded during his lifetime. He spent nine of his last years in a mental institution. After his release in 1946, he lived only two years. His posthumous recognition might be credited to Peter Brook whose 1964 production of *Marat/Sade* was influenced by Artaud's theories. Artaud was also a major influence on the direction of French theater in the decade following the events of May 1968.

EXPRESSIONISM

Like symbolism and surrealism, expressionism is a highly subjective approach to art, as implied in its capsule definition: *die Ausstrahlungen des Ichs* (the outflinging of the self, or radiation of the ego). The expressionist artist projects his own emotional state onto objective reality, and this effects a subjective distortion of that reality. The earliest works in such a heightened, personal vein (even before the word "expressionist" began to be used) were certain plays by August Strindberg and the paintings of Vincent van Gogh and Edvard Munch. Munch's 1893 painting *The Scream* might be seen as emblematic of the expressionist aesthetic; the central figure on a bridge holds his face in his hands and cries out, a scream that seems to send all of nature—the vivid blue water, the orange-streaked sky—into a responding swirl that echoes the intensity of the subject's emotion. (Indeed, *Schrei*, meaning "scream," was to become a key term in the German expressionist drama of the World War I period.) Other groups of painters adopted Munch's and van Gogh's use of bright colors, uneven or violent applications of pigment, and departures from realism: *Les Fauves* (Wild Beasts), a group led by Henri Matisse, whose controversial Paris exhibition of 1905 shocked the public and critics alike; *Die Brücke* (The Bridge), founded in Dresden in 1905 and moved to Berlin in 1911, including, most notably, the intense, brooding work of Emil Nolde; and *Der Blaue Reiter* (Blue Rider), which made Munich into the center of modern art from 1911 until World War I. Wassily Kandinsky, leader of the Blue Rider group, published an influential treatise, *Über das Geistige in der Kunst* (On the Spiritual in Art, 1912), which promulgated an abstract "art of internal necessity" arising from the *existentielle Angst* of the artist concerned about a spiritually bankrupt bourgeoisie controlling an overindustrialized world.

A comparable preexpressionist aesthetic in dramatic literature might be discerned as early as Georg Büchner's *Woyzeck* (1836; first produced in 1913); the play is an accumulation of fragmented glimpses of the impersonal social forces in which the title character is helplessly caught up. Similarly, Frank Wedekind's *Spring's Awakening* (1891; first produced 1906) presents a dehumanized vision of hypocritical middle-class adults in contrast to the emotional warmth of the confused adolescents who are the focal point of the play. Much influenced by Wedekind, Carl Sternheim mocked the shallow values of the bourgeoisie by reducing his characters' dialogue to clichés in "telegrammatic" style. Beginning with *Die Höse* (The Underpants, 1909), which was banned for "immorality" after Max Reinhardt staged it in Berlin, Sternheim traced the fortunes of the Maske family through a series of comedies collected under the title *Aus dem bürgerlichen Heldenleben* (Scenes from the Heroic Life of the Middle Classes). The grotesque effects of Sternheim's handling of language and character were to have a telling impact on the expressionists.

The defining characteristics of early expressionist drama are prefigured in August Strindberg's autobiographical trilogy *Nach Damascus* (To Damascus, 1898–1901) and in his *Ein Traumspiel* (A Dream Play, 1901). These plays feature episodically constructed plots, abstract characters, and distortions of reality calling for elaborate scenic effects, to express the inner man (or woman, as in *A Dream Play*) on a spiritual journey. Strindberg's preface to *A Dream Play* sums up the playwright's techniques for expressing reality with dreamlike subjectivity. He wrote (as translated by Harry G. Carlson):

> In this dream play, as in his earlier dream play *To Damascus,* the author has attempted to imitate the disconnected but seemingly logical form of a dream. Anything can happen, everything is possible and plausible. Time and space do not exist. Upon an insignificant background of real life events, the imagination spins and weaves new patterns: a blend of memories, experiences, pure inventions, absurdities, and improvisations. The characters split, double, redouble, evaporate, condense, fragment, cohere. But one consciousness is superior to them all: that of the dreamer.

The central, superior consciousness of the dreamer represents the creative vision of the artist. In many expressionist plays, the central character is an archetypal figure, and the other characters are projections of his or her consciousness. Like the Blue Rider painters who wanted to transfer musical dynamics into visual terms, the early expressionist playwrights attempted to create verbal harmonies and dissonances to evoke subjective experience. Strindberg applied this principle in the dialogue of *To Damascus,* and he referred to the play's arrangement of scenes as a "contrapuntal" or "polyphonic" form. But he also structured *To Damascus I* with reference to the stations of the cross on the road to Calvary, thus giving rise to the expressionist practice of conceiving plays as a series of *Stationen.*

It is a painter, Oskar Kokoschka, who has usually been credited with having written the first expressionist play. The twenty-two-year-old Austrian art student had already flouted the decorative conventions of the Viennese *Jugendstil* in his 1908 Kunstschau exhibit, but it was his first play, *Mörder Hoffnung der Frauen* (Murderer Hope of Women, 1907), which he produced himself in a small outdoor theater in July 1909, that earned him the epithet "Scourge of the Bourgeoisie" *(Bürgershreck)*. This short drama uses visceral imagery and violent action to express the simultaneous sexual attraction and emotional antagonism between Woman and Man. Although Kokoschka remains best known as a painter, he wrote several other expressionist plays, including *Sphinx und Strohmann* (1907, Sphinx and Strawman), which was performed by the Dadaists in Zurich in 1917, and *Der brennende Dornbusch* (The Burning Bush, 1913).

The early phase of German expressionist drama lasted into World War I and produced such works as Reinhard Sorge's *Der Bettler* (The Beggar, 1912), Ernst Barlach's *Der tote Tag* (The Dead Day, 1912), Paul Kornfeld's *Die Verführung* (The Seduction, 1913) and Walter Hasenclever's *Der Sohn* (The Son, 1914). In general, these plays focused upon the individual's need for spiritual rebirth. Like surrealist plays, they manifest a Freudian influence in their techniques of free association, repetitions of key concepts, and various other psychological phenomena. Hasenclever's *The Son* adumbrated a new direction in expressionist drama, which became evident during the latter part of the war. This play's theme of the rebellious son, whose actions precipitate his father's death, rallied the war-weary and disillusioned German youth of the day, promoting a revolutionary zeal to overthrow the hidebound conventions of the previous generation.

In its later phase, expressionist drama's area of concern expanded from the individual to society as a whole. The allegorical hero gave way to the concept of a social collective. The urgency of the impulse for social change coupled with the experience of the war led to the use of increasingly violent images and action. The subjective distortions of objective reality revealed the threatening nature of that reality. The rapid development of wartime technology was perceived as one of the greatest threats to man's spiritual striving. Reduced to cannon fodder or to automatonlike subservience before a goal of mass production, man himself became a mere cog in a vast social machine. Man's depersonalization was dramatized by the kind of staccato language that Sternheim had pioneered and by frantic, disjointed action that obviated character development as well as well-made-play conventions like exposition, narrative continuity, rising action, and the logical denouement.

The shift in emphasis within the expressionist movement is evident—within a slightly later time frame—in a number of silent films from Germany's famous Ufa studio, which played an important role in rehabilitating the country's postwar image on the international scene. In Robert Wiene's 1919 film *The Cabinet of Dr. Caligari,* the narrative unfolds from the point of view of a would-be romantic hero; thus the dangers this character faces in order to rescue the woman he loves are exagger-

August Strindberg's A Dream Play *(1901) prefigures the expressionist movement that was to become important in the theater fifteen years later. In 1917 Svend Gade (1877–1952) designed an expressionist production of the play for Copenhagen's Dagmarteatret. Courtesy of the Teatermuseet, Copenhagen.*

Else Lasker-Schüler's Die Wupper *(The River Wupper; written 1908, produced 1919) was a naturalistic play criticizing social conditions, but it has often been produced expressionistically. The distorted angles in the setting of this prize-winning Wuppertal production suggest an expressionist approach. Courtesy of the German Information Center.*

atedly threatening—the evil aspect of Dr. Caligari, the deep shadows in the narrow streets, the dangerously angled rooftops—as shown through his perspective. The 1922 film *Nosferatu* might also be tied to early expressionism because of its dreamlike imagery. The preoccupations of later expressionism come to the fore in Fritz Lang's *Metropolis* (1927), which shows the downtrodden masses in subservience to a machine with an almost human face; furthermore, the heroine is reproduced as a robot, so that the good woman and her demonic clone appear indistinguishable. The word "robot" (from the Czech *robota*, meaning hard labor) had made its first appearance in a 1920 play entitled *R. U. R.* (for Rossum's Universal Robots) by Czechoslovakian dramatist Karel Čapek. In his variation on the theme of technology's threat to human values, Čapek shows the man-made, soulless, artificial creatures achieving the total destruction of humanity.

Two dramatists are outstanding in the latter period of German expressionism: Georg Kaiser and Ernst Toller. Author of seventy-four plays, Kaiser was the most prolific of the expressionist playwrights and one of the most troubled in his personal life. He abandoned a career in business in order to write, but his work was largely ignored for a decade. With the 1917 production of his pacifist play *Die Bürger von Calais* (The Burghers of Calais, 1914), Kaiser vaulted to prominence. His career and the movement itself peaked during the next six years with numerous German productions of his greatest play *Von Morgens bis Mitternachts* (From Morn to Midnight, 1916). In this *Stationendrama*, a bank cashier absconds with some funds in hopes that this will enable him to achieve a higher purpose with his life, but his various encounters over the next twelve hours lead only to disillusionment and a Christ-like death. *From Morn to Midnight* more than any other play brought international recognition to German expressionism, especially after its 1922 New York production by the Theatre Guild. Kaiser's other most important work is his "Gas trilogy," again dealing with a money-based society in conflict with what Kaiser regarded as his fundamental theme, *die Erneuerung des Menschen* (the regeneration of man). Comprising the trilogy are *Die Koralle* (The Coral, 1917), *Gas I* (1918), and *Gas II* (1920). Despite the popularity of his work, Kaiser's financial difficulties led him to sell the furniture that came with his rented apartment, for which he spent six months in prison in 1920. With Hitler's rise, his books were banned and burned. After 1938 Kaiser lived in exile in Switzerland.

Ernst Toller too was an idealist whose writing was a product of his disillusionment and was banned by Hitler. His own wartime experience as an army volunteer became the basis for his first play, *Die Wandlung* (Transfiguration, 1919), which he wrote—like his other major plays—while serving a five-year prison sentence for his part in a Communist uprising in Munich. Published and produced with great success that year, *Transfiguration* was quickly followed by his major work, *Masse Mensch* (Man and the Masses, 1920). Both plays alternate scenes of dream and reality. Friedrich, the young soldier in *Transfiguration*, and The Woman in *Man and the Masses* struggle with a violence-prone society for a new order based upon peace and love. However, Toller's political activism colored his artistry, taking the plays away from the raw emotion of early expressionism and onto a more intellectual plane. The suicide of the disillusioned central character in his *Hoppla: Wir Leben!* (Hoppla! Such is Life, 1927) foreshadowed Toller's own self-inflicted death in New York in 1939.

The theatrical advances engendered by German expressionism ultimately outweigh the movement's literary importance. The distortions of reality, the onstage transformations (like the snow-covered tree that takes the shape of a skeleton in *From Morn to Midnight*), the rapid succession of disjointed episodes—all required innovations in lighting, scene shifting, and other scenic effects. In their book *Continental Stagecraft* (1922), Kenneth Macgowan and Robert Edmond Jones described in detail the striking theatrical effects achieved in Jürgen Fehling's 1921 Berlin production of *Man and the Masses*. Among the techniques that impressed them were a choral voice "coming out of a darkness in which faces vaguely begin to hover," a song mounting up against the distant rattle of machine guns, and "the rejection of every shred of actuality that stands in the way of inner emotional truth." Acting, too, was affected by the demands of expressionist texts. Beginning with Paul Kornfeld's "Epilogue to the Actor" (1916), the expressionists poured forth a stream of theoretical statements on acting to express the spirit of the "new man." The stylized abstraction of plays featuring archetypal characters seemed to require exaggeration and distortion in performance (mechanical movements, the face as mask, a rhetoric of gesture, vocal work to approximate the range and variety of music). At the same time, however, expressionism by its very subjective nature called for "ecstatic acting," the actor's baring of his *Seele* (soul) in the intensity of the universal emotions aroused in performance. Austrian actor Fritz Kortner embodied all of these features in his acting of Shakespearean roles in the 1920s, just as American theater artists subsequently experimented with applying expressionist production techniques to standard plays. One of the most noteworthy of such efforts was a 1921 New York production of *Macbeth* directed by Arthur Hopkins and designed by Robert Edmond Jones. The theatrical distortions of reality in Jones's setting expressed the psychological grip of the witches over Macbeth's increasingly unstable outlook.

Expressionism generated many such innovative approaches to scene design and stage lighting in the American theater, but only two playwrights won lasting recognition for their work in this vein. Elmer Rice is remembered for two of his many plays, the expressionist *Adding Machine* (1923), in which Mr. Zero falls victim to the dehumanizing conditions of the machine age, and *Street Scene* (1929), a quasi-lyrical look at the social collective in a New York slum. Eugene O'Neill, who always acknowledged the profound influence of Strindberg on his work, tried his hand at expressionism early in his career, with mixed results. *The Emperor Jones* (1920) and *The Hairy Ape* (1922) certainly rank among the finest expressionist plays anywhere and were remarkably successful in production. In *The Fountain* (1925) and *The Great God Brown* (1926), O'Neill borrowed from expressionism the use of masks without entirely succeeding in meshing them with the dominant modes of those plays. Finally, the melodramatic *Dynamo* (1929), dramatizing the idea of a symbiotic relationship of man and machine, was a failure in production.

One important Austrian writer must be mentioned in conjunction with expressionism, although he did not identify himself with the movement. Karl Kraus, poet, journalist, and satirist, published his own pe-

Robert Edmond Jones's famous expressionistic design for the banquet scene in Macbeth *emphasized the supernatural with three masks suspended overhead. This 1921 New York production was directed by Arthur Hopkins and starred Lionel Barrymore. From* Theatre Arts Prints: Stages of the World.

riodical *Die Fackel* (The Torch) in Vienna from 1899 until his death in
1936. His early contributors included Strindberg, Wedekind, and Oscar
Wilde, but after 1911 he wrote it all himself. Kraus's masterpiece of social
and literary criticism is an 800-page documentary and satirical tragedy
of mankind in dialogue form: *Die letzten Tage der Menschheit* (The Last
Days of Mankind, 1919). Never intending it for the stage, Kraus poured
into it his uncompromising antimilitarism (a lonely and courageous
stand during World War I) and his concern that the erosion of standards
in language—particularly as affected by journalistic usage—inevitably
meant a decline in conceptual thought, morality, and the arts. Like
expressionist drama, *The Last Days of Mankind* is composed of disjointed
short scenes; they range from the farcical to sequences composed of
quotations from published sources. The characters include actual public
figures as well as archetypes like the Patriot, the Psychiatrist, the Prussian
Rifleman, the German Bookseller, the War Correspondent. Interspersed throughout are dialogues between the Grumbler (Kraus's
mouthpiece) and the Optimist. It has been said that the play's protagonist is European mankind. It opens on Vienna's Ringstrasse in 1914,
where a Newsboy's cry heralds the advent of war. The last of the 259
scenes presents a harrowing sequence of images culminating in a vision
of a mound of corpses and an endless procession of pale women; the
final voice is that of the Unborn Son asking not to be born.

The Bauhaus, founded in 1919 by Walter Gropius as a school for the
unified study of all the fine and decorative arts, has been at least ten-
uously linked to expressionism. The first head of the Bauhaus theater
program, Lothar Schreyer, drew upon his background as an expressionist playwright of the early spiritually inclined variety, as exemplified by his very short play *Crucifixion* (1920). His inclination toward
mysticism, however, put him at odds with the functionalism stressed by
his colleagues in their first public exhibition, entitled "Art and Technology—A New Unity," in 1923. Schreyer resigned, to be replaced by
painter-sculptor Oskar Schlemmer. Schlemmer's productions used a
variety of materials—puppets, screens with shadow play, colored lights,
furniture, wooden slats, glass tubes, wires, soft padding, cardboard,
musical instruments, and everyday household objects—to explore "the
stage as the arena for successive and transient action" through abstraction, mechanization, and "new potentials of technology and invention."
Schlemmer's internationally renowned *Triadisches Ballet* (Triadic Ballet,
1922) remained in the repertoire until the closing of the Bauhaus in
1932, and represented the culmination of his experiments in choreographing abstract figures. Although it was said that students went to the
Bauhaus to be "cured of expressionism," Schlemmer's stage designs for
the commercial theater showed clear evidence of the expressionist influ-

ence. Indeed, by expanding the public's latitude of acceptance for departures from realism, expressionism must be considered a seminal influence on the development of theater in the twentieth century.

THE SOVIET GOLDEN AGE

Most Russian artists—symbolists and decadents included—welcomed the October Socialist Revolution of 1917. Besides a general expectation that the "dictatorship of the proletariat" would mean a better life for everyone, they were encouraged by the lifting of the Imperial censorship and bureaucratic controls that had hampered much initiative in the arts. When the Bolsheviks signed the Treaty of Brest-Litovsk with the Germans in 1918, thus betraying Russia's allies in order to spare the hard-hit country further suffering, the theaters were suddenly crowded with enthusiastic new audiences of ragged, hungry soldiers home from the front, as well as factory workers. No matter if they came to the theater primarily as an escape from their unheated apartments in that time of severe shortages of fuel and food, their unstudied involvement with the action on stage and their spontaneous responses were tonic for artists accustomed to the jaded, upperclass prerevolutionary audiences. It was heartening also that this revolution, unlike most, did not bring systematic destruction of the great works of art created under the hated old regime. Playwright Maxim Gorky carried out an instrumental role in the protection and nationalization of tsarist art and architecture. But while the goal of making art available to the masses was an idealistic one for artists, it was a coldly calculated effort on the part of Vladimir Ilich Lenin.

Lenin's plan to exploit the arts in support of his totalitarian government began with the establishment of the People's Commissariat for Enlightenment *(Narkompros)*. His appointment of Anatoly Lunacharsky as its first commissar (1917–29) was one of the most fortunate policy implementations of his despotic career. The humane and cultured Lunacharsky has been described as "an intellectual among Bolsheviks, and a Bolshevik among intellectuals." Lunacharsky's championship of proletarian art and realism in the theater did not preclude a benign tolerance of the avant-garde experimentation that was to blossom in the 1920s. One of Lenin's first directives to Lunacharsky initiated a program of "monumental propaganda," rapidly created public sculptures—necessarily in perishable materials like plaster of Paris—of revolutionary heroes to inspire the public. Graphic artists responded with particular vigor to the propaganda needs of the Bolsheviks; posters from the first decade after the revolution remain one of the most exciting products of the period. Agitprop trains and river steamers, their exteriors painted with bright, bold revolutionary images and slogans, carried propaganda leaflets to remote provincial towns. These vehicles, equipped with their own electrical generators, also functioned as mobile auditoriums where the locals could view silent films. Even porcelain was designed to incorporate the hammer and sickle motif within their abstract patterns. Theater people contributed their share of agitprop works, including animated posters, skits, and the staging of newspaper reports in a manner not unlike the American theater's "living newspapers" of the 1930s.

One of the most vivid manifestations of art for the masses was the "mass spectacles," open-air reenactments of revolutionary events, staged in various cities during the first few years after the revolution. The most renowned of these occurred in Petrograd (formerly St. Petersburg; renamed Leningrad after Lenin's death in 1924). In *The Mystery of Liberated Toil* on May 1, 1920, a cast of two thousand used the steps of the Stock Exchange as a scenic metaphor for the struggle between capital and labor; an audience numbering about thirty-five thousand stood on the square in front of the Stock Exchange. The same location held an estimated forty-five thousand spectators for *In Favor of a World Commune* on July 19, 1920, during which their attention was also directed by means of spotlights to action occurring on nearby bridges over the River Neva, on battleships on the river, and at the Fortress of Saints Peter and Paul. The most grandiose of the mass spectacles, *The Storming of the Winter Palace* (November 7, 1920), commemorated the third anniversary of the October Revolution (which had occurred on October 25 by the old Julian calendar then used in Russia, or on November 7 by the Gregorian calendar). As director-in-chief, Nikolai Evreinov commanded a cast of eight thousand plus a five-hundred member orchestra; he maintained contact with his assistants—including those on remote locations like battleship *Aurora*, whose guns were fired on cue—by field telephone and messengers on motorcycles. The one hundred thousand spectators stood in the center of Palace Square watching an allegorical struggle between the Reds and the Whites on two huge platforms. Culminating the evening, performers costumed as soldiers and armed workers stormed the palace. Thousands of voices sang the "Internationale" as an illuminated red star appeared in each window of the vast facade of the Winter Palace and a red banner was raised aloft. Such spectacles, enacted by underrehearsed factory workers, soldiers, and students, could not hold the public's interest indefinitely. Although mass spectacles died out around 1921, Frantisek Deák sees their continuing influence in environmental staging, audience participation, and mass action in both the theater and cinema of the 1920s.

The so-called Proletcult (proletarian culture) movement, celebrating

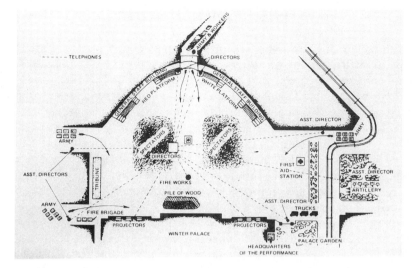

In Petrograd, the huge courtyard framed by the Winter Palace and the semicircular General Staff building was the site of The Storming of the Winter Palace, a mass spectacle directed by Nikolai Evreinov. The diagram shows the 100,000 spectators clustered near the center of the square. The platforms on which the struggle between the Reds and the Whites was enacted are set before the façade of the General Staff building.

Yuri Annenkov's watercolor shows the platforms with settings erected in front of the General Staff building for the 1920 production of The Storming of the Winter Palace. The Red platform on the left has industrial buildings, whereas the White platform on the right is a largely sterile space.

working-class art, flourished from 1917 until about 1923. Its original impetus, articulated by Alexander Bogdanov, was to break with and even suppress the "bourgeois culture" of the past in favor of a "pure" or undiluted art created exclusively by members of the proletariat without reference to the dominant cultural heritage. However, Lenin and Lunacharsky—partly in order to retain the allegiance of the intelligentsia—reined in the iconoclastic Proletcult, making it subordinate to the People's Commissariat of Enlightenment in 1920. Lunacharsky's concern with protecting diverse traditions in the arts is evident in his "Theses . . . concerning Basic Policy in the Field of Art" (1920): "All fields of art must be utilized in order to elevate and illustrate clearly our political and revolutionary agitational/propaganda work." The Proletcult movement and its successor, the Blue Blouse (*Sinyaya Bluza*, 1923–28), quickly spawning over twenty thousand playreading circles and amateur theater groups all over the country, not only spread interest in theater, but also contributed significantly to the fight against illiteracy. The decline of those efforts after 1928 might be attributed to a general exhaustion of interest in the crude Communist party literature distributed by the Department of Agitation and Propaganda.

The golden age in Soviet theater lasted only a few years, roughly 1921 to 1928, but the quantity, quality, and rich variety of the work produced in that period gave it a brilliance equal to any other great period in world theater. It is no coincidence that such dazzling achievements in the arts began in the same year that Lenin announced his New Economic Policy (NEP), a limited return to private enterprise in order to jolt the collapsing economy. The government's focus on economic conditions left artists free to experiment. While capitalism brought rapid improvement to the economy, it also opened the door to a generation of unscrupulous entrepreneurs dubbed "nepmen." The gap between Communist ideals and gritty reality inspired a plethora of NEP satires, comedies, and lively melodramas, including such outstanding plays as Nikolai Erdman's *Mandat* (The Mandate, 1924) and *Samo-ubitsa* (The Suicide, 1928), Aleksey Faiko's *Uchitel' Bubus* (Bubus the Teacher, 1924) and *Chelovek s portfelem* (Man with a Briefcase, 1928), Mikhail Bulgakov's *Zoykina kvartira* (Zoya's Apartment, 1926), Valentin Kataev's *Rastratchiki* (Embezzlers, 1928), and Vladimir Mayakovsky's *Klop* (The Bedbug, 1929). Although Lenin died in 1924, the NEP was allowed to continue until 1928, when Stalin replaced it with the first Five-Year Plan. That year also brought the abolition of private publishing and—through much stricter control by Glavrepertkom (the censorship committee for theater, established in 1923)—the end of freedom to experiment in the arts. From there it was only a short step to the imposition of the doctrine of Socialist Realism on art and literature in 1934, and to the purges of artists and intellectuals in 1936.

While it lasted, the Soviet golden age was distinguished above all by its stage directors, and their work was enhanced by a generation of superb designers. One director, Vsevolod Meyerhold, outshone all the others and indirectly influenced the course of twentieth-century theater. In 1896 he abandoned his law studies at Moscow University to join Nemirovich-Danchenko's Philharmonic Dramatic School. At his graduation two years later, the silver medals in acting went to him and Olga Knipper; both were invited to join Nemirovich-Danchenko and Stanislavsky as original company members of the Moscow Art Theatre. In his four seasons with the company, Meyerhold played eighteen roles, most notably Konstantin Treplev in Chekhov's *The Seagull*. But, growing impatient with what he perceived as limited acting opportunities and an unconcern for social implications in production, Meyerhold left to form his own theater group in the Ukraine. Although the struggle to keep his company afloat from 1902 to 1904 took a toll on his finances and his health, Meyerhold gained from it his first experience as a director. After some tentative imitations of Stanislavsky's methods, he began experimenting with departures from realism and found himself particularly drawn to the dramatic theories of the symbolists. Unable to sustain his own venture, in 1905 he accepted Stanislavsky's invitation to return to Moscow as the head of a studio theater organized under the aegis of the Moscow Art Theatre for the purpose of exploring the potential of "The New Drama" of the symbolists. Meyerhold's work at the studio never reached the public, not only because the 1905 strikes and workers' rebellions undermined much theatrical activity that year, but also because Stanislavsky grew nervous about the amount he was investing in an endeavor that proved artistically alien to his own inclinations. Meyerhold wrote in a letter to his wife: "The collapse of the Studio was my salvation—it wasn't what I wanted, not what I wanted at all. It is only now that I realise how fortunate its failure was."

Meyerhold accepted an invitation from actress Vera Komissarzhevskaya to serve as artistic director of her theater company in St. Petersburg. His opening production of Ibsen's *Hedda Gabler* in 1906 heralded the defiance of realistic stage conventions that would mark the rest of his career. Against a beautiful but unrealistic setting designed by Nikolai Sapunov, Meyerhold directed his actors to speak their lines facing the audience. There was almost no movement, gesture, facial expression, or pantomimic business, and yet—to some observers—the stylization allowed an "inner dialogue of presentiments and emotions" to surface. The general public's lack of appreciation did not deter Meyerhold from further forays into symbolist production with plays like Maeterlinck's *Sister Beatrice* and *Pelléas and Mélisande*, Andreyev's *The Life of Man*, and Blok's *Little Fairground Booth*. The latter production caused considerable critical turmoil, but for Meyerhold—who played the role of

Pierrot—it marked a turning point, as it led him away from static symbolism and toward the lively artifice of commedia dell'arte. Meyerhold had begun his second season with Komissarzhevskaya when she dismissed him on the grounds that their goals for the theater were incompatible and that his direction could lead only to puppet theater.

With the 1908 season, Meyerhold began a ten-year engagement as a stage director and actor in the Imperial Theater system in St. Petersburg. He understood the necessity to work in a more conventional vein when he staged plays at the Alexandrinsky Theater and operas at the Maryinsky. Thus he sought other outlets for his creative needs by working on the side in various studio theaters. At the request of the Imperial Theaters' administration, he took a pseudonym, Doctor Dappertutto, for use in his private experimental work. It was under this alter ego's name that in 1914 he staged *Little Fairground Booth* for the second time, now incorporating many elements of popular theater, such as the *lazzi* of commedia dell'arte. That year he also began publishing a periodical entitled *The Love for Three Oranges: The Journal of Doctor Dappertutto*. At the Alexandrinsky, Meyerhold's most famous production was Mikhail Lermontov's romantic melodrama *Maskarad* (Masquerade, 1836), which included over 150 extras in the two ballroom scenes. The lavishly mounted production—for which Aleksandr Golovin designed not only the settings, but also the furniture, chandeliers, proscenium mirrors, and even the china used on stage—turned out to be a final dazzling display of the Russian aristocracy's profligate extravagance. The production seemed to mock reality, for as the wealthy patrons left the theater on opening night, February 25, 1917, they heard the sound of gunfire and the cries of demonstrators for "bread." The February uprising was a prelude to the October revolution.

Although he had worked for a tsarist institution, Meyerhold espoused the revolutionary cause, and in 1918 he joined the Bolshevik party. Meyerhold became excited at the prospect of directing Valdimir Mayakovsky's "Heroic, Epic, and Satiric Representation of our Era," *Mystery-Bouffe,* a farcical, allegorical struggle between the Cleans (royalty and bureaucrats) and the Uncleans (workers and soldiers). However, such "futurist" fare ("futurism" having become a blanket term for leftist avant-garde art of any kind) could not be tolerated in an Imperial Theatre. For the first anniversary of the October Revolution, Meyerhold staged the play under Bolshevik sponsorship, with sets and costumes designed by the suprematist painter Kasimir Malevich. (Suprematism aspired to achieve the "supreme" liberation from old art by a reduction of literal content and feelings to geometric forms.) Although that 1918 production did not cause much of a stir, it was significant in inaugurating the outstanding director-playwright collaboration of the Soviet golden age, that of Meyerhold and Mayakovsky.

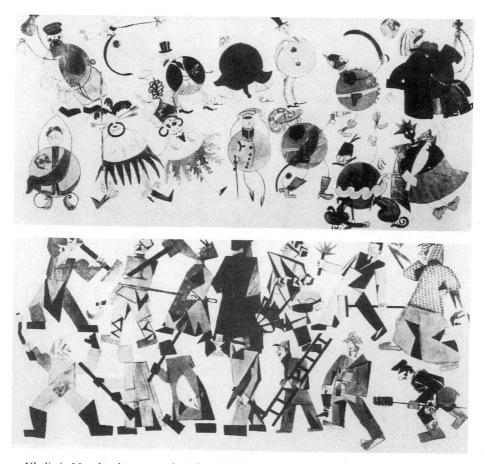

Vladimir Mayakovsky was a talented graphic artist as well as a poet and playwright. In 1919 he made his own designs for his play Mystery Bouffe, *which had previously been staged with designs by Malevich. These costume renderings are done in watercolor on large sheets of brown paper. (a) The "Clean" include well-fed foreigners, a speculator, a priest, and a diplomat. (b) The "Unclean" include a soldier of the Red Army, a lamplighter, a truck driver, a miner, a baker, a laundress, a fisherman, and others.*

Meyerhold went to Yalta in 1919 to get treatment for tuberculosis. There he got caught up in the civil war, was arrested and nearly executed by the Whites, but survived to support the Reds when they recaptured the area. Appointed by Lunacharsky to head the Theater Section of the Commissariat for Enlightenment, Meyerhold promoted "October in the Theater." This initiative was particularly aimed at established theaters like the Moscow Art Theater, which had not altered their repertoires or production approaches to reflect postrevolutionary reality. To set an example of the vigorous new propagandist theater he advocated, Meyerhold took over the artistic direction of a Moscow theater, which he named R.S.F.S.R. Theater No. 1. However, Lunacharsky's and Lenin's conservative tastes in art were vindicated when, under the New Economic Policy, many theaters returned to a profit-making status and demonstrated that the general public preferred the tried and true in art as opposed to the avant-garde. Meyerhold resigned his Theater Section post in 1921. Later that year he became director of Moscow's state-sponsored theater training workshops; one of his pupils in the first two-year directing class was Sergei Eisenstein, who would later become the greatest of the Soviet film directors. All his life, Eisenstein professed the profound influence of Meyerhold on his own work and declared that he had "never loved, revered, and respected anyone as much" as his teacher Meyerhold.

In his workshops, Meyerhold began developing an approach to acting that he called "biomechanics." Proceeding from the premise that emotion could be expressed through physical means, he focused on "the mechanics of the body." The body's resources should be exercised and utilized according to scientific principles, like a technically proficient machine. His actors were trained in the skills of circus performers, athletes, dancers, acrobats, fencers. In 1922 he staged a production of Belgian dramatist Fernand Crommelynck's Le Cocu magnifique (The Magnanimous Cuckold, 1920) with a cast composed entirely of his workshop students. The setting, designed by Lyubov Popova, was intended to serve as a "machine for acting" that would offer opportunities for biomechanical performance, as well as allow economies in construction and backstage personnel. The result was a stage-filling, unpainted wooden construction with a number of moving parts as well as ramps, platforms, stairs, a ladder, a slide, and a revolving door. The huge disk and wheels on the upstage side of the framework revolved at varying speeds to suit the tempo of the scenes, and they suggested metaphorically the waterwheels of the play's millhouse setting. Popova had already won recognition for her constructivist sculptures and "architectronic" paintings, but it was her setting for The Magnanimous Cuckold—as well as Meyerhold's brilliant utilization of its possibilities—that initiated constructivism as a major production style in Soviet golden age theater.

In 1923 Meyerhold formed his Meyerhold Theater company and achieved popular success with Sergei Tretyakov's Strana perekrestok (Earth Rampant, adapted from Marcel Martinet's La Nuit; 1923), which he staged as a revolutionary drama. Motorcycles and cars were driven down the aisles of the auditorium and onto the stage; civil war slogans were projected on screens; spotlights were visibly operated from the auditorium; farce and tragedy overlapped in the action. Earth Rampant rescued the Meyerhold Theater from a financial condition so precarious that its electricity had been cut off for nonpayment on the very day that Meyerhold was honored as the sixth "People's Artist of the Republic"; he

The constructivist setting designed by Lyubov Popova for Meyerhold's production of The Magnanimous Cuckold *featured a rotating disk on which were painted all the consonants from the Belgian dramatist Crommelynck's name.*

This moment in the action of Meyerhold's The Magnanimous Cuckold *suggests the use of the setting as a "machine for acting."*

In response to Lunacharsky's 1923 slogan "Back to Ostrovsky!," Meyerhold staged his own adaptation of Ostrovsky's The Forest *in a constructivist setting.*

Erast Garin played a bespectacled Khlestakov and Zinaida Raikh played the Mayor's wife in Meyerhold's 1926 production of Gogol's The Inspector General.

was the first stage director to be so recognized. 1923 was also the centenary of the birth of Alexander Ostrovsky, and Lunacharsky took the occasion to issue an official slogan: "Back to Ostrovsky!" The idea was to encourage a return to realism as the artistic mode that would be most directly appealing to the masses. Meyerhold's response was to stage Ostrovsky's *Les* (The Forest, 1871) as a series of blackout scenes, the title of each scene projected on a screen above the stage. The actors were costumed not for verisimilitude, but as "social masks." Elements of the unit setting and incongruous props were also used nonrealistically. According to Edward Braun, it was the most popular Soviet production of the period, remaining in the repertoire fourteen years, with over seventeen hundred performances.

Another of Meyerhold's greatest productions was Gogol's *The Inspector General*, which unleashed a storm of controversy in 1926. Some defended Meyerhold's right to interpret Gogol's comedy as a tragedy; others—including leftists who normally supported his work—saw his innovations as "decadent." Most were unable to grasp all the complexities of Meyerhold's interpretation—the interplay of stereotype and psychological subtext, interpolated pantomimic business, the famous bribery scene in which a hand holding a wad of bills was thrust through each of eleven doors arranged in a semicircle on stage, the "musical" form applied to the action—in a performance that ran over four hours. *The Inspector General* remained in the repertoire until 1938. On the basis of these and his many other exciting productions, there can be no doubt that all of the theatrical innovations with which Bertolt Brecht has long been credited were originated by Meyerhold.

Meyerhold continued to follow his own road in the 1930s, but was increasingly subjected to criticism for his "formalist" tendencies. Formalism, or an emphasis on form over content, was condemned in the Stalinist period as antithetical to the doctrine of socialist realism, which demands realistic content in harmony with the spirit of socialism. Meyerhold staged Mayakovsky's *The Bedbug* in 1929 and *Banya* (The Bathhouse) in 1930. Both plays satirically reflect the former revolutionary idealist's growing disillusionment with the direction in which the new society was heading, and both were criticized by the Russian Association of Proletarian Writers (RAPP). The satire of Soviet bureaucracy in *The Bathhouse* drew such fire from the critics that many of the artists' friends prudently stayed away. Mayakovsky, further depressed by the public's shunning of a twenty-year retrospective exhibit of his graphic art, committed suicide in 1930 at the age of thirty-six.

The Meyerhold Theater was liquidated in 1938. It was thanks to Sergei Eisenstein's courageous secreting of Meyerhold's papers that they have survived. And Konstantin Stanislavsky demonstrated considerable courage and generosity by offering Meyerhold a job at the Moscow Art

Theater. Before Stanislavsky died later that year, both men had the satisfaction of knowing—despite the years of striving in apparently opposite directions—the depth of respect that each felt for the other's work. On June 17, 1939, Meyerhold spoke at the All-Union Conference of Stage Directors. No transcript of his remarks has been verified as authentic, but it is believed that he began with a scripted speech recanting his formalist tendencies, but ultimately broke away from that text to uphold the principle of free artistic expression in all its variety. Three days later he disappeared. Although his fate remained a mystery for many years, the savage murder and mutilation of his wife, actress Zinaida Raikh, was reported in the *New York Times* a month later (July 18, 1939). It is now known that Meyerhold endured seven months of interrogation and torture in Moscow's Butyrsky prison, and was executed by firing squad at Lefortovo prison on February 2, 1940.

Sergei Eisenstein's stage and film directing must be counted as one of the glories of the Soviet golden age. He started out as a scenic designer at the Moscow Proletcult Theatre in 1920. His success in that capacity—and his creativity fueled on the side by two years of workshop sessions with Vsevolod Meyerhold—led to Eisenstein's appointment as director of his own Proletcult Theatre workshop. His very popular 1923 production of Ostrovsky's *The Diary of a Scoundrel* was adapted to a circus setting and incorporated acrobatics, juggling, a trapeze, a tightrope, and even a short film. The influence of Meyerhold is clear in Eisenstein's rationale: "A gesture expands into gymnastics, rage is expressed through a somersault, exaltation through a *salto-mortale,* lyricism on 'the mast of death.' The grotesque of this style permitted leaps from one type of expression to another, as well as unexpected intertwinings of two expressions." The production also tested Eisenstein's theory of "montage of attractions" that was to inform his subsequent innovations in film editing. Eisenstein became best known as the director of such extraordinary silent films as *Battleship Potemkin* (1925), *October* (1927), *Alexander Nevsky* (1938), and *Ivan the Terrible* (1945).

Evgeny Vakhtangov's work has been characterized as the successful synthesis of Stanislavsky's realism and Meyerhold's theatricality. Stanislavsky regarded Vakhtangov as his most brilliant pupil, and Vakhtangov always revered Stanislavsky, even as his directorial style was moving ever closer to that of Meyerhold. Vakhtangov joined the Moscow Art Theater as an actor in 1911, but he pursued many simultaneous teaching and directing opportunities almost from the beginning. He headed the Moscow Art Theater's First Studio while working with his own student group, the Mansurov Studio, which eventually became the Third Studio. There he developed the distinctive style that he called "fantastic realism": an acting style that recognized the importance of the character's inner reality blended with such creative distortions as grotesque makeup, expressive movement, eclectic costuming, and dropping character to commune with the audience briefly before resuming, with total inner belief, the persona of the character. In simple terms, he combined character psychology with theatrical stylization.

Vakhtangov directed his two most famous productions during the last year of his life, shortly before he died of cancer in 1922. These were S. Ansky's *The Dybbuk* at the Habimah Theater and Carlo Gozzi's *Turandot* at the Third Studio, (which became the Vakhtangov Theater in 1926). In a deliberate counterpoint to the dark mysticism of the Jewish folk play and the privations suffered by the public in those difficult times, he chose to stage the Chinese fairy-tale play *Turandot* in a lively commedia dell'arte style, with an air of improvisatory spontaneity, masks, brightly colored costumes, and a fanciful abstract setting by Ignati Nivinsky. "We need a festival," he said. Rehearsals were held late at night, after the theater's regular performances, with the mortally ill director on a daybed in the auditorium. Its success was legendary, and it remained in the Vakhtangov Theater repertoire for over fifty years.

Vakhtangov's direction of *The Dybbuk* gave the Habimah Theater its greatest success. Written by Solomon Ansky in 1914, the mystical tale of a young Jewish bride possessed by a *dybbuk* (spirit) was first produced in its original Yiddish by the Vilna Troupe in 1920, and it eventually became a staple of the Yiddish-language popular theaters everywhere. The Habimah Theater, however, was organized by Nahum Zemach expressly for the purpose of producing plays in the rarely spoken Hebrew language. Determined that his production standards would be higher than those of the Yiddish theaters, Zemach went to Stanislavsky for advice in 1917. His timing was fortuitous, as the new revolutionary government not only abolished censorship in the theater, but was encouraging the revival of minority languages and cultures. Stanislavsky took a personal interest in Zemach's cause; he appointed Vakhtangov to head a studio for the group, and he himself conducted over twenty classes there. The Habimah premiered in 1918 with an evening of four Jewish one-acts directed by Vakhtangov. For the Hebrew-language premiere of *The Dybbuk*, Vakhtangov studied Jewish folklore and religion. Although he worked from a Russian translation of the play, he was sensitive to the musical rhythms of Hebrew. His "fantastic realism" allowed him to incorporate many expressionistic elements. Nikolai Evreinov commented on the production: "To take this folklore, all this humor of Jewish life, and make of it an integral, deeply moving, organic part of a mystery play, calls not for ability, but—and I say this without hesitation—genius. For me the ultimate demonstration of Vakhtangov's genius lies in the fact that, though I do not understand Hebrew, I was

Aleksandr Ostrovsky would not have recognized his own 1868 play The Diary of a Scoundrel *in Sergei Eisenstein's 1923 theatricalist interpretation at Moscow's Proletcult Theater.*

Evgeny Vakhtangov's 1922 production of Gozzi's Turandot *mingled commedia del-'arte, art deco, and Chinese fantasy. The long white beard of the old man at center is improvised from an ascot worn with a dinner suit in the prologue.*

constantly excited, and my excitement rose and fell with the rhythm of the plot." Vakhtangov died four months after the opening, but the production remained in the Habimah's repertoire for forty-three years. The Habimah left Russia in 1926, toured Europe and the United States for several years, and settled in Palestine in 1931. In 1949 it became a state theater of Israel.

Another Jewish theater that contributed significantly to the Soviet golden age was the Moscow Jewish State Theater, founded in 1917 by Alexander Granovsky. It is believed that this theater was originally encouraged by the Bolsheviks to divert attention from the Habimah, which was associated with Zionism. The sophisticated Granovsky had traveled in western Europe and was drawn to experimentations in nonrealism. He explored a variety of material, from Jewish biblical and folk plays to Maeterlinckian symbolism. He gathered some extraordinary talent, including designers Marc Chagall, Mstislav Dobouzhinsky, and Natan Altman, and the great actor Solomon Mikhoels. Perhaps the outstanding work of the Granovsky years was the 1922 production of Avrom Gold-fadn's *Koldunye* (The Witch, 1877), which might be described as a joyous Purim carnival on a constructivist setting (designed by Isaak Rabinovich). The performances of Mikhoels as the peddler and Benjamin Zuskin as the witch established them as among the finest actors in Moscow. During the company's 1928–29 tour of Europe, Granovsky defected to the west. Mikhoels assumed the directorship just when Stalin was beginning his crackdown on the arts. By steering a careful course with the authorities, Mikhoels kept his theater alive for twenty years. His greatest role during that period was King Lear, of which Edward Gordon Craig said: "Since the time of my teacher, the great Henry Irving, I do not remember an actor who has touched me to the very bottom of my soul as Mikhoels did with his King Lear." The short, unregal-looking Mikhoels achieved "shocking" poignancy with surprising gestures like the final one, described by Ludmila Kafanova: "He lay down beside the dead Cordelia and tried to kiss her. Unable to reach, he kissed his fingers and touched them to his daughter's lips. His hand flew up and, uttering an abrupt laugh, he died." With Zuskin in the role of the Fool and Alexander Tishler's metaphorical fairground-booth setting, that 1935 production was the brightest spot in a culturally wasted decade. However, Stalin's anti-Semitic campaign finally destroyed the Jewish State Theater; in 1948 Mikhoels was lured to the outskirts of Minsk, beaten, and thrown in front of an oncoming truck.

Only recently has the directorial achievement of the 1935 *King Lear* been properly credited, according to Konstantin Rudnitsky. The explanation for a production that so far surpassed anything that the supposed director Sergei Radlov had previously done is that it was actually conceived by the Ukrainian director Les Kurbas. Kurbas's Berezil Theater, which he founded in Kiev in 1922, is now recognized as one of the most innovative of the Soviet golden age. Much influenced by Max Reinhardt and other western European theater he had seen, Kurbas developed his own brand of expressionism with strong emphasis on musical elements. He used a constructivist setting for Kaiser's *Gas I* and for a dramatization of Upton Sinclair's *Jimmie Higgins,* both in 1923. His 1924 "tragi-farcical" *Macbeth,* regarded as one of the best Shakespeare productions of the decade, had a coronation finale that was widely imitated: a clownlike bishop crowned Malcolm, who was immediately stabbed by a new pretender to the throne. After the bishop calmly picked up the crown and placed it on the assassin's head, that king in turn was stabbed. And so on through a whole line of kings.

If there is one other golden age director who would rank on a par with Meyerhold, Vakhtangov, and Stanislavsky, it is Aleksandr Tairov. With his wife, actress Alice Koonen, he opened the Kamerny Theater in Moscow in 1914. There he worked meticulously through a variety of plays to define and refine what he called a "synthetic theater." This idea called for a fusion of popular and decorative arts with dance and drama. From his inaugural production, the Sanskrit drama *Shakuntala* by Kalidasa, Tairov used the actor's body as his primary expressive instrument. Against Pavel Kuznetsov's colorful backdrops based upon ancient Hindu motifs, the half-naked actors conveyed emotion through gesture and dance movement while creating aesthetically beautiful compositions. Tairov's most famous prerevolutionary production, Isidor Annensky's *Thamyris Kitharodos* (Famira Kifared, 1906; produced 1916), marked the stage design debut of avant-garde artist Aleksandra Ekster. The irregular floor of her setting and the costumes she conceived as "living sculptures" were integral to Tairov's use of distinctive rhythms and patterns of movement for the bacchanalian Dionysians as opposed to the orderly Apollonians. Tairov and Ekster achieved similarly successful organic relationships between the actor-dancer and the "rhythmically organized space" of the stage with Oscar Wilde's *Salomé* in 1917 and Shakespeare's *Romeo and Juliet* in 1921. Among the other outstanding designers with whom Tairov collaborated were Natalia Goncharova, Alexander Vesnin, and Vadim Ryndin. In the 1920s, Tairov produced more foreign plays—including plays by American authors Eugene O'Neill and Sophie Treadwell—than any other Soviet director. In the 1930s, his preoccupation with form and feeling put him at odds with the regime's insistence on social content presented in a realistic vein. His tenuous survival might be attributed to the success of his earlier foreign tours, which had given him an international reputation, and to the remarkable triumph of his production of Vsevolod Vishnevsky's *Optimisticheskaya Tragediya* (Optimistic Tragedy, 1932), a socialist realist drama about the civil war. Although Tairov was honored as a "People's

The legendary 1935 production of King Lear *at Moscow's State Jewish Theater featured Benjamin Zuskin as the Fool and Solomon Mikhoels as Lear.*

Aleksandra Ekster designed this cubist-influenced formal setting for Tairov's 1921 production of Romeo *and* Juliet. *The steps, ramps, bridges, and balustrades provided abundant opportunity for the choreographed movement that was a signature of the Kamerny Theater.*

Artist" in 1935, he continued to come under attack for his formalist tendencies, and in 1937 his theater was forcibly merged with that of another prominent director, Nikolai Okhlopkov. However, the union of their two contrasting personalities and artistic credos was not successful. The Kamerny was closed in 1949, and Tairov died in 1950.

An amazing amount of talent flourished in the 1920s, only to be wásted after Stalin came to power. Director Nikolai Evreinov emigrated to Paris in 1925. Michael Chekhov, an outstanding actor, made a narrow escape to the west in 1928 and enjoyed a long, successful career as an actor-director-teacher in the United States. Filmmaker Vsevolod Pudovkin's best work ended with *Storm Over Asia* in 1928, Alexander Dovzhenko's with *Earth* in 1930. Sergei Eisenstein's filmmaking was severely hampered in his last years before he died in 1948, and his *Ivan the Terrible, Part II* was not released until 1958. Among the finest playwrights, there were other tragic losses besides that of the dynamic poet-playwright Vladimir Mayakovsky. Sergei Tretyakov, whose dramatizations of revolutionary fervor—most notably *Ruchi, Kitai* (Roar, China!, 1926)—were second only to those of Mayakovsky, turned to translation in the 1930s, but was arrested in 1937 and died in a prison camp. Nikolai Erdmann, who had been hailed for *The Mandate* and *The Suicide* as "the new Gogol," had his plays suppressed in 1932. For having "calumnied Soviet reality," he was restricted to the city of Kalinin and prohibited from literary activity; it was reported that he never again spoke above a whisper. After three superb plays—*Zagovor chuvstv* (The Conspiracy of Feelings, 1929), *Tri tolstyaka* (Three Fat Men, 1930), *Spisok blagodeyanii* (A List of Assets, 1931)—as well as some short stories, Yuri Olesha fell silent. The short fiction writer Isaak Babel, author of two plays, *Zakat* (Sunset, 1928) and *Marya* (Maria, 1935), owed his survival into the thirties to the protection of Maxim Gorky. He was arrested in 1939, and all his unpublished writing was destroyed; he is believed to have died in prison in 1941.

Finally, one playwright of the era must be signaled above all others: Mikhail Bulgakov. After completing a degree in medicine at the University of Kiev in 1916, he witnessed the numerous changes of government as that city was taken over in successive waves by Ukrainian nationalists, Germans, Poles, and the Red Army. This experience resulted in his novel *The White Guard* (1925), which he dramatized at Stanislavsky's invitation as *Dni Turbinikh* (Days of the Turbins, 1926). The difficulties that Bulgakov encountered in rehearsal eventually impelled him to write a novel satirizing the Moscow Art Theatre personnel, *Black Snow: A Theatrical Novel* (1937; published 1965). *Days of the Turbins* opened to a hostile press, which attacked Bulgakov as an "internal emigré," because he did not affect proletarian dress or abandon his prerevolutionary, polite forms of speech. For the public, however, the play was a revelation, as it

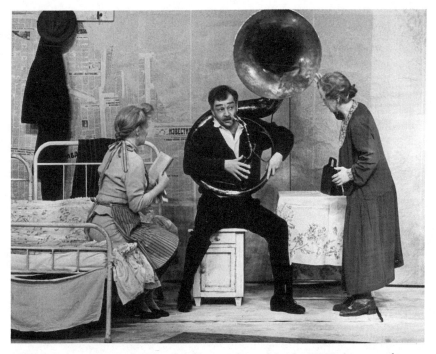

Nikolai Erdmann's comedy The Suicide *was banned in the USSR in 1932, but re-discovered and produced all over the world in the 1970s. Manfred Wekwerth directed this production at the Berliner Ensemble in East Berlin. Photograph by Vera Tenschert, courtesy of the Berliner Ensemble.*

Days of the Turbins *by Mikhail Bulgakov dramatized events of the civil war period in postrevolutionary Russia. It opened at the Moscow Art Theater in 1926 to harsh critical reaction, but the public loved it. Stalin reportedly attended fifteen performances of it over the years. In 1935 the company toured it to New York.*

depicted a family of White Russians as sympathetic human beings instead of perpetuating the Red propaganda image of Whites. *Days of the Turbins* was one of the Moscow Art Theater's most popular postrevolutionary productions.

Bulgakov wrote a total of thirty-six plays, but only five were produced during his lifetime. In 1929 all of his plays were banned from the stage and from publication. Bulgakov then wrote a daring letter to Stalin protesting the regime's reprisals against the intelligentsia; Stalin's response was to appoint Bulgakov to the literary staff of the Moscow Art Theater. There he worked on adaptations and translations of classic plays, and in 1936 saw a final attempt to stage one of his plays. That play, *Kabala sviatosh* (Cabal of Hypocrites; or Molière, 1931), was given three hundred rehearsals, but the brilliant production had only seven performances before the all too evident allegorical meaning caused it to be suppressed. Perhaps the most powerful theatrical images in Bulgakov's drama occur in *Beg* (Flight, 1928), a strangely disturbing depiction of moral degeneration among White Russians as they flee further and further from their homeland. In 1937 Bulgakov diagnosed himself and realized that his neurosclerosis left him little time to live, so he put all his effort into finishing his great novel *The Master and Margarita*. With its first Soviet publication in 1966–67, Bulgakov's reputation was rehabilitated. The steady growth of appreciation for his work has led also to dramatizations of a number of his works of fiction, most notably *The Heart of a Dog* (1925).

BRECHT AND DIALECTICAL THEATER

In the 1920s and early 1930s, there was a free flow of information and frequent contact between Soviet and German theater artists. For example, a Blue Blouse troupe performed in Berlin in 1927, and Meyerhold's company toured there in 1930. Many German periodicals regularly provided in-depth reporting on Soviet theater; among others, *Das neue Russland* published detailed reviews of a number of Meyerhold's productions of the 1920s. Living in Berlin at the time was a young playwright-theater critic whose eventual impact on world theater would be assessed thus by Peter Brook (in *The Empty Space*, 1968): "No one seriously concerned with the theatre can by-pass Brecht. Brecht is the key figure of our time, and all theatre work today at some point starts or returns to his statements and achievement."

Bertolt Brecht's achievements were considerable indeed, but—as Katherine Bliss Eaton and other scholars have demonstrated—they were built directly upon ideas that Brecht appropriated from Meyerhold. Before moving to Berlin in 1924 to work as dramaturg in Max Reinhardt's Deutsches Theater, Brecht had written three full-length plays, which might generally be described as expressionist impulses weighted with leftist politics. He then initiated a lifelong practice of rewriting classic plays by such authors as Christopher Marlowe, Sophocles, Molière, Shakespeare, and George Farquhar. The most famous of these, *Die Dreigroschenoper* (The Threepenny Opera, 1928), used the plot and characters from John Gay's *Beggar's Opera* (1728), with a heavy added dose of Marxist ideology. Accused of plagiarism, Brecht replied: "Copying is not easier; it is an art in itself. . . . The pitiful fear of members of our society that one could question their originality is closely connected with their shabby concept of property." Despite his declared scorn for the concept of "intellectual property," he sued the company that made a film version of the popular play, because the filmmaker preferred not to alter it, as Brecht wanted, to reflect Brecht's increasingly radical political views. The enormously successful production of *The Threepenny Opera* at Berlin's Theater am Schiffbauerdamm (where today's Berliner Ensemble is housed) brought together such talents as composer Kurt Weill, scenic designer Caspar Neher, and actress Lotte Lenya. And it helped to shape many of the ideas that Brecht was soon to schematize as what he called "epic theater." Many of those ideas were also tested in the productions of Erwin Piscator, who directed plays of political commitment at Berlin's Volksbühne from 1924 and at the Theater am Nollendorfplatz from 1927 to 1930. Brecht worked with Piscator at the latter theater and was strongly influenced by Piscator's awareness of the most recent developments in Soviet theater as well as by his interest in technology. Piscator had been, as early as 1924, one of the first directors to use filmed sequences within a play.

Brecht's essay "Notes on the Opera," published with the text of Brecht and Weill's *Aufstieg und Fall der Stadt Mahagonny* (The Rise and Fall of the City of Mahagonny, 1930), includes a chart setting forth some distinctions between the "dramatic theater," which he regarded as old-fashioned, and the "epic theater," which he proposed as an alternative. He would later expand upon his concept of epic theater in his most important theoretical work, *A Short Organum for the Theater* (1948). However, his posthumous notes (1956) reveal that he intended to substitute the term "dialectical theater" for "epic," apparently because "epic" suggested formalism, whereas "dialectical" would emphasize the constant process of change in man and society that is an important feature of Marxist ideology. In essence, Brecht wanted to use the theater to put social conditions on trial. This could not be done effectively in the "dramatic theater," which still embraced the precepts of Aristotle's *Poet-*

Mack the Knife visits the brothel in this scene from the original 1928 Berlin production of The Threepenny Opera *by Bertolt Brecht. Courtesy of the German Information Center.*

Erich Engel directed the 1960 revival of The Threepenny Opera *with sets by Karl von Appen. This scene shows the arrival of the Mounted Messenger just in time to save Macheath from hanging. Courtesy of the German Information Center.*

The Theater am Schiffbauerdamm, where The Threepenny Opera *premiered in 1928, today houses the Berliner Ensemble. Photograph courtesy of Ute Eichel.*

Brecht's folk play Puntila and His Hired Servant Matti *was written in 1941 and first performed in Zurich in 1948. This is a scene from the 1956 production at the Stadttheater in Bonn. Courtesy of the German Information Center.*

ics, because such theater depends upon the spectator's willing suspension of disbelief, which is achieved by drawing him into the plot and making him care about the characters. According to Brecht, the spectator's investment of emotion and his eagerness to learn the outcome of the story obstruct his ability to analyze objectively what he sees on stage. Brecht's epic or dialectical theater, on the contrary, would confront the spectator with the plot rather than drawing him into it. The use of such devices as narration, arguments, placards announcing each episode's action in advance, screens with projected images that comment on the action—all would help the spectator to remain objective, to think rather than feel, and to evaluate what happens on stage.

The key concept in Brecht's theory is what he called *Verfremdungseffekt,* which might be roughly translated as an effect of alienation or distanciation. There can be little doubt that Brecht educed this idea from the Russian formalist Viktor Shklovsky's *ostranenie* (estrangement). Brecht undoubtedly became familiar with it through his friend, Soviet dramatist Sergei Tretyakov, who had worked closely with Meyerhold since 1922. Brecht proposed the term *Verfremdungseffekt* only after his 1935 visit to Moscow, when he stayed in Tretyakov's apartment. The idea of "alienation" or "distanciation" is to remind the spectator constantly that what he is seeing is not real life but a theatrical construct; thus the spectator will watch critically rather than empathically. Some specific techniques for achieving this have become quite commonplace in the modern theater: exposed lighting instruments, episodic action, the incorporation of slides and filmed sequences, grotesque costumes or makeup, props that show the wear and tear of frequent use, songs and narration that interrupt suspenseful sequences, acting techniques borrowed from Chinese theater, exaggerated gestures, music that comments on the action. Although there are occasional references to Meyerhold in Brecht's writings, Eaton points out that "by 1939, the year Meyerhold was arrested. Brecht was giving himself and Piscator credit for pioneering epic theater." Certainly, Brecht must be credited with winning broad, international acceptance for this kind of socially conscious theatricalism—something that Meyerhold might have achieved only through years of touring his productions outside Russia. Brecht did it largely through self-promotion and by writing good plays.

It was the brilliant theatricality and intellectual provocativeness of Brecht's plays—even in those with borrowed plots—that sold the theory. The best of his fifty or so plays, besides *The Threepenny Opera,* are: *Mutter Courage und Ihre Kinder* (Mother Courage and Her Children, 1939), *Leben des Galilei* (The Life of Galileo, 1939), *Der Gute Mensch von Sezuan* (The Good Person of Setzuan, 1940), and *Der Kaukasische Kreidekreis* (The Caucasian Chalk Circle, 1945). The latter play was written in California, where Brecht and his wife, Austrian actress Helene Weigel,

Manfred Wekwerth directed the 1959 production of The Resistible Rise of Arturo Ui *at the Berliner Ensemble. Courtesy of the German Information Center.*

Brecht's The Resistible Rise of Arturo Ui *(written 1941, first performed 1948) is a parable—using Chicago gangsters and businessmen—of Hitler's rise to power. Courtesy of the Berliner Ensemble.*

Above, Brecht's version of Shakespeare's Coriolanus *was produced at the Berliner Ensemble in 1964 under the direction of Manfred Wekwerth and Joachim Teñschert. The major scenic unit was the huge revolving gate, one side of which represented Rome (shown here) and the other Corioli. Courtesy of the German Information Center.*

Right, the Austrian actress Helene Weigel, who was Brecht's wife, played the title role in Mother Courage and Her Children *at the Berliner Ensemble under the direction of Erich Engel and Brecht. Photograph by Hainer Hill, courtesy of the Berliner Ensemble.*

Robert Pinget (b. 1919) is usually identified as an absurdist, and his plays are often compared to those of Samuel Beckett. This 1977 production of his Paralchimie *(1972) was produced at the Petit Odéon in Paris. Shown here are Raymond Acquaviva, Michel Aumont, and Catherine Salviat. Courtesy of French Cultural Services.*

had taken refuge in 1941 after years of exile. After they left Germany in 1933, Brecht's citizenship was revoked and his books were banned. For a time, they found temporary refuge in Denmark, Sweden, and Finland. In 1941 the Brecht family obtained American immigration visas and traveled, just ahead of the invading Nazis, to Moscow, thence by Trans-Siberian railway to Vladivostok and across the Pacific to California. Hollywood had lured many other German exiles, including Brecht's sometime collaborator Lion Feuchtwanger, novelist Thomas Mann, film-maker Fritz Lang, and actor Peter Lorre. In 1947 Brecht was summoned to testify before the House Un-American Activities Committee. He left the United States immediately afterward. In 1949 he settled perma-nently in East Berlin, where he founded the Berliner Ensemble. Despite the difficulties presented by the Communist imposition of socialist real-ism as the only acceptable approach to art, over the years the Berliner Ensemble presented most of Brecht's plays, featuring the superb scenic designs of Karl von Appen. Brecht died in 1956, but that theater con-tinues to profess his legacy.

THE THEATER OF THE ABSURD

During the 1950s in Paris, several iconoclastic playwrights first saw their plays produced. Besides the fact that they all wrote in French, the Romanian-born Eugène Ionesco, the Irish-born Samuel Beckett, the Russian-born Arthur Adamov, the Spanish-born Fernando Arrabal, and Frenchman Jean Tardieu displayed certain common characteristics in their early plays. None of them, however, saw himself as part of a larger aesthetic movement unless it was something vaguely referred to as *le nouveau théâtre* (new theater). Indeed, it was only toward the end of the decade that a pattern became evident in retrospect and was dubbed "theater of the absurd." So imprecise were its boundaries, however, that Martin Esslin's 1961 book *The Theatre of the Absurd* (which contributed more than any other work to the popularization of the term) included almost every out-of-the-mainstream dramatist who had come to prominence in the 1950s. Other avant-garde dramatists produced in Paris from the late 1940s to early 1960s, whose plays exhibit some but not all aspects of the absurd, are Jean Genet, Boris Vian, Georges Schéhadé, Henri Pichette, Robert Pinget, Jacques Audiberti, Jean Vauthier. Some critics have even made a case for Belgian dramatist Michel de Ghelderode as an absurdist, although much of his work was written earlier, and his Flemish inspiration puts him in a class by himself. A second wave of absurdists, who wrote in languages other than French, appeared in the early 1960s—Americans Edward Albee and Arthur Kopit, England's N. F. Simpson and Harold Pinter, Germany's Wolfgang Hildesheimer and Günter Grass, Spain's Lauro Olmo and José-María Bellido, Poland's Slawomir Mrozek and Tadeusz Różewicz, Czechoslovakia's Vaclav Havel, and Andrei Amalrik in the USSR—but changing times soon carried their work in other directions.

The forerunners of theater of the absurd can be readily identified: Alfred Jarry and his Père Ubu, the surrealists, and the existentialists. Existential philosophy, first formulated by the nineteenth-century Danish philosopher Søren Kierkegaard, takes as its fundamental concern the nature of existence, as opposed to the search for transcendent essences. The nature of a human being is not simply to be what one is, but constantly to achieve self-definition by what one thinks—or, in other words, by the choices one makes. Because of its focus on the individual and on making choices, there is a natural affinity between existentialism and the drama. The two leading French existentialist philosophers, Jean-Paul Sartre and Albert Camus, were also playwrights, as was the Christian existentialist philosopher Gabriel Marcel. In such plays as *Les Mouches* (The Flies, 1943), *Huis Clos* (No Exit, 1944), *Les Mains sales* (Dirty Hands, 1948), and *Les Séquestrés d'Altona* (The Condemned of Altona, 1959), Sartre dramatized his famous precepts: "A man is the sum of his actions"; "Hell is other people"; "Man is condemned to be free." The difficult situations depicted in his plays carried strong resonances for a public that had recently lived through the horrors of World War II in Europe. Albert Camus exercised an even more direct influence on the dramatists of the 1950s through his famous essay *Le Mythe de Sisyphe* (The Myth of Sisyphus, 1942). Subtitled *Essai sur l'absurde* (Essay on the Absurd), it took as a metaphor of modern existence the endless, meaningless task to which the gods condemned Sisyphus: repeatedly pushing a huge boulder to the peak of a mountain, only to see it roll back again to the bottom. Condemned to carry out the task of existence in a universe where the fundamental questions are never answered, modern man feels cut adrift and any action seems meaningless or absurd.

A number of other factors contributed to the sense of absurdity that was crystalized in so much art of the 1950s, like the dribbled abstract expressionist painting of Jackson Pollock or the poetry of Jack Kerouac, Gregory Corso, Allen Ginsberg, and others of the "beat generation," or the French "new novel" and *nouvelle vague* cinema (1958–62). Rapid economic recovery from the war brought a decade of unprecedented prosperity. A home with a picture window, a pink convertible with spaceshiplike tail fins, patio barbeque equipment, and a television set—all came within the reach of the middle classes; and along with it, critics said, came rampant materialism and mindless conformity. The novelty of television meant that the traditional family dinner turned into a group of viewers seated in a semicircle, eating "frozen TV dinners" on rickety metal "TV tables;" a bombardment of images replaced the art of conversation. At the same time, a deep-seated fear of Communism, nurtured by the cold war, led many families to build and stock backyard bomb shelters. Perhaps most absurd of all was the continued atmospheric testing of the atomic and hydrogen bombs. In assimilating all these factors, the theater of the absurd neither preached nor proposed solutions; it merely responded to conditions as they were.

The perceived meaninglessness of human existence was reflected in the breakdown of traditional dramatic structure. Instead of building a narrative logically through cause and effect to a satisfying *dénouement*, the absurdists merely depicted a static situation like the one in Beckett's *Waiting for Godot*, or—as in Ionesco's *The Bald Soprano* and *The Lesson*—used a circular construction to avoid arriving at a conclusion. Character psychology was abandoned; now the persons of the drama functioned solely as vehicles for action. Their language was often nonsensical, or tended to garble ideas more often than communicate them. Tardieu's *L'A.B.C. de notre vie* (The ABC of Our Life, 1959) uses a largely unintelligible chorus murmuring under the speeches of The Protagonist. Finally—perhaps in response to the materialism of the decade, or perhaps as a reification of the television-induced cult of the image in place of language—objects became an important focus of the theater of the absurd. Objects multiply, to highly theatrical effect, in a number of Ionesco's plays, as in *The Chairs* and *The New Tenant*. In Beckett's plays, objects—like the contents of Winnie's handbag in *Happy Days,* or Estragon's boot in *Waiting for Godot*—are examined with great meticulousness. A pinball machine is the central concern of Adamov's *Le Ping Pong.* In Jean Vauthier's *Le Personnage combattant* (The Character against Himself, 1955), the action derives from a typewriter, the contents of a suitcase, and the furnishings of a hotel room.

Two plays may be said to have launched absurdism in the theater. The first was Eugene Ionesco's *La Cantatrice chauve* (The Bald Soprano, 1949), which Nicholas Bataille staged in Paris in 1950. Although that production angered its audiences, a revival not long afterward on a bill with *La Leçon* (The Lesson, 1950) in a tiny left-bank theater achieved a run of over four decades. The second play that signaled the theater of the absurd as a phenomenon deserving of serious attention was Samuel Beckett's *En attendant Godot* (Waiting for Godot, 1952), which was first staged by Roger Blin in 1953. Even more remarkable than that production's success with the general public has been the play's staying power. Forty years later, *Waiting for Godot* continues to be revived in dozens of languages, as have many of Beckett's other plays. This "tragicomedy" in which two interdependent tramps, Vladimir and Estragon, pass the time while waiting for a Godot who never comes, is undoubtedly the single most significant and influential piece of dramatic writing of the twentieth century. As a metaphor for the human condition, it unflinchingly depicts the bleakness of existence, as exemplified by the play's most famous line: "They give birth astride of a grave, the light gleams an instant, then it's night once more." And yet, that sober vision gives rise to exquisite comedy as well as the thought that the very ability to wait for something, whether it ever comes or not, is cause for celebration. *Waiting for Godot* transcends the absurdist aesthetic that it defined.

Beckett's other important plays of the 1950s were *Fin de partie* (Endgame, 1957) and *La dernière bande* (Krapp's Last Tape, 1958). Like his novels, they exhibit his characteristic purity of style tinged with bawdy Irish humor. After his *Oh! les beaux jours* (Happy Days, 1963), his plays became increasingly brief, as if to demonstrate how few resources are necessary to sum up the meaning of existence. Ionesco, in contrast, became increasingly verbose after a long succession of short pieces in the 1950s. His full-length allegorical comedy *Rhinocéros* (1960) might be

The Pedestrian of the Air (1963) by Eugène Ionesco had its world premiere in Dusseldorf. Beringer, the title character and Ionesco's alter ego is able to stroll about in midair, but he cannot win the understanding of his contemporaries. Photograph by Inter Nationes/Rabanus, courtesy of the German Information Center.

considered a turning point in Ionesco's evolution. Although rhinoceroses multiply throughout the play and the central character can only be called an "antihero," it departs from absurdism in its use of a conventional dramatic structure, and it even went to Broadway without being stigmatized as avant-garde.

Although many critics attempt to classify Jean Genet as an absurdist, his plays—like *Les Bonnes* (The Maids, 1947) and *Le Balcon* (The Balcony,

Samuel Beckett stands at center between Erich Schröder and Hoor Bollwann, two actors from the production of his play Endgame, *which he directed at the Schiller Theater in Bonn. Courtesy of the German Information Center.*

In Beckett's Endgame, *Nagg and Nell are a married couple who live in side-by-side garbage cans. In the background are Hamm and Clov. Courtesy of the German Information Center.*

Madeleine Renaud played Winnie in Samuel Beckett's Oh! les beaux jours *at the Odéon in Paris during the 1960s. It is virtually a one-woman play. In Act 1, Winnie is buried up to her waist in sand; in Act 2, she is buried up to the neck. Photo Lipnitzki, courtesy of French Cultural Services.*

Tadeusz Lomnicki, Poland's outstanding contemporary actor, played the title role in Beckett's Krapp's Last Tape *at the Theater Studio in Warsaw under the direction of Antoni Libera. Photograph by Zygmunt Rytka, courtesy of the Art Center Studio Theater.*

Jean-Louis Barrault played the title role in Jean Vauthier's strenuous one-man play Le Personnage combattant *(The Character against Himself). Courtesy of French Cultural Services.*

Fernando Arrabal was considered an absurdist early in his career. Today he is one of the most produced playwrights in the world. Photograph courtesy of Fernando Arrabal.

1956)—differ from absurd drama in their multileveled but coherently plotted action and in their richly textured language. Furthermore, Genet's bountiful scenic metaphors coupled with an undercurrent of violence and sensuality would seem to place his work more in the tradition of Antonin Artaud.

Fernando Arrabal's traumatic childhood during the Spanish civil war was the major source of the grotesque imagery and bizarre outlook in his plays. Since those characteristics have remained constant in the steady stream of plays he continues to write, it is tempting for critics to see him as a perennial absurdist. He wrote his first plays in 1952–53 with no knowledge of Beckett or Ionesco, but those one-acts were received as theater of the absurd when produced in Paris at the end of the decade. Arrabal subsequently fell in with the aging surrealists, but then founded his own artistic movement, which he called panic theater after the Greek god Pan. The approach is best described in his own words: "I dream of a theatre in which humor and poetry, panic and love are united. The theatrical rite would then be transformed into an *opera mundi*. It would be just like the fantasies of Don Quixote, the nightmares of Alice, the delirium of K, indeed the humanoid dreams that haunt the nights of an IBM machine." On a return visit to Franco's Spain in 1967, Arrabal was arrested and imprisoned for three weeks. After that, he rejected panic theater in favor of what he called guerrilla theater, and he wrote his best work, *Et ils passèrent des menottes aux fleurs* (And They Put Handcuffs on the Flowers, 1969). Chief among his numerous other plays is *L'Architect et l'Empereur d'Assyrie* (The Architect and the Emperor of Assyria, 1967). In Paris and New York, Arrabal's plays have been staged by such outstanding directors as Victor Garcia, Jerome Savary, Jorge Lavelli, and Tom O'Horgan.

Edward Albee's fling with theater of the absurd was brief. His early one-acts, including *The Sandbox* (1959) and *The American Dream* (1960), introduced the little-known aesthetic to American audiences and made his reputation. His masterpiece *Who's Afraid of Virginia Woolf?* (1962) took him to Broadway and headed an outstanding record of subsequent plays. Arthur Kopit's *Oh Dad, Poor Dad, Mama's Hung You in the Closet and I'm Feelin' So Sad* (1960) is one of the most popular absurdist plays that have continued to be staged long after the "movement" has run its course. In addition to the wealth of dramatic literature it engendered, theater of the absurd provided a healthy impetus for greater variety and daring in theatrical production.

THE POLISH AVANT-GARDE

Perhaps the longest continuing tradition of experimental theater in the twentieth century has been that of Poland. The strength of Polish avant-garde theater is the more remarkable in that it has all occurred in government-subsidized or "establishment" theaters; indeed, there was virtually no other kind of theater in Poland from World War II until the severing of former ties to the USSR in 1989. Two related factors are responsible for the many provocative departures from realism in a country within the orbit of the USSR, where formalism in the arts was being treated as a capital offense. One factor was the public's interest in detecting supratextual political meaning in their theater; audiences felt rewarded when they could read into a production some commentary that could not have passed the mass media censors. Although theater censorship was never as severe in Poland as in the USSR (the most serious restriction being against any unfavorable depiction of the Soviets), it was safest not to rely upon the spoken text to carry a message, but to focus upon the communicative power of the visual. Thus, theater artists had a strong incentive to exploit to the fullest the metaphorical possibilities of the elements of production, whether the play was a classical or a contemporary work. The second impetus for the vitality of the avant-garde was the Polish cult of the director. "It is characteristically Polish that the director should be allowed a free hand," states Bohdan Drozdowski, who noted in 1979 that "the number of bizarre, wildly-interpreted productions is always on the increase."

The century's first great innovator, Stanisław Wyspiański, was a poet, dramatist, graphic artist, set designer, stage director, and maker of stained-glass windows and books. Trained as a painter, he expressed himself most readily in images. Drawing upon a solid education in the classics, he wrote his earliest plays on subjects from Greek mythology. After travels in Europe that took him to the theater in Bayreuth, he adopted Richard Wagner's idea of theater as a synthesis of all the arts and expounded it in an influential *Study of Hamlet* (1905). Edward Gordon Craig, Adolph Appia, and the folk heritage of the area around his native Krakow were also important influences. From his study of the Polish Romantics, especially Mickiewicz and Slowacki, Wyspiański learned to incorporate the fantastical in his own plays, a number of which focus upon historical events in medieval Krakow or at the time of the 1830 November Insurrection or the 1848 Spring of Nations. Thematically, all of his plays deal with the problem of Polish liberation; and yet he never allowed his text to dominate in production. To Wyspiański, who directed and designed his own plays (as well as, in 1901, the premiere of Mickiewicz's *Forefathers' Eve*), the poetic dialogue was merely an outline to be scored both visually and musically by actors, costumes, setting, and sound effects. His scenic designs were considered revolutionary in their day.

Wyspiański's most important play, indeed the seminal work for an understanding of modern Polish dramatic literature, is *Wesele* (The Wedding, 1901). The inspiration for this tragicomedy in verse came when Wyspiański attended—in the nearby village of Bronowice, along with various artists, journalists, and aristocrats from the city—the wedding of a Krakow poet and a peasant girl. *The Wedding* suggests that such unity across the social spectrum provided the best hope for the Polish nationalist cause. As the merrymaking continues through the night, underscored by haunting folk melodies, fantastic creatures appear. A fiddle-playing Straw-Man (a figure composed of mulch from the garden) casts a spell on hosts and guests alike, so that the action culminates in a hypnotic dance, symbolic of the people's inability to take concerted action in the nationalist cause. At the 1901 premiere, many Krakovians recognized themselves and took offense at what they perceived as a lampoon; but the play has since served as a source of powerful images and recognizable allusions in Polish drama up to the present day.

Wyspiański's most fantastic play, *Akropolis* (Acropolis, 1903), includes no human characters at all. The dreamlike action occurs in Krakow's historic Wawel castle on a night when statues and figures from the tapestries come to life. This encounter of men, gods, and mythological figures from Polish, classical Greek, and biblical history culminates at sunrise with the arrival of a triumphal figure representing both Apollo and the resurrected Christ. *Acropolis* was not performed in its entirety until 1926, long after Wyspiański's untimely death in 1907 at the age of

In 1901 in Krakow, playwright Stanislaw Wyspianski staged the premiere of Adam Mickiewicz's 1832 drama of Polish nationalism, Forefather's Eve. *Shown here is the ritual of calling forth the ghosts of the dead. Photograph by Tadeusz Kazmierski, courtesy of the Laboratory of Theater Documentation, Polish Academy of Sciences.*

Wyspianski collaborated on the staging and scenic design for the 1901 production of his masterpiece, The Wedding, *in Lvov. Near the end of the play, just before dawn, all the wedding guests are listening to the sound of phantom hoofbeats. Photograph by Tadeusz Kazmierski, courtesy of the Laboratory of Theater Documentation, Polish Academy of Sciences.*

The great Polish director Leon Schiller staged Forefather's Eve *in 1934. Edmund Wiercinski played the priest and Józef Wegrzyn was Konrad in this exorcism scene. Photograph by Tadeusz Kazmierski, courtesy of the Laboratory of Theater Documentation, Polish Academy of Sciences.*

Schiller directed Shakespeare's The Tempest *in 1947 in Lodz. The set was by Wladeslaw Dasewski. Photograph by S. Brzozowski and J. Malarski, courtesy of the Laboratory of Theater Documentation, Polish Academy of Sciences.*

thirty-eight. His theatrical vision was instrumental in the founding in 1913 of Warsaw's Polski Theater, which long held a fine reputation for avant-garde work. It was there that Leon Schiller began his theater career in the position of dramaturg. Schiller, the greatest Polish director of the first half of the century, based his work on Wyspiański's concept of "monumental theater" and was instrumental in keeping Wyspiański's reputation alive in the following decade. Schiller too came under the influence of Edward Gordon Craig and contributed to Craig's periodical *The Mask*. After directing for a time at Juliusz Osterwa's Reduta Theater, in 1924 Schiller founded his own Bogusławski Theater in Warsaw, where he staged an important production of Krasinski's *The Un-Divine Comedy*. His brilliant use of lighting, music, rhythmic gesture and movement animated a wide variety of plays. Despite the militant leftist political tendencies of his work in the 1930s, he never abandoned the poetic atmospheric quality for which he was renowned. As a director, composer, essayist, and teacher, he influenced an entire generation of Polish directors, including such leading directors of the 1940s—60s as Erwin Axer and Kasimierz Dejmek.

Like Wyspiański, Stanislaw Ignacy Witkiewicz was a painter-playwright who achieved his full measure of recognition only posthumously. During his lifetime, the superior reputation of his father's realistic paintings impelled Witkiewicz to explore a more abstract style and to assert his individuality by taking the name Witkacy. In his youth he traveled abroad and fought in the Russian army, then returned to Poland in 1918 to take up his prolific painting and writing of philosophical essays and "comedies with corpses." His mature artistic activity thus coincided exactly with the twenty-one years of Poland's existence as an independent nation, for he committed suicide on September 18, 1939, the day after Russian troops invaded Poland once again. Witkacy expounded his highly developed views on art in essays like his "Introduction to the Theory of Pure Form in the Theater" (1920). He rejected the contemporary theater of his day and proposed instead a theater that would be analogous to painting, one in which form is experienced for its own sake and functions like "an abstract 'drug' enabling us to experience metaphysical feelings." He set out to enlarge the boundaries of the drama by eliminating logic. His nonrealistic use of time and space allows startling juxtapositions, reverse action, repetitions, but always with a sense of the aesthetic harmony of the whole. Among Witkacy's major plays are *Tumor Mózgowicz* (Tumor Brainerd, 1920), *Kurka wodna* (The Water Hen, 1921), *Wariat i zakonnica* (The Madman and the Nun, 1923), and *Szalona lokomotywa* (The Crazy Locomotive, 1923). Few of his forty or so plays were published or produced during his lifetime. Rediscovered in 1955 when his 1922 play *Matwa* (The Cuttlefish) was produced in Krakow, he has come to be regarded as a precursor of the theater of the absurd and, along with Mrozek, one of the century's greatest Polish dramatists.

Witold Gombrowicz, in the preface to his play *Slub* (The Marriage, 1946; published 1953), makes an analogy between Witkacy's "pure form" and his own idea of the life process by which "each person deforms other persons, while being at the same time deformed by them." Such dual deformation is not only a reciprocal struggle but an act of creation that serves merely as a pretext for producing an ultimately unpredictable effect. Jan Kott refers to Grombrowicz's theater as "a duel of grimaces." Czeslaw Milosz describes his "crazy" method as "a game of constant provocation, cornering the reader into an admission of unpalatable truths." Besides *The Marriage*, two other plays by Gombrowicz have continued to hold an important place in the contemporary Polish theatrical repertoire: *Iwona ksiezniczka Burgunda* (Ivonna, Princess of Burgundia, 1935) and *Operetka* (Operetta, 1966).

World War II brought six years of suffering under the brutal Nazi occupiers. Despite the closure of all theaters except those offering light collaborationist entertainment, clandestine theater groups continued to offer avant-garde performances, including a student production of Witkacy's *Madman and the Nun* in 1942. One of the actors in that endeavor was Andrezej Trzebinski, who also edited an underground resistance journal, *Art and the Nation*. The twenty-year-old poet wrote a play, *Aby podniesc róze* (To Pick up the Rose, 1942), in the grotesque tradition of Witkacy and Gombrowicz, about history running amok, but did not live to see its postwar publication (1955) and production (1970). He was shot by the Nazis in 1943 in a random street execution.

After the war, major efforts went into the reconstruction of theaters all over the country; indeed, at the war's end, not a single theater had been left standing in Warsaw. Most were rebuilt by 1949, ironically just in time for the imposition of socialist realism as the only acceptable approach to the arts. Meanwhile, another antiestablishment writer published a series of hundreds of intentionally unstageable miniplays under the title *Teatryzk "Zielona Ges"* (The Little Theater of the Green Goose, 1946–49). The wildly imaginative Konstanty Gałczynski mocked intellectual pretensions in those playlets ranging from a few lines to a couple of pages in length, with titles like *The Atrocious Uncle* (1946), *Hamlet and the Waitress* (1948), and *The Tragic End of Mythology* (1949). In a half-page play entitled *The Flood That Failed in Winter* (1947), for example, Noah announces to his wives, children, and animals that the waters have frozen over, and he asks their consent to turn the ark into a sleigh. The curtain comes down on the ensemble riding up Mount Ararat on a sleigh with bells. Such creativity was suppressed during the Stalinist period, and even the Polish romantic plays were banned once again. However, 1956 marked the beginning of a thaw in the arts and a new blossoming of

The Shoemakers *by Stanislaw Ignacy Witkiewciz (Witkacy) was staged by Jerzy Krasowski at the Polski Theater in Warsaw in 1983. Photograph by Myszkowski.*

This 1932 production of Juliusz Slowacki's Samuel Zborowski *in Lvov was directed by Waclaw Radulski. Tadeusz Bialoszcynski, at center, played Lucifer. Photograph by Tadeusz Kazmierski, courtesy of the Laboratory of Theater Documentation, Polish Academy of Sciences.*

A 1976 production in Gdansk of Tadeusz Różewicz's White Marriage *was directed by Ryszard Major, with scenography by Marian Kolodziej. Photograph by Tadeusz Link.*

Kristian Lupa directed and designed Slawomir Mrozek's On Foot *at the C. K. Norwid Theater in Jelenia Góra in 1982. Photograph by Leszek Strzelec.*

experimental theater, which lasted until 1968. The well-subsidized theaters attracted poets whose ability to use drama as parable stimulated directors and designers to ever greater innovations with scenic metaphor.

Two major dramatists came to the fore in the 1960s. Tadeusz Różewicz was already known as a poet and short story writer when he turned to the theater, beginning with *Kartoteka* (The Card Index, 1960). The fragmentation of reality, and even of human identity, in that and other plays of the 1960s categorized him as an absurdist. However, his outrageous style found fuller and more accessible expression in later plays like *Biale malzenstwo* (White Marriage, 1974) and *The Trap* (1982). Sławomir Mrozek also displayed strong affinities with theater of the absurd in his early short pieces like *The Police* (1958) and *Charlie* (1961). Mrozek gained an international reputation with his first full-length play, *Tango* (1964), which uses a quasi-absurd intergenerational conflict as political allegory. Mrozek's denunciation of the Soviet invasion of Czechoslovakia in 1968 resulted in his exile from Poland. He has continued to write prolifically; *Emigrés* (1974), *On Foot* (1980), and *The Ambassador* (1981) are but a few of his plays that are most frequently staged in Europe.

Several of the leading directors since the 1960s have also been accomplished painters and scene designers. Tadeusz Kantor worked as a stage designer before 1956, when his paintings could not be exhibited. In 1956 he opened his own theater, Cricot 2, with the production of *The Cuttlefish* that revived Witkacy on the Polish stage. His efforts to break away from an overly self-conscious avant-garde led him to concentrate on producing "happenings" in the 1960s. With the publication of his manifesto "The Theater of Death" in 1975, he embarked upon what have been his most internationally renowned productions: *Umarla klasa* (The Dead Class, 1975), *Wielopole, Wielopole* (1980), *Let the Artists Die* (1985), and *I'll Never Go Back* (1988). Jozef Sjana, a painter, narrowly survived death in a concentration camp in his youth, an experience that found expression in his most famous production, *Replika*, in 1971 at Warsaw's Art Center Studio Theater. For this production the audience was seated around a mound of rubble and junk; items like gas masks, bicycle wheels, the leg of a mannequin, and an empty picture frame served as the basis from which a mounting effect of horror was created. Another scenographer-painter, Jerzy Grzegorzewski, was one of the most original directors of the 1970s; his productions of *The Slow Darkening of the Painting* and Brecht's *Threepenny Opera*, both in 1986, combined striking stage images and innovative sound effects. Konrad Swinarski started as a stage designer in 1953 and, until 1975, when he was killed in a plane crash, he was regarded as the leading Polish director of the postwar period. Among his outstanding productions were Büchner's

Jozef Sjna's 1973 production, Replika, *remained in the repertoire of the Art Center Studio Theater of Warsaw repertoire for many years. Photograph by Wojciech Plewinski, courtesy of Polish Academy of Sciences.*

Jerzy Grzegorzewski, one of Poland's most innovative contemporary directors, staged The Slow Darkening of the Painting, *based upon the work of Malcolm Muggeridge, at the Art Center Drama Studio in Warsaw in 1985. Photograph by Wojciech Plewinski, courtesy of Art Center Studio Theater.*

In 1987 Warsaw's Art Center Studio Theater produced variations on Poland's national drama by Mickiewicz. Entitled Forefather's Eve—Improvised, *it was directed by Grzegorzewski. Photograph by Wojciech Plewinski, courtesy of Art Center Studio Theater.*

A popular premiere at Warsaw's Art Center Studio Theater in 1988 was the musical Lips are Silent, but the Soul Sings, *directed and designed by Grzegorzewski and composed by Irina Kluk-Drozdowska. Photograph by Wojciech Plewinski, courtesy of Art Center Studio Theater.*

Pilgrims and Voyagers, *directed and designed by Jerzy Kalina, with music composed by Jan Kaczmarek, at Warsaw's Art Center Studio Theater in 1989, was a succession of powerful images, performed entirely without dialogue, on the theme of Poland's recreation of itself as a nation. Photograph by Zygmunt Rytka, courtesy of Art Center Studio Theater.*

The great postwar designer–director Konrad Swinarski staged Peter Weiss's The Persecution and Assassination of Jean-Paul Marat at the Asylum of Charenton under the Direction of the Marquis de Sade *at the Schiller Theater in West Berlin in 1964. Shown here are Liselotte Rau as Charlotte Corday and Peter Mosbacher as Marat. Courtesy of the German Information Center.*

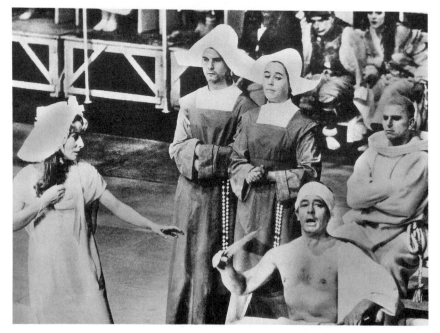

Woyzeck in 1966, Weiss's *Marat/Sade* in 1967, and Mickiewicz's *Forefathers' Eve* in 1973, as well as other Polish Romantic dramas and several plays of Shakespeare. Some other innovative Polish directors of the 1970s and 1980s include Zygmunt Huebner, Jerzy Jarocki, Janusz Warminski, Adam Hanuszkiewicz, Kasimierz Braun, and Andrejz Wajda.

Perhaps the most internationally known Polish director since the 1960s is Jerzy Grotowski. From his early work in theater in Krakow, he theorized about what theater should be. In 1959 he took over the directorship of a small theater in Opole, which was designated as a professional experimental theater. There he explored the dynamics of the actor-audience relationship through unconventional uses of theatrical space, worked on freeing the actor from intellectual biases, and began his probes into the nature of ritual in the theater. In 1962 his company became the Polish Laboratory Theatre. His production of Wyspianski's *Akropolis* in collaboration with Sjana marked a new departure for him. His work became increasingly painstaking, especially with respect to the rigorous training program he developed for his actors. His 1963 production of Christopher Marlowe's *Tragical History of Dr. Faustus* placed the actors on long trestle tables with audience members seated along both sides as if they were guests at a ritual banquet. With the international attention his work was attracting, the company was moved to the larger town of Wrocław in 1965. That year's production of Calderón de la Barca's *The Constant Prince* became one of the Laboratory Theatre's most acclaimed works. The culmination of Grotowski's work in Wrocław was *Apocalypsus cum Figuris* (1968), based upon the Gospels of the Bible and created by the company over a three-year period. That year also saw the publication of Grotowski's theoretical book, *Towards a Poor Theatre*. Its title refers to his belief that the theater should avoid reliance upon artifice and technical devices like makeup and recorded sound, by putting the focus solely on the actor. Grotowski envisioned the actor's work in spiritual terms, but based it in intense physicality: the actor gives of himself totally in performance in order to achieve communion with the spectator. In 1970 Grotowski gave up his directorship of the company in order to pursue the paratheatrical activities that have been his primary focus since then.

OTHER EXPERIMENTAL WORK SINCE THE 1960s

Pluralism and experimentation took many forms in the 1960s and 1970s, especially in the United States, as the art world became centered more in New York than in Paris and as the polemics generated by American involvement in Vietnam more and more found theatrical forms of expression. In New York there was a general sense that off-Broadway theater had become just as commercialized as a Broadway that was increasingly dominated by musical comedy. An off-off-Broadway movement began with the informal presentation of plays at Cafe Cino in 1961; other such ventures quickly followed, providing needed forums for new plays and young talent that might otherwise not get a hearing. The most durable of these was Ellen Stewart's LaMama Experimental Theatre Club, which began in a basement in 1961 and moved five times in the next eight years. She provided a home for a variety of innovative endeavors and formed a permanent company directed by Tom O'Horgan. By 1965 the company was taking productions like Jean-Claude Van Itallie's *America Hurrah,* with its oversized puppets designed by Robert Wilson, on international tours. The rock musical *Hair* originated in 1967 and moved to Broadway; it was staged by O'Horgan, who also directed the English-language premieres of many plays by Fernando Arrabal.

Although founded in 1947, the Living Theatre won little recognition for its radical mingling of art and anarchy until its 1961 tour to Paris, where it won the grand prize at the Festival of Nations. Constantly courting difficulties in the United States for nonpayment of taxes and other assorted infractions, founders Julian Beck and Judith Malina remained in Europe from 1964 to 1968, where their productions of Kenneth Brown's *The Brig* (1963) and the company-developed *Frankenstein* (1965) were their most popular productions. Their experimental work with Artaud's theories culminated in the intentionally provocative *Paradise Now* (1968), which used nudity and general chaos in an attempt to incite audiences to protest the conditions of American life. The Living Theatre announced its demise in 1970: since its credo called for opposition to all institutions, the company could no longer tolerate itself as an institution. Artistic quality was never an important factor in the work of the Living Theatre, but it did spawn a number of individual artists and companies whose work had a major impact. Joseph Chaikin acted in several Living Theatre productions before founding his own company, The Open Theatre, in 1964. Using an improvisational approach, Chaikin's company developed important works like Megan Terry's *Viet Rock* (1966) and Jean Claude Van Itallie's *The Serpent* (1968). Other politically committed groups that were inspired by the Living Theatre include the San Francisco Mime Troupe, founded in 1959, and Peter Schumann's Bread and Puppet Theatre, founded in 1961. The San Francisco Mime Troupe in turn gave rise to El Teatro Campesino, which was founded in 1965 by Luis Valdez with the idea of applying the Mime Troupe's lively, irreverent outdoor production style to the social problems of Chicano farmhands. After a number of ethnically grounded and politically simplistic productions, Valdez wrote a play of broader appeal: *Zoot Suit* (1978) became the first Chicano play on Broadway.

Like the Living Theatre, Richard Schechner's Performance Group, founded in New York City in 1967, emphasized social concerns and used nudity and audience participation as major production values. Citing also a debt to Grotowski, Schechner called his approach "environmental theater." The most notorious of his rough-edged productions at The Performing Garage was *Dionysus in 69* (1968), based upon Euripides' *The Bacchae*. Two of his company members, Elizabeth LeCompte and Spalding Gray, began producing their own work in 1975. Renaming their company The Wooster Group in 1980, they went on to win recognition not only for their meticulously articulated presentations (through constant reworking), but also for their ability to sustain their collaborative methods throughout the 1980s.

By the mid-1970s, the political focus of most American avant-garde theater was overshadowed by what Bonnie Marranca dubbed "the theater of images." Robert Wilson's originality derived from having conquered a speech impediment that left him scarcely capable of conversation until he was seventeen. He was helped over it by Miss Byrd Hoffman, a dancer-teacher in her seventies, who showed him how to eliminate physical tension through relaxation. Wilson went on to become a painter and a therapist for children with learning disabilities and other brain disorders. In 1966 he founded the Byrd Hoffman School for Byrds, where he developed slow-motion exercises to help the patients' concentration. This work coupled with a chance encounter on the street in Brooklyn—a black child who had been mute ever since he witnessed the murder of two babies—led to Wilson's first major production, *Deafman Glance* (1970), an "opera of images" that took Europe by storm. Using his slow-motion technique, he created marathon sequences of elaborate stage pictures that underwent constant, subtle transformations in the movement of the performers, in the setting, in the lighting, and in the sound patterns of spoken "arias" written by his autistic collaborator Christopher Knowles. Philip Glass composed the music for several of Wilson's productions. Among Wilson's better known works are: *The Life and Times of Joseph Stalin,* a performance lasting twelve hours (1973); *A Letter to Queen Victoria* (1974), *Einstein on the Beach* (1976), and *I Was Sitting on My Patio This Guy Appeared I Thought I Was Hallucinating,* in collaboration with Lucinda Childs (1977). Wilson spent much of the 1980s working on an epic production, different parts of which would be prepared by different opera companies around the world, to be eventually brought together under the title *The CIVIL WarS.*

In contrast to Wilson's gradual changes in the stage picture, Richard Foreman's use of images is rapid and disrupted. He founded his Ontological-Hysteric Theatre in New York in 1968. Among his productions, using such "signature" elements as a character named Rhoda and strings stretched across the stage at various angles, are *Pain(t)* (1974) and *Pandering to the Masses: A Misrepresentation* (1975). Mabou Mines, founded in

1970 by Lee Breuer, JoAnne Akalaitis, and Ruth Maleczech, has tended to produce works with a stronger narrative while incorporating a variety of mixed media elements. Besides such original collaborative efforts as Breuer's series of *Animations* in the 1970s, Mabou Mines excelled at producing works by Samuel Beckett, including adaptations of novels like *The Lost Ones,* in which David Warrilow established himself as an outstanding interpreter of Beckett. Breuer has also worked with other groups, as when he staged *The Gospel at Colonnus* (1983) for the Brooklyn Academy of Music. Squat Theatre began as an amateur group in Budapest. The forced exile of those collaborators in 1977 took them to New York, where they acquired a performance space with a storefront window. There they offered image-based works like *Pig, Child, Fire!*, *Andy Warhol's Last Love,* and *Mr. Dead and Mrs. Free.* The window at the back of the stage framed a vista of street life behind the action of the play; thus pedestrians who paused to peer in the window became a part of the performance.

The young, outspoken, and flamboyant director Peter Sellars began generating controversy from his freshman year at Harvard where he was given the unprecedented opportunity of directing on the Loeb Theatre's main stage; although that production of William Walton and Edith Sitwell's *Façade* flopped, Sellars continued his outrageous experiments with the classics, culminating in his senior-year production of *King Lear* in which the title character, played by himself, arrived on stage in a luxury car symbolizing power and status; the car disintegrated in the course of the play. This brought him an invitation, even before he graduated, to direct Gogol's *The Inspector General* at American Repertory Theatre in 1980. During the next ten years Sellars dazzled the world with a string of unconventionally interpreted operas like his Mozart series at the Pepsico Summerfare: *Così fan tutte* (1986) set in a diner, *Don Giovanni* (1987) set in Spanish Harlem, and *The Marriage of Figaro* (1988) set in New York's Trump Tower. His most renowned and internationally acclaimed work was his staging of the original opera *Nixon in China* (1987), composed by John Adams with a libretto by Alice Goodman. Sellars's longtime collaborators Adrianne Lobel, Dunya Ramicova, and Jim Ingalls designed the sets, costumes, and lighting respectively. During his two-year tenure as artistic director of the American National Theater in Washington DC, 1984–86, Sellars's attempts to invent a new American theater style—in productions like Alexander Dumas *père's The Count of Monte Cristo* (1985) and Robert Sherwood's *Idiot's Delight* (1986)—were misunderstood by many. In 1987 he took a ten-year appointment as director of the Los Angeles Festival.

From the late 1970s the American theatrical avant-garde embraced many performing artists whose work blurs the boundaries between music, dance, painting, and mime. Chief among them are Laurie Anderson, Trisha Brown, Meredith Monk, and Ping Chong. The 1980s have also seen the rise of experimental work in various parts of the country, not only in California and New York. In the south, an umbrella organization called Alternative ROOTS (Regional Organization of Theatres South) fosters thirty different performing organizations. Chicago became a hotbed of activity, with dozens of small companies providing production opportunities for new playwrights. From her base at the Omaha Magic Theatre, Meagan Terry sends original community action dramas on the road. Pluralism has manifested itself in hundreds of special-interest theaters defined by ethnic group or sexual preference. Minneapolis boasts one of the premiere feminist theaters, At the Foot of the Mountain.

While the normal pattern is for an alternative theater to begin with experimental work that gradually adapts itself to a broader constituency, one of the world's leading directors has traveled decidedly in the other direction. Britain's Peter Brook began his career as a Shakespearean director during the war and soon joined the Royal Shakespeare Company. From his charming 1946 *Love's Labour's Lost* to a renowned *King Lear* in 1962 to the thoroughly iconoclastic and internationally acclaimed *Midsummer Night's Dream* in 1970, he expanded the scope of classical production. His move toward experimentalism was signaled in 1964 when his production of Peter Weiss's *Marat/Sade* revived interest in Artaud's idea of a "theater of cruelty." In 1970 he moved to Paris and founded the International Center for Theatre Research with the idea of bringing together performance artists from many cultures to explore new relationships between theater and life. One of the first projects was a production entitled *Orghast* in an artificial language invented by poet Ted Hughes. Twenty-five actors of nine different nationalities came together on a mountainside in Persia for a ritualistic enactment on a vast scale. That work has been documented in the book *Orghast at Persepolis* by A. C. H. Smith. Brook continued his intercultural explorations with *The Ik* (1975) and *The Conference of the Birds* (1976). Perhaps his most remarkable effort was the nine-hour production of the Indian classic *The Mahabharata* (1985), as adapted by Jean-Claude Carrière.

Experimentation in departures from realism has been a prominent feature of postwar German-language theater. In the German Democratic Republic (East Germany), the well-subsidized theater has only gradually shaken off its respectful allegiance to Brechtian dramaturgy. Playwrights, directors, and audiences continue to acknowledge the theater's major function as an instrument of social change, but have shown increasing tolerance for unconventional methods of fulfilling that function. Three disciples of Brecht gained recognition as the leading postwar

East German directors: Benno Besson, Manfred Wekwerth, and Peter Palitzsch. Besson's 1969–77 tenure at Berlin's Volksbühne—where he collaborated often with designer Ezio Toffolutti—gave that theater its period of greatest glory; both artists then emigrated to the west. Wekwerth worked closely with Brecht and designer Karl von Appen; after directing at various other theaters, he returned to the Berliner Ensemble in 1977 to succeed Ruth Berghaus as *intendant* (artistic director). Palitzsch staged one of the Berliner Ensemble's most important productions, *The Resistible Rise of Arturo Ui* by Brecht, in 1955, but has worked exclusively in the west since 1960. With designer Wilfred Minks, Palitzsch concentrated on discovering fresh approaches to Brecht and other "classic" authors, especially through his emphasis on physical action. Directors and scenographers of the subsequent generation have made a specialty of reinterpreting the classics through striking abstract design to reveal new shades of social content.

East German dramatists too have long worked in the shadow of Brecht, as did Heiner Müller in his early plays like *Der Lohndrücker* (The Scab, 1956). During his travels in the west in the 1970s, however, Müller saw Robert Wilson's and Richard Foreman's "theater of images," which helped him to break away from an orderly dramatic structure and to take up a disjointed, apparently formless writing that—he believes—more nearly approximates modern reality, as in his *Germania Tod in Berlin* (Germania Death in Berlin, 1976) or *Die Hamletmaschine* (The Hamletmachine, 1977). According to Müller: "The fragmenting of an event emphasizes its process-character; it prevents the production's disappearance in the product which is simply marketed, and turns the presentation of the event into an experimental experience in which the audience can participate in a productive way." East Germany's other outstanding dramatists—Volker Braun, Ulrich Plenzdorf, Peter Hacks, and Christoph Hein—offer intellectually and aesthetically challenging plays, often taking as a theme the relationship of the individual to the collective.

For at least two decades after the war, drama in the German Federal Republic (West Germany) reflected a need to come to terms with the past. While some plays dealt directly with wartime events, most were allegorical. The latter tendency may be seen even in plays by Swiss dramatist Max Frisch, for example, in *Die chinesische Mauer* (The Chinese Wall, 1946) or *Biedermann und die Brandstifter* (The Firebugs, 1958). Austrian playwright Friedrich Dürrenmatt wrote obliquely political "tragic comedies" that eschewed realism by incorporating grotesque elements. The original German text of *Der Besuch der alten Dame* (The Visit, 1955) is considerably more bizarre than the translation that is normally used for American productions. The 1960s brought a spate of "documentary dramas," including Rolf Hochhuth's *Der Stellvertreter* (The Dep-

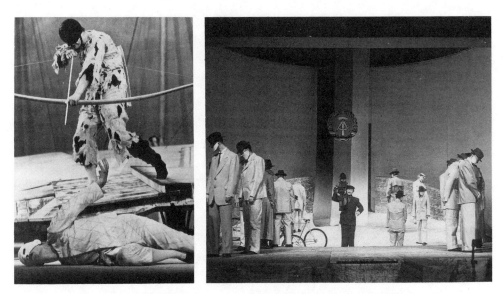

Above, left, Heiner Müller borrowed the subject of his 1966 play Philoctetes *from Sophocles, but took it to a different conclusion. This East German play premiered in West Germany, at Munich's Residenz Theater, under the direction of Hanns Lietzau. Here, Helmut Griem as Philoctetes aims his magic bow at Martin Benrath, who plays Odysseus. Courtesy of the German Information Center.*

Above, right and below, Germania Death in Berlin *by Heiner Müller was produced at the Berliner Ensemble, directed by Fritz Marquardt, with sets and costumes by Karl Kneidel. Photograph by Vera Tenschert, courtesy of the Berliner Ensemble.*

In Friedrich Dürrenmatt's The Visit, *the richest woman in the world succeeds in buying the death of her former small-town sweetheart. This 1958 production was at the Städtische Bühnen in Münster. Photograph by Heinz Koschinski, courtesy of the German Information Center.*

Erwin Piscator directed Rolf Hochhuth's The Deputy, *below, left, at the Theater am Kurfürstendamm in 1963. From left to right are Dieter Borsche as the Pope, Günter Tabor as Riccardo, and Hans Nielsen as the Cardinal. Photograph by Heinz Köster, courtesy of the German Information Center.*

Right, Heinar Kipphardt based his documentary drama In the Matter of J. Robert Oppenheimer *on the 3,000-page transcript of the proceedings of the US Atomic Energy Commission. As "the father of the atom bomb," Oppenheimer was investigated for his deliberate delaying of its development. Courtesy of the German Information Center.*

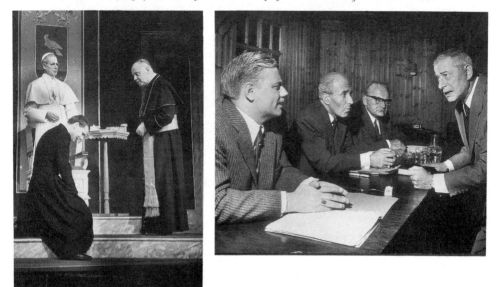

uty, 1963), Heinar Kipphard's *In der Sache J. Robert Oppenheimer* (In the Matter of J. Robert Oppenheimer, 1964), and Peter Weiss's *Die Ermittlung* (The Investigation, 1965). New explorations of dramatic form came out of the 1970s trend toward greater subjectivity: delving into personal memories and other aspects of the inner life of the individual. Botho Strauß's *Gross und Klein* (Big and Little, 1978), a long sequence of disjointed scenes that cumulatively portray the emotional life of the lonely central figure Lotte, cries out for a stage setting that depicts metaphorically an environment of spiritual alienation. Thomas Bernhard, Peter Handke, and Wolfgang Bauer have also developed individualistic, highly iconoclastic techniques for theatricalizing the workings of the mind. Although Franz Xaver Kroetz identifies himself as a realist, his plays exhibit a realism unlike any other, using a paucity of dialogue and an absence of apparent motivation in his depictions of underclass characters who erupt into violence.

By the end of the 1970s, West German theater was signaled as the most dynamic in the world. The "German theater miracle" has been attributed to a constellation of inventive directors as well as to generous government subsidies that amount to as much as 80 percent of a state theater's budget. The per capita amount of government subsidy for the theater has been the highest in the world. In a country roughly the size of the stage of Oregon, seventy-five cities boast permanent theater companies in addition to a number of other opera and ballet companies. Flourishing alongside the state and municipal theaters are numerous private theater companies, and there are some so-called free groups that usually originated as amateur special-interest theaters. West German theater is distinguished not only by the quantity and quality of innovative work as opposed to conventional realism, but by the fact that such theater is supported by a mainstream audience—an anomalous condition that might be called "avant-garde for the masses."

Leading the distinguished pack of directors who helped to create this situation, Peter Stein came to prominence with his 1967 production of Edward Bond's *Saved* at the Munich Kammerspiele. After directing in Bremen and Zurich, Stein settled in Berlin as artistic director of the Schaubühne am Halleschen Ufer from 1970 to 1985. He gets away with heavy-handed exploitation of the text for antiestablishment propagandistic purposes only because the quality of the work is at a level that Volker Canaris describes as "faultlessly, almost frighteningly perfect, each as beautiful and clever as the last." Working with his cast and production staff as a collective, Stein proceeds from a thoroughly researched grounding in the historical, social, and political context of the play, even when he stages a farce like Eugene Labiche's *La Cagnotte* (The Kitty, 1864) in 1973. The dialectical nature of his productions is manifested in their implied commentary on current conditions, in the way

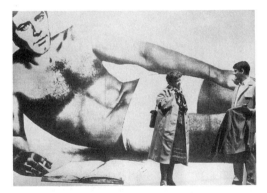

Mensch Meier (1978) by Franz Xaver Kroetz premiered at three theaters simultaneously. The Düsseldorf Schauspielhaus version, shown here, was performed by Ruth Drexel and Hans Brenner as Mr. and Mrs. Meier. Courtesy of the German Information Center.

The innovativeness of West German playwriting and staging is exemplified by this production of Tankred Dorst's The Forbidden Garden. Pictured are Gottfried Lackmann as Gabriele D'Annunzio and Stefan Wieland as Cockerel. Photograph by Ludwig Binder, courtesy of the German Information Center.

Peter Stein directed The Bacchae by Euripides in 1974 at the Schaubühne am Halleschen Ufer. For this "Antiquities Project," spectators were expected to attend on two successive evenings. The first night was devoted to grappling with the text and its original context through a series of exercises for actors; the play itself was performed on the second night. Pictured are Edith Clever as Agave holding the head of Pentheus, and Peter Fritz as Kadmos. Courtesy of the German Information Center.

An unusual interpretation of Ibsen's Peer Gynt *was staged by Peter Stein at the Schaubühne am Halleschen Ufer in 1971. Courtesy of the German Information Service.*

Directorial innovation is apparent in George Tabori's staging of Hans Magnus Enzensberger's The Sinking of the Titanic *at Munich's Kammerspiele. Courtesy of the German Information Center.*

Although Günter Grass remains better known as a novelist, he has written several successful plays, most notably The Plebeians Rehearse the Uprising *(1966), which examines Bertolt Brecht's apparent condoning of the Soviet suppression of striking East German workers in 1953. This production was staged at the Schiller Theater in Berlin. Courtesy of the German Information Center.*

Elfriede Zelinek's Illness *was staged by Jean-Claude Riker and Peter Echsberg at the Stadttheater of Bonn in 1987. Courtesy of the German Information Center.*

his·actors seem to comment upon the characters they portray, and in his frequent use of simultaneous action on different parts of the set. Among Stein's many important productions are Ibsen's *Peer Gynt* (1971), Kleist's *The Prince of Homburg* (1972), *Shakespeare Memory* (1976) which was developed from the background materials for his *As You Like It* (1977), and Chekhov's *Three Sisters* (1984).

Peter Zadek's childhood and early career were spent in England, where his Jewish parents had immigrated in 1933, but he has enlivened the West German theater scene since 1960, especially with his unorthodox stagings of Shakespeare. Both his 1961 and 1972 productions of *Merchant of Venice* were attacked as anti-Semitic; in other works too, Zadek made a practice of challenging expectations. During the 1960s his spectacular productions in Bremen were designed by Wilfred Minks. He served as *intendant* at the Bochum theater from 1972 to 1975, and subsequently became a free-lance director based in Hamburg. Minks later turned to directing with considerable success. Other exciting directorial work in West German theater has been done by Klaus Michael Grüber, Hansgünther Heyme, Hans Hollman, Claus Peymann, Hans Neuenfeld, and choreographer Pina Bausch. Mention must also be made of the striking reinterpretations of the classics by Roberto Ciulli at the Theater an der Ruhr, which he founded in 1980. That theater very quickly established an international reputation with plays by authors ranging from Sophocles to Woody Allen. Despite its challenging material, one of Ciulli's most admired productions is *Der kroatische Faust* (The Croatian Faust, 1987) by Yugoslavian dramatist Slobodan Snajder.

The broad pattern that emerges from this cursory survey of experimental theater in the twentieth century is a passing of leadership from the dramatist to the director-designer team. Early in the century, the avant-garde was identified with specific aesthetic movements that were defined by playwrights. Starting in the 1960s, theatrical innovation was more often something that the director did, usually in concert with a designer, to an existing text. For this reason, it becomes almost impossible after that time to make a hard and fast distinction between avant-garde and "mainstream" theater. There is a certain arbitrariness about designating the German theater's departures from realism as experimental while consigning to the mainstream the director-centered theater that emerged in France after the events of May 1968. By definition, however, the avant-garde is always in advance of the main body of work being done. By the time the main body begins to absorb elements of the avant-garde, the advance patrol has moved still further ahead. The French directors after 1968 took their cues from the theories of Brecht and Artaud, but by that time the German directors had moved beyond Brecht and were exploring dynamic new uses of stage space along with challenging scenic metaphors.

Currents in the Mainstream

DIAGHILEV AND HIS INFLUENCE

France was the original home of classical ballet, which reached a peak of development there in the 1840s. When the French dancer-choreographer Marius Petipa left for Russia in 1847, no one suspected that he would take a golden age of ballet with him. Petipa rose to the position of ballet master for the Imperial Theatres of St. Petersburg and dominated Russian ballet for fifty years, until his retirement in 1903. He is credited with establishing the standard form of the five-act story-telling ballet that featured virtuoso set pieces connected by pantomime in a visually spectacular framework. At about the time Petipa retired, Michel Fokine became the youngest dancer ever appointed to the faculty of the Imperial Ballet School. He soon began creating original ballets and introducing his ideas for reform: the elimination of pantomime, a greater variety of styles, and greater unity within a chosen style. He was also much impressed by the natural expressiveness of American dancer Isadora Duncan. However, the Imperial Ballet could not offer the opportunities he craved to develop his creativity to the fullest. Fokine's decision to join forces with Serge Diaghilev in 1909 was instrumental in returning the world's most exciting ballet to France.

Serge Diaghilev grew up with constant exposure to all the arts. He hoped first to make a career in music, then painting, but finally faced the fact that he had no talent for either. Taking stock of himself, he wrote: "I am first a great charlatan—but with flair; second, a charmer; third, inordinately pushy; fourth, a man of much logic and few scruples; fifth, sadly lacking any artistic gifts of my own. So I think I have found my vocation—artistic patronage. For that, I've got all the right qualities, except money—and that will come." In 1898 he and painter Alexander Benois founded a carefully designed and lavishly illustrated periodical, *Mir Isskustvo* (The World of Art, 1898–1904), which both celebrated the richness of Russia's own artistic heritage and promoted European modernism. Soon Diaghilev was organizing exhibits of Russian painting and concerts of Russian music to show in Paris. Next he decided to show off Russian opera in Paris; in 1908 he took an elaborately mounted production of Mussorgsky's *Boris Godunov* with Fyodor Chaliapin in the title role. The success of such undertakings established the tour as an annual event in the summer when the performers' regular season had ended.

It was Benois who suggested adding a ballet to the 1909 opera tour and inviting Fokine to stage it. Because of last-minute budgetary problems, the planned repertoire of five full-length operas and one program of short ballets had to be drastically reduced. Instead, Diaghilev presented one full opera and two other programs, each composed of one act of opera and two short ballets. The unexpected emphasis on ballet, which had long fallen out of favor in Paris, meant that the company could not get booked into the Opera. Diaghilev remodeled the Châtelet Theater, replacing its muted color scheme with vivid red upholstery and carpeting in keeping with the saturated hues on stage. The Russian company's triumph launched a new fashion for bright colors and pattern in Parisian interior decor. As the French poet Anna de Noailles described it, "everything dazzling, intoxicating, enchanting, seductive had been assembled and put on that stage." The designers for that season included Benois, Léon Bakst, Nikolai Roerich, Konstantin Korovin, and Ivan Bilibin. The real significance of the 1909 season, however, was its revival of interest in the ballet in Paris as well as a definitive change of direction, from opera to ballet, for Diaghilev.

Parisians hailed dancer Vaclav Nijinsky as a genius. Although he looked stolid in ordinary life, his appearance was transformed on stage by his instinctively fine acting, his charismatic presence, and, most of all, his thrilling leaps that seemed almost superhuman in elevation and weightlessness. He and Fokine and several others brought the male dancer back to prominence, although the company also included the brilliant ballerina Tamara Karsavina as well as Anna Pavlova, Aleksandra Baldina, and the exotic Ida Rubinstein. The 1910 season was noteworthy for *Sheherazade*, which established Léon Bakst as the designer of sets and costumes most readily identified with the Russian ballet. That season also marked the first full ballet that Diaghilev commissioned Igor Stravinsky to compose, *L'Oiseau de feu* (The Firebird, 1910). Diaghilev premiered other Stravinksy ballets also: *Petroushka* (1911), *Le Sacre du printemps* (Rite of Spring, 1913), *Pulcinella* (1919), and *Les Noces* (Wedding Rites, 1923).

By 1911 Diaghilev was able to form his own permanent company with Fokine as chief choreographer and Nijinsky as principal dancer. Nijinsky's great roles with *Les Ballets russes* included the Golden Slave in *Sheherazade,* and the title roles in *Petroushka* and *Le Spectre de la Rose*

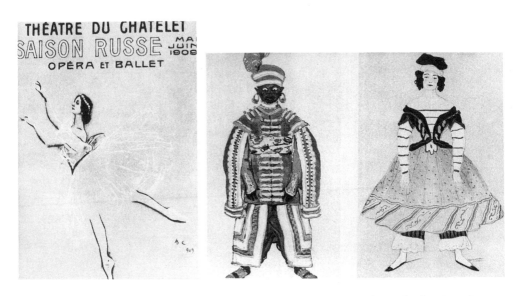

The poster and program for Diaghilev's 1909 season in Paris, left, featured a drawing of Anna Pavlova by Valentin Serov.

Right, Benois's renderings for the costumes of the Blackamoor and Columbine in Petrushka *were published in the Parisian journal* Comoedia Illustré *in 1911.*

Below, Stravinsky's 1911 ballet Petrushka *captured the spirit of a St. Petersburg fair, as evoked in this setting—with the show booth at center—for scenes 1 and 4, designed by Alexandre Benois. Vaclav Nijinsky danced the title role.*

Above, Aleksandr Golovine contributed to the Ballets Russes's reputation for opulent orientalism with his sets and costumes for Stravinsky's The Firebird *in 1910.*

Below, Michel Fokine and Tamara Karsavina danced the principal roles in The Firebird in 1910. Fokine also choreographed the ballet to Stravinsky's music.

Below, right, Vaclav Nijinsky choreographed and danced the title role in the Ballets Russes production of Debussy's Afternoon of a Faun *(1912). The set and costumes were by Leon Bakst.*

(1911). Fokine resigned at the end of the 1912 season, but Diaghilev had already determined that Nijinsky would branch into choreography. Nijinsky's first choreographic effort, Claude Debussy's *L'Après-midi d'un faune* (Afternoon of a Faun, 1912), caused a scandal less for the unconventional and hypnotic angularity of the movement than for Nijinsky's sexual explicitness in the title role. Nijinsky also choreographed *Rite of Spring* and Debussy's *Jeux* (Games, 1913) before sailing with the company on a tour to South America. Diaghilev, who had stayed behind, was infuriated when he learned of Nijinsky's marriage on the tour to Romola de Pulszka, a Hungarian woman who traveled with the tour. He dismissed Nijinsky from the company. Nijinsky continued to perform and choreograph elsewhere, but within a few years he was diagnosed as schizophrenic; much of the rest of his life was spent in institutions.

Diaghilev constantly attracted new talent, including Russian designers Mstislav Doboujinsky, Natalia Goncharova, and Mikhail Larionov. Nijinsky's sister Bronislava Nijinska, who had danced opposite him in *The Afternoon of a Faun,* choreographed a number of ballets in the 1920s. After the 1917 revolution in Russia, Diaghilev's company remained in the west, making its headquarters in Monte Carlo. Over the years, many leading non-Russian artists worked with Diaghilev. Jean Cocteau wrote his surrealist ballet *Parade* (1917) for the company, with music by Erik Satie and scenography by Pablo Picasso. Other easel painters who designed for *Les Ballets russes de Monte Carlo* included Henri Matisse, Georges Braque, Marie Laurencin, Maurice Utrillo, Georges Rouault, and Giorgio De Chirico. With the work of those foreign artists, the general look of the ballets evolved away from folklore and exoticism and toward modernism, as exemplified in Jean Cocteau's *Le Train bleu* (The Blue Train, 1924), composed by Darius Milhaud, with choreography by Nijinska. Named after the fast train between Paris and the Riviera, this ballet incorporated acrobatic movements—suggesting seaside activities—by dancers in bathing costumes. Léonide Massine choreographed most of Diaghilev's ballets from 1915 to 1920. In 1925 George Balanchine joined the company and formed his style there before moving to New York in 1933.

Serge Diaghilev died in 1929. His work represents the culmination of a process begun by Richard Wagner fifty years earlier, to achieve a synthesis of all the arts. Diaghilev probably did more than any other artist to overcome Russia's cultural isolationism. His death resulted in the dispersal of Russian dancers, composers, choreographers, and designers all over the world, carrying with them the Russian style, which strongly influenced the development both of the ballet and of decorative arts, especially in France, England, and the United States. In England, Ninette de Valois applied her experience with Diaghilev to founding and nurturing the Vic-Wells Ballet, which eventually became the Royal Ballet. Balanchine founded the School of American Ballet and the New York City Ballet. Charles Spencer sees a continuity of Diaghilev's influence in the work of modern American choreographers like Jerome Robbins and Alvin Ailey. At least a dozen of the ballets premiered by Diaghilev have entered the world's permanent ballet repertoire. Although much of the work was innovative, and some of it quite shocking, its rapid acceptance by general audiences places it distinctly in the mainstream of twentieth-century theater art.

Natalia Goncharova designed vivid, warm-toned sets and costumes for the opera–ballet The Golden Cockerel *(1914). This is her rendering for act 1.*

THE IRISH RENAISSANCE

From the seventeenth century, Ireland produced a steady stream of talent for the theater. But William Congreve, George Farquhar, Peg Woffington, Richard Brinsley Sheridan, Oliver Goldsmith, Dion Boucicault, Bernard Shaw, Oscar Wilde, and others achieved their creative goals only by leaving Ireland. Thus their accomplishments are credited to the English theater. Even the thriving theaters of Dublin and various provincial towns housed English companies performing English plays. There was no native drama on Irish subjects either in English or in the Gaelic language. The first step toward such a drama was taken by yet another Irishman who had gone to live in England: William Butler Yeats. In 1891 Yeats helped to found the Irish Literary Society in London. The following year, Yeats published his first play, *The Countess Cathleen* (1892), an Irish verse drama that mingles Christian and pagan folk elements. He also participated in Dublin's National Literary Society, which sponsored a lecture by Douglas Hyde on "The Necessity of De-Anglicising Ireland."

The first practical steps toward organizing a theater for Irish plays in Dublin were taken in 1897 when Yeats met with Lady Gregory (*née* Isabella Augusta Persse in County Galway) and another west-Ireland landowner, Edward Martyn, to plan a project that would "build up a Celtic and Irish School of dramatic literature." They began soliciting funds and added a fourth founder, George Moore, the only one of the group who could boast some actual experience in theater, having had a play of his produced in London by J. T. Grein's Independent Theatre Society in 1893. Because Dublin's theaters were completely booked to English troupes, the fledgling Irish Literary Theatre rented the Antient Concert Rooms for three performances by actors who had been hired in England. They presented Yeats's *Countess Cathleen* on May 8 and Edward Martyn's *The Heather Field*, an Ibsen-influenced play with an Irish setting, on May 9 and 10, 1899. Some were scandalized by what they perceived as morally, politically, and religiously offensive attitudes in Yeats's play, but the yet-unknown James Joyce joined the enthusiastic applause of the majority. For the second season, in February 1900, three plays were performed on two evenings at a real theater, the Gaiety, again by English actors. For the third season, also at the Gaiety, in October 1901, English actors performed Yeats's and Moore's *Diarmuid and Grainne,* but an afterpiece—Douglas Hyde's *Casadh an tSugáin*—was offered in Gaelic by local amateur actors.

Two Irish music hall performers, brothers William and Frank Fay, boosted the professionalism of the endeavor when they joined in 1902. The group presented a series of performances under different rubrics and finally settled on the name Irish National Theater Society. By then all plays were performed by Irish actors. In 1903 the company produced its first play by John Millington Synge, who was to emerge as the leading light of the renaissance in Irish drama. That same year, two invited performances in London earned a warmly favorable public response and the financial support of an Englishwoman, Miss Annie Horniman, who bought and remodeled a concert hall on Abbey Street in Dublin. The Abbey Theater opened on December 27, 1904, with three short plays, *On Baile's Strand* and *Cathleen ni Houlihan* by Yeats and *Spreading the News* by Lady Gregory. Despite numerous setbacks—riots in the theater in 1907 and 1926, Miss Horniman's withdrawal of subsidy in 1910, the death of an actor in the 1916 Easter week uprising, severe financial troubles in 1921–22, and partial destruction of the theater by fire in 1951—the Abbey Theatre has survived. On the positive side, the Abbey has made a number of very successful American tours, the first in 1911, the most extensive in the 1930s. With the award of an annual subsidy from the Irish Free State in 1924, the Abbey became the first government-subsidized theater in the English-speaking world. An auxiliary space for experimental work, the Peacock Theatre, opened in 1927. In 1966, fifteen years after the fire, a new Abbey Theatre opened on the site, and the following year brought the opening of a new Peacock Theatre. Above all, the Abbey brilliantly fulfilled the Irish Literary Theatre's original purpose of developing some world-class Irish playwrights.

Although better known as the greatest English-language poet of the first half of the twentieth century, William Butler Yeats wrote over twenty-five plays (some in several drastically revised versions) and worked with the Abbey Theatre until his death in 1939. From his earliest mystically inclined, romantic plays of the "Celtic twilight" to the spare, abstract verse drama of the end of his life, Yeats demonstrated an aversion to realism; despite considerable variety within the canon, Yeats's plays could be broadly categorized as symbolist. Yet he championed Synge's realist dramas of Irish life, although they represented the antithesis of his own work. Yeats's romanticism ended abruptly in 1903 when Maud Gonne—the actress and ardent Irish nationalist revolutionary whom he had loved unrequitedly for fourteen years—married another. Always fascinated by Irish folk legends, Yeats wrote several plays about the epic hero Cuchulain of iron-age Ireland: *On Baile's Strand* (1903), *The Green Helmet* (1910), *At the Hawk's Well* (1917), *The Only Jealousy of Emer* (1919), *Fighting the Waves* (1934), and *The Death of Cuchulain* (1939). Some of his plays, influenced by the Japanese Noh theater, were collected as *Plays for Dancers* in the 1920s. Because of the hermetic nature of his verse dramas, they had little popular appeal for audiences at the Abbey. Yeats won the Nobel Prize for Literature in 1923.

Over thirty plays by Lady Gregory were produced at the Abbey Theater, beginning with her first one-act comedy (apart from two earlier plays written in collaboration with Yeats), *The Twenty-Five* (1903). Most of her plays were one-acts of Irish life and lore like *Spreading the News* (1904), *Hyacinth Halvey* (1906), *The Jackdaw* (1907), *The Workhouse Ward* (1908), and *Hanrahan's Oath* (1917). The popularity of her work is suggested by the fact that by 1912 there had been 600 performances of her plays at the Abbey, but only 245 performances of Yeats's plays and 182 of Synge's. Lady Gregory also translated four plays by Molière into the Galway dialect, and these were very successful in performance.

William Butler Yeats's At the Hawk's Well *(1917) was revived in 1969 at the Peacock Theatre, an auxiliary stage of the Abbey Theatre. Sara-Jane Scaife played the Woman of the Sidhe in that production, directed by James W. Flannery. Courtesy of the Abbey Theatre.*

John Millington Synge was only thirty-eight when he died of Hodgkin's disease in 1909, yet he had written the best and most enduring plays that came out of the Abbey Theatre. After completing his studies at Trinity University, he traveled in Germany and settled in Paris, where he studied literature and wrote for the newspapers. There he met Yeats, who urged Synge to return to Ireland, to immerse himself in the life of the people of the Aran Islands. From 1898 until 1902, Synge spent every summer on those rocky islands, and the journal he kept became a source for his great one-act tragedy *Riders to the Sea* (1902; produced 1904). In the preface to his masterpiece *The Playboy of the Western World* (1907), Synge acknowledges the sources of his rich, poetic prose dialogue:

> Anyone who has lived in real intimacy with the Irish peasantry will know that the wildest sayings and ideas in this play are tame indeed, compared with the fancies one may hear in any little hillside cabin in Geesala, or Carraroe, or Dingle Bay. . . . When I was writing *The Shadow of the Glen* some years ago, I got more aid than any learning could have given me from a chink in the floor of the old Wicklow house where I was staying, that let me hear what was being said by the servant girls in the kitchen. . . . In a good play every speech should be as fully flavoured as a nut or apple.

Synge further commented that "on the stage one must have reality, and one must have joy." The joy in *The Playboy of the Western World* is its blend of humor, fantasy, and sentimentality. It was the reality—his unflinching portrayal of Irish character and the strong language—that provoked "the Playboy riots." One review of the opening-night performance called the play "a libel upon Irish peasant men, and worse still upon Irish peasant girlhood." Police were hired to keep order at subsequent performances. Yeats's defense of the play in news stories and radio interviews turned the brouhaha to advantageous publicity. The Abbey's inclusion of the play in the repertoire for the 1911 tour to the United States led to the arrest of the entire cast in Philadelphia for presenting an "immoral and indecent" play. Synge's fiancée Molly Allgood (who acted under the name Máire O'Neill) directed his posthumous play *Deirdre of the Sorrows* in 1910. Synge's style influenced a number of other writers whose peasant dramas were produced at the Abbey, most notably Padraic Colum and George Fitzmaurice. A strong current of political drama is also exemplified in plays by William Boyle, T. C. Murray, Denis Johnston, Paul Vincent Carroll, and Sean O'Casey.

O'Casey had a doubly disadvantaged childhood: he was a Protestant in Catholic Dublin and his family was desperately poor. Because of weak eyesight he could not attend school and soon went to work as a manual laborer. His political commitments—first to Irish nationalism, which he abandoned in favor of the Irish Labour movement after experiencing the ugliness of class conflict during the Dublin strike of 1913—generated the material for his plays. The first three—known as "the Dublin trilogy"—were produced at the Abbey: *The Shadow of a Gunman* (1923), the long-popular *Juno and the Paycock* (1924), and *The Plough and the Stars* (1926). The latter production aroused the wrath of audiences sensitive to what they considered a defamation of Ireland's national honor. Set at the time of the 1916 Easter week rebellion, the four-act tragedy (interlarded with raucous comedy) portrayed a working class that was deemed insufficiently heroic. The press played up the protests, but Yeats and Lady Gregory once again defended a play that was not particularly to their own tastes. Successfully revived as early as 1928, *The Plough and the Stars* became the Abbey's most revived play. O'Casey, however, emigrated to England, and his subsequent plays premiered at other theaters.

In 1928 director Hilton Edwards and actor–designer Micheál Mac-Liammóir founded the Dublin Gate Theatre with the goal of presenting a broader repertoire with more emphasis on production values than the Abbey. Although the Gate did do many foreign plays, particularly in the expressionist vein, it also introduced Irish playwright Denis Johnston, producing in 1929 his first play *The Old Lady Says "No!";* (rejected by the Abbey, the script had been returned to Johnston with that oblique reference to Lady Gregory written across the cover).

A second wave of developments in Irish theater began in the 1950s with the establishment of professional theaters in Belfast and Cork, the 1957 inauguration of the Dublin International Theatre Festival, the rise to international prominence of the Irish-born Samuel Beckett, and the appearance of a new generation of dramatists, most notably Brendan Behan, author of *The Hostage* (1958), and Hugh Leonard, who began writing plays in the 1950s, but was little known outside of Ireland before his 1973 play *Da*.

Northern Ireland's theatrical renaissance began at the end of World War II with the founding of Belfast's Ulster Group Theatre and the Belfast Arts Theatre, followed by Mary O'Malley's Lyric Players Theatre in 1951. Before that, the two best authors of "Ulster comedies," George Shiels and Rutherford Mayne, had their first plays produced by the Abbey Theatre. More recent Northern Irish dramatists have gravitated toward political drama; among these are David Rudkin, Graham Reid, Ron Hutchinson, and Anne Devlin. Frank McGuinness's important play *Observe the Sons of Ulster, Marching Towards the Somme* (1985) premiered in Dublin. Outstanding among contemporary playwrights of Northern Ireland is Brian Friel. *Philadelphia Here I Come!* (1964) exemplifies his early "comfortable" plays. In the 1970s he took a broader social and historical perspective in plays like *Aristocrats* (1979), *The Faith Healer* (1979), and his superb *Translations* (1980). The latter play inaugurated the Field Day Theatre, founded by Friel and Stephen Rae to tour Irish plays both in Northern Ireland and the Republic of Ireland.

Friel settled in the Republic, in County Donegal, just across the border from Derry, where the Field Day Theatre productions are premiered. Similarly, a number of other playwrights have been drawn to the west of Ireland. Among them is Field Day member Thomas Kilroy,

The Shadow of a Gunman, *the first play in Sean O'Casey's "Dublin trilogy," was produced at the Peacock Theatre in 1989. Pictured are Garrett Keogh and Johnny Murphy. Courtesy of the Abbey Theatre.*

Godfrey Quigley, at left, played Dada in the Abbey Theatre's 1987 production of A Whistle in the Dark *by Tom Murphy. Critic Michael Coveney called this study of contemporary Irishmen in England a "clenched fist of a play." Courtesy of the Abbey Theatre.*

author of *Talbot's Box* (1977), who lives in County Galway. Galway is also the home of the internationally renowned Druid Theatre Company, founded in 1975 by Garry Hynes. The Druid has nurtured the careers of, among others, Geraldine Aron and Thomas Murphy. Murphy is, along with Brian Friel, one of the two leading contemporary Irish dramatists. The Galway-born Murphy has been a writer-in-association with both the Druid and the Abbey theaters. His award-winning plays include *The Gigli Concert* (1983), *Bailegangaire* (1985), and *Conversations on a Homecoming* (1985). County Kerry is represented by the popular John B. Keane and a woman dramatist who writes in Gaelic, Siobhan O Suilleabhain. Finally, mention must be made of the politically radical and provocative work of Dublin-born Margaretta D'Arcy and her English husband John Arden, whose collaborative efforts have included the 26-hour-long *Non-Stop Connolly Show* (1974).

SPAIN: '98, '27, POST-WAR, AND POST-FRANCO

By the late nineteenth century, Spanish drama and theater had long been stagnating in a comfortable symbiosis with conservative middle-class theatergoers who demanded nothing more than traditional light entertainment. In such a climate, José Echegaray stood out not for any innovation but for the intensity with which he reaffirmed bourgeois values. This math professor, economist, engineer, founder of the Bank of Spain, and politician pleased audiences with his bombastic rhetoric, clever twists of plot, and moral themes in Ibsen-influenced melodramas like *El Gran Galeoto* (The Great Galeoto, 1881). Somehow he won the Nobel Prize for Literature in 1905. It was partly in reaction against Echegaray's heavy-handed moralizing that a fresh current in the drama found acceptance around the turn of the century. The new literary movement, called *modernismo,* was introduced in poetry by the Nicaraguan Rúben Darío. His opulent, exotic, erotic mingling of images and themes borrowed from French symbolism and baroque painting, and expressed with great musicality of poetic sound values, served an escapist function in counterpoint to Spain's humiliating defeat in the Spanish-American War of 1898. Several dramatists—including Juan Ramón Jiménez and Ramón del Valle-Inclán—embraced *modernismo* during its brief vogue, but later returned to a more sober literary vein. The theatrical figure who remains most identified with *modernismo* is Gregorio Martínez Sierra, director of Madrid's Eslava Theater from 1917 to 1925. However, as Patricia O'Connor has shown, the authorship of plays like the popular *Canción de cuna* (Cradle Song, 1911)—long credited solely to him—was in great measure the work of his wife María Martínez Sierra. Yet Gregorio Martinez Sierra's *modernismo* extended also to the visually exquisite, imaginative, and original staging of an interesting range of plays by his Compañía Comico-Dramática. One critic called him "the Spanish Lugné-Poe" and the Eslava "the only art theater in Spain." Much of his success stemmed from his efforts to recognize and assemble extraordinary talents like designers Manuel Fontanals, Rafael Barradas, and Sigfredo Burmann, and actress Catalina Bárcena. It was Martinez Sierra who urged the young poet Federico García Lorca to write his first play, *El maleficio de la mariposa* (The Butterfly's Evil Spell, 1920), which he produced at the Eslava.

The first major impetus for a revitalization of Spanish literature and arts came from a brilliant group of writers whose work achieved maturity between 1890 and 1905. Known as the Generation of 1898, they represented a variety of individual styles but were united in their rigorous intellectualism and in their not uncritical patriotism. They were rallied by Angel Ganivet, whose 1897 tract *Idearium español* called for intellectual and spiritual regeneration through a strengthening of national will and a synthesis of tradition with innovation. Saddened by Spain's long decline in prestige among the community of nations, the *Generación de '98* promoted awareness of Spain's illustrious history and pride in the unique aspects of its heritage. Although many of them were primarily novelists and essayists, they saw the theater as a valid literary platform on which to express their aspirations for the nation. The leading intellectual among them was the philosopher, novelist, and poet Miguel de Unamuno. In 1906 he wrote an important essay on "The Regeneration of the Theater," which he saw as the task of the poet. Beginning with his tragedy *Fedra* (Phaedra, 1908), he sustained an active interest in theater and wrote eleven plays, most importantly *El Otro* (The Other, 1926). His 1938 play *El Hermano Juan* (Brother John) is a variation of the traditional Spanish Don Juan theme. Unamuno's own poetic dramas are spare and idea-oriented. At the same time, however, a trend labeled *teatro poético* (poetic theater) brought together elements of *modernismo*, Maurice Maeterlinck's dramatic symbolism, and historical subjects. Chief among those who contributed to the "poetic theater" were Eduardo Marquina and the Machado brothers, Antonio and Manuel. Antonio Machado, the leading poet of the generation, collaborated with his brother on seven plays. Another pair of brothers represent a parallel subcurrent of the Generation of 1898: Joaquín and Serafín Alvarez Quintero excelled at *costumbrismo*, that is, the use of folk customs and local color. Beginning in the 1880s, when they were in their teens, the Alvarez Quintero brothers wrote over two hundred plays, mostly short pieces, many of them incorporating song and dance. These warmly humorous comedies set in sunny Andalusía found an international audience in the 1920s. Carlos Arniches continued in that vein, but took a darker tone with his urban *costumbrismo*.

Of the three best dramatists in the Generation of 1898, only one, Jacinto Benavente, won substantial recognition in his lifetime. Winner of the 1922 Nobel Prize for Literature, Benavente wrote about 170 popular plays in various genres ranging from *Los Intereses creados* (The Bonds of Interest, 1907), a satire on business, using commedia dell'arte characters, to the erotic rural tragedy *La Malquerida* (The Passion Flower, 1913). Overshadowed by Benavente, Jacinto Grau has never been given the attention deserved by his very original and stageworthy plays like *El señor de Pigmalión* (Mister Pigmalion, 1921) and the century's best Don Juan play, *El burlador que no se burla* (The Trickster Untricked, 1930). In contrast, the plays, novels, and poetry of the brilliant eccentric Ramón del Valle-Incán have earned posthumous critical accolades that place him as one of the great writers of the century. Born in Galicia (a romantically isolated province where mystery and superstition flourish in local legends) on the northwestern coast of Spain, Valle-Inclán cultivated a mysterious persona in turn-of-the-century bohemian Madrid. The one-armed poet of aristocratic temperament looked so idiosyncratic with his long beard and huge round spectacles that one friend described him as "a mask on feet." His early dramatic writing, which he called *comedias bárbaras* (barbaric plays), centers upon on a Galician family and conveys a nightmarish atmosphere, combining horrific supernatural elements and luxuriant poetry; among these is *Romance de lobos* (Ballad of Wolves, 1907). After touring in South America and Spain with the company of Maria Guerrero and Fernando Mendoza, he became disillusioned with commercial theater and ceased all dramatic activity for seven years. But in 1920 he suddenly published four plays: two farces, a tragicomedy—*Divinas palabras* (Divine Words)—that has become his most produced play, and *Luces de Bohemia* (Bohemian Lights), the first of a new dramatic genre that he called *esperpentos*. One of the characters in *Bohemian Lights* describes *esperpentismo* as the kind of distortion that is produced when classical heroes are reflected in concave mirrors. Valle-Inclán apparently intended these plays for a puppetlike style of performance, to reveal the comic side of life's tragedy. They mingle elements of farce, squalor, brutality, and a strange poetry of images. Although his *esperpentos* were virtually ignored during his lifetime, *Los Cuernos de Don Friolera* (Don Friolera's Horns, 1921) and others have in recent decades been found as stageworthy as they are exemplary of literary excellence.

Many members of the Generation of '98 continued writing as late as the 1950s, but their artistic leadership had waned by the 1920s, especially as a new generation of writers became prominent around 1927.

The year was significant as the three-hundredth anniversary of the death of the Spanish poet Luís de Góngora, whose metaphorically rich poetry, dense with allusions to classical mythology, strongly influenced the new generation of poets, many of whom lived in the famous *Residencia de Estudiantes* in Madrid at that time. The Generation of 1927 showed little interest in traditional themes of religion and love, preferring to explore the nature of art itself in all its departures from reality. They were more cosmopolitan in outlook than their predecessors; without sacrificing their "Spanishness," they took an active interest in artistic developments in Europe and the Americas. Identifying themselves primarily as poets, only three of the Generation of '27 wrote also for the theater: Rafael Alberti, Alejandro Casona, and Federico García Lorca. Two others, Luis Buñuel and Salvador Dalí, went to Paris and made two surrealist films together. Buñuel went on to make an outstanding career in films, while Dalí became one of the great painters of the century. Several of this generation, unfortunately, were silenced by death, exile, or political repression in 1936 and after.

Alejandro Casona chose exile in Latin America when Franco came to power in the Spanish civil war. It was in Buenos Aires that he wrote *La Dama del alba* (The Lady of the Dawn, 1944), the most popular of his numerous internationally successful, humanistic plays of poetic fantasy. The play was premiered there by an outstanding theater company, that of Margarita Xirgu, and, like his other plays, has subsquently been produced in many languages. Federico García Lorca not only excelled as a lyric poet and playwright, but also composed music, played the piano and guitar as easily as he made conversation, exhibited his drawings and paintings, designed scenery and costumes, produced puppet theater, and from 1932 to 1936 directed a touring company called La Barraca. Like several others of the Generation of '27, he flirted with surrealism, most notably in his play *Así que pasen cinco años* (When Five Years Pass, 1931). Apart from his much-loved lyric poetry, he is best known for his three tragedies of rural Spanish womanhood: *Bodas de sangre* (Blood Wedding, 1933), *Yerma* (1934), and *La Casa de Bernarda Alba* (The House of Bernarda Alba, 1936). His dramatic masterpiece is undoubtedly *Doña Rosita la soltera* (Doña Rosita the Spinster, 1935). However, he also wrote a play, *El Público* (The Audience, written 1930; published 1976) so avant-garde in technique and so daring in its homosexual thematic content that it was withheld from publication for forty years after his death. Lorca was shot and buried in an unmarked grave in the first month of the civil war.

Although theater during the Franco era in Spain, 1939–75, was inhibited by strict censorship, the number of theaters and audiences for them gradually increased as production values steadily improved. The way to higher standards had been paved in the prewar period by two outstanding theater companies directed by women, Lola Membrives and Margarita Xirgu. In 1939, two Madrid theaters were designated as national theaters, the Teatro Español and the Teatro Maria Guerrero. Between them they generated audiences for the classics, foreign plays in translation, and new Spanish drama. Over the years others were added to the national theater network. Plays from the post-civil-war period fall into roughly three categories: *teatro de evasión* (escapist drama), realistic drama, and underground or "new wave" drama. Plays of the first category—innocuous light comedies that pandered to the desire of conservative middle-class audiences to see the bright side of things—dominated the commercial and state theaters. Enrique Jardiel Poncela's comedies of the 1940s enjoyed a spectacular revival of interest in the 1970s and 80s. So popular and ubiquitous were plays by the prolific Alfonso Paso in the 1950s that theatergoers often phrased their invitations to the theater as *"Vámonos al Paso!"* The actor-journalist-screenwriter Miguel Mihura found his true calling in the theater when he won his first *Premio Nacional de Teatro* (National Prize for Theatre) in 1953 with a comedy written much earlier, *Tres sombreros de copa* (Three Top Hats, 1932). Another frequent prizewinner, Joaquín Calvo-Sotelo, achieved over five thousand performances of one play, his *La Muralla* (The Wall, 1954).

At the same time, another group of playwrights followed the more daring path of writing plays of honest appraisal of Spanish life in their own time. This group, called the "realistic generation," rallied around Antonio Buero Vallejo, whose steady output during more than three decades has secured his reputation as Spain's greatest dramatist of the second half of the century. Buero Vallejo had intended to be a painter; indeed, many of his plays—for example, *Las Meninas* (The Maids of Honor, 1960) and *El sueño de la razón* (The Sleep of Reason, 1970)—take painters and painting as subjects. During the civil war, he fought on the Republican side, was captured, heard a death sentence pronounced against him, and spent six years in prison. Not long after his release, he wrote two plays, both of which were produced and won prizes in 1949. One of those plays, *Historia de una escalera* (Story of a Staircase, 1947), marks a turning point in Spanish drama; its impact cannot be overestimated. Set in the stair hall of a rundown Madrid tenement building, it depicts—without overtly criticizing—the difficult social conditions under which four families live over a period of thirty years. In the 1970s Buero Vallejo developed a technique that he called *efecto de inmersión* (immersion effect), by which the spectator experiences reality in much the same way as does a central character. In *The Sleep of Reason*, for example, whenever the deaf painter Goya is on stage, the audience sees characters moving their mouths but hears no dialogue. In *La Fundación* (The

Federico García Lorca's long-suppressed play El Público *(The Audience) finally premiered in Spain in 1988 at the Centro Dramático Nacional, under the direction of Lluis Pascual. Pictured are Juliet and the White Horses in "the theater under the sand." Courtesy of the Centro de Documentación Teatral, Ministerio de Cultura.*

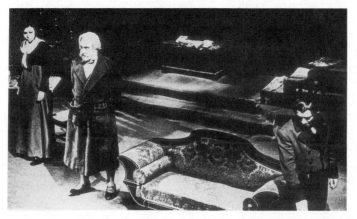

The Sleep of Reason *by Antonio Buero Vallejo was produced at Madrid's Teatro Reina Victoria in 1970. Courtesy of the Centro de Documentación Teatral, Ministerio de Cultura.*

Nuria Espert appears in the foreground in the poignant final scene of Federico García Lorca's Doña Rosita the Spinster, *in which Espert played the title role. Courtesy of the Centro de Documentación Teatral, Ministerio de Cultura.*

Foundation, 1974), the audience sees a stripping away of decorative elements and comforts as the prisoner Tómas is forced to give up his fantasies. Other playwrights of the Realistic Generation followed Buero Vallejo's example, carefully remaining within the formal censorship guidelines set forth in 1963 (the harsher and more capricious censorship prior to 1963 had been in the hands of priests responsible to a repressive Ministry of Information) while presenting realistic studies of the serious social problems in Franco's Spain. Those writers include Alfonso Sastre, Lauro Olmo, José Martín Recuerda, and Carlos Muñiz.

A generation of dramatists who began writing in the 1960s rejected realism and experimented with a variety of techniques that would enable them to express their frustration with conditions and yet not lose too much text to the censor. The plays tended to be short, with few characters, utilizing pantomimic business or scenic metaphors to communicate as much as the dialogue. That is, the form of these plays showed the influence of Theatre of the Absurd writers like Ionesco and Beckett, while the content was geared to protest existing conditions. In a sense, these writers were "silenced" by a double barrier of their own making: even if the content of their plays survived censorship, the nonrepresentational form would alienate producers and theatergoers. "Underground theater" seemed an appropriate appellation for such plays that rarely got produced. Among the numerous authors in this vein are Antonio Martínez Ballesteros, Manuel Martínez Mediero, José Ruibal, Eduardo Quiles, Francisco Nieva, José María Bellido, and Luís Riaza. With the death of Franco in 1975 and the abolition of government censorship in 1978, the "new wave" dramatists expected to come into their own. However, productions of those plays failed to attract audiences, who were more prone to be distracted by the frequent nudity on the stage. For several seasons, the theater seemed most bent upon testing the limits of its new freedom, and the result was what many regarded as pornography. It was said, too, that both artists and audiences were so creatively repressed that they simply did not know what best to do with their sudden freedom. The new government-subsidized Centro Dramático Nacional, opened in 1978, became a target of criticism for not doing more to promote the work of innovative young playwrights. This led to the establishment of two additional government-subsidized companies in Madrid: the Centro Nacional de Nuevas Tendencias Escénicas for new work, and the Compañía Nacional de Teatro Clásico for Spanish classics.

By the early 1980s the Spanish theater seemed to be finding its way, and hovered possibly on the verge of greatness. The new Ministry of Culture made giant strides in encouraging the development of regional theaters, even Catalonian-language theater in Barcelona, in contrast to the Franco era's centralized theater in Madrid. A new generation of Spanish dramatists has managed to combine popular appeals with serious subjects. Among these are Antonio Gala, Ana Diosdado, Jaime Salom, Fernando Fernán Gómez, and José Luís Alonso de Santos. Besides the well-established Diosdado, a number of women dramatists are beginning to make their mark: Lidia Falcón, Paloma Pedrero, María Manuela Reina, and Carmen Resino.

One actress-producer deserves special mention for her role in broadening the public's latitude of acceptance, beginning even before Franco's death. Nuria Espert had been acting since childhood in Barcelona. In 1959, when she was twenty-one, she and her husband Armando Moreno founded the Compañia Nuria Espert, which they toured successfully to Madrid. For the next fifteen years, they depended entirely upon the box office to sustain the company. Espert played title roles ranging from *Gigi* to *Hamlet*. In the 1960s the company won permission to stage the first Spanish productionsof plays by Brecht and Sartre. The production that made her internationally famous, Genet's *Les Bonnes* (The Maids), directed by Victor García, won the grand prize at the 1969 Belgrade International Theatre Festival and subsequently toured to other festivals, to ecstatic reviews. García also directed her in the title role of Lorca's *Yerma*, set on a gigantic undulating, elastic membrane that took different contours for various scenes. Police injunctions delayed the Spanish premiere three times, but the obstacles only rallied an audience. Following its Madrid triumph, Espert toured *Yerma* in Europe and the Americas for four years. Her next production, Valle-Inclán's *Divine Words* toured the world for two years, 1975–77, and subsequent productions were similarly acclaimed. In 1986 Espert made her directorial debut with Lorca's *House of Bernarda Alba* in London, and she continues to be much in demand as a director of opera.

A significant independent theater movement has contributed to Spain's theatrical renaissance in the 1980s. Madrid's Tábano company, for example, works collectively in a Brechtian style. Some of the most exciting work originates in Barcelona and is performed in Catalán: Els Joglars, directed by Albert Boadella; Els Comediants, offering theater in a spirit of festival; Josep María Flotats's company in the Teatro Poliorama; and the superb Teatre Lliure. Lluis Pascual, founder of the Teatre Lliure, left for Madrid in 1983 to head the Centro Dramático Nacional, and in 1990 he joined Giorgio Strehler as co-director of the Odéon-Théâtre de l'Europe in Paris.

MAINSTREAM MAVERICKS

During the early decades of the twentieth century, while such avantgarde movements as futurism, dada, surrealism, and expressionism were both shocking the bourgeoisie and preparing the way for popular acceptance of departures from realism, certain other artists saw their mission as one of refreshing and revitalizing the theater from within the mainstream. These efforts, which were often perceived as avant-garde in their day, took a variety of forms: drawing additional segments of the population to the theater, raising production standards, reawakening appreciation for the classics and for poetic language, forging links among the theaters of different nations.

One such maverick began his long-unheralded crusade before the turn of the century in England. William Poel (a stage name taken by William Pole) made his acting debut in 1876 in Charles Mathews's company and learned the various crafts of theater during two seasons of touring. The cause for which he is remembered came to the fore as early as 1879 when he organized The Elizabethans, "professional ladies and gentlemen whose efforts are specially directed towards creating a more general taste for the study of Shakespeare." Their tours of excerpts from Shakespeare taught Poel that the texts contain their own scenery, that the plays were not enhanced but diminished by the then-current practice of staging Shakespeare with lavish "realistic" settings confined within a proscenium arch. Poel tested his ideas in an 1881 production of the first quarto version of *Hamlet*, his debut as a Shakespearean director. Throughout the rest of his long career, as the director of numerous readings and independent productions from 1884 until his death in 1934, Poel never wavered from his self-appointed mission to demonstrate that the plays' action flows most effectively on an uncluttered stage, unpunctuated by the drop of a curtain after each scene. He also advocated a style of line delivery that he called "exaggerated naturalness." To further the cause of reintroducing Elizabethan staging as it was then understood, Poel founded the Elizabethan Stage Society in 1894, and this was his producing arm until 1905. Besides his numerous presentations of Shakespeare and other Elizabethans in many different lecture halls and courtyards, Poel won particular acclaim—and the only money he ever made on a production—for his austerely beautiful staging of *Everyman*, the medieval play's first performance in four hundred years.

When financial difficulties forced Poel to disband the Elizabethan Stage Society in 1905, it was immediately succeeded by the English Drama Society. Founded by Nugent Monck, who had acted in Poel's *Everyman*, the latter company carried on Poel's reforms until 1909. Poel and Monck worked together on a 1910 production of *Two Gentlemen of Verona* for an annual Shakespeare festival organized by Sir Herbert Beerbohm Tree at His Majesty's Theatre. Beerbohm Tree's visually extravagant approach to Shakespeare represented the antithesis of what Poel was working for; and yet the innovations introduced by Poel on that occasion—the extension of the apron over the orchestra pit to create a playing space allowing greater intimacy with the audience, and the installation of lighting instruments on the balconies for frontal illumination of the new playing space—were adopted by Beerbohm Tree for his own production of *King Henry VIII* two years later. Monck went on to direct the Norwich Players, which he founded in 1911 as a pretext for his

This 1906 production of Shakespeare's Antony and Cleopatra *at His Majesty's Theatre exemplifies Sir Herbert Beerbohm Tree's lavish production style. From* Play Pictorial.

simplified stagings of both classic and modern plays. In 1921 he acquired a former chapel in Norwich and remodeled it according to the best available knowledge in his day of what an Elizabethan stage might have been. At that Maddermarket Theatre (as well as a brief stint at the Abbey Theatre School in Dublin), Monck directed over five hundred productions, including many revivals of thirty-seven of Shakespeare's plays, in forty-one years, until his retirement in 1952.

Although Poel was regarded somewhat as a crackpot, his influence extended also through the work of Henry Granville-Barker, who performed the title role in Poel's *Richard III* in 1899 and ever afterward credited Poel for showing him the basics of staging Shakespeare. In 1912–14 Granville-Barker directed a landmark series of Shakespeare plays at the Savoy Theatre: *The Winter's Tale, Twelfth Night,* and *A Midsummer Night's Dream.* Espousing Poel's insistence on the uncut text, simplicity of staging, continuous action, and emphasis upon the actor's speech, Granville-Barker added strikingly stylized elements of design. His "post-impressionist" settings merely suggested the time, place, and mood of the action: "a simple harmony of white pilasters and dead gold curtain" for Leontes's palace in *The Winter's Tale,* a pink pagoda and futuristic cone-shaped trees "of most unnatural green" for Olivia's formal garden in *Twelfth Night,* and golden woods against which flitted a scarlet-clad Puck in *A Midsummer Night's Dream.* From 1900 Granville-Barker led a campaign for a national theater, an effort that was not fulfilled in his lifetime; but the National Theatre that was finally formed at the Old Vic in 1963 and moved into its present South Bank complex in 1976 certainly owes much to his groundwork.

Like Poel, whose ideas he deeply respected, Edward Gordon Craig was, in Hugo von Hofmannsthal's words, a "lonely pioneer." Although few of Craig's lofty dreams of scenic visions were realized (scarcely two dozen productions in thirty-five years), his influence was such that Marsden Hartley could claim in 1924: "There is no theatre in existence which is not a Gordon Craig theatre, since every prevailing genius of the stage has at one time or another made reference to and direct use of the Craig idea of space and mass and movement." The British designer began as an actor under Henry Irving in the 1890s, but rebelled against the Lyceum Theatre's brand of painted realism in 1900, when he directed and designed Henry Purcell's opera *Dido and Aeneas.* Using little more than colored lights, backcloths, and gauzes to create atmospheric effects of great beauty, Craig also patterned the performers' movements to accentuate the musical moods. That synthesizing approach, in the tradition of Richard Wagner and the symbolists, led him to emphasize the role of the director as the visionary creator of all aspects of production; it was such a view of himself as directorial mastermind that caused problems when he was hired to design for other directors in England, on the Continent, and in the United States. Most controversial was his apparent disregard for the actor's creative contribution, as when he conceived of replacing actors with *über-marionettes* that could be fully controlled by the director. At his studio in Florence, Craig experimented with his concept of settings composed of movable screens; these were first tested in a production of William Butler Yeats's *The Hour Glass* at the Abbey Theatre (1911) and subsequently used in the famous *Hamlet* directed by Stanislavsky at the Moscow Art Theatre (1911). In 1913 Craig founded The School for the Arts of the Theatre in Florence. Over the years he enunciated his theories in numerous publications: an important essay "The Art of the Theatre" (1905); *The Mask,* a quarterly journal he published from 1908 to 1929; and books like *Towards a New Theatre* (1913) and *Scene* (1923).

One contributor to *The Mask* was the outstanding Hungarian direc-

Edward Gordon Craig's characteristic emphasis of the vertical line in his scenic designs is exemplified in this sketch made by a member of the Moscow Art Theater staff for the famous 1911 Hamlet *on which Craig collaborated with director Konstantin Stanislavsky. The sketch was published in* Teatr i Isskustvo *(1912).*

In 1908 Sándor Hevesi directed the great Hungarian national drama, The Tragedy of Man, *by Imre Madách, at the National Theater in Budapest. Hevesi was obsessed with the play and was to direct it again in 1923, 1926, and 1929. Courtesy of Hungarian Centre of the International Theatre Institute.*

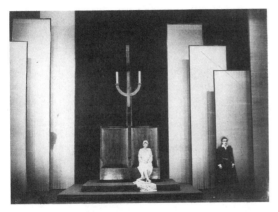

Karel Hugo Hilar directed and Vlastislav Hofman designed this 1926 Hamlet *at Czechoslovakia's National Theater in Prague. Pictured are Leopolda Dostalova as Gertrude and Eduard Kohout as Hamlet. Courtesy of the Hungarian Centre of the International Theatre Institute.*

This photograph of Hofman's setting for Hilar's 1926 Hamlet *clearly reveals the influence of Edward Gordon Craig. At center is Eduard Kohout as Hamlet. Photograph by Karel Vána, courtesy of Art Centrum, Czechoslovak Center of Fine Arts.*

The final scene of Hilar's modernist Hamlet *shows Horatio with the dying Hamlet at center. Laertes lies to one side, while Gertrude and Claudius have died in their thrones. Photograph by Karel Vána, courtesy of Art Centrum, Czechoslovak Center of Fine Arts.*

In 1934 Hilar directed a renowned production of Eugene O'Neill's Mourning Becomes
Electra *at Czechoslovakia's National Theater. Hofman designed the settings. In this scene,
Lavinia confronts her mother in Christine's bedroom. Courtesy of Art Centrum, Czechoslo-
vak Center of Fine Arts.*

Hofman's setting for Ezra Mannon's study in Hilar's production of Mourning Becomes
Electra *is dominated by the quasi-expressionistic portrait of Mannon, who lies in the coffin.
Courtesy of Art Centrum, Czechoslovak Center of Fine Arts.*

Max Reinhardt inaugurated the annual Salzburg festival in 1920 with his production of
Jedermann *performed in front of the cathedral. His second Salzburg production, also
using a script by Hugo von Hofmannsthal, was an allegorical spectacle entitled* The
Great Salzburg World Theater, *based upon a play by Calderón de la Barca. This
photograph shows a 1965 production of the latter work in front of St. Michael's Church in
the town of Schwäbisch-Hall, staged in the manner of Reinhardt. Courtesy of the German
Information Center.*

tor Sándor Hevesi, whose article "Shakespeare as Scenographer" advocated compromise between Poel's search for archaeological accuracy in production and the needs of a contemporary audience. Hevesi's career had progressed from theater criticism to running a small independent theater, the Thália Society (1904–07), to directing at the National Theater in Budapest. When he was appointed artistic director of the latter theater, he launched a cycle of Shakespearean productions. His directorial approach owed much to Stanislavski's example of realistic ensemble acting as well as to Edward Gordon Craig's sense of theatricality in the visual aspects of production.

The influences of Stanislavsky and Craig merged also in the Czechoslovakian theater. After his early infatuation with expressionism at the Prague Municipal Theatre, Karl Hugo Hilar became director of the National Theater in 1921 and mounted many stylish productions from the world repertoire, including a notable staging of O'Neill's *Mourning Becomes Electra* in 1934. The influence of Craig is especially evident in the clean, vertical lines of Vlastislav Hofman's designs for Hilar's 1926 *Hamlet*. Another Czech director, E. F. Burian, emulated Craig in his masterminding of all aspects of production, including writing the scenario, composing and conducting the music, and animating his company as a collective, which he called Divadlo 34 (Theater 34, founded in 1934 and renamed each year: D 35, D 36, etc. until 1941). Each member of the collective was required to study a foreign language, take training in choreography, and attend weekly lectures on the arts and humanities. Burian and his designer Miroslav Kouril used Craig-like screens, curtains, and dramatic lighting effects, but also experimented with multimedia effects that may be seen to have prepared the way for the great Czech designer of the 1970s, Josef Svoboda.

Max Reinhardt acknowledged the inspiration he took from Edward Gordon Craig; "he has swallowed Craig," commented American producer Arthur Hopkins, "but he has not digested him." And it was said that Reinhardt's famous outdoor courtyard production of Hugo von Hofmannsthal's *Jedermann* for the 1920 Salzburg Festival owed much to Poel's *Everyman*, which Reinhardt had seen. By the 1910s, however, the Austrian was well established as the most exciting director in Europe. He had begun his career as a character actor in Otto Brahm's company at Berlin's Deutsches Theater in the 1890s. In 1902 he turned to directing, both in the intimate Kleines Theater and at the Neues Theater; in his first two seasons he mounted three plays by Wedekind as well as numerous others ranging from Lessing to Oscar Wilde. On the basis of that acclaimed work, Reinhardt succeeded Brahm in 1905 as director of the large Deutsches Theater, where he installed a revolving stage and mounted Shakespeare and the German classics. Soon he opened the adjoining Kammerspiele for modern plays on a smaller scale. Directing regularly on both stages, with scenic designs by Karl Walser, he demonstrated the principle that different plays require a different scope of production. On the whole, however, Reinhardt tended toward large-scale undertakings like his famous stagings of Karl Vollmöller's *The Miracle,* with music by Engelbert Humperdinck. For the 1911 London production, he transformed the Olympia sports arena into a Gothic cathedral surrounding the audience as well as the dramatic action. He again directed *The Miracle* in Vienna in 1912, in Leipzig and other German cities in 1913, in Berlin in 1914, in Stockholm and other Swedish cities and in Bucharest in 1917, and, with the American designer Norman Bel Geddes, in New York in 1924. Indeed, one of Reinhardt's most important contributions to the art of directing was the example he set for close collaboration between director and designer.

Reinhardt's largest theater was the Grosses Schauspielhaus, which opened in 1919 and which seated three thousand; architect Hans Poelzig innovatively combined an open stage with a U-shaped thrust. With the idea of letting "the theatre become a festival again," Reinhardt founded the Salzburg Festival in 1917 and ran it for several years. Both the choice of plays and the attraction of theatergoers from afar promoted awareness of theater as an international art. His directing could not be defined in terms of a "Reinhardt style," because the most characteristic feature of his work was that each production had its own inherent style. Ludwig Lewisohn commented: "The essence of this man's work is not to be sought in his revolving stages, his tiny or gigantic playhouses, or even in the unexampled wealth of great dramatic literature which he persuaded his public to accept. His secret is his inner and initial conception of his task; his triumph is in the lonely hours of contemplation before his vision was transferred to the theatre . . . a vision of the play's soul, of its innermost nature in terms of images and sounds." All the details of each Reinhardt production—directorial interpretation of the text, blocking, vocal intonations, lighting changes, and so on—were recorded in a production book or *Regiebuch;* those manuscripts provide invaluable historical records. Reinhardt's 1935 movie version of *A Midsummer Night's Dream* was based upon his stage interpretation of the play. In 1938 Reinhardt emigrated to the United States.

An early admirer of Reinhardt, the drama critic and theorist Georg Fuchs founded the Munich *Künstlertheater* (Artists' Theatre) in 1908 with the idea of awakening the general public's latent appetite for culture by giving them the classics in a festival spirit. Max Littmann built the lovely theater in Austellungs (Exposition) Park, drawing upon the architectural ideals of Karl Friedrich Schinkel and Gottfried Semper as well as his own experimentation with aspects of scenic architecture at Munich's Prince

Regent's Theater. Fuchs opened the Artists' Theater with a visually simple, but strikingly beautiful production of Goethe's *Faust* designed by Fritz Erler; it quickly achieved international renown. On the shallow stage, the pictorial compositions looked like a frieze in relief. A few prismlike scenic units moved into various configurations as the action flowed from one locale to another. The visual harmony of these effects was enhanced by the exquisitely modulated lighting from hidden sources; it was, as a Paris critic noted, "light that liberates the imagination." At the end of the first season, Fuchs published his influential book *Die Revolution des Theaters* (Revolution in the Theater, 1908), in which he drove home his motto: *"Rethéâtraliser le théâtre!"* (Retheatricalize the theater!).

That rallying cry was picked up in France by Jacques Copeau, but the concepts were demonstrated even earlier in the short-lived Théâtre des Arts (1910–13), founded in Paris by Jacques Rouché. Copeau was the drama critic for Rouché's periodical *La Grande Revue,* and the two discovered that they shared a distaste for the facile acting, shallow content, and painted-canvas drawing rooms of the commercial theater. On his return from a trip to Italy, Germany, and Russia, Rouché published a book, *L'Art théâtral moderne* (Modern Theatrical Art, 1910), in which he called attention to the work being done by Appia, Craig, Reinhardt, Fuchs, Stanislavski, and Meyerhold. Not content simply to prescribe remedies, Rouché opened his own theater. The inaugural production, *Carnaval des enfants* (Children's Carnival, 1910) by Saint-Georges de Bouhélier, made his point; Maxime Dethomas's settings accentuated line and color instead of painted details and endless props. Against the blue gray, steel, and ochre settings, the black-costumed characters created striking pictorial compositions in lighting effects that "varied like inflections in a conversation." The Théâtre des Arts presented nearly twenty plays, including Jacques Copeau's adaptation of Dostoevski's *Brothers Karamazov* in 1911. Although it had won critical praise and found an audience, the small theater could not continue to meet expenses. Hired to direct and design at the Opéra, Rouché and Dethomas continued to offer fresh interpretations of old material and to make inroads against stale scenic conventions. It is safe to say that without Rouché the more widely known work of Copeau could not have been done. And Copeau in turn influenced two generations of theater artists.

In 1913 Jacques Copeau published a manifesto in the *Nouvelle Revue Francaise* (a journal he had cofounded in 1908) on artistic renewal in the theater; and he opened his Théâtre du Vieux Colombier, deliberately choosing a Left Bank location rather than the commercial theater district on the other side of the Seine. Like Fuchs, Copeau proposed a *rethéâtralisation du théâtre.* The director's job would be to serve the author's intention by translating the script as faithfully as possible into move-

The trend toward simplification and stylization in twentieth-century set and costume design originated in Germany. The 1908 Munich Künstlertheater production of Faust, *directed by Georg Fuchs and Albert Heine and designed by Fritz Erler, is typical.*

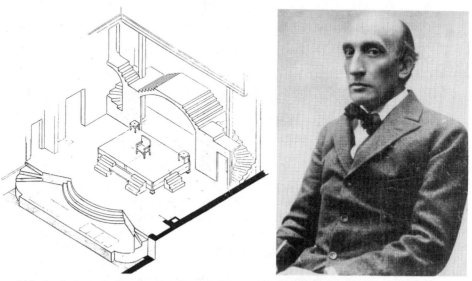

Left, Louis Jouvet's drawing for the remodeling of the Théâtre du Vieux Colombier in 1919 shows the open stage and the upstage architectural unit that could be used in various configurations for different productions.

Jacques Copeau (1879–1949), right, was one of the most influential French men of theater in the twentieth century. Courtesy of French Cultural Services.

ment, gesture, vocal inflections, silences, and rhythms, through the living presence of the actor. He repudiated the commercial theater's reliance on a star system, frequent scene changes, and hack writing, proposing instead an ensemble, a *tréteau nu* (bare stage), and a repertoire in which the classics would provide an example and antidote to *faux goût*. Like his idol Stanislavski, Copeau took his company to the country to live and rehearse together for the summer before opening the theater. Among the ten young actors, several were to become great names in the French theater of subsequent decades: Charles Dullin, Louis Jouvet, Suzanne Bing, Valentine Tessier. Copeau proved to be a strict disciplinarian with uncompromisingly high standards. The eclectic inaugural season included plays by Molière, Musset, Thomas Heywood, Henry Becque, Paul Claudel, and a revival of Rouché's production of *The Brothers Karamazov,* but critics remained largely indifferent until the final production of the season: Shakespeare's *Twelfth Night.* With this unqualified triumph, the company truly became an ensemble. Copeau's staging struck just the right balance of poetry and bawdy comedy. Of this landmark in French Shakespearean production, Harley Granville-Barker reputedly exclaimed, "I was astonished to see French actors performing Shakespeare better than ours normally do." Two months later, World War I began, Dullin and Jouvet were drafted, and the company disbanded.

Invalided from the army in 1915, Copeau made pilgrimages to Italy to meet Craig and to Switzerland to meet Jacques Dalcroze, who introduced him to Adolph Appia. Even before the war's end, Copeau's company was reconstituted when the French government sent it on a cultural mission to the United States. Using New York's Garrick Theatre, the company gave three hundred performances in French of forty-four different plays during two seasons (1917–19). Returning to Paris in 1919, Copeau and Jouvet oversaw the remodeling of the Vieux Colombier. To achieve a sense of communion between actors and audience, they removed both footlights and proscenium arch and carried the auditorium's vaulted ceiling design into the stage area. At the back of the stage was constructed a formal arrangement of stairs with a central arch inspired by the idea of the Elizabethan "inner stage." Now that the Théâtre du Vieux Colombier had earned critical respect, Copeau initiated a project that was especially dear to his heart: he opened the Vieux Colombier Theater School in 1920. Like Stanislavski, he believed that actor training should be a continuing process alongside performance. This principle, along with exercises he developed in improvisation, mime, use of masks and other commedia dell'arte techniques, constitute one of Copeau's major legacies to twentieth-century theater. In 1924 Copeau abruptly closed both the school and the theater, but took several members from both to form a new kind of troupe in a village in

The historic Théâtre du Vieux Colombier was photographed in 1977. Courtesy of French Cultural Services.

The four members of the Cartel des Quatre were photographed together: Charles Dullin (kneeling), Georges Pitoëff, Gaston Baty, and Louis Jouvet.

One of Charles Dullin's most famous productions at the Théâtre de l'Atelier was an adaptation by Jules Romains and Stefan Zweig of Ben Jonson's Volpone *in 1928. From* Settings and Costumes of the Modern Stage *(1933).*

Burgundy. Named Les Copiaus by the locals, they developed small-scale works to be presented in neighboring towns and at local festivals. Although Copeau withdrew from the project in 1929, the ensemble work continued under the leadership of his nephew Michel de Saint-Denis, who called the troupe La Compagnie des Quinze.

Copeau was the moral presence behind the work of four leading directors of the 1930s. In 1927, these directors—Louis Jouvet, Charles Dullin, Georges Pitoëff, and Gaston Baty—formed a loose association known as the Cartel des Quatre. The Cartel issued no manifesto; it simply offered a mechanism for mutual support in their uphill battle to sustain viable theater operations without resorting to the cheap appeals of the Parisian boulevard theaters. While each of these directors represented a unique artistic style, all were devoted to Copeau's idea that the theater's revitalization would come about not through avant-garde experimentation, but through a return to theatricalism at the highest level of artistry. Their association would allow them to coordinate publicity, selection of plays, and tours. Through two of these directors, Copeau's legacy was passed along to the two outstanding actor-directors of the 1950s and 1960s: Jean-Louis Barrault, who trained under both Jouvet and Dullin, and Jean Vilar, who trained under Dullin. (It might be noted in passing that Dullin also helped to launch the career of Antonin Artaud.) Besides Copeau, one other influence touched all four directors of the Cartel, that of Jacques Hébertot. He ran the Théâtre des Champs-Elysées, where he attempted, in the early 1920s, to create a center for international art that would showcase the leading theater, ballet, and opera companies and artists from all over the world.

Charles Dullin regarded himself primarily as an actor and a teacher of actors, even when he was directing his own theater, the Atelier, from 1921 to 1941, and the larger Théâtre de la Cité (also known as Théâtre Sarah-Bernhardt) from 1941 to 1947. His great roles included the title characters of Molière's *L'Avare* (The Miser), Ben Jonson's *Volpone,* and Shakespeare's *Richard III.* An especially gifted mime, Dullin trained a generation of actors, including the great mime Marcel Marceau, in the school he ran for twenty-eight years. As a director, his style evolved from a Copeau-influenced austerity to more lavish settings designed by painters like Jean Hugo, André Barsaq, and André Masson. The 1930 Paris tour of Meyerhold's company influenced Dullin toward greater theatricality, which he described as "poetry of the stage."

Like Dullin, Louis Jouvet remained best known as an actor. His deadpan manner gave an interesting edge to his great roles, Dr. Knock in Jules Romains's *Knock* and Arnolphe in Molière's *L'Ecole des femmes* (School for Wives); the latter production also featured a famous setting by Christian Bérard. After working with Copeau and Hébertot, Jouvet opened his Théâtre de l'Athénée in 1934. There he developed a close working relationship with Jean Giraudoux, the finest French playwright between the wars. As the Cartel director most passionate about language, Jouvet was the perfect director to premiere Giraudoux's linguistically brilliant plays like *Siegfried* (1928), *Intermezzo* (Intermezzo, 1933), *La Guerre de Troie n'aura pas lieu* (Tiger at the Gates, 1935), *Ondine* (1939), *La Folle de Chaillot* (The Madwoman of Chaillot, 1943), and many others.

The tall, dark Russian-born actor-director-designer Georges Pitoëff made his acting debut in Vera Kommissarzhevsky's St. Petersburg theater in 1908. In Geneva during World War I, he opened the Théâtre Pitoëff, which gained a fine enough reputation that Hébertot brought him and his company to Paris and installed them in the Comédie des Champs-Elysées. From 1934 until his death five years later, Pitoëff ran his precariously financed company at the Théâtre des Mathurins. The more than one hundred plays he staged in Paris, designed by himself, introduced more foreign dramatists to French audiences than any other theater had done, including those of Antoine and Lugné-Poe. One of Pitoëff's most celebrated productions was the French-language premiere of Luigi Pirandello's *Six Characters in Search of an Author* in 1923. He also presented eight plays by Bernard Shaw, five by Henrik Ibsen, and many Russian plays as well as numerous others including Eugene O'Neill, Arthur Schnitzler, Gabriele D'Annunzio, and Rabindranath Tagore; and he helped launch the career of French dramatist Jean Anouilh. Pitoëff's closest collaborator was his wife, the lovely actress Ludmilla Pitoëff, opposite whom he played Romeo at fifty. Their son Sacha Pitoëff became a leading actor-director in the 1950s.

Gaston Baty, the only member of the Cartel who was not an actor, was the least obsessed with the primacy of the dramatic text, which he mockingly referred to as *"Sire le Mot"* (His Majesty, The Word). At his Théâtre Montparnasse from 1930 to 1947, Baty staged an often esoteric repertoire using stylized settings with dramatic effects of light and shadow. He often focused on visual evocations of historical periods, and he dramatized two historical novels, Dostoevski's *Crime and Punishment* and Flaubert's *Madame Bovary*. His leading actress Marguerite Jamois, who took over the administration of the company in 1943, was renowned for the roles of the bride in *The Dybbuk* and two breeches roles, Musset's *Lorenzaccio* and Shakespeare's *Hamlet*.

While Copeau and his disciples devoted their small independent theaters to pursuing an ideal of total revitalization of all aspects of dramatic art, a European-influenced renewal in scenic art swept the American commercial theater. The so-called "new stagecraft" encompassed a revolt against stale conventions in acting and directing, but its major impact was in the area of design. This rejection of scenery as literal illustration comprised two overlapping trends. The first was exemplified best in the stage designs of Joseph Urban, who emigrated from Vienna in 1911 to become artistic director and designer at the Boston Opera Company. By 1915 he had begun designing the annual Ziegfeld *Follies* on Broadway and, by 1917, for the Metropolitan Opera in New York, followed by numerous Broadway musicals in the 1920s. From a lesser artist, Urban's contribution might have represented a step backwards, for it meant a return to painted-canvas scenery. However, instead of the long-standard box sets with elements of painted realism, Urban excelled at stylization; he used portals within the proscenium arch to give each setting its individual frame; he emphasized beauty of line: and he set a new standard for scene painting that applied the atmospheric qualities and techniques of the French impressionists to the stage picture.

In contrast to Urban's decorative approach, most American designers of the new stagecraft movement opted for the kind of visual simplification that had been pioneered by Adolph Appia, Edward Gordon Craig, Georg Fuchs, Jacques Rouché, Jacques Copeau, and others. It should be stressed that the two trends within the American new stagecraft were not mutually exclusive. The leader in the latter approach, Robert Edmond Jones, graduated *cum laude* from Harvard in 1910, and went to Europe in 1913, hoping to study under Edward Gordon Craig in Florence, but was not accepted. He saw a production by Appia and Dalcroze at Hellerau that much impressed him, and he settled in Berlin to serve an apprenticeship at the Deutsches Theater under Max Reinhardt and his designers. Jones launched the new stagecraft on Broadway in 1915 with his sets and costumes for Anatole France's *The Man Who Married a Dumb Wife*, produced by Harley Granville-Barker. The simplicity of the almost-abstract, gray and black setting kept the emphasis on the actors in their colorful medieval costumes. In the 1920s Jones designed the sets for three important Shakespeare productions on Broadway, all directed by Arthur Hopkins: *Richard III* (1920), starring John Barrymore; *Macbeth* (1921), starring Lionel Barrymore; and *Hamlet* (1922), starring John Barrymore. Hopkins's directorial approach complemented Jones's constant effort to capture the essence of a period or place without tying it down to a specific reality. Hopkins worked to eliminate superfluous activity and handling of props on stage. Jones's expressionistic settings for *Macbeth* were among his least appreciated in their day, but they appear remarkably original seventy years later. Against a black background Jones set an open structure composed of angular arches that took different configurations in different scenes; as Macbeth became ever more steeped in blood, the arches tilted crazily. In addition, Jones suspended three masks above the stage and beamed strong shafts of light through the eyeholes whenever the three witches appeared on stage.

Louis Jouvet (1887–1951), at center, played the Ragpicker in Jean Giraudoux's The Madwoman of Chaillot. *He worked closely with Giraudoux and directed all his important premieres. Marguerite Moreno played the Madwoman. Photo Lipnitzki, courtesy of French Cultural Services.*

Christian Bérard designed sets and costumes for The Madwoman of Chaillot *at the Théâtre de l'Athénée. This rendering shows costumes and a set piece for act 2. Courtesy of French Cultural Services.*

Another important Giraudoux play produced by Jouvet was Ondine, *the tale of a water sprite who loves a human. This is Pavel Tchelitchew's rendering for the act 2 setting of the 1939 production. Courtesy of French Cultural Services.*

These sketches by Christian Bérard show his famous setting for Jouvet's 1937 production of The School for Wives *by Molière. Street scenes were played with the walls closing off access to Arnolphe's house. Those walls could swing open to reveal Arnolphe's garden courtyard. Courtesy of French Cultural Services.*

One of Gaston Baty's most renowned productions was an adaptation of Flaubert's novel Madame Bovary, *produced at the Théâtre Montparnasse in 1936. Marguerite Jamois played the title role. Courtesy of French Cultural Services.*

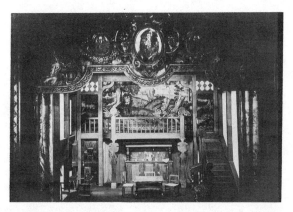

The theatricalism of Gaston Baty (1885–1952) is evident in this setting designed by Emile Bertin for a 1938 production of Lenormand's adaptation of Arden of Feversham. *Courtesy of French Cultural Services.*

Robert Edmond Jones (1887–1954), one of America's most influential scene designers, was a leader in the New Stagecraft movement, advocating artistic selectivity and simplification of elements in place of the standard romantic realism. This 1915 design for The Man Who Married a Dumb Wife *is one of his earliest. From* Stages of the World: Theatre Arts Prints.

Pirandello takes a bow with the cast of the Odescalchi company from Rome in a 1932 revival of Six Characters in Search of an Author, *at the Théâtre Edouard VII in Paris. From* Scenario *(1933).*

In 1922 Robert Edmond Jones and Kenneth Macgowan spent ten weeks traveling in Europe to see plays in France, Sweden, Germany, Czechoslovakia, and Austria. Jones made sketches of numerous stage settings, and he and Macgowan together published their impressions in an enormously influential book, *Continental Stagecraft* (1922). Jones later published *The Dramatic Imagination* (1941). In Jones's own settings there was, according to John Mason Brown, a "lustrous" quality and an "exaltation"; Brown wrote of his ability to create a kind of beauty even in a sordid milieu: "The beauty he created was never sentimental, vapid, or self-advertising in its prettiness. It had the dignity that comes from a fine sense of selection, the strength of simple emphasis, and a purity of design that gave glory to daily things." Other American designers associated with the new stagecraft include Lee Simonson, Norman Bel Geddes, and Jo Mielziner.

The work of all the "mainstream maverick" directors and designers might be summed up as explorations of ways to create a theatricalized reality, which is not the same as realism. They wanted to heighten dramatic effects without losing (as so many avant-garde experimenters had done) the human element at the core of the work. Certain dramatists also sought to transcend realism within a context that could be understood and appreciated by commercial theater audiences. The single most influential one of these dramatists, Luigi Pirandello, questioned the very nature of reality. He played with the conventions of theater to demonstrate that reality depends upon one's point of reference, that there is no single reality but many different ones; and he applied this multiple vision to human identity. A professor of Italian literature in Rome, Pirandello took refuge in writing his intellectual comedies during the difficult years when his wife was undergoing a mental breakdown, making home life miserable for Pirandello and their three children. Living with his wife's madness gave him an immediate awareness of the multiplicity of aspects of the human personality; in this regard it is significant that his plays were collected under the title *Maschere Nude* (Naked Masks).

The 1921 premiere of Pirandello's *Sei Personaggi in Cerca d'Autore* (Six Characters in Search of an Author) in Rome so outraged the audience by its confusing defiance of convention that he and his daughter had to be rescued from the crowd. But within a few years the play had been translated into two dozen languages and performed in every major city. It was this play, with its complex dialectic between life and art, between reality and illusion, that challenged all previous notions of verisimilitude in art. *Six Characters in Search of an Author* is one of a Pirandellian trilogy of plays about the theater, the other two being *Ciascuno a suo modo* (Each in His Own Way, 1924) and *Questa sera si recita a soggetto* (Tonight We Improvise, 1930). In 1925 Pirandello founded his own Teatro d'Arte in Rome. His subsequent work owed much to the help and inspiration he gained from his leading actress Marta Abba. Their tours of Europe, along with Actor Ruggero Ruggeri, were highly acclaimed, and in 1934 Pirandello—author of forty-four plays, six novels, and many volumes of short stories, poetry, and criticism—won the Nobel Prize for Literature.

It was in the 1920s and 1930s too that Eugene O'Neill wrote most of his plays that changed the course of American drama. Perhaps his greatest contribution was simply to be the internationally respected dramatist that the United States had awaited for over a century. His recognition as such began with his first Broadway production, *Beyond the Horizon,* which won the Pulitzer Prize in 1920, and it was confirmed with three additional Pulitzer Prizes, for *Anna Christie* (1920), *Strange Interlude* (1928), and the posthumous *Long Day's Journey into Night* (1957). Although he remains best known for such realistic plays as his one comedy *Ah! Wilderness* (1933) or his late tragedy of hope *The Iceman Cometh* (1939; produced 1946), O'Neill experimented with a variety of styles that expanded the boundaries of mainstream theater. His early expressionistic plays prompted such innovations as the first American use of a plaster sky dome, installed by designer Cleon Throckmorton for *The Emperor Jones* (1920). This play broke new ground also by putting most of the action in the form of a monologue, by running without intermission as a full-length play, and by featuring a black character as protagonist. Most significantly, O'Neill's insistence that a black actor be found to play the title role—a break from the standard practice of using white actors in blackface for Negro speaking parts—initiated the racial integration of the American stage. (The title role of *The Emperor Jones* was created by Charles Gilpin; Paul Robeson took the role in the 1924 revival and on tour to London.) In contrast to his short full-length plays like *The Hairy Ape* (1921), O'Neill also tested his audience's endurance with long plays like the tremendously successful *Mourning Becomes Electra* (1931), composed of three full-length plays—a total of thirteen acts—presented as a single production. The Pirandellian concern with discrepancies between the mask and the self was explored through the use of masks in *The Great God Brown* (1925) and through thoughts spoken aloud in the nine-act *Strange Interlude*. O'Neill won the Nobel Prize for Literature in 1936.

England's leading dramatist of the age wrote in a very different spirit from the gloomy O'Neill and yet he too was a theatricalizer of reality. Noël Coward highlighted the "hectic and nervy" momentum of the 1920s and the sleek, sophisticated modernism of the 1930s in a long string of successes both as performer and playwright. He had sung, danced, and acted from childhood, and began acting the witty leading roles in his own plays in 1920. *The Vortex* (1924), which opened on his

Eugene O'Neill's earliest productions were his one-act plays of the sea staged by the Provincetown Players. This one, The Moon of the Caribbees *(1918) was performed in New York under the direction of Thomas Mitchell. The setting, representing the deck of the USS Glencairn, was designed by Cleon Throckmorton. Photograph by Francis Bruguiere, from Sheldon Cheney,* Stage Decoration.

Ben Halley, Jr., played the title role in The Emperor Jones, *produced at Missouri Repertory Theatre in 1988 for the centennial of Eugene O'Neill's birth. George Keathley directed, John Ezell designed the sets, and costumes were by Baker S. Smith.*

Noël Coward's Hay Fever *(1925) is a perennial favorite of professional and community theaters everywhere. Pictured in this 1982 Missouri Repertory Theatre production are Ellen Baker as Jackie, Peg Small as Judith Bliss, Richard Gustin as Richard Greatham, Kevin Paul Hofeditz as Sandy Tyrell, Cynthia Rendlen as Sorel Bliss, and Rob Knepper as Simon Bliss. Francis J. Cullinan directed. The set was by Wray Steven Graham, with costumes by John Carver Sullivan.*

T. S. Eliot's poetic drama Murder in the Cathedral *was produced at the Comédie Française in 1978. The British director Terry Hands staged it. Shown here are Michel Etcheverry and Francois Beaulieu. Courtesy of French Cultural Services.*

twenty-fifth birthday, catapulted him to fame with its suave treatment of a daring subject: an aging woman seeks reassurance of her charm by taking a young lover, while her son turns to drugs as an antidote to his mother's indifference. In sixty plays and over three hundred songs, Coward captured the hard-edged cynicism of his time while celebrating frivolity. His fast-paced repartee in plays like *Hay Fever* (1925), *Private Lives* (1930), and *Design for Living* (1932) prompted Somerset Maugham's observation that he wrote dialogue to be "eked out with shrugs, waves of the hand and grimaces," which he saw as "another nail in the coffin of prose drama." Mrs. Patrick Campbell thought that Coward's characters "talked like typewriting."

At the same time, the 1930s brought a revival of poetic drama in England. It began in 1928 when John Masefield's religious verse drama *The Coming of Christ* was produced in Canterbury Cathedral with sets and costumes by the Appia-influenced designer Charles Ricketts. For several years afterward, there was an annual Canterbury Festival featuring classic plays like the *Everyman* produced by Nugent Monck. After seeing T. S. Eliot's pageant play *The Rock* in London in 1934, the dean of the cathedral commissioned Eliot to write an original play in verse, on a subject from the cathedral's history, for the 1935 festival. The result was *Murder in the Cathedral*, which also initiated the Christian verse drama movement in England. In an essay entitled "The Aims of Christian Drama," Eliot stated: "What poetry should do in the theatre is a kind of humble shadow or analogy of the Incarnation, whereby the human is taken up into the divine." Other poets who followed Eliot in using Christian themes in plays that combined poetic purity of form with visual pageantry included Charles Williams, Dorothy Sayers, Christopher Hassall, and Christopher Fry. After the church had reintroduced the poet into the theater, the professional theater took up the cause. Outstanding among the nonreligious verse plays were *The Dog Beneath the Skin* (1935) and *The Ascent of F6* (1938) by W. H. Auden and Christopher Isherwood. After World War II, a number of poets turned to the commercial theater, most notably Eliot with *The Cocktail Party* (1949) and Christopher Fry with *The Lady's Not for Burning* (1948) and *Venus Observed* (1949).

France also produced a great poet-dramatist of deep religiosity: Paul Claudel. A mystical experience in Notre Dame Cathedral on Christmas 1886, when he was eighteen, awakened Claudel's fervent Roman Catholicism. At the same time he began frequenting symbolist literary circles. These persuasions, which found expression in his unique poetic line—*le vers claudélien*, an unrhymed, unmetered verse based upon breath groups—infused the plays he began writing in the 1890s. "Poetry is the realm of the visible to which Faith adds the invisible," he stated. Entering the diplomatic service, he was posted to China where he experienced an adulterous love affair that became the subject of his most personal play, *Partage de midi* (Break of Noon, 1905). This spare, four-character lyrical tragedy distills Claudel's most characteristic themes, the opposing pulls of carnal and spiritual desires, the harmonious complexity and unity of the universe, the attainment of the absolute through self-renunciation. Because of its intimate nature, Claudel withheld *Break of Noon* from production until 1948 when he authorized a production directed by Jean-Louis Barrault, who also acted in it. Barrault had staged a brilliant premiere of Claudel's *Le Soulier de satin* (The Satin Slipper, 1924; produced 1943) at the Comédie Française during the Nazi occupation of Paris; the play's soaring affirmation of faith had strengthened the morale of the French resistance. As dramatist and director, Claudel and Barrault complemented each other in much the same way that Giraudoux and Jouvet enhanced each other's work. Claudel's over two dozen plays, several of which exist in more than one version, continue to hold the stage in France at the end of the twentieth century.

The Belgian playwright Michel de Ghelderode often used religious subjects, but his impetus was more superstition than faith. Although he wrote in French, he took his inspiration from Flemish sources, including painters Pieter Breughel and Hieronymus Bosch. His sense of theatricality grew out of his early love for marionette theater coupled with an interest in the violence of Elizabethan theater; it is typical that he often characterized Death as a figure of farce. From 1927 to 1930, he wrote for the Flemish Popular Theater, where the young actor Renaat Verheyen played the leading roles in plays like *Pantagleize* (1929); Verheyen's untimely death caused Ghelderode to abandon active participation in the theater. He remained little known outside Belgium until the 1940s, when a Frenchwoman, Catherine Toth, discovered his plays and brought them to the Paris stage, where his *Fastes d'enfer* (Chronicles of Hell, 1929) outraged audiences in 1949. Although Belgian theater is not widely known outside that country, it comprises abundant work in Dutch as well as French. Of the Flemish writers, Hugo Claus is outstanding; others are Lucienne Stassaert and Ivo Van Hove. Prominent among the postwar French-language Belgian dramatists are René Kalisky, Jean Louvet, Jean Sigrid, and Paul Willems.

DECENTRALIZATION OF THE THEATER

At the beginning of the twentieth century, the playhouses of most nations were concentrated in the capital cities, but nowhere was the theater so highly centralized as in France and the United States, where professional theater meant Paris and New York. Touring companies, less prevalent than they had been in the nineteenth century, rarely appeared in towns without railway connections. Although the international workers' movement considered theater a tool of public instruction, the numerous French socialist theater initiatives of the 1890s occurred either in Paris or in its working-class suburbs. One early provincial theater success story was the long-lived Théâtre de Bussang, an outdoor theater in the Vosges, founded by Maurice Pottecher in 1895. The idea of a "people's theater" gained greater currency after novelist-playwright Romain Rolland articulated a populist ideal in his 1903 book *Le Théâtre du peuple* (People's Theater) Thus, in France the geographical decentralization of the theater was linked with the idea of reaching new audiences across the social spectrum.

That process was given its major impetus by a largely unsung hero of the modern theater, Firmin Gémier. After a stint in the working-class neighborhood melodrama theaters, the self-taught actor joined André Antoine's Théâtre Libre in 1892 and gained a following there before moving on to Aurélien Lugné-Poe's Théâtre de l'Oeuvre, where he created the title role in Jarry's *Ubu roi*. Turning to free-lance directing in 1900, he focused on works that would appeal to broadly based audiences, including Rolland's populist history play *Le 14 juillet* (Bastille Day) in 1902 and a commemorative mass spectacle (2,500 performers for an audience of 20,000) in Lausanne, Switzerland, in 1903. Gémier took over the direction of the Théâtre Antoine after Antoine moved to the Odéon, and there, from 1906 to 1921, Gémier offered an eclectic repertoire to a receptive public. However, he dreamed of reaching much larger audiences and soon began to wage a campaign for public funding for a national touring company to take theater to culturally deprived provincial towns. Although he did not get a government subsidy, Gémier attracted private funding and inaugurated his Théâtre National Ambulant in 1911. Eight steam-engine tractors pulled a caravan of thirty-seven trailers that carried the sets, costumes, lighting equipment, electric generator, seating for 1,650 people, portable stage and proscenium arch, and the double-walled tent—supported by five seventeen-meter steel towers—that housed the stage and auditorium. The enterprise was enormously successful in drawing enthusiastic mass audiences in every part of the country, but its finances were undermined by constant breakdowns of the tractors and by the longer-than-anticipated setup time of the tent. After two seasons, Gémier ended his noble experiment.

In 1919 Gémier tried a new tactic for broadening the base of the theatergoing public. He commissioned Saint-Georges de Bouhélier to write a pageant-spectacle based upon the myth of Oedipus, and staged it in Paris's Cirque d'Hiver. The sixty-four performances of *Oedipe roi de Thèbes* (Oedipus, King of Thebes), in which Gémier played the title role, were seen by a total of fifty-thousand people. This clear triumph of theater for a mass audience was certainly a factor in his obtaining government subsidization in 1920 to found a national popular theater. Gémier's populist spirit is evident in his choice of a national holiday, November 11, to open the Théâtre National Populaire (T.N.P.). Furthermore, his inaugural production was not a play but a show, *Les Chants de la République* (Songs of the Republic), composed of song, dance, mime and spectacle. The five-thousand-seat Trocadéro auditorium posed considerable problems, but it remained the home of the T.N.P. until 1935, when the building was razed to make way for the Palais de Chaillot international exposition hall. The T.N.P. ceased to exist until its 1951 revival by Jean Vilar. While remaining at the helm of the T.N.P. until his death in 1933, Gémier also took on the direction of the Odéon from 1922 to 1930. There, often professing his interest in American theater, he introduced the plays of Eugene O'Neill to French audiences. An ardent admirer of Shakespeare's plays, he founded the Société Shakespeare and acted many Shakespearean roles, most notably a highly acclaimed Shylock. Gémier's last great undertaking was international in scope. He worked for many years to realize his dream of establishing a world organization of theater artists. The Société Universelle du Théâtre, founded in 1926, became the prototype for today's International Theatre Institute sponsored by UNESCO. In 1927 he presided over the first International Congress of the Theater, which attracted such notable artists as Pirandello, Meyerhold, and Reinhardt. Held annually in different cities, the congress not only showcased interesting international productions, but also provided a venue for lively exchanges of information among artists in all areas of theater.

The next step in the decentralization of French theater occurred almost immediately after World War II. At that time there were fifty-two theaters in Paris as opposed to fifty-one theaters for all the rest of the country; the latter group—mostly poorly equipped municipal theaters—depended heavily upon touring productions from Paris. Appointed to the theater and music section of the new government bureau of arts and letters, Jeanne Laurent took the initiative to create combinations of government, local, and municipal subsidization that would permit the establishment of five regional dramatic centers, each with a permanent theater company and drawing its clientele from the surrounding area. Within six years after the end of the war, companies were established in Toulouse in the southwest, Strasbourg in the east, Saint-Etienne in the south central region, Rennes in the north, and Aix-en-Provence in the southeast. By 1951 a government report could claim: "The success of the regional dramatic centers proves . . . that it is possible to reach a popular audience with works, classic or modern, of high quality."

That postwar wave of decentralization must also include the inauguration in 1947 of what was to become an annual summer festival of

Left, among the many Shakespearean roles acted by Firmin Gémier was Shylock. This 1915 production of The Merchant of Venice *in Paris was directed by Gaston Baty. Courtesy of French Cultural Services.*

Right, the decade after World War II saw the revival of many classic plays, perhaps as an expression of longing for stability. The Comédie Française produced Pierre Corneille's Nicomède *in 1951, directed by Jean Debucourt. Courtesy of French Cultural Services.*

Below, an all-star cast performed Jean Racine's Britannicus *in 1952. The production was directed and designed by Jean Marais. On stage from left to right are Roland Alexandre, Renée Faure, and Jean Marais. Courtesy of French Cultural Services.*

The enormous theater in the Palais de Chaillot became the home of the Théâtre National Populaire under Jean Vilar (1912–71). Courtesy of French Cultural Services.

Jean Vilar's production of Shakespeare's A Midsummer Night's Dream *(Le Songe d'une nuit d'été) at the Théâtre National Populaire was designed by Léon Gischia, with music by Maurice Jarre. In this scene, Vilar played Oberon to the Titania of Maria Casarès. Courtesy of French Cultural Services.*

Molière's Dom Juan *was produced at the Théâtre National Populaire in 1953 under the direction of Jean Vilar. Shown here are Vilar in the title role, Monique Chaumette as Elvire, and Daniel Sorano as Sganarelle. The half-Senegalese Sorano (1920–62) was one of the finest actors on the twentieth-century French stage. Courtesy of French Cultural Services.*

Daniel Sorano played Figaro in the T.N.P.'s 1956 production of The Marriage of Figaro *by Beaumarchais. He is shown here with Catherine Le Couey. Courtesy of French Cultural Services.*

theater in Avignon. It began when Jean Vilar won the support of the municipal government to present the French premiere of Shakespeare's *Richard II* and two previously unproduced French plays in the courtyard of the Palace of the Popes. On a vast bare stage—in the tradition of Copeau's *tréteau nu*—before the outer walls of the fourteenth-century palace, Vilar developed the "Avignon–T.N.P. style" of production: characters entered from darkness into pools of light that isolated the focal elements for each scene; Leon Gischia's period costumes used vivid colors and large-scale patterns that would make a statement even to the last row of the two thousand seats; drum rolls bridged the scene changes. *Richard II,* with Vilar in the title role, was performed in Paris the following season and revived at Avignon in 1948, 1949, and 1952. When the T.N.P. was resuscitated in 1951 and given the three-thousand-seat theater in the Palais de Chaillot, Vilar was the obvious choice to head it. Besides carrying over the production style he had developed in Avignon, he inaugurated several policies that were intended to draw popular audiences to see his repertoire of classics mingled with some Brecht, O'Casey, and Valle-Inclán. Ticket prices were significantly lower than those of other theaters. An early curtain time and an inexpensive buffet at the theater made it easy for workers to come directly from their jobs to the theater. Tipping was abolished. He also instituted "artistic weekends" as a way of taking theater directly to the people. The first of these, a legendarily successful two-day festival in the industrial suburb of Suresnes, offered a package of two plays, a concert, discussions with the cast, three meals, and a dance, all for twelve-hundred francs, at a time when a single ticket to a commercial play cost around eight hundred francs. Never did Vilar forget his maxim, "Theatre is a public service." His brilliant company, performing in Paris during the theater season and in Avignon in the summer, included many who would rise to international stardom: Gérard Philipe, Jeanne Moreau, Silvia Monfort, Germaine Montéro, Michel Bouquet, Georges Wilson. Maurice Jarre composed music for the company. Vilar ran the T.N.P. until 1963, when he resigned to protest certain government policies toward the theater. However, he continued to direct the Festival d'Avignon until his death in 1971, but he did not personally stage any more productions after the infamous events of May 1968.

Between the postwar and the 1960s waves of decentralization was founded the provincial theater that would eventually, in 1972, replace the Paris venue as the Théâtre National Populaire. The founder, Roger Planchon, had been working with an amateur group called the Comédie de Lyon. The quality of their work and their efforts to reach working-class audiences brought them an invitation in 1957 to move into a large theater in Villeurbanne, an industrial sister-city to Lyon. Planchon adopted many of Vilar's techniques and took advantage of his working-class location to keep in close touch with his public. By 1959 Planchon's Théâtre de la Cité de Villeurbanne was granted government subsidization along with designation as a *troupe permanente* (permanent company); in 1963 its level of subsidy was upgraded to that of a *centre dramatique* (regional dramatic center).

The 1960s wave of decentralization resulted from President Charles DeGaulle's 1959 appointment of André Malraux to head a newly created Ministry of Cultural Affairs apart from the Ministry of Education. Proclaiming "every French citizen's right to culture," Malraux set forth on a mission to "make the great works of humanity, and especially those of France, accessible to the greatest number of French people; to introduce the widest audience to the cultural patrimony and to support the creation of works of art and a mentality that enriches it." He created a new category of government-supported theater complex that would rank above the *troupes permanentes* and the *centres dramatiques;* this was the *maison de la culture* (house of culture). Twenty of these were planned, but only seven had been built before the events of May 1968. A theater is at the heart of each *maison de la culture,* which also incorporates a lecture hall, movie theater, concert hall, recording and book lending libraries, cafeteria, nursery, and areas for socializing or listening to poetry readings. In addition to the *maisons de la culture* in provincial cities, one theater in Paris became a part of the decentralization process: the Théâtre de l'Est Parisien (T.E.P.), which had begun as a small independent troupe operating on a shoestring budget in a former movie house on the working-class east side of Paris, was granted the status of a *maison de la culture* in 1963. Its director, Guy Rétoré, built up a large subscription audience for a repertoire of classics and contributing activities.

Despite Malraux's herculean efforts, his Ministry's budget was never adequate to the task, and two-thirds of it went for simple maintenance of museums and historical monuments. Furthermore, the three national theaters—the Comédie Française, the Odéon, and the T.N.P.—received as much as all other subsidized theaters combined. And there were some who criticized the very concept of the *maisons de la culture* as tools for imposing a bourgeois cultural patrimony that was irrelevant to the lives of working-class French people. At the same time, the plays of the Theatre of the Absurd were criticized as "closed theater," because they posited the futility of existence. Brecht became the model for an "open theater" that would promote social change through *réalisme engagé* (committed realism). Indeed, the seed had been planted as early as 1954, when the Berliner Ensemble, on its first tour outside the "iron curtain," performed Brecht's *Mother Courage* in Paris. Roger Planchon subsequently directed Brecht's *Good Person of Setzuan* (1954) and applied Brecht's theories to his politicized interpretations of the classics, like his

Gérard Philipe (1922–59), kneeling, played the title role in the T.N.P.'s 1951 production of The Cid *by Pierre Corneille. Philipe was a superb actor who won a large following as a matinee idol. Courtesy of French Cultural Services.*

Philippe Noiret and Maria Casarès were among the outstanding actors who performed the classics for popular audiences at the T.N.P. They are shown here in Victor Hugo's Marie Tudor *in 1955. Courtesy of French Cultural Services.*

Roger Planchon (b. 1931) attracted popular audiences to his theater in Villeurbanne with productions like The Three Musketeers, *which entered his repertoire in 1958. Courtesy of French Cultural Services.*

1962 and 1973 versions of Molière's *Tartuffe*. This was the cultural climate in which the events of May 1968 occurred.

The unrest began in March at Nanterre University, not far from Paris, when students led by Daniel Cohn-Bendit ("Danny the Red") demonstrated to protest capitalism, imperialism, and university paternalism. Students at the Sorbonne in Paris, disgruntled by chronically overcrowded classrooms and what they perceived as "élitist art," joined the cause in May. The street demonstrations soon involved workers who went on strike for better working conditions and higher wages. For several days, France was virtually paralyzed by work stoppages. In order to keep the workers from returning out of boredom to their jobs, the protesters created street entertainments of all kinds; they sent performers and discussion leaders to lend moral support to the workers occupying their factories. Theaters suspended performances, in part as a declaration of solidarity based upon the idea that artists are workers too, and in part because audiences were forsaking theatergoing in favor of the livelier action in the streets.

The theater also figured prominently in the events of May 1968 when the Odéon was overrun by insurgents who chose it as a symbol of the bourgeois culture they execrated. The government-subsidized Odéon-Théâtre de France had been under the artistic direction of Jean-Louis Barrault since 1959. Barrault had made a distinguished stage and film career since his training in mime under Charles Dullin. After acting and directing at the Comédie Française during the war years, he and his wife, actress Madeleine Renaud, formed their own company in 1946. The first home of the Compagnie Renaud-Barrault was a boulevard theater, the Marigny. There they produced an eclectic repertoire—characteristic of his entire career—ranging from classics to the avant-garde, and they embarked upon frequent international tours. When Barrault moved the company to the Odéon, he accepted an unrealistically low level of subsidy, but succeeded beyond all expectations in attracting an ardent following from the Latin Quarter in addition to the fashionable theatergoers who had supported him at the Marigny. David Whitton describes Barrault's approach to acting and directing as "combining the beauty of the text with a physical musicality based on bodily expression."

The rabble that occupied the Odéon for a month destroyed not only state property but also the entire costume stock and equipment owned by the Compagnie Renaud-Barrault, amounting to nineteen full productions. When Barrault attempted to engage in a dialogue with the demonstrators he was hooted down and insulted. Barrault suggests in his memoirs, *Memories for Tomorrow* (1972), that he was used by the government as a scapegoat. The entire episode—the wasting of twenty years of his work for no clear purpose—was deeply dispiriting to Barrault. He

One of the Barrault-Renaud productions at the Marigny was Malatesta *by Henry de Montherlant. They are shown here as Malatesta and Isotta. Barrault directed, with sets and costumes by Ariano Andreu. Courtesy of French Cultural Services.*

Madeleine Renaud and Jean-Louis Barrault display the poster for their first season at the state-subsidized Odéon-Théâtre de France, little suspecting how their efforts would be betrayed in May 1968. Courtesy of French Cultural Services.

Rabelais, *a production created by Jean-Louis Barrault, based upon the works of François Rabelais, premiered at the Elysée-Montmartre in Paris in 1968. Its phenomenal success revived the Compagnie Madeleine Renaud-Jean-Louis Barrault. Courtesy of French Cultural Services.*

had embraced all forms of theater as possible avenues of communication among all people, but now he observed that "political theatre is in reality class theatre attacking another class." Barrault and Renaud resolutely began afresh. Barrault rented a theater and created a production, *Rabelais,* based upon the rollicking, irreverent work of the sixteenth-century author; its success was phenomenal, and the company was launched anew. After performing from 1972 to 1981 in the Gare d'Orsay (the former railway terminal that is today a museum of nineteenth-century art), the company moved into the Théatre du Rond Point, a lovely complex built into a former skating rink on the Champs-Elysées; it is scarcely two hundred meters from the Marigny, where the Compagnie Renaud-Barrault had been born thirty-five years earlier.

The events of May 1968 had serious repercussions not only for Barrault but on all of French theater for the next decade. That same month Roger Planchon called a general meeting of artistic directors at his theater in Villeurbanne to consider various demands to politicize French theater. On May 25, forty-two directors signed a "Declaration of the rights of the public and the duties of producers." It pointed up such real problems as inadequate funding and excessively centralized control over the organization of individual theaters, but it also went so far as to define theater as a "political instrument." The directors set themselves the challenge of reaching the "non-audience," the great segment of the population whose lives were untouched by cultural institutions. They determined that they would change the repertoires that had been announced for the following season to reflect a new populism that would arouse the political consciousness of the "non-audience"—even if it meant losing their traditional subscribers. Planchon, for example, wrote and staged *La Mise en pièces du Cid* (The Tearing to Pieces of *The Cid,* 1969), a satirical treatment of Corneille's classic play intertwined with a topical consideration of the role of theater in society. Although Planchon's inventive staging put the material across to his working-class constituency, most directors were less skilled at transforming current events into spectacle. The 1968–69 season brought the first decrease in total theater attendance in a decade.

Avignon, too, was affected by the course of events. The annual summer festival had grown enormously over the years. While the T.N.P. productions in the courtyard outside the Palace of the Popes remained the centerpiece of the festival, numerous other companies were presenting invited productions in various locations around the town in addition to concerts, films, dance programs, and lectures. At the twentieth annual Avignon festival, several hundred leftists gathered to denounce the event as a "supermarket of culture" that encouraged passive consumption of art. Among the disrupters of the festival were the Americans

Julian Beck and Judith Malina, who had also been present at the occupation of the Odéon. Their company, the Living Theatre, was an invited participant at the 1968 Avignon festival; however, they began demanding the right to present their production of *Paradise Now* not only in their assigned theatrical space but also as a free street performance at one o'clock in the morning. Vilar refused them permission out of consideration for the rights of the residents in those streets. For this Vilar was reviled as a member of the establishment, attacked and insulted by people who could only have been ignorant of everything he had stood for during his career. Jean Vilar died in 1971.

Few playwrights were prepared in 1968 to write plays based upon the headlines of the day, but this did not particularly concern the directors who met at Villeurbanne. They felt that the theater had too long been dominated by *"Sire le Mot,"* and that they could best attract the nonaudience away from their television by offering a theater of images and action rather than mere dialogue. A new generation of directors known as the *jeunes loups* (young wolves)—influenced by Brecht, Artaud, and the movies—started making waves around 1968. Like Planchon, they were not content merely to direct an established text. They wanted to create the entire show: scenario, leading role, sets, costumes, and lighting; that is, they deemphasized the playwright's text or *écriture dramatique* in favor of an *écriture scénique* (stage language) that was largely visual. The result was the antithesis of Copeau's *tréteau nu* and Vilar's "T.N.P. style;" it was a theater of neobaroque spectacle. Among the directors who might be called *jeunes loups* were Patrice Chéreau, André Benedetto, Gabriel Garran, Gérard Gélas, Georges Lavaudant, Marcel Maréchal, Daniel Mesguich, Jean-Pierre Vincent, Antoine Vitez, and several directors of Latin American origin: Jérome Savary, Victor Garcia, Jorge Lavelli, and Alfredo Arias.

An overlapping tendency that further suppressed the art of the dramatist for nearly a decade was a production approach called "collective creation." This practice grew out of attempts to organize theater companies like workers' cooperatives with all members of the company sharing in the backstage tasks and in the creative process. Once the company had decided on the subject for a production, everyone would contribute background research. Through a process of improvisation and general give-and-take, a show would be developed. One troupe managed to create works of exceptional artistic quality by this method, undoubtedly due to the sure guiding hand of its director, Ariane Mnouchkine. She founded her company, Le Théâtre de Soleil, in Paris in 1964. Their first production that captured a great deal of attention, a French version of Arnold Wesker's *The Kitchen* in 1967, was revived after the events of May 1968 and often performed in factories. In 1969, their

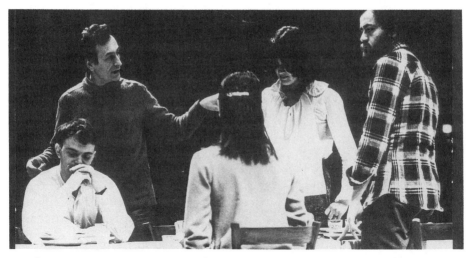

Above, Antoine Vitez (1930–90) made his reputation as a leading French director at the National Theater in the Palais de Chaillot. In 1988 he was appointed to head the Comédie-Française. In this 1977 photograph, Vitez (standing at left) directs a rehearsal of Iphigénie Hotel *by Michel Vinaver. Courtesy of French Cultural Services.*

Below, left, like many of the directors known as the "young wolves," Roger Planchon wrote his own script, directed the production, and played a leading role. Planchon, seated, appears with Jean Boise in La Remise *(1963). Courtesy of French Cultural Services.*

Below, right, Jorge Lavelli is one of several outstanding Argentine directors who have made their careers in Paris since the 1960s. Lavelli is shown here rehearsing a scene from La Mante polaire *(The Polar Cap, 1979) by the French–Russian–Iranian playwright Serge Rezvani. Spanish-born actress María Casarès is seated at center. Courtesy of French Cultural Services.*

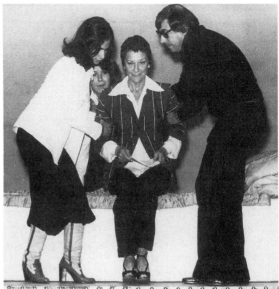

Above, Pierre Bourgeade's Palazzo Mentale, *which won the French theater critics' prize for 1977, exemplifies the beginning of a return to respect for the spoken word while retaining all that had been learned since 1968 about stage imagery and strong lighting effects. The production was directed by Georges Lavaudant. Courtesy of French Cultural Services.*

Below, left, in the 1970s, playwright Jean-Paul Wenzel countered the theater of neo-baroque spectacle with what he called le théâtre du quotidien *(theater of ordinary life). His spare and intimate study of boredom,* Loin d'Hagondange *(Far from Hagondange, 1977), directed by Patrice Chéreau, was performed by François Simon and Tatiana Moukhine. Courtesy of French Cultural Services.*

Below, right, Hélène Cixous, a novelist turned playwright, wrote a dramatic deconstruction of Freud's case study of Dora. Le Portrait de Dora *was directed by Simone Benmussa at the Théâtre d'Orsay in 1976. Courtesy of French Cultural Services.*

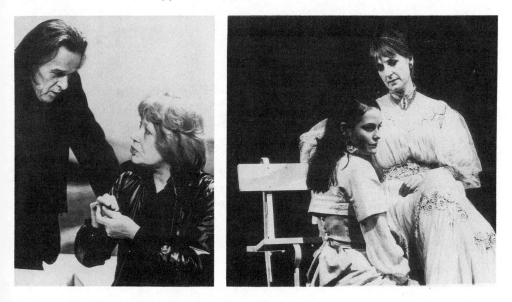

first collective creation, *Les Clowns* (The Clowns), explored the relationship of the artist to society and of art to politics. The company then acquired a permanent home in a former munitions factory, the Cartoucherie de Vincennes, on the outskirts of Paris, and inaugurated it with what remains their most famous production: *1789: La révolution doit s'arrêter à la perfection du bonheur* (1789: The Revolution Must Stop when Complete Happiness is Achieved, 1970). The French Revolution was chosen as a topic that would be meaningful to every French citizen. Through six months of research and improvisation, the actors invented a retelling of the revolution using the devices of popular street entertainment. Most of the audience milled about in a space surrounded by several connected platform stages on which simultaneous action occurred. Thus the spectators were made to feel as if they were a part of the events. *1789* achieved a total attendance of 281,370 and could have run longer, but the company was eager to create anew. In 1972 they premiered a sequel, *1793*, followed by *L'Âge d'or* (The Golden Age, 1975) and Mnouchkine's own adaptation of Klaus Mann's novel *Mephisto* (1979).

By the end of the 1970s, French theater people were realizing how much had been lost by the decade of neglect of the dramatist. Mnouchkine's effort to recover the verbal element took the form of a brilliant series of Shakespeare productions: *Richard II* (1981), *Twelfth Night* (1982), and *Henry IV, Part I* (1984). Besides a renewal of respect for the classics, there was a concerted effort on the part of many directors to discover and nurture new playwrights. Many had begun writing before 1968, but found their audiences in the 1980s, including Michel Vinaver, Romain Weingarten, Jean-Paul Wenzel, Marguerite Duras, Nathalie Sarraute, Andreé Chedid, Jean-Claude Grumberg, Serge Rezvani, and others.

The American theater's decentralization away from Broadway proceeded quite differently. One early impetus was the introduction of dramatic literature courses into the college curriculum. In the nineteenth century, many universities had extracurricular literary clubs that sponsored performances, but it was not until Columbia University gave Brander Matthews the title of Professor of Dramatic Literature in 1902 (the first such appointment in the United States) that the study of plays as literature began to be taken seriously. Matthews understood that plays exist more fully in performance than as literature, but it was left to George Pierce Baker to win acceptance for that view. In his course on medieval and renaissance English drama at Harvard University in the 1890s, Baker incorporated material on the plays as vehicles for the stage. By the turn of the century he was offering courses in the contemporary drama at Harvard and at Radcliffe. In 1903 he taught the first college course in playwriting at Radcliffe, and his English 47 course introduced techniques of dramatic composition into the Harvard curriculum. One of his first students, Edward Sheldon, wrote a full-length play, *Salvation Nell* (1908), that was produced by Minnie Maddern Fiske. Realizing the need to test the new writing in production, Baker organized an extracurricular laboratory for English 47. Beginning in 1912, the 47 Workshop nurtured such theater artists as playwrights Eugene O'Neill, S. N. Behrman, Sidney Howard, and Josephine Preston Peabody; critics John Mason Brown and Robert Benchley; producers and academics Hallie Flanagan and Frederick Koch; designers Lee Simonson and Robert Edmond Jones; directors George Abbott, Alexander Dean, and Theresa Helburn. In 1925, unable to expand his program at Harvard, Baker moved to Yale University, where a new playhouse was built to support a full curriculum of graduate studies in drama under his direction. The first Master of Fine Arts degree in theater was awarded at Yale University in 1931.

Other university theater programs followed. As early as 1914, a degree-offering department of dramatic arts was established at Carnegie Institute of Technology under Thomas Wood Stevens; later he became director of the Goodman Memorial Theatre of the Chicago Art Institute. After producing plays for thirteen years at the University of North Dakota, Frederick H. Koch moved to the University of North Carolina, where in 1919 he founded the famed Carolina Playmakers to produce original folk plays. Thomas H. Dickinson of Wisconsin, Alexander Drummond of Cornell, Hallie Flanagan at Vassar, and E. C. Mabie of Iowa also pioneered dramatic arts in the college curriculum.

A second factor contributing to the decentralization of American theater was the little theater movement. The original impetus for the proliferation of amateur community theaters across the country in the 1910s may have been the example of the European independent theaters, which received widespread coverage in the American press. Dissatisfaction with the commercial theater is evident in the fact that many groups were started as "art theaters" to present foreign plays in translation or to experiment with production styles, as did Maurice Browne's Chicago Little Theatre, an amateur avant-garde troupe founded in 1912. In communities rarely visited by traveling companies, there was an element of civic pride about participation in such an endeavor. The Northampton Municipal Theatre, founded in 1912 by Jessie Bonstelle, was one of the first of these, and it was one in which students and professionals worked side by side. Bonstelle, a successful stock company manager, artistic director, and actress, espoused populist ideals for her theater where, for five years, she produced a repertoire ranging from light comedies to Shakespeare. "It comes so close to being the right idea," she wrote in 1912, "that every city should have at least one theatre of its own." Soon she was envisioning a national theater, and later she advocated a network of civic theaters, starting in eight representative cities. She proposed that these be modeled after the Detroit Civic Theatre, which she founded in 1928 and ran until her death in 1932.

The traditional date for the beginning of the little theater movement is 1915, the year in which the Washington Square Players, the Neighborhood Playhouse, and the Provincetown Players were all founded. Under the leadership of Lawrence Langner, the Washington Square Players in New York City's Greenwich Village presented an ambitious repertoire of American and foreign plays, paying neither salaries nor royalties, but upholding high standards of production. Before they disbanded in 1918, the Washington Square Players had produced sixty-two one-act and six full-length plays. After the war, many of that group came together again to form The Theatre Guild, which has achieved a long history of producing good plays, although it did not maintain a permanent company. A splinter group from the Theatre Guild became The Group Theatre (1931–41); among the outstanding talents associated with the Group were its three founding directors Harold Clurman, Lee Strasberg, and Cheryl Crawford; playwrights Clifford Odets, Paul Green, Irwin Shaw, and Sidney Kingsley; designer Mordecai Gorelik; director Robert Lewis; and actors Morris Carnovsky, Elia Kazan, John Garfield, Lee J. Cobb, Franchot Tone, and Luther and Stella Adler. The Neighborhood Playhouse was founded at New York's lower east side Henry Street Settlement House by Irene and Alice Lewisohn, with a goal of producing ethnic plays to instill pride in individual national heritages. Its success brought unexpected growth and attracted such talents as Richard Boleslavski and Martha Graham. Although the theater closed in 1972, the Neighborhood Playhouse School of Theatre was founded the following year. There, as head of the acting program since 1935, Sanford Meisner trained one of the most impressive rosters of actors in the American theater.

The Provincetown Players began as an informal gathering of artists vacationing in Provincetown, Massachusetts, in the summer of 1915. Two one-act plays—including *Suppressed Desires* by the group's leader George Cram "Jig" Cook and his wife Susan Glaspell—were staged in a private home. The interest generated led to additional performances in a fish house on a wharf and an expanded endeavor the following summer. Eugene O'Neill joined them in the summer of 1916, and they produced his one-act sea play *Bound East for Cardiff* in the fish house, which had been remodeled as the Wharf Theatre. With water lapping beneath the tiny theater and a foghorn sounding in the harbor, the mood of O'Neill's play was perfectly captured. This play and others were revived in a

Greenwich Village space in the fall, and the company was launched on a club membership or subscription basis. Besides its opposition to Broadway commercialism, the guiding principle was to encourage good new American play writing. The major talents to emerge from the endeavor were Eugene O'Neill and designer Robert Edmond Jones. The Provincetown Players peaked with O'Neill's *Emperor Jones* (1920), but the pressure to move uptown and to attain greater professionalism led to its demise in 1922. By that time the company had produced ninety-seven new plays by forty-seven American writers.

Bridging the long hiatus between the little theater movement and the 1960s proliferation of regional professional theaters, the Cleveland Play House began as an amateur theater group in 1915 and was reorganized as a professional company under Frederic McConnell in 1921. It remains today the oldest continuously producing professional theater in the United States. Chicago's Goodman, founded in 1925 as a professional theater adjunct of the Art Institute, functioned only as a theater training school for three decades after the depression. In 1969, however, the school's director John Reich—responding to the city's embarrassing lack of a resident Equity company—returned the Goodman to a fully professional status. Under Reich's leadership, attendance more than quadrupled within a few seasons, thus paving the way for a remarkable growth of professional theater throughout the city. By the late 1980s, stimulated by the biennial International Theatre Festival and by a host of small professional theaters nurturing new playwrights, Chicago had emerged as perhaps the liveliest metropolitan theater center in the United States.

During the depression, the Federal Theatre Project of the Works Progress Administration also gave an important impetus to decentralization. Under the leadership of Hallie Flanagan, the Federal Theatre Project (1935–39) sponsored over 1,200 productions of 830 plays in forty states, as well as over six thousand radio plays. Employing as many as twelve thousand people in theatrical jobs at its peak, the government-sponsored project provided abundant "free, adult, uncensored" theater, including landmark productions like New York's Negro theater production of a "voodoo *Macbeth*" set in Haiti, produced and directed by John Houseman and Orson Welles, with a musical score by Virgil Thomson. The seven-month run of *Macbeth* at Harlem's Lafayette Theatre encouraged Negro theater units in other cities to perform the classics. Another unit produced the popular "living newspapers," which dramatized current events and problems like the housing shortage, as dramatized in *One-Third of a Nation* (1938). Flanagan's vision and commitment are evident in her statement: "While our immediate aim is to put to work thousands of theatre people, our more far-reaching purpose is to orga-

Orson Welles directed Macbeth *in a Caribbean setting designed by Nat Karson for New York's Negro theater division of the Federal Theater Project in 1930. From* Stages of the World: Theatre Arts Prints.

nize and support theatrical enterprises so excellent in quality and so low in cost and so vital to the communities involved that they will be able to continue after federal support is withdrawn." Federal support was withdrawn sooner than expected, because some members of congress feared political repercussions from productions like Marc Blitzstein's *The Cradle Will Rock* as produced in New York by Houseman and Welles in 1937. Despite the closure of that production and the abrupt ending of the Federal Theatre Project in 1939, the four-year experiment in government subsidy of the arts laid the groundwork for many important future developments in American theater, including the 1965 congressional legislation that created the National Endowment for the Arts and the National Endowment for the Humanities.

Despite formidable obstacles, black Americans had built a distinguished record of theatrical activity even before the opportunities that were opened up by O'Neill's *The Emperor Jones* and the Federal Theatre Project. The achievements of the African Company and Ira Aldridge have been touched upon in the fourth chapter, The Drama Sobers Up: Realism and Naturalism. William Wells Brown, an escaped slave who became a professional lecturer and historian, wrote the earliest known play by a black author in America. *The Escape; or, A Leap to Freedom,* based upon Brown's own experience, was published in 1858, and Brown often gave readings of it "with telling power," but it was never fully produced. Henrietta Vinton Davis specialized in platform readings of Shakespeare in the 1880s and performed once with the

Astor Place Company of Coloured Tragedians (1884–86), an important Shakespearean troupe headed by black actor-manager-journalist J. A. Arneaux. Davis later produced and starred in black dramatists' plays, including William Edgar Easton's historical dramas *Dessalines* (1893) and *Christophe* (1912). Bob Cole, a playwright, director, and song-and-dance man, sometimes described as a "black George M. Cohan," ran the Negro Stock Company at Worth's Museum in New York, but his rise to prominence began with his authorship of and starring role in *A Trip to Coon Town* (1898), the first black musical comedy with a story line, thus breaking the pattern that confined black artists to the minstrel tradition. Cole and his partner, composer J. Rosamond Johnson, wrote songs for a string of popular musicals in the 1900s, including the first black operetta, *The Shoo-Fly Regiment* (1907). Angelina Weld Grimke's *Rachel* (1916) heads a long list of plays by black women dramatists, perhaps most notably those of Georgia Douglass Johnson in the 1920s, Lorraine Hansberry in the 1950s, Adrienne Kennedy in the 1960s, and Ntozake Shange in the 1970s. Actress Anita Bush organized the Lafayette Players in Harlem in 1915; the company's condensed versions of popular Broadway fare won mixed audiences during the Harlem Renaissance, on the road, and—from 1928 until its demise in 1932—in Los Angeles.

The widespread interest in black American culture that generated the "Harlem Renaissance" of the 1920s rested in great part upon recognition by both blacks and whites of the black contribution to the World War I effort. Not only did Harlem become a fashionable mecca for musical entertainment, but at the same time black arts moved downtown with several original black productions on Broadway. The first big hit, *Shuffle Along* (1921), with songs by Eubie Blake and Noble Sissle, ran 502 performances. Subsequent black musicals on Broadway made stars of Florence Mills, Josephine Baker, Ethel Waters, and Bill Robinson. Garland Anderson's *Appearances* (1925) was the first full-length drama by a black author produced on Broadway; it was revived in the 1929–30 season. W. E. B. DuBois encouraged black playwrights with the Krigwa Playwriting Contest in 1925, and this led him to form the Krigwa Players as the flagship of what he hoped would be a nationwide black little theater movement. This period also saw the beginning of such illustrious careers as those of poet-dramatist Langston Hughes, actor-singer-social activist Paul Robeson, and actress Rose McClendon.

An idealistic vision of a theatrical enterprise "national in scope, professional in standing: a people's project, organized and conducted in their interest, free from commercialism, but with the firm intent of being as far as possible self-supporting" resulted in the 1935 congressional chartering of the American National Theatre and Academy (ANTA). Without federal funding, however, and falling behind wartime priorities, ANTA languished until 1946. Then Robert Breen made it into a clearinghouse for new playscripts, a source of information and advice for theater people across the country, and—under the title Experimental Theatre—a producer of twenty-five new plays in three years (1946–49). According to Brooks Atkinson, ANTA became, by default, "an unofficial branch of the State Department, which was trying to improve international relations." It was Breen who ensured the inclusion of theater in UNESCO's arts program. In 1948 UNESCO's first director general, Julian Huxley, met in Paris with Jean-Louis Barrault, J. B. Priestley, and ANTA board member Rosamond Gilder to establish the International Theatre Institute. From the original eight participants, the International Theatre Institute has grown to over seventy national centers. ANTA served for a time as I.T.I.'s United States Center. ANTA's function as a purveyor of information for a national network of theaters has been superseded by Theatre Communications Group.

The American regional theater network may be said to have begun with Margo Jones in Dallas in 1947. It was then that "the Texas tornado" opened her Theatre '47, which the following year became Theatre '48, and so on until her death in 1955. Jones's book *Theatre-in-the-Round* (1951) chronicles the realization of her vision of a permanent, professional, repertory theater with the purpose of discovering and producing the best new American plays alongside the classics of all countries. Among the playwrights whose early work she nurtured were Tennessee Williams (she premiered *Summer and Smoke* in 1947), William Inge (*Farther Off from Heaven*, 1947; later retitled *The Dark at the Top of the Stairs*), and Jerome Lawrence and Robert E. Lee (*Inherit the Wind*, 1955). In the wake of Margo Jones, a number of regional professional theaters were founded by women; these included Nina Vance's Alley Theatre in Houston (1947), Zelda Fichandler's Arena Stage in Washington, DC (1950), Mary John's Milwaukee Repertory Theatre (1954), Patricia McIlrath's Missouri Repertory Theatre in Kansas City (1964), and JoAnn Schmidman's Omaha Magic Theatre (1969). The concept could even be adapted to New York City, as in the case of Rosetta LeNoire's multiracial, musical AMAS Repertory Theatre (1969).

Some of the leading American dramatists of the twentieth century worked in a strongly regional idiom. William Saroyan used his California background in plays like *The Time of Your Life* (1939). Although Thornton Wilder was born in Wisconsin, his plays—*Our Town* (1938), *The Matchmaker* (1957), and others—are infused with a New England sensibility. Arthur Miller's working-class Brooklyn formation informed dramas like *All My Sons* (1947), *The Death of a Salesman* (1949), and *A View from the Bridge* (1955). Lillian Hellman's *The Little Foxes* (1939) and other plays use Southern settings, as do Beth Henley's *Crimes of the Heart* (1979)

Patricia McIlrath is one of the great guiding lights of the American regional repertory theater movement. She founded Missouri Repertory Theatre in 1964 and served as its artistic director until her retirement in 1985. She personally directed over one-hundred productions at The Rep and for the University of Missouri–Kansas City Department of Theatre, which she simultaneously chaired. Her contribution to the American theater has been recognized through numerous honorary doctorates and other awards.

and others. The South was also a pervasive influence on Tennessee Williams, as exemplified in *A Streetcar Named Desire* (1947), *Cat on a Hot Tin Roof* (1955), and *Vieux Carré* (1977). Ranking alongside O'Neill at the peak of American playwriting, Williams broadened his range to include such works as a Sicilian comedy, *The Rose Tattoo* (1950); the expressionist *Camino Real* (1953); a searing and lyrical drama set in Mexico, *The Night of the Iguana* (1961); and the much-revised *Two-Character Play* (1967–75). William Inge drew upon his Kansas roots in *Come Back, Little Sheba* (1950), *Picnic* (1953), and *Bus Stop* (1955). Lanford Wilson's Missouri is the setting for *The 5th of July* (1978), *Tally's Folly* (1979), and others. Sam Shepard and William Hauptman both celebrate the open road of the American west; Shepard's *Fool for Love* (1979) and *A Lie of the Mind* (1985) are typical.

The number of nonprofit professional theaters increased most dra-

The Magrath sisters—Lenny (Ewa Wielgat), Babe (Laura San Giacomo), and Meg (Susan Warren)—constantly shift between tears and laughter in Beth Henley's comedy Crimes of the Heart. *Missouri Repertory Theatre's 1985 production was directed by Pamela Hawthorn. Vincent Scassellati designed the costumes.*

The Glass Menagerie *(1945) is perhaps the popular favorite of all Tennessee Williams's immortal dramas. In Missouri Repertory Theatre's 1987 production, Tracey Ellis played Laura and Jim Birdsall played The Gentleman Caller. George Keathley directed and John Carver Sullivan designed the costumes.*

Wiliam Inge's Come Back, Little Sheba *(1950) featured Jonathan Farwell as Doc and Barbara Houston as Lola in Missouri Repertory Theatre's 1984 production, directed by Patricia McIlrath, with a set by Robert Moody and costumes by Baker S. Smith.*

Left, with Talley's Folly, *the second of Lanford Wilson's plays set in Lebanon, Missouri, the playwright said he "set out to write a Valentine." The two-character romance won the Pulitzer Prize for 1980. David Schuster and Jeannine Hutchings played Matt and Sally in Missouri Repertory Theatre's 1981 production. John Ezell designed the set and Michelle Bechtold designed costumes.*

Brothers Austin and Lee, right, were played by Mark Robbins and Jim Birdsall in Missouri Repertory Theatre's 1984 production of True West *by Sam Shepard. Albert Pertalion directed and Harry Feiner designed the set.*

Sam Shepard's Fool for Love *is set in a motel on the edge of the Mojave Desert. Richard McWilliams and Caryn West played Eddie and May in the 1986 Missouri Repertory Theatre production, directed by Peter Bennett, with set by David Wallace and costumes by Gwen Walters.*

matically in the 1960s. Prominent among the many outstanding companies launched in that decade, the Minnesota Theater Company (later known as The Guthrie Theater) was founded in 1963 by Tyrone Guthrie, Oliver Rea, and Peter Zeisler, who had conducted a systematic nationwide search for the right city in which to establish an exemplary alternative to New York's commercial theater. Minneapolis proved an excellent choice; over the years, the presence of a nationally recognized company spawned a number of other professional theaters in the city, and The Guthrie set a fine example for other cities. By 1966 the number of professional actors working in regional theaters surpassed those on Broadway. By the 1980s nonprofit theaters employed three times as many actors as did commercial theaters. Furthermore, most of the new American plays were being generated by regional theaters like Gordon Davidson's Mark Taper Forum, which opened in Los Angeles in 1967, or Actors Theatre of Louisville, under the direction of Jon Jory since 1969. A number of theaters established close ties with certain playwrights, which enabled the writers to develop their work in a supportive atmosphere. Among these were Preston Jones at Dallas Theater Center, Megan Terry at Omaha Magic Theatre, Sam Shepard at San Francisco's Magic Theatre, Marsha Norman at Actors Theatre of Louisville, Mark Medoff at New Mexico Repertory Theatre, David Mamet at The Goodman Theatre, and August Wilson at Yale Repertory Theatre.

Even as professional theaters proliferated across the nation, Broadway was being challenged at closer range: the 1950s saw the rise of off-Broadway theater. In 1949, the response to frequent "moonlighting" by Equity actors in New York's nonprofessional theaters, the Off-Broadway Theater League was formed to professionalize those theaters that had no more than 299 seats. Lower salary scales were set, allowing off-Broadway theaters to employ theater professionals in riskier endeavors than the commercial pressures of Broadway would allow. The Circle in the Square, founded in 1951 by Ted Mann, José Quintero, and others, was one of the great success stories of the off-Broadway movement. The company eventually obtained an arena-stage Broadway house, which operates as a nonprofit theater, along with its original off-Broadway venue. Another nonprofit venture in New York, Lincoln Center Repertory Company in the Vivian Beaumont Theatre, has had a more checkered history, with numerous changes of leadership interspersed by dark periods. As the financial risk of theatrical production increased, off-Broadway had become by the end of the 1960s virtually indistinguishable from Broadway in terms of the kinds of plays being offered. Meanwhile, the off-off-Broadway theater emerged as the alternative to commercialism, as described in chapter 5.

The summer Shakespeare festival might be seen as another chapter in the saga of decentralizing the American theater. The oldest continuously operating Shakespearean company in America, the Oregon Shakespeare Festival, was founded in Ashland, Oregon, in 1935 by Angus L. Bowmer. From its earliest summer productions on a simple wooden platform, it grew to a complex of three theaters offering a year-round repertory of a variety of plays, among which Shakespeare remains the centerpiece. The American Shakespeare Theatre in Stratford, Connecticut, opened in 1955 in a fifteen-hundred-seat Elizabethan-style theater; it won particular renown for the many celebrated performers—like Katharine Hepburn, James Earl Jones, Morris Carnovsky, and others—who accepted low salaries for the opportunity to play Shakespearean roles in rotating repertory. Joseph Papp's New York Shakespeare Festival has offered free summer productions of Shakespeare in Central Park since 1956, as well as other productions at the Public Theatre, which he opened in the old Astor Library with the original production of the rock musical *Hair* in 1967. In addition, Papp organized a mobile theater to tour Shakespeare productions to parks and schools in the five boroughs of New York City.

Shakespeare production was also a major impetus for the blossoming of Canadian theater in the latter half of the twentieth century. Journalist Tom Patterson persuaded Tyrone Guthrie to spearhead the founding of an annual summer festival in Stratford, Ontario, beginning in 1953. With his designer Tanya Moiseiwitsch, Guthrie presented three seasons of plays in a tent. Attendance for the first six-week season (*Richard III* electrifyingly performed by Alec Guinness, and *All's Well That Ends Well*) reached 68,000. By 1990 the Stratford Festival had expanded to fifteen productions in three theaters for a season running from April to November. Michael Langham took over the artistic directorship in 1956. His tenure, which lasted until 1968, saw the opening of a permanent Festival Theatre in 1957. The Stratford Festival seemed to catalyze Canadian theater in general. Besides setting a high standard of production, it generated a healthy nationalistic sense of identity for the theater of Canada. A regional theater movement began with the 1958 founding of the Manitoba Theatre Centre, followed by a strong "alternate theatre" movement in the 1960s and 1970s. Toronto's Tarragon Theatre, founded in 1970 by Bill Glassco, has nurtured such outstanding Canadian playwrights as David French, David Fennario, Sharon Pollack, James Reaney, John Murrell, Joanna Glass, and George F. Walker. The Tarragon has also been the leading English-language producer of plays originally written in French by Quebec writers like Michel Tremblay, author of *Les Belles-Soeurs* (Sisters-in-Law, 1968), *A toi, pour toujours, ta Marie-Lou* (Forever Yours, Mary Lou, 1973), and *Bonjour, là, bonjour* (1974). Other leading French Canadian dramatists include

Left, Actors Theatre of Louisville premiered several plays by Marsha Norman. Lynn Cohen and Susan Kingsley appeared in her 1978 drama Getting Out. *Photograph by David S. Talbott, courtesy of Actors Theatre of Louisville.*

Right, the Goodman Theatre in Chicago premiered David Mamet's Pulitzer Prize-winning play Glengarry Glen Ross *in 1984 under the direction of Gregory Mosher. This scene from act 1, set in a Chinese restaurant, shows Robert Prosky and T. J. Walsh. Photograph by Brigitte Lacombe, courtesy of The Goodman Theatre.*

Mike Nussbaum and Joe Mantegna created their roles in Mamet's Glengarry Glen Ross *at the Goodman Theatre and went with the production to Broadway, where the play won the Pulitzer Prize for 1984. Photograph by Brigitte Lacombe, courtesy of The Goodman Theatre.*

Above, luminaries from seven decades of Broadway theater gathered at Great Lakes Theater Festival in Cleveland in 1987 to celebrate "Classic Broadway" and the one-hundredth birthday of George Abbott, who has been writing, directing, and producing Broadway shows since the 1920s. Pictured are (top row) Garson Kanin, Joe Bova, Donald Saddler, Stanley Green, Robert Sklar, Nancy Walker, Eddie Albert, Joy Abbott, Betty Comden, Dorothy Hart, Oliver Smith, John Ezell; (bottom row) Harold Prince, Gerald Freedman, George Abbott, Sheldon Harnick, and Adolph Green. Photograph by Ki Ho Park, courtesy of Great Lakes Theater Festival.

By the 1980s most new American plays were coming out of the regional professional theaters. A leader in the nurturing of playwrights has been Actors Theatre of Louisville through its annual Humana Festival of New American Plays. Among the premieres at the eighth Humana festival was John Patrick Shanley's Danny and the Deep Blue Sea. *Pictured are June Stein and John Turturro. Photograph by David S. Talbott, courtesy of Actors Theatre of Louisville.*

Marie-Claire Blais, Jean-Claude Germain, and Jean Barbeau. Edmonton's Citadel Theatre, the largest regional theater in Canada, was founded in 1965, but came to prominence under the artistic direction of John Neville from 1973 to 1978. James Roy founded the Blyth Festival in that tiny Ontario community in 1975 in order to encourage new work by regional playwrights, most notably that of Anne Chislett, who wrote *The Tomorrow Box* (1980) and *Quiet in the Land* (1981).

Although London remains the focal point of British theater, two postwar developments have contributed toward making theater more accessible to all. One was a new kind of voice that began to be heard on the British stage after the 1956 production of John Osborne's *Look Back in Anger* at the Royal Court Theatre. The general rage against the establishment that is vented by the play's central character, Jimmy Porter, incited a generation of playwrights who became known as "the angry young men." Among these Beckett-influenced rebels against the genteel drawing-room stage tradition were John Whiting, John Arden, Arnold Wesker, Shelagh Delaney, and John Mortimer. Director Joan Littlewood also expressed dissatisfaction with London's commercial (West End) theater by establishing her Theatre Workshop (1953–73) in East London and producing lively works of social criticism like *Oh, What a Lovely War!* (1963). The Royal Court's English Stage Company—under the artistic direction of George Devine from 1956 to 1965, his successor William Gaskill (1965–72), and subsequently, with provocative works like Tariq Ali and Howard Brenton's *Iranian Nights* (1989)—continued to produce new and often controversial plays. The second development was the so-called repertory movement, a network of new theaters built outside London. Beginning with the Belgrade Theatre in Coventry in 1958, twenty new facilities were constructed by 1970, fifteen of them purposely designed for producing plays in rotating repertory. Such construction continued in the 1970s and after, and included two major complexes in London: the three performance spaces in the National Theatre on London's South Bank (1976) and the two theaters administered by the Royal Shakespeare Company in The Barbican Arts Centre (1982). According to Anthony Jackson, the regional repertory network is now "the main provider of theatre in Great Britain at large—indeed in most areas outside London the sole provider."

One of the most important, if short-lived, efforts to decentralize a nation's theater occurred in Spain during the Republican period before the civil war that began in 1936. In 1932 Federico García Lorca founded La Barraca, a student theater group that toured the classics to rural areas of Spain. During the next four years, the government-subsidized troupe made twenty-two excursions, taking a repertoire of mostly Spanish Golden Age plays, directed by Lorca, to people who had never before seen live theater. A similar venture, the Teatro del pueblo (1931–36),

Above, left, Toronto's Tarragon Theatre produced John Murrell's Farther West *in 1986. Pictured left to right are Mary Haney, Denise Naples, Diana Leblanc, and Nora McLellan. Photograph by Michael Cooper, courtesy of the Tarragon Theatre.*

Above, right, Tom Stoppard launched his outstanding playwriting career with Rosencrantz and Guildenstern Are Dead *(1967). The 1979 Missouri Repertory Theatre production, directed by Gerald Gutierrez, featured Richard C. Brown as Guildenstern, Robert Lewis Karlin as the Player, and Michael Haney as Rosencrantz.*

Peter Shaffer is well established as one of England's leading dramatists with plays like The Royal Hunt of the Sun *(1964),* Amadeus *(1979), and—shown here—*Equus *(1973). In Missouri Repertory Theatre's 1986 production, Christopher Cull played Alan Strang and Martin Coles played the horse, Nugget.*

was directed by playwright Alejandro Casona. He had previously operated a children's theater entitled *El pájaro pinto* (Painted Bird).

In 1947 Paolo Grassi and Giorgio Strehler founded Italy's first postwar *teatro stabile* (permanent theater), the Piccolo Teatro di Milano. The example set by the Piccolo's highly acclaimed work was enormously inspiring and led to the founding of other *stabili* such as those of Genoa (1951) and Turin (1955). Subsidized by the state and municipal governments, such theaters were intended to reach a wide audience with productions of high quality. By 1958 Italy was enjoying a boom in theatrical production. The increasing number of productions for a growing provincial theater audience provided opportunities for many excellent directors. Besides Grassi and Strehler, major figures included Luchinbo Visconti, Luigi Squarzina, Franco Zeffirelli, Gianfranco De Bosio, Franco Enriquez, and Luca Ronconi.

Sweden has one of the most successfully decentralized theaters in Europe, with about 150 companies (including three state theaters and twenty-three regional and city theaters) reaching a total annual attendance of four and a half million in a country whose total population is eight million. The Riksteatern, founded in 1934, operates out of a huge complex in a Stockholm suburb and reaches over 500,000 people annually with its two thousand performances in over three hundred locations throughout the country. The Riksteatern produces adult plays (including works by the controversial contemporary dramatist Lars Norén), children's theater, musical comedy, opera, ballet, theater for the deaf, and theater in prisons. Norway's National Theatre also sends out touring productions, giving over six hundred performances a season. Opened in 1899, the National Theatre in Oslo still keeps the plays of Henrik Ibsen at the core of its repertoire. Oslo is also home to Det Norske Teatret (The Norwegian Theater), founded in 1913 to perform plays in Nynorsk, the more indigenous of the two official forms of the Norwegian language. Its attractive and modern facility, opened in 1985, incorporates a technologically superb main stage with an eight-hundred-seat auditorium plus two studio theaters. Denmark too has expanded its theater network, beginning with provincial theaters in Aarhus and Odense early in the century and achieving international renown in the 1960s with Eugenio Barba's Odin Teatret in Holstebro.

FROM SOCIALIST REALISM TO PERESTROIKA IN THE USSR

The period of Stalin's first Five-Year Plan (1928–32) was a transitional phase in the theater, as formalism was condemned and yet few

Swedish playwright Lars Norén has been widely performed throughout Europe in the 1980s. This production of his Autumn and Winter *was produced at Det Norske Teatret in Oslo in 1989. Photograph by Leif Gabrielsen, courtesy of Det Norske Teatret.*

The main auditorium of Det Norske Teatret's 1985 facility seats eight-hundred and features a front curtain designed by Jan Groth. Teigens Fotoatelier, courtesy of Det Norske Teatret.

The Pretenders *by Henrik Ibsen was a much acclaimed production at Det Norske Teatret in Oslo in 1989. Courtesy of Det Norske Teatret.*

good new plays had been written to present reality as the Bolsheviks would have it. Many plays from the 1920s and 1930s were historical melodramas—like Vishnevsky's *Optimistic Tragedy*—about the 1917 revolution and the civil war. The All-Union Association of Proletarian Writers (VAPP) and the Russian Association of Proletarian Writers (RAPP) promoted proletarian art as a weapon against the "capitalist, decadent, and formalist spirit in literature and the theater," but their crude methods alienated many. In 1932 those two bodies were dissolved and replaced by the Union of Soviet Writers, which held its first congress in 1934. There, Andrei Zhdanov's definition of socialist realism was approved, and it remained the officially sanctioned doctrine for all creative and critical work—although the rigidity of its interpretation varied over the decades—until the advent of *glasnost* (openness) in the 1980s. According to the definition, socialist realism "demands of the artist the truthful, historically concrete representation of reality in its revolutionary development. Moreover, the truth and historical completeness of the artistic representation of reality must be combined with the task of ideological transformation and education of the working man in the spirit of Socialism." Thus, all the arts were to employ realistic content for the pedagogical (propagandistic) purpose of building communism. If communism is the happy ending to be achieved through socialism, then a realistic depiction of life must take a positive attitude and conclude happily. The superfluous man of Russian literature was replaced by the Soviet "positive hero." The problem for playwrights was how to introduce conflict into such work. From the 1930s until Khrushchev's "thaw" in 1956, Soviet drama tended to focus on such dilemmas as whether to plant corn or wheat. Some westerners have facetiously described it as "boy meets tractor." In addition, there were plays that mythologized Lenin, like Nikolai Pogodin's "Lenin trilogy" (1937–58).

Under such conditions, few artists managed to create work of exceptional interest or lasting value. Evgeny Shvarts did it by writing what were ostensibly children's plays, but those folk-fantasy dramas often carried oblique meanings. Of his "adult fairy tales," *Drakon* (The Dragon, 1944) most enchantingly warns against the acceptance of tyranny as the apparent path of least resistance. The text was passed by the censors in 1944, but after one performance the play was removed from the repertoire of Leningrad's Comedy Theater, which had premiered it. Although *The Dragon* was soon widely produced throughout Europe and the United States, it was prohibited in the USSR until 1962, when the Comedy Theater revived it—but again the run was oddly curtailed. Nikolai Akimov, who directed both *The Dragon* and Shvarts's *Ten'* (The Shadow, 1940), was one of the most brilliant theater artists of that long, difficult era. Perhaps best remembered today for his set, costume, and poster designs, Akimov launched his directorial career with a controversial, irreverent interpretation of *Hamlet* at Moscow's Vakhtangov Theater in 1932. Thereafter, he spent most of his career, until his death in 1968, as artistic director of the Comedy Theater in Leningrad.

Soviet drama and theater reached new lows of mediocrity during the years following World War II, when "Zhdanovism" meant tighter controls on artistic work, and propaganda fueled anti-Western sentiment. Furthermore, Stalin's World War II ban on many of Shakespeare's plays continued until his death. Even *Hamlet,* a perennial Russian favorite, was proscribed, because its portrait of a man who hesitates (and thinks too much) was deemed contrary to the spirit of the socialist positive hero. In the 1953–54 theater season, immediately following Stalin's death, virtually every city in the USSR saw a production of *Hamlet.* Outstanding among all of these was the so-called iron curtain *Hamlet* directed by Nikolai Okhlopkov at the Mayakovsky Theater in Moscow in 1954. V. F. Ryndin's design for the setting took its cue from Hamlet's line, "Denmark's a prison." The basic setting was a heavy-bolted, massive iron gate that filled the entire width of the stage. It could

Plays about revolution were encouraged in the USSR in the 1920s. Y. Shaporin's The Decembrists *(1925) was based upon the 1825 Decembrist uprising. In this scene, those "first martyrs of the Russian revolution" are being sent off to Siberian exile.*

Roar, China! *(1926) by Sergei Tretyakov was one of the more successful revolutionary plays of the 1920s, especially in this production directed by Vsevolod Meyerhold.*

Among the socialist-realist dramas of the 1930s, Platon Krechet *by Aleksandr Korneichuk was a favorite.*

Nikolai Akimov directed and designed sets and costumes for The Shadow *(1940), an adult allegorical fairy tale by Evgeny Shvarts.*

Akimov served as artistic director of the Comedy Theatre, located on Nevsky Prospekt in Leningrad, for over thirty years.

serve as a dark, forbidding palace wall, or it could swing slowly open to reveal other settings within. The bars in the facade of the iron curtain also formed the frames for twelve separate cubicles or prison cells—four blocks across and three blocks high—which could be opened to the view of the audience. Members of the court sat in these cells to watch the Players' dumb show performed on the shallow apron.

The "thaw" introduced by Khrushchev's denunciation of the crimes of the Stalin era at the Twentieth Party Congress in 1956 opened the way for a drama with greater psychological interest. While innovation in form continued to be discouraged, the latitude of acceptable content was broadened. Outstanding among those who began to explore personal feelings in the drama were Viktor Rozov and Alexei Arbuzov. Two of the latter's plays—*Irkutskaya istoriya* (It Happened in Irkutsk, 1959) and *Moi Bedni Marat* (The Promise, 1965)—were successfully produced in New York as well as in numerous theaters in the USSR. Among the other important Soviet dramatists from the 1960s to the 1980s are Aleksandr Vampilov, Edvard Radzinsky, Mikhail Roshchin, Mikhail Shatrov, Aleksandr Galin, Aleksandr Volodin, Ludmila Petrushevskaya, and Mark Rozovsky. Rozovsky's *Istoria Loshchad* (Strider, 1975) reached Broadway in 1980.

Natalia Sats established the world's first professional theater for children, Moscow Children's Theater, in 1921. Located in a former movie house, it was attended by five million spectators in fifteen years and inspired the founding of dozens of such theaters worldwide as well as in the USSR. In 1936 the government changed the troupe's name to Central Children's Theater and installed it in a large, well-equipped theater on Sverdlov Square next to the Bolshoi Theater of Opera and Ballet. Natalia Sats's artistic directorship at the new facility lasted little over a year; in August 1937 she was arrested on trumped-up charges (stemming from the American ambassador's attendance at a performance) and sent to the Siberian labor camps for five years. Not until two years after Stalin's death was her name cleared and permission given for her to return to Moscow. Sats spent the next decade working toward her dream of a children's musical theater and was finally allowed to establish a company in 1965. In 1979 the Children's Musical Theater moved into the strikingly designed Palace of Children's Opera that was constructed especially for the company in the southwestern section of Moscow. There, young audiences attend lavishly staged operas like Mozart's *Bastien und Bastienne*, Puccini's *Madame Butterfly*, Eduard Khagagortian's *The Hat with Ear-flaps*, and Shirvani Chalaev's *Mowgli*. Adult musical theater in the USSR also advanced rapidly after the 1960s, when a number of American musical comedies were produced in Moscow. The first Soviet rock musical, *Avos*, composed by Aleksei Rybnikov, was produced in 1981 at Moscow's Lenin Komsomol Theater.

Strider: The Story of a Horse, *a musical drama by Mark Rozovsky, was produced at Missouri Repertory Theatre in 1984, with Jonathan Farwell (center) in the title role. James Assad directed; sets were by Herbert L. Camburn; costumes were by Vincent Scassellati.*

Below, left, Yuri Liubimov played a leading role in Alexei Arbuzov's It Happened in Irkutsk *(1959), one of the most successful plays that treated love interest on a par with heroism in daily life.*

Below, right, a dramatization of Tolstoy's Anna Karenina *(1937) was typical of the unadventurous repertoire of the Moscow Art Theater during the Stalin era.*

In 1956 Oleg Efremov founded the Sovremennik (Contemporary) Theater, the first new theater in Moscow in twenty years. Many of his company members came from the Moscow Art Theater's training school, but joined Efremov in rebelling against the venerable theater's stale, unadventurous repertoire. The Sovremennik's inaugural production, *Vechno zhivie* (Alive Forever!, written 1943; produced 1956) by Viktor Rozov, illustrated its goal of creating a kind of theater analogous to the cinema of Italian neorealism: gritty and bold in the acknowledgment of social problems while focusing upon real (unheroic) people. The Sovremennik's leadership in expanding the repertoire and raising the quality of production had a tremendously salutary effect on Soviet theater as a whole. The 1960s saw the founding of a number of new theaters. In 1970 Efremov was asked to take over the moribund Moscow Art Theater. Under his artistic directorship, it regained much of its old prestige and in 1973 moved its operations into a newly constructed facility on Tverskoi Boulevard. The original theater continued to be used as a second stage and eventually had its backstage area modernized while the front of the house was restored to its former art nouveau beauty. By 1985, however, Efremov was calling for a reorganization of the huge company, which had so grown in size that many actors rarely got to perform. Finally, the Moscow Art Theater was split into two autonomous units with Efremov at the head of the company using the "old" Moscow Art Theater and Tatiana Doronina running the company in the modern building on Tverskoi Boulevard. The two companies were quickly dubbed the "male" and "female" Moscow Art Theaters.

Despite the cumbersome bureaucracy that controlled the arts and despite the hardships of the so-called period of stagnation under Brezhnev, Soviet theater was often brilliant. Audiences learned to glean dissident ideas from theatrical metaphors in the productions of outstanding directors like Anatoly Efros and Georgi Tovstonogov, both of whom died in the 1980s, and especially in those of Yuri Liubimov. A period of rapid changes occurred with the introduction of *glasnost* and *perestroika* (restructuring). The "revolution from above" initiated by Mikhail Gorbachev in 1985 took effect in the theater late in 1986 when theater professionals suddenly set up their own Union of Theatrical Workers. Within the next three years, over three hundred small, independent (unsubsidized) theater groups appeared all across the country, especially in Moscow and Leningrad. Also indicative of the rapid pace of change was the publication of Vladimir Gubaryev's play *Sarkofag* (Sarcophagus, 1986) about the aftermath of a nuclear disaster like the one at Chernobyl; indeed, the play appeared less than six months after the April 1986 explosion. Scholars too have been eagerly investigating hitherto closed chapters in Soviet theater history; our understanding of the theatrical past may well be modified as previously suppressed documentation surfaces on subjects like Stanislavsky's last years, as well as the underanalyzed works and mystery-shrouded deaths of Meyerhold, Mikhoels, Les Kurbas, and Andrei Amalrik. The theater's new freedom from censorship surely heralds enough promise to outweigh the economic hardships to be endured in the 1990s. Much hope for the future of Soviet theater lies with a new generation of imaginative directors: Robert Sturua, Roman Vitiuk, Lev Dodin, Eimuntas Nekroshius (of Lithuania), Yuri Pogrebnichko, and Anatoly Vasiliev.

INTERNATIONALLY RENOWNED DIRECTORS

In an age of increasing interdependence among all nations, the theater world's relative neglect of new foreign plays in translation defies explanation. Contemporary foreign plays are almost never produced commercially in the United States and only rarely in the nonprofit theaters, despite such efforts as Theatre Communications Group's Latin American play project or Ubu Repertory Theatre's dissemination of plays in English translation from France and French Africa. It required Vaclav Havel's election to the presidency of Czechoslovakia to arouse widespread interest in his plays, although they have been available for twenty years—much of which time the author spent in prison for his dissident views. The British stage has proved itself more hospitable than the American to foreign plays, but rediscoveries of neglected classics (especially Russian works like those of Ostrovsky, Gorky, and Erdmann) have clearly outnumbered modern selections. In continental Europe, the greatest effort to reach out to the rest of the world has occurred in the French theater. For example, a randomly chosen week (June 7–13, 1989) in the Paris theater season shows performances of plays by Americans A. R. Gurney, Jr., Neil Simon, and Kevin Wade; Argentine Kado Kostzer; Polish Slawomir Mrozek; and English Alan Ayckbourn. In addition to those contemporary dramatists, one could see plays by Eugene O'Neill, Luigi Pirandello, Carlo Goldoni, Anton Chekhov, Jacob Lenz, and Stanislaw Witkiewicz, all during that same week, in Paris. No other world capitol can boast as much. A few living playwrights might be considered international superstars whose work is known and regularly produced in translation: Sam Shepard and Woody Allen from the United States, Fernando Arrabal from Spain via Paris, England's Peter Shaffer, Harold Pinter, and Edward Bond, South Africa's Athol Fugard, East Germany's Heiner Müller, Poland's Slawomir Mrozek, Italy's Dario Fo, Nigeria's Wole Soyinka, and perhaps France's Marguerite Duras.

Eimuntas Nekroshius, artistic director of the State Theater of Lithuania, has been hailed as a rising star among international directors. His energetic and unorthodox interpretation of Chekhov's Uncle Vanya *is suggested in these two photographs of Doctor Astrov (played by K. Smoriginas) with the long-braided Sonya (D. Overaite) and with a sensual Elena (Dalia Storik).*

Paris has proved especially hospitable to new works by foreign playwrights. Groupe TSE, an Argentine company, has produced a number of Argentine plays there. This one, God Save the Queen *(1989) by Kado Kostzer, is a one-woman play performed by Marilù Marini. Photograph by Marc Gaubert, courtesy of Kado Kostzer.*

One example of the international orientation of Paris theater was this 1978 production of Boat for Lipaia *by Soviet dramatist Alexei Arbuzov, a great success starring Edwige Feuillère and Guy Tréjean. Courtesy of French Cultural Services.*

Athol Fugard of the Union of South Africa has written many powerful plays about interracial relationships, including what is perhaps his masterpiece, Master Harold . . . and the Boys *(1981). George Keathley directed it at Missouri Repertory Theater in 1986 with Herbert Mark Parker as Sam and Christopher Cull as Hally. Harry Feiner designed the set.*

On the whole, however, the most active and visible international liaisons in the theater today are the foreign residencies of renowned directors. The hiring of a distinguished foreign director to stage a single production has been a growing practice since the 1960s in Europe and the Americas, but it almost invariably involves the production of a classic play, most often one by Shakespeare or Chekhov. Working with a script that is a known quantity perhaps best enables the director to demonstrate an original approach to and handling of universal themes. Of the dozen or so leading directors in the world today, the one "director's director" is surely the Italian Giorgio Strehler. At the Piccolo Teatro di Milano, Strehler created innovative *mises-en-scène* for a wide range of classic plays, but above all he reinvigorated Italian Shakespearean production, beginning with his 1948 version of *Richard II*. One critic called it "the best production I have ever seen in Italy." That same year, Strehler staged an enchanting outdoor production of *The Tempest* in Florence's Boboli Gardens, using fountains, fireworks, and a boat on the lake. Thirty years later, Strehler was still astonishing the world when his new and equally brilliant 1978 interpretation of *The Tempest* toured Europe and the United States. Plays by Goldoni, Pirandello, and Brecht have also figured strongly in Strehler's repertoire. He describes his approach to directing as assembling a totality the way one would put together "three Chinese boxes," the innermost of which contains the true depiction of how people live; that box nests inside the historical-context box, which in turn is contained by the box of life itself, the eternal parabola of human adventure. In the 1980s, Strehler divided his time between Milan and Paris, serving as artistic director of the Odéon-Théâtre de l'Europe as well as continuing to direct at the Piccolo.

The work of Soviet director Yuri Liubimov became widely known in the west during his years of exile, 1983–88. He began his theater career as an actor, playing romantic leads at Moscow's Vakhtangov Theater. In 1953, when he was thirty-six, Liubimov turned to teaching and directing at the Vakhtangov theater school. In 1963, the last year of Khrushchev's "thaw," Liubimov obtained—with difficulty—permission to direct Brecht's *Good Person of Setzuan* as the diploma production of the 1964 class. The production quickly became a sensation among theatergoers and gave Liubimov the prestige he needed to get his own theater. He was assigned the small, run-down Taganka Theater far from the central theater district of Moscow, but he was allowed to bring along eight actors from the graduating class to combine with the Taganka's older resident company. In the lobby Liubimov placed blown-up photographs of his theater's "artistic godfathers": Stanislavsky, Meyerhold, Vakhtangov, and Brecht. Their example influenced Liubimov in his twenty years of producing what was consistently the best theater in the USSR. Although his poetic collages and his revolutionary plays always made a powerful

Reaching an international theater audience across language barriers often means offering the classics. This production of Aristophanes' The Birds *at the Bad Hersfeld Festival is typical. Courtesy of the German Information Center.*

Giorgio Strehler's 1948 production of Shakespeare's The Tempest *was staged in the Boboli Gardens of Florence in an outdoor fairy-tale like decor designed by Gianni Ratto. From* World Theatre *(1951), published by the International Theatre Institute; with the permission of* World Theatre.

impact, it was his fresh approach to the classics that won the most renown. Molière's *Tartuffe,* Shakespeare's *Hamlet,* Chekhov's *Three Sisters,* and others, staged in collaboration with designer David Borovsky, used minimal scenic elements incorporating powerful stage metaphors to convey an uncompromising personal statement. Liubimov's famous 1971 production of *Hamlet,* for example, featured an open grave at center stage and a proliferation of skulls. In addition, a huge curtain of tangled wool hung on a swivel, which allowed it to move noiselessly in any direction across the stage, even diagonally; it seemed to function as an accomplice of evil, supporting Claudius and Gertrude, allowing Polonius to eavesdrop behind it, and sweeping corpses aside. The role of Hamlet was played by the popular, gravel-voiced balladeer Vladimir Vysotsky; when he died in 1980, the production was withdrawn from the repertoire. In 1982 Liubimov was refused permission to open his fully rehearsed production of *Boris Godunov* at the Taganka, and yet he was allowed to accept an invitation to guest direct his version of Dostoevsky's *Crime and Punishment* in London. After he made some uncautious remarks about Soviet censorship to a British reporter, Liubimov was *in absentia* removed from his directorship of the Taganka, expelled from the Communist Party, and stripped of his Soviet citizenship; subsequently his name was even expunged from Soviet theater history books. Although he had not defected, he could not return to his homeland. However, theaters all over Europe and America vied to hire him as director. He worked everywhere and eventually settled in Israel. Finally, Soviet Premier Mikhail Gorbachev's reforms made it possible for Liubimov to return to his former position as head of the Taganka Theater in 1989.

In 1982, Liubimov gave Vysotsky's guitar to Robert Sturua, artistic director since 1962 of the Rustaveli Theater of Tblisi, the capitol of the Soviet republic of Georgia. It was a symbolic gesture of recognition of the remarkable quality of Sturua's work, which Alan Smith has described as a "fusion of Brecht and the bard." Sturua's three stunning Shakespeare productions, performed in Georgian—*Richard III, King Lear,* and *As You Like It*—have all been seen in the west, where his haunting stage images (like a silent jester figure interpolated into *Richard III* to mock the tyrant) made a strong impact, even if their political subtext was less accessible. Sturua's international guest-directing credits include innovative interpretations of *Mother Courage* in Buenos Aires, *Tartuffe* in Tel Aviv, and *Three Sisters* in London.

Czechoslovakian director Otomar Krejca, by contrast, achieved his international prominence by remaining utterly faithful to the text, trying to discover the playwright's original intention through a method he calls "empirical analysis." Krejca became chief director at Czechoslovakia's National Theater in 1956. There, with designer Josef Svoboda and

Yuri Liubimov's 1967 production of Pugachev *at the Taganka Theater was based on a work by the turn-of-the-century "peasant poet" Sergei Essenin. Strong ensemble work and minimalist scenic elements with dramatic lighting are characteristic of Liubimov's directorial style.*

Czechoslovakian director Otomar Krejca and designer Josef Svoboda collaborated on this beautiful 1963 production of Shakespeare's Romeo and Juliet *at the National Theater in Prague. Photograph by Dr. Jaromir Svoboda.*

Krejca has won international renown for his direction of plays by Anton Chekhov. Svoboda designed this production of The Seagull. *Photograph by Dr. Jaromir Svoboda.*

Left, Ingmar Bergman directed Strindberg's Miss Julie *at the Dramaten in Stockholm in 1985 with set and costumes designed by Gunilla Palmstierna-Weiss. Pictured are Marie Göranzon as Miss Julie and Peter Stormare as Jean. Photograph by Bengt Wanselius, courtesy of the Dramaten.*

Right, Ingmar Bergman's acclaimed and controversial production of Shakespeare's Hamlet *premiered at Stockholm's Dramaten in 1986 and then toured internationally. Shown here are Börje Ahlstedt as Claudius, Peter Stormare as Hamlet, and Gunnel Lindblom as Gertrude in costumes by Göran Wassberg. Photograph by Bengt Wanselius, courtesy of the Dramaten.*

dramaturg Karel Kraus, he provided a major impetus for new Czechoslovakian playwriting alongside such internationally renowned productions as their 1963 *Romeo and Juliet,* using kinetic architecture to create a "psycho-plastic space" or environment reflective of the emotion of a scene. In 1965 he and his collaborators founded the Divadlo za branou (Theatre behind the Gate) in Prague in hopes of evading some of the harassment that censors directed against the more visible National Theater. Krejca directed seven premieres at the Gate, most notably Chekhov's *Three Sisters* and Musset's *Lorenzaccio,* before the theater was forcibly closed in 1972. Since then, Krejca has been in demand as a director all over Europe, especially for productions of Chekhov's plays.

Erik Vos, artistic director of The Appel in The Hague, directs Juliet Randall and Claude Woolman in Shakespeare's Antony and Cleopatra *at Missouri Repertory Theatre in 1982. Costumes are by Tom Schenk, also of The Appel company.*

Olivia Virgil Harper was a powerful Cassandra in Agamemnon *by Aeschylus as directed by Erik Vos for Missouri Repertory Theatre in 1985. The set and costumes were by Niels Hamel.*

Although he has directed each of Chekhov's full-length plays (except *Platonov*) several times, each production is different, as he says he continues to find new meanings in the texts themselves. Svoboda, who designed for Krejca in Czechoslovakia, has also made an international career, although he retains a base of operations in Prague, where he is artistic director of Laterna Magica, a theater that ingeniously integrates live and filmed performances. Designer of over five hundred stage productions as well as the film *Amadeus*, Svoboda is considered by many to be the foremost designer in the world today.

After Strehler, Liubimov, and Krejca, several other directors rank close to the top on the international scene. Swedish director Ingmar Bergman may be better known as a film director, but his stage direction both at Stockholm's Dramaten and abroad has brought fresh and exciting interpretations of Shakespeare, Molière, Strindberg, and Ibsen as well as less well known dramatists like Yukio Mishima. Erik Vos of the Netherlands began directing in 1954 and moved quickly through positions at the Nieuwe Komedie, the Municipal Theater of Amsterdam, the National Theater in The Hague, and numerous guest residencies abroad, to founding his own company, The Appel, in 1972; he has dedicated himself to making the classics—including the Greeks—come alive for contemporary audiences. Ying Ruocheng of China has devoted most of his career to acting, but he also founded the Beijing People's Art Theater where he has directed his own translations of Shakespeare as well as modern classics like Peter Shaffer's *Amadeus*. Ying's position as his country's vice minister of culture has led him to focus his attention on bringing about reforms that will give Chinese theaters greater independence from party control, but he remains in demand as a director and actor in the United States and Europe. Other directors whose work is of this same high caliber have been discussed elsewhere: Ariane Mnouchkine, Patrice Chéreau, Peter Sellars, Robert Wilson, Lluis Pascual, Tadeusz Kantor, Michael Langham, Peter Brook, and Roberto Ciulli. Mention must also be made of the Hungarian director Tamás Ascher, Scottish director Philip Prowse, and Romanians Livieu Ciuli, André Serban, and Lucien Pintilie, all of whose work has been seen internationally. Four British directors brought the Royal Shakespeare Company to its international prominence: Peter Hall, John Barton, Terry Hands, and Trevor Nunn. In addition, Michael Bogdanov toured his English Shakespeare Company's magnificent seven-play cycle *The Wars of the Roses* to Hong Kong, Tokyo, Chicago, Hamburg, Berlin, Frankfurt, and several cities in Australia; then he accepted a position as artistic director at the Deutsches Schauspielhaus in Hamburg.

Finding common ground in the classics is undoubtedly one of the easiest routes to international awareness, especially when guided by a

Ying Ruocheng as Willy Loman advises his sons Biff (Li Shilong) and Happy (Mitiezeng) in a scene from Death of a Salesman *by Arthur Miller, as produced by the Beijing People's Art Theater in 1983. Courtesy of Ying Ruocheng.*

director who brings a different national perspective to bear on the text. Increasingly, designers are following directors in working with theater companies of different countries. For performers and theatergoers too, the crossing of national borders is facilitated and encouraged by the proliferation of international theater festivals—Avignon, Edinburgh, Chicago, Belgrade, Madrid, the rotating Festival of Nations, to name a few—and these world-class showcases can only have the effect of stimulating more meaningful interaction and raising production standards everywhere. As Giorgio Strehler said at the fortieth anniversary of the Avignon festival in 1987, "Theater rests upon a sense of responsibility to the human community. It is a form of permanent discourse among fellow men."

Epilogue: Converging Theaters around the Globe

Until the twentieth century, theater in the eastern and southern hemispheres developed largely within discrete cultural traditions. Certainly, there were isolated instances of the cross-cultural plantation of alien modes. There were, for example, the eighteenth-century fads for *chinoiseries* and *turqueries* in France and England, a French-influenced Egyptian theater in the aftermath of Napoleon's occupation, performances amalgamating native Indian languages and traditions with Spanish golden age models in colonial Latin America, and so on. But such cultural transferrals rarely went beyond a superficial homage or the straightforward adaptation of texts. For the most part, the serious examination and appropriation of basic elements of an exotic performance tradition by another culture awaited artists like William Butler Yeats, with his application of features of the Japanese Noh to his dance dramas; or Antonin Artaud, who developed a dramatic theory inspired by Balinese dancers; or Peter Brook, with his experiments drawing upon multicultural cross-fertilization in the creative process. With modern technology's reduction of the international community of nations to a so-called global village, such cultural transmutations are certain to occur with increasing frequency. While they can be enriching, there is at the same time the danger that cultural homogenization will lead to the extinction of certain slowly evolved and long-cherished modes of performance. It will take a third volume to cover adequately those continuing theatrical traditions as well as the new directions being explored in Africa, Asia, the South Pacific, the Arabic world, and South and Central America. Here space permits little more than acknowledgment of the vitality and promise of the theater of various nations in those parts of the world.

564

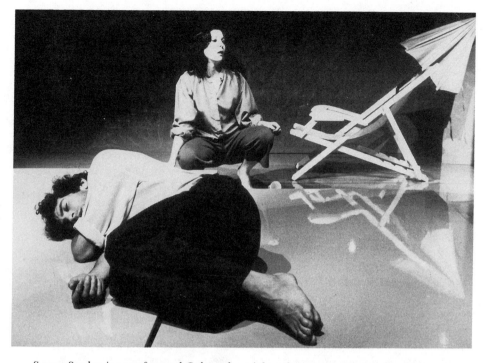

Severo Sarduy is one of several Cuban playwrights whose works were produced interna-tionally beginning in the 1970s. La Playa (The Beach), a suite of variations on fantasies of memory, was staged at the Théâtre d'Orsay in Paris by Simone Benmussa in 1977.

The cultural diversity of the countries of Central and South Amer-ica can scarcely be suggested in a brief overview. Evidence of the exis-tence of pre-Columbian Indian theatricals is ample, but their sup-pression by the Spanish conquistadores left little trace of what those performances may have been like. The earliest example of an indige-nous drama that has been accepted as authentic is *Rabinal Achí* (Rabinal Warrior), a Mayan dance-drama in the Quiché language; the piece survived, apparently, because it was dictated to a priest by his Indian servant in 1856. The Jesuits who came to South America in the sixteenth century not only staged Spanish *autos sacramentales* as instruments of religious and moral instruction, but they also learned the native lan-guages—such as Aymara and Quechua in the area around Lima—and borrowed local traditions to create new plays for performance by In-dians. Although the colonial period brought mostly imported Spanish plays, some *criollo* dramatists (Creole; of Spanish descent, but born in the new world) achieved renown for plays reflecting local color and con-cerns. Among them were Mexico's Fernán González de Eslava in the sixteenth century and, a century later, the talented young nun Sor Juana Inés de la Cruz, who wrote eighteen poetic dramas. The major theatrical centers during the colonial period were Lima, Mexico City, and Havana.

Romanticism came to the theaters of Latin America in the first half of the nineteenth century, during the period of the wars for independence, but it produced no important native dramatists. The late nineteenth century brought realism and was especially characterized by an appetite for frivolity in the theater. Argentina and Mexico embraced the Spanish *género chico,* small-scale programs of light variety fare, sometimes using material by major writers like the turn-of-the-century Nicarauguan poet Rubén Darío. Circuses and other tent shows were popular, especially in Argentina, where the Italian circus was warmly welcomed. Brazilian theatergoers proved notably receptive to French operettas and vaudevilles, into which the stock character of *le brésilien,* a spendthrift ladies' man, was often interpolated. Theaters with names like Variétés and Bouffes-Parisiennes were constructed in Rio de Janeiro and Sao Paulo, and French headliners were imported to play there. *Costumbrismo* flourished in light comedies that served as vehicles for the observation of local color and customs in the ethnically mixed national cultures of all South American countries. In Argentina, a special type of *costumbrista* drama developed in the 1880s when a widely popular dramatization of Eduardo Gutiérrez's novel *Juan Moreira* (1886) launched a vogue for plays about the violent lives of the gauchos on the vast pampas. Local color was employed to more serious purpose in most of the twenty-three plays by Latin America's greatest dramatist, Florencio Sánchez, whose plays belong to Argentina's "golden decade," 1900–1910. A Uruguayan who devoted most of his career to Argentine theater, Sánchez focused on social themes in plays like *M'hijo el dotor* (My Son the Lawyer, 1903), which illuminates tensions between urban and rural society and between first- and second-generation immigrants; *La gringa* (The Immigrant Girl, 1904), a conflict between an Argentine *criollo* and Italian *gringos;* and *Barranca abajo* (Down the Gully, 1905), a tragedy that is considered to be his masterpiece.

In the twentieth century, a group of seven Mexican playwrights (*El Grupo de los Siete,* 1925) charted a course of renewal, taking international models like Chekhov, Pirandello, and O'Neill, but seeking to establish a Mexican national identity distinct from the Spanish heritage. For example, they advocated a Mexican Spanish stage diction as opposed to the Castilian that had previously been standard in the theater. The Group of Seven's efforts at reform were expanded and carried to greater success by experimental groups like the Teatro de Ulises (1928) and, most notably, the Teatro de Orientación, founded in 1932 by Celestino Gorostiza. Of many Mexican dramatists who were encouraged by the independent theater movement of the 1930s, Rodolfo Usigli was outstanding. Politically daring and exquisitely crafted, his serious but non-didactic plays like *El gesticulador* (The Imposter, 1937) and *Corona de sombra* (Crown of Shadow, 1943) won permanent places in the Mexican repertoire. One avant-garde group, Poesía en Voz Alta (Poetry Out Loud, 1956–63), was particularly influential in promoting the work of new dramatists and expanding the range of Mexican drama beyond the realistic mode. Mexico's finest contemporary dramatist, Emilio Carballido, has led the way in departures from realism. Other important Mexican playwrights include Elena Garro, Luisa Josefina Hernández, Carlos Solórzano, and—now living in the United States—Guillermo Schmidhuber de la Mora. In addition, novelist Carlos Fuentes has written three plays.

Argentina's independent theater movement began with the founding of the Teatro del Pueblo in 1930 and lasted until the 1960s; among the outstanding dramatists it produced were Roberto Arlt, Osvaldo Dragún, and Griselda Gambaro. As noted elsewhere, a number of Argentine directors and playwrights have made successful careers in Paris. Playwright Kado Kostzer's work is often produced on both continents. Eugenio Griffero has successfully directed a number of his own plays of the 1980s. The development of Uruguayan theater is closely linked to that of Argentina; together they are called "River Plate theater." Prominent among Uruguayan dramatists after Florencio Sánchez were Ernesto Herrera, Vicente Martinez Cuitiño, and Carlos Maricio Pacheca. Brazil's renowned director and dramatic theorist Augusto Boal worked at the Teatro Arena in Sao Paolo until the changing political climate suppressed that and other such innovative theaters, and drove Boal into exile.

Chilean theater developed more slowly than that of other countries due to economic and political problems. A major impetus came from the establishment of two university theater groups: a group formed in 1941 and later renamed Instituto de Teatro de la Universidad de Chile (ITUC Teatro Experimental de la Universidad Católica [TEUC, 1943]). The dramatists of the resulting "generation of 1950" included several women, but Chile's three finest dramatists flourished in the 1960s: Luis Heiremans, Egon Wolff, and Alejandro Sieveking. The great poet Pablo Neruda wrote one play before his death in 1973, the year of the coup that initiated a period of severe political and artistic repression in Chile. Neruda appears as a character in *Ardiente paciencia* (Burning Patience, 1982), a deeply moving and warmly humorous play by Chilean playwright-in-exile Antonio Skármeta. Since 1984 the arts have been allowed greater freedom in Chile, and the theater has flourished correspondingly. Venezuelan theater gained momentum in the 1930s; its best playwrights since the 1950s are César Rengifo and Isaac Chocrón. Theater in Colombia of recent decades has been distinguished by collective creation and social concern; playwright Enrique Buenaventura's Teatro Experimental de Cali (1969) is prominent among the approximately one hundred such groups. Peruvian novelist Maria Vargas Llosa wrote two plays in the 1980s. Outstanding Central American dramatists are José Triana of Cuba and René Marquès of Puerto Rico. Recent years have seen increasing interest in defining national identity through the theater and a proliferation of festivals of theater throughout Central and South America. This part of the globe is likely to produce some of the twenty-first century's liveliest theater.

In Africa, traditional indigenous ritual performances coexist alongside the more conventional scripted drama that has been propagated by the universities since the various nations achieved their independence in the 1950s and 1960s. The skills of African singers, dancers, drummers, magicians, acrobats, and storytellers that have been passed across the generations for five centuries form the basis of the loosely structured traditional entertainment. It differs from European theater in many respects, most notably in the active communion between performer and spectator. Scott Kennedy emphasizes the direct connection between this traditional music-drama and the everyday life of the people, as opposed to theater art for art's sake. "These dramatic expressions associated with social rituals or ceremonial occasions and narrative drama, including dialogue, music, dance and mime with more spontaneity than formality, and dance-drama movements may all be well known and expected by the audience," writes Kennedy. "And this audience-ritual-identification may keep the spectators involved for days or weeks without their becoming bored."

With the nineteenth-century colonization of Africa, public schools were established. Although primarily intended to provide a European concept of education, such institutions—like the Ecole Normale William Ponty (opened by the French in Dakar, Sénégal, in 1913) or the Arts Theatre (founded by British lecturers Martin Banham and Geoffrey Axworthy in 1958) at the University of Ibadan, Nigeria, or the University of Ghana at Legon, Accra, or the University of Dar es Salam in Tanzania, among others—took an active role in studying and encouraging traditional African theater. The wealth of written drama in recent decades—in English, French, Swahili, Yoruba, and other languages—was largely spawned by the universities. Nigeria has long been in the forefront of African drama. Chief Hubert Ogunde began his professional career as a playwright, producer, and performer of Yoruba plays and operas in 1944. His tours of the thirty-eight productions he mounted in twenty-eight years established his reputation as the father of Nigerian theater. Other Yoruba opera companies followed, most notably Kola Ogunmola's Travelling Theatre, which offered Ogunmola's very popular dramatization of Amos Tutuola's novel *The Palm-wine Drinkard.* John Pepper Clark wrote a number of successful plays in English in the 1960s, and James Ene-Henshaw excelled in naturalism. The most internationally renowned of all African dramatists, Nigeria's Wole Soyinka, won the Nobel Prize for Literature in 1986. Among his numerous plays, written in English, are *A Dance of the Forests* (1963), *The Lion and the Jewel* (1964), *The Trials of Brother Jero* (1964), *Madmen and Specialists* (1971), and *Death and the King's Horseman* (1975).

The leading figures in the theater of Ghana, both women, have been affiliated with the Ghana Drama Studio in Accra, which Efua Theodora Sutherland founded in 1957. A playwright and director as well, Sutherland has been tireless in her efforts to promote a national theater in Ghana. Ama Ata Aidoo is also a playwright and has served as Ghana's Secretary of Education. Although he is from the Ivory Coast, playwright Bernard Dadié is a product of the William Ponty School in Sénégal; one of his first plays produced there was subsequently staged at the Studio des Champs-Elysées in Paris in 1937. Among his many French-language plays, *Monsieur Thôgô-gnini* (Mr Opportunist, 1969) is considered to be the best. Other important West African dramatists writing in French include Sénégal's Cheik Aliou Ndao, the Congolese Sony Lab'ou Tansi, the Cameroon's Guillaume Oyônô-Mbia, and Algeria's Kateb Yacine. Although Aimé Césaire is from Martinique in the Caribbean, he is strongly identified with African theater in his choice of subjects and incorporation of an African poetic idiom in his use of language; he wrote *La Tragédie du roi Christoph* (the Tragedy of King Christoph, 1964), *Une Saison au Congo* (A Season in the Congo, 1967), and an "adaptation for a black theater" of Shakespeare's *The Tempest,* entitled *Une tempête* (1969).

East Africa was more sparsely populated than West Africa, but was more heavily settled by Europeans. Thus the amateur theatricals and school dramas of the colonists remained more isolated from native traditions. Interchange was further delayed by the greater violence of the East African struggles for independence. The 1970s finally saw the emergence of a generation of talented playwrights: James Ngugi and Kenneth Watene of Kenya, John Ruganda and Robert Serumaga of Uganda, and David Pownall of Zambia. In addition, Tanzania's President Julius Nyere has made translations of Shakespeare into Swahili.

Precolonial theater in South Africa embraced a variety of forms, including solo narratives in Nguni, Sotho praise poems, as well as Hottentot and Bushman amalgamations of mime, music, and dance. The first European theater was built in Cape Town in 1801 for touring performers from England. Afrikaans plays (in Dutch) began to be produced at the turn of the century. As the English and Afrikaans theaters blossomed, so did native African work. In 1929, a professional black company called the Lucky Stars began offering comedies with music, in Zulu, for both white and black audiences. Although English-speaking theater dominated the cultural scene, a black musical *King Kong* (1959), starring Miriam Makeba, gained international renown. In 1963 the Afrikaaner government passed its most sweeping law against racially mixed audiences at public entertainments. Athol Fugard, a playwright of Afrikaans descent who writes in English, began his longstanding defiance of such restrictions in 1958 when he worked with black actors to stage his play *No-Good Friday*. While Fugard gradually rose to international prominence with plays like *The Blood Knot* (1961), *Sizwe Bansi is Dead* (1972), *A Lesson from Aloes* (1978), and others, black South African theater was also finding a place in commercial theater abroad. Among the productions that toured to New York or London were *Sponono* (1964), *Ipi Tombi* (1973), *Woza Albert* (1982), and *Asinamali!* (1986). The catalyst for much of that kind of activity is Gibson Kente, who has been since the 1960s Africa's leading black theatrical entrepreneur as well as a playwright, director, and choreographer.

There has always been a strong tradition of oral recitation or storytelling in Arabic cultures, but the boundary between storytelling and full-fledged dramatic enactment has wavered according to religious interpretation, and thus the development of dramatic art in the Middle East has been erratic. Beyond the coverage of early Islamic performance in volume 1, the most important developments in Arabic drama have occurred in Egypt. Various reports by European travelers in Egypt in the late eighteenth and early nineteenth centuries confirm the existence there of lively, costumed dramatic performances in informal settings. A European influence began with the French theatricals enjoyed by Napoleon's occupying forces, who even built a theater in Cairo in 1800. The earliest literary Arabic play using a European dramatic structure was written by Maroun al-Naqqash, a Maronite Christian from Lebanon, who had traveled in Italy. His first play, *al-Bakhil* (The Miser), much inspired by Molière, was staged in the garden of his house in Beirut in 1847. Its enthusiastic reception prompted him to write two more plays before his death at thirty-eight. Maroun al-Naqqash's family sporadically continued their theatrical presentations, and in 1872 his nephew Salim al-Naqqash took the troupe to Egypt. By then, Egyptian theater had already been given a strong impetus by the Khedive Isma'il, whose interest in attracting European visitors and business led him to build a magnificent Cairo Opera House (1869) for the opening of the Suez Canal. He also encouraged Ya'qub Sanu (James Sanua), who put together and trained a company of actors to perform in the local dialect his own short, humorous musical plays on contemporary subjects. Dubbed "the Molière of Egypt," Sanu enjoyed a popular following until his satire offended the khedive and brought the closure of his theater in 1872. Salim al-Naqqash experienced political difficulties too, but his troupe persevered under the management of its leading actor Yusuf Khayyat. One of Khayyat's players, Sulayman al-Qardahi, in turn formed a troupe that toured to North Africa and Paris before settling in Tunisia. Ahmed Abu Khalil al-Qabbani introduced professional theater to Syria, but religious objections forced his emigration to Egypt in 1884. Al-Qabbani succeeded there, not only because he was an excellent performer, but also because of his emphasis on music and on Arabic themes. Although a fire destroyed his Cairo theater and ruined him financially, his influence continued to be felt through the work of a generation of actors who had performed with him.

The most important Egyptian troupe of the early twentieth century was that of Jurj Abyad, who was born in Beirut, studied in Paris, and came to Egypt in 1910 at the head of a French company. By 1912 he had formed an Arabic-language troupe and began a long successful career of touring European classics in translation throughout the Arab world. Active until the 1950s, he remains a seminal figure in the establishment of a tradition of serious legitimate drama. Abyad's contributions in classical theater were paralleled by the achievements of Naguib al-Rihani in comedy. An actor-manager whose career also began in the 1910s and spanned four decades, al-Rihani became famous for the stock character he invented and with whom he was always closely identified in the popular mind: Kishkish Bey. Al-Rihani's Kishkish was a good-hearted but cunning figure; his adventures in a series of comic sketches and longer plays generally involved his being taken advantage of by foreigners, but Kishkish would ultimately outsmart them. Other important troupes were those of Yusuf Wahbi and actress Fatima Rushdi. Among the three outstanding playwrights of the century, Tawfiq al-Hakim is considered to be the father of modern Egyptian drama. He studied in Paris, returned to Egypt in 1927, worked several years as a court prosecutor, and began getting his plays produced in the 1930s. Among his seventy plays are *The Sultan's Dilemma* (1960), Egypt's first absurdist play *The Tree Climber* (1962), and the brilliantly imaginative philosophical drama *Fate of a Cockroach*. A Chekhovian influence permeates the socially conscious plays of Nu'man 'Ashur, including *The People Upstairs* (1956) and *The People Downstairs* (1958). Perhaps the most outstanding of Egypt's living dramatists, Rashad Rushdy moved from his early plays of poetic realism like *Butterfly* (1959) to politically conscious plays like *Egypt, My Love* (1967).

The turmoil in the Middle East during the 1970s and 1980s has retarded theatrical development in most Arabic countries. Although western-influenced theater in Turkey can be traced back to 1859, it truly flourished only after the proclamation of the Republic in 1923. That period brought government support for both traditional Turkish theater forms and modern dramas of psychological realism, as well as the removal of all restrictions against the appearance of Turkish women on stage. Modern Turkish theater reached a peak in the decade of the 1960s, before social problems began to take their toll on live theater attendance. In East Jerusalem, the first professional Palestinian theater company, El-Hakawati, has attracted some Israeli theatergoers by its artistic quality and high ideals. Its mission, according to director François Abu Salem is "to bring more understanding not only between Israelis and Palestinians but between the Middle East and the West."

The British conquest of India in 1818 superimposed a culture that left its influence long after the departure of the British in 1947. Indians began staging Shakespeare in English as early as 1831 and were soon translating the plays into Bengali. Of the sixteen major Indian languages, Bengali and Marathi most readily absorbed the English influence. Some Indian artists worked toward a synthesis of Indian and western dramatic form, but this was eventually countered by an effort to revive Sanskrit drama and the various traditional forms of dance-drama. Undoubtedly the greatest literary figure of modern India was Rabindranath Tagore, winner of the Nobel Prize in 1913. He wrote over sixty Bengali plays between 1884 and 1939, many of which he directed himself, especially as he became fascinated with creating a new poetic form of dance-drama. The great film director Satyajit Ray was one of Tagore's pupils. In 1954 the Indian government established the Sangeet Natak Akademi (National Academy of Music, Dance, and Drama) to foster such a national dramatic art. However, there is little government subsidization for theater in India and surprisingly little commercial theater. It is the countless amateur companies that nurture new dramatists and provide the most employment opportunities for performers. Reportedly, there are about three thousand registered amateur companies in Calcutta and five hundred in Bombay. Among the best known of the Calcutta groups since the 1950s are Uptal Dutt's Marxist-oriented Little Theatre Group; Sombhu Mitra's Bohurupee, which excels at productions of Tagore's plays featuring one of India's finest actresses, Tripti Mitra; Ajitesh Bannerji's Nandikar, offering Brecht, Chekhov, and other foreign plays in Bengali; and the Theatre Centre, which specializes in plays by its director Torun Roy. In Delhi, Habib Tanvir has explored folk elements in Sanskrit dramas at his Naya Theatre, and Rajinder Nath's Abhiyan company presents plays from other Indian languages in Hindi.

Ghashiram Kotwal, *a Marathi play by Vijay Tendulkar (b. 1928), was performed by the Theatre Academy of Pune, under the direction of Jabbar Patel. This tale of greed and corruption, blending historical fact and fiction, is set in eighteenth-century Pune. Courtesy of the Sangeet Natak Akademi, New Delhi.*

Ghashiram Kotwal *combined Indian classical tradition with modern production techniques. It included song, dance, and mime from various types of folk theater. Courtesy of Sangeet Natak Akademi, New Delhi.*

Andha Yug, *a Hindi play by Satayadev Dubey (b. 1936), is based upon the last part of the* Mahabharata. *Directed by Dharamvir Bharati, it was produced in 1989 by two Bombay theater groups, Samvardhan and Arpana. Courtesy of Sangeet Natak Akademi, New Delhi.*

Ratan Thiyam founded Chorus Repertory Theatre in 1976 to explore the theater forms based upon the arts and lore of Manipur. Their 1989 production of Chakravyuha, *written and directed by Thiyam, evolved out of workshop study of the* Mahabharata. *Courtesy of Sangeet Natak Akademi, New Delhi.*

A flier for Arrabal's production in Japan reproduces one of the famous portraits of him that incorporate many personal symbols. Courtesy of Fernando Arrabal.

French–Spanish playwright Fernando Arrabal directed his own play Grand Ceremonial *in Tokyo in 1987. In Japan, as elsewhere in Asia, contemporary western theatrical forms find a place alongside the traditional. Courtesy of Fernando Arrabal.*

In Bombay, Vijay Mehta's Rangayan has presented Sanskrit classics in Marathi.

Aspects of Indian culture are evident in the myriad theatrical modes of southeast Asia, but the complexity of the many variations of shadow puppet theater and dance-drama in that region make it difficult to summarize. The combination of highly inflected gestures and movement with song, spoken dialogue, and narration are designed to create multiple impressions on several levels at once. In general, the western influence has been minimal on the mainland nations: Burma, Thailand, Kampuchea, Laos, and Vietnam. Attempts to synthesize Asian and western theatrical elements have occurred largely in the peninsular and island countries of Malaysia, Indonesia, and the Philippines. Indonesian playwright W. S. Rendra, for example, in the 1970s reworked plays like *Oedipus Rex, Oedipus at Colonus,* and *Waiting for Godot* to place them in a Javanese cultural context, using a performance style based on traditional folk elements. In the 1980s, his work became increasingly political, and this has limited his ability to reach wide audiences. A number of southeast Asian playwrights have focused on questions of national identity, and this has led them back to native theatrical modes.

The founding of the People's Republic of China in 1949 brought fifteen years of theatrical vitality, as both traditional and modern drama were encouraged, theaters were built, and theater schools were opened. At Beijing's Central Dramatic Institute, opened in 1950, Soviet teachers were brought in to train students in the Stanislavsky system of acting. At the same time, the National School of Beijing Opera and similar institutes in Shanghai and elsewhere were offering intensive training in the intricacies of traditional musical forms. Building upon the momentum generated during China's war against Japan—when anti-Japanese propaganda plays performed in the streets and rural villages had helped to unify the people in their common cause—Mao Zedong encouraged amateur theater as a spare-time activity for peasants and workers. By 1960 it was estimated that approximately eight million Chinese were participating in amateur theater groups, fulfilling the slogan "small in scale, rich in variety." The masses' preference for music and spectacle meant that traditional drama predominated, even though many of the old Beijing and other regional operas had been revised to purge them of feudalistic content. Modern "spoken" dramas continued to be performed, including those of China's first and greatest modern dramatist, Cao Yu, author of *Leiyu* (Thunderstorm, 1935), *Richu* (Sunrise, 1936), and others. The Hundred Flowers Movement (named for Mao Zedong's call to "let a hundred flowers bloom, let a hundred schools of thought contend," 1956–57) brought revivals of some traditional pieces that had previously been banned. In Beijing in 1957 one could see forty-two Beijing operas, six spoken dramas, and two Soviet plays in translation.

Ying Ruocheng, Li Shilong, and Mitiezeng in a happier moment in the 1983 production of Death of a Salesman *at the Beijing People's Art Theatre. Courtesy of Ying Ruocheng.*

The Shanghai Youth Drama Troupe presented Shakespeare's Much Ado About Nothing *in a lovely interpretation of Western theatrical style in 1978. Courtesy of Wang Yiqun.*

Tibetan students at the Shanghai Drama Institute presented Romeo and Juliet *in 1981. The success of the production enabled it to tour to Beijing and to Lhasa, Tibet. Chinese theatergoers in the capital found it so moving that they long recalled "when Tibet brought tears to Beijing." Courtesy of Wang Yiqun.*

The traditional operas were suppressed, as were all foreign plays, when Mao's wife Jiang Qing assumed control over the Chinese repertoire during the harrowing decade of the Cultural Revolution (1966–76). Conceiving of theater only in terms of its potential as an instrument for the radical transformation of society, Jiang Qing (who had been an unsuccessful actress) established a repertoire of "model" operas that demonstrated the revolutionary ideology. Only eight approved works could then be seen in the theaters or heard on the radio for a five-year period. The smashing of the Gang of Four (Jiang Qing and three others) in October 1976, a month after the death of Mao Zedong, brought a return of the "hundred flowers" policy. New spoken dramas were written and foreign plays again reached the stage. London's Old Vic Company performed *Hamlet* in China in 1979. In 1983 Authur Miller directed

Chinese actors at the Beijing People's Art Theatre in a production of his own *Death of a Salesman,* featuring the internationally renowned actor-director Ying Ruocheng as Willy Loman. The following year Ying directed *Fifteen Strings of Cash,* a seventeenth-century Kunchu drama, at Missouri Repertory Theatre, and in 1986 he directed his own Chinese translation of Peter Shaffer's *Amadeus* in Beijing. A 1986 Shakespeare festival held in both Beijing and Shanghai brought together a total of twenty-eight productions, some performed as spoken drama, others adapted into various traditional opera forms. Although the tragic events in Tiananmen Square in June 1989 clouded the arts along with all other aspects of life in China, it is to be hoped that a Shakespeare festival planned for 1991 will help to renew the international bonds among artists that reinforce a nation's humanistic values.

It is only in the last thirty-five years that Australian drama has achieved a national identity distinct from English, Irish, and continental European influences. Imported successes filled most of the theaters throughout the nineteenth century, although there was a following for homegrown melodramas featuring Australian character types like the

The international prestige of Australian theater has increased rapidly since the 1970s. David Williamson is one of the better known of a generation of outstanding playwrights. This picture, from the film version of his play Don's Party, *shows Ray Barrett, Graeme Blundell, and Jeanni Drynan. Courtesy of Australian Information Service.*

Jorn Utzon of Denmark won the 1956 international competition for the design of the Sydney Opera House (1960–73). It stands as an internationally recognized symbol of the vitality of Australian arts. Courtesy of Australian Information Service.

bushranger. In the 1910s and 1920s Louis Esson succeeded in creating a drama of realistic Australian content with literary status. His attempt to run a theater presenting only Australian plays lasted only four seasons, but the influence of his plays is considered seminal. Some historians date modern Australian drama from Ray Lawler's *Summer of the Seventeenth Doll* (1955), a play based upon the traditional outback concept of "mateship" (male friendship). Produced first in Melbourne and Sydney, it went on to become the country's first international success. The election of the Whitlam Labor Government in 1972 marks another turning point, as the last two decades have seen a tremendous flourishing of all the arts in Australia from the construction of great cultural centers to the remarkably successful film industry. The leading contemporary dramatist, David Williamson, came to prominence with *The Removalists* in 1971 and has continued to write plays and film scripts that analyze Australian society and behavior, as in *Don's Party* (1971) and *Travelling North* (1980).

Other important playwrights include Alexander Buzo, Thomas Keneally, Louis Nowra, Alma De Groen, and the first major Aborigine dramatist, Jack Davis.

The experience of Australia and other nations has shown that the theater can make a unique contribution to establishing a nation's self-definition, examining its problems, and focusing its aspirations. The task of the theater in the twenty-first century will be to preserve all the flavor and individuality of the various theatrical traditions while opening up our theaters and expanding our audiences' interests to encompass the plays in translation that can contribute so much to our understanding of our neighbors on this planet.

Bibliography

General Works

Banham, Martin, ed., *The Cambridge Guide to World Theatre*. New York, 1988.
Benson, Eugene and L. W. Conolly, eds., *The Oxford Companion to Canadian Theatre*. Oxford, 1989.
Berthold, Margot, *The History of World Theater: From the Beginnings to the Baroque*. New York, 1991.
Brockett, Oscar G., *History of the Theatre*, fifth edition. Boston, 1987.
Bronner, Edwin J., *The Encyclopedia of the American Theatre, 1900–1975*. San Diego, 1980.
Cheney, Sheldon, *Stage Decoration*. New York, 1928.
Couty, Daniel and Alain Rey, eds., *Le Théâtre*. Paris, 1984.
Hartnoll, Phyllis, ed., *The Oxford Companion to the Theatre*, fourth edition. Oxford, 1983.
Harvey, Sir Paul and J. E. Heseltine, eds., *The Oxford Companion to French Literature*. Oxford, 1959.
Hochman, Stanley, ed., *McGraw-Hill Encyclopedia of World Drama*, 5 vols. New York, 1984.
Kirkpatrick, D. L., ed., *Contemporary Dramatists*, fourth edition. London, 1988.
Leiter, Samuel L., ed., *Shakespeare Around the Globe: A Guide to Notable Postwar Revivals*. New York, 1986.
Kirstein, Lincoln, *Movement and Metaphor: Four Centuries of Ballet*. New York, 1970.
Kolin, Philip C., ed., *American Playwrights since 1945: A Guide to Scholarship, Criticism, and Performance*. New York: Greenwood Press, 1989.
Kullman, Colby H. and William C. Young, eds., *Theatre Companies of the World*, 2 vols. New York, 1986.
Matlaw, Myron., *Modern World Drama: An Encyclopedia*. New York, 1972.
Rischbieter, Henning, *Theater-Lexikon*. Zurich, 1983.
Terras, Victor, ed., *Handbook of Russian Literature*. New Haven, 1985.
Thorlby, Anthony, ed., *The Penguin Companion to European Literature*. New York, 1969.

The Stuart Court and Restoration England

Arrowsmith, Joseph, *The Reformation: A Comedy*. Introduction by Deborah C. Payne. Los Angeles, 1986.

Avery, Emmett L., and Scouten, Arthur H., eds., *The London Stage 1600–1700: A Critical Introduction.* Carbondale, 1968.

Barbeau, Anne T., *The Intellectual Design of John Dryden's Heroic Plays.* New Haven, 1970.

Barker, Felix, and Jackson, Peter, *London: 2,000 Years of a City and Its People.* New York, 1972.

Behn, Aphra, *The Lucky Chance; or, The Alderman's Bargain.* Edited by Fidelis Morgan. New York, 1984.

———, *The Rover (The Banished Cavaliers).* A program/text with commentary by Simon Trussler. London, 1986.

Boswell, Eleanore, *The Restoration Court Stage (1660–1702): With a Particular Account of the Production of Calisto.* New York, 1965.

Brown, John Russell, and Harris, Bernard, eds., *Restoration Theatre.* New York, 1965.

Brown, Laura, *English Dramatic Form, 1660–1760: An Essay in Generic History.* New Haven, 1981.

Butler, Martin, *Theatre and Crisis 1632–1642.* Cambridge, 1984.

Cibber, Colley, *An Apology for the Life of Mr. Colley Cibber Written by Himself.* 2 vols. Edited by Robert W. Lowe. London, 1889.

Clark, Constance, *Three Augustan Women Playwrights.* New York, 1986.

Clark, Sir George, *The Illustrated History of Britain.* Edited and with additional material by Dr. J. N. Westwood. New York, 1982.

Coate, Mary, *Social Life in Stuart England.* Westport, 1971.

Cohen, J. Bernard, *Revolution in Science.* Cambridge, 1985.

Coleman, Antony, and Hammond, Antony, editors, *Poetry and Drama 1570–1700: Essays in Honour of Harold F. Brooks.* London, 1981. "The Restoration: Age of Faith, Age of Satire" by Earl Miner; "Securing a Repertory: 156 Plays on the London Stage 1660–1665" by Robert D. Hume.

A Comparison between the Two Stages: A Late Restoration Book of the Theatre. Edited by Staring B. Wells. New York, 1971.

Congreve, William, *Complete Plays.* Edited by Alexander Charles Ewald. New York, 1963.

DeMarly, Diane, "The Architect of the Dorset Garden Theatre," *Theatre Notebook,* 1975, pp. 119–124.

Dennis, John, *The Critical Works of John Dennis.* Edited by Edward Niles Hooker. Vol. 1: 1692–1711, Vol. 2: 1711–29. Baltimore, 1943.

Dent, Edward J., *Foundations of English Opera: A Study of Musical Drama in England During the Seventeenth Century.* Cambridge, 1928.

Dibdin, Charles, *A Complete History of the English Stage.* Vol. 4. New York, 1970.

Dobbs, Brian, *Drury Lane: Three Centuries of the Theatre Royal 1663–1971.* London, 1972.

Dobrée, Bonamy, *John Dryden.* London, n.d.

———, *Essays in Biography 1680–1726.* Freeport, New York, 1967.

Downes, John, *Roscius Anglicanus.* Edited by Judith Milhous and Robert D. Hume. London, 1987.

Doyle, Anne T., *Elkanah Settle's "The Empress of Morocco" and the Controversy Surrounding It: A Critical Edition.* New York, 1987.

Dryden, John, *Three Plays*. Edited, with an introduction and notes by George Saintsbury. New York, 1957.

———, *Dramatic Essays*. London, 1921.

Etherege, Sir George, *The Man of Mode*. Edited by W. B. Carnochan. Lincoln, 1966.

Falkus, Christopher, *The Life and Times of Charles II*. New York, 1972.

Farquhar, George, *The Recruiting Officer, The Beaux Stratagem, The Constant Couple, The Twin Rivals*. Edited by William Archer. New York, 1959.

———, *The Recruiting Officer*. Edited by Peter Dixon. Dover, N.H., 1986.

Festival Designs by Inigo Jones: An Exhibition of Drawings for Scenery and Costumes for the Court Masques of James I and Charles I. Introduction and catalogue by Roy Strong, 1967.

Furfey, Paul Hanley, *A History of Social Thought*. New York, 1946.

Gardner, William Bradford, *The Prologues and Epilogues of John Dryden: A Critical Edition*. New York, 1951.

Giesbrecht, Martin Gerhard, *The Evolution of Economic Society: An Introduction to Economics*. San Francisco, 1972.

Goreau, Angeline, *Reconstructing Aphra: A Social Biography of Aphra Behn*. New York, 1980.

Greene, Graham, *Lord Rochester's Monkey: Being the Life of John Wilmot, Second Earl of Rochester*. New York, 1974.

Hanson, Michael, *2000 Years of London: An Illustrated Survey*. London, 1967.

Harris, Bernard, *Sir John Vanbrugh*. London, 1967.

Harris, John; Orgel, Stephen; and Strong, Roy, *The King's Arcadia: Inigo Jones and the Stuart Court*. Arts Council of Great Britain, 1973.

Harwood, John T., *Critics, Values, and Restoration Comedy*. Carbondale, 1982.

Hart, Roger, *English Life in the Seventeenth Century*. London, 1970.

Highfill, Philip H., Jr.; Burnim, Kalman A.; and Langhans, Edward A., *A Biographical Dictionary of Actors, Actresses, Musicians, Dancers, Managers and Other Stage Personnel in London, 1660–1800*. Carbondale, 1984.

Hill, Christopher, *The Century of Revolution 1603–1714*. Edinburgh, 1961.

Hobbes, Thomas, *Leviathan*. Introduction by A. D. Lindsay. New York, 1950.

Hook, Judith, *The Baroque Age in England*. London, 1976.

Hotson, Leslie, *The Commonwealth and Restoration Stage*. New York, 1962.

Hume, Robert D., *The Development of English Drama in the Late Seventeenth Century*. Oxford, 1976.

———, "The Dorset Garden Theatre: A Review of the Facts and Problems," *Theatre Notebook* 33 (1979): 4–17.

———, "Elizabeth Barry's First Roles and the Cast of *The Man of Mode*," *Theatre History Studies* 5 (1985): 16–19.

———, "*The Maid's Tragedy* and Censorship in the Restoration Theatre," *Philological Quarterly* 61 (1982): 484–90.

———, "The Nature of the Dorset Garden Theatre," *Theatre Notebook* 36, no. 3 (1982): 99–109.

———, *The Rakish Stage: Studies in English Drama, 1660–1800*. Carbondale, 1983.

———, ed., *The London Theatre World, 1660–1800*. Carbondale, 1980. Includes "Company Management" by Judith Milhous; "The Theatres" by Edward A.

Langhans; "Scenery and Technical Design" by Colin Visser; "Performers and Performing" by Philip H. Highfill, Jr.; "The Making of the Repertory" by George Winchester Stone, Jr.; "The Changing Audience" by Harry William Pedicord; "Political and Social Thought in Drama" by John Loftis.

Jordan, R., "Observations on the Backstage Area in the Restoration Theatre," *Theatre Notebook* 38, no. 2 (1984): 66–68.

Joseph, Bertram, *The Tragic Actor.* New York, 1959.

Kenny, Shirley Strum, ed., *British Theatre and the Other Arts, 1660–1800.* Washington, D.C., 1984. Includes "Theatre, Related Arts, and the Profit Motive: An Overview" by Shirley Strum Kenny; "The Multimedia Spectacular on the Restoration Stage" by Judith Milhous; "Opera in London, 1695–1706" by Robert D. Hume; "The Anti-Evolutionary Development of the London Theatres" by Arthur H. Scouten.

Koon, Helene, *Colley Cibber: A Biography.* Lexington, 1986.

Langhans, Edward A., "A Conjectural Reconstruction of the Dorset Garden Theatre," *Theatre Survey* 13 (1972): 74–93.

———, *Restoration Promptbooks.* Carbondale, 1981.

Latham, Robert, ed., *The Illustrated Pepys: Extracts from the Diary.* Berkeley, 1978.

Leacroft, Richard and Helen, *Theatre and Playhouse: An Illustrated Survey of Theatre Building from Ancient Greece to the Present Day.* New York, 1985.

Lebrun, Charles, *A Method to Learn to Design the Passions* (1702). Introduction by Alan T. McKenzie. Los Angeles, 1980.

Limon, Jerzy, *Gentlemen of a Company: English Players in Central and Eastern Europe 1590–1660.* London, 1985.

Lindley, David, ed., *The Court Masque.* Manchester, 1984. Includes "The French Element in Inigo Jones's Masque Designs" by John Peacock; "Dryden's *Albion and Albanius:* The Apotheosis of Charles II" by Paul Hammond.

Loftis, John; Southern, Richard; Jones, Marion; and Scouten, A. H., *The Revels History of Drama in English.* Vol. 5: 1660–1750. London, 1976.

Lowe, Robert W., *Thomas Betterton.* New York, 1971.

McCollum, John I., ed., *The Restoration Stage.* Boston, 1961.

Milhous, Judith, and Hume, Robert D., "An Annotated Guide to the Theatrical Documents in PRO LC 7/1, 7/2 and 7/3," *Theatre Notebook* (n.d.): 25–31.

Milhous, Judith, "Elizabeth Bowtell and Elizabeth Davenport: Some Puzzles Solved," *Theatre Notebook* 39 (1985): 124–34.

———, *Thomas Betterton and the Management of Lincoln's Inn Fields 1695–1708.* Carbondale, 1979.

———, *Producible Interpretation: Eight English Plays 1675–1707.* Carbondale, 1985.

Morgan, Fidelis, *The Female Wits: Women Playwrights on the London Stage 1660–1720.* London, 1981.

Mullin, Donald C., *The Development of the Playhouse.* Berkeley, 1970.

Nettleton, George H., and Case, Arthur E., eds., *British Dramatists from Dryden to Sheridan.* Boston, 1939.

Nicoll, Allardyce, *British Drama.* Revised by J. C. Trewin. New York, 1978.

Opper, Jacob, *Science and the Arts: A Study in Relationships from 1600–1900.* Rutherford, 1973.

Orgel, Stephen, and Strong, Roy, *Inigo Jones: The Theatre of the Stuart Court*. 2 vols. Berkeley, 1973.

Orrell, John, "Scenes and Machines at the Cockpit, Drury Lane," *Theatre Survey* 26, no. 2 (November 1985): 103–19.

———, *The Theatres of Inigo Jones and John Webb*. New York, 1985.

Parry, Graham, *The Golden Age Restor'd: The Culture of the Stuart Court, 1603–1642*. Manchester, 1981.

Penzel, Frederick, *Theatre Lighting before Electricity*. Middletown, 1978.

Pepys, Samuel, *The Diary of Samuel Pepys: A New and Complete Transcription*. Edited by Robert Latham and William Matthews. Berkeley, 1970.

Pix, Mary, and Trotter, Catherine, *Plays*. 2 vols. Edited by Edna L. Steeves. New York, 1982.

Polwhele, Elizabeth, *The Frolicks; or, The Lawyer Cheated* (1671). Edited by Judith Milhous and Robert D. Hume. Ithaca, 1977.

Powell, Jocelyn, *Restoration Theatre Production*. London, 1984.

Price, Curtis A., *Music in the Restoration Theatre*. Ann Arbor, 1979.

Reik, Miriam M., *The Golden Lands of Thomas Hobbes*. Detroit, 1977.

Rosenfeld, Sybil, *Foreign Theatrical Companies in Great Britain in the 17th and 18th Centuries*. London, 1955.

Sawyer, Paul, *Christopher Rich of Drury Lane: The Biography of a Theatre Manager*. Lanham, Maryland, 1986.

Silvette, Herbert, *The Doctor on Stage: Medicine and Medical Men in Seventeenth-Century England*. Knoxville, 1967.

Smith, Dane Farnsworth, *The Critics in the Audience of the London Theatres from Buckingham to Sheridan: A Study of Neoclassicism in the Playhouse, 1671–1779*. Albuquerque, 1953.

Southern, Richard, *Changeable Scenery: Its Origin and Development in the British Theatre*. London, 1951.

Spingarn, J. E., ed., *Critical Essays of the Seventeenth Century*. Vol. 3, 1685–1700. Oxford, 1909. Includes "Preface to *Prince Arthur*" by Sir Richard Blackmore; "From *A Short View of the Immorality and Profaneness of the English Stage*" by Jeremy Collier.

Spring, John R., "The Dorset Garden Theatre: Playhouse or Opera House?" *Theatre Notebook* 34 (1980): 60–69.

———, "Platforms and Picture Frames: A Conjectural Reconstruction of the Duke of York's Theatre, Dorset Garden, 1669–1709," *Theatre Notebook* 31 (1977): 6–19.

Stone, George Winchester, Jr., and Highfill, Philip H., *In Search of Restoration and Eighteenth-Century Biography*. Los Angeles, 1976.

Strong, Roy, *Van Dyck: Charles II on Horseback*. New York, 1972.

Styan, J. L., *Restoration Comedy in Performance*. Cambridge, 1986.

Summers, Montague, *The Playhouse of Pepys*. New York, 1964.

Tidworth, Simon, *Theatres: An Architectural and Cultural History*. New York, 1973.

Vanbrugh, Sir John, *The Provoked Wife*. Edited by Antony Coleman. Dover, New Hampshire, 1982.

Van de Bogart, Doris, *Introduction to the Humanities: Painting, Sculpture, Architecture, Music, and Literature*. New York, 1968.

Van Lennep, William, ed., *The London Stage 1660–1800*. Part 1: 1660–1700. Carbondale, 1965.

Visser, Colin, "*The Descent of Orpheus* at the Cockpit, Drury Lane," *Theatre Survey* 24 (May and November 1983): 35–53.

———, "The Killigrew *Folio:* Private Playhouses and the Restoration Stage," *Theatre Survey* 19 (November 1978): 119–38.

Ward, Adolphus William, *A History of English Dramatic Literature to the Death of Queen Anne*. Vol. 3. New York, 1970 (from the edition of 1899).

Waterhouse, Ellis, *Painting in Britain 1530 to 1790*. New York, 1978.

White, Eric Walter, *A History of English Opera*. London, 1983.

Wickham, Glynne, *Early English Stages 1300 to 1660*. Vol. 2: 1576 to 1660, parts 1 and 2. New York, 1971, 1972.

Wilson, John Harold, *All the King's Ladies: Actresses of the Restoration*. Chicago, 1958.

———, *A Preface to Restoration Drama*. Boston, 1965.

Wykes, David, *A Preface to Dryden*. London, 1977.

The Eighteenth Century

Alasseur, Claude, *La Comédie francaise au 18e siècle*. Paris and La Haye, 1967.

Albert, Maurice, *Les Théâtres des boulevards 1789–1848*. Paris, 1902.

Allen, John J., *The Reconstruction of a Spanish Golden Age Playhouse: El Corral del Príncipe 1583–1744*. Gainesville, Florida, 1983.

Alvarez-Detrell, Tamara, and Paulson, Michael G., *The Gambling Mania On and Off the Stage in Pre-Revolutionary France*. Washington, D.C., 1982.

Andioc, René, *Sur la querelle du théâtre au temps de Leandro Fernandez de Moratín*. Tarbes, 1970.

Andrews, Stuart, ed., *Enlightened Despotism*. London, 1967.

Avery, Emmett L., *The London Stage 1700–1729*. Carbondale, 1968.

Bains, Yashdip Singh, "Canada's First Professional Company," *Theatre Survey* 18 (May 1977): 84–98.

Bapst, Germain, *Essai sur l'histoire de théâtre*. New York, 1971 (reprint of 1893 edition).

Barnett, Dene, *The Art of Gesture: The Practices and Principles of 18th Century Acting*. Heidelberg, 1987.

Baur-Heinhold, Margarete, *The Baroque Theatre: A Cultural History of the 17th and 18th Centuries*. New York, 1967.

Beijer, Agne, *Court Theatres of Drottningholm and Gripsholm*. New York, 1972.

———, *Drottningholms slottsteater på Lovisa Ulrikas och Gustaf III:s tid*. Stockholm, 1981.

Bellermann, Ludwig, *Schiller*. Leipzig, 1901.

Bernier, Olivier, *The Eighteenth-Century Woman*. Garden City, 1981.

Bevis, Richard W., ed., *Eighteenth Century Drama: Afterpieces*. London, 1970.

Biermann, Berthold, *Goethe's World as Seen in Letters and Memoirs*. New York, 1949.

Bjurstrom, Per, *Slottsteatern på Gripsholm*. Stockholm, 1982.

Bogard, Travis; Moody, Richard; and Meserve, Walter J., *The Revels History of Drama in English.* Vol. 8: "American Drama." New York, 1977.

Boileau, Nicolas, *Le Lutrin* and *L'Art poétique.* Paris, 1933.

Boncompain, Jacques, *Auteurs et comédiens au XVIIIe siècle.* N.p., 1976.

Booth, Michael R.; Southern, Richard; Marker, Frederick and Lise-Lone; and Davies, Robertson, *The Revels History of Drama in English.* Vol. 6, 1750–1880. London, 1975.

Braham, Alan, *The Architecture of the French Enlightenment.* Berkeley, 1980.

Brenner, Clarence D., and Goodyear, Nolan A., eds., *Eighteenth-Century French Plays.* New York, 1927.

Brookner, Anita, *Jacques-Louis David.* London, 1980.

Brown, F. Andrew, *Gotthold Ephraim Lessing.* New York, 1971.

Brown, Jane K., *Goethe's Faust: The German Tragedy.* Ithaca, 1986.

Browning, J. D., ed., *The Stage in the Eighteenth Century.* New York, 1981.

Bruford, W. H., *Theatre, Drama, and Audience in Goethe's Germany.* Westport, Connecticut, 1974.

Bruntière, Fernand, *Les Epoques du théâtre francais (1636–1850).* Paris, 1892.

Burnim, Kalman A., *David Garrick, Director.* Carbondale, 1973.

Carlson, Marvin, *The German Stage in the Nineteenth Century.* Metuchen, New Jersey, 1972.

——, *Goethe and the Weimar Theatre.* Ithaca, 1978.

——, *The Theatre of the French Revolution.* Ithaca, 1966.

——, *Theories of the Theatre.* Ithaca, 1984.

Centre National de la Recherche Scientifique, *Victor Louis et le théâtre: Scénographie, mise en scène et architecture théâtrale aux XVIIIe et XIXe siècles.* Paris, 1982.

Chapman, P. A.; Cons, Louis; Levengood, S. L.; Vreeland, W. U.; Wade, Ira O., compilers, *An Anthology of Eighteenth Century French Literature.* Princeton, 1930.

Charlton, David, *Grétry and the Growth of Opéra-Comique.* New York, 1986.

Charlton, D. G., *France: A Companion to French Studies.* London, 1979.

Chevally, Sylvie, *La Comédie-francaise hier et aujourd'hui.* Paris, 1970.

Clark, Barrett H., *European Theories of the Drama.* Edited by Henry Popkin. New York, 1965.

Clark, William Smith, *The Early Irish Stage: The Beginnings to 1720.* Westport, Connecticut, 1973.

Clunes, Alec, *The British Theatre.* London, 1964.

Cobban, Alfred, ed., *The Eighteenth Century: Europe in the Age of Enlightenment.* New York, 1969.

Cohen, Selma Jean, ed., *Dance as a Theatre Art: Source Readings in Dance History from 1581 to the Present.* New York, 1974.

Cohen-Stratyner, Barbara, ed., *Scenes and Machines from the 18th Century: The Stagecraft of Jacopo Fabbris and Citoyen Boullet.* Translated by C. Thomas Ault, in *Performing Arts Resources.* Vol. 11. New York, 1986.

Cook, John A., *Neo-Classic Drama in Spain: Theory and Practice.* Dallas, 1959.

Copin, Alfred, *Talma et la révolution.* 2nd ed. Paris, 1888.

D'Amico, Silvio, *Storia del teatro drammatico.* 3: *L'Ottocento.* Milan, 1958.

Délégation à l'action artistique de la ville de Paris/Théâtre National de l'Odéon, *Théâtre de l'Odéon 1782–1982*. Paris, 1981.

"Les demeures de la Comédie-Française (2)," *Comédie-Française* 92 (October 1980): 38–41.

DeRitter, Jones, "A Cult of Dependence: The Social Context of *The London Merchant*," *Comparative Drama* 21 (Winter 1987–88): 374–86.

Diderot, Denis, and d'Alembert, Jean le Rond, eds., *Theatre Architecture and Stage Machines: Engravings from the Encyclopédie, ou Dictionnaire raisonné des arts, des sciences, et des métiers*. New York, 1969.

Divertissmens du théâtre des petits appartemens pendant l'Hiver de 1749 à 1750. N.p., 1750.

Dobbs, Brian, *Drury Lane: Three Centuries of the Theatre Royal 1663–1971*. London, 1972.

Doebber, A., *Lauchstädt und Weimar: Eine theaterbaugeschichtliche Studie*. Berlin, 1908.

Donnert, Erich, *Russia in the Age of Englightenment*. Leipzig, 1986.

Doucette, Leonard E., *Theatre in French Canada: Laying the Foundations 1606– 1867*. Toronto, 1984.

Drogheda, Lord; Davison, Ken; and Wheatcroft, Andrew, *The Covent Garden Album: Three Centuries of Theatre, Opera, and Ballet*. London, 1981.

Dubech, Lucien, *Histoire Générale Illustré du Théâtre*. Tome 4. Paris, 1933.

Dukore, Bernard E., *Dramatic Theory and Criticism: Greeks to Grotowski*. New York, 1974.

Dumont, Gabriel Pierre Martin, *Parallèle de plans des plus belles salles de spectacles d'Italie et de France, avec des détails de machines théâtrales*. New York, 1968 (reprint of 1774 Paris edition).

Dumur, Guy, ed., *Histoire des spectacles*. Paris, 1965.

Dunbar, Janet, *Peg Woffington and Her World*. Boston, 1968.

Edwards, Murray D., *A Stage in Our Past: English-Language Theatre in Eastern Canada from the 1790s to 1914*. Toronto, 1968.

Egan, Pierce, *The Life of an Actor*. London, 1892.

Eklund, Hans, and Stribolt, Barbro, *Bolhuset och Dramaten Kungliga teaterbyggen Fran Adelcrantz till Lilljekvist 1753–1908*. Stockholm, 1978.

Farber, Marvin, ed., *Philosophic Thought in France and the United States*. Albany, 1968.

Fargher, Richard, *Life and Letters in France: The 18th Century*. New York, 1970.

Filippi, Joseph, *Parallèle des principaux théâtres modernes de l'Europe et des machines théâtrales francaises, allemandes, et anglaises;* drawings by Clément Contant. New York, 1968 (reprint of 1860 edition).

Fitz-Simon, Christopher, *The Irish Theatre*. London, 1983.

Fonteneau, Jean-Marie, "Le Palais-Royal a deux cents ans," *Palais-Royal*. Paris, 1986.

Fonvizin, Denis, *The Political and Legal Writings*. Translated with notes and an introduction by Walter Gleason. Ann Arbor, 1985.

Forsstrom, Lars, and Rangstrom, Ture, eds., *Drottningholms Slottsteater*. Stockholm, 1985.

Friedenthal, Richard, *Goethe: His Life and Times*. Cleveland, 1963.

Fuchs, Max, *La Vie théâtrale en province au XVIIIe siècle* and *Lexique des troupes de comédiens au XVIIIe siècle*. Geneva, 1976.

Gaiffe, Felix, *Le Drame en France au XVIIIe siècle*. Paris, 1910.

Gay, Peter, ed., *The Enlightenment: A Comprehensive Anthology*. New York, 1973.

Gay, Peter, *The Enlightenment: An Interpretation*. Vol. 1: *The Rise of Modern Paganism*. New York, 1966. Vol. 2: *The Science of Freedom*. New York, 1969.

————, *The Party of Humanity: Essays in the French Enlightenment*. New York, 1964.

Gerard, Alexander, *An Essay on Taste: To Which Are Annexed Three Dissertations on the Same Subject by Mr De Voltaire, Mr D'Alembert, and Mr De Montesquieu*. New York, 1970 (facsimile of the 1764 edition).

Gerould, Daniel, ed., *Gallant and Libertine: Divertissements and Parades of 18th Century France*. New York, 1983.

Giesbrecht, Martin Gerhard, *The Evolution of Economic Society*. San Francisco, 1962.

Goethe, Johann Wolfgang von, *Faust: A Tragedy*. Translated by Walter Arndt. *Backgrounds and Sources, The Author on the Drama, Contemporary Reactions, Modern Criticism*. Edited by Cyrus Hamlin. New York, 1976.

————, *Faust, Parts One and Two*. Translated by Robert David MacDonald. Birmingham, 1988.

————, *Götz von Berlichingen*. Translated by Charles E. Passage. New York, 1965.

————, *Plays*. Translated with introductions by Charles E. Passage. New York, 1980.

Golding, Alfred S., *Classicistic Acting: Two Centuries of a Performance Tradition at the Amsterdam Schouwberg, to Which Is Appended Translation of the "Lessons on the Principles of Gesticultation and Mimic Expression" of Johannes Jelgerhuis*. Lanham, Maryland, 1984.

Graham, Franklin, *Histrionic Montreal*. New York, 1969.

Gray, Charles Harold, *Theatrical Criticism in London to 1795*. New York, 1964 (reprint of 1931 edition).

Grendel, Frédéric, *Beaumarchais: The Man Who Was Figaro*. Translated by Roger Greaves. New York, 1977.

Hannaford, Stephen, "The Shape of Eighteenth-Century English Drama," *Theatre Survey* 21 (November 1980): 93–103.

Harrison, Robin, *Lessing: Minna von Barnhelm*. London, 1985.

Hautecour, Louis, *Histoire de l'architecture classique en France*. Vols. 3, 4. Paris, 1950.

Hawkins, Frederick, *The French Stage of the Eighteenth Century*. Vol. 2: 1750–1799. New York, (reprint of 1888 edition), 1968.

Hazard, Paul, *La Crise de conscience européenne, 1680–1715*. Paris, 1961.

————, *European Thought in the Eighteenth Century*. Cleveland, 1963.

Herzfeld-Sander, Margaret, ed., *Essays on German Theater*. New York, 1985.

Hewitt, Barnard, *Theatre U.S.A. 1665–1957*. New York, McGraw-Hill, 1969.

Hibbert, Christopher, *The Days of the French Revolution*. New York, 1981.

Hill, Aaron, and Popple, William, *The Prompter: A Theatrical Paper (1734–1736)*. Selected and edited by William W. Appleton and Kalmin A. Burnim. New York, 1966.

Hornblow, Arthur, *A History of the Theatre in America*. Vol. 1. New York, 1965.

Hume, Robert D., *Henry Fielding and the London Theatre 1728–1737*. Oxford, 1988.

Izenour, George C., *Theater Design*. New York, 1977.

Jauffret, E., *Le Théâtre révolutionnaire (1788–1799)*. Paris, 1869.

Jomaron, Jacqueline de, *Le théâtre en France*, I: "du Moyen Age à 1789." Paris, 1988.

———, *Le théâtre en France*, II: "de la Révolution à nos jours." Paris, 1989.

Jordain, Eleanor F., *Dramatic Theory and Practice in France, 1690–1808*. New York, 1968.

Jullien, Adolphe, *Histoire du théâtre de Madame de Pompadour; Les Grandes nuits de Sceaux: Le théâtre de la Duchesse de Maine; L'Opéra secret au XVIII siècle (1770–1790)*. Geneva, 1978.

Kahan, Gerald, "The American Career of George Alexander Stevens' Lecture on Heads," *Theatre Survey* 18 (November 1977): 60–71.

Kalnein, Wend Graf, and Levy, Michael, *Art and Architecture of the Eighteenth Century in France*. Translation of part 2 by J. R. Foster. Hammondsworth, 1972.

Karlinsky, Simon, *Russian Drama from Its Beginnings to the Age of Pushkin*. Berkeley, 1986.

Kelly, Linda, *The Kemble Era: John Philip Kemble, Sarah Siddons, and the London Stage*. New York, 1980.

Kendall, ed. and intro., *Love and Thunder: Plays by Women in the Age of Queen Anne*. London, 1988.

Kindermann, Heinz, *Theatergeschichte der Goethezeit*. Vienna, 1948.

———, *Theatergeschichte Europas*. Vols. 1–10, 1957–74. Salzberg, 1974.

Kindleberger, Charles P., *A Financial History of Western Europe*. London, 1984.

Kirstein, Lincoln, *Movement and Metaphor: Four Centuries of Ballet*. New York, 1970.

Koon, Helene, *Colley Cibber: A Biography*. Lexington, 1986.

Lagarde, André, and Michard, Laurent, *XVIIIe siècle: Les grands auteurs francais du programme*. Bordas, 1962.

Lamport, F. J., *Lessing and the Drama*. Oxford, 1981.

Laver, James, *Drama: Its Costume and Décor*. London, 1951.

Leacroft, Richard and Helen, *Theatre and Playhouse*. New York, 1985.

Lebrun, Charles, *A Method to Learn to Design the Passions* (1734). Los Angeles, 1980.

Ledoux, C. N., *Architecture*. Princeton, 1983.

Leith, James A., *The Idea of Art as Propaganda in France 1750–1799: A Study in the History of Ideas*. Toronto, 1965.

Lekain, Henri Louis, *Mémoires*. Paris, 1801.

Lessing, G. E., *Hamburg Dramaturgy*. Translated by Helen Zimmern. New York, 1962.

Lewes, George Henry, *Life of Goethe*. 3rd edition. New York, 1902.

Ley, Charles David, "The Spanish Dramatist Moratín and the London Theatres 1792–1793," *Theatre Notebook* 42 (1988): 37–38.

Liesenfeld, Vincent J., *The Licensing Act of 1737*. Madison, 1984.

Loftis, John, *Comedy and Society from Congreve to Fielding*. Stanford, 1959.

————, ed., *Essays on the Theatre from Eighteenth-Century Periodicals*. Los Angeles, 1960.

————; Southern, Richard; Jones, Marion; and Scouten, A. H., *The Revels History of Drama in English*. Vol. 5, 1660–1750. London, 1976.

Lough, John, *Paris Theatre Audiences in the Seventeenth and Eighteenth Centuries*. London, 1965.

McKechnie, Samuel, *Popular Entertainments through the Ages*. New York, 1969.

McKee, Kenneth N., *The Theater of Marivaux*. New York, 1968.

Mackintosh, Iain, *The Georgian Playhouse: Actors, Artists, and Architecture, 1730–1830*. London, 1975.

McNamara, Brooks, *The American Playhouse in the Eighteenth Century*. Cambridge, 1969.

Majewski, Henry F., *The Preromantic Imagination of L.-S. Mercier*. New York, 1971.

Manvell, Roger, *Sarah Siddons: Portrait of an Actress*. New York, 1971.

Marker, Lise-Lone, and Marker, Frederick J., "William Bloch and Naturalism in the Scandinavian Theatre," *Theatre Survey* 15 (November 1974): 85–104.

Mason, Eudo C., *Goethe's Faust; Its Genesis and Purport*. Berkeley, 1967.

Mason, Haydn, *Voltaire: A Biography*. London, 1981.

Mayor, A. Hyatt, *The Bibiena Family*. New York, 1945.

Mercier, Louis-Sébastien, *Tableau de Paris*. Édition abrégé. Paris, n.d.

Meserve, Walter J., *An Emerging Entertainment: The Drama of the American People to 1828*. Bloomington, 1977.

————, *An Outline History of American Drama*. Totowa, New Jersey, 1970.

Milhous, Judith, and Hume, Robert D., "David Garrick and Box-Office Receipts at Drury Lane in 1742–1743," *Philological Quarterly* 67 (1988): 323–41.

Mitford, Nancy, *Frederick the Great*. New York, 1984.

————, *Madame de Pompadour*. New York, 1984.

Mittman, Barbara G., *Spectators on the Paris Stage in the Seventeenth and Eighteenth Centuries*. Ann Arbor, 1984.

Moody, Richard, ed., *Dramas from the American Theatre 1762–1909*. With introductory essays. Cleveland, 1966.

Morwood, James, *The Life and Works of Richard Brinsley Sheridan*. New York, 1985.

Moses, Montrose J., and Brown, John Mason, *The American Theatre as Seen by Its Critics*. New York, 1967.

Mullin, Donald C., *The Development of the Playhouse*. Berkeley, 1970.

————, "Lighting on the Eighteenth-Century London Stage: A Reconsideration," *Theatre Notebook* 34, no. 2 (1980): 73–85.

Nicoll, Allardyce, *The Development of the Theatre*. New York, 1966.

————, *The Garrick Stage: Theatres and Audience in the Eighteenth Century*. Edited by Sybil Rosenfeld. Manchester, 1980.

Norman, Hilda Laura, *Swindlers and Rogues in French Drama*. Chicago, 1928.

Ogden, Dunbar H., *The Italian Baroque Stage; Documents by Giulio Troili, Andrea Pozzo, Ferdinando Galli-Bibiena, Baldassare Orsini*. Berkeley, 1978.

Opper, Jacob, *Science and the Arts: A Study in Relationships from 1600–1900*. Rutherford, 1973.

Parfaict, E. and C., *Histoire du théâtre francais depuis son origine jusqu'à présent*. Vols. 14, 15. New York, 1968 (reprint of 1748 Paris edition).

Pedicord, Harry William, *The Theatrical Public in the Time of Garrick*. Carbondale, 1954.

Penzel, Frederick, *Theater Lighting before Electricity*. Middletown, Connecticut, 1978.

Pitou, Spire, *The Paris Opera: Genesis and Glory, 1671–1715*. Westport, Connecticut, 1983.

Pollock, Thomas Clark, *The Philadelphia Theatre in the Eighteenth Century*. New York, 1968.

Price, Cecil, *Theatre in the Age of Garrick*. Totowa, New Jersey, 1973.

Pry, Kevin, "Theatrical Competition and the Rise of the Afterpiece Tradition, 1700–1724," *Theatre Notebook* 36, no. 1 (1982): 21–27.

Rangstrom, Ture, ed., *Drottningholms Slottsteater Program 1989*. Stockholm, 1989.

Rankin, Hugh F., *The Theatre in Colonial America*. Chapel Hill, 1960.

Rémy, Tristan, *Jean-Gaspard Debureau*. Paris, 1954.

Reynaud, Charles, *Musée rétrospectif de la classe 18, Théâtre, à l'exposition universelle internationale de 1900, à Paris*. Saint Cloud, n.d.

Rice, Howard C., Jr., *Thomas Jefferson's Paris*. Princeton, 1976.

Rice, Paul F., *The Performing Arts at Fontainebleau from Louis XIV to Louis XVI*. Ann Arbor, 1989.

Richards, Kenneth, and Thomson, Peter, eds., *The Eighteenth-Century English Stage; Proceedings of a Symposium Sponsored by the Manchester University Department of Drama*. London, 1972.

Richtman, Jack, *Adrienne Lecouvreur: The Actress and the Age*. Englewood Cliffs, 1971.

Roach, Joseph R., *The Player's Passion: Studies in the Science of Acting*. Newark, 1985.

Roberts, Warren, *Morality and Social Class in Eighteenth-Century French Literature and Painting*. Toronto, 1974.

Robertson, J. G., *Lessing's Dramatic Theory: Being an Introduction to and Commentary on His Hamburgische Dramaturgie*. New York, 1965.

Rogers, Pat, *The Augustan Vision*. London, 1974.

———, ed., *The Eighteenth Century*. New York, 1978.

Root-Bernstein, Michèle, *Boulevard Theater and Revolution in Eighteenth-Century Paris*. Ann Arbor, 1984.

Rosenfeld, Sybil, *Georgian Scene Painters and Scene Painting*. Cambridge, 1981.

———, *The Georgian Theatre of Richmond, Yorkshire, and Its Circuit*. London, 1984.

Roth, Georges, ed., *Chefs-d'oeuvre comiques des successeurs de Molière*. Vol. 1: Baron et Dufresny; Vol. 2: Dancourt. Paris, ca. 1916.

Saisselin, R. G., *Taste in Eighteenth Century France*. Syracuse, 1965.

Sambrook, James, *The Eighteenth Century: The Intellectual and Cultural Context of English Literature, 1700–1789*. New York, 1986.

Schnapper, Antoine, *David*. New York, 1982.

Scouten, Arthur H., *The London Stage 1729–1747: A Critical Introduction*. Carbondale, 1968.

Seebohm, Andrea, ed., *The Vienna Opera*. New York, 1987.

Shillingsburg, Miriam J., "The West Point Treason in American Drama, 1798–1891," *Educational Theatre Journal* 30 (March 1978): 73–89.

Shvedova, Irina, "Fyodor Volkov's 250th Birth Anniversary," *Soviet Theatre* 1 (1979): 9–13.

Silverman, Kenneth, *A Cultural History of the American Revolution*. New York, 1976.

Sitwell, Sacheverell, ed., *Great Houses of Europe*. London, 1970.

Slonim, Marc, *Russian Theater: From the Empire to the Soviets*. New York, 1962.

Smith, Dane Farnsworth, *The Critics in the Audience of the London Theatres from Buckingham to Sheridan: A Study of Neoclassicism in the Playhouse, 1671–1779*. Albuquerque, 1953.

Southern, Richard, *The Georgian Playhouse*. London, 1948.

Speck, W. A., *Stability and Strife: England, 1714–1760*. Cambridge, 1977.

Starikova, Ludmila, *Teatral'naya zhizn' starinnoi moskvi*. Moscow, 1988.

Starobinski, Jean, *1789: The Emblems of Reason*. Translated by Barbara Bray. Charlottesville, 1982.

Steele, Richard, *The Theatre: 1720*. Edited by John Loftis. Oxford, 1962.

Stone, George Winchester, Jr., ed., *The Stage and the Page: London's "Whole Show" in the Eighteenth-Century Theatre*. Berkeley, 1981.

———, and Kahrl, George M., *David Garrick, A Critical Biography*. Carbondale, 1979.

Stribolt, Barbara, "Eighteenth-Century Stage Settings at the Court Theatres of Drottningholm and Gripsholm," *Performing Arts Resources*. Vol. 8. New York, 1983.

Striker, Ardelle, "A Curious Form of Protest Theatre: the *Pièce à écriteaux*," *Theatre Survey* 14 (May 1973): 55–70.

Strohm, Richard, *Essays on Handel and Italian Opera*. Cambridge, 1985.

Taylor, S. S. B., ed., *The Theatre of the French and German Enlightenment: Five Essays*. New York, Barnes and Noble, 1978.

Tidworth, Simon, *Theatres: An Architectural and Cultural History*. New York, 1973.

Touchard, Pierre-Aimé, *Histoire sentimentale de la Comédie-Francaise*. Paris, 1955.

Trott, David, and Boursier, Nicole, eds., *L'Age du théâtre en France / The Age of Theatre in France*. Edmonton, 1987. Includes "A dramaturgy of the unofficial stage: The non-texts of Louis Fuzelier" by David Trott; "Garrick's Role in the Shakespeare Controversy in France" by Frances Wilkshire; "Des bancs et du parterre: la réception du spectacle dramatique au 18e siècle" by Derrick de Kerckhove.

———, "Pour une histoire des spectacles non-officiels: Louis Fuzelier et le théâtre à Paris en 1725–1726," *Revue d'histoire du théâtre* 3 (1985): 255–75.

Usigli, Rodolfo, *Mexico in the Theatre*. University, Mississippi, 1976.

Van der Kemp, Gérard, *Versailles*. New York, 1978.

Vaughn, Jack A., *Early American Dramatists: From the Beginnings to 1900*. New York, 1981.

Vbovin, G., *Ostankino*. Moscow, 1988.

Vince, Ronald W., *Neoclassical Theatre: A Historiographical Handbook*. New York, 1988.

Walsh, T. J., *Opera in Dublin 1705–1797: The Social Scene*. Dublin, 1973.

Waterhouse, Betty Senk, trans., *Five Plays of the Sturm und Drang*. Lanham, Maryland, 1986.

Wegelin, Oscar, *Early American Plays 1714–1830*. New York, 1970.

Weiss, Jonathan M., *French-Canadian Theater*. Boston, 1986.

White, Eric Walter, *A History of English Opera*. London, 1983.

Williams, Simon, *German Actors of the Eighteenth and Nineteenth Centuries: Idealism, Romanticism, and Realism*. Westport, Connecticut, 1985.

Wilson, Garff B., *Three Hundred Years of American Drama and Theatre*. Englewood Cliffs, New Jersey, 1973.

Woods, Leigh, *Garrick Claims the Stage: Acting as Social Emblem in Eighteenth-Century England*. Westport, Connecticut, 1984.

Wright, Richardson, *Revels in Jamaica, 1682–1838*. New York, 1969.

Zielske, Harald, "Some Original Early Nineteenth Century Stage Decorations in the Ludwigsburg Court Theatre: Problems of Conservation and Presentation," *Performing Arts Resources*. Vol. 8. New York, 1983.

The Romantic Impulse and Popular Offshoots

Albert, Maurice, *La Littérature francaise sous la révolution, l'empire, et la restauration (1789–1830)*. Geneva, (reprinted from 1898 edition), 1970.

———, *Les Théâtres des boulevards 1789–1848*. Paris, 1902.

Allen, Shirley S., *Samuel Phelps and Sadler's Wells Theatre*. Middletown, Connecticut, 1971.

Bassan, Fernande, *Alfred de Vigny et la Comédie-Francaise*. Paris, 1984.

Betti, Franco, *Vittorio Alfieri*. Boston, 1984.

Bogard, Travis; Moody, Ricard; and Meserve, Walter J., *The Revels History of Drama in English*. Vol. 8: *American Drama*. London, 1977.

Booth, Michael R., *Prefaces to English Nineteenth Century Theatre*. Manchester, n.d.

———, *Victorian Spectacular Theatre 1850–1910*. Boston, 1981.

———; Southern, Richard; Marker, Frederick and Lise-Lone; and Davies, Robertson, *The Revels History of Drama in English*. Vol. 4: "1750–1880." London: Methuen, 1975.

———, ed., *Victorian Theatrical Trades: Articles from "The Stage" 1883–1884*. London, 1981.

Borgerhoff, Joseph L., ed., *Nineteenth Century French Plays*. New York, 1931.

Brazier, *Histoire des petits théâtres de Paris depuis leur origine*. Vols. 1–2. New York, (reprint of 1838 edition), 1969.

Briggs, Asa, ed., *The Nineteenth Century*. New York, 1970.

Brown, Frederick, *Theater and Revolution: The Culture of the French Stage*. New York, 1980.

Brown, T. Allston, *History of the American Stage; Containing Biographical Sketches of Nearly Every Member of the Profession That Has Appeared on the American Stage, from 1733 to 1870*. New York, (reprint of 1870 edition), 1969.

Bruntière, Fernand, *Les Epoques du Théâtre Francais (1636–1850)*. Paris, 1892.

Butler, Marilyn, *Romantics, Rebels, and Reactionaries: English Literature and Its Background 1760–1830*. Oxford, 1981.

Carlson, Marvin, *The French Stage in the Nineteenth Century*. Metuchen, New Jersey, 1972.

————, *The German Stage in the Nineteenth Century.* Metuchen, New Jersey, 1972.

————, *The Italian Stage: From Goldoni to D'Annunzio.* Jefferson, North Carolina, 1981.

Cave, Richard Allen, ed., *The Romantic Theatre: An International Symposium.* Totowa, New Jersey, 1986.

Charlton, D. G., ed., *France: A Companion to French Studies.* 2nd ed. London, 1979.

Clarke, Mary, and Crisp, Clement, *Ballet Art: From the Renaissance to the Present.* New York, 1978.

Cohen, Selma Jean, ed., *Dance as a Theatre Art.* New York, 1974.

Cooper, Joshua, trans. and intro., *Four Russian Plays.* New York, 1972.

Csida, Joseph, and Csida, June Bundy, *American Entertainment: A Unique History of Popular Show Business.* New York, 1978.

Daniels, Barry Vincent, "Shakespeare à la Romantique: *Le More de Venise* d'Alfred de Vigny," *Revue d'Histoire du théâtre* 27 (April–June 1975): 125–55.

Delgado, Alan, *Victorian Entertainment.* New York, 1971.

Disher, Maurice Willson, *Blood and Thunder: Mid-Victorian Melodrama and Its Origins.* London, 1949.

Donnet, Alexis, *Architectonographie des théâtres de Paris.* Paris, 1840.

Donohue, Joseph, *Theatre in the Age of Kean.* Oxford, 1975.

Dorman, James H., Jr., *Theater in the Ante-Bellum South.* Chapel Hill, 1967.

Dowd, David Lloyd, *Pageant-Master of the Republic; Jacques-Louis David and the French Revolution.* Lincoln, 1948.

Dubech, Lucien, *Histoire générale illustrée du théâtre.* Vol. 5. Paris, 1934.

Dumas *pére,* Alexandre, *The Great Lover and Other Plays.* Translated by Barnett Shaw. New York, 1979.

Fabre, Jean, *Lumières et romantisme; energie et nostalgie de Rousseau à Mickiewicz.* 2nd ed. Paris, 1980.

Fenger, Henning, and Marker, Frederick J., *The Heibergs.* New York, 1971.

Furnas, J. C., *Fanny Kemble: A Biography.* New York, 1982.

Gade, Svend, *Mit Livs Drejescene; 50 Aar i Teatrets og Filmens Tjeneste.* Copenhagen, 1941.

Gascar, Pierre, *Le Boulevard du crime.* Paris, 1980.

Gerould, Daniel, ed., *Melodrama.* New York, 1980.

————, *Theatre and Politics in Nineteenth-Century Spain: Juan de Grimaldi as Impresario and Government Agent.* Cambridge, 1988.

Gilbert, Douglas, *American Vaudeville; Its Life and Times.* New York, 1940.

Godechot, Jacques; Hyslop, Beatrice F.; and Dowd, David L., *The Napoleonic Era in Europe.* New York, 1971.

González Lopez, Emilio, *Historia de la literatura española: la edad moderna.* New York, 1965.

Gottlieb, Vera, *Chekhov and the Vaudeville: A Study of Chekhov's One-Act Plays.* Cambridge, 1982.

Granjean, Lisbet, *Teatermuseet 1912–1987.* Copenhagen, 1987.

Grillparzer, Franz, *Plays on Classic Themes.* Translated with introduction by Samuel Solomon. New York, 1969.

Grimsted, David, *Melodrama Unveiled: American Theater and Culture 1800–1850.* Berkeley, 1987.

Hautecoeur, Louis, *Histoire de l'architecture classique en France*. Vol. 5: *La Restauration et le gouvernement de juillet 1815–1848*. Paris, 1955.

Havens, Daniel F., *The Columbian Muse of Comedy: The Development of a Native Tradition in Early American Social Comedy, 1787–1845*. Carbondale, 1973.

Hemmings, F. W. J., *Alexandre Dumas: The King of Romance*. New York, 1979.

Hewitt, Barnard, *Theatre U.S.A. 1665 to 1957*. New York, 1959.

Hoover, Kathleen O'Donnell, *Makers of Opera*. New York, 1955.

Howarth, W. D., *Sublime and Grotesque: A Study of French Romantic Drama*. London, 1975.

Howell, Margaret J., *Byron Tonight: A Poet's Plays on the Nineteenth Century Stage*. Windlesham, 1982.

Hughes, Langston, and Meltzer, Milton, *Black Magic: A Pictorial History of the Negro in American Entertainment*. Englewood Cliffs, New Jersey, 1967.

Hugo, Victor, *Hernani*. Edited with notes by Pierre Richard and Gérard Sablayrolles. Paris, 1965.

———, *Préface de "Cromwell"; suivi d'extraits d'autres préfaces dramatiques*. Edited with notes by Pierre Grosclaude. Paris, 1949.

———, *Ruy Blas*. Edited with notes by Francis Lafon. Paris, 1966.

———, *Ruy Blas*. Edited with notes by Gérard Sablayrolles. Paris, 1965.

———, *Le Théâtre en liberté; L'Intervention; Les Jumeaux*. Introduction by Jeanlouis Cornuz. Lausanne, 1962.

Hyde, Ralph, *Panoramania!: The Art and Entertainment of the 'All-Embracing' View*. London, 1988.

Jefferson, Joseph, *The Autobiography of Joseph Jefferson*. Edited by Alan S. Downer. Cambridge, Massachusetts, 1964.

Jiji, Vera, ed., *Showcasing American Drama: George L. Aiken/Harriet B. Stowe, "Uncle Tom's Cabin."* Brooklyn, 1983.

———, *Showcasing American Drama: A Handbook of Source Materials on "The Lion of the West" by J. K. Paulding*. Brooklyn, 1983.

Johnson, Diana L., *Fantastic Illustration and Design in Britain, 1850–1930*. Providence, 1979.

Jomaron, Jacqueline de, *Le Théâtre en France*, vol. 2: de la Révolution à nos jours. Paris: Armand Colin, 1989.

Jones, Eugene H., *Native Americans as Shown on the Stage 1753–1916*. Metuchen, New Jersey, 1988.

Jones, Louisa E., *Sad Clowns and Pale Pierrots; Literature and the Popular Comic Arts in 19th-Century France*. Lexington, 1984.

Karlinsky, Simon, *Russian Drama: From Its Beginnings to the Age of Pushkin*. Berkeley, 1986.

Kauver, Gerald B., and Sorenson, Gerald C., eds. and intro., *Nineteenth-Century English Verse Drama*. Rutherford, 1973.

Kemble, Frances Anne, *Journal of a Residence on a Georgian Plantation in 1838–39*. New York, 1863.

———, *The Journal of Frances Anne Butler, Better Known as Fanny Kemble*. New York, (reprint of 1835 edition), 1970.

Kennett, Victor and Audrey, *The Palaces of Leningrad*. New York, 1973.

Kilgarrif, Michael, ed. and intro., *The Golden Age of Melodrama: Twelve Nineteenth Century Melodramas*. London, 1974.

Kirstein, Lincoln, *Movement and Metaphor: Four Centuries of Ballet.* New York, 1970.

Kridl, Manfred, ed., *Adam Mickiewicz: Poet of Poland.* New York, 1951.

Krzyzanowski, Julian, *History of Polish Literature.* Warsaw, 1978.

Lagarde, André, and Michard, Laurent, *XIXe siècle: Les grands auteurs français du programme V.* Paris, 1962.

Larra, Mariano Jose de, *Artículos de costumbres.* Edited by Azorín. Buenos Aires, 1963.

———, *Macías.* Edited and introduced by Benito Varela Jacome. Madrid, 1967.

Laufe, Abe, *The Wic¹ ᵈd Stage: A History of Theater Censorship and Harassment in the United States.* New York, 1978.

LeBreton, André, *Le Théâtre romantique.* Paris, 1935.

Lermontov, Mikhail, *A Lermontov Reader.* Edited, translated, and introduced by Guy Daniels. New York, 1965.

Ludlow, Noah, *Dramatic Life as I Found It.* St. Louis, 1880.

McClelland, I. L., *The Origins of the Romantic Movement in Spain.* New York, 1975.

McCormick, John, *Melodrama Theatres of the French Boulevard.* Cambridge, n.d.

Macready, William Charles, *The Journal of William Charles Macready, 1832–1851.* Abridged and edited by J. C. Trewin. Carbondale, 1967.

Magarshack, David, *Pushkin: A Biography.* New York, 1967.

Malnick, Bertha, "The Theory and Practice of Russian Drama in the Early Nineteenth Century," *The Slavonic Review* 34 (1955–56): 10–33.

Mankowitz, Wolff, *Mazeppa; The Lives, Loves, and Legends of Adah Isaacs Menken.* London, 1982.

Marker, Frederick J., *Hans Christian Andersen and the Romantic Theatre.* Toronto, 1971.

———, and Marker, Lise-Lone, *The Scandinavian Theatre: A Short History.* Oxford, 1975.

Matlaw, Myron, ed., *The Black Crook; and Other Nineteenth-Century American Plays.* New York, 1967.

Meserve, Walter J., *An Emerging Entertainment: The Drama of the American People to 1828.* Bloomington, 1977.

———, *Heralds of Promise: The Drama of the American People in the Age of Jackson 1829–1849.* Westport, Connecticut, 1986.

Migel, Parmina, *The Ballerinas: From the Court of Louis XIV to Pavlova.* New York, 1972.

Milosz, Czeslaw, *The History of Polish Literature.* 2nd edition. Berkeley, 1983.

Miquel, Pierre, *Le Second Empire.* Paris, 1979.

Moody, Richard, *America Takes the Stage; Romanticism in American Drama and Theatre 1750–1900.* Bloomington, 1969.

———, *The Astor Place Riot.* Bloomington, 1958.

Moses, Montrose J., *The American Dramatist.* New York, (reprint of 1925 edition), 1964.

———, and Brown, John Mason, eds., *The American Theatre as Seen by Its Critics 1752–1934.* New York, 1967.

Musset, Alfred de, *Oeuvres complets.* Edited by Philippe van Tieghem. Paris, 1963.

———, *Théâtre complet.* Edited by Maurice Allem. Paris, 1958.

Naess, Trine, *Teatermuseet i Oslo.* Oslo, 1985.

Neiiendam, Klaus, *Hofteatret og Teatermuseet ved Christiansborg.* Copenhagen, 1982.

Norman, Axel Otto, *Johanne Dybwad: Liv og kunst.* Oslo, 1950.

Noyes, George Rapnall, trans. and intro., *Masterpieces of the Russian Drama.* Vol. 1. New York, 1961.

Otten, Terry, *The Deserted Stage: The Search for Dramatic Form in Nineteenth-Century England.* Athens, 1972.

Paskman, Dailey, *"Gentlemen, Be Seated!": A Parade of the American Minstrels.* Revised ed. New York, 1976.

Peers, E. Allison, *The Romantic Movement in Spain.* Liverpool, 1968.

———, *Historia del movimiento romántico espanol.* 2 vols. Madrid, 1954.

Perugini, Mark Edward, *The Omnibus Box: Being Digressions and Asides on Social and Theatrical Life in London and Paris, 1830–1850.* London, 1946.

Playfair, Giles, *The Flash of Lightning: A Portrait of Edmund Kean.* London, 1983.

———, *The Prodigy: A Study of the Strange Life of Master Betty.* London, 1967.

Pougin, Arthur, *Dictionnaire historique et pittoresque de théâtre et des arts qui s'y rattachent.* Paris, 1885.

Pougnard, Pierre, *Théâtres: 4 siècles d'architecture et d'histoire.* Paris, 1980.

Pushkin, Alexander, *The Bronze Horseman and Other Poems.* Translation and introduction by D. M. Thomas. New York, Penguin Books, 1982.

———, *Mozart and Salieri: The Little Tragedies.* Translated by Antony Wood; foreword by Elaine Feinstein. London, 1987.

———, *The Poems, Prose, and Plays.* Edited and introduced by Avrahm Yarmolinsky. New York, 1964.

Rahill, Frank, *The World of Melodrama.* University Park, 1967.

Reeve, F. D., trans. and intro., *Nineteenth-Century Russian Plays.* New York, 1973.

Robertson, E. G., *Mémoires récréatifs scientifiques et anecdotiques du physicien-aéronaute E. G. Robertson, connu par ses expériences de Fantasmagorie, et par ses Ascensions Aérostatiques dans les principales villes de l'Europe.* 2 vols. Paris, 1831, 1833.

Rosenfeld, Sybil, *A Short History of Scene Design in Great Britain.* Oxford, 1973.

Rowell, George, *The Victorian Theatre 1792–1914.* Cambridge, 1978.

Roy, Donald, ed., *Plays by James Robinson Planché.* Cambridge, 1986.

Sampson, Henry T., *The Ghost Walks: A Chronological History of Blacks in Show Business, 1865–1910.* Metuchen, New Jersey, 1988.

Sands, Mollie, *The Eighteenth-Century Pleasure Gardens of Marylebone 1737–1777.* London, 1987.

Saxon, A. H., *The Life and Art of Andrew Ducrow and the Romantic Age of the English Circus.* Hamden, Connecticut, 1978.

Segal, Harold B., *Polish Romantic Drama: Three Plays in English Translation.* Edited and introduced by Harold B. Segal. Ithaca, 1977.

———, "Polish Romantic Drama in Perspective," *Theater Three* 6 (Spring 1989): 129–44.

Senelick, Laurence, *The Age and Stage of George L. Fox: 1825–1877.* Hanover, 1988.

———, intro., trans., and ed., *Russian Dramatic Theory from Pushkin to the Symbolists: An Anthology.* Austin, 1981.

———, intro., trans., and ed., *Russian Satiric Comedy: Six Plays*. New York, 1983.
———, "Russian Serf Theatre and the Early Years of Mikhail Shchepkin," *Theatre Quarterly* 10 (1980): 8–16.
———, *Serf Actor: The Life and Art of Mikhail Shchepkin*. Westport, Connecticut, 1984.
Sharma, Kavita A., *Byron's Plays: A Reassessment*. Salzburg, 1982.
Shelley, Percy Bysshe, *The Poetical Works, Vol. 2: Plays, Translations, and Longer Poems*, New York, 1910.
Smith, Sol, *Theatrical Management in the South and West*. New York, 1868.
Spitzer, Marian, *The Palace*. New York, 1969.
Stanton, Stephen S., ed., *Camille and Other Plays*. New York, 1968.
Stein, Charles W., ed., *American Vaudeville: As Seen by Its Contemporaries*. New York, 1984.
Stendhal, *Racine et Shakespeare*. Edited with notes by René Ternois. Paris, 1936.
Stribolt, Barbara, ed., *The Drottningholm Theatre Museum*. Stockholm, 1984.
Subirá, José, *Historia y anecdotario del Teatro real*. Madrid, 1948.
Tapia, John Reyna, *The Spanish Romantic Theatre*. Lanham, Maryland, 1980.
Terras, Victor, *Belinskij and Russian Literary Criticism: The Heritage of Organic Aesthetics*. Madison, 1974.
———, ed., *Handbook of Russian Literature*. New Haven, 1985.
Toll, Robert C., *On with the Show; the First Century of Show Business in America*. New York, 1976.
Troyat, Henri, *Pushkin; A Biography*. New York, 1975.
Ullman, Pierre L., *Mariano de Larra and Spanish Political Rhetoric*. Madison, 1971.
Van Tieghem, Philippe, *Le Romantisme français*. Paris, 1963.
Wells, George A., *The Plays of Grillparzer*. London, 1969.
Whittall, Arnold, *Romantic Music*. London, 1987.
Wroth, Warwick, *The London Pleasure Gardens of the Eighteenth Century*. Hamden, Connecticut, (reprint of 1896 edition), 1979.

The Drama Sobers Up: Realism and Naturalism

Amiard-Chevrel, Claudine, *Le Théâtre artistique de Moscou (1898–1917)*. Paris, 1979.
Antoine, André, *Memoires of the Théâtre Libre*. Edited by H. D. Albright; trans. by Marvin Carlson. Coral Gables, 1964.
Appia, Adolphe, *Music and the Art of the Theatre*. Edited by Barnard Hewitt. Coral Gables, 1962.
———, *Oeuvres complètes, II: 1895–1905*. Edited by Marie L. Bablet-Hahn. Bonstetten, 1983.
———, *The Work of Living Art and Man Is the Measure of All Things*. Edited by Barnard Hewitt. Coral Gables, 1960.
Appignanesi, Lisa, *Cabaret: The First Hundred Years*. New York, 1985.
Archer, William, *William Archer on Ibsen: The Major Essays, 1889–1919*. Edited by Thomas Postlewait. Westport, Connecticut, 1984.
Auerbach, Nina, *Ellen Terry: Player in Her Time*. New York, 1987.

Bairati, Eleonora, Julian, P., Falkus, M., Monelli, P., Riesz, J., and Vigezzi, B., *La Belle Epoque: Fifteen Euphoric Years of European History*. New York, 1978.

Beacham, Richard C., *Adolphe Appia; Theatre Artist*. Cambridge, 1987.

Beales, Derek, *From Castlereagh to Gladstone 1815–1885*. London, 1969.

Benedetti, Jean, *Stanislavski: A Biography*. London, 1988.

Bentley, Eric, *Bernard Shaw*. New York, 1985.

———, *The Theory of the Modern Stage*. Baltimore, 1968.

———, ed., *Let's Get a Divorce! and Other Plays*. New York, 1964.

Bernard, Isabelle, *Le Théâtre de Courteline*. Paris, 1978.

Binns, Archie, *Mrs Fiske and the American Theatre*. New York, 1955.

Blum, Daniel, *A Pictorial History of the American Theatre 1860–1970*, third edition. New York, 1972.

Booth, Edwin and Winter, W., *Between Actor and Critic; Selected Letters*. Edited with an introduction and commentary by Daniel J. Watermeier. Princeton, 1971.

Booth, Michael, ed., *The Magistate and Other Nineteenth-Century Plays*. London, 1974.

———, *Prefaces to English Nineteenth-Century Theatre*. Manchester, 1980.

Bristow, Eugene K., "Let's Hear It From the Losers: or, Chekhov, Kom misarzhevskaya, and *The Seagull* at Petersburg in 1896," *Theatre History Studies* 2, 1982, pp. 1–13.

Bryan, George B., *An Ibsen Companion; A Dictionary-Guide to the Life, Works, and Critical Reception of Henrik Ibsen*. Westport, Connecticut, 1984.

Büchner, Georg, *The Complete Collected Works*. Translated with an introduction by Henry J. Schmidt. New York, 1977.

———, *Complete Works and Letters*. Edited by Walter Hinderer and Henry J. Schmidt. New York, 1986.

———, *Complete Plays and Prose*. Translated with an introduction by Carl Richard Mueller. New York, 1963.

———, *Plays*. Translated and introduced by Victor Price. London, 1971.

Carlson, Marvin, *The German Stage in the Nineteenth Century*. Metuchen, New Jersey, 1972.

———, *The Italian Shakespearians; Performances by Ristori, Salvini, and Rossi in England and America*. Washington, 1985.

Chekhov, Anton, *The Brute and Other Farces*. Edited by Eric Bentley. New York, 1985.

———, *Letters of Anton Chekhov*. Selected and edited by Avraham Yarmolinsky. New York, 1973.

———, *Anton Chekhov's Plays*. Translated and edited by Eugene K. Bristow. New York, 1977.

———, *The Selected Letters of Anton Chekhov*. Edited and introduced by Lillian Hellman. New York, 1984.

Claus, Horst, *The Theatre Director Otto Brahm*. Ann Arbor, 1981.

Crawford, Mary Caroline, *The Romance of the American Theatre*. New York, 1940.

D'Amico, Silvio, *Storia del Teatro Drammatico*, 2, 3. Milan, 1950.

Davies, Frederick, trans. and intro., *Three French Farces*. Harmondsworth, 1973.

DeHart, Steven, *The Meininger Theater 1776–1926*. Ann Arbor, 1981.

Donaldson, Frances, *The Actor-Managers*. Chicago, 1970.

Downs, Brian W., *Ibsen: The Intellectual Background*. New York, 1969.

Edwards, Christine, *The Stanislavsky Heritage; Its Contribution to the Russian and American Theatre.* New York, 1965.

Emeljanow, Victor, *Victorian Popular Dramatists.* Boston, 1987.

Fanger, Donald, *The Creation of Nikolai Gogol.* Cambridge, 1979.

Fido, Martin, *Oscar Wilde: An Illustrated Biography.* New York, 1985.

Forbes, Bryan, *That Despicable Race; A History of the British Acting Tradition.* London, 1980.

Gassner, John, *Directions in Modern Theatre and Drama.* New York, 1966.

Gippius, V. V., *Gogol.* Edited and translated by Robert A. Maguire. Ann Arbor, 1981.

Glasstone, Victor, *Victorian and Edwardian Theatres.* Cambridge, 1975.

Gogol, Nikolai, *Marriage.* Translated and introduced by Bella Costello. New York, 1969.

Gorky, Maksim, *Reminiscences of Tolstoy, Chekhov, and Andreyev.* New York, 1966.

Gottlieb, Vera, *Chekhov and the Farce-Vaudeville: A Study of Chekhov's One-Act Plays.* Cambridge, 1982.

Grabbe, Christian Dietrich, *Jest, Satire, Irony, and Deeper Significance.* Trans. and intro. by Maurice Edwards. New York, 1966.

Grimm, Reinhold, *Love, Lust, and Rebellion; New Approaches to Georg Büchner.* Madison, 1985.

Grube, Max, *The Story of the Meiningen,* trans. Ann Marie Koller. Coral Gables, 1963.

Guilleminault, Gilbert, *La Belle Epoque.* Paris, 1958.

Hatch, James V., ed., *Black Theater U.S.A.: 45 Plays by Black Americans 1847–1974.* New York, 1974.

Hays, Michael, *The Public and Performance: Essays in the History of French and German Theatre 1871–1900.* Ann Arbor, 1981.

Heiberg, Hans, *Ibsen: A Portrait of the Artist.* Translated by Joan Tate. Coral Gables, 1969.

Hemmings, F. W. J., *The Life and Times of Emile Zola.* New York, 1977.

Henderson, Mary, *The City and the Theatre; New York Playhouses from Bowling Green to Times Square.* Clifton, New Jersey, 1971.

Hibbert, Christopher, *Gilbert and Sullivan and Their Victorian World.* New York, 1976.

Hill, Errol, *Shakespeare in Sable; A History of Black Shakespearean Actors.* Amherst, 1984.

Hilton, Julian, *Georg Büchner.* New York, 1982.

Hingley, Ronald, *A New Life of Anton Chekhov.* New York, 1976.

Hobson, Sir Harold, *French Theatre since 1830.* Dallas, 1979.

Holroyd, Michael, ed., *The Genius of Shaw; A Symposium.* London, 1979.

Howard, Diana, *London Theatres and Music Halls 1850–1950.* London, 1970.

James, Burnett, *Wagner and the Romantic Disorder.* New York, 1983.

Jefferson, Alan, *The Complete Gilbert & Sullivan Opera Guide.* New York, 1984.

Jelavich, Peter, *Munich and Theatrical Modernism: Politics, Playwriting, and Performance 1890–1914.* Cambridge, 1985.

Johnson, Claudia D., *American Actress: Perspectives on the Nineteenth Century.* Chicago, 1984.

Johnston, Brian, *Text and Subtext in Ibsen's Drama.* University Park, 1989.

Johnston, William M., *Vienna Vienna: The Golden Age, 1815–1914.* New York, 1980.

Jomaron, Jacqueline de, ed., *Le Théâtre en France, Vol. 2: de la Révolution à nos jours.* Paris, 1989.

Kaufmann, Friedrich Wilhelm, *German Dramatists of the 19th Century.* Freeport, N.Y., 1970.

Kaufmann, R. J., *G. B. Shaw: A Collection of Critical Essays.* Englewood Cliffs, New Jersey, 1965.

Kennedy, Dennis, *Granville-Barker and the Dream of Theatre.* New York, 1985.

Knepler, Henry, *The Gilded Stage; The Years of the Great International Actresses.* New York, 1968.

Koht, Halvdan, *The Life of Ibsen,* trans. Clara Bell. London, 1890.

Koller, Ann Marie, *The Theatre Duke; Georg II of Saxe-Meiningen and the German Stage.* Stanford, 1984.

Koteliansky, S. S., ed. and trans., *Anton Tchekhov: Literary and Theatrical Reminiscences.* New York, 1965.

Kracauer, S., *Orpheus in Paris: Offenbach and the Paris of His Time.* New York, 1972.

Laver, James, *Manners and Morals in the Age of Optimism, 1848–1914.* New York, 1966.

Lindenberg, Daniel, "Dossier *Les Corbeaux;* Un dissident théâtral: les luttes d'Henry Becque," *Comédie Francaise* 109, May 1982, pp. 7–12.

Londré, Felicia Hardison, "Eleonora Duse: An Italian Actress on the American Stage," *Studies in Popular Culture* 8, 2, 1985, pp. 60–70.

———, "Ermolova's Revolutionary Realism Before and After the Revolution," *The Theatre Annual* 30, 1985, pp. 25–39.

———, "The Snowmaiden That Came in from the Cold," *Theatre History Studies* 1, 1981, pp. 64–80.

MacKaye, Percy, *Epoch—Life of Steele MacKaye,* 2 vols. New York, 1927.

Maguire, Robert A., ed., trans., and intro., *Gogol from the Twentieth Century; Selected Essays.* Princeton, 1974.

Malyusz, Edith Csaszar, *The Theater and National Awakening.* Atlanta, 1980.

Mander, Raymond and Mitchenson, J., *The Wagner Companion.* New York, 1977.

Manvell, Roger, *Ellen Terry.* New York, 1968.

Marker, Frederick J. and Marker, L.-L., *The Scandinavian Theatre: A Short History.* Oxford, 1975.

———, "William Bloch and Naturalism in the Scandinavian Theatre," *Theatre Survey* 15, November 1974, pp. 85–104.

Marshall, Herbert, and Stock, M., *Ira Aldridge: The Negro Tragedian.* Carbondale, 1968.

May, Keith M., *Ibsen and Shaw.* New York, 1985.

McArthur, Benjamin, *Actors and American Culture, 1880–1920.* Philadelphia, 1984.

Meisel, Martin, *Shaw and the Nineteenth Century Theatre.* New York, 1968.

Meyer, Michael, *Ibsen: A Biography.* Garden City, New York, 1971.

Miller, Anna Irene, *The Independent Theatre in Europe; 1887 to the Present.* New York, 1931.

Molnár, Ferenc, *All the Plays of Molnár,* with a foreword by David Belasco. New York, 1937.

Moore, Sonia, *The Stanislavsky System*. New York, 1967.

Morgan, Joyce Vining, *Stanislavski's Encounter with Shakespeare: The Evolution of a Method*. Ann Arbor, 1984.

Moses, Montrose J., *The American Dramatist*. New York, 1964.

—— and Brown, John Mason, *The American Theatre as Seen by its Critics, 1752–1934*. New York, 1967.

Munk, Erika, ed., *Stanislavski and America*. Greenwich, Connecticut, 1967.

Nabokov, Vladimir, *Nikolai Gogol*. New York, 1961.

Nemirovich-Dantchenko, Vladimir, *My Life in the Russian Theatre*, trans. by John Cournos. Boston, 1936.

Nestroy, Johann, *Three Comedies*. Translated by Max Knight and Joseph Fabry. Foreword by Thornton Wilder. New York, 1967.

Newman, Ernest, *Wagner as Man and Artist*. New York, 1985.

Nietzsche, Friedrich, *The Birth of Tragedy and The Genealogy of Morals*, trans. by Francis Golffing. Garden City, 1957.

Nightingale, Benedict, "In Life, Ibsen *Was* 'The Master Builder,'" *New York Times*, October 16, 1983, section 2, pp. 3, 4.

Nohain, Jean, and Caradec, F., *Le Pétomane, 1857–1945*. New York, 1985.

Normann, Axel Otto, *Johanne Dybwad*. Oslo, 1950.

Oberthur, Mariel, *Cafés and Cabarets of Montmartre*. Salt Lake City, 1984.

Osborne, Charles, *Wagner and His World*. New York, 1977.

Osborne, John, *The Nationalist Drama in Germany*. Totowa, New Jersey, 1971.

Ostrovsky, Alexander, *Five Plays*. Trans. and ed. by Eugene K. Bristow. New York, 1969.

——, *Plays*. Introduced and translated by Margaret Wettlin. Moscow, 1974.

Pandolfi, Vito, *Storia universale del teatro drammatico*, 2. Torino, 1966.

Pearson, Hesketh, *The Last Actor-Managers*. London, 1974.

Penzel, Frederick, *Theatre Lighting Before Electricity*. Middletown, 1978.

Perry, John, *James A. Herne; The American Ibsen*. Chicago, 1978.

Pinero, A. W., *Plays*. Edited by George Rowell. Cambridge, 1986.

Pitcher, Harvey, *Chekhov's Leading Lady: A Portrait of the Actress Olga Knipper*, London, 1979.

Polyakova, Elena, *Stanislavsky*. Moscow, 1982.

Pontiero, Giovanni, *Eleonora Duse: In Life and Art*. Frankfurt-am-Main, 1986.

Postlewait, Thomas, *Prophet of the New Drama: William Archer and the Ibsen Campaign*. Westport, Connecticut, 1986.

Pronko, Leonard, *Eugene Labiche and Georges Feydeau*. New York, 1982.

Quéant, Gilles, ed., *Encyclopédie du théâtre contemporain, Vol. 1: 1850–1914*. Paris, 1957.

Rearick, Charles, *Pleasures of the Belle Epoque; Entertainment and Festivity in Turn-of-the-Century France*. New Haven, 1986.

Rich, Norman, *The Age of Nationalism and Reform, 1850–1890*. New York, 1977.

Richardson, Joanna, *Sarah Bernhardt and Her World*. New York, 1977.

Robertson, Tom, *Plays*. Edited by William Tydeman. Cambridge, 1982.

Rose, Jonathan, *The Edwardian Temperament: 1895–1919*. Athens, Ohio, 1986.

Rowell, George, ed., *Late Victorian Plays 1890–1914*. London, 1972.

——, *Nineteenth Century Plays*. London, 1972.

——, *Queen Victoria Goes to the Theatre*. London, 1978.

———, *Theatre in the Age of Irving*. Totowa, New Jersey, 1981.

———, *The Victorian Theatre 1792–1914; A Survey*. Cambridge, 1978.

Salomé, Lou, *Ibsen's Heroines*. Translated and introduced by Siegfried Mandel. Redding Ridge, Connecticut, 1985.

Schanke, Robert A., *Ibsen in America: A Century of Change*. Metuchen, New Jersey, 1988.

Schelde, Per, "Missing the Mermaids of *Rosmersholm*," *The Drama Review*, 33, 3 (T123): 8–10.

Schenkan, Arlette, *Georges Feydeau*. Paris, 1972.

Schorske, Carl E., *Fin-de-Siècle Vienna: Politics and Culture*. New York, 1981.

Senelick, Laurence, trans. and ed., *Russian Dramatic Theory from Pushkin to the Symbolists*. Austin, 1981.

Shattuck, Charles H., *The Hamlet of Edwin Booth*, Urbana, Illinois, 1969.

———, *Shakespeare on the American Stage; From the Hallams to Edwin Booth*. Washington D.C., 1976.

———, *Shakespeare on the American Stage; From Booth and Barrett to Sothern and Marlowe, Vol. 2*. Washington, 1987.

Shaw, George Bernard, *The Quintessence of Ibsenism*. New York, 1957.

———, *Shaw's Dramatic Criticism (1895–1898)*, selected by John F. Matthews. New York, 1959.

Seigel, Jerrold, *Bohemian Paris: Culture, Politics, and the Boundaries of Bourgeois Life, 1830–1930*. New York, 1986.

Skavlan, Einar, "Johanne Dybwad," *The American–Scandinavian Review* 20, June–July 1932: 327–338.

Skinner, Corneila Otis, *Madame Sarah*. Boston, 1966.

Solovieva, I. N. and Shitova, V. V., *K. C. Stanislavsky*. Moscow, 1985.

Stanislavski, Constantin, *My Life in Art*. Translated by J. J. Robbins. New York, 1952.

———, *Selected Works*. Compiled by Oksana Korneva. Moscow, 1984.

———, *Stanislavsky's Legacy: A Collection of Comments on a Variety of Aspects of an Actor's Art and Life*, edited and translated by Elizabeth Reynolds Hapgood. New York, 1968.

Sukhovo-Kobylin, Alexander, *The Trilogy of Alexander Sukhovo-Kobylin*. Translated by Harold B. Segal. New York, 1969.

Taine, Hippolyte, *Histoire de la littérature anglaise*, Vol. 1. Paris, 1877.

Taylor, Tom, *Plays*. Edited by Martin Banham. Cambridge, 1985.

Taylor, John Russell, *The Rise and Fall of the Well-Made Play*. New York, 1967.

Terry, Ellen, *Memoirs; Being a new edition of "The Story of My Life" by Ellen Terry*. New York, 1969.

Tidworth, Simon, *Theatres; An Architectural and Cultural History*. New York, 1973.

Troyat, Henri, *Tchekhov*. Paris, 1984.

Traubner, Richard, *Operetta: A Theatrical History*. New York, 1983.

Turgenev, Ivan, *Three Famous Plays*. Westport, Connecticut, 1977.

Urbach, Reinhard, *Arthur Schnitzler*. New York, 1973.

Volbach, Walther, *Adolphe Appia: Prophet of the Modern Theatre*. Middletown, Connecticut, 1968.

Von Eckardt, Wolf, Gilman, Sander L., and Chamberlain, J. Edward, *Oscar Wilde's London: A Scrapbook of Vices and Virtues, 1880–1900*. New York, 1987.

Wagner, Richard, *Wagner on Music and Drama; A Compendium of Wagner's Prose Works,* selected with intro. by Albert Goldman and Evert Sprinchorn. New York, 1964.

Watermeier, Daniel J., ed. and intro., *Between Actor and Critic; Selected Letters of Edwin Booth and William Winter.* Princeton, 1971.

―――― and Ron Engle, "The Dawison-Booth Polyglot *Othello,*" *Theatre Research International* 13, Spring 1988, pp. 48–56.

――――, "Edwin Booth's Iago," *Theatre History Studies* VI, 1986, pp. 32–55.

――――, ed. and annot., *Edwin Booth's Performances: The Mary Isabella Stone Commentaries.* Ann Arbor, 1989.

――――, "Edwin Booth's Richelieu," *Theatre History Studies* 1, 1981, pp. 1–19.

Waxman, Samuel Montefiore, *Antoine and The Théâtre-Libre.* New York, 1968.

Weaver, William, *Duse: A Biography.* San Diego, 1984.

Weber, Eugen, *France: Fin de Siècle.* Cambridge, 1986.

West, Rebecca, *1900.* New York, 1982.

Wilmeth, Don B., *The Language of American Popular Entertainment.* Westport, Connecticut, 1981.

Witkowski, Georg, *The German Drama of the Nineteenth Century.* New York, 1968.

Woodard, Debra J., "The Mackaye Collection: A Wealth of Americana," *Theatre Survey,* May 1982, pp. 108–111.

Zograf, N. G., *Maly Teatr b kontse XIX–nachale XX veka.* Moscow, 1966.

Pluralism and Experimentation

Artaud, Antonin. *Oeuvres complètes,* tomes IV and V. Paris, 1964.

――――. *The Theater and Its Double,* trans. by Mary Caroline Richards. New York, 1958.

Ashton, Dore, Steve Harvey, Neal Oxenhandler, Arthur Peters, Ned Rorem, Roger Shattuck, and Francis Steegmuller. *Jean Cocteau and the French Scene.* New York, 1984.

Bablet, Denis. *Le Décor de théâtre de 1870 à 1914.* Paris, 1963.

――――, ed. *Le Théâtre d'agit-prop de 1917 à 1932,* 2 vols. Lausanne, 1977.

Balakian, Anna. *Surrealism: The Road to the Absolute.* New York, 1970.

Barna, Yon. *Eisenstein: The Growth of a Cinematic Genius.* Boston, 1973.

Barr, Alfred H., Jr. *Fantastic Art, Dada, Surrealism.* New York, 1936.

――――. *The Symbolist Movement: A Critical Appraisal.* New York, 1967.

Bauer, Wolfgang. *Change and Other Plays,* intro. by Martin Esslin. New York, 1973.

Beaumont, Keith. *Alfred Jarry: A Critical and Biographical Study.* New York, 1985.

Beckett, Samuel. *Waiting for Godot.* New York, 1954.

Béhar, Henri. *Etude sur le théâtre dada et surréaliste.* Paris, 1967.

――――. *Vitrac, théâtre ouvert sur le rêve.* Paris, 1980.

Beigbeder, Marc. *Le Théâtre en France depuis la libération.* Paris, 1959.

Benedikt, Michael and George E. Wellwarth, eds. *Modern French Theatre: An Anthology of Plays.* New York, 1966.

――――. *Modern Spanish Theatre: An Anthology of Plays.* New York, 1969.

――――. *Postwar German Theatre: An Anthology of Plays.* New York, 1968.

Benson, Renate. *German Expressionist Drama: Ernst Toller and Georg Kaiser.* New York, 1984.

Block, Haskell M. *Mallarmé and the Symbolist Drama.* Detroit, 1963.

Bojko, Szymon. *New Graphic Design in Revolutionary Russia.* New York, 1972.

Bowlt, John E., ed. and trans. *Russian Art of the Avant Garde: Theory and Criticism 1902–1934.* London, 1988.

———. *Russian Stage Design: Scenic Innovation, 1900–1930.* Jackson, Miss., 1982.

Braun, Edward. *The Theatre of Meyerhold: Revolution on the Modern Stage.* New York, 1979.

Brecht, Bertolt. *Brecht on Theatre: The Development of an Aesthetic,* trans. by John Willett. New York, 1964.

Brecht, Stefan. *The Theatre of Visions: Robert Wilson.* Frankfurt am Main, 1978.

Breton, André. *Manifestes du surréalisme.* Paris, 1966.

Brockett, Oscar G. and Robert R. Findlay. *Century of Innovation: A History of European and American Theatre and Drama since 1870.* Englewood Cliffs, New Jersey, 1973.

Brook, Peter. *The Empty Space.* New York, 1968.

Bulgakov, Michail, *Black Snow,* trans. and intro. by Michael Glenny. London, 1986.

Calandra, Denis. *New German Dramatists.* New York, 1983.

Camus, Albert. *Le Mythe de Sisyphe: Essai sur l'absurde.* Paris, 1942.

Carrière, Jean-Claude. *The Mahabharata,* trans. by Peter Brook. New York, 1987.

Conroy, William T. *Viliers de l'Isle Adam.* Boston, 1978.

Constantine, Mildred and Alan Fern. *Revolutionary Soviet Film Posters.* Baltimore, 1974.

Contemporary Arts Center, Cincinnati. *Robert Wilson: The Theater of Images.* New York, 1980.

Dahlström, Carl Enoch William Leonard. *Strindberg's Dramatic Expressionism.* New York, 1968.

Dasgupta, Gautam. "Squat: Nature Theatre of New York," *Performing Arts Journal* 19 (1983).

Deák, Frantisek. "Russian Mass Spectacles," *The Drama Review* T66 (June 1975), pp. 7–22.

Dukore, Bernard F. and Daniel C. Gerould, eds. *Avant Garde Drama: A Casebook, 1918–1939.* New York, 1976.

Durpzoi, Gérard and Bernard Lecherbonnier. *Le Surréalisme: Théories, thèmes, techniques.* Paris, 1972.

Eaton, Katherine Bliss. *The Theater of Meyerhold and Brecht.* Westport, Connecticut, 1985.

Elliott, David. *New Worlds: Russian Art and Society 1900–1937.* New York, 1986.

Esslin, Martin. *The Theatre of the Absurd.* Garden City, 1969.

Ewen, Frederic. *Bertolt Brecht: His Life, his Art, and his Times.* New York, 1969.

Filler, Witold. *Contemporary Polish Theatre.* Warsaw, 1977.

Gambit 33–34: Special Double Polish Theater Issue. London, 1979.

Garten, H. F. *Modern German Drama.* New York, 1962.

Gerould, Daniel, ed. *Doubles, Demons, and Dreamers: An International Collection of Symbolist Drama.* New York, 1985.

————, ed. *Twentieth-Century Polish Avant-Garde Drama: Plays, Scenarios, Critical Documents.* Ithaca, 1977.

————. *Witkacy: Stanislaw Ignacy Witkiewicz as an Imaginative Writer.* Seattle, 1982.

Glover, J. Garrett. *The Cubist Theatre.* Ann Arbor, 1980.

Godard, Colette. *Le Théâtre depuis 1968.* Paris, 1980.

Goldberg, RoseLee. *Performance: Live Art 1909 to the Present.* New York, 1979.

Golub, Spencer. *Evreinov: The Theatre of Paradox and Transformation.* Ann Arbor, 1984.

Gorchakov, Nikolai A. *The Theater in Soviet Russia,* trans. by Edgar Lehman. New York, 1957.

Gordon, Mel, ed. *Expressionist Texts.* New York, 1986.

Green, Michael, ed. and trans. *The Russian Theatre: An Anthology of Plays and Critical Texts.* Ann Arbor, 1986.

Greene, Naomi. *Antonin Artaud: Poet without Words.* New York, 1970.

Grodzicki, August. *Polish Theatre Directors.* Warsaw, 1977.

Grossvogel, David I. *Twentieth Century French Drama.* New York, 1967.

Grotowski, Jerzy. *Towards a Poor Theatre.* New York, 1969.

Guerman, Mikhail. *Art of the Russian Revolution.* New York, 1979.

Guicharnaud, Jacques, with June Beckelman. *Modern French Theatre: From Giraudoux to Beckett.* New Haven, 1961.

Hagemann, E. R. *German and Austrian Expressionism in the United States, 1900–1939: Chronology and Bibliography.* Westport, Connecticut, 1985.

Hayman, Ronald, ed. and intro. *The German Theatre: A Symposium.* London, 1975.

Hippius, Zinaida. *Between Paris and St. Petersburg: Selected Diaries of Zinaida Hippius,* trans. and ed. by Temira Pachmuss. Urbana, Illinois, 1975.

————. *Selected Works,* trans. and ed. by Temira Pachmuss. Urbana, Illinois, 1972.

Huettich, H. G. *Theater in the Planned Society: Contemporary Drama in the German Democratic Republic in its Historical, Political, and Cultural Context.* Chapel Hill, North Carolina, 1978.

Innes, Christopher. *Holy Theatre: Ritual and the Avant Garde.* New York, 1981.

Jacquot, Jean, ed. *Le Théâtre moderne II: Depuis le deuxième guerre mondiale.* Paris, 1967.

Jarry, Alfred. *The Ubu Plays,* trans. by Cyril Connolly and Simon Watson Taylor. New York, 1968.

Jelavich, Peter. *Munich and Theatrical Modernism: Politics, Playwriting, and Performance, 1890–1914.* Cambridge, Massachusetts, 1985.

Kafanova, Ludmila. "Remembering Solomon Mikhoels," *The New Leader* (March 13, 1978), pp. 16–17.

Kaiser, Georg. *The Coral, Gas I,* and *Gas II,* introductions by Victor Lange. New York, 1963.

Kirby, Michael. *Futurist Performance.* New York, 1971.

Knapp, Bettina L. *Antonin Artaud: Man of Vision.* New York, 1969.

————, ed. *The Contemporary French Theater.* New York, 1973.

Kozloff, Max. *Cubism/Futurism.* New York, 1973.

Kraus, Karl. *The Last Days of Mankind,* abridged and ed. by Frederick Ungar. New York, 1974.

————. *No Compromise,* ed. by Frederick Ungar. New York, 1977.

Kristiansen, Donna M. "What is Dada?" *Educational Theatre Journal* 20 (1968), pp. 457–62.

Kumiega, Jennifer. *The Theatre of Grotowski*. New York, 1985.

Lagercrantz, Olof. *August Strindberg*, translated by Anselm Hollo. New York, 1984.

Landis, Joseph C., ed. and trans. *The Great Jewish Plays*. New York, 1974.

Levy, Emanuel. *The Habima—Israel's National Theater 1917–1977*. New York, 1979.

Marranca, Bonnie, ed. *The Theatre of Images*. New York, 1977.

Maslenikov, Oleg A. *The Frenzied Poets: Andrey Biely and the Russian Symbolists*. New York, 1968.

Matthews, J. H. *Theatre in Dada and Surrealism*. Syracuse, 1974.

Mayakovsky, Vladimir. *The Complete Plays*, trans. by Guy Daniels. New York, 1968.

McConachie, Bruce A. and Daniel Friedman, eds. *Theatre for Working-Class Audiences in the United States, 1830–1980*. Westport, Connecticut, 1985.

McNamara, Brooks and Jill Dolan, eds. *The Drama Review: Thirty Years of Commentary on the Avant-Garde*. Ann Arbor, MI, 1986.

Melzer, Annabelle. *Latest Rage the Big Drum: Dada and Surrealist Performance*. Ann Arbor, Michigan, 1980.

Meyerhold, Vsevolod. *Meyerhold on Theatre*, translated and edited with a critical commentary by Edward Braun. New York, 1969.

———. "Petition," *Soviet and East European Performance* 9 (Summer 1989), pp. 19–22.

Milosz, Czeslaw. *The History of Polish Literature*. Berkeley, CA, 1983.

Mortenson, Brita and Brian Downs. *Strindberg: An Introduction to His Life and Work*. Cambridge, Massachusetts, 1965.

Natan, Alex, ed. *Expressionism and After; German Men of Letters, Vol. III*. London, 1979.

Osinski, Zbigniew. *Grotowski and His Laboratory*, trans. by Lillian Vallee and Robert Findlay. New York, 1986.

Oxenhandler, Neal. *Scandal and Parade: The Theater of Jean Cocteau*. New Brunswick, NJ, 1957.

Patterson, Michael. *German Theatre Today: Post-War Theatre in West and East Germany, Austria and Northern Switzerland*. London, 1976.

Penrose, Roland. *Man Ray*. Boston, 1974.

Piotrowski, Piotr. *Stanislaw Ignacy Witkiewicz*. Warsaw, 1989.

Pittock, Malcolm. *Ernst Toller*. Boston, 1979.

Proffer, Ellendea. *Bulgakov*. Ann Arbor, Michigan, 1984.

———. *Evreinov: A Pictorial Biography*. Ann Arbor, Michigan, 1981.

———. *A Pictorial Biography of Mikhail Bulgakov*. Ann Arbor, Michigan, 1984.

Pronko, Leonard C. *Théâtre d'avant-garde: Beckett, Ionesco et le théâtre expeérimental en France*. Paris, 1963.

Ramsey, Roger. "The Death of the Living Theatre," *Research Studies* 45 (March 1977), pp. 14–29.

Read, Herbert. *A Concise History of Modern Painting*. New York, 1963.

Ribemont-Dessaignes, Georges. *Théâtre*. Paris, 1966.

Rice, Martin P. *Briusov and the Rise of Russian Symbolism.* Ann Arbor, Michigan, 1975.

Ries, Frank W. D. *The Dance Theatre of Jean Cocteau.* Ann Arbor, Michigan, 1986.

Rischbieter, Henning. *Art and the Stage in the Twentieth Century: Painters and Sculptors Work for the Theater.* Greenwich, Connecticut, 1970.

Ritchie, J. M. *German Expressionist Drama.* Boston, 1976.

Robichez, Jacques. *Le Symbolisme au théâtre: Lugné-Poe et les débuts de L'Oeuvre.* Paris, 1957.

Roose-Evans, James. *Experimental Theatre from Stanislavsky to Peter Brook.* New York, 1984.

Rudnitsky, Konstantin. *Meyerhold, the Director.* Ann Arbor, Michigan, 1981.

―――. *Russian & Soviet Theatre: Tradition and Avant Garde,* trans. by Roxane Permar. London, 1988.

Russell, Robert, *Russian Drama of the Revolutionary Period.* Totowa, New Jersey, 1988.

Sainer, Arthur. *The Radical Theatre Notebook.* New York, 1975.

Sandrow, Nahma. *Vagabond Stars: A World History of Yiddish Theater.* New York, 1977.

Savran, David. *The Wooster Group, 1975–1985: Breaking the Rules.* Ann Arbor, Michigan, 1986.

Savona, Jeannette L. *Jean Genet.* New York, 1983.

Schlemmer, Oskar. *The Letters and Diaries,* selected and edited by Tut Schlemmer; trans. by Krishna Winston. Middletown, Connecticut, 1972.

Schmidt, Paul, ed. *Meyerhold at Work.* Austin, Texas, 1980.

Schumacher, Claude. *Alfred Jarry and Guillaume Apollinaire.* Basingstoke, 1984.

Schvey, Henry I. *Oskar Kokoschka: The Painter as Playwright.* Detroit, 1982.

Sebald, W. G., ed. *A Radical Stage: Theatre in Germany in the 1970s and 1980s.* New York, 1988.

Sellin, Eric. *The Dramatic Concepts of Antonin Artaud.* Chicago, 1975.

Senelick, Laurence, ed. and trans. *Russian Dramatic Theory from Pushkin to the Symbolists: An Anthology.* Austin, Texas, 1981.

Shattuck, Roger. *The Banquet Years: The Origins of the Avant-Garde in France, 1885 to World War I.* New York, 1968.

Slavic and East European Arts. Special Issue: Recent Polish and Soviet Theatre and Drama. (Winter/Spring 1985).

Smith, A. C. H. *Orghast at Persepolis: An International Experiment in Theatre.* New York, 1972.

Sokel, Walter H., ed. *Anthology of German Expressionist Drama,* revised and abridged edition. Ithaca, New York, 1984.

Stapanian, Juliette R. *Mayakovsky's Cubo-Futurist Vision.* Houston, Texas, 1986.

Steegmuller, Francis. *Cocteau.* New York, 1970.

Stewart, Ellen. "La Mama Celebrates 20 Years," *Performing Arts Journal* 17 (1982).

Stourac, Richard and Kathleen McCreery. *Theatre as a Weapon: Workers' Theatre in the Soviet Union, Germany and Britain, 1917–1934.* London, 1986.

Strauss, Botho. *Big and Little,* trans. by Anne Cattaneo. New York, 1979.

Strindberg, August. *Five Plays,* trans. by Harry G. Carlson. Berkeley, California, 1983.

———. *Plays of Confession and Therapy: To Damascus I, To Damascus II, To Damascus III*, trans. and intro. by Walter Johnson. Seattle, 1979.

Surer, Paul. *Le Théâtre francais contemporain*. Paris, 1964.

Symons, Arthur. *The Symbolist Movement in Literature*. New York, 1958.

Szydlowski, Roman. *The Theatre in Poland*. Warsaw, 1972.

Tairov, Alexander. *Notes of a Director*, trans. with intro. by William Kuhlke. Coral Gables, Florida, 1969.

TDR: The Drama Review. Special Issue: German Theatre. T85 (March 1980).

———. Special Issue: Poland: From the Love Affair with Communism to Theatre under Martial Law. T111 (Fall 1986).

TheaterWeek. Samuel Beckett commemorative issue. Vol. 3, no. 21 (January 8, 1990).

Tkacz, Virlana. "Les Kurbas and the Actors of the Berezil Artistic Association in Kiev," *Theatre History Studies* VIII (1988), pp. 137–155.

Toller, Ernst. *Seven Plays*. New York, n.d.

Tzara, Tristan. *Seven Dada Manifestos* and *Lampisteries*, trans. by Barbara Wright. New York, 1981.

Veinstein, André. *Du Théâtre Libre au Théâtre Louis Jouvet: Les Théâtres d'art à travers leurs périodiques (1887–1934)*. Paris, 1955.

Villiers de l'Isle Adam, Philippe Auguste. *Axël*. Intro. by Pierre Mariel. Paris, 1960.

Vitrac, Roger. *Théâtre*. Paris, 1946.

Vogker, Henryk. *Rozewicz*. Warsaw, 1976.

Völker, Klaus. *Brecht Chronicle*, intro. by Carl Weder. New York, 1975.

Weber, Carl. "Heiner Müller: The Despair and the Hope," *Performing Arts Journal* 12, no. 3 (1980), pp. 135–46.

Wedekind, Frank. *The Lulu Plays*, trans. and intro. by Carl Richard Mueller. Greenwich, Connecticut, 1967.

———. *Spring Awakening*, trans. by Tom Gordon. New York, 1985.

Wellwarth, George E. *The Theater of Protest and Paradox: Developments in the Avant Garde Drama*. New York, 1965.

Willett, John. *The Theatre of Bertolt Brecht: A Study from Eight Aspects*. New York, 1968.

Wilson, Edmund. *Axel's Castle: A Study in the Imaginative Literature of 1870 to 1930*. New York, 1959.

Woroszylski, Wiktor. *The Life of Mayakovsky*, trans. by Boleslaw Taborski. New York, 1970.

Worrall, Nick. *Modernism to Realism on the Soviet Stage: Tairov, Vakhtangov, Okhlopkov*. Cambridge, Massachusetts, 1989.

———, ed. *Theatrefacts* IV, no. 1. Theatre Checklist No. 13: Vladimir Mayakovsky (1977).

Wright, A. Colin. *Mikhail Bulgakov: Life and Interpretations*. Toronto, 1978.

Zadek, Peter. "Radical Stagings of Shakespeare," *Performing Arts Journal* 12 (1980), pp. 106–21.

Zlobin, Vladimir. *A Difficult Soul: Zinaida Gippius*, ed. and intro. by Simon Karlinsky. Berkeley, California, 1980.

Currents in the Mainstream

Abramson, Doris E. *Negro Playwrights in the American Theatre 1925–59*. New York, 1969.

Akimov, Nikolai. *Teatralnoe nasledie*, vols. 1 and 2. Leningrad, 1978.

Almansi, Guido. "Writing Like Tickling: On Noel Coward," *Encounter* 48 (May 1977), pp. 71–78.

Amoia, Alba. *The Italian Theatre Today: Twelve Interviews*. Troy, New York, 1977.

Andrews, John and Ossia Trilling, eds. *International Theatre*. London, 1949.

Arnott, Brian. *Edward Gordon Craig and Hamlet*. Ottawa, Canada, 1975.

Auden, W. H. and Christopher Isherwood. *Two Great Plays: The Dog Beneath the Skin, The Ascent of F5*. New York, 1937.

Ayling, Ronald, ed. *Sean O'Casey*. Nashville, 1970.

Ballester, G. Torrente. *Teatro español contemporáneo*. Madrid, 1968.

Barrault, Jean-Louis, ed. "Connaissance de Paul Claudel," *Cahiers Renaud-Barrault* 12. Paris, 1955.

———. *Memories for Tomorrow*, trans. by Jonathan Griffin. New York, 1974.

Beigbeder, Marc. *Le Théâtre en France depuis la libération*. Paris, 1959.

Berenguer, Angel. *El teatro en el siglo XX (hasta 1939)*. Madrid, 1988.

Bleiberg, Germán and E. Inman Fox, eds. *Spanish Thought and Letters in the Twentieth Century*. Nashville, 1966.

Bourges, Hervé, ed. *The French Student Revolt: The Leaders Speak*. New York, 1968.

Bradby, David. *Modern French Drama, 1940–1980*. New York, 1984.

Brown, Langdon. "Firmin Gémier's *Cirque d'Hiver* Production of *Oedipe roi de Thèbes*," *Theatre Journal* 31 (October 1979), pp. 370–85.

———. "Firmin Gémier's *Théâtre National Ambulant*," *Theatre Survey* 21 (May 1980), pp. 33–48.

———. "Gémier and Baty's *La Grande Pastorale:* A Medieval Mystery Play for the Twentieth Century," *Theatre History Studies* 2 (1982), pp. 69–82.

Buckle, Richard. *Nijinsky*. New York, 1971.

Burian, Jarka. *The Scenography of Josef Svoboda*. Middletown, Connecticut, 1974.

Caputi, Anthony. *Pirandello and the Crisis of Modern Consciousness*. Champaign, Illinois, 1988.

Castle, Charles. *Noël*. Garden City, 1973.

Centro Español del Instituto Internacional del Teatro. *Panorámico del teatro en españa*. Madrid, 1973.

Champagne, Lenora. *French Theatre Experiment since 1968*. Ann Arbor, Michigan, 1984.

Clark, Barrett H. *Eugene O'Neill: The Man and His Plays*. New York, 1947.

Claudel, Paul. *Théâtre*, vols. 1 and 2, ed. by Jacques Madaule. Paris, 1956.

Cooper, Roberta Krensky. *The American Shakespeare Theatre: Stratford, 1955–1985*. Washington, 1986.

Copfermann, Emile. *Théâtres de Roger Planchon*. Paris, 1977.

Craig, Edward. *Gordon Craig: The Story of His Life*. New York, 1985.

Daoust, Yvette. *Roger Planchon, Director and Playwright*. Cambridge, Massachusetts, 1981.

Davis, Lenwood G. *A Paul Robeson Research Guide: A Selected Annotated Bibliography.* Westport, Connecticut, 1982.

Dejean, Jean-Luc. *Le théâtre francais depuis 1945.* Paris, 1987.

Domenech, Ricardo, ed. *Ramón del Valle-Inclán.* Madrid, 1988.

Edwards, Gwynne. *Dramatists in Perspective: Spanish Theatre in the Twentieth Century.* New York, 1985.

Eliot, T. S. "The Aims of Poetic Drama," *Adam International Review* 200 (November 1949), pp. 10–16.

Etherton, Michael. *Contemporary Irish Dramatists.* New York, 1989.

Etkind, Mark. *N. P. Akimov—Khudozhnik.* Leningrad, 1960.

Faust, Richard and Charles Kadushin. *Shakespeare in the Neighborhood.* New York, 1965.

Feinsod, Arthur B. "Stage Designs of a Single Gesture: The Early Work of Robert Edmond Jones," *The Drama Review* 28 (Summer 1984, T102), pp. 102–20.

Ferreras, Juan Ignacio. *El teatro en el siglo XX (desde 1939).* Madrid, 1988.

"Firmin Gémier, French Actor, Producer, Dies," *New York Herald Tribune* (November 22, 1933).

Fitz-Simon, Christopher. *The Irish Theatre.* London, 1983.

Flanagan, Hallie. *Arena: The Story of the Federal Theatre.* New York, 1985.

Floyd, Virginia. *The Plays of Eugene O'Neill: A New Assessment.* New York, 1987.

Fowlie, Wallace. *Dionysus in Paris: A Guide to Contemporary French Theater.* New York, 1960.

Frank, André. *Jean-Louis Barrault.* Paris, 1971.

Fuchs, Georg. *Revolution in the Theatre: Conclusions concerning the Munich Artists' Theatre,* trans. and adapted by Constance Connor Kuhn. Ithaca, New York, 1959.

Fry, Christopher. *The Lady's Not for Burning, A Phoenix Too Frequent, and an Essay, An Experience of Critics.* New York, 1977.

Fuerst, Walter René and Samuel J. Hume. *Twentieth-Century Stage Decoration,* 2 vols. New York, 1967.

Gard, Robert E., Marston Balch, and Pauline Temkin. *Theater in America.* New York, 1968.

Gershkovich, Alexander. *The Theater of Yuri Lyubimov: Art and Politics at the Taganka Theater in Moscow,* trans. by Michael Yurieff. New York, 1989.

Ghelderode, Michel de. *Seven Plays,* Vols. 1 and 2, trans. by George Hauger. New York, 1964.

Godard, Colette. *Le Théâtre depuis 1968.* Paris, 1980.

Gorelik, Mordecai. *New Theatres for Old.* New York, 1962.

Gregory, Lady. *Our Irish Theatre,* intro. by Daniel J. Murphy. New York, 1965.

Gubaryev, Vladimir. *Sarcophagus: A Tragedy,* with a preface by Robert Peter Gale. New York, 1987.

Halsey, Martha T. and Phyllis Zatlin, eds. *The Contemporary Spanish Theater: A Collection of Critical Essays.* Lanham, Maryland, 1988.

Hansen, Robert C. *Scenic and Costume Design for the Ballets Russes.* Ann Arbor, Michigan, 1985.

Hardison, Felicia. "Valle-Inclán and Artaud: Brothers Under the Skin," *Educa-

tional Theatre Journal 19 (December 1967), 455–66.

Hatch, James V., ed. *Black Theater U.S.A.: 45 Plays by Black Americans 1847–1974.* New York, 1974.

Hildy, Franklin J. *Shakespeare at the Maddermarket: Nugent Monck and the Norwich Players.* Ann Arbor, Michigan, 1986.

Hill, Errol, ed. *The Theater of Black Americans,* Vol. 1. Englewood Cliffs, New Jersey, 1980.

———. *Shakespeare in Sable: A History of Black Shakespearean Actors.* Amherst, Massachusetts, 1984.

Holme, Geoffrey, ed. *Design in the Theatre.* London, 1927.

Holt, Marion P. *The Contemporary Spanish Theater (1949–1972).* Boston, 1975.

Hort, Jean. *La Vie héroïque des Pitoëff.* Geneva, 1966.

Horwitz, Dawn Lille. *Michel Fokine.* Boston, 1985.

Jomaron, Jacqueline de, ed. *Le Théâtre en France,* Vol. 2: De la Révolution à nos jours. Paris, 1989.

Kennedy, Dennis. *Granville Barker and the Dream of Theatre.* Cambridge, Massachusetts, 1985.

King, Mary C. *The Drama of J. M. Synge.* Syracuse, New York, 1985.

Kochno, Boris. *Diaghilev and the Ballets Russes,* trans. by Adrienne Foulke. New York, 1970.

Kohfeldt, Mary Lou. *Lady Gregory: The Woman Behind the Irish Renaissance.* New York, 1985.

Kolin, Philip C. *Shakespeare in the South: Essays on Performance.* Jackson, Mississippi, 1983.

Kraft, Irma. "Firmin Gemier: Strolling Actor and International Impresario," *New York Herald Tribune* (December 3, 1933).

Krause, David. *The Profane Book of Irish Comedy.* Ithaca, New York, 1982.

Kucharenko, Ilya. *Natalia Satz.* Moscow, 1989.

Lahr, John. *Coward: The Playwright.* New York, 1982.

László, Anna. *Hevesi Sándor: Második, Atdolgozott Kiadás.* Budapest, 1973.

Lebon, Joel, ed. *Barrault, Renaud: Paris, notre siècle.* Paris, 1982.

Leclerc, Guy. *Le T. N. P. de Jean Vilar.* Paris, 1971.

Lederman, Minna, ed. *Stravinsky in the Theatre.* New York, 1975.

Lieven, Prince Peter. *The Birth of the Ballets-Russes,* trans. by L. Zarine. New York, 1973.

Lima, Robert. *Valle-Inclán: The Theatre of His Life.* Columbia, 1988.

Little, Stuart W. Little. *Off-Broadway: The Prophetic Theatre.* New York, 1972.

Londré, Felicia Hardison. "Evgeny Shvarts and the Uses of Fantasy in the Soviet Theatre," *Research Studies* 47 (September 1979), pp. 131–44.

———. *Federico García Lorca.* New York, 1984.

———. *Tennessee Williams.* New York, 1979.

Lowery, Robert G., ed. *A Whirlwind in Dublin: "The Plough and the Stars" Riots.* Westport, Connecticut, 1984.

Lyon, John. *The Theatre of Valle-Inclán.* Cambridge, 1983.

Macgowan, Kenneth and Robert Edmond Jones. *Continental Stagecraft.* New York, 1964.

Macgowan, Kenneth. *The Theatre of Tomorrow.* New York, 1921.

Martínez Sierra, Gregorio, ed. *Un teatro de arte en españa, 1917–1925*. Madrid, 1926.

Maxwell, D. E. S. *A Critical History of the Modern Irish Drama, 1891–1980*. New York, 1985.

McConachie, Bruce A. and Daniel Friedman, eds. *Theatre for Working-Class Audiences in the United States, 1830–1980*. Westport, Connecticut, 1985.

Mikhail, E. H., ed. *The Abbey Theatre: Interviews and Recollections*. Totowa, New Jersey, 1988.

———. *A Bibliography of Modern Irish Drama, 1899–1970*. Seattle, 1972.

Mitgang, Herbert. "516 Pirandello Letters Donated to Princeton," *New York Times* (December 29, 1986), p. C13.

Musset, Alfred de. *Lorenzaccio*, ed. by Géray, Christian and Catherine VandelIsaakidis. Paris, 1985.

Nadel, Norman. *A Pictorial History of the Theatre Guild*. New York, 1969.

Novick, Julius. *Beyond Broadway: The Quest for Permanent Theatres*. New York, 1968.

O'Connor, Garry. *French Theatre Today*. Bath, 1975.

O'Connor, John and Lorraine Brown, eds. *Free, Adult, Uncensored: The Living History of the Federal Theatre Project*. Washington, DC, 1978.

O'Connor, Patricia W., ed. and trans., *Contemporary Spanish Theater: The Social Comedies of the Sixties*. Madrid, 1983.

———. *Gregorio and María Martínez Sierra*. Boston, 1977.

———. *Dramaturgas españolas de hoy*. Madrid, 1988.

———, ed. and trans., *Plays of Protest from the Franco Era*. Madrid, 1981.

Oenslager, Donald. *Stage Design: Four Centuries of Scenic Invention*. New York, 1975.

O'Riordan, John. *A Guide to O'Casey's Plays*. New York, 1985.

Patterson, Lindsay, ed. *Anthology of the American Negro in the Theatre: A Critical Approach*. New York, 1967.

Peacock, Ronald. *The Poet in the Theatre*. New York, 1946.

Pendleton, Ralph, ed. *The Theatre of Robert Edmond Jones*. Middletown, Connecticut, 1958.

Percival, John. *The World of Diaghilev*. New York, 1979.

Pirandello, Luigi. *Naked Masks*, ed. and intro. by Eric Bentley. New York, 1952.

Popkin, Henry. "A Georgian Lear: The Political Theater of Robert Sturua," *Theater Week* (April 30–May 6, 1990), pp. 23–24.

Propert, W. A. *The Russian Ballet in Western Europe, 1909–1920*. New York, 1972.

Puaux, Paul. *Avignon en Festivals; ou, les utopies nécessaires*. Paris, 1983.

Rabey, David Ian. *British and Irish Political Drama in the Twentieth Century*. New York, 1986.

Ranald, Margaret Loftus. *The Eugene O'Neill Companion*. Westport, Connecticut, 1984.

Reiss, Francoise. *Nijinsky ou la grace: Esthétique et psychologie*. Paris, 1957.

———. *La Vie de Nijinsky*. Paris, 1957.

Rollins, Ronald Gene. *Divided Ireland: Bifocal Vision in Modern Irish Drama*. Lanham, Maryland, 1985.

Rouché, Jacques. *L'Art Théâtral moderne*. Paris, 1910.

Rowell, George and Anthony Jackson. *The Repertory Movement: A History of Regional Theatre in Britain*. New York, 1984.

Rudlin, John. *Jacques Copeau*. Cambridge, 1986.

Ruiz Ramón, Francisco. *Historia del teatro español: Siglo XX*. Madrid, 1981.

Saint-Denis, Michel. *Theatre: The Rediscovery of Style*. New York, 1961.

Salino, Brigitte, ed., with Emmanuelle Klausner and Claire Baldewyns. *Avignon 88: Histoire d'une génération, Les metteurs en scène vingt ans après*. Paris, 1988.

Sarlós, Robert Károly. *Jig Cook and the Provincetown Players*. Amherst, 1982.

Sayler, Oliver M., ed. *Max Reinhardt and His Theatre*. New York, 1968.

———. *Our American Theatre*. Westport, Connecticut, 1970.

Seller, Maxine Schwartz. *Ethnic Theatre in the United States*. Westport, Connecticut, 1983.

Sheaffer, Louis. *O'Neill, Son and Artist*. Boston, 1973.

Shuvalova, M. A., ed., *Leningradskii Gosudarstvenni Teatr Komedii*. Leningrad, 1964.

Siliunas, Vidas. *Ispanskaya drama: XX veka*. Moscow, 1980.

Simmons, James. *Sean O'Casey*. New York, 1983.

Simon, Alfred. "The Theatre in May," *Yale French Studies* 46 (1971), pp. 139–48.

Simonson, Lee. *The Stage is Set*. New York, 1963.

Skelton, Robin, ed. *The Collected Plays of Jack B. Yeats*. Indianapolis, 1971.

———. *The Writings of J. M. Synge*. Indianapolis, 1971.

Smelyansky, Antoly. "'Glasnost' Produces a Cultural Revolution," *World Press Review* (February 1990), pp. 32–34.

———. *Oleg Yefremov*. Moscow, 1988.

Smith, Alan. "Retrospective on the Rustaveli," *Theatre International* 10 (1983), pp. 13–25.

Spanos, William V. *The Christian Tradition in Modern British Verse Drama: The Poetics of Sacramental Time*. New Brunswick, New Jersey, 1967.

Speaight, Robert. *William Poel and the Elizabethan Revival*. Cambridge, Massachusetts, 1954.

Spencer, Charles, with contributions by Philip Dyer and Martin Battersby. *The World of Serge Diaghilev*. Chicago, 1974.

Stevens, Franklin. *Dance as Life: A Season with the American Ballet Theatre*. New York, 1976.

Strehler, Giorgio. *Un Théâtre pour la vie*. Paris, 1980.

Surer, Paul. *Le Théâtre français contemporain*. Paris, 1964.

Synge, J. M. *The Playboy of the Western World* and *Riders to the Sea*. New York, 1962.

Szafkó, Péter. "Sándor Hevesi and the Thália Society in Hungary," *Theatre History Studies* II (1982), pp. 115–24.

Taylor, John Russell. *Anger and After*. Baltimore, 1963.

Theatre Research International, "Irish Issue," Spring 1990.

Travail Théâtral, "*Différent: le théâtre du soleil*" (numéro spécial, February 1976).

———, "Otomar Krejca et le Théâtre Za Branou de Prague" (supplement to *Travail Théâtral*, 1972).

Triplett, Lori L. *Jessie Bonstelle: A Biography* (unpublished M.A. thesis, University of Missouri-Kansas City, Missouri), 1981.

Victorov, Victor. *The Natalia Sats Children's Musical Theatre*. Moscow, 1986.

Vilar, Jean. *De la tradition théâtrale*. Paris, 1955.

Vizcaino, Juan Antonio. "El teatro a escena," *Prólogo* 2 (March–April 1989), pp. 16–22.

Volz, Jim. *Shakespeare Never Slept Here: The Making of a Regional Theatre: A History of the Alabama Shakespeare Festival*. Atlanta, 1986.

Wagner, Anton, ed. *Contemporary Canadian Theatre: New World Visions*. Toronto, 1985.

Wehle, Philippa. *Le Théâtre populaire selon Jean Vilar*. Le Paradou, 1981.

Western European Stages, vols. 1 and 2. (Fall 1989, Spring 1990).

Whitton, David. *Stage Directors in Modern France*. Manchester, England, 1987.

Willinger, David, ed. *An Anthology of Contemporary Belgian Plays, 1970–1982*. Troy, New York, 1984.

Wilson, Garff B. *Three Hundred Years of American Drama and Theatre*. Englewood Cliffs, New Jersey, 1973.

Woll, Allen. *Dictionary of the Black Theatre: Broadway, Off-Broadway, and Selected Harlem Theatre*. Westport, Connecticut, 1983.

Yeats, William Butler. *The Collected Plays*. New Edition, with Five Additional Plays. New York, 1952.

———. *Eleven Plays*, ed. with introduction and notes by A. Norman Jeffares. New York, 1966.

Young, Howard T. *The Victorious Expression: A Study of Four Contemporary Spanish Poets*. Madison, Wisconsin, 1966.

Zatlin Boring, Phyllis. "Theatre in Madrid: The Difficult Transition to Democracy," *Theatre Journal* (December 1980), pp. 459–74.

Ziegler, Joseph Wesley. *Regional Theatre: The Revolutionary Stage*. New York, 1977.

Epilogue: Converging Theaters around the Globe

Australian Drama Studies 11, October 1987.

Badawi, M. M. *Modern Arabic Drama in Egypt*. Cambridge, 1987.

Banham, Martin, with Clive Wake. *African Theatre Today*. London, 1976.

Brandon, James R. *Theatre in Southeast Asia*. Cambridge, Massachusetts, 1974.

Brisbane, Katharine, ed. *New Australian Drama*. London, 1989.

Carballido, Emilio. *The Golden Thread and Other Plays*, trans. by Margaret Sayers Peden. Austin, Texas, 1970.

Carroll, Dennis. *Australian Contemporary Drama 1909–1982*. New York, 1985.

Casas, Myrna, ed. *Teatro de la vanguardia: Contemporary Spanish American Theatre*. Lexington, Massachusetts, 1975.

Colecchia, Francesca and Julio Matas, eds. and trans. *Selected Latin American One-Act Plays*. Pittsburgh, 1973.

Cuadernos de la Comedia Nacional, vol. 1, nos. 2–3 (May–June 1984). Buenos Aires.

Dolby, William. *A History of Chinese Drama*. New York, 1976.

Escenarios/Scenarios, vols. 1–3 (1985–87). New York.

Etherton, Michael. *The Development of African Drama*. New York, 1982.

Goodman, David G., trans. with introduction. *After Apocalypse: Four Japanese Plays of Hiroshima and Nagasaki.* New York, 1986.

Al-Hakim, Tewfik. *Fate of a Cockroach and Other Plays,* trans. by Denys Johnson-Davies. London, 1977.

Holt, Marion Peter and George W. Woodyard, eds. *Drama Contemporary: Latin America.* New York, 1986.

Hammouda, Abdel-Aziz. "Modern Egyptian Theatre: Three Major Dramatists," *World Literature Today* 53 (Autumn 1979), pp. 601–5.

Howard, Roger. *Contemporary Chinese Theatre.* Hong Kong, 1978.

Irvin, Eric. *Theatre Comes to Australia.* St. Lucia, Australia, 1971.

Jones, Eldred Durosimi. *The Writing of Wole Soyinka,* revised ed. Portsmouth, New Hampshire, 1984.

Jones, Willis Knapp. *Behind Spanish American Footlights.* Austin, Texas, 1966.

———. *Breve historia del teatro latinoamericano.* Mexico City, 1956.

Kapeliuk, Olga. "The Theater in Egypt," *New Outlook* 1 (Tel Aviv, October 1957), pp. 32–38.

Kavanagh, Robert Mshengu. *Theatre and Cultural Struggle in South Africa.* London, 1985.

Kennedy, Scott. *In Search of African Theatre.* New York, 1973.

Larlham, Peter. *Black Theater, Dance, and Ritual in South Africa.* Ann Arbor, Michigan, 1982.

Litto, Fredric M., ed. *Plays from Black Africa.* New York, 1968.

Love, Harold, ed. *The Australian Stage: A Documentary History.* Kensington, New South Wales, 1984.

Lyday, Leon F. and George F. Woodyard, eds. *Dramatists in Revolt: The New Latin American Theater.* Austin, Texas, 1976.

Mackerras, Colin, ed. *Chinese Theater: From Its Origins to the Present Day.* Honolulu, 1983.

———. "Chinese Theatre and Social Change since Mao," *Asian Theatre Reports* (1978), pp. 3–8.

Manzalaoui, Malmoud, ed. *Arabic Writing Today: The Drama.* New York, 1986.

McDougall, Bonnie S., ed. *Popular Chinese Literature and Performing Arts in the People's Republic of China 1949–1979.* Berkeley, California, 1984.

Miller, Arthur. *Salesman in Beijing.* New York, 1984.

Mishima, Yukio. *Five Modern No Plays,* trans. with introduction by Donald Keene. Tokyo, 1980.

"Notes and Comment" (Palestinian theatrical troupe El-Hakawati), *The New Yorker* (August 28, 1989), pp. 23–24.

Orenstein, Gloria Feman. *The Theater of the Marvelous.* New York, 1975.

Qu Liu Yi. "The Tibetan Theatre of China," *Theatre International* 6 (2/1982), pp. 12–20.

Rea, Kenneth. "Theatre in India: the Old and the New, Part 1," *Theatre Quarterly* 8 (Summer 1978), pp. 9–23.

Robertson, Malcolm. "The Australian Theatre: The Situation in the Seventies," *Biala* (Prahran College of Advanced Education, Victoria, Australia, 1976), pp. 7–14.

Scolnicov, Hannah and Peter Holland, eds. *The Play Out of Context: Transferring Plays from Culture to Culture.* Cambridge, 1989.

Scott, A. C. *The Theatre in Asia.* New York, 1972.

Tagore, Rabindranath. *Three Plays,* trans., with an introduction by Ananda Lal. Calcutta, 1987.

The Unesco Courier, special issue on world theater (April 1983).

Unger, Roni. *Poesía en Voz Alta in the Theater of Mexico.* Columbia, Missouri, 1981.

Usigli, Rodolfo. *Mexico in the Theater,* trans. by Wilder P. Scott. University, Mississippi, 1976.

Vandenbroucke, Russell. *Truths the Hand Can Touch: The Theatre of Athol Fugard.* New York, 1985.

Walder, Dennis. *Athol Fugard.* New York, 1985.

Waters, Harold A. "Black French Theatre: The Latest Plays," *World Literature Today* (Summer 1981), pp. 410–12.

Wolfe, George C., preface. *Afrique: New Plays.* New York, 1987.

Woodyard, George W., ed. *The Modern Stage in Latin America: Six Plays.* New York, 1971.

Zhao Xun. "The Present State of Chinese Theatre," *Theatre International* (3–4/1981), pp. 69–83.

Index

Abba, Marta, 509
Abbey Theater, 476–82
Abington, Frances, 93
absurd, theater of the, 437, 438–45, 453, 488, 520
Achard, Marcel, 382
Ackermann, Konrad, 144–47
acrobats, 68, 71, 72, 280
acting, 43, 74, 156, 312–26, 346, 367, 408
  classic style, 222, 230–31, 323, 325
  Delsarte system, 346
  Hamburg and Weimar styles, 151, 153, 156
  heroic style, 88, 89, 96
  Leipzig style, 143, 146
  melodramatic, 205, 298
  "method," 368, 374
  natural, 84, 86–88, 90, 93, 146, 180, 185, 227, 297, 298–99, 306, 308, 323, 325, 353–54, 357, 359, 372, 422, 423
  plasticity in, 318, 322
  Romantic, 98, 220, 221, 222, 224, 319
  standards of, 141, 142
  Stanislavsky system, 367, 368, 372, 576
actors, 140, 196, 205, 312–26, 344, 408, 492, 510–11, 555
  American, 162–71, 207, 209–14, 224–25, 325, 345–46, 381, 536, 537, 540, 541, 561
  black, 278–79, 312–13, 314, 509, 532–33, 570
  in blackface, 212, 276, 509
  children as, 70, 72, 185, 195, 203

Chinese, 562, 563, 577, 579
comic, 63, 140, 141, 186–87, 327, 361, 363
East European, 313, 443, 448, 451, 494, 554–55
English, 16–19, 32, 33, 37, 38–46, 63, 71, 73, 86–98, 217–23, 301–2, 312
in female roles, 16, 134
French, 62, 64, 67, 68, 80, 81–82, 91, 117, 174, 177, 180–85, 218, 228, 235–38, 242, 298, 321, 380–81, 437, 500–3, 516–24
German, 132, 139–46, 149, 154, 159, 191–92, 288, 437, 463, 464, 466
Irish, 88, 166, 172, 478, 481
Italian, 50–51, 308–10
persecution of, 10, 162, 183–84, 374, 479
Russian, 134, 260, 262–63, 307, 359–61, 365–67, 369, 370, 372, 420, 425, 551, 558
Scandinavian, 125–27, 264–65, 266
social status of, 10, 143, 144, 217, 325
strolling, 139, 140, 142, 150, 153, 164
training of, 17, 180, 262, 288, 297, 311, 326, 327–29, 345, 346, 360, 361, 368, 374, 418, 500, 502, 530
See also names of actors
actors' rebellions, 39, 71, 75
actresses, 4–5, 14, 18, 25, 48, 81–82, 147, 312–26, 572

Rich, Christopher, 39, 42, 71–73
Rich, John, 265
Rihani, Naguib al-, 571
riots and disturbances, theatrical, 323,
   479, 508
   in America, 223, 224
   in England, 62, 91, 97, 98, 103
   in France, 118, 174, 184, 227,
      230–31, 232, 234, 385, 393,
      394
Risner, John, 63
Ristori, Adelaide, 308, 309, 312,
   314
Rivas, Duque de (Angel de Saavedra),
   243, 244
Rivière, Henri, 376
Roach, Joseph, 88
Robert, Etienne-Gaspard (Robertson),
   267–69
Robertson, T. W., 298, 301, 302, 345
Robeson, Paul, 509, 533
Robespierre, Maximilien, 189
Roe, William, 10
Rogers, Robert, 166
Rolland, Romain, 514
Romanian theater, 310, 311
Romanticism, 191, 200, 214–85, 339,
   566
   in America, 207, 223–25
   in ballet, 272–75
   in Denmark, 215–16
   in England, 216–22
   in France, 226–43, 256–58, 287–
      88
   in Germany, 215, 216
   idealism of, 285, 288
   reaction against, 285–88, 294
   in Russia, 246–51
   in Spain, 243–46
Ronsin, Eugène, 390
rope-dancers, 68, 71, 172, 198, 280,
   282, 422
Różewicz, Tadeusz, 438, 452, 453
rosserie, 352, 385
Rossi, Ernesto, 308, 309
Rostand, Edmond, 256–58
Rouché, Jacques, 498–500, 504

Rowe, Nicholas, 88
Rowson, Susanna, 172
Rozov, Viktor, 550, 552
Rubé, Alfred, 295, 297
Rudnitsky, Konstantin, 425
Ruggeri, Ruggero, 509
Ruocheng, Ying, 562, 563, 577, 579
Rushdy, Rashad, 571
Russian theater, 58, 130–38, 202,
   302–8, 359–74, 411–30, 544–
   53
   and ballet, 275, 470
   propaganda in, 411–14, 417, 430
   puppetry in, 66, 67
   Romanticism in, 246–51
   tsars' involvement in, 131–33
   and variety entertainment, 260–
      64
Ryndin, V. F., 547

Saint-Denis, Michel, 502
Salis, Rodolphe, 375–76
salons, 55, 375
saloons. *See* Cabaret theater
Saltykov-Shchedrin, Mikhail, 304
Salvini, Tommaso, 308, 309, 314, 323,
   360
Salvo y Vela, Juan, 269
Sánchez, Florencio, 566
Sand, George, 241, 284
Sandford, Samuel, 46
Sanquirico, Alessandro, 201, 225
Santelli, Claude, 62
Sanu, Ya'qub, 570–71
Sapunov, Nikolai, 391, 415
Sardou, Victorien, 260, 291, 295, 297,
   298, 322, 382
Sarduy, Severo, 565
Saroyan, William, 534
Sassinot, Yvonne, 62
Satie, Erik, 398, 399, 474
satire, 392, 414, 421, 484
   American, 163, 166, 211
   English, 2, 56, 72, 75, 219
   French, 57, 377
Sats, Natalia, 550
Saxe, Maréchal Maurice de, 63